This Sporting Life

This Sporting Life

Sport and Liberty in England, 1760–1960

ROBERT COLLS

OXFORD
UNIVERSITY PRESS

OXFORD
UNIVERSITY PRESS

Great Clarendon Street, Oxford, OX2 6DP,
United Kingdom

Oxford University Press is a department of the University of Oxford.
It furthers the University's objective of excellence in research, scholarship,
and education by publishing worldwide. Oxford is a registered trade mark of
Oxford University Press in the UK and in certain other countries

First Edition published in 2020

Impression: 3

Published in the United States of America by Oxford University Press
198 Madison Avenue, New York, NY 10016, United States of America

British Library Cataloguing in Publication Data

Data available

Library of Congress Control Number: 2020932447

ISBN 978-0-19-820833-4

Printed and bound in Great Britain by
CPI Group (UK) Ltd, Croydon, CR0 4YY

For Leo and Rosa, Annika and Eddie, with love

... so much a part of us that we barely notice it is the addiction to hobbies and spare-time occupations, the privateness of English life. We are a nation of flower-lovers, but also a nation of stamp-collectors, pigeon-fanciers, amateur carpenters, coupon-snippers, darts-players, crossword-puzzle fans. All the culture that is most truly native centres round things which even when they are communal are not official— the pub, the football match, the back garden, the fireside and the 'nice cup of tea'. The liberty of the individual is still believed in, almost as in the 19th century. But this has nothing to do with economic liberty, the right to exploit others for profit. It is the liberty to have a home of your own, to do what you like in your spare time, to choose your own amusements instead of having them chosen for you from above . . . It is obvious, of course, that even this purely private liberty is a lost cause. Like all other modern peoples, the English are in the process of being numbered, labelled, conscripted, 'co-ordinated'. But the pull of their impulses is in the other direction.

(George Orwell, 'The Lion and the Unicorn', 1941)

Preface and Acknowledgements

This book would never have been started without a Visiting Fellowship at St. John's College Oxford and it would never have been completed without an invitation to join De Montfort University Leicester. In between, a Senior Research Fellowship from the Leverhulme Trust and a Mellon Fellowship at Yale gave me opportunities to go deep.

My time at St. John's was the best of times. By day, the College allowed me to discover the Bodleian's John Johnson Collection of Printed Ephemera, a truly outstanding source for the social history of this country. In the evenings, David Coleman, Rosalind Harding, Ross McKibbin, and William Whyte were especially good fellows. De Montfort, on the other hand, Leicester's other university, provided opportunities in a place I knew already, giving me the space to pursue my research across a wider range of interests. The Leverhulme Trustees showed extraordinary maturity in dealing with a wilful researcher. I wanted to explore sports history my way and they let me. Nothing more to be said. I hope this repays their Trust. The Yale Centre for British Art was more than a lot of valuable drawings and paintings. It was a six weeks centre of operations for an historian who wanted to learn how to learn, from art. That this was facilitated at every turn, and done so with the utmost grace and forbearance by everybody, every day, was a minor Yallie miracle. Over the road from the Centre, Keith Wrightson's Yale History Seminar survived my early thoughts on boxing and asked questions that were certainly better and probably longer, than the paper itself. At the end of a hard day in the galleries (somebody has to do it) New Haven was a great place for Mr. Mrs. Colls to go honky tonkin' (round this town). Back home, Stephen Hatcher showed me the museum that he built at Englesea Brook. The librarians at Leicester and De Montfort continued to be one of the best reasons for going to these universities, even as their institutions get less and less like libraries. As a try out for one of the chapters, I was glad to give a paper on Tom Cribb and Tom Sayers to one of Ross McKibbin's *festschrift* seminars.

Then there were all those places that looked after me no matter how anonymous the visit, including Abingdon Public Library, the Bodleian Library Oxford, the British Library London, Carlisle Record Office, Cheltenham Ladies' College, Chigwell School, the National Newspaper Library Colindale, Durham County Record Office, Palace Green Library Durham, the Football Association, the Harris Library Preston, Lancashire Record Office, Laygate Lane School, Leicestershire Leicester and Rutland Record Office, the Women's Library at London Metropolitan University, the John Rylands Library Manchester, the

National Archives at Kew, the Royal Society for the Prevention of Cruelty to Animals Archive at Horsham, Newcastle Central Library, Northumberland Estates Alnwick, Northumberland Archive Service Woodhorn, South Shields Public Library, Stamford Mercury Archive Trust, Stamford Town Hall, Sussex University Mass Observation Archive, Tyne and Wear Museums, Uppingham School Library and Archive, and Worksop College.

My week at Carlisle Record Office was a breakthrough and it happened on Matthew Constantine's watch. Julie-Anne Lambert at the John Johnson drew me in at the start of the day and managed to get me out at the end. Chris Hunwick at Alnwick advised on Bill Richmond. Janice Norwood opened my eyes to the *The Brit*, Hoxton. Peter Morritt and Squire de Lisle granted permission to quote from the Quorn minute books. Jerry Rudman at Uppingham found me a quiet corner. As well as being a genial host, Michael Winstanley advised on the Butterworth and Baines Papers in Preston. Many years ago Christine Hiskey found me some wonderful Weardale material in the Durham County Record Office, which I remembered for a rainy day. I had a very nice root round Stamford Town Hall with Bob Williams, and the Town Clerk Patricia Stuart-Hogg got me the painting in a time of lockdown. Paul Rafferty introduced me to the kids at Laygate Lane and couldn't do enough for me, or them. Rachel Roberts at Cheltenham was an unfailing guide and correspondent. Membership of the historians' 'boot room' at the old Newcastle Central Library was a rare privilege. Archivists and librarians tend to prefer anonymity but I thank them all, named or not, archivists or not.

My hometown of South Shields was one of the birthplaces of British social democracy but it was not until later that the idea of writing the history of so-called 'ordinary' people who lived in so-called 'ordinary' places like Shields became clear to me, and Sussex University in the 1960s was the place for that. Stephen and Eileen Yeo provided the push, Donald Winch the pull, and all intellectual currents seemed to flow in the direction of social history. E P Thompson's *The Making of the English Working Class* was the book that mattered while, up at York, my doctoral supervisor Gwyn Williams touch lit his own Welsh fireworks display to light up (for me) the regional sky. Gwyn, author of *Proletarian Order*, responded to Jim Walvin's pioneering researches into Proletarian Football with bafflement and wonder. But the message was the same. Look for the people and bring them on.

All this went in various directions until in 2012 I joined the International Centre for the History of Sport and Culture at DMU. The bibliography at the back lists some of the numerous papers delivered by the Centre, and given to the Centre, including important work by Emma Griffin which stretched the time-line of serious sport history, seminars by Dominic Sandbrook and Prashant Kidambi which stretched the imagination on how to think about Wolverhampton Wanderers and Indian cricket (though not necessarily in the same direction), and a powerful set of papers given by Gavin Kitching on the origins of football and the meaning of things. Then there are all those friends and colleagues at Leicester University whom I played football with over the years who know my own sporting life did not go unblemished. Thanks then to them for the old times, and more recently to my ICSHC colleagues across town for the new: to Neil Carter, Tony Collins, Mike Cronin, Jeremy Crump, Heather Dichter, Dick Holt, Gavin Kitching, Tony Mason, James Panter, Martin Polley, Dil Porter, and Matthew Taylor. Here's the book guys. I hope it adds to the kicking power of a sports history outfit that is already the best in the world.

As usual, the people at Oxford University Press were great to work with. Cathryn Steele was there at the beginning, and at the end. Matt Cotton patiently explained to me what I'd done right. Fiona Tatham found what I'd missed, and some more. Nivedha Vinayagamurthy worked hard in the engine room, Katie Bishop steadied the ship. Together they brought many years work home and I am grateful for their professionalism. For those who like footnotes, there's plenty here. Same for those who like Introductions. For those who don't like, or need, either, I suggest you move straight to Chapter one and stick with the story.

Finally, there's my personal trainers. David Storey wrote the first *This Sporting Life* in 1960 and gave me something to think about in the years in between. Dick Holt got me playing in the first place, and the thanks are all mine. Jeremy Crump put the manuscript through its paces, and made some telling observations. Nobody does it tougher. Ron Greenall explained the real rules of rugby (both types) and much besides. Paul Rouse encouraged me to be audacious and defensive at the same time. My brother Graham saved me from danglers and other literary injuries. As usual, John Gray, out on the wings, has been more influential than he knows. Karl Ove Knausgaard made a late surge into the box.

This Sporting Life is dedicated to my grandchildren Leo Colls Moore, Rosa Kington-Colls, Annika Kington-Colls, and Eddie Colls Moore, and it is offered to Becky and Amy, and to Rosie, my best and most beautiful friend since 1972 and a real cool grandma now. She advised and consented on this book more than anyone else.

Robert Colls

Leicester
1 May 2020

Contents

List of Figures and Plates

Figure

Plates

Plates section is found in the middle of the book

Introduction

If you say how the world is, that should be enough.

(Ken Loach, BBC2, 30 July 2016)

The human personality is a drama not a monologue.

(Clive James, *Unreliable Memoirs*, 1980)

In 1948 the social research organization Mass Observation estimated that 22 per cent of the population played games of various sorts. If football was the most popular, cricket was the best regarded. A previous report had advised that even though it was impossible to imagine sport in England without gambling, amateurs were the real sportsmen.[1]

My first game of football must have been around 1954 when I was old enough to join the rough and tumble of the back lane. Right by the lane, between our block and the next, was a large patch of open waste which we called 'the back field' but which was in fact an old waggonway that used to run from the local pit to the railway at the top of the street. There was always a game of football simmering here, and all kinds of other games as well—from cricket and hand ball in the summer to chucks and handies, hide and seek, skipping, and roller skating all the year round. Boys dominated the back field, flicked marbles along the gutter, and played 'ciggie cards' against the wall. Girls held their own territory, most of the lane and all the backyards, with a whole medley of games that involved being in or out or up or down. Plenty play involved both tribes as well, including 'chasies', 'kick the tin', and 'in the wall'. One favourite was to throw a ball over the entire block so that what came from the back lane bounced over the roof down into the front street where a posse of kids waited to catch it. I can't remember the girls being any less strong in the arm, or the eye, in this. But for me football was king. Apart from a few weeks' cricket in the warm dusty days of August, we played football all day every day until the ball burst or the Mams appeared out of the dusk to haul us in.

This book has two aims, first to try and say something about England's sporting life as it was lived and played, and second, slightly more formally perhaps, to dwell on what Ross McKibbin meant when he called sport 'one of the most powerful of England's civil cultures'.[2]

---

[1] University of Sussex, MO Archive: file 3045 October 1948; file 6 October 1939.

[2] McKibbin, *Classes and Cultures* (1998) p.322.

My methods have more or less adhered to what the primary sources have allowed. That said, you will find very few football results and no batting averages in these pages. You will find, however, a tonne of ethnographic description showing the sporting life across a range of 'sports' (usually competitive), and 'sport' (giving pleasure or amusement), over about 200 years. Not exactly 200 years because cultures are no respecters of historical periods, and not definitively 'sport' or 'sports' because I have not spent too long on definitions. I have tried instead to follow what contemporaries meant, whether or not they were consistent.[3] *Chambers' Twentieth Century Dictionary* for 1908 defines 'sport' as mainly frolic and amusement. At one end of the spectrum, any old bit of fun could be sport. At the other, competitive sport could be serious business. And yet, when the business stopped, the fun went on. The world was hit by coronavirus in 2020 and the business-end of sport with it, but all sorts of new sport emerged from what was near to hand, just like the old times, from forward rolls to toilet rolls. "A whole world of nonsense", according to Andy Bull on April Fool's Day in *The Guardian*.[4]

The idea of *Sport and Liberty* suffuses the whole work. I could have subtitled it something more general like 'Sport and Society' or 'Sport and Culture', words that embrace all aspects of life. Or I could have dropped the subtitle altogether and let the chapters speak for themselves. But I have emphasized liberty because that is what came first. Without it, all other meanings would fall. As George Orwell remarked in 'The Lion and the Unicorn', the liberty of the individual is a natural impulse in England.

There are eight loosely related chapters, each one a case study that widens out to consider the sporting life more generally. If you read the footnotes, please be aware that where there is more than one reference in a single footnote, I have started that note with the last textual reference first.

Chapter one, 'Land of Liberty', starts in 1909 with Minna Burnaby of Baggrave Hall in Leicestershire. No English sporting life was more fashionable than fox-hunting. For over 200 years it identified England to itself and others as a cheery olden-time rural sort of place. But fox-hunting was not just a question of good cheer. In order to hunt, you had to have land or access to land, you had to have influence or access to influence, and you had to have the time and the money. At the very least you had to have a horse. Masters of hounds had all these things, and authority. They rode at the front, made the rules, led the county, and claimed their place in that wider horsey world of pony clubs and gymkhanas, point to point and passing cavalry regiments. Young men would come up from London to show what they could do. Women too. Everybody loved a lord and at the hunt there was every chance of meeting one. The gentry were as devoted to their horses and hounds almost as much as to their acres, and by putting one with the other in

---

[3] McKibbin, *Democracy and Political Culture* (2019) p.117.
[4] 'From marble racing to balcony marathons':*The Guardian* 1 April 2020.

pursuit of the little red fox, they showed, to their own satisfaction at least, what it was to be free.

The Poor hunted too. If they hunted foxes, it was not for fun and never on a horse. But 'game' they could eat, or sell, or gift. So when the gamekeepers turned up to deny them their sport, hunting turned into poaching and poaching could turn into transportation and exile. Chapter 2, 'Bonny Moor Hen', describes how what was sport for one class could mean the far end of the world for another.

Chapter 3, 'Bottom', gets into the boxing ring early one morning in Hampshire in 1860. A lot of people have come down from London to see two hard men, one English, one Irish-American, fight it out. Billed as one of the first 'international' or 'world championship' contests, this match was driven by newspapers on both sides of the Atlantic. Heenan, the American, was younger, taller, heavier, stronger, louder. Sayers, the Englishman, was more experienced, not one for talking much, and known to have 'bottom', said to be a peculiarly English fighting quality much prized in the army and not unknown among Irishmen. Prize fights sometimes happened on the sly at race meetings, or in out of the way corners well away from magistrates, but mainly they take us into a half-world of intense violence and gentlemanly *hauteur*. Along with fox-hunting, prize fighting represented the nation to itself. The heavy-set stoicism of one stood sharp against the showy-red of the other.

Chapter 4, 'Custom', begins in the streets of a Lincolnshire market town. Every November for 600 years (or so), the people of Stamford (or some of them), believed that 'they' (meaning their forbears) had run a bull to death. Attempts by metropolitan liberals in the 1830s to stop it were met with stubborn resistance. Minna Burnaby rode for fun. Sayers fought for money. Stamford ran the bull because that is what Stamford thought it was. It was a straight constitutional question therefore, and when Stamford stopped running the bull many thought it stopped running some part of itself. This is only one example of what happened in many places in many ways to the country's amusements, festivals, pastimes, sports, and so forth, all of them involving profound changes in how people thought about who they were. Once the bull-running was over, Stamford was open to new forms of authority. Once people lost their right to be the People, on the street, according to custom, the constitution opened itself to new forms of interpretation, mainly by lawyers. Once upon a time the middle class had the vote and the people had the constitution. By the 1930s, the people had the vote and the middle class, now called 'public opinion', had the constitution.

Chapter 5, 'Home', begins with Edwin Butterworth on his tour of the Lancashire parishes. Butterworth was using his local connections in the service of Edward Baines, his employer. Baines, editor of the *Leeds Mercury*, was writing a county history. One of his key questions was how parish sports and customs had survived in a county which Marx and Engels were soon to describe as the raging heartland of the world's first Industrial Revolution. By way of the parish, and the legal privileges of 'settlement' which it bestowed, people had reason to think they belonged. But as parish privileges were removed or forgotten, people lost their old sense of place. Playgrounds were built over, pathways blocked, boundaries eroded, streams diverted, lands and rivers polluted. Not that everyone accepted parish belonging. The Methodists came to declare their own particular war on the parish—an attack from modern Puritans who rejected sports and games, especially when played on Sundays. But the old need to belong never faded. People felt they must belong and modern sport was a way that even the Methodists came to embrace. When in 1992 Nick Hornby explained how he belonged to a football pitch, no less, he was saying something important about a quality of community many thought had been extinguished. And when *Fever Pitch* became a Penguin Modern Classic in 2012, Lambeth Council were learning how difficult it was to evict skateboarders from the South Bank Undercroft. Refusing not to belong, they said it was their 'sanctuary' and 'second home'.[5]

Chapter 6, 'New Moral Worlds', goes to Uppingham School to meet the cricketers. It is 1858 and the headmaster Rev. Edward Thring is struggling to make these boys come to heel. His predicament introduces us to a broader Church of England campaign to change the nature of elite young men. In doing so headmasters and mistresses reinvented two key institutions of the modern world, the school and the university. From horseplay to cadging, the Student Rag blended a public school sense of what it was to be youthful, with a parish festival sense of what it was to play the fool.[6] For over a century, this new moral ethos shaped a large swathe of student life. Less well known is the part students played in that life, the subject of chapter 7, 'Bloods'. Whether they played or not, whether they ragged or not, undergraduates built their identity on college fun and friendship, badges and scarves, 'propping' and 'prepping'—a sporting ethos that co-existed with the altogether more aristocratic notion of being a bit mad, of doing as you pleased, of being a 'Blood'.

The last chapter, 'Moderns', begins with the first football craze. Football was codified in the 1860s by one of the boys we met in the Uppingham cricket XI. He, along with a few other young men representing a number of London clubs, got together to call themselves the Football Association. By 1914 their playing of the game had become a British working-class obsession and by the 1930s it was probably the world's most popular sport. We ask why the girls did not play. Some say it was because football took on industrial forms of labour. But girls took on industrial forms of labour. Some say it was because football lived on the streets and back lanes. But girls lived on the streets and back lanes. Some say it was because the FA banned women from affiliated grounds. But since when did anyone need an affiliated ground to play? Whatever the reason, most

---

[5] Whitter and Madgin et al., vimeo, *You Can't Move History* (AHRC 2016). Snell, *Parish and Belonging 1700–1950* (2006); Nick Hornby, *Fever Pitch* (1992, 2012).

[6] *The Guardian*, 1 March 1962.

girls did not play football and by the time they were women they had made other arrangements. There were, however, exceptions.

As for the boys, after the factory reforms of the 1850s, and the new FA code from the 1860s, football took off to be *the* game for moderns. The sporting life did not die. Football inherited all the old sporting qualities to be played in a way that made liberty out of movement, that required courage and 'bottom', that was learnt by custom and practice and continued to happen in places—from pieces of waste to old park goal posts—that were accessible and meaningful. No word means more to football clubs than 'Home'. Football teams were new moral worlds too, facilitating new ways of being together and different ways of being violent. At its best, football could be sublime, joyful, fluent, and aesthetic. Men felt more alive. They recalled a beautiful goal better than they recalled a good result.

A more modest title for this book might have been 'eight essays on some aspects of sport and amusement'. But apart from lacking a certain dash, this would not have caught my wider intention to look at the sporting life as something absorbed by whole societies.

I started the research knowing some social history, knowing something about Englishness and suspecting that there was something more interesting to see in sport and national identity than eleven people in national colours.[7] However, unlike national identity, which can be researched through the richly representative institutions of the state, sports reports can look pretty scant. I scanned the football results to little avail. I looked at photographs of boys in blazers and girls in boaters and wondered why. I considered histories of the FA and the MCC and, to say the least, wondered who.

Orwell thought representative institutions misrepresented as much as they represented. He hardly wrote a word about governments, even though he was a prolific political writer. He barely wrote a word about the Spanish Civil War, even though he never forgot his comrades. I wanted to do what he did and catch the flavour of life on the ground. But he, afer all, had his art. All I had were my footnotes.

In one sense, sports historians are spoilt for choice. There are any number of record offices and every modern newspaper has its sports page. But which record office? Which sports page? Which sport? How do you link up a thousand weekend games? That they were all called 'sport' does not guarantee their homogeneity or similarity. Even if it was possible to research them all, and turn them into one thing called 'sport', you would still have to find words to describe what they meant, a task not made easy by the fact that sport expresses itself first in actions.

---

[7] Hobsbawm thinks not: 'the imagined community of millions seems more real as a team of eleven named people': *Nations and Nationalism* (1990) p.143. Holt wrote the pioneering work on the subject, *Sport and the British* in 1990. See also McKibbin, *Classes and Cultures* (1998) and Rouse, *Sport in Ireland* (2015).

Not everything is measurable and sometimes the best things are only measurable in deeds. I spent the first two months of my research reading other people's histories feeling more and more bereft as to my own.

Then I went to Cumbria on a whim. A few days in Carlisle Record Office while staying at The Oddfellows Arms in Caldbeck convinced me that the project could move forward. I saw, for instance, that although fox-hunting in Cumbria and fox-hunting in Leicestershire were two different things, knowing about one helped me see what mattered in the other. I gave up planning in the head and started putting documents in front of my eyes. I gave up fretting about difference and embraced it. I decided to start with the activity itself, not its place in some idea of what sport is. The idea of living in a 'history' or a 'culture' is supposed to tell us who we are. So it does, but never wholly so because the idea of a history or a culture is never whole any more than we are whole.

Novelists understand how this works better than historians, and prefer to let the people speak first. William Faulkner deliberately built human contradiction and obscurity into his histories. His *Absalom, Absalom* (1936) offers no completed 'history' or 'culture' that was nineteenth-century Mississippi or, if it does, it does so only by tacking back from the present taking in contradictions and obscurities as they were passed down along the way. People expect tricks from writers of fiction in a way they do not expect tricks from historians. I have tried, therefore, to avoid contradiction and obscurity. At the same time, I have tried to build my subject out of different human experiences, out of the detail, putting it together as I went forward rather than looking for it entire as I looked back. (Strangely, that which was most unreliable for contemporaries, the betting, operates as a proxy fact- straightener for historians. The more money involved, the greater the effort to make sure what was said to have happened did happen).

After coming alive in Cumbria, I needed a set of sports rich in detail but not so different or diffuse as to be unmanageable. I needed to remember also that looking is not the same as finding. There was nothing much I could do about the over-bearing weight of historical evidence in favour of men.

Social theories are designed to help us make sense of the detail by positing what is whole. Darbon's five and Guttmann's seven defining features of modern sport helped me think in general terms about what had seemed otherwise hopelessly diffuse. Yet once I came upon an actual sport and tried to identify its defining features, those features only held by not allowing the exceptions to intrude.[8] Huizinga's notion of 'play' for instance, or Geertz's notion of 'deep play,' or

---

[8] Modern sport is defined by Darbon as universal, institutional, equal, specifically spatial and equally durational: *Les Fondements du Systeme Sportif* (2014). Modern sport is defined by Guttmann as secular, equal, specialist, rational, bureaucratic, skilled, and rewarded: *From Ritual to Record. The Nature of Modern Sport* (1978).

Wahrman's notion of 'playfulness', or Piaget's notion of learning through play, all involve generalizations that overrule the exceptions. As they must. But where does that take the practical historian? Even two sports as alike as Rugby League and Rugby Union are so different in who plays, how they play, and where they play, that you ask what is the point of generalizing? From up in the stands, the two games look roughly the same. Up close, looking roughly the same loses much of its point. It is in the differences that we come see to what matters. All generalizations to some extent anonymize and, when it comes to history, every anonymization is a small death. What is more, historians have to be constantly on the look out for change. Everything changes. Sport itself changes, its meaning changes, and the meanings that are applied to its meanings change. What is vaguely similar one decade can look strikingly different the next, and social theories have no obvious way of dealing with this. At the same time, the historian is charged with making overall sense of something that is supposed to be unchanging.

Academic theories of sport history generally fall into two main camps. First, there are those to do with gradual processes that see sport as evolving into ever more complex or refined conditions of play. Second, there are those that see sport essentially as a controlling or repressive activity carried out in the interests of the existing order.

Theories of complexity and refinement move in evolutionary stages. These can include for instance stages of 'institutionalization' or 'modernization', or 'democratization', or 'commodification', or 'civilization' and the rest, and they all point to an increasing complexity or refinement according to the feature, or the set of features, the theorist has decided to track. Turn of the century sociologists saw modern sport as degenerate because they thought it was destroying the playful element in society. Huizinga wrote in praise of traditional sport as a playful and civilizing counterpoint to modern degeneracy. Elias on the other hand saw modern sport as *regenerative*, part of the civilizing process. McKibbin tried to disentangle the various lines of argument to come up with a 'fairly minimalist' theory of sport resting on a crucial distinction between what is 'play' and what is 'system', something Darbon calls 'sportization', another version of the same debate, but still he found definitional difficulties in the difference between sport for the individual and sport for the collective.[9] All these abstract features are only *names* of course and what they feature always contains internal differences. All models are wrong but some are useful, and whether we call them (very properly) 'names', or (very reasonably) 'features', or (very grandly) 'theories', they are all capable of making sense here and there and I have drawn on them as appropriate.

Theories of social control on the other hand tend to explain whole systems acting in concert. For instance, there are theories of control appertaining to sport

---

[9] Elias, *The Civilizing Process* (1939); Huizinga, *Homo Ludens* (1938); McKibbin, *Democracy & Political Culture* (2019) p.119.

as alienated labour, or over-disciplined bodies, or stolen rights, or sublimated psychologies, or sport in the service of imperialistic, capitalistic, misogynistic or racist power structures. And so on. At their heart lies a soft Marxism where an overarching theory of economic exploitation has been replaced by an overarching theory of cultural exploitation. Although I was by no means dead to the attraction of applying powerful critical theory to the 1001 peculiarities of England's class-race-gender inflected sporting life, I have to confess that although some of these ideas appealed here and there, no theory of social control appealed across the board. Only very occasionally is sport deliberately controlling or repressive in itself, and even when it is, outcomes rarely match intentions. My point is: not all social theories are easy to apply, and some are not worth applying at all.

In any case, as Gavin Kitching remarked, when we are trying to understand human experience, we should not *apply* anything. We have to communicate instead. It is worth remembering that academics are quite capable of applying descriptions far less useful than those that were used by the people they study.[10]

So, rather than apply a general theory outside my subject (in order to see it whole and value free), I have chosen to step inside and communicate from there. I have tried, in other words, to do without the 'isms', to write about their lives not mine, to be a neighbour not a stranger, to bear in mind the whole and remember that everything counts.[11] Working from the inside-out rather than outside-in appeals to the workaday historian in me and is, in fact, nearer to how most people see their lives. The worst history I have written has directly applied theory or ideology. The best has described how things actually work.

I have tried, therefore, to understand the absorption of sport into our common life and, although I have avoided too many abstract agents ('Culture', 'Power' 'Progress' 'Urbanization', etc) along the way, I have tried to pick up on any patterns or syndromes that seemed helpful. Some will be obvious to the reader. There is evidence of 'institutionalization' and 'modernization' (the founding of the Football Association for instance). There is evidence of 'democratization' and 'commodification' (the new leisure economy for instance). There is evidence of repression and control, or at any rate the *intention* to repress or control (aspects of fox-hunting for instance, or the game laws, or women's sport). But there is also evidence of the breakdown of institutions, of times when the things that should have died out did not die out, when women found their liberty, when modern sport stood for drive and passion, not control.

---

[10] Kitching, 'Mrs Thatcher, Ludwig Wittgenstein and Social Science', Ms paper, ICSHC, DMU, January 2019.
[11] David Storey's *This Sporting Life* (1960) goes inside that which, he says, presented itself to him as something immediate and exterior: *The Times*, 23 November 1963. For anthropological insights for historians see: Thomas, 'History and Anthropology', *Past & Present* 24 (1963) p.4, p.17.

Other syndromes presented themselves. I noted that in spite of Darbon's theory of sport and 'sportization', there never was a time when people played without some sort of system. What was done traditionally in the name of custom, for instance, was itself a system of expectation. Another syndrome is the way in which sport was seen as constitutive of the country and its people. Many saw it as fundamental to being 'freeborn' just as they saw being freeborn as fundamental to being English. Sport was therefore a means of self expression, of affiliation, of showing that everything wasn't just politics and politics wasn't just words. Like everything else in life sport lives off words. When play is over and the bat and ball have been taken away, sports journalism has claim to be the first modern writing, sportsmen the first modern celebrities.

Most striking of all perhaps, there was no sudden transition from the 'traditional' to the 'modern'. There is a sense in which football helped invent the modern world but there was no obvious rupture, for example, between what we might label 'pre-industrial' and 'industrial', and it was never clear at either point where the future lay. There was change yes, but only when seen from two points on the map. England in 1960 can still be regarded as a land that saw itself as free, where 'bottom' or what we would now call 'heart' remained widely regarded, where many aspects of life were still learned by custom, where play continued to harbour strong feelings of belonging, where the need to create close moral bonds and friendships was still a social given, and where football had never stopped standing for what was mass and modern. Most people in these islands continued to see themselves as national peoples although by the 1960s they seemed to have surrendered their sense of entitlement to the constitution. In the end, the biggest syndrome was sport as an expression of liberty and belonging—only names of course, and not always naming the same thing, but powerful undercurrents all the same.

The book was built up from a wide network of sources, at the last count including the histories of over 60 schools, over 120 newspapers and journals, and over 30 primary collections covering everything from personal diaries to national newspapers, to courts and commissions, to walls and walls of some of the most valuable oil paintings in the world at Yale, to boxes and boxes of scraps of paper miraculously saved, stamped, and made available to the public in the Bodleian.

This project came alive when I stopped worrying about diffusion and learned to love peculiarity. In order to explore part of what it felt like to be alive, in England, between 1760 and 1960, *This Sporting Life* is a detectorist not a drone. Not in ideas but in things. At first I struggled with old photographs of men in shorts and girls in boaters. Now that I can put some meaning to them suggests at least that something has been achieved.

I played my last game of football on 12 December 1993 for Leicester Academicals in the local Sunday League. I took a heavy challenge in the sleet and the mud and that, as they say, was that. I was 44 years old and the surgeon told me to take up something more civilized, like rugby.

Everybody knows a sporting story or two. They might be light on the facts, heavy on the detail, and not know the difference between a leg break and a broken leg, but chances are they can tell the story or at least voice an opinion, which is a story of sorts.

Sport is a story the country tells itself but it is not the only one and not the most important one. At times I must confess to wondering how my mention of the young Stanley Matthews kicking a football with a tea cosy on his injured foot dared inhabit the same intellectual space as histories of war and peace, death and disease, trade and technology. Reading David Edgerton's superb *The Rise and Fall of the British Nation* (2018) provoked doubts in me about the significance of the foot in the tea cosy. Then we went to the match and spun new stories out of old after it without so much as a mention of GDP or ECB or WTO or any of the big stuff that is supposed to matter when it comes to what we tell ourselves. Even as we know sport to be trivial, we know we are trivial, or can be, and so, *ergo*, are some of the histories we write. It's not as if the economists do not tell stories. Our capacity for play, for nuance and swerve and taking on opponents, stretches beyond sport. Sport is only a physical contest in the first place. It becomes a story immediately after and stories, as any poet will tell you, know how to play. Even this book comes out to play sometimes. For six hours before the Battle of Trafalgar, one of the greatest in Britain's long history, Stephen Taylor's *Sons of the Waves* tells us how Nelson's fleet cruised in the breeze while ship bands played and sailors danced the hornpipe.

'Jack Tar' was eighteenth-century England's foremost patriot—a heart of oak and a hero. But a people's hero only. Maritime art did not include him. Like the poachers and the pugilists whose company he kept, Jack existed not in art but in cheap pot and print, in tickets and tattoos, in songs and stories. *This Sporting Life* has given me the opportunity to delve into his world in order to put its dog-eared ephemera up against the official record, and the official record up against him. I wanted to salute these sort of people and the things they knew and the life they made, and show how aspects of that life shaped them to think of themselves not as victims or inferiors, or God forbid, inert masses, but winners, the people on whom the country depended for its strength and liberty.

The sporting life is one of those things in our history that has been neglected by scholars out of all proportion to the love and attention lavished on it by those who lived it. Now that they have gone and the coal and the ships and the regiments have gone with them, I am drawn to these people first because once upon a time they were alive like I am alive and now they are not; second because I am curious about the life they lived and what they thought of it; and third because I am interested in civil society for all sorts of reasons, not all past participle. Which is to say, I wrote this book first for them, second for me, and third for all of us. I hope it works for you.

1

Land of Liberty

The English invented personal liberty without any theories about it.
They value liberty because it is liberty.

(Alexander Herzen, in Tom Stoppard's *The Coast of Utopia* 2002)

Thoroughly Modern Minna

Minna Burnaby had a good season in 1909–10. On 25 October she enjoyed 'two
nice gallops' at Ashby and on 29th she took a 'nice little turn around the Vale' at
Dalby. In November she hit a 'good hunt' at Long Clawson, a 'capital 40 minutes'
at Wymeswold, and 'top speed' in 'glorious country' at Seagrave. December saw
a 'splendid day' at Ab Kettleby, a 'capital day' at Hungarton, a 'Bully Day' at
Goadby, and a 'topping day...fast up to Halstead' on New Year's Eve. On 14
January she went full tilt for seven minutes in a high wind at Quenby before
finding the scent again at Baggrave and running up to Ashby Pastures 'then right
handed missing Thorpe ran fast up to Barsby and along the brook...'[1] Over the
year Minna was pleased to report that *The Kid* had gone 'divinely', *Repidan*
'deliciously', and *Bodkin* 'top hole'. In eighty-two days' fox-hunting she took
eight falls.

The Leicestershire parishes that marked Minna's glory days were small and, in
the winter months, obscure. The landscape, by any measure, was modest. The fox
she hardly mentions, dead or alive. What Minna liked was what Minna did:
chatting at the meet, walking the hounds, 'lots of jumping', and clear runs on
cold sunny days. What Minna did not like was anything that clogged the scent or
slowed the field: road, frost, rain, snow, wind, fog, fence wire, steep hills, stiff
hedges, too many riders, too few foxes, ploughy fields, rabbit holes, woodland, and
'coffee shop' at the covert ('did nothing but stand about...while a wholesale
slaughter of cubs went on'). Minna was not one to hide her feelings. It was a
'poisonous' day for her when her horse went lame at the Noel Arms, and 'vile',
'dreadful', 'miserable', and 'absolute Brute' at other times. Yet it was 'joyous' for
her when her horse 'jumped at least 100 fences' in one outing and there were other
moments when it was impossible to know what Minna really liked except the risk

---

[1] Minna Burnaby's Hunting Diary, 1909–10: Leicestershire Record Office (LRO), DG 51/2.

of not knowing what will happen next. She had 'real folly on the new mare' [who is] 'a clinking hunter and jumps too beautifully', while *The Kid*, one of her favourites, 'nearly sacked me off! Was as near the floor as makes no matter'.[2]

Fox-hunting was never as fast and flowing as its writers and artists liked to depict, but Leicestershire had achieved a reputation for style and speed long before Minna Burnaby. In 1843 the great sports journalist 'Nimrod', a tad too eager perhaps, said it was 'as nearly approaching perfection as nature and art can make it, and its fame may be said to have reached the remotest corners of the civilized world'.[3] The least we can say is that Leicestershire's notorious 'double oxter' fences were a long leap into the unknown. When the Pytchley Hunt's 16 stone Waterloo veteran went over no matter what ('Where's Wyndham?'), the county's reputation for risk and excitement was safe for another day.[4]

There had been a time when hunting foxes had been, and still was in many places, an unseemly scramble. Riders kicked along, or got off and went on foot, or did a bit of each. Leicestershire on the other hand was famous for light riding over fast, open country, country as near to aristocratic parkland as could be expected. Expert horsemen like Osbaldeston, Caprilli, and Nolan made the ride quick (knees high, stirrups short), enclosure and the shift to grazing made it firm, and a low undulating country made it pleasant.[5] Traditional fox-hunting, according to Beckford in 1798, depended upon the hounds and, 'it may be objected', upon the huntsman who, 'generally speaking, is an illiterate fellow'. For Siegfried Sassoon in 1928, fox-hunting was 'lyrical, beautiful, ecstatic'.[6]

Leicestershire took the cream of wealth and fashion.[7] There is no mention of fox-hunting in Burton's 1777 *Description* of the county, but in that same year Charles Dormer was joshing Fortescue Turville that his Warwickshire hounds were 'even' as good as Turville's Leicestershire hounds, and in 1782 we find the Leicestershire man being told by a London friend how he 'longed many a one of these fine mornings to have been with them a galloping over that fine country of Leicestershire'. Three years later we find the Prince of Wales trying to establish a hunt at Woburn 'more fashionable then *even* Mr. Meynell's' in Leicestershire, and by 1795 Nichols' county history described it as 'celebrated for hunting'.[8]

---

[2] ibid, DG 51/4, 51/3. Ethel Greene's Northumberland Hunting Diary (1895–1901) shares much the same hunting likes, dislikes, and adjectives: LRO DE 2101/128.

[3] Nimrod, *Hunting Reminiscences* (1843) p.26; Cecil, *Records of the Chase* (1854) pp.115, 148–51.

[4] Carr, *English Fox Hunting* (1976) p.87. 'Double oxters' had two rails, two hedges and a ditch. High blackthorn hedges were called 'bullfinches'.

[5] Hoskins, *One Man's England* (1978): 60 per cent Leicestershire enclosure was mainly pre-parliamentary for fatstock in the north and east of the county (p.82).

[6] Sassoon, *Fox Hunting Man* (1928) p.274; Beckford, *Thoughts on Hunting* (1798) p.5.

[7] Nimrod, *The Chace* (1837) p.14.

[8] Nichols, *History and Antiquities of County of Leicester* (1795) vol. i, p.lxci; Burton, *Leicestershire* (1777); letter, Charles Dormer, Warwickshire, to Fortescue Turville, Leicestershire, 11 January 1777: LRO DG 39/1096; letter, George Talbot, London, to Fortescue Turville, 12 March 1782: LRO DG 39/

Leicestershire was on its way to be being not only fashionable but legendary. Around the same time that Robert Lowth (1800) made fun of the crowds of riders who came jostling for a place at the meet, John Hawkes (1808) began the great tradition of Leicestershire fox hunters talking about each other. His book went through six editions up to 1936. Page's *Victoria County History* defined Edwardian Rutland (adjoining Leicestershire) as an earthly paradise, 'famous in the annals'. Nimrod had spotted its raw appeal early on:

> I repeat, it is some trial of nerve... to look before us at a strong blackthorn hedge, five or six feet high, with a rail or wide ditch to boot, and 'who knows what' on the other side; but still more so, if at this time we look behind us, and see two or three of our friends running away with their horses, or their horses running away with them – for the difference matters not – roaring out at the top of their voices, 'Go along Sir; pray go along! We shall be left half a mile behind!!'[9]

Leicestershire had coal mines in the north-west, textile factories in the towns, and village manufacturing all round, but to the riding fraternity it was above all the home of five great fox-hunting 'countries'. Their borders could change but generally speaking to the south there was the Pytchley near Lutterworth, to the west the Atherstone near Market Bosworth, and in the east three hunts, the Cottesmore, north of Uppingham, the Belvoir, near Belvoir Castle, and the Quorn near Loughborough stretching north over the Soar into Nottinghamshire. Melton Mowbray served as an eastern hub, its national communications network (turn-pike 1760s, canal 1790s, rail 1830s) good enough to supply hunt tourists with all the food and fodder they could manage. When it came to reputation, no hunt matched the Quorn. In 1912 its 300 riders crashed through into the fourth great network of national communication, the cinematograph.[10]

To be the master of fox hounds (MFH) was a mark of extraordinary distinction. Hunts knew their masters by name, rank, and the order in which they followed one another. The Quorn started with the founder, Boothby, in 1698 (obscure); Meynell in 1753 (legendary); Sefton in 1800 ('polestar of fashion'); Assheton-Smith in 1812 (hundred falls a season); Osbaldeston in 1817 (hundred fights a season); Goodricke in 1831 (died hunting Irish otters); Suffield in 1838 (hopeless

---

111; letter, Mr. T. Potts to 'Mons Turville Gentilhomme Anglais, Nancy', 27 September 1785: LRO DG 39/1158.

[9] Nimrod, *Hunting Reminiscences* (1843) pp.36, 48; Robert Lowth, 'Billesdon Coplow Hunt' (1800) 4pp; Hawkes, *Meynellian Science* (1809); Cecil, *Records of the Chase* (1854) p.115; Page, *VCH Rutland* (1908) p.305. There was usually a lot of reference to having the 'nerve' to ride. Alice Hayes told her lady readers that a Master of Hounds had once told her 'that his nerve was so bad that he positively prayed for frost': Hayes, *The Horsewoman* (1903) p.245. p. lxci.

[10] In 'a sort of hunting Saturnalia': Bradley, *Shire to Shire* (1912) p.135.

but not desperate); and Sir Harry Greene in 1843 (first county man).[11] Developed through Sir Thomas Boothby, his wife's grandfather, by Sir Hugo Meynell, a Derbyshire landowner and MP, the Quorn became famous on a rising tide of moneyed young men looking for fast packs and high performance horses. Nimrod, who had never seen him hunt, said Meynell was a great rider, a sort of Beau Nash of the saddle, part of the eighteenth-century taste for fashion.[12] Commonly known as 'thrusters', young men came up from London to ride hell for leather.[13] By the time of his retirement in 1800, and contrary to legend, Meynell had not invented fox-hunting, or made it scientific, or showed it how to go, but had succeeded in turning Quorndon Hall ('neither very large or magnificent') into a 'first rate London Tavern'.[14] He called himself, or got others to call him, the first fox hunter in the land,[15] and he let it be known that this was the place where between November and March every year, London 'poured forth her abundance'.[16] To Scarth-Dixon in 1921, the Quorn was so fast you could fly. To Arthur Mee in 1937, fox-hunting was born there, although actually it wasn't.[17]

In 1832, England's first sporting journalist, Pierce Egan, dedicated his book on sport as 'the Mirror of Life' to George Osbaldeston, twice Master of the Quorn. Osbaldeston was a difficult man, deeply unpopular in Leicestershire. But it was said that his most redeeming feature was that he had the mark of a 'True Meltonian', 'bang up' to it, an 'Out and Outer' and an 'Out and Out Meltonian' at that.[18] Egan was followed, as the doyen of sports journalists, by Charles Apperley, or 'Nimrod'. Mighty Hunter, Son of Cush, and Grandson of Noah, Nimrod was a former cavalryman turned horse dealer who thought Meltonians were the best and wasted no opportunity in saying so at a guinea a page.[19]

[11] Scarth-Dixon, *Quorn* (1921) provides the full list, pp.24–30; Cecil, *Records of the Chase* (1854) pp.126–34; Nimrod, *Hunting Reminiscences* (1843) p.30.

[12] Nimrod, *The Chace* (1837) p.310.

[13] And were 'content to be strangers': *The Times*, 7 March 1952.

[14] Throsby, *Selected Views* (1791) p.310.

[15] Nichols, *History and Antiquities of County of Leicester* (1800), vol. iii, p.101.

[16] Throsby, *Selected Views* (1791) p.311.

[17] There is plenty of evidence that medieval lords hunted foxes for pleasure as well as vermin: Middleton, 'The Myth of Hugo Meynell and the Quorn', *Sport in History* (2005) pp.2–8; Scarth-Dixon, *Quorn* (1921) p.10; Mee, *Leicestershire and Rutland* (1937) pp.1–2.

[18] Egan, *Book of Sports* (1832) pp.223–4. Pierce Egan (1772–1849) was a London compositor before becoming the country's first pre-eminent sporting journalist. His popular series *Life in London* (1821) tells us half the story in its sub-title: *Life in London or, the Day and Night Scenes of Jerry Hawthorn Esq and his elegant friend Corinthian Tom, accompanied by Bob Logic, the Oxonian, in their rambles and sprees through the Metropolis*. Well served by George and Robert Cruikshank's illustrations, *Pierce Egan's Life in London* (1824) eventually merged with *Bell's Life in London* (1822) to become 'the most voluminous single record of 19th century sport': Denis Brailsford, 'Pierce Egan', *Oxford Dictionary of National Biography* (ODNB). Egan is an under-rated writer and we will return to him later.

[19] Nimrod, *Hunting Tours* (1903) pp.2–5; Nimrod, *Hunting Reminiscences* (1843) p.26; Itzkowitz, *Peculiar Privilege* (1977) pp.14–15. Apperley (1778–1843), or 'Nimrod' went to Rugby School and served in the Light Dragoons. He followed Egan after his first piece, 'Fox-Hunting in Leicestershire' (1822), doubled the sales of *The Sporting Magazine*. The *Magazine* paid him large sums to act as a gentleman correspondent. He was known as 'Pomponius Ego' to his rival Robert Surtees: Norman

Henry Dixon, or 'Druid', represented the next generation of hunting journalists paid large sums to massage rich men's egos. Although the Druid preferred to bump along in a gig, not on horseback, he understood the hunt's 'immense scope for anecdote and disquisition' and, along with mid-century sports writers such as R S Surtees, George Whyte Melville, and Bromley Davenport, he spread the story far and near.[20]

There was only one story: faintly mocking and adoring at the same time it was all about English hunting heroes. Their stories were almost as long as their runs:

> Racing men are bad enough but I have heard ladies, who are perhaps the best judges of volubility, affirm that for energy, duration, and the faculty of saying the same thing over and over again, a dialogue between a couple of fox hunters beats every other kind of discussion.[21]

Robert Surtees' 'Mr. Sponge' is fiction's most famous Meltonian even though he is a fraud. Whyte-Melville's novelettish comedies are full of men riding big horses with clumsy feet and cigars sticking out of their mouths (the men's, not the horses'). Sir Samuel Stuffy, Hon Crasher, Major Brush and Captain Struggles all like the simple things of life, especially themselves. Sassoon remembered how he and his hunting cronies took their names out of *Mr Sponge's Sporting Tour* (1853)—from Lord Scamperdale to Jogglebury Crowdey. Every page of Whyte-Melville's *Market Harborough* (1861) was an opportunity for the hunt to see itself through its own cigar smoke.[22]

Gash, 'Charles James Apperley', *ODNB*. Chapter 39 of Surtees' heavily satirical *Mr Sponge's Sporting Tour* is called 'Writing a Run'.

[20] Druid, *Post and the Paddock* (1856) p.116. Henry Hall Dixon (1822–70), or 'The Druid', Rugby School and Trinity College Cambridge, chose racing as his sport and Newmarket as his town, but did much for fox-hunting too. A practising lawyer, Dixon wrote mainly for *Bell's Life* and *The Sporting Magazine*.

[21] Mr. Sawyer in Whyte Melville's *Market Harborough* (1861) p.42. George Whyte-Melville (1821–78), Eton College and Coldstream Guards, was a Scottish comic novelist and poet who wrote indefatiguably about hunt heroes and heroines from *Digby Grand* (1853) onwards. He died riding with the Vale of White Horse.

[22] ibid, p.139; Sassoon, *Fox Hunting Man* (1928) p.167. Sassoon said he knew an elderly colonel who 'modelled himself on ... the Whyte Melville standard ... and coloured prints of a slightly earlier period' (p.180). Robert Smith Surtees (1805–64) was a Durham landowner and fox hunter. Although he never acknowledged writing as a profession he was one of the most influential comic writers of the century, succeeding Nimrod as hunting correspondent for *The Sporting Magazine* in 1830, and, supported by John Leech's illustrations, inventing those irrepressible hunters 'Soapy' Sponge and John Jorrocks. We can see the origins of his Mr. Sponge in Peter Pasquin's *Day's Journal of a Sponge* (1824). As well as Egan, Nimrod, Surtees, and the Druid, there was Cornelius Tongue, or 'Cecil' (1800–84), now forgotten, who spent his life turning sport into literature, including the *Fox Hunter's Guide* (1847) and *Records of the Chase* (1854).

Sports writers had their own way of writing and were known for it.[23] Assisted by a burgeoning sporting press keen on saddle room sayings, old saws and tall stories, hunts fostered their own mythologies.[24] On 24 February 1800 the Quorn ran twenty-eight miles at Billesdon Coplow and never forgot it. A generation later, Nimrod could say that he thought the best introduction for any young man of fashion was to be found at Billesdon Coplow (population: two), and in 1912 Bradley was recalling the run as if it had happened only yesterday.[25] Occasionally, readers were reminded that long runs could kill horses as well as riders. Nimrod put 'The Death of Edwin' down to a true Meltonian:

> The scent appeared better and better; indeed, the pace had been awful since the check in the wind-mill field. I looked back twice and could only see four, and then there were but five besides myself with the hounds. 'This is beautiful' I said. 'Divine!' shouted L. I could not help giving them a cheer which I don't often do. Ten minutes more, however, began to tell tales. We crossed the brook under Norton-by-Galby, and went as straight as a line for Rolleston Wood. 'Ha! Ha! Another ox fence' said I to myself as we rose the hill in Galby field... catching fast hold of his head I sent him at it manfully: but the ditch was broad and deep, the hedge thick and plashed, and the rail beyond them strong. Neither was this all ... the drop must have been seven feet at the least, and he had to struggle to keep his legs, for he must have cleared more than seven yards in length, or he would not have got over it at all. It told upon him but I soon got him upon a headland and standing up in my stirrups took a pull at his head, which recovered him wonderfully before he got to the end of the ground, which was 60 acres or more. In short, he cleared a high gate into the Uppingham and Leicester road, a little to the right of Billesdon, and a large straggling black thorn-hedge and ditch out of it with apparent ease to himself. 'This cannot last long', I said, 'I wish the fox would die or that *Footpad* [his second horse] would make his appearance... [26]

Places mattered in hunting legend that wouldn't matter anywhere else.[27] Billesdon Coplow, Oadby Toll Bar, Tilton Wood, John O'Gaunt's, Ram Jam Inn, and a score of other Leicestershire meeting points appear again and again, while revolutions in printing technique took hunt prints (penny plain, tuppence coloured) into almost every home and public house.[28] The Alken family were the little masters of hunting art, Henry popularly known as 'Ben Tally Ho'. Thomas Bewick's first

[23] Both sentimental and sporting ways of writing were acknowledged popular forms: see trade cards, Thomas Rowlandson engraving, in John Johnson Collection, Bodleian Library, Sport Box 9.
[24] Quorn Hunt Scrapbook: LRO, DE 3030/29.
[25] Nimrod, *Hunting Tours* (1903) frontispiece; Bradley, *Shire to Shire* (1912) p.153, p.115, p.172.
[26] Nimrod, *Hunting Reminiscences* (1843) p.51.
[27] From among the many: Pennell-Elmhirst, *Cream of Leicestershire* (1883).
[28] Ray, *Illustrator and the Book* (1976) pp.178–81; Snelgrove, *British Sporting and Animal Prints* (1981) pp. ix–x.

important wood cut 'Old Hound' was presented to the Royal Society when he was just 22. His famous *History of Quadrupeds* (1790) featured Northumbrian hunt tales. The celebrated engraver John Scott made his bread and butter out of hunting scenes. If not all of the scenes were polite ('just get over the gate'), they were popular. Manufacturers sold their pots and plates through a lot of olden time good cheer featuring hunting horns and punch bowls. By the 1840s fox-hunting was a mainstay of adult light fiction, and by the 1860s it was being rewritten as an English Tory idyll.[29] When linocut appeared as a modernist art form in the 1920s, it did fox hunters too.[30]

So popular was the genre, sometimes horses and riders were painted with their faces left blank.[31] Who hadn't heard of the Donnington Run or Baggrave Spinney? Who didn't know that all riders wore pink (even though they didn't)? Who doubted that double-oxters were difficult and only to be found in Leicestershire?[32] So strong was the hunting hold on the upper class nation, some declared its wiles and ways part of the constitution.[33] Mr. Churchill became Prime Minister in 1940 in a race against a man who said he'd rather be an MFH.[34]

First came the MFH, usually rich if not titled, and very much the dignified part of the constitution. Colonel in chief and paymaster general, he was, for the day, lord of all he surveyed. Then came the huntsman, usually the only professional in the field, the efficient part of the constitution and responsible for the hounds, which he counted in couples. It was his business to make the pack physically fit and biddable, and convention had it that he blew the horn.[35] Then came the whippers-in, answerable only to the huntsman, breaking up riots and generally enforcing order in the pack. Then the field, anything from a dozen to a few hundred riders, all under the MFH and not allowed to pass him or cross him. Then the hunt servants, who did what they were told, including 'stopping earths'

---

[29] *Sporting Magazine*, 1863, p.450; May, *Fox-Hunting Controversy* (2013) p.125. On the Alkens and other hunt artists, including Henry Thomas and Henry Gordon, see Ralph Nevill in *The Connoisseur*, August 1905, and Alken (YCBA 1949); Bewick in Uglow, *Nature's Engraver* (2006) p.275; Scott in Welford, *Men of Mark* (1895) p.358; and generic scenes in John Johnson, Bodleian, Trade Cards.

[30] Sybil Andrews, 'Full Cry': 'Modernist British Printmaking' at Dulwich Picture Gallery, *New Statesman*, 2–15 August 2019.

[31] 'Blank: The Property of his Grace the Duke of Ancaster' (Bowles & Carver, St Paul's Churchyard, nd): John Johnson, Bodleian, Trade in Print and Scraps, vol. ii.

[32] Four plates, colour, Alken Jnr., engraver Charles Hunt (London, Laird, Leadenhall Street, nd).

[33] 'Hunting, unlike other forms of sport [but just like the British Consitution], has no written rules of its own for the guidance of the uninitiated': de Broke, *Sport of Our Ancestors* (1921) pp.18–20, and Hayes, *The Horsewoman* (1903) p.309.

[34] Edward Wood, Lord Halifax, in Shakespeare, *Six Minutes in May* (2017) p.325. Lord Hartington said he'd rather win the Derby than be Prime Minister: Strachey, *Eminent Victorians* (1918) p.246.

[35] The huntsman was a 'menial servant' earning £100 to £130 a year, and used to being patronized. He was better off than local domestics however and, with house and regular wages, better off than many skilled workers in the towns. But he had no independence. Dick Burton was a long-lived and much honoured Quorn Huntsman who rode with Assheton-Smith and Nimrod. *Eclipse* magazine remembered him as a 'great favourite' forced by a bad back into retirement 'to his little property . . . *we forget which*, at Quorn' (*Eclipse*, 5 January 1863). [Italics mine].

(denying the fox the chance of going to ground the night before). Last came the hunt followers; on foot, unnoticed, and unmentioned. Apart from the huntsman who earned a little bit more than the servants, and the farmers, who earned about five times more, those in the saddle earned at least twenty times more than those who ran behind.[36]

Lady riders, who found themselves hobbled by a fiendish saddle and a mass of buckles and pins, did not wear red and were generally invited to keep out of the way.[37] Nimrod once heard a female rider rebuked by the master for calling a hound 'pretty'. 'Handsome' does it, she was told.[38]

For a long time sporting ladies were seen as oddities. Gravelot's picture of a woman out hunting for game makes her look every inch a gallant in her long coat and boots until we realize that the gun over her shoulder is cocked and everyone ought to keep his head down. Mrs. Inge inherited the mastership of the Atherstone Hunt from her father in 1914, and other women took leadership roles during the war too, but instruction manuals for lady hunt riders were as much about how to look as how to ride. Not that men were unconcerned about how men looked, but mostly they made the rules.[39] Munkwitz reckoned there were twenty-five female MFHs before 1914, and thirty-three by 1918. Every woman who rode was supposed to be grateful as well as graceful.[40] There's no sign of it in Minna's journals it has to be said, but then Minna had married the MFH. Not one to call a hound 'pretty' in the first place, no one was going to rebuke her if she did.

In spite of fox-hunting's reputation for male boorishness, women loved to ride. Thomas Turner's sister wrote to him from Sapcote. In a letter full of horses and hounds ('We have a new hound. Its name is Matcham') she had to tell him that she'd got bold at leaping and didn't mind going at a stile.[41] Manuals came to

---

[36] These figures are based on agricultural rents only, and exclude urban rents and non-agricultural investments, which were high, and in 1867, getting higher: Allen, *Industrial Revolution* (2017) pp.65–6.

[37] Women usually wore blue or grey, very subdued: Hayes, *The Horsewoman* (1903) pp.309–11, 90–124. Most women rode side-saddle. Designed by men but never used by them, it must have taken women hours to get ready and if they were going to do it according to the manual they needed assistance. Mrs. Hayes does not spare the details. She does however show Miss Emmie Hayes of New Zealand jumping an appalling vertiginous wire fence side-saddle (fig. 102).

[38] Pittman *Nimrod's Hunting Tours* (1835) p.688.

[39] May, *Fox-Hunting Controversy* (2013) p.41. Gravelot, 'Sporting Lady' (YCBA, nd); Mrs. Inge took over accompanied by her son in law for the duration of the war and was followed by her daughters: Page, *VCH Rutland* (1908) pp.279–80. Munkwitz: paper, 'Riding Habits', CESH, De Montfort University, 6 September 2016.

[40] Stirling Clarke, *Ladies Equestrian Guide* (1857), Greville, *Ladies in the Field* (1894), Hayes, *The Horsewoman* (1903). Women comprised about 10 per cent of the daily turnout in Leicestershire in 1878 according to Itzkowitz, *Peculiar Privilege* (1977) p.56. The *Manchester Guardian* thought the growing presence of female riders was deplorable (12 December 1900). Yet according to *The Times* (7 March 1952) women and girls were a tiny minority of riders until the growth of subscription packs and pony clubs from the 1920s.

[41] Letter to Thomas Turner, nd (eighteenth century): LRO DE 718/D/96/iii.

recognize that riding a horse was good for your health.[42] They sometimes recognized that women brought special qualities of horsemanship.[43] Fox-hunting was modern and euphoric and dangerous and so too, on occasion, were young women who were instructed how to compel the horse, to animate him, and make him do it.[44]

That all this was personally liberating rather complicated matters. Horse riding offered women the freedom to go where they pleased.[45] Free from prying eyes and flapping skirts, where else could a young woman—or indeed an older one—find the same excitement?[46] Later on, a small coterie of young women would find it climbing Alpine peaks (club founded 1907) and many more would eventually find it playing school lacrosse or college cricket, but when girls really wanted to fly, they went as *riders*. In jumper and jodphurs Amy Johnson was the most famous woman in the world. She carried a Browning and a hundred rounds in her bag.[47]

Hunt convention had it that skirts and riding aprons must not show that the lady had legs, while side-saddles offered the slightly contradictory view that if she did have legs she must not open them. George V banned army officers' wives riding astride, and by the 1930s it was still uncommon enough to be noticed. Women were advised that although 'riding astride has become popular with some', 'the breeches should be exactly like a man's and show four buttons above the boots'.[48] Minna's friend Lady Warrender rode long legged.[49] But none of this mattered once a woman was up and riding. 'Seated as we are high in the air, surrounded by the pure atmosphere, and inhaling it, our elasticity is increased, and an indescribable sense of happiness pervades the whole frame'.[50]

Equestrian guides talked about a lady's 'seat' but Catherine Walters talked about her 'bloody arse'.[51] Hyde Park was the place to take it.[52] Courtesans rode there every day except on Sundays. Walters, or 'Skittles' to her friends, stitched into a riding habit that had been made to measure against her naked body, rode

---

[42] 'After which a cigarette in a lounge on the verandah may be indulged in': Mrs. Martell, 'Riding in Ireland and India', in Greville, *Ladies in the Field* (1894) p.21; Stirling Clarke, *Ladies Equestrian Guide* (1857) p.36.

[43] Stirling Clarke, ibid, p.49.

[44] 'Let's face it, given the chance, who would not want to go really fast on a horse?': Victoria Pendleton, World and Olympic cycling champion, *Sunday Telegraph*, 13 March 2016. It seems all hunts had two or three women who could do these things: Stirling Clarke, *Ladies Equestrian Guide* (1857) p.181, p.212.

[45] From Mary Braddon's *Lady Audley's Secret* (1862), and Dorre, *Cult of the Horse* (2006) p.81.

[46] Ladies were advised to sew lead into their skirts: Carr, *English Fox Hunting* (1976) p.174; Greville, *Ladies in the Field* (1894) Preface. In India, 'you'd go through the villages...': MacMillan, *Women of the Raj* (1988) p.158. Just at the point that fox-hunting was banned, riding and hunting changed Jane Shilling's life with a passion she didn't expect: *The Fox in the Cupboard* (2005).

[47] Amy Johnson, Photo Collection Box 4: Women's Library, London Metropolitan University.

[48] 'Women's Kit' by 'G.G', *Polo and Hunting Journal*, Sept 1925.

[49] Minna's Journal and Scrapbook: LRO DG 51/19.

[50] Stirling Clarke, *Ladies Equestrian Guide* (1857) p.36.   [51] Blyth, *Skittles* (1970) pp.170–2.

[52] *Sporting Magazine*, 1862, p.119.

the finest horses prostitution could buy.[53] Born into a poor family in Toxteth, she was famous in riding circles for her daring (she was said to have taken a Hyde Park railing for £100) and for turning up at the Quorn in 1861 complete with male entourage. The subject of pornographic fiction, Catherine had her moments. Riding a woman was the oldest sexual metaphor. A woman riding took it further. In his 'The Shrew Tamed' at the Royal Academy, Landseer put them together in a single picture.[54] Visiting Frenchman Hyppolyte Taine could hardly take his eyes off the Hyde Park girls, short coats 'well cut to the figure'. That some smoked made the prospect even more exciting. Along with tight collars and stiff wrists, the hunt enjoyed an erotic charge.[55] Riding and smoking were each one of the 'bad paths' a girl could take. Sexual freedom went with personal liberty, and always had done.[56]

We can only speculate about things which even in their own day were not openly talked about. Yet the implication was there all the time. The company was 'racy' as well as horsey. The 'season' was as sexual as well as sporting. Harrods and Harvey Nicks provided the shopping. *Aquascutum* (1853), *Gabardine* (1880), and *Slazenger* (1881) provided the materiel. Early 'pin ups' included female riders and sporting beauties. Splendidly mounted, they go at great pace, stop at nothing, never refuse, and hand the hat round at the end (never looking 'at anything but paper'). 'Ain't he a daisy?' said Lottie to Tottie and Dottie.[57] Written by 'Lilly White' and 'Georgie Shelley', this is the sort of literature where you can never tell if it is written for the amusement of a certain kind of man or a certain kind of woman. Or both. Along with spa towns, free and easy music halls, seaside hotels, French sorties, and country house weekends, fashionable fox-hunting was free from chaperones and, given the opportunity, there was always the chance that women would encounter men behaving badly or at least, extra-maritally: steady drinking, heavy chaffing, kissy games, pranks, and what not.

[53] Taine referred to London's 'meagre' supply of courtesans compared to Paris. London had large numbers of part-time prostitutes however. Friday night in the Strand he referred to as 'a march past of dead women': *Notes on England* (1860–70) p.31. McCreery reckons that prostitution was the most common subject in 18th- and 19th-century prints of women: *Satirical Gaze* (2004) p.49.

[54] Edwin Landseer (1802–73) 'The Shrew Tamed' or 'The Pretty Horsebreaker': Royal Academy (RA) 1861. He said the breaker was Annie Gilbert, who was well known. Others said it was Catherine Walters. On Walters: Anon, *Skittles. Biography of a Fascinating Woman Never Before Published* (1864). The novel ends with Sir Frederick going hunting with 'Carry' Waters and giving her 'the brush' (fox tail) before they slip off to Brussels. 'A List of Sporting Ladies' (Newcastle upon Tyne, D Bass, 1804) surveys the field of local hacks and fillies. Surtees did not like hunt vulgarity but put women into two camps, 'bolters' and 'rearers' all the same: Bradshaw, 'Surtees' (2002) pp.66–8.

[55] *Sporting Magazine*, 1862, p.263; Taine, *Notes on England* (1860–70) p.20, p.70.

[56] Dabhoiwala, 'Lust and Liberty', *Past & Present* (2010) p.108; on bad paths and good paths, *Girls' Own* (1894) and *Seed Time & Harvest* (1908), in Olsen, *Juvenile Nation* (2014) pp.61–4, p.105. On hunting in an erotic way: Nicolson, *The Gentry* (2011) p.110.

[57] Lottie Tottie and Dottie in *The Joker*, 1, i, Saturday 18 July 1891. Beauties included in *The Girl of the Period Almanack* (1869) price 3d: 'Diana Hunting Club' for November ('very few men can live' with the pace; 'most are found wanting at the kill'); 'Atalanta Swimming Club' for January ('leg gracefully extended'), the 'Hero Rowing Club' for June (thirty-five strokes per minute) and others.

There's not much sign of this in a jolly photograph of the Cumberland Hunt Ball at Armathwaite Hall, Bassenthwaite in 1931. A man at the front holds up a fox skin as the sign of a good day out, and the black ties and ball gowns show a lot of effort went into the evening, but this is a formal picture taken before things started to warm up.[58]

We have to allow for the possibility that for all the young women who chose to attend gatherings of this kind who did not know what they were doing, there were those who did. It's not as if hunts lacked a reputation. It's not as if the county didn't talk. According to Whyte-Melville, Cecilia Dove 'would have passed muster as good looking in London' so 'she ought to have been placarded "dangerous" in Leicestershire'. Jane Shilling found her first hunt euphoric, 'same as being in love'. Rachel Johnson provided the more experienced view of what to expect from a country weekend.[59] If Mrs. Stirling Clarke could worry about how a girl might fall into the arms of the wrong sort (the groom) in the yard, it is unlikely that she did not worry about the right sort in the field. For a certain sort of cad, girls and horses went together.[60]

Even so, riding bestowed power.[61] Thorneycroft's small bronze 'Queen Victoria on Horseback' (1853) is a young woman sitting side-saddle. But look again as she trots forward; her riding crop is a sceptre and her small brimmed hat a crown. Above all, she is in control.[62] Margot Tennant, sixth daughter of Sir Charles and Lady Tennant, attended the Beaufort Hunt in 1880. Riding out, she says she went where she wanted. After dinner, she says she was no longer an innocent.[63] Like Minna, Margot went hunting and how she fell was her business.[64]

Devoted to the Horse

In 1854 there were about one hundred top-class packs in Great Britain and Ireland, rising to about 150 by the end of the century. Each hunt met five or six times a week. Subscription packs made it considerably cheaper for all concerned,

[58] Tullie House, Carlisle Record Office (CRO), Acc. No 169.1978.1.

[59] Johnson in *The Guardian*, 20 August 2008; Whyte-Melville, *Market Harborough* (1861) p.68; Shilling in *The Sunday Telegraph*, 9 May 2004.

[60] 'The Pious Horse to church may trot / A maid may work a man's salvation / Four horses and a girl are not / However, aids to reformation': Kipling, in Nicholson, *Almanac of Twelve Sports* (1898) p.3; Stirling Clarke, *Ladies Equestrian Guide* (1857) p.75. Morland painted sportsmen coming upon vulnerable women in darkened woodsides: 'The Lucky Sportsman', Snell, *Spirits of Community* (2016) pp.65–72.

[61] Dorre's *Cult of the Horse* (2006) explores its multiple meanings, some contradictory (p.163).

[62] Thomas Thorneycroft, bronze sculpture: 'Queen Victoria on Horseback' (YCBA 1853).

[63] Ellenberger, *Balfour's World* (2015) p.90–1, p.120.

[64] Mrs. Musters, 'The Wife of the MFH', in Greville, *Ladies in the Field* (1894) p.86.

but still you had to have the time and right connections.[65] Even if a rider just turned up at 11am (no point starting early), he or she would have preferred an invitation or some sort of acknowledgement from the MFH. Some hunts delivered calling cards. Some printed fixtures. Others advertised in the local press.[66] Whatever the method—and invitations to hunt could result in invitations to dine—most people knew what was expected. Willoughby de Broke was right. As an expression of a class that liked to think it ruled by personal relationships, not written rules, the hunt was part of the constitution.[67]

In any case, what else was there to do in the country? Over a long winter season, there was always cards, or sewing, or reading or, for outdoor types, looking out of the window. Everyone had dinner and drinks of course, but hunting sharpened the appetite and brought life to short winter days. Richard Jeffries saw it as a 'gallant show' followed by a 'splendid burst'.[68] Friedrich Engels thought riding with the Cheshire the greatest joy of his life. Henry Greene, another socialist son of the factory-owning classes, concurred. A long hot bath at the end of the day was his luxury of luxuries.[69]

Painters and engravers loved the hunt just as much as they loved the race meeting. You could never go near a hunt in your life and still know that it entailed a Hearty Breakfast, an Excitable Meet, Drawing the Fox, Cracking the Whip, Blowing the Horn, Taking a Gate, Clearing a Bank, Full Cry, Kill, and Coming Home.[70] What to wear? Craxwell's for boots, but brown or cream for tops? Kipward's for coats, but single or double breast? 'A slang looking red coat is the greatest abomination', thought Cecil. Sassoon said he kept to 'the Melton Mowbray standard of smartness'.[71] Scarlet (not for the beginner) looked stunning

[65] Cecil, *Records of the Chase* (1854) pp.407–8; 431–2; *Bailey's Magazine of Sports and Pastimes' List of Hounds* (1895). Subscriptions varied enormously. Against the Quorn's 1919 rate of £35 a day, the Pytchley charged £25 a year for gentlemen and £10 for ladies: Hayes, *The Horsewoman* (1903) p.306. Munkwitz ('Women and Fox Hunting', *Sport in History*, 2017) thinks there were about 400 hunts in 1913–14, which means she must be including lower-grade packs (p.400).

[66] Hunt calling cards: 18th and 19th century: John Johnson, Bodleian, Sports Box 9, and LRO DG 51/109–21. Hunt advertisements, for example: *Newcastle Chronicle*, 1810–11 and *Newcastle Courant* 1820–22.

[67] de Broke, *Sport of Our Ancestors* (1921) p.3; Sassoon, *Fox Hunting Man* (1928) frontispiece. On the iconic status of the country estate to a class who spent a lot of their time in London: Ian Warren, 'English Landed Elite', *English Historical Review*, February 2011.

[68] Jeffries, *Hodge and His Masters* (1949) p.96.

[69] Greene, *Pack My Bag* (1952) p.60; Engels, in Ashton, *Little Germany* (1986) p.62. Dormer wrote to Turville at Bosworth Hall asking what young Mr. George did through the winter: 'does he give the preference to his Gun or his Hunter?': LRO DG 39/1542. See Janet Mullin, *Gaming and the English middle classes 1680–1830* (2015).

[70] Henry Thomas Alken specialized in the full day out, see for instance his *Hunt in Five Prints*, with C. Bentley (London, S & J Fuller, Sporting Gallery, Rathbone Place 1828): John Johnson, Bodleian, Sport Large Box, and Trade Cards Box. See numerous works, for instance in the Yale Centre for British Art (YCBA), by, among others, Neil Cawthorne (1936–), John Dalby (active 1826–53), Lionel Edwards (1878–1966), John Ferneley (1782–1860), Edward Hull (1823–1906), Benjamin Marshall (1767–1835), Francis Calcraft Turner (1782–1846), and John Wootton (1682–1764).

[71] Cecil, *Records of the Chase* (1854) p.389; Sassoon, *Fox Hunting Man* (1928) p.171.

in a frosty landscape. Black looked marvellous against a steel blue sky. Out with the hunt, gentlemen had a chance of resembling a natural aristocracy: widest view, bravest mount, not a creditor in sight.[72]

Slightly downmarket, Surtees' Mr. Jorrocks was President of a Free and Easy at The Pig in Trouble in Oxford Street where 'members may take all sorts of liberties with each other'... 'all sorts of jokes'... 'call each other names, play tricks and practical jokes—like the officers of the 46th'. Jorrocks, the Cockney Grocer & Tea Dealer turned MFH, first appeared in *The New Sporting Magazine* in 1831. A figure of fun who was also capable of seeing things as they actually were, he thought fox-hunting was the sport of kings and the office of MFH 'the highest pinnacle of exhibition'. But 'enough of the rhapsodies let us come to the melodies... *wot will it cost?*'[73]

Riding was the first division of labour. The sports and pastimes of the poor simply did not include it.[74] The sports and pastimes of the rich most certainly did, and they did not go quietly.[75] Alken's *Six Meltonians* (1811) had them 'slapping' and 'swishing' their way across the country. According to Keith Thomas, riding well and bearing arms was early modern England's 'supreme proof of manhood' and there can be no doubt that that didn't change for most of our period.[76] Strutt put gracefulness at its heart. (Rowlandson put weak knees and falling off.) Matthew Arnold recognized field sports as the pre-eminent sign of gentlemanliness in the 1860s. Everyone could forgive a man who rode well.[77]

Most people did not ride. Some worked with horses and enjoyed them, some contrived to work with horses in order to enjoy them, but rarely for sport. There were an estimated 200,000 pit ponies in British coal mines in 1900. Boys were not allowed to ride them (though they did).[78] The regular army's crack regiments were cavalry and its most modern regiments were horse-drawn (by 1917, it stabled

[72] Burke, 'Appeal to the Whigs' (1791) pp.100–1.
[73] Surtees, *Hunts with Jorrocks* (1854) p.66, p.500, p.62. Jorrocks asked 'vot's an MP compared to an MFH?' (p.87).
[74] Strutt, *Sports and Pastimes* (1801) p.19.
[75] See Gould's 1895 cartoon of the 'Tory Village': Readman and Cragoe, *Land Question* (2010) fig 10.1, p.191.
[76] Thomas, *Ends of Life* (2009) p.44. He identifies riding and bearing arms as the supreme virtues to be replaced by the 'technical qualifications of an occupational group'—in other words, professional soldiers (p.69).
[77] Jeffries, *Hodge and His Masters* (1949) p.99; Arnold, *Culture and Anarchy* (1867–9) p.105; Strutt, *Sports and Pastimes* (1801) p.9; Rowlandson, 'Horses and Riders' (1799): John Johnson, Trade & Print Scraps Box 2.
[78] The partial exceptions were stable lads, jockeys, cavalry regiments, and members of the Royal Company of Artillery. It's unlikely that boys went down the pit to ride ponies although working with horses was always a good reason to take an apprenticeship: see the obituary of Albert Marshall (1897–2005), last British survivor of the battle of the Somme, who joined the Essex Yeomanry under age in order to ride, and went on to work for the Essex and Suffolk Hunt: *The Guardian*, 21 June 2005. For the early life of a Georgian stable lad: Holcraft, *Memoirs* (1816). On horses down the mine: Kirkup, *Pit Ponies* (2008). Animal inspections were authorized under the 1911 Coal Mines Act. Very occasionally someone painted a working horse: Charles Towne, 'Billy a Draught Horse age 62', small oil on panel (YCBA 1823).

591,000 horses).[79] It's true that Nimrod and Alken liked to include the occasional mail coach in their gallery of sporting heroes—the men sitting tough, the horses like titans—but this was not riding or sport. It was hard graft.[80]

From the first European cavalry schools in the seventeenth century, horseman-ship was a seen as a gentlemanly performance.[81] But there were no cavalry schools in England and riding drew its best men, and its best mounts, from hunting and racing. In England, it was the Light Brigade not the Heavy that stirred the heart.[82] When the French traveller Taine thought of English power he thought of 'muck foul'd hind quarters'.[83] When the poet spoke of 'Desire', he was not talking of women.[84]

Every town and city had its park or common to ride on. Leicester's Victoria Park was the subject of a furious mid-century spat between the county gentry (Tory) who wanted somewhere to ride, and the municipal authorities (Unitarian) who wanted somewhere to stroll.[85] Fox-hunts and horse races (followed by gangs of riders) could look and sound like military manoeuvres. John Wootton's *George I at Newmarket* (1717) in red coat and sash with riding crop for a field marshal's baton, resembles some of Philippe de Hondt's (1663–1740) pictures of the Duke of Marlborough at war. Wootton's *A Fox Hunt* (1730–40) is also Dutch influenced, and note the touch of menace. Peter Tilleman's *Foxhunting in Wooded Country* (1730) and George Stubbs' *Reapers* (1795) carries the same threat.[86] What Minna liked most certainly did not include violence, but she enjoyed the distinction of not having to worry about it.[87]

Nimrod knew all about this and was careful to bathe it in a patriotic light. Of the Quorn in 1837 he said 'Bonaparte's Old Guard would not have stopped such men as these'.[88] And it is worth remembering that as he said these words the Leicestershire Yeomanry (with many Hunt members) was actively repressing radical and trade union movements in the county, and had been doing so since 1794.[89] The part-time Yeomanry had a poor reputation. In times of trouble,

[79] Rising from 25,000 in 1914, plus 213,000 mules and 47,000 camels: Singleton, 'Britain's Military Use of Horses 1914-18', *Past & Present* (1993) p.178.

[80] Nimrod, *The Chace* (1837) pp.83–4; Alken, 'The Driver of 1832', *Fores's Contrasts* (YCBA 1852).

[81] Worsley, 'Cavaliers', *History Today* (2004) p.9. 17c 'manege' is now called 'dressage'.

[82] Abler, *Warriors* (1999) p.2.   [83] Taine, *Notes on England* (1860–70) p.100.

[84] 'I saw her at Four running loose in a field': Fothergill, *Twenty Sporting Designs* (1911).

[85] Jeremy Crump, 'Horse-racing and liberal governance', *Sport in History* (2016).

[86] On raiders: 'under cover of a great hunting' Sir William Selby organized 'a great assembly' to confront Border robber gangs: letter, Selby to Sir William Lawson, 19 May 1606: CRO D PEN/216. See also 'Surveys of Reivers 1542-1550', in Charlton, *North Tyndale* (1871) p.31. Wootton's *Fox Hunt* and *George I at Newmarket* are to be seen in the YCBA. See also Egerton, *British Sporting and Animal Painting* (1978).

[87] 'Those who are held to be distinguished have the privilege of not worrying about their distinc-tion": Bourdieu, *Distinction* (1979) p.246.

[88] Nimrod, *The Chace* (1837) pp.35–7.

[89] Raised to repel French invaders, the Yeomanry's six troops (300 men) spent most of their time repelling Leicestershire bread rioters (1795), Luddites (1811), Hampden Clubs (1817), Radical Reformers (1819,1832), Chartists (1842, 'Battle of Mowmaker Hill'), and workhouse rioters (1848):

magistrates preferred regulars. In Birmingham, calling out volunteers, they thought, would look 'highly improper ... particularly obnoxious ... [and] inflame the minds of the people'.[90] As for the infamous activities of the Manchester and Salford Yeomanry at 'Peterloo' in Manchester on Monday 16 August 1819, their attack on the crowd was in print almost as soon as it happened. Tegg's 'Britons Strike Home!', shows fat soldiers on horses hacking away at thin people on foot: 'Down with 'em! Chop 'em down my brave boys! give 'em no quarter'. Henry Hunt, the speaker, recalled them slicing into the demonstrators. Samuel Bamford, one of the sliced at, remembered them dismounting, easing their saddle girths, and carefully wiping the blood from their sabres.[91]

Fox-hunting represented the power of the county at its most vivid. Assheton-Smith returned to his old mastership of the Quorn and a brigade of two thousand hunters turned up to cheer.[92] Count Ernst Saxe Coburg, who didn't understand these things, thought they were cheering him. Assheton-Smith had been introduced to Napoleon's officers in 1802 as 'le premier chasseur de l'Angleterre'. Wellington during the French campaign unkenneled his hounds twice a week, 'as if he had been a denizen of Leicestershire'. There was hardly a cavalry regiment in the British Empire that did not hunt when it could.[93] In battle, the cavalry charge was deemed ineffectual without the Full Cry.[94] Wolseley's description of a cigar-smoking staff officer in battle riding in full view of the line—up and down, 'cool to the utmost extent'—was a Meltonian as Meltonians liked to see themselves.[95] Heavy cavalry was a one way smash.[96] Light cavalry, like the hunt, was alert, all seeing, free to turn and chase. The hunt knew its power, and cast it across the land. When George Berkeley saw hunters, he thought he saw raiders.[97] When Daniel Defoe saw dragoons, he thought he saw huntsmen. The British army

---

Temple Patterson, *Radical Leicester* (1954). Sometimes the Yeomanry caused disturbances rather than quelled them—as for instance, when drunk at the theatre (p.377). Meanings change. On 25 September 1916 Capt. Breacher of 8th Battalion Leicestershire Regiment rallied the ranks by sounding the Quorn Hunt Tally Ho! at Guendecourt, Battle of the Somme: Ts account, LRO DE 6007/376. Leicester City Football Club adopted the Post Horn Gallop before home games in 1941, and the 'Fox and Crop' badge in 1948.

[90] To deter food riots: letter to Home Department (later Home Office), 2 March 1815: Home Office (HO), National Archives 42/143.

[91] Hunt, *Memoirs* (1822) vol. iii, p.615; Bamford, *Life of a Radical* (1848) p.153. 'The Peterloo Massacre' as it was called, saw eleven to eighteen killed and over 400 wounded. Tegg's print claimed to be published on the same day as the massacre: S. Tegg, 'Britons Strike Home!' (Cheapside, 16 August 1819).

[92] 20 March 1840: Itzkowitz, *Peculiar Privilege* (1977) p.86.

[93] ibid; MacFarlane, *Life of Wellington* (1886) p.114.

[94] Glover, *Peninsular Preparation* (1963) p.137.

[95] 'It is an indispensable qualification for a staff officer that he should be able to ride well': Wolseley, *Soldier's Pocket Book* (1869) p.15, 28, 10.

[96] Just prior to the General Strike in May 1926 the 2nd Battalion Leicestershire Regiment was put on full alert but instructed to be low key and cautious: no machine guns, no swords, and no officer's chargers: LRO DE 6007/175.

[97] Quiller Couch, ed., *Oxford Book of English Prose* (1925) p.376.

remained devoted to the horse well into the 1930s. Right into the 1950s, military men dominated field sports.[98]

Not that Minna and friends wanted to ride Leicestershire hosiery workers into the ground. It was just the fox they wanted, and on 8 January 1919 at a meeting in the County Assembly Rooms, the Quorn was reconstituted after a break of five years. Minna's husband Algernon and Mr. Paget of Nanpantan Hall were accepted as joint masters. A month later, Algy thanked the hunt for the honour: no better sport, jolly good fun, must keep the farmers happy, and so on. Both masters had county pedigrees. William Edmund Paget, formerly of the Leicestershire Yeomanry, was the son of a former Master of the Quorn. Algernon Edwyn Burnaby, acting Master of the Quorn, formerly of the Royal Horse Guards, had served on hunt committees since 1905, was the grandson of a former High Sheriff, and son of the man who had given a famous hunt breakfast for the Prince of Wales. Subscriptions were agreed (regulars £35 per day per week, occasionals £50, strangers up to £100), and so were subsidies to the tune of £4,000 a year to Paget and Burnaby apiece.[99] These were huge sums. First meet would be at Kirby Gate in November, which was accompanied by a nice photograph in *The Daily Graphic*. There's no sign of Minna, but we can see the joint masters and their huntsman paying a lot of attention to the camera; horses and hounds not paying any.[100]

As a county councillor and the member for Gaddesby, as a magistrate and occasional supporter of Melton Conservative Association, Burnaby represented his county in the only way he knew but not really in a way that was to his taste. When he talked about the burden of public service etc, this is what he meant: not his bag, do it all the same. As the owner of historic Baggrave Hall however, and as a soldier who had served his country in youth and middle age, and as a gentleman farmer and spokesman for county agriculture through lean times, and as a loyal supporter of the parish church, the village hall, and the Royal British Legion, and as Master of the Quorn—a dashing role which brought all the other roles to life— in all these things Algy was playing to his strengths. In a town and county that could still with some justification claim to be founded on small family firms, and farms, Tory paternalism had, as the sociologists used to say, a material base. Algy's social round was one of a thousand small exchanges, shakes of the hand, looks in the eyè, mutterings of encouragement, and so forth, life and soul of a national Conservative and Unionist Party of one and a half million members but many, many more supporters. How he dressed mattered, and was noted. How he spoke mattered, and was noted. How Minna dressed and spoke mattered just the same.

---

[98] On the British Field Sports Society: May, *Fox-Hunting Controversy* (2013) p.44. Defoe, *Tour* (1724–26) p.139.

[99] Quorn Hunt Minute Book, 26 January 1905, 8 January, 5 February 1919: LRO DE 857/1, DE 857/4; *Star*, 27 January 1919; *Sporting Life* (25 January 1919); *Melton Times* (14 February 1919); *Handbook Quorn Hounds* (Melton 1918): LRO DG 51/109–21.

[100] *Daily Graphic* (11 November 1919).

How they spent their money and where they put themselves were not things of small moment although of course that is exactly what they were and why they mattered so much. His family had been there forever. Their wedding anniversary filled Baggrave Hall with guests, not all of them rich. Like Marx's unalienated man, Algy filled his diary with business in the morning, hunting in the afternoon, and public life in the evening. He got around. In a country busy putting up war memorials his record was impeccable, his style Meltonian, his humour droll. As a young army officer he had steeple-chased through the night in a lady's nightdress. As MFH, the nightdress had been discarded but Algy still liked to banter with the ladies: 'don't mind jumping on that hound there! Plenty more in the kennel'.[101]

Most Conservative supporters were women and, like them, Minna knew how to keep up. Minna knew how to keep up. Small and sharp and American, there was hardly a hair of her head that the local press did not notice. She opened grand bazaars and sales of work. She arrived at garden fetes in a hat and left dinner dances in a shawl. She lined up with the District Nursing Board. She visited Leicester Prison. She judged puppy shows, pony shows, and baby shows, and she enjoyed her more egregious moments in the enclosure at Leicester Races, or being fined £1 for speeding in her coupe in Spencefield Lane. Minna played her part. She rode with the best, learned to fly in jodphurs, played golf in flatties, raised money, distributed alms, and kept a pet fox. When the occasion demanded it, she led the ladies: 'Leicestershire's hard riding women, clad in saturated habits and heavily plastered with mud which made them almost unrecognizable, were nevertheless thoroughly happy when they dismounted at Twyford yesterday'.[102]

It was a full life poured into short winter days, right across the country, a thousand hunts a week, every winter.[103] It wasn't only about earning a living, or having fun, or patrolling the land, and it wasn't at all about keeping the fox population down. A class that Thorstein Veblen called 'the leisure class' with its roots in 'the higher stages of the barabarian culture' now preferred to see itself as the up-to-date sporting set.[104] What Minna liked was the beginning of the modern era.

Fay ce que voudras

English counties were governed by overlapping circles of landowners, parish officials, clerics, and justices of the peace. In 1884–85 these circles were ruptured, in theory at least, when the franchise was extended to agricultural labourers. Local government Acts in 1888 and 1894 went on to democratize county

---

[101] Obituary, Minna's Journal and Scrapbook, inc. *Horse and Hound,* 31 January 1931 and note, Claridge's 1937: LRO DG 51/19. On inter-war Conservatism: Ball, *Portrait of a Party* (2013) ch 3.
[102] 'Modern Dianas Revel in Mud': ibid.
[103] On ritual as legitimation: Langford, *Eighteenth Century* (2002) p.208.
[104] Veblen, *Leisure Class* (1899) p.1.

administration. Elected councillors stepped forward and county grandees stepped back.[105] But these were also times of agricultural depression and as the value of the land fell and the authority of the gentry wilted, it was one of the great paradoxes of English life that the land came to seem even more important and its symbolic power, perforce, took on extra meaning.[106] In a country rarely given to excessive displays of national identity, the MFH was rural England's prime sporting ornament. Where he led, others followed. When the hunt swept up to the brow of a hill, England belonged to them.[107]

Aristocrats were used to going where they liked, and their parks and estates were designed to give them the feeling that they could. The four hundred peers and 1288 great landowners who owned 40 per cent of England and Wales in 1875 certainly didn't lack land or liberty.[108] The Duke of Beaufort's 700 square miles was all a freeborn Englishman could ride in a day. Sir Richard Sutton was fond of saying 'I go where I like' and the Quorn pretty much gave him the opportunity. Four earls of Lonsdale said the same of the Cottesmore.[109]

In 1782 the young Prussian clergyman C P Moritz was shocked at the free and easy behaviour of MPs in the House of Commons. They cracked nuts, peeled oranges, called out, stood up, sat down, waved, and generally did what they liked in front of the Speaker.[110] Do as you like, go where you like, *Fay ce que voudras* as you like, words carved above the front door of Hambleton Hall in Rutland, built in 1881 as a hunting lodge for Walter Marshall, shipping magnate.[111] This was a liberty founded on land: not fancy, or an opinion, but something grounded, like the country itself, in what these people owned. For Matthew Arnold, 'Doing As One Likes' was the main theme of English life and part of the anarchy that typified it.[112] 'Town Spy' thought if every lady and gent was fined 5s for swearing as they liked, the National Debt could be cleared, with further fines 'for all Oaths at the Groom-porters and at the Horse racing, Prize-fighting, and Cocking...'.[113] Tories claimed any Englishman could do as he liked be he a lord or a tinker, and this was

---

[105] Joanna Innes, in Langford, *Eighteenth Century* (2002) p.131; Cannadine, *British Aristocracy* (1990) refers to 'the inexorable dilution of patrician society' in this period (p.353).

[106] As 'the new rich continued to pour into the countryside': Cannadine, ibid, p.367; Readman, *Land and Nation* (2008) pp.86–94.

[107] For England as an Arcadian ideal and the English gentry as its custodians: Nicolson, *Earls of Paradise* (2008) and *The Gentry* (2011).

[108] Based on Bateman's Land Return, based in turn on Parliamentary Return of Owners of Land, 1875–6, Table 3/2, Land Ownership by Class 1872: Cahill, *Who Owns Britain?* (2001) p.45.

[109] Carr, *English Fox Hunting* (1976) p.115; Page, *VCH Rutland* (1908) p.302. Under the 5th Earl, the Cottesmore comprised 360 square miles.

[110] Moritz, *Travels in England* (1782) p.43.

[111] Words from Rabelais and the Hell Fire Club, Marshall was a sometime member of the Quorn, the Cottesmore, the Belvoir, and the Fernie.

[112] Arnold, *Culture & Anarchy* (1867–69) p.83.

[113] Anon., or 'The Town Spy', *View of London and Westminster* (1728) p.4.

undoubtedly true.[114] All the tinker required to hunt was a horse, a meet, a certain distinction, £50, and the train fare home.

All was not what it seemed however. Behind the gentry's commanding prospects lay all who would bar their way—from vexed farmers and cussed gamekeepers to angry villagers, huffy landowners, rival hunters, awkward riders and, according to Sassoon, a vicar who stood by his garden gate shouting 'Brutes!' George Osbaldeston's entire mastership seems to have been a battle with those who cut him or crossed him. 'It is almost impossible to give universal satisfaction to the Meltonian', he thought.[115] Lord Lonsdale told the Quorn that the first duty of mastership was not sport but managing other landowners:

> I should like to lay plainly before before you my views as to the position and the duties I am undertaking, that there may be no mistake hereafter. I by no means place the actual fox-hunting as the first of such duties, rather that all consideration and consulting of their convenience be paid to landlords and covert owners, equally to all tenants and occupiers of land. Subject to this, I will try all means in my power to show you sport.[116]

Which is to say, whatever sport these people enjoyed, it rested upon landlordism.[117] Whole estates could be turned to fox-hunting and in the face of all the money and effort that went into it, one shot fox was a violation. Sportsmen called it 'vulpicide', a crime followed in hunt loathing only by 'chopping', which killed them in their covert, or 'bagging', which brought them in in a bag. Why shoot the fox when we want to chase it? Why chop it when we want to kill it? Why have a hunting policy at all when you can bring it in a bag?[118]

Masters faced an endless stream of bills for covert rents, road tolls, fence damage, drainage, wire, stabling, kenneling, licensing, feeding, vets, tradesmen, and hunt servants, not to mention the boots and bridles, whips and saddles, caps and jackets, and all the dinners that were as much a part of the show as the chase itself. In 1837 master's costs were estimated at a minimum of £2,235 a year or, to put it in perspective, being willing and able to fork out £52 (or a year's income for a farm labourer) to host a champagne lunch in the Bull's Head, Loughborough.[119]

---

[114] Anthony Trollope, quoted in Carr, *English Fox Hunting* (1976) pp.72–4.

[115] Osbaldeston, *Autobiography* (1856) p.110 and pp. 52, 93, 115.

[116] Hugh Lowther, 5th Lord Lonsdale, to Quorn Hunt Committee, County Assembly Rooms, Leicester, 1 January 1897 Quorn Hunt Minutes: 1884–1913: LRO DE 857/1. See also Sassoon, *Fox Hunting Man* (1928) p.207.

[117] Wentworth Fitzwilliam to Lord Lowther, 25 December 1880: CRO D Lons/21/2/54.

[118] For examples of 'vulpicide': *Sportsman's Magazine* (23 January 1847); 'Atrocity in Hunting Field', *Eclipse* (5 January 1863); 'Fox Murder in Herts', *Bell's Life* (13 June 1868). The calling card of the City Hounds promised a bagged fox on 10 April 1799: John Johnson, Bodleian, Sport Box 9.

[119] Lunch bill to Capt. Warner, Joint Master of the Quorn, 23 October 1868: LRO, DE 3030/148; for all the bills and all the worries, Quorn Hunt Minutes, 1884–1913: LRO DE 857/1. For costs: Nimrod, *The Chace* (1837) p.15.

The Quorn and Cottesmore were subscription packs where subscribers guaranteed a certain subsidy to the master who in turn paid the kennel bills and managed the country. When he became MFH, Mr. Jorrocks promised to take his hat off only to *paying* subscribers, and was roundly cheered for it, though how strict masters were, or could be, is open to question. The Cottesmore's subscriptions were written up in an old school exercise book. In 1919 the Quorn adopted a complex fee structure that proved ineffectual.[120] In any case, fashionable hunts didn't really need accounts because they could usually clear debts in a day. In 1884 the Quorn raised £680 at one go in the Bell Hotel Leicester, and £1,000 in the County Rooms the following year. In 1889 the Cottesmore resolved to build new stables and cottages and £7,000 was guaranteed there and then from ten members. A £60 whip round for 'Drew the Jockey', who broke his neck at Brighton Races riding *Pellucid*, finished the matter in moments. He was 21 years old.[121]

Algy accepted his Quorn mastership with a gracious speech thanking the farmers for not making too many claims. Mr. Crawford responded on behalf of the farmers.[122] Disagreements usually turned on the fundamental problem of rearing and protecting animals in order to kill them. No farmer liked foxes (in 1897 the Quorn had to stand a £300 poultry bill), not to mention the associated problem of horses trampling crops, frightening livestock, and getting tangled up in wire. In 1886, two farmers got themselves elected to the Quorn Hunt Committee. At first, they were ignored, then they were resisted, Mr. Roberts carrying the meeting in his view that 'it was better that these matters should be left in the hands of the gentry'. He didn't want any unpleasantness. Neither did the farmers. That is why they persisted although to what end it is difficult to say.[123] In 1894, an Old Dalby farmer took MFH Warner and Huntsman Firr to Court of Queen's Bench for trespass and damage after a hundred riders trampled his winter wheat and frightened his sheep and cattle. He claimed the loss of three ewes and thirty-five calves and it would appear that at first the hunt had been unwilling to negotiate—which was unusual because all hunting, not just fox-hunting, was underwritten by a complex web of negotiation and consent.[124]

As for hunting with firearms, up in Cumberland Will Tinker and Norman Parker did not have permission to shoot on Lord Lonsdale's land; but Wilfred Lawson did. James Stainbank had 'a great desire' to keep a greyhound; but Lord Lowther had a greater desire that he didn't. Lord Lowther kept dogs; but couldn't

---

[120] There were constant short falls in payment. The hunt did not exist only to chase foxes: eg Quorn Hunt Minutes, 1919: LRO 857/14; and Surtees, *Handley Cross* (1854) p.87.

[121] *Eclipse*, 10 August 1863; Quorn Hunt Minutes, 5 April 1884, 27 February 1885: LRO DE 857/14; Cottesmore Hunt Minutes, 24 July 1889: LRO DG 37/194.

[122] *Leicestershire Mail*, 6 February 1919.

[123] Farmers, Quorn Hunt Minutes, 28 April–19 June 1886: LRO DE 857/1.

[124] Poultry, Quorn Hunt Minutes, 27 October 1897: LRO DE 857/1; documents relating to high court action of William Willoughby, 21 February 1894: LRO DE 603.

keep them off his tenants' sheep.[125] Wire fencing was an especially cheap and effective guard for the farmer; but invisible and treacherous for horse and rider. No farmer liked foxes. No hunter liked wire. In December 1903 the Quorn entered into one of its many wire negotiations, this time at Ashby Folville. When negotiations broke down, there was always the ultimate threat of changing tenancy agreements because, in the end, fox-hunting depended upon the deference of English tenant farmers[126] A country of stroppy peasants would have made it impossible. In February 1915 the British army stopped fox hunting in France after complaints from *les paysans*.[127]

Farmers could be awkward, but in the end, like the hounds, they were usually biddable. The labouring poor showed little interest in fox-hunting except as a chance to earn a few shillings. It was difficult to know why they would want to chase foxes anyway, except as vermin. Whatever the reason, '... as of late it has been a very general Practice of the Labourers and Idle People to take foxes, greatly to the injury of Sir H Harpur's Hunt'.[128] But some landowners could be very difficult, daring to disoblige other landowners, and rival hunts could be worse. There were bitter disputes during the 1880s between the Quorn and the South Quorn, later called The Fernie.[129] Disputes like these were almost colonial, centring on borders and resources, particularly covert rights. Cecil laid it down that 'a gentleman resident in the country would be very reluctant to render himself so unpopular [to refuse use of his covert] even if he were not on friendly terms with the master of hounds'. Equally, he opined that no gentleman could be made MFH without 'the consent of the majority of the most influential owners of coverts'. A man who could not bear to see horsemen on his land ought to give up his land, thought Trollope.[130]

But what if Trollope was wrong? What when gentlemanliness failed? What if the landowner did not feel that which all landowners were meant to feel? Given that the fox did not understand the laws of trespass and went where it willed, and given that it was the will of the hunt (an Englishman's liberty) to follow, then the outcome was usually a question of who could get their way—the obliging hunt or the disobliging landowner? In 1820, Mr. Legh-Keck of Stoughton Grange in Leicestershire admitted to the Earl of Denbigh that it was perfectly true that Mrs. Legh-Keck had objected to the Quorn drawing their fox in her spinney.

---

[125] Permissions to shoot: CRO D LONS L1/3/9/34–177; letters, Mr. Sowden to Mr. Armitage, 22, 24 September 1750: CRO D LONS/L5/2/11/251.

[126] Quorn Hunt Minutes, December 1903: LRO DE 859/1; on tenancies, printed letter from MFH to all members and landowners, Blackmore Vale Hunt, Stourhead, 27 May 1896: John Johnson, Bodleian, Sport Box 9.

[127] Riedi & Mason, 'Leather', *Canadian Journal* (2006) p.492.

[128] Letter on behalf of Sir H Harpur, Calke, Derbyshire to Mrs. Curzon, Breedon on the Hill, Leicestershire, 13 March 1770: LRO DE 1536/390.

[129] 'unexampled bitterness': Page, *VCH Rutland* (1908) pp.273–5; Quorn Hunt Minutes, 16 February to 7 June 1888: LRO DE 857/1.

[130] Trollope, *British Sports* (1868) p.74; Cecil, *Records of the Chase* (1854) pp.49–50.

But it was indubitably not the case that her gamekeeper had shot their fox (if indeed it was their fox). Writing to a peer of the realm, Mr. Legh-Keck assured his correspondent that they were loyal supporters of the hunt &c &c but as a substantial landowner, a longstanding MP for the county, and Lt. Col. Commandant of the Leicestershire Yeomanry, he was clearly not going to be pushed around. Legh-Keck's politics were almost as Tory as the noble Earl's and, firing salvoes on his wife's behalf from the battlements of their Leicestershire castle, he must have thought that he had won the day. Not a bit of it. A few days later, the letter from Hell arrived. It came, according to *Bailey's*, from none other than 'the greatest sportsman the world ever knew since the days of the Assyrian Nimrod'. Mr. George Osbaldeston, expelled from Eton, recipient of a good 4th at Oxford, and one day to be thrown out of the MCC but for the time being Master of the Quorn, informed the Legh-Kecks that he was pleased to hear they supported the hunt, that he looked forward to testing their facilities 'in every possible shape', and that he would call upon them at the earliest opportunity.[131]

The story of George Osbaldeston's rushing of the Legh-Kecks can be contrasted with the story of Lord Lonsdale's two letters. Lonsdale's pack had been hunting in the Tring and Woburn area (they'd travelled down from Cumberland by train) and had run a fox to ground in another hunt's covert. The local gamekeeper had not minced his words and in their subsequent exchange of letters the two masters disagreed as to what precisely happened next. Major Hope, writing on behalf of the Oakley, accused Lonsdale's party of violating hunt law by digging the fox out. Lonsdale, writing from Carlton House Terrace, St James's, drafted two letters. One said sorry, never do it again, deep regret, *all that*. The other accused Hope's gamekeeper of a fondness for drink and fisticuffs and hinted that even if the fox had been dug out, it was not he the MFH who had ordered it but the Master of Harriers—in hunt etiquette, a completely different thing.[132] Not every dispute was so finely tuned. In 1860 Mr. Clowes asked the well-named Mr. Packe to contribute £500 towards Lord Stamford's Quorn. Packe took his time before writing back to say no.[133]

There had been legal judgements in 1786 and 1809 on the line between consent granted and assumed, but sporting men preferred to sort it out for themselves. The

---

[131] G. A. Legh-Keck to Denbigh, 11 February 1820, and Osbaldeston of Quorndon Hall to Legh-Keck, 20 February 1820: LRO DE 2515, Bewicke Ms; *Bailey's Magazine*, Itzkowitz, *Peculiar Privilege* (1977) p.103. Col George Anthony Legh Keck (1774–1860), of Stoughton Grange, Leicestershire, and Bank Hall, Bretherton, Lancashire, had been forced to abandon his Leicestershire parliamentary seat in 1818 due to his opposition to popular radicalism in the county: Simon Harrett, in Fisher, ed., *History of Parliament 1820–32* (2009). Osbaldeston was in the process of squandering a fortune while living the sporting life.

[132] Hope to Lonsdale, 28 November 1849, and Lonsdale, draft letters, 30 November 1849: CRO D LONS L1/2/154.

[133] Mr. Clowes of Woodhouse Eaves to Charles William Packe, Branksome Towers, Poole, Dorset and Prestwold Hall, Leicestershire, 21 December 1860; Packe to Clowes, 5 January 1861: LRO DE 5047/113/1–2.

Jockey Club and the Pugilistic Society had each been founded to control their own sports in their own way but hunting countries were far more difficult to manage.[134] An informal hunt arbitration committee was set up at Boodles in 1856 that eventually became The Hunt Masters' Association in 1881, but with no great success. And no wonder. Rules on digging and drawing admitted that drawing was not necessarily the same thing as digging but drawing without digging might require the use of a terrier (which could not be borrowed).[135]

In the end, the hunt's desire to go where it will was not restricted to set permissions inside carefully delineated boundaries. It depended on the dynamic interplay of occasionally head-strong gentlemen managing land they knew and owned, or managing others to manage it for them.[136] That success in these matters could not always be guaranteed paved the way for more convenient equestrian events in the form of 'Point to Point', or Gymkhana, or National Hunt. Point to Point is cross country racing over fences for amateur riders, often farmers. The phrase was first used in *Bell's Life* in 1874 concerning a meeting convened by the 9th Lancers. Gymkhana, usually for children, or 'eventing', usually for serious riders, is competitive jumping. National Hunt was and is the professional version of Point to Point where race courses are built to resemble hunting countries with water jumps, high fences, dead drops and all the chance of a fall.[137] Flat racing remained the supreme English sport well into the 1930s, but if the Epsom Derby (1780) brought all sorts of people together, fresh out of London, the Grand National (1839) brought the whole nation together, fresh out of the bookies. Everyone knew about Becher's Brook and Valentine's even if the nearest they came to these jumps was losing a bet.[138]

In a similar vein, 'coursing' (two greyhounds matched cross country against a hare), emerged as another version of hunting without the difficulty, just as greyhound track racing was the urban version of coursing without the hare. Based on betting and breeding but with hounds, both sports dressed in the horsey fashion, raced in the horsey fashion, and bestowed names in the horsey fashion—a mixture of the classical ('Leander'), the popular ('Toddlin Hame'), and the exemplary ('Beeswing'). Cumbrian coursing was dominated by farmers but could be grand enough for gentlemen (Waterloo Cup) and cheap enough for labourers

---

[134] Henricks, *Disputed Pleasures* (1991) ch 6. Jockey Club was founded in 1750, Pugilistic Society in 1814.

[135] Itzkowitz, *Peculiar Privilege* (1977) pp.68–74.

[136] The fourteen hunting packs of the British Army of the Rhine were disbanded in October 1952 after the Prime Minister acceded to local demands about to be reflected in the Bundestag. British army officers, in other words, could not manage their estates. In 1948 Mr. Churchill had turned out with the Old Surrey and Burstow Hunt on his 74th birthday.

[137] Cheltenham Steeple Chase, five miles distant, described by Rev. Witts in the 1830s: Witts, *Cotswold Parson* (1979) p.134.

[138] Horse racing still dominated the front and middle pages of the sporting press into the 1920s. The *Daily Telegraph* said it witnessed an 'annual intermixture of all classes unknown beneath the sun' at The Derby (26 May 1864).

(2s 6d to join a subscription club in 1821). At a meeting at Brampton in 1870, entry fee was 5s on a horse and 1s on foot. If you challenged the judge, fine £5. If your dog got loose, fine 10s. It cost 7 guineas to have your bitch 'served' at a stud in 1905.[139]

Classic racing was on the flat by young horses over short distances, headquarters at Newmarket. National Hunt racing was over jumps by older horses over longer distances, headquarters at Cheltenham. Both depended for their popularity on betting and betting depended for its national popularity on rapidly published results, provided by newspapers, including penny results papers like *Sporting Snips* and *Turf Times*. A minor industry of form books and racing manuals allowed punters to repent at their leisure. If National Hunt was fox-hunting without the fuss, or the fox, fox-hunting was National Hunt without the *hoi poloi*.[140] Apart from the betting, racing and hunting had a lot in common, including hard caps, the chance of injury, and aristocratic patronage—especially at the most fashionable venues. Nimrod thought racing, for all its high style, induced anxiety and bad company while hunting induced health and happiness. McKibbin thinks that without the betting, there would have been almost no interest in racing.[141] The 1925 Ascot Gold Cup attracted owners Lords Astor, Derby, Rosebery, H. H. Aga Khan, and H. H. Maharaja of Rajpipla. The owner of the winning horse 'Santorb' was Mr. Barclay Walker of the Liverpool brewing family. (James) Rhodes was named as trainer and the jockey (Steve Donaghue) wasn't mentioned at all. In 1932 the Quorn Annual General Meeting attracted a field only slightly less distinguished, including HRH Prince of Wales, Earl Lonsdale, the Marquis of Blandford, Lord Crawshaw, and Miss Fox, naturally.[142]

---

[139] Race cards, CRO D/CL/P/9/2 and D/ING/164; studbooks, Wilson, *VCH Cumberland* (1905) pp.457–61; Wensleydale subscription rules 1821: John Johnson, Bodleian, Sport Box 2.

[140] John Johnson, Bodleian, Sport Box 11 and 12; Quorn AGM: LRO DE 857/14. The racing press and art market made much of the crowds: Derby Day was the biggest in the calendar (*Sportsmen's Magazine*, 7 June 1845) but see Charles Turner (1773–1857), 'An Extensive View of the Oxford Races' (YCBA nd), and Thomas Rowlandson, 'A Crowded Race Meeting' (YCBA 1805–10).

[141] McKibbin, *Classes and Cultures* (1998) p.355; Huggins, *Horse Racing* (2003) pp.8–31; and Eadie, 'English Horse Racing 1830-60', Oxford DPhil (1993). Racing sought to encourage gentry money into the towns. See for instance notes on racing in Abingdon borough and at Oxford Port Meadows: Challenor, *Borough of Abingdon* (1898), and *Oxford Journal* (7 August 1819). Nimrod's reflections on health and stress: *The Chace* (1837) p.119. On hard caps, Alphabet book, *Trades and Characters* (nd 1850s?), John Johnson, Bodleian, Sport Box 10: ' "H" is for Hunts-man, "J" is for Jockey'. When sportsmen competed for stakes and wagers, riding or walking, they did so in jockey silks and caps. See for instance: Thomas Rowlandson, 'Capt Barclay's Rally Match—the Finish' (YCBA 1809), when the celebrated Barclay wagered W. W. Webster that he could walk 1,000 miles in 1,000 hours for 1000 guineas; and Henry Alken, 'G Osbaldeston Esq Performing His Wonderful and Unprecedented Feat of 200 Miles against Time', which he did in ten hours (YCBA 1831).

[142] Ascot Gold Cup official programme 18 June 1925: John Johnson, Bodleian, Sport Box 11; Quorn Minutes, 22 March 1932: LRO DE 857/14.

In hunting, disputes over honour could linger on for years. In racing, turf accountants settled matters in minutes as only money can.[143]

Masters

Masters of Fox Hounds usually put themselves near the upper reaches of a county hierarchy that started with the lord lieutenancy at the top and ended with a seat on the magistrates' bench near the bottom. In Warwickshire, MFH de Broke put himself second after the Lord Lieutenant—higher than all the big landowners and clergy, and way higher than MPs. Many saw the MFH as an idealization of the independent propertied Englishman, 'one in blood and interest with his tenants' and simple in his tastes even if, being at liberty, 'occasionally running riot a little'.[144]

There was no shortage of obituaries that reflected the type. Farquharson of the Dorset, Williams Wynn of the Shropshire, Fane of the South Oxfordshire, Priestman of the Braes of Derwent, Greenall father and son of the Belvoir, Annely of the Pytchley, Col. Alan Percy of the Percy, and Lord Lonsdale of the Cottesmore (and the Pytchley, the Blankney, and the Quorn) were all portrayed as born leaders, usually with an army background, embedded in their own counties if not always to be found there.[145] Percy rode with his own hounds in his own earldom, but Greenall the Lancashire brewer and Lonsdale the Cumbrian coal-owner hunted far from home. The Quorn specialized in non-Leicestershire men but that didn't matter as long as they were gentlemen.[146] Reciprocity was part of the business.[147] Gifts of game were powerful signifiers; as were fox cubs.[148] Sometimes, gentlemen raised their fists, as when MFH Lord Daresbury (Toby Greenall), formerly of the Lifeguards, took on MFH Captain Filmer-Sankey, same

---

[143] Tattersall's was the clearing house for bets on 'Settling Day': Egan, *Book of Sports* (1832) p.184. Pollard's 'Epsom Races. The Betting Post' (YCBA 1834–5) shows hundreds of mounted men jostling each other and bookies alike.

[144] Nimrod, *Life of a Sportsman* (1842) p.349. On being one blood with his tenants, see obituary of Maj Thomas Guy Paget, *The Times*, 13 March 1952. Willoughby de Broke is cited in Cannadine, *British Aristocracy* (1990) p.356.

[145] Farquharson's obituary praised him as a 'landlord, father, magistrate and friend' who hunted at his own expense: *Bell's Life*, 14 February 1858; Williams Wynn, *Eclipse*, 12 January 1863; Col. John Fane, *Sporting Chronicle*, 24 November 1875; Priestman, Greenall, and Annely, in Bradley, *Shire to Shire* (1912) pp.34–40, 115, 227–30, 172; Percy is in *Newcastle Journal*, 4 October 1930.

[146] Page, *VCH Rutland* (1908) pp.270–1.

[147] We find the Duke of Beaufort asking Fortescue Turville for that 'sole Priviledge' (sic) to hunt which his father had enjoyed: letter, from Gosport camp to Turville at Bosworth Hall. 5 November 1803: LRO DG 39/1602. When the younger Turville was denied hunting rights by Lord Shrewsbury ('answered very coolly') he grumbled at length to his father: letter, 15 October 1808: LRO DG 39/1763.

[148] For example, H. Ainslie to Lord Lowther, 12 September 1829, 23 August 1830, 9 October 1833, and special gift of deer, W. Armitage to Sir James Lowther, and Robert Marker to W. Armitage, 20 September 1750: CRO L1/2/63.

regiment, in a Leicestershire covert, one in collar and tie, the other in flannels and tennis shoes.[149]

Not all masters conformed to the hero myth. Hunt mythology worked in its favour, but self-deprecating hunt banter worked against. Many riders were freeloaders out for the day. They may have paid their fees, but not their dues. Worse, they might be poor riders liable to lose face in front of bumpkins on a gate looking for a laugh. Although the main thing was not to be laughed at, or censured, in the land of the Charge of the Light Brigade it was difficult to tell where brave riding ended and risky riding began.[150] Sometimes the chaffing was so strong that those who could ride called those who couldn't Meltonians too, but whatever they were called ('Meltonians', 'Sporting Men', 'Snobs', 'Funkers', 'Foreigners', 'Macadamizers', 'Cockneys', 'Grocers') bad Meltonians were only there to be compared with true Meltonians. As Alken painted it: 'How to Qualify for a Meltonian?' 'Some Do and Some Don't. It's All a Notion'.[151] There was a right way to dress (not flash), to take a gate (don't funk), and mix (right tone). You must never get too near the hounds or go in front of the Master. Being unhorsed was the ultimate disgrace, but naturally there was a right and a wrong way to fall.[152] Wrong was all down the horse's neck.[153] Right was 'fall cool'. *Funny Folks* (12 December 1874) offered 'The Whole Art of Falling from a Horse' in three pages. 'Fall only to rise' it advised, and don't for a minute give the impression of being dead, even if you are.[154] According to Alken, 'Funks' and 'Macadamizers' didn't fancy jumping and went the long way round, very bad funks funked in front of the ladies, while sporting Cockneys got hoff and jumped over themselves (not exactly), letting the horse follow on.[155] Osbaldeston got off his horse to fight with stockingers over a badger at Hallaton, with drunks at Sileby, and with an unrepentant vulpicide at Ashby. 'One of the greatest difficulties to be contended with in the Quorn ... was the behaviour of the stocking-makers and weavers who used to assemble in crowds at the covert side'[156] When things got really bad, the

---

[149] *Daily Telegraph*, 19 February 1990.

[150] 'the hero ambitious of riding fame, if he should have assisted in passing the hounds beyond the line ... has not only defeated his own purpose but also interrupted the sport of his companions': Cecil, *Records of the Chase* (1854) p.406. Contrast Nimrod's ideal MFH of the quick eye and gentle pace, with all the miseries that can befall even the best: Nimrod, *Hunting Reminiscences* (1843) p.27; Anon, *Book of Sports* (1843) pp.81–4.

[151] Alken, 'How to Qualify for a Meltonian' (YCBA 1819, six plates); 'Some Do and Some Don't: It's All a Notion' (YCBA 1820, seven plates); 'Comparative Meltonians, as they Are and as they Were' (YCBA 1832, six plates). Other nicknames are to be found in Cecil, *Records* (1854) p.242, p.400, p.410; Beckford, *Thoughts on Hunting* (1798) in his Letter XIV, made the same comparisons as Cecil; Barrett Davis (YCBA 1840), 'Fox Hunting: Rural Riders or Funkers?'; Ferneley (YCBA 1829); Johnson Payne (YCBA early 20c); Hall (YCBA 1835); Alken (YCBA nd) 'Quorn Hunt Snob is Beat'; Nimrod (YCBA nd) on being 'Macadamized'.

[152] Aspin, *Ancient Customs* (1832) p.93.

[153] 'the great difficulty is how to fall well': Alken, 'Some Do'.

[154] Cecil, *Records of the Chase* (1854) p.383.

[155] Alken (YCBA nd) 'Set of 12 Sporting Satirists'.

[156] Osbaldeston, *Autobiography* (1856) p.97, p.99, p.101.

humour turned droll, redolent of the battle field. Overtaken and bumped by a thruster, Earl Spencer asked him if he'd come far to do it. Surtees' MFH Jorrocks caught the mood:

> You 'airdresser on the chestnut horse', he roars during a check to a gentleman with a very big ginger moustache. 'Pray 'old 'ard!
>
> 'Hairdresser?' replies the gentleman, turning round in a fury. 'I'm an officer in the 91st regiment.
>
> 'Then you hossifer in the 91st who looks like an 'airdresser. '*Old 'ard'.*[157]

Algy and Minna, then, were master and mistress of a strange kingdom adjoining other strange kingdoms. *Sporting Life* (21 August 1847) chose yachting, fox-hunting, and horse racing as the national sports, but of the three, betting on the horses was the only one most people understood. Algy claimed to speak for Leicestershire yet most Leicester people did not know where his kingdom began, or ended, or what really went on there. He claimed his birthright to a kind of liberty they could not know, but liberty was a good place to start in the national story, whoever claimed it. That which the political class claimed for themselves, made it harder to deny for others. Knowing such things was one of 'the secret rules of upper classness'.[158]

In 1928 the Quorn's joint master Paget died in a riding accident and his place was taken by Algy and Minna's near neighbour, Harold Nutting. The deal was sealed over lunch at Quenby Hall with Sir Harold and Lady Enid.[159] The Burnabys stayed on for one more season as master and first lady. On Algy's death in 1938, Minna sold the farm. The funeral oration was read by Major Guy Paget, Paget's son (who was himself to die of a fall in 1952). He told of Algy's hatchet face and bright blue eyes, his saddle humour and liking for the ladies, how he puffed but never huffed even though he commanded the largest and most difficult field in the country. Unlike some, he said, Algy was a man who never took his pack home. 'Algy. Was ever a man so mis-named? He was neither bearded nor the Algy of the Music Hall, the effeminate pseudo aristocrat'.[160]

All those years ago, in the days of Sir Hugo Meynell, Beckford recognized that fox-hunting was a trifle only to those who did not do it. So it was with the Burnabys. As gentry, their love of honour and horses was the sum of all they

---

[157] Surtees, *Hunts with Jorrocks* (1854) quoted in Lord Charles Cecil, Lecture to R. S. Surtees Society (2014); Carr, *English Fox Hunting* (1976) p.159.

[158] McKibbin, *Classes and Cultures* (1998) p.2.

[159] Nutting to Burnaby, by hand, 8 December 1930: LRO DG 51/31. Nutting joined on a subsidy of £4,500 a year.

[160] Unlike Lord Lonsdale, that is, Minna's Diary, 14 January, 5 April 1911: LRO DG 51/2; eulogy, Maj Guy Paget, LRO DG 51/36.

pretended to be. Algy wrote himself a note headed 'The Christian Knight'. 'Unless natural', he said, 'he may be a good man but not necessarily a gentleman'.[161]

As a postscript: Algy and Minna could not have known John Peel and he was no Christian Knight. But he was the most famous fox hunter in the world. A failing Cumbrian farmer who hunted his own small pack with his boon companions, Peel was not even a Blencathrian let alone a Meltonian.[162] In his old grey coat and cross-bred pony, he hunted a world away from the Quorn, and only became celebrated after his death (the *Carlisle Patriot* only gave him eleven lines) when a song about him, *D'ye Ken John Peel?* written in Cumbrian phonetic by John Woodcock Graves sometime between 1825 and 1830, found its way into George Coward's 1866 *Songs and Ballads of Cumberland*. By 1910, a time of intense English regionalism, we find The Border Regiment having adopted the song as its regimental quick march and Cumbrian patriots singing it all over the world, even in Newcastle.[163]

It was the rousing chorus that did it. In response to the call, the singer swears his intention to roam free: 'For the sound of his horn cawd me frae my bed / And the cry of his hounds has me oft times led...' In the higher ground of the Lake District, Peel and his men oft times had to get off and walk. In 1818, they walked all through the night.[164] In John Peel country the terrain was badly mapped and hard to cross.[165] It wasn't the same land of liberty as Leicestershire, but it was a land of liberty all the same.

[161] A. E. Burnaby, 'The Christian Knight' (nd): LRO DG 51/32.

[162] John Peel, born Caldbeck 1776, farmed Ruthwaite, Ireby, died 13 November 1854, buried Caldbeck parish church. The Blencathra Hunt (f.1838) was the most prestigious in the Lake District, too grand for Peel, but not too grand for his hounds, who were related: Machell, *John Peel* (1926) Foreword. In 1816 Peel and his wife Mary mortgaged their 200 acres, and in 1845 had to sell meadow and waste. In 1860, two of their sons auctioned what was left at the Sun Inn, Ireby, for £1,020: 1816 indenture and 1860 auction: CRO D/IG/31; 1845 title deeds: CRO D/IG/8. That he was the 'Nimrod of the North' but never a Meltonian is the point of the piece in the *Monthly Chronicle of North Country Lore and Legend*, June 1887.

[163] *Carlisle Patriot*, 18 November 1854. In 1910, along with the sentimental 'The Labourer's Noon Day Hymn' ('each field a hallowed spot'), the Cumberland and Westmorland Association hammered home how well they knew *John Peel* at a patriotic supper in Newcastle: programme, CRO DSO 34/17.

[164] Mitchell, *Men of Lakeland* (1966) pp.42–3, as reported in the *Sporting Magazine*, March 1818.

[165] Rollinson, *Man in the Lake District* (1967) p.121, pp.129–30.

2

Bonny Moor Hen

Just think, when we're goin' up t'woods, tha'll be goin' down in t' cage.
Ar, just think; an' next year tha'll be coming down wi' me.

(Barry Hines, *A Kestrel for a Knave* 1968)

Land of Liberties

The buying and leasing of land in England often included 'liberties'. A liberty was
a franchise, or a right, originally in the king's gift devolved onto private property
and usually associated with manors. Blackstone's legal *Commentaries* dealt with
liberties under the heading of 'Incorporeal Hereditaments', or franchises, or rights
that arose out of the ownership of a thing, like a permission, but not ownership of
the thing itself. Thus, a man called East 'who did keep and use a ferret' did not
have the right to use it where he did use it, because he did not own the land, or
lease it, *and* because he carried no ancient entitlement, or warrant, or permission,
or franchise, or right, *or liberty*, to use it.[1]

Liberties were many and various. They could involve, for instance, the right to
dig turf or take wood, or, in the sporting life, the right to cross land not your own.
The liberty granted to mine lead in Wirksworth, or dance in Winster, or play
football in Ashbourne, was not matched by the equal liberty to hunt or hawk in
Kirkby Thore, or fish off Great Crosby foreshore.[2] When people talked of England
as a land of liberty, it is as well to remember that even at its most exalted as in the
case of fox-hunting, most sport rested upon *entitlements* which in turn rested
upon who owned the land and how they managed it. That this was obvious might
go without saying, but it made less sense when it was extended to the landlordship
of birds in the sky, or fish in the river, all the less so when it was extended to those
who made their sport, or their living, hunting those animals. Against all that
'circumscribed locomotion', or unfreedom, which he so deplored in other

---

[1] Man called East, Herefordshire summons, 11 December 1827: John Johnson, Bodleian, Sport
Box 7.
[2] Porteous, *Ancient Customs of Derbyshire* (1976) pp.22–3; Kirkby Thore parish, 1844 deed: Kendal
Record Office (KRO), WPR 36/2/7; legal documents appertaining to liberties of Great Crosby putative
anglers: Ince Blundell Papers, Lancashire Record Office (LaRO), Preston, DDWW/3/3/1.

countries, Rt. Hon. Earl of Wilton neglected to mention that much of that English liberty he so admired depended, for the most part, on struggles to cross land owned by other people.[3]

"The Bonny Moor Hen" was a song probably written in 1818 by Thomas Coulson, a Weardale schoolmaster. It tells the story of how the Bishop of Durham ('the fat man of Oakland') laid claim to his grouse only to find he was opposed by local men who took a different view of what that liberty entailed.[4] In the song, they take the Bishop's game and run rings round his special constables who, according to William Egglestone sixty years later, had boasted they could take the dale with a black pudding. In the song, having dealt with them finally, the poachers declare their right to the bonny moor hen and call for a pudding to be made with the constables' own blood.[5]

Oh this bonny moor hen, as it plainly appears
She belonged to their fathers some hundreds of years;
But the miners of Weardale are all valiant men,
They will fight till they die for their bonny moor hen.

Court records are full of sporting disagreements of this kind, also known as trespass and affray, also known as offences under the game laws. Up on the fells, sportsmen whatever their stripe were on a land pitted with claims where one man's property abutted other men's properties all carrying varying degrees of entitlement. For example, in the relatively simple case of the unlawful possession of two hare skins on the land he leased, John Smith of Unthank could say without fear of contradiction that the skins had been found at mowing time by his dog and had nothing to do with him.[6] One might reasonably ask in what sense two leaping hares could possibly belong to anyone, including the person or the persons who owned the lands across which they leapt, but Smith had his story ready because that was the claim that had been put him in court. In another case, at Bowes, the witnessing of two men crossing land other men thought they did not have the liberty to cross made for more legal complexity.[7] First, there was the magistrate, Robert Dinsdale, who brought the case. Second there was the defendant, Peter Dent, farmer, of Bowes, who was appealing against his conviction and £2 fine plus 11s costs for crossing land he allegedly had no entitlement to cross. Third there was Jonathan Ireland, Dent's accomplice, also fined. Fourth there was Richard

---

[3] 'Circumscribed locomotion' he ascribed to other countries: Wilton, *Pursuits of the English* (1868) p.26.
[4] Written by Coulson 'in all probability': Egglestone, *Stanhope* (1882) pp.1–8. 'Oakland' is the Bishop's residence Auckland Castle.
[5] Egglestone, who based his account on living memory, told the pudding story. There are various versions of the song. I have not been able to find reference to black pudding in the primary sources. See Canaan, 'Battle of Stanhope' (1997).
[6] Deposition of John Smith, yeoman, 30 November 1747: Carlisle Record Office (CRO) H HUD 8/10/9.
[7] Case of trespass in pursuit of game in the manor and parish of Bowes, 5 September 1836, North Riding Michaelmas Sessions 1836: Durham County Record Office (DCRO) D/HH/2/13/4-67.

Guy, assistant keeper, who saw Dent and Ireland not just crossing the land but 'ranging with their guns and dog' across it. Fifth there was Adam Bonsfield, tenant, who farmed the land the defendants ranged across. He claimed neither man had consent from him or from his landlord. Sixth there was Charles Davis the landlord, who claimed it was his right to give consent, not Bonsfield's, and that he did give it, but only after the trespass had occurred, not before. In reply Bonsfield the tenant claimed that the land had been contracted to him three years before at £40 a year with no mention of needing any special entitlements to take game and that he had let it to a third party without Davis the landlord complaining. Then there was the lawyer, trying to reduce all this to something simple. Then there were the lords of the manor of Bowes, the third parties to whom Bonsfield had let the land in order that they might employ keepers upon it, as they had the right to do. Finally, there were the witnesses, the keeper and his colleague, plus Calvert, a former tenant, who testified that Peter Dent and Jonathan Ireland did have permission to cross the land in question.

All Smith of Unthank had to do in 1747 was explain why he was found in possession of two hare skins. All Dent of Bowes had to do in 1836 was explain the whole of the law of incorporeal hereditaments.

It wasn't all down to the letter of the law either. In a famous case of 1857 over Holt Common, Tillett the lawyer had to argue that the right of commoners (to take rabbits) had been transferred from them to the charity trustees under the enclosure award of 1807, and from the charity trustees to Mr. Barker in a legal agreement of 1855, in contravention of *expectation*, and, prior to 1855, in contravention of *custom*.[8] These were all after the fact. When the poaching gangs tramped the moor lifting crescents of gun fire in their path, the only question was who could stop them?[9]

The first game law of 1671 set a property qualification of £100 for entitlement to hunt. Passed by the landed gentry on behalf of the landed gentry, the Act applied to partridges, pheasants, moor fowl, and hares. It did not apply to deer and rabbits, which were covered by other laws. Foxes, badgers, and otters were left unprotected. In 1831 the property qualification to take game was removed and it became the property of those who owned the land on which it was found. Given that the law of trespass remained, and given that land leases involved a myriad of clauses and entitlements, and given that up on the moor, game was deemed 'property' whether it was owned by a whole class of property owners or just one, and bearing in mind that animals didn't take much notice of whose property it was anyway, it's hard to see the law making much difference once guns were levelled.[10] When the chief constables of four counties were asked by a government select committee in 1872 how could they know that a hopping hare or a random rabbit belonged to a

---

[8] Lee, *Unquiet Country* (2005) ch.7.   [9] Anon, *Book of Sports* (1843) p.34.
[10] Munsche, *English Game Laws 1671-1831* (1981) pp.1–3, pp.5–6.

certain piece of land and its owner, they couldn't rightly say. One thought it depended on the circumstances. One thought it depended where it was taken. One didn't know what to think. One thought he wasn't clever enough to answer.[11] One thing is for sure. Fox-hunters claimed the fox was theirs no matter where it ran. That was the point. As freeborn Englishmen it was their country, and great effort went into making sure that it, and they, could go where they pleased.

Game laws of increasing vindictiveness followed the 1671 Act. Once wild and vagrant things, game birds were now plumped and protected on huge reservations. Historians have studied slavery, tobacco, sugar, tea, coffee, cotton, and music as part of an eighteenth-century consumer revolution—and game was part of the same growing market.[12] True, it is impossible to judge the size of a black market in game produced by a 1755 ban on trade in it, which drove demand, and frustration, on all sides. But basically a gentleman seen on the fells with a dog was a sportsman and a poor man seen on the fells with a dog was a felon.

With the frustration came a rising tide of punishment—summary justice in 1770, whipping and imprisonment in 1800, capital offence in 1800, up to seven years transportation for night work in 1816, up to fourteen years in 1828 and so on, all at the magistrates' discretion.[13] Printers published wall charts indicating each Act and what it said. Based on property qualifications, natural seasons, legal entitlements, types of bird, degrees of fine and forfeiture, and the like, it was easy to show the technical details. But the politics of game was a different matter because the laws were upheld by a landed class to whom was afforded enormous discretion in their capacity as sportsmen, property owners, and magistrates.[14] From their point of view, not unreasonably, bands of armed men traversing the land, their land, by night was unacceptable.[15] Seen from the poachers' point of view, the game laws were in the interests of property pure and simple, and broke the notion of reciprocity on which rural society depended. As Robert Lee observed: 'just as the rights of the Poor only had meaning when they were

---

[11] Q 804 to chief constables of Somerset, Derbyshire, Lincolnshire, and Staffs: Report of Select Committee on the Game Laws (1872) p.31.

[12] Hammonds, *Village Labourer* (1911) pp.132–4; Berg, 'Consumption in Britain', in Floud and Johnson, eds., *Cambridge Economic History of Modern Britain* (2004) vol. i, 1700–1860. Berg's key theme on the extent to which the labouring classes took part in the consumer revolution applies equally to game (p.375). She describes it as a revolution in 'the material products…of fashion and global commerce' (*Luxury and Pleasure*, 2005, p.6), while McKendrick notes how the commodities were 'crucially' identified 'with Britishness' (*Birth of a Consumer Society*, 1982, p.189).

[13] The 1816 Act referred to 'habits of luxury and indulgence' fuelling the market. If it wasn't so much a black market; it was a gift relationship, also impossible to measure.

[14] In 1876 it was estimated that 710 persons owned 25 per cent of Britain and 5,000 persons owned 75 per cent: Readman, *Land Question* (2010) pp. 257–76.

[15] The inhabitants of Wharton Hall, Westmorland claimed to feel 'in great Danger of our Lifes' on seeing a poaching gang enter Lowther's park: Hugh Wharton to W. Atkinson, 3 January 1680: CRO D/Lons/L1/3/2.

responded to by elites, so the laws of the ruling class only had meaning when they were recognized by the Poor'.[16]

At a casual level there was the opportunity to pocket a rabbit. It is impossible to measure the extent of sport as near to hand as that. Then there was the local man who went out with his dog and gun, usually at night, to bring something home for the pot. And maybe something for the local market too, which preferred one shot birds, which kept better, to the mutilated birds of the big gentry shoot, or *battue*, where thousands were blasted out of the sky in a week.[17] In this kind of arrangement, many poachers could be called work-a-day sportsmen, living off mixed economies in diverse environments. Up in the Pennines, men went hunting the red grouse. Along the Essex and Suffolk coast, in and around the marshlands and the Norfolk broads, they went punting for wildfowl. Then there were the large gangs who took from large protected game areas to sell on to a commercial market.[18]

'Poaching' was just another word for the sporting life of the rural poor, but when the two sides clashed you could be forgiven for seeing it as war. In 1819 *The Edinburgh Review* could talk of 'village guerillas' in 'a rivalry of courage' with the keepers. Given the vindictiveness of the laws, the keepers were generally detested, but on sight you could hardly tell a poacher and a keeper apart. Earl Lonsdale reviewed his keepers in 1863 and what was said of them could have been said of any group of working men. Coward was 'worn out'. Rudd 'has been good'. Thornborrow is 'a most active, powerful and resolute young man'. All for £41 a year. The self-styled 'King of the Norfolk Poachers' liked his sport—from tying a cat's tail, to blocking the neighbour's chimney, to moving around the country with his common law wife, 'my pall' as he put it—but best of all he enjoyed taking from the rich and giving to himself.[19] It was no small thing for this Swaffham boy to feel he was forcing the gentry to disgorge. The Bishop of Durham presided over the richest diocese in the country. Those who poached his moor took from him some part of his massive £87,500 a year and rewarded themselves with the money, and the thrill, of doing so. In a single year, two leadminers 'expert in their native hills' according to the *Tyne Mercury*, took 600 brace off Alston Moor.[20]

Keepers complained like any other worker about their pay and conditions, yet went cap in hand to their employer. Poachers did not go cap in hand, hence the

---

[16] Lee, 'Encountering and Managing the Poor', Leicester PhD (2003) pp.257–76; Anon, *Compleat Sporting Table* (1741); Anon, *Concise Table* (1773): John Johnson, Bodleian, Sport Book Large. Wilson noted how much sport could be spoiled if tenancy relations broke down: Wilson, *VCH Cumberland* (1905) p.431.

[17] *Sporting Magazine*, 1862, p.317.

[18] Winstanley, 'Rural and Urban Poaching', *Rural History*, 2006, p.202. On East Anglian fowling and the works of James Wentworth Day: Snell, *Spirits of Community* (2016) ch.7.

[19] Anon, *I Walked By Night* (1935) p.111; *Edinburgh Review*, 3 March 1819; 2nd Earl Lonsdale to George Lumb, agent, 2, 11 March 1863, and Lumb to Lonsdale, 12 March: CRO D/Lons/L1/3/486.

[20] *Tyne Mercury*, 12 February 1819; on the bishop: Lambert, *Local Government Board* (1873) vol. i. Major Landowners in Durham & Northumberland.

respect shown to them.[21] Their boldness was a popular ballad cliché. Blake's watercolour the 'Poacher's Progress' shows tense and silent men lifting nets in the darkness. Lifting nets meant you didn't have to risk carrying firearms.[22] But one night on the North Yorkshire moors in 1837 Ainsley and Barker were caught firing their guns and keeper Cox confronted them: 'John thou wilt not deny but this is a fair catch... I saw thee shoot fair enough... It'll be a bad job for thee [if you don't come quietly]'. Ainsley's reply was unequivocal: 'Don't be saucy or I'll pummell thee'. One nation divided by a single sport, the newspapers called these encounters 'desperate affrays'. For over a hundred years they were the country's undeclared civil war.[23]

Many affrays were between men who knew each other already. Few were as good natured as that between Mr. Bowes' watcher William Miller and the defendant Richard Beadle.'"Good morning William!" "Good morning Richard. I shall be forced to bring you up". "Well you can if you like"'.[24] But increasingly severe penalties raised the threshold of risk and therefore the level of violence. In a deposition taken at Barnard Castle in 1850, keeper Longstaff told how he heard the defendant Robert Thirlkeld fire his gun and then proceeded to stalk him down the opposite side of a dry stone wall until he made himself known and the defendant started to run. Ten yards from the gate, Thirlkeld turned and faced the keeper, levelling his gun. Longstaff heard the click. 'Rob thou had better mind thyself', he warned. But Thirlkeld fired anyway and Longstaff took shot to the arm, face, hand, and shoulder. No poacher or keeper wanted an affray. They preferred the light foot to the heavy hand. From the moment he is first accosted, we find the Leicestershire poacher James Hawker estimating how hard the opposition can run. Cross country running with heavy bag, long coat, and valuable firearm, was one of England's lesser known popular sports. It was vital to keep an even pace and a steady distance until a smart disappearance at the finish.[25] 'Him who can't run can't poach'.[26]

The rural elite had all the land and all its pleasures—gardens, parks, fountains, rivers and lakes, horses, and houses. Between them and the labouring poor stood the hedgerow or the wall, the dog or the keeper, the informant or the small printed warning to keep off, delivered in person to the suspect's door.[27] Poachers usually worked by night, their faces blackened. Sometimes, to hide themselves, they wore

[21] Hawker, *Poacher* (1961) p.141.

[22] For examples of poacher lads in ballads: Nevill, *Sporting Days* (1910) p.242; and John Johnson, Bodleian, Ballads 13; Blake (YCBA 1830s).

[23] Hopkins, *Long Affray* (1986) p.6; prosecution of John Barker, North Riding Epiphany Sessions 1837: DCRO D/HH/2/13/75.

[24] Deposition of William Miller, 26 May 1895, Greta Bridge: DCRO D/HH/2/13/116-131.

[25] Hawker, *Poacher* (1961) p.31. See Hammonds, *Village Labourer* (1911) p.137.

[26] Anon (Lilias Haggard), *I Walked by Night* (1935) pp.69–83; deposition of J. S. Longstaff, 1850, Barnard Castle: DCRO D/HH/2/13/145.

[27] For warnings delivered by hand: John Johnson, Bodleian, Law Box 7. On the buying up of small freeholds, the closing of long-term beneficial leases, and the eighteenth-century growth of the 'great

women's bonnets, or women's clothing (or were women).[28] If they were valued at all, keepers were valued for their attachment to the family that employed them.[29] Poachers too were known for their attachment to land they knew (but where strangers roamed).[30] Big landlords saw poachers as a minor irritant. Lord Lonsdale's correspondence with his agent is full of rents and leases, not poachers. Game comes up only now and then.[31] Poachers on the other hand, from their point of view, put their lives on the line. We find John Burn of Keld in hiding because he took a brace or two. Fearing transportation, 'he faithfully promises he will give up poaching...so long as he may continue in England'. Thomas Keighley was doing six months hard for the same privilege. As he told his brother: 'I am on the wheel...I can hardly walk...Servear paine In my back...You must pay the interest for my coat that is in pledge'.[32]

Battle of Stanhope 1818

In 1797 the new Bishop of Durham, the Rt. Rev. & Hon. Shute Barrington, proclaimed his intention to defend Weardale from the people who lived there. The richest tithe in the richest diocese in England, Weardale also mined lead with high levels of profit, mortality, and environmental damage. Here, the Bishop was not only a priest, but a landlord and owner of mineral rights. To outsiders, this dale, hunting ground of bishops since 1183, was a vast sporting arena. To the people who lived there, it was exactly the same.[33]

estate': Allen, 'Agriculture 1700-1850', in Floud and Johnson, *Cambridge Economic History* (2004) p.100.

[28] On 'scuttle caps' to hide the face: Dixon, 'Old Coquetdale', *Archaelogia Aeliana* (1892); on blacking up: William Whelans, Newcastle Assizes 3 August 1838: Assizes Papers (ASSI, National Archives) 45/24; on a man's bulldogs and the Romford overseer's reluctance to confront them, or him: Sokoll, *Essex Pauper Letters* (2001) 3 February 1831, p.545. Martin Amis' Lionel Asbo is a 'desperate fellow' who keeps a bulldog. On 'Rebecca's Daughters', who liked dressing up, and the links between popular protest and transgressive behaviour: Jones, 'Women, Community and Collective Action', in John, *Mother's Land* (1991).

[29] Sir Edward Blackett's 100-year-old keeper John Armstrong was regaled on his birthday for his strong sense of family attachment: Richardson, *Table Book* (1843) p.181. See Mrs. F Hudleston letter to her husband, 26 December 1827: CRO D HUD/15/5.

[30] The Alston miners bound themselves to William Marshall of Patterdale Hall for £50 to refrain from poaching while at the same time Mr. John James of Leeds bought the privilege not to: 'Bond to refrain from poaching', 24 December 1830: CRO D/WAL/2.

[31] Letters, to and from Lord Lonsdale and George Lumb, 1863: CRO D Lons/L1/3/486.

[32] Thomas Keighley to Joseph Keighley, Catherstone, Barnard Castle, 5 November 1842: DCRO D/HH/2/13/151. See also petition of Rev. John Rowlandson, 26 December 1833, and Walter Parker in mitigation, to Lord Lowther: CRO D Lons/L5/2/36/29.

[33] He called them 'Dog-breakers and Pretended Game-Keepers'. The Bishop was simultaneously appointing new keepers and paying indemnities to allotment holders under the 1773 Act of Enclosure: DCRO Quarter Sessions Order Books (QSOB), 29 May 1813 (Q/D/EC 1-12), 15 July, 21 December 1816. His 1797 proclamation appears in Devey, *Records of Wolsingham* (1926) pp.229–30, made in the

In August 1814 Arthur Aylmer was appointed gamekeeper of Low Coniscliffe Manor, property of Henry Howard. That Aylmer had served as a general in the army and lived in a castle rather clarifies the significance of his appointment. A build-up of keepers began that same year and went on for the next five. All the great northern landowners—the earls of Durham and Carlisle, the Dean & Chapter of Durham Cathedral, the coal barons Lambton, Ellison and Carr—as lords of the manor of various sporting estates, started swelling their forces until it became clear that General Aylmer was their unofficial commander-in-chief.[34] Also in 1814, Shute Barrington stiffened his pastoral visitations. Asking about those who absented themselves from worship, parish officers told him about Methodists.[35]

In October 1816, a time of post-war labour disputes in Newcastle and Sunderland that would rumble on for another four years, we find General Byng, commander of northern regular forces, visiting the region, and the lord lieutenants of Northumberland and Durham building up their Yeomanry strength.[36] November 1816 saw two direct attacks on magistrates. First, on the evening of 13 November, a shot gun blasted the upstairs window of Whickham House where George Leaton, the resident magistrate, was sitting with his wife. He had no doubt, he said, that 'it was done by a poacher'.[37] Two weeks later, on 30 November, a dozen armed masked men burst into 'Riddlehamhope' near Hexham, the home of Charles Clavering, another resident magistrate. They had come, they said, in order to liberate a gun and the eleven birds he had confiscated from James Gregg, one of their number. Clavering and his family (who locked themselves in the upstairs dressing room) were frightened in their home in ways that magistrates and their families were not supposed to be frightened in their homes. Edward Johnson, a Royal Navy lieutenant who was staying with the Claverings, confronted the intruders at a bend in the upstairs passage. In the scuffle that ensued Johnson dropped his pistol but managed to get away. The household found the gun next morning with a message in the pan. Mr. Clavering must not suppose his position would shield him from justice, it said, for

> Under what Law, or what Act of Parliament, did you act in detaining an industrious Man's Gun, whose sole view was to relieve a few Hungry Children, and who had not fired one Shot in any part of your Ground...the Crime

same year that 'Lover of Freedom' called the game laws 'Badges of Slavery': *Poetical Remarks on the Game Laws* (1797).

[34] DCRO QSOB 18, 20 August 1814. For the build-up: DCRO QSOB 18, M 7/4 microfilm, and QSOB 19. The other way to pressure poachers was through voluntary associations of landowners bound to prosecute: eg 'A Country Gentleman', 'A Letter on the Game Laws' (1815).
[35] Bishop's Visitations 1814, University of Durham Palace Green Library: DDR/UP/1806/4.
[36] Byng to Lord Sidmouth, Home Department, 1 October 1816: HO 42/153–4.
[37] George Thomas Leaton, Whickham House, to Sidmouth, 24 February 1817: HO 42/160.

imputed to us is merely killing a Bird—where is your Mark? How do you know them? Remember Sir, God is no respecter of Persons.[38]

In January 1817 Northumberland magistrates put in force the Night Poaching Act, originally passed in 1816. As the Lord Lieutenant explained to the Home Secretary: 'in consequence of the attack made upon Mr Clavering's house', and in view of the 'daring manner' of poaching gangs across the county, including the prisoner Thomas Low's refusal to give information about the attack on Riddlehamhope, he felt it was time to make example. Two brothers, Joseph and Christopher Fawcett, labourers of Chollerton and Humshaugh Fell, had been convicted at Northumberland Quarter Sessions under the Act, and he wanted them in the hulks and transported as quickly as possible 'lest in the present disposition of the County, an attempt should be made to rescue them'.[39] In the light of further threats and outrages, Northumberland had already put the Yeomanry on full alert and introduced a night curfew, and here he is on 22 January, just over two weeks after the convictions, pushing Sidmouth to get the Fawcetts out of the county and half way across the world before things got out of hand.

But things had already got out of hand. The Fawcetts had been treated monstrously. The bill against them is signed off as a 'true bill', but it lacks names of witnesses or officers of the court (except for the foreman of the jury) and contains no reference whatsoever to the evidence. At law, a true bill was supposed to be followed by a trial but this one merely indicates the sentences. The brothers are recorded as pleading not guilty at the bottom of the bill, and someone has written the sentence under that.[40] All very odd. Seven years' transportation not for the 'questionable crime' (according to Blackstone) of poaching, but for *intending* to poach, was a cruel and unusual punishment. Under the Act, to be decided in a petty court by a jury but sentence to be given by a magistrate, transportation was rare, less than 10 per cent of all convictions. But the Lord Lieutenant couldn't get them onto the hulks fast enough and his magistrates acted accordingly. We can be sure they were not rescued. Finally departing on the ship *Larkins* on 24 July, they arrived in New South Wales on 22 November 1817. For inflicting such punishments, magistrate Clennell received a letter threatening him and other 'paltry gents'. What to Clennell was a crime, to his correspondent, 'Poacher', was merely a matter of supply and demand:

---

[38] Deposition of Edward Johnson, RN, 2 December 1816; Duke of Northumberland to Sidmouth, 7 December 1816, containing information from George Johnson, butler, taken 3 December: HO 42/156.

[39] Duke of Northumberland to Sidmouth, 22 January 1817: HO 42/158; information on Low[e], Northumberland to Sidmouth, 24 December 1816: HO 42/157.

[40] True Bill, Northumberland Archives Service [NAS] QS1/521/36, Northumberland Quarter Sessions, 1817. Quarter Sessions are organized into Order Books, Bundles, and Indictments. A True Bill is an Indictment. This Order Book merely contains an abridged version of the Bill. Northumberland Archives has no Bundles, that is, no additional documentary evidence, for 1817.

... for nothing more than taking that which belongs to them by the laws of God while you and such like encourage it yourselves, you constantly send to shops for all kinds of Game, you must know that it is poached, and when you ... go to an Inn, you ask for Game ... *Monster*, I write this as a warning to you other people must live as well ... you (and many others) shall be watched ... we shall not remain idle, show this to your fellow *Monsters* ... I have read the Scriptures and understand them ... there's not a poacher in England that has not as good a Conscience in the sight of God as you and such like who pretend to administer justice ... beware thou art in a perilous situation, I don't mean your Body or anything in that way ... your most Obed Servant, 'Poacher'.[41]

In June 1818 the trouble started all over again, this time over another two brothers, Charles and Anthony Siddle of St. John's Chapel, Weardale. A party having arrested Charles for non-payment of a poaching fine was repelled on St. John's Chapel bridge when men whose names had appeared before in the Clavering incident rescued him from a constable and four assistant constables. Thomas Low[e] and James Craggs (or Gregg, or Greg) were charged, along with the two Siddles (or Sidall), Emmerson Featherston[e], John Kidd, Dixon Watson, and John Curry (or Currah) for riot, rescue, and assault.[42] Come August, Charles Siddle and his rescuers were still at large and we find General Aylmer and the magistrates imploring local worthies to support Francis Johnson, the parish constable, to make arrests, a task not helped by Johnson's evident reluctance to risk it.[43] By October, Siddle and friends still had not been brought in, the leadminers of the dale were in dispute with their employers ('controlled by what they call a Committee') and threatening to march on Bishop Auckland and Durham, and, according to Col. Beaumont of Blackett Beaumont lead mines, '[making] different attempts on my moor'.[44] Anyone who didn't know English history better might suppose Weardale was in a state of rebellion.[45] The Home

---

[41] Anon to Thomas Clennell JP, Harbottle, Northumberland, 20 January 1817: HO 42/158. The Yeomanry had gone on full alert 13 January and Sidmouth was pressed further on the Fawcett case 22 January: Duke of Northumberland to Sidmouth, 13, 22 January 1817: HO 42/158. For other local 'outrages', magistrates Newburn, Richmond, Dent and Shafto, to Northumberland, 3 December 1816: HO 42/156. Blackstone, *Commentaries on the Laws and Constitution* (1820) put 'game' under 'Public Wrongs' and judged it the subject of 'numerous and confused' legislation (p.443). Under the Night Poaching Act, less than 10 per cent of convictions resulted in transportation over the period of the Act 1816–27: Munsche, *English Game Laws* (1981) p.103. On the Fawcetts' transportation: British Transportation Registers 1787–1867: HO 11/2/357–63.

[42] On non-payment of fine: Aylmer to Sidmouth, 21 December 1818: HO 42/182; on the rescue: DCRO QSOB 18, June 1818, Michaelmas Sessions 19 October 1818.

[43] Aylmer and six JPs to principal inhabitants of Stanhope, 6 August 1818: DCRO D/X 1369/122.

[44] On the leadminers' Committee, Joseph Forster, Mayor of Newcastle, to Sidmouth, 6 October 1818: HO 42/181; Col. Beaumont, Hexham Abbey, to Aylmer, 4 October 1818: DCRO D/X 1369/25. Fear of marching gangs came from Auckland Castle: T. H. Faber to Aylmer, 20 September 1818: DCRO D/X 1369/22-7.

[45] Though not by looking at the Criminal Registers, according to which County Durham had no game law offences in 1818 and Northumberland only two: HO Criminal Registers HO 27/15. On the

Secretary reminded the Mayor of Newcastle of the land forces at his disposal with Marines on their way to Shields by sea.[46]

Sport and the law were the two great obsessions of the landed gentry.[47] Flagrant humiliation in their own territory was intolerable. Further warrants were issued on 19 October stemming from the June warrants, but by December, a full six months after the rescue, they were gathering dust and the wanted men were still at large. A new plan was in the offing and T H Faber at Auckland Castle, on behalf of the Bishop, and Aylmer, gamekeeper-in-chief and (in the conspicuous absence of the Earl of Darlington) seemingly acting lord lieutenant, agreed that a posse would be raised in Darlington to make its way up the dale to be passed keeper to keeper until, 'by a back way into Dawson's house' at Stanhope (Dawson was the St. John's Chapel publican assaulted along with Johnson the parish constable in June), they would rest and wait until eight watchers were ready to take them on across the moor by night. Faber and Aylmer were aware of the risks for the plan, like the dale, was long and difficult. What if the Siddles weren't in? What if the terrain was too rough? What if the watchers didn't show up? What about Dawson, a key witness, now apparently 'full of fears'?[48]

The plan was implemented on Monday 7 December 1818. While Darlington the Lord Lieutenant was still in bed with that morning's fox-hunting to look forward to, the posse alighted on St. John's Chapel out of the night and took the Siddles by surprise. They were then taken eight miles down the dale to Stanhope where, quite unbelievably, a second rescue took place freeing the Siddles, wounding four constables, and leaving the rest barricaded up in the Black Bull.[49] In the view of the resident magistrate, in their march up the dale and down again the posse had behaved like braggarts and anyway, in his view, the leadminers would have been a match for a party four times their number.[50] This was the Battle of Stanhope as recorded in 'The Bonny Moor Hen'.

Aylmer called immediately for a general meeting of magistrates in Durham (the minute book read 'Outrage in Weardale') and turned his attention to his man on the spot, resident magistrate Rev. W Wilson, Rector of Wolsingham.[51] Aylmer asked Wilson if he was active? Had he gathered information on the rescue? Could he muster the civil power? Could he come to the magistrates' meeting in Durham

---

southern 'Swing' disturbances of 1831, preceded by 'constant and habitual offences against the game laws': Hobsbawm and Rude, *Captain Swing* (1973) p.57.

[46] Sidmouth to Forster, 10 October 1818: HO 41/4; DCRO QSOB 18, 7 October 1818.
[47] Hay, in Hay, *Albion's Fatal Tree* (1975) p.248.
[48] Faber to Aylmer, 4 December 1818: DCRO D/X 1369/24 (ii); warrants, 19 October 1818: DCRO QSOB 18.
[49] *Durham County Advertiser*, 12, 19 December 1818.
[50] Rev. W. Wilson to Aylmer, 15 December 1818: DCRO D/X 1369/23 (iii).
[51] Aylmer to Wilson, 15 December 1818: DCRO D/X 1369 (i); adjourned Michaelmas Sessions, 19 December 1818: DCRO QSOB 18.

and explain? Wilson respected his parishioners as law abiding and independent communities. The very nature of their work (they contracted 'bargains' directly with the lead companies) demanded it.[52] He wrote back to say that he couldn't attend the meeting (the meeting in turn reported that he had been 'unable or unwilling' to act); that he had never stopped gathering information; that he was not and never had been in favour of using force; that Anthony Siddle had been reluctant to be rescued, an astonishing admission, and that now was time for reconciliation. Although Aylmer never admitted it, and although he remained critical not to say libellous of the Rector, the Rector's advice prevailed.[53]

First, although the magistrates had called in the army, by the time the 18th Hussars arrived at Durham on 2 January, they didn't want them anymore. Aylmer had made it clear to General Byng, army man to army man, the day before, that the dale was nineteen miles long and lacked any effective auxiliary power, added to which everyone knew the Hussars were coming and there could be no question of surprise. Byng replied assuring Aylmer that once he had the Hussars he wouldn't need any auxiliaries because they were equal to any task.[54] Second, although it was not true that Wilson was a soft or inactive magistrate (in January he fined Jasper Hogarth of Stanhope £1 for shooting a pigeon), sometime between 7 and 11 December, Wilson and Brignall, the new man appointed to implement the warrants, met representatives of the wanted men in St. John's Chapel, where they secured promises that the men would present themselves at the next Quarter Sessions on trust that Wilson would secure what was in effect a pardon.[55] Third, it is hard to remember that all this was a question of sport. While the St. Leger was running at Doncaster in one great northern sporting contest, in quite another cavalry were clattering up the Great North Road, Lord Lambton was recruiting more keepers, Col. Beaumont was loading more spring guns, and Durham magistrates were running hither and thither trying to arrest half a dozen young leadminers.[56]

[52] Hunt, *Lead Miners of the Northern Pennines* (1970) pp.222–8.

[53] Wilson to Aylmer, 15 December 1818: DCRO D/X 1369 23 (iii); Aylmer to Sidmouth, 21 December 1818: HO 42/182; report, meeting of twenty-three magistrates at Durham, 19 December 1818: HO 42/182.

[54] Aylmer to Sidmouth, 21 December 1818 and Byng to Aylmer, 25 December 1818: HO 42/182; Aylmer to Byng, 1 January 1819 and Byng to Aylmer, 3 January 1819: HO 42/182 (iii). Over the same period, Lord Lieutenant Darlington changed his mind about the use of force. At first he doesn't want the army, then he wonders if he has the power to use at least the Yeomanry 'respecting the lawless Delinquents in Weardale': letter from Raby Castle to Sidmouth, 7 January 1819: HO 42/183; to Aylmer, 14 December 1818: DCRO D/X 1369/26.

[55] On the pigeon: *Durham County Advertiser*, 9 January 1819; on the plan: ibid, 30 January 1819 and *Tyne Mercury*, 2 February 1819. Given their situation it was incumbent on the poachers to deny any such 'deal' or 'plan' and they did so in a staunch statement to the *Advertiser* on 27 February—'Please no meddling' signed by Thomas Low (his mark), James Craggs (his mark), John Kidd, John Curragh, William Bell the Younger, and Dixon Watson.

[56] *Newcastle Weekly Chronicle*, 26 December 1818, 23 January 1819; *Newcastle Chronicle*, 16 January 1819.

Brignall testified in court that the men had been 'much misrepresented' and Wilson kept to the agreement. Siddle and Featherston were fined 6d each, for assault. Low, Kidd, Curragh, Craggs, Bell, and Dixon Watson were fined one shilling each, with £50 sureties.[57] A mix of miners and publicans stood surety. Only John Kidd, inexplicably, was left out, and he was sentenced to twelve months in Durham gaol.

James Losh, the prosecuting lawyer, and Rev. William Nesfield, the chairman of the bench, were sympathetic and experienced arbitrators. Nesfield had played a key role in settling the Tyne Wear pitmen's dispute of 1810–11 (a dispute Bishop Shute Barrington had graced by turning his palace stables into a gaol) and was as trusted as the Bishop was hated. In 1815 he had been requested to arbitrate for a second time, this time by Tyne seamen. Not that he was entirely a friend of the Poor. In 1816 he crushed a strike at Newbottle and Rainton collieries when he judged the men to be in the wrong.[58] Either way, it is hard to believe that Wilson had not been in touch with him in a personal capacity. Losh on the other hand belonged to a family of Tyneside entrepreneurs and radical lawyers. Both spoke highly, too highly, of the defendants. 'Daring mountaineers in arms' they called them and, while they talked in session about inflicting 'severe and exemplary' punishments, the deal had been struck and sixpence it was.[59]

Efforts at social control followed immediately after, starting with the famous Shute Barrington church schools built in seven parishes including St. John's Chapel. The Primitive Methodists surfaced in Teesdale and Weardale the following year and by 1822 they were in full revival mode.[60] We will see more of them in chapter 5, but the 'Prims' were not only on the side of the poor, they *were* the poor, and not in favour of sport either, much less poachers, whose souls they liked to canvass. E P Thompson, who had much to say on Whigs, hunters, and Methodists alike, famously showed how the notorious 'Black Acts'—involving fifty new capital offences between 1720 and 1723 for taking deer and game—were prompted by the 'repeated public humiliation' of the authorities by poachers in Windsor Forest.[61] He blamed the severity of the Acts on the legislators' 'mental distance' from ordinary life. All one can say of events in Weardale one hundred years later is that not much had changed except Revs. Wilson and Nesfield and their impressive willingness to see that if this was just sport and a little business, not rebellion, peace was something that could be managed.

Not that the sport ceased. In 1822 at York Lent Assizes one Thomas Low[e] and John Curry (or Curragh), along with two other Durham men, were charged for

---

[57] Durham Epiphany Sessions, 11 January 1819, Easter Sessions, 19 April 1819: DCRO QSOB 18.

[58] Colls, *Pitmen* (1987) p.82; Rev. Robert Gray JP to Sidmouth, 3 November 1815: HO 42/147; Nesfield to William Hutchinson, High Sheriff Co. Durham, 6 June 1816: HO/42/151.

[59] *Durham County Advertiser*, 24 April 1819. Hannah More's tract 'Black Giles. The Poacher' (Cheap Depository Publications 1820) showed how little she knew.

[60] Colls, *Pitmen* (1987) p.148.   [61] Thompson, *Whigs and Hunters* (1975) p.190.

gathering at Grinton to take game, resist the law, commit menace, threaten others, and making intimidatory gestures. Low was clearly incorrigible. He was also missing his front teeth (which had been originally noted by the butler in his deposition after the attack on Clavering's house in 1816). We can suppose that he excelled in intimidatory gestures.[62]

Poaching didn't figure in the county's three leading public order issues for 1840 but that did not mean the game wars were over. Nineteenth-century England found class struggle in the towns, 'landlordism' in the country, and 'big game' in the colonies. Cobbett saw the game laws as part of 'Old Corruption'. Aspin's history of sport thought the game laws denied poor people their land and liberty. Chartists used the game laws to demean the aristocracy. John Bright told parliament that for the sport of the forty thousand few, the whole country was 'insulted and oppressed'. The right of constables to search on suspicion of contravening the game laws caused a massive outcry among Radicals in 1862.[63] 'The Shooter's Diary', meanwhile, advertised great shooting opportunities abroad: a whole world made to be shot at for £600.[64]

Ireland politicized the 'Land Question' after 1846, but clearly England and Scotland had their own land questions. Rev. Edward Thring, headmaster of Uppingham School, knew all about the local gentry. He reckoned a man may be excellent, 'but if he is a landowner and you have not tried him on land and game, you know nothing of him'.[65] The Land Nationalization Society in 1881, the English Land Restoration League in 1884, the Scottish Land Restoration League in the same year, and the English Land Colonization Society in 1893, all reflected the radical land value theories of Henry George. When Masterman wanted to highlight 'The Conquerors' in his 1909 *Condition of England*, he chose a rich, sporting plutocracy who had turned half of Scotland into a game reserve.[66] Lloyd George's famous Limehouse speech of 1909 called for a tax on sales of land previously used for sport. It was argued that the urban unemployed, victims of untaxed land values, were the descendants of freeborn Englishmen pushed off the land to make room for game.[67] It was argued that the rural unemployed were the descendants of freeborn Englishmen who had stayed on the land only to suffer

[62] York Lent Assizes 1822: DCRO D/HH/2/13/130. On Low's front teeth: Northumberland to Sidmouth, 7 December 1816: HO 42/156.

[63] Convictions went up from 2642 in 1839 to 10659 in 1880: *Anti Game Law League* (1880). Cobbett, *Newcastle Chronicle* 21-24 September 1832; Aspin, *Ancient Customs* (1832) p.105; Northern Political Union, 'Address to the Middle Classes of the North of England' (1839): HO 40/42; Edwards, *Game Laws* (1862); Newton, *Game Laws* (1862); John Bright, Commons Sitting, *Hansard*, 23 March 1848, c.945. Bright was presenting a bill for the repeal of all game laws from 48 George III to 3 William IV.

[64] *The Shooter's Diary* (1866) 'Abyssinia': John Johnson, Bodleian, Sport Box 10.

[65] Thring's Diary, 30 May 1865: Parkin, *Thring* (1900) p.132.

[66] Masterman, *Condition of England* (1909) p.26.

[67] Edwards, *Landholding in England* (1909) p.21; Lloyd George, 'Limehouse Speech' (1909) p.13: John Johnson, Bodleian, Land and People Box 2.

humiliation and distress.[68] The Cooperative Wholesale Society was told by the president of the Free Land League at its annual congress in Manchester in 1887 that private property separated the land from its people, including 'the frequent sacrifice of agriculture to sport'.[69] Alexander Mackenzie, a Scottish highlander, called landlordism exterminism. Henry George called it barbarous.[70] Joseph Arch told the Select Committee that he had had enough 'teeth locking' for one life. 'Game! Game! We have heard too much and had ... too little'. To get land, Arch was in favour of emigration. It was as if land was all the nation could see.[71] Apart from William Bell, who emigrated to the USA, the Weardale men lived out their lives in their native dale. In spite of all evidence to the contrary, people still believed England belonged to them.[72]

Framing Land and Liberty

Who did it really belong to? The national story told the tale of freeborn Englishmen who saved their liberties in the 'Glorious Revolution' of 1688–89 and consolidated them in the 'Whig Settlement' that followed. Both were carried out in the name of England's ancient liberties, but as the eighteenth century wore on and the Whig party found itself hampered by military failure abroad and corruption at home, a new Tory patriotism emerged.[73] High fashion and metro-politan tastes, which were Francophile, didn't quite cut it for the new Tory patriots, and one way of looking at the rising popularity of hunting in the national consciousness is to see it, and the small industry of prints and pictures which promoted it, as part of a deliberately provincial patriotic counter-culture that emerged from the 1760s: the landed gentry at home.[74]

In these culture wars between metropolitan and provincial tastes, Addison and Steele's 'Sir Roger De Coverley' (*The Spectator* 1711) and Henry Fielding's 'Squire Western' (*The History of Tom Jones* 1749) made mock of the hunting booby whose gross rural habits were contrasted with the *macaroni*, delicate victims of continental pleasures. Cobbett liked rustic village sports, but showed his

---

[68] Williamson, *Life in a Devon Village* (1947) p.7.

[69] Arnold, *The Land and the People* (1888) p.14.

[70] Mackenzie, 'Highland Clearances' (1881) p.31, John Johnson, Bodleian, Land & People Box 9. Henry George, 'True Conservatism' (1884) p.104, John Johnson, Bodleian Land & People Box 1.

[71] Rendering the part played by business and capital invisible: Edgerton, *Rise and Fall* (2018) pp.107–8, and George, *Progress and Poverty* (1883) p.273; Arch, *Joseph Arch* (1898) p.157.

[72] Thompson, *Making of the English Working Class* (1963) p.222.

[73] *Blackwell's Magazine* built a Tory revival in the 1820s out of what was taken as English country bluffness: Borsay in Langford, *Eighteenth Century* (2002) p.207; Hoppitt, *Land of Liberty?* (2002) p.419.

[74] Francophilia and the patriotic reaction to it: Newman, *English Nationalism* (1987) pp.28–64. For eighteenth-century wars with the French and the patriotic reaction to them: Colley, *Britons* (1992) chs. 7, 8.

displeasure at the landed variety by seeing them as little more than metropolitan riff raff mixing with vengeful gamekeepers and installers of man-traps. His *Rural Rides* includes sporting ne'er do wells of every type—from Indian nabobs and West Indian 'negro-drivers', to stock-jobbers and loan-sharks, 'not to mention the long and *black list* in gowns and three-tailed wigs'.[75] Against them stood traditional squires and loyal tenants. In time, even the fox, now miraculously able to speak, would join their freeborn ranks.[76]

Baudelaire said that a good picture had meaning before you could see its subject.[77] With hunting and racing there was never any doubt about the subject. Often called 'pictures of record', a valuable horse was a valuable horse, a trusty dog a trusty dog, a beautiful park a beautiful park—and a record was required. But this did not mean, as some art experts have taken it to mean, that these pictures bore 'no allegorical or secondary purpose'.[78] Far from it. Hunting and racing pictures showed a new political class that espoused land and liberty under a constitutional monarchy but had no intention of sharing it, a class that had taken power at the end of the seventeenth century for the most part by stealth, with no great battles or campaigns, no popular movements, no barricades or stormings—only the dealings of state and nation that went on, mercifully, largely without strife. William III replaced James II in 1688 as a Protestant monarch willing to abide by parliament and as such represented a turn in English history. But he was only remembered as a name, not a hero. They called his 1688 *coup d'etat* 'The Glorious Revolution' but they also called it 'bloodless', meaning negotiated by lawyers rather than won by the people. No great royal palaces or glittering court, no great moment of victory—the Houses of Orange and Hanover lived largely unspectacular lives.[79]

What was there to picture? Seventeenth-century Puritanism had its civil war heroes it is true, and some of them—Cromwell of course—lingered on into nineteenth-century dissenting traditions, but Dissent was never entirely popular or decisive. True, there had been momentary excitements. The Jacobites had got as far south as Derby and 'Bonnie Prince Charlie' was eventually seen as romantic, but only in retrospect, and only on behalf of a Stuart dynasty dead-headed and gone. American revolutionaries were clearly not acceptable heroes for English

---

[75] Cobbett, *Rural Rides* (1830. 1912) vol. i, p.38. For Meynell, 'Prince of Fox Hunters': Throsby, *Selected Views* (1791) pp.301–11.

[76] Smith, *Life of a Fox* (1843) p.ix; 'Mind of the Hunted Fox', *Hunting and Polo Journal*, October 1925, vol. I, 4.

[77] David Sylvester, *London Review of Books*, 18 May 2000.

[78] Brigstocke, *Western Art* (2001) p.714; Egerton, *British Sporting and Animal Painting* (1978) p.viii. Pictures of record were not always accurate: eg 'Coursing at Ashdown', CRO D/ING/164.

[79] It took a long time before what came to be called 'Whig History' emerged in Macaulay's (*History of England* 1848–55) narrative of a country saved by the accession of William III, and in Carlyle's advocacy of Puritanism as a preceding act of national salvation (*Letters and Speeches of Oliver Cromwell* 1845). As we will see in chapter 4, eighteenth-century popular constitutionalism was the radical forerunner of Whig History, itself a Victorian interpretation of the progress of English liberty after 1688, finally labelled as such by Herbert Butterfield in 1931 as *The Whig* interpretation of history.

liberty either, though they had their supporters. The consumer revolution was not at first glance heroic, and slave owners were generally despised. Nor were the early engineers and industrialists seen as heroes. George Stephenson, indubitably one of the greatest, was considered an idiot by the scientific establishment.[80] Britannia and the Union Flag were icons of the state, not representations of the people.[81]

Without great heroes or popular movements, how could the Glorious Revolution be shown? Occasionally, shooting parties were made to look like a good day out, but only that, and no one, not even landlords, saw the raising of a landlord's gun as any kind of patriotic gesture.[82] But *equestrian* sporting art, particularly pictures of the thoroughbred racer in a tranquil, law-abiding landscape, was a different matter. Not the rocking horse sort. Rocking horse figures were sometimes painted to represent the folksy side of horse racing, but for all its fun, this was not dignifying.[83] Rather there was that kind of equestrian art which, in Hawkes' words, represented sport as 'a peculiar privilege'. Conventionally seen as 'conversation pieces', these were paintings of the new civil society, based on family groups dispersed across their estates, close to their servants and the land, enjoying the fruits of liberty but at the same time showing who held them.[84]

It is true that horses were painted as soon as they were famous and doomed to hang in gloomy corridors ever after.[85] But it is not true that these paintings were simply pictures of record. Horse pictures sometimes gave you the breeding as well as the name, and therefore the worth, but in Baudelaire's sense you would be able to make out the meaning long before you read the name: a silky race horse, usually in full frame, generally still, possibly with a handsome stable boy, white shirt, the sky luminous, the land utterly free from obstruction (or invasion), or allotments or workers, or children playing, the whole bathed in a brilliant light and colour all brushed down to a cool painterly shine. Down market, Trollope noted how the 'flyers' as he called them appeared as prints on every pub wall and were 'better known ... than the names and deeds of our most eminent statesmen'.[86]

A world away from events in Weardale, the shining horse picture was the aristocracy's view of itself as a class perpetrated by breeding, standing mysteriously as an object of power and refinement in its own right, in its own land, on its

---

[80] For the President of the Royal Society's attacks on the 'ignorant mechanic' George Stephenson: Cantor, 'Humphrey Davy: a study in Narcissism?', *Notes and Records* 72, September 2018, p.230. I am grateful to Prof Ken Pounds for this reference.

[81] Groom, *Union Jack* (2006) p.194.

[82] Blackstone saw the game laws as breeding a little tyrant in every manor. See Page Wood's invocation of Judge Blackstone in the debate to the introduction of John Bright's bill for the repeal of the game laws: Commons Sitting, *Hansard*, 23 March 1848, vol. 97, cc.960.

[83] See for instance Alken, 'Drawing a Cover' or 'The Meet' (YCBA nd), or Dalby, 'Quorn Hunt' (YCBA 1835).

[84] Hawkes, *Meynellian Science* (1809) pp.47–8.

[85] Reynolds charged 35 guineas for a head, 70 guineas down to the knees: *The Connoisseur*, xii, 48, August 1905, p.252. Ruskin on gloomy corridors in Hewison, *Ruskin* (2000) p.12; 'The Present State of the Arts in England' (1755), in John Johnson, Bodleian, Sport Box 11.

[86] *British Sports* (1868) p.21. On cool surfaces: Prown, *Winterthur Portfolio* (1980) p.205.

own authority. Ideas of the 'picturesque' even gave artists the right to change the record and to 'picture things unseen'. (Throsby thought that gravel pits ought to be removed from pictures of Leicestershire.)[87] In one sense, this new genre offered vistas of unimaginable open-ness. What could be more open and stable than a park? On the other hand, the horse, object of power and the principal means of being free to ride to the farthest corners of freedom, remained tethered or reined, saddled or bridled. Power and restraint equalled liberty, one and the same, personified in a horse in a landscape.[88]

English Horse Paintings

English horse paintings were emotional images before they were pictures of record. But they were also neo-classical, with clarity of order and line, perfectly composed, showing the natural order of things.[89] Wootton's Newmarket race horses—'Bonny Black' (1715), 'Lamprey' (1723), and the grey 'Victorious' (1725)—differ from his fox-hunting pictures in that they fill the frame.[90] James Seymour's 'Othello' (1741–45) shows that he too was painting differently for racing than for hunting. But the big breakthrough came in the 1760s with George Stubbs. Stubbs broke the tethering rule with his giant painting of the mighty, rearing, 'Whistlejacket'. Robert Tombs cites Charles Watson-Wentworth, 2nd Marquess of Rockingham, who commissioned the painting, as a key figure in the new ruling class:

> ...a prime example of the wealthy, cultivated and public-spirited Whig oligarchy ...a fellow of the Royal Society and the Society of Antiquaries, a member of the Society of Dilettanti, a trustee of Westminster School, vice-admiral of Yorkshire and Lord Lieutenant of the West Riding: he owned broad acres in Yorkshire, Northamptonshire and Ireland, and controlled several parliamentary seats; and he was a member of Whites and the Jockey Club, a horse lover and a patron of the arts.[91]

---

[87] Gilpin, *Observations* (1786) Introduction. Throsby, *Selected Views* (1791) pp. i-iii. On the thoroughbred as a luxury object in a consumer culture: Podeschi, *Books on the Horse* (YCBA 1981) p. ix.

[88] 'the pictorial tradition of the imperial prince on his charger...had gone...But the horses hadn't': Schama, *Face of Britain* (2015) p.64.

[89] Horse pictures could show people at work. Grooms, jockeys, stable lads, and trainers can be seen mounted or leading or looking on: race cards 1813–1903, John Johnson, Bodleian, Sport Box 12. It was not unusual for race cards not to mention jockeys. J F Herring's 'Study of Three Steeplechase Cracks [top jockeys]' (YCBA 1846) was a turning point.

[90] John Wootton, 'Duke of Rutland's Bonnie Black' (YCBA 1715), 'Lamprey with his owner Sir William Morgan' (YCBA 1723), 'Duke of Hamilton's Grey Victorious, at Newmarket' (YCBA 1725).

[91] Tombs, *English and their History* (2014) p.348.

Stubbs' powerful thoroughbreds—'Lustre', 'Scrub', 'Gimcrack', 'Turf', 'Eclipse'—took the genre to another level of natural order, a tradition carried on by Benjamin Marshall and G. F. Herring before reaching, in the 1930s, that other genius of neo-classical equestrian painting, Alfred Munnings.[92] Munnings' two great hunt pictures—'Portrait of a Sporting Lady' (1929) and 'Paul Mellon on Dublin' (1933)—followed Stubbs and Marshall in the high racing style long after the Whigs had been forgotten.[93]

Early hunting pictures are more difficult to interpret. Wootton's 'Preparing for the Hunt' (1740–50) for instance, and Seymour's 'Sir Roger Burgoyne Riding Badger' (1740), are heavily Dutch influenced. Wootton's is full of clutter: no land, no liberty, no movement or promise of movement. Seymour's 'Badger' is a big grey carrying a stiff-backed rider. Similar with the early hunting on-foot pictures, Closterman's 'John, 1st Earl Poulett' (1680) and Wissing's 'Portrait of a Boy' (1685) show hunters emerging out of dark woods, neither open nor free, their clothes unsuitable, the gun too long and the spear carrier looking for a better part. Later hunting on-foot pictures, more Tory provincial than Whig metropolitan, settled on generic English landscapes with varying degrees of realism—sportsman with son, sportsman with wife, sportsman with dog, gun, pony, brace of pheasant etc—but with no great painterly or allegorical power other than the way back through the woods.[94]

Late eighteenth-century fox-hunting pictures liked to show land and liberty but only reached the high racing ideal with Benjamin Marshall, who could paint the Stubbs way whether for hunting or for racing ('George 5th Duke of Gordon on Tiny', 1806; and 'Diamond', 1799), as could Edwin Cooper ('A Sportsman with Pony and Dogs', 1832), Richard Davis ('George Mountford et al', 1836), and Lionel Edwards ('Taking Out the Hounds', nd). But fox-hunting, as we have seen, trumpeted its own version of land of liberty by other means—in prints and engravings, on pots and mugs, through comic stories, popular ballads, and light fiction.

[92] Starting with James Seymour's, 'Othello' (YCBA 1741–45); George Stubbs, 'Whistlejacket' (National Gallery 1762); Stubbs, 'Lustre, held by a Groom' (YCBA 1760–62); Stubbs, 'Turf, with jockey up, at Newmarket' (YCBA 1765). See essays by Blake on Stubbs and servants, and Stubbs and politicians, in Warner and Blake, *Stubbs and the Horse* (2004) chs. 3, 5. 'He perfected an immaculate clarity': Prodger, 'What Lies Beneath?', *New Statesman*, 18 October 2019. For fine examples of the style after Stubbs, with jockeys 'up', see paintings by Benjamin Marshall ('Diamond with Dennis Fitzpatrick Up', YCBA 1799), G F Herring ('Memnon with William Scott Up' YCBA 1825), and 'Margrave with James Robinson Up' (YCBA 1833).

[93] Although not to historians. Alfred Munnings, 'Portrait of a Sporting Lady' (YCBA 1929) and 'Paul Mellon on Dublin' (YCBA 1933). Mellon, whose collecting made some of this book possible, is interesting in his own right as man who found liberty through riding: Mellon, *Treasures* (2001) p.22, p.74.

[94] Edward Hartley, 'A Sportsman' (YCBA 1752); Francis Wheatley, 'Portrait of a Sportsman with his Son' (YCBA 1779); James Ward, 'Portrait of Rev T Levett and Favourite Dogs, Cock-shooting' (YCBA 1811); Edwin Cooper, 'Sportsman with Shooting Pony and Gun Dogs' (YCBA 1832).

Thomas Gainsborough's 'Mr and Mrs Andrews' (1750) is probably the most famous English picture of the eighteenth century, and although it has no horse or rider it is a land and liberty sporting picture nevertheless. Light and spacious, the estate runs as far as the eye can see, and the artist lets you see that by keeping his figures well to the side. Mrs. Andrews sits in a bower of blue silk. Mr. Andrews casually carries a gun, faithful dog looking up.[95] There are no mantraps and there's not a poacher to be seen, let alone one without his teeth making intimidatory gestures. By contrast, William Henry Hunt's 'The Gamekeeper' (1834) puts land and liberty squarely in the gamekeeper's hands. A picture of a free man, he is young, hardy, armed, and ready. But he stands like no servant stands and could just as easily be a poacher. There could even be something in his bag, but a strong left arm is not going to let you look.[96] You have to judge.

Not that everybody judged these pictures positively. There were many *anti-horsey* pictures. You discover that your horse has the reins under his tail. You discover that he wants to go the other way. You discover (alas too late and out of sight) a small post. These are 'The Miseries of Driving'. Out hunting, the parson discovers another form of baptism, in the river. And so on. In 1854 a London theatre ran a sketch called 'The Parlour of a Sporting House' where a stupid sportsman loses his gun to a safety-conscious clown who promptly blows the head off a member of the audience. No doubt everybody knew what they were laughing at.[97]

Everything about hunting was to do with land but everything to do horses and hounds was a matter of *judgement*. The gentry built their authority on it. Horse breeders built their reputations on it. Algy and all the great MFHs built their masterships on it. In 1921 the Prince of Wales and the Duke of York joined Minna and Algy and the Quorn for a few days in the saddle. Like Paul Mellon, Minna was an American who had acquired that habit of cool side-on judgement (for horses, for cattle, for hounds, for people, for paintings) expected of her. She wanted the royals to have it too, and was surprised they didn't.[98] In 1921 Ireland was in a state of revolution and John Butler Yeats painted 'On the Old Racecourse, Sligo'. Taken from an Irish point of view of horse and rider going hard at it, not the English point of looking side-on at a reined or tethered animal, Yeats' rider holds on for dear life behind a shaggy main pounding across a rough course.[99] This is the

---

[95] Gainsborough (National Gallery 1750).   [96] Hunt (YCBA 1834).

[97] Norwood, 'Britannia Theatre, Hoxton', Leicester PhD (2006) ch. 6. See also Alken, 'Sporting Discoveries', nd, graphite; Hablot Knight Brown, 'The Sporting Parson', nd, black chalk, and works by, among others, Cruikshank. Mary Darly, Gillray, Jones, Rowlandson, and Smith: Paul Mellon Collection, YCBA, and John Johnson, Bodleian, Sport Box 10.

[98] According to Minna, Prince Edward rode badly on ill-considered horses and both princes showed bad manners by keeping the hunt waiting: Hunting Diary, February to March 1921: LRO DG 51/9. On the importance of good judgement, Henry Field, Ts, 'The Quorn Hunt', 11 March 1954: LRO DG 51/123.

[99] J B Yeats, 'On the Old Racecourse, Sligo' (YCBA 1921). The English painter 'Snaffles', (Charles Johnson Payne) answered Yeats with a similar picture, also from the rider's point of view, only this time

framing of land and liberty in an Irish idiom. You can only know the real meaning of something by opposing it.

This Sporting Life

Orwell got it wrong. Hunting was never 'merely a fetish of the aristocracy'. The country life, and regard for the country life, was apparent to all classes. Fox hunters traversed the country while other classes looked on. Legal hunters went out by day. Illegal hunters went out by night. While the game laws cut across rural life like a knife, fox-hunting ran across it like a mob.[100] Sport did not have to wait until the modern era in order to become important.

Of all the peculiar privileges of the old ruling class—their money and wealth, their homes and pictures, their travel and taste—sport was the most public and the most publicized. But working with dogs and horses and breeding birds and rabbits and taking down game and lifting fish was part of a working-class sporting life too, and it never faded. In the country, people kept their tools sharp and straight, loved their dogs, mended their nets, and knew their terrain. In the towns people loved the Arcadian ideal, even if they could not always imagine what it might mean to them.[101] They loved horse racing, even though most of them had never been near a race horse.[102] They loved fighters and jockeys, horses and greyhounds, like old friends and put their money on them. McKibbin makes the chastening point that the middle classes had never heard of 'Mick the Miller' (Irish brindle, 1926–39, sixty-one wins in eighty-one races, £20,000 lifetime prize money).[103]

In any case, the difference between town and country was not always so obvious. In Alan Sillitoe's *The Loneliness of the Long Distance Runner* (1959), Smith is townie locked up in a borstal but when he runs, he runs free and loves the land. In Melvyn Bragg's *Crossing the Lines* (2003), Joe goes scavenging the fells with local poachers, men from the poorer end of town, 'always with dogs,

coming up to a jump, in Leicestershire, on a beautiful day. He called it 'The Finest View in Europe' (YCBA 1926). When fox-hunting was banned in 2005, the *Daily Mirror*, which had campaigned for the ban, offered a photograph of a hunt from the unflattering back rather than the all-powerful front— 'Tally Ha Ha ha' 'Now Fox Off!' (18 February 2005).

[100] Orwell, *Tribune* 10 March 1944. The wrestler William Litt ('whose name will ever live on in the annals of Cumbrian sport') thought fox-hunting 'a work of blood and murder': Caine, *Cleator and Cleator Moor* (1916) p.400.

[101] The 'Arcadian' ideal, invented 1520–1650, is seen by Nicolson as an organic, patriarchal, libertarian natural world fit for human life spreading its ideological wings into Romanticism, Marxism, Environmentalism, and Americanism: *Earls of Paradise* (2008) p.5. Thomas explains the natural world as a sort of liberty: *Man and the Natural World* (1984) pp.15–18.

[102] Vamplew calls the thoroughbred race horse 'little more than a betting mechanism' but in this he is surely missing something: 'Horse Racing', in Mason, ed., *Sport in Britain* (1989) p.215.

[103] *Classes and Cultures* (1998) p.362.

always with each other, the last of a deeply persistent tribe' trusting their living to the land itself.[104]

People admired poachers in England like they admired social bandits in other countries.[105] People grew giant onions and marrows too, and brought home from the garden bunches of beetroot hanging from their handlebars. They showed everything and turned it into a contest—from leek shows and flower shows to brass bands and pigeon fancying. Grinning and baking made sport, and in order to be able to ride and shoot they joined the Volunteers and the Territorials. It is a mistake to see land and liberty as cut off from the everyday lives of an industrial people. Barry Hines' Billy Caspar scuffs along the back fields of a Yorkshire mining village dreaming of a new life and finds it in a young hawk which he names Kes. That the sport he and Kes make has got absolutely nothing to do with the football or anything else Billy does at school makes it all the more high and wondrous. Not every kid played to the teacher's whistle.[106]

And it is a mistake to see field sports as either 'traditional' or 'modern'. Leicestershire fox-hunting was modern in the sense that it was quick, smart, and consumable. Certainly it was radically different from what had gone before, just as the rapid breech loading rifle was different from the old Brown Bess. Yet modern as fox-hunting could be, hunting on horseback was as old as horseback and hunting with a weapon was as old as hunting. People hunted for all sorts of reasons.

Finally, fox-hunting and poaching had much in common. Both were wrapped in territorial control, in military analogy, symbolic mastery, personal identity, courage, skill, and sensation. Both got tired and wet, miserable and hot, lost their way, lost their judgement, found nothing, caught a cold, had a bad day.[107] It's true that poachers were on the wrong side of the law, but there was sport in that too. Beating the keepers took some nerve and skill. As for fox hunters and wealthy shooting parties who had paid for their right to sport, both groups were criticized for destroying agriculture, raising prices, criminalizing the poor, and being foolish when they were supposed to be sensible. Both were associated with the worst excesses of landlordism and croneyism while working-class race-goers were criticized for their debauchery on exactly the same terms as aristocrats.[108] In England, the red vans of the Land Nationalization Society drew large crowds in the agricultural villages. In Wales, Lloyd George built his reputation on addressing the land problem and the sporting gentry who had created it. In Scotland, deer-

---

[104] Bragg, *Crossing* (2003) p.168; Sillitoe, *Loneliness* (1959) p.10.

[105] Hobsbawm, *Bandits* (1969) p.13.

[106] ' "It's fierce an' it's wild, an' it's not bothered about anybody, not even me right? And that's why it's great" ': Hines, *Kestrel* (1968) p.146, and movie *Kes* directed by Ken Loach (1969). Harry Pearson does the northern round: horses (Appleby Fair), flowers (Malton Show), fruit (Egton Gooseberry Fair), birds (Sedgefield Show), pigs (Bellingham Show), sheep dogs (Kildale Show), onions (Harrogate Show), and rabbits (North East Rabbit Championships): *Racing Pigs and Giant Marrows* (1966).

[107] Henry Alken, 'Grouse Shooting: The Right Sort, The Wrong Sort', 'Partridge Shooters: The Right Sort, The Wrong Sort' (YCBA *c.*1815).

[108] Newcastle races in 1847 hosted 128 publicans' tents and the day finished with a riot: Newcastle Races Herbage Committee List of Tents and Stands 1847 (NCL).

hunting was equated with desolation. In Ireland, the Englishness of sport played its part in fomenting a revolution.[109] In time, people would win their right of way over footpaths and bridleways, and the National Trust and National Parks would expand the right to roam. In a democracy, it was difficult for landowners to deny others that liberty which they claimed as quintessentially English for themselves. And yet, whatever their class or nationality, fox-hunters and game-hunters alike knew their high days and holidays, days of action and repose, days they would never forget.[110] Sport was big, and people knew about it. It promised a land of liberty in ways they understood.

[109] It's an interesting question whether country house fox-hunting, the sport of the colonizer, or the Gaelic Athletic Association, the sports of the Gael, contributed more to nationalism in Ireland: Rouse, *Sport in Ireland* (2015) ch. 3. 'In the absence of the lords of the parish the labourers would often manifest the liveliest appreciation': 'Among the Agricultural Labourers' (London, Land Restoration League 1893) p.10; George, 'The Rural Land Problem' (London, Liberal Publication Department 1913); Stewart, 'Deer Forests, National Wastefulness' (Liverpool, Financial Reform Association 1888) and Outhwaite, 'Deer and Desolation. The Scottish Land Problem' (London, United Commission to Tax Land Values 1910): John Johnson, Bodleian, Land and People, Box 3.
[110] George Stubbs, 'Two Gentlemen Going a Shooting with a View of Creswell Crags' (YCBA nd).

3

'Bottom'

> *Bottom*: a courage equally active and passive—the safest man to back
> in the universe
>
> (Dowling, Fistiana, 1841)

Deep Play

In his depiction of a Balinese cock-fight, the American anthropologist Clifford
Geertz tried to understand what was happening beyond the fight itself. He
concluded that cocks fought while men gambled in order to express their deepest
'inner affiliations'. The real meaning of the cock-fight, therefore, lay not in what
you could see, only in what you couldn't see; in what Geertz famously called 'deep
play'.[1]

Whatever Tom Sayers and John Heenan thought they were doing in a
Hampshire field early one April morning in 1860, they were not playing at it,
deeply or otherwise. They were there to fight with their bare hands for as long as it
took one to inflict such injuries on the other that he was rendered incapable of
standing up like a human being. On the face of it, you might think that no sane
person would want to do or witness such a thing. This was not the case, and this
chapter is an attempt to explain why.

The fight had started twelve months before in the New York newspaper offices
of *Porter's Spirit of the Times* and in the London offices of *Bell's Life*.[2] In the
English champion Sayers, *Bell's* thought they had an English sporting hero, or at
any rate the chance of making one at a time when prize-fighting was in low
regard.[3] In the challenger Heenan, *Porter's* thought they had a big Irish-American
who could relieve the English of their own championship. In the event, both sides
were wrong, but from the moment Heenan got off the boat and Sayers turned up

---

[1] In the Balinese cock-fight 'ordinary everyday experience [is rendered] comprehensible': Geertz,
'Thick Description', *Interpretation of Cultures* (1958) pp.8–9, p.443.

[2] Modelled on *Bell's Life in London*, *The Spirit of the Times* was founded by William Porter in 1831.
Porter's Spirit of the Times split from the original in 1858.

[3] 'By the 1830s prize fighting was a farce': Anderson, 'Prize Fighting and the Courts', *Sports
Historian*, 2001, p.37. By the 1840s, English prize-fighting was not even making the front page of
journals named after prize-fighters: *Tom Spring's Life in London*, 6 June 1841 to 18 June 1843. *The
Northampton Herald* said it preferred 'the boat, the bat and the rifle ground' to the prize-ring (21 April
1860).

to meet him at Owen Swift's public house in Tichborne Street, *Bell's Life* reported that interest in the fight was 'unusually deep and extensive'.[4] Newspapers on both sides of the Atlantic ran the story at least once a week in a four month run-up, and newspapers all over the English speaking world were running it for months after. Readers learned that nothing stood between the two men and the championship belt other than Tom's 'consumate generalship' on the one hand and Heenan's 45 inch chest on the other.[5]

Who was John Heenan? John Camel Heenan was a New York strong boy, born to Irish parents in West Troy on 2 May 1833. When John was 14 the family moved to California, where he was apprenticed as a blacksmith in the Benicia shipyards of the Pacific Mail Steamship Company. But Heenan's real talent was for violence and next we find him back home, with a manager, living in Park Row, one of the notorious Five Points intersections of New York City. Here he appears to have had connections with the Irish interest at Tammany Hall, running a sporting house with various associates, and working in a privileged position for the Customs House. That was the day job, but the inference was that Heenan also worked as a minder and enforcer when required.[6] In October 1858, age 25, he was tempted into proving how hard he really was by agreeing to have a proper fight with another Tammany Hall hard man, John Morrissey. Morrissey had been implicated in a spate of attacks and assassinations directed against 'Nativist' New York gangs led by Tom Hyer and Bill Poole, at whose hands the Irishman had suffered a terrible waterfront beating in 1855.[7] But Morrissey had been around the ring too long for Heenan and it only took him twenty minutes to stop the challenger in what by now he and his backers were calling the American Heavyweight Championship. That Heenan knew bad men and was not unacquainted with large sums of money ($5,000 stake against Morrissey), or show girls (he was married briefly to the actress Adah Menken), does not in itself tell us much about him other than that his world did not much resemble that of his English opponent. When they met, Sayers had had fifteen official fights (won fourteen) to Heenan's one, and plenty others before that. His last fight had been only for a few hundred pounds, and the nearest (so far as we know) he got involved with show business women was when his former common law wife hit him in the face near a theatre. Sarah was bound over for £10 (paid by her father) after confronting

[4] *Bell's Life* 15, 29 January 1860. The two men met at Swift's on 17 December 1859.
[5] *Bell's Life* 1 January 1860.
[6] Anon, *Prize Ring Heroes* (1889) p.63; Anon, *Death and Memoir of J C Heenan* (1873) pp.1–2. The Five Points intersection contained 3,435 Irish families in 1860 according to Asbury, *Gangs of New York* (1927) p.6.
[7] Asbury, ibid, p.21, pp.82–91; Gorn, 'Prize Fighting', in Pope, ed., *New American* (1997) p.231. Morrissey was arrested in 1855 as an accessory in the murder of Poole, or 'Bill the Butcher'. The trial collapsed and Morrissey walked free. Arrested again in 1856 for the attempted murder of two waiters, it was rumoured that Tammany Hall's influence with the District Attorney's Office got him off: *New York Clipper, Life and Battles of John Morrissey* (1879) p.13. On Nativists and Irish American fighters: Anon, *Prize Ring Heroes* (1889) pp.47–51.

Sayers in the street with his stage mules at half past midnight after a performance at *The Britannia* music hall. Accompanied by some other men, she also knocked his hat off. Tom had custody of the children. 'I don't know where she lives and I don't want to know for 1000 years' he told the magistrate.[8] Above all, Sayers was the best prize-fighter in England and Heenan was not only not the best prize-fighter in the United States, he was not even the best prize-fighter in West Troy.[9]

The most important point about Tom Sayers was that he was an out and out professional who beat much bigger men not only because he had 'bottom'—that is, the capacity to take punishment and give it—but because prize-ring rules allowed him to fight tactically. That there were no official weight divisions, only 'matches', and the fact that there was no points scoring, or medical supervision, might have led to ludicrous encounters except that money, not daring, decided whether a fight happened, and once it did happen, strength and size did not always decide the outcome.[10] The 1839 London Rules (themselves a refinement of Broughton's 1743 Rules) allowed a man to 'drop' (go on one knee) in order to end one round before coming back to 'scratch' (a mark in the middle of the ring) in order to start another. The thirty-second break in between was vital to men in trouble or in need of a rest. It is true that fighters were not supposed to drop without an effective blow having been struck, but what was an effective blow? They dropped all the same, and anyway, bare fists were neither so hard nor so swingeing that one could be sure whether they alone put the man down.[11] In 1853 the 'Pugilistic Benevolent Association', so called, revised London Rules by limiting the size of boot spikes for outdoor fights, but nothing major. Sayers fought classically according to the rules, punching straight and short, moving gamely in spiked boots, and ending most rounds either wrestled to the ground or going down on one knee, but always able to make it back to his corner and up to scratch again. Lane Jackson saw Sayers fight Bob Brettle in the street in 1859: a sudden commotion, hundreds of carts and barouches, a 'perfunctory handshake', a quick lead-off and, for this schoolboy at least, more dropping than fighting.[12]

Sayers had his first proper prize-fight in 1848, soon after his move to north London. Born in the back lanes of Brighton in 1826, he started fighting age 16 in

---

[8] British Library Theatre Cuttings Box 65, newspaper cutting, 31 March 1863. Heenan met the actress Adah Menken at the *Clipper* offices and they married in 1859. Like her English contemporary Catherine Walters, Menken understood the sexual allure of women on horseback: cover photograph, Fleischer, *Reckless Lady* (1941). On the stake money: *Porter's Spirit of the Times*, 19 October 1858.

[9] Morrissey also came from West Troy. *Troy Daily Arena*, 23 January 1860 accounts for its two home town boys.

[10] The National Sporting Club in London introduced seven mandatory weight divisions in 1904, and an eighth, 'light heavyweight', in 1914. Broughton's Rules identified 'heavy' 'middle', and 'light' in 1746, but only as a guide for punters.

[11] Dowling, *Fistiana* (1846) pp.105–6. London Rule 7 said that dropping without being hit meant disqualification: Rodriguez, *Regulation of Boxing* (2008) p.26.

[12] Lane Jackson, *Sporting Days* (1932) pp.144–5. There were rumours of duplicity (a 'cross') in this fight.

casual wagers at the town races. The editor of *Bell's* claimed that his parents were from County Kerry, making him as Irish as Heenan, but this was wrong.[13] His father and mother were Sussex people, William a shoemaker. Sayers said he was a bricklayer by trade[14] (and Heenan the brick) but publicans ran the London fight game so, after laying bricks on the railway in the 1840s, we find him in the early 1850s with a growing reputation keeping house with Sarah Henderson at *The Laurel Tree* in Bayham Street, Camden, and after that at *The Bricklayers' Arms*, also in Camden.[15] Dickens described Camden at that time as 'an unsettled neighbourhood', unsettled by 'THE RAILROAD', and Tom came with the railroad.[16] Though church people they were not, he and Sarah married with their two children in tow at St. Peter's Church, Islington, on 8 March 1853.

Tom was barely 11 stone but he couldn't get 11-stone men to fight him. Or, more accurately, they couldn't get anyone to back them to fight him. No stake, no match, so he was usually over-matched against bigger men in long, tactical encounters. Fight details vary but it seems he went nearly two hours with Dan Collins in 1850, two and a half hours with Jack Grant in 1852, over two hours with Nat Langham in 1853, over three hours with Harry Paulson in 1856, five hours over two fights with Aaron Jones in 1857, and over an hour giving away four stone against the 'The Tipton Slasher', Bill Perry, in a boat off Southend Pier also in 1857, where he was presented with his championship belt.[17] When he was matched against Heenan, Sayers' last big fight had been two years before against Paddock of Redditch, winning in one hour twenty, dropping three times but nevertheless, by all accounts, 'a picture to behold'. At his benefit night in St George's Hall, Southwark, in March 1860, Sayers showed his belt and was presented with the old time champion Tom Cribb's cup and lion's skin 100 gram silver belt just to remind him, as if he needed reminding, in whose steps he trod.[18]

The Englishman had the experience and the American had the chest. Odds are always short in boxing matches unless there's talk of a mismatch, or a 'cross', and in this regard Tom was not naive. His fight with William Bainge, fighting name 'Benjamin', in 1858, was so mismatched *Bell's* said it was 'an insult'. Bainge was a novice who had no idea what he was in for. The fight lasted six minutes with no tactics and plenty of 'ruby'.[19]

[13] Editor of *Bell's Life, The Championship of England* (1860) p.8.   [14] *The Times*, 31 May 1860.

[15] Public houses were 'bulkheads' of popular culture, says Stan Shipley, in "Tom Causer", *History Workshop Journal* (1983) p.30. The connection between drink and sport continued long after publicans stopped being patrons. See adverts for beers and ales—Flowers' IPA? 'invaluable tonic'; Waltham's Ale? 'great strength'; Elliott's Ale? 'splendid condition': John Johnson, Bodleian, Beer Box 1.

[16] Dickens, *Household Words*, 11 November 1854, in Slater, ed., *Dickens' Journalism* (1998) p.244. Dickens knew Bayham Street. He'd lived there as a child in 1823.

[17] *Bell's Life*, 20 June 1858.   [18] *Bell's Life*, 4 March 1860.

[19] Or blood. *Bell's Life*, 10 January 1858 referred to the fight's perversion of the betting with rumours that Sayers was intending to 'chuck it'.

As the big fight approached, the odds on a Sayers victory lengthened from 7/4 to 2/1, although it's fair to say there were different betting markets depending on how much you were prepared to lose.[20] Stake money was different from betting, and in this case was set at £500 apiece to be deposited in £50 instalments, the final £50 at Swift's *Horseshoe*.[21] *Bell's* noted a gathering surge of excitement 'more than anything... in modern times'. Do or die, it predicted that if the fight was badly conducted, it would 'put an end to pugilism in this country'.[22]

Both men went into training in February—Tom back on home turf on the breezy Sussex Downs; Heenan and entourage braving it in deepest Wiltshire. Training was serious because money was serious. Working within a tradition that advocated the balancing of the body's natural 'humours' (blood, phlegm, bile), old ring hands advocated three salts, three sweats, and three sicks (vomits) a day, plus lots of walking and lean meat, no fats, no oils, no puddings, pastries, tea, coffee, sex, masturbation, or constipation. A blue pill as big as a pea did the trick (apparently).[23]

In March, the Sayers camp moved to Newmarket, sticking with the racing fraternity, while Heenan found himself not welcome wherever he went. From Wiltshire to Somerset, from Cambridge to Northamptonshire to Leicestershire, county constabularies told him to move along. After some pushing and shoving at his Trent Lock training camp, he was arrested only to be released by Derby magistrates on bail bigger than the stake money.[24]

If there were plenty of people in authority who turned a blind eye to the ring's depredations, there were those who didn't and tried to stop it as a breach of the peace, or a riot, or common assault, or, if it turned for the worse, manslaughter.[25] The main legal objection was not physical injury but the risk of social disorder. In 1825 judges were encouraging magistrates to apply the criminal law after two deeply unpleasant manslaughter cases had come to the fore, one involving a carter (guilty), the other involving two Eton schoolboys 'not the least discomposed' (acquitted).[26] The courts tried again in the 1830s under the 1828 and 1837 Offences Against the Person Act which allowed convictions against all involved in the common enterprise of organizing a fight, not just the fighters, gaining convictions for manslaughter in 1838 and 1839. But no matter how hard judges

---

[20] *Bell's Life*, 1, 8 April 1860.   [21] *Bell's Life*, 26 February, 25 March, 8 April 1860.

[22] *Bell's Life*, 8 April 1860.

[23] 'Pupil', *British Boxer* (1850) p.11; Dowling, *Fistiana* (1846) pp.133–6. On traditional and modern fitness regimes, see Carter, *Medicine, Sport and the Body* (2012) p.15.

[24] *Bell's Life*, 26 February, 6 March, 15 April 1860.

[25] 'the beating or it may be only the striking or touching of a person, or putting him or her in fear': 'Common Assault' as defined in Vincent, *Police Constables' Manual* (1912) 15th edition. The 1839 Metropolitan Police Act allowed constables to take custody of anyone suspected of disturbing the public peace.

[26] *Bell's Life*, 30 January, 13 March 1825. Lord Shaftesbury's younger brother died after an organized fight with an older boy at Eton that lasted two hours, or sixty rounds: Hammonds, *Shaftesbury* (1923) p.265.

pressed, magistrates continued to turn a blind eye. Of the thirty men tried at the Old Bailey for prize-fighting manslaughter charges between 1856 and 1875, thirteen were acquitted and of the seventeen who were convicted, no one got more than six months. In 1875 Judge Bent called the prize-ring 'brutal and disgraceful' but superior persons had been calling it that for a hundred years and by then the ring, a hole-in-corner affair anyway, was being driven into ever darker places.[27]

Heenan was no stranger to dark places. Prize-fighting was illegal in New York too. Big matches there, like big matches in London, popped up at safe or secret venues—across the state line, on boats, or over in Canada.[28] In England, Tom's first fight with Collins had started in Kent, moved to Surrey, and ended at Gravesend docks six months, two counties and ninety-two rounds later. Sir George Lewis, Home Secretary, said that the Heenan fight, once it happened, would be treated as a breach of the peace. Sir Richard Mayne, Commissioner of Metropolitan Police, said the same and issued his constables with cutlasses just as he had during the Chartist disturbances. In the week before, nobody knew where Sayers Heenan was going to take place but everybody knew where to buy a ticket. On the night before, nobody was sure where to find Heenan but everyone knew he was at Nat Langham's.[29] On the morning of the fight, Tuesday 17 April, everybody knew that it wasn't going to happen but everyone knew when and where the trains left (4am, London Bridge), how many (two, thirty-five carriages apiece), and whether rugs and hampers were available (they were).[30] Dickens sent his best man, Hollingshead, who wondered whether the early morning crowds had come to go with him or see him go. He shared a compartment, he said, with a lord, a baronet, an MP and a famous poet; but named no names.[31] *The New York Times* correspondent had never seen so many thieves and pickpockets in one place and wondered at so many wanting to know the time, so few able to give it.[32] Constables were stationed at every railway station out of Surrey, but the train took the Dover line before turning south and swinging west at Reigate. Once out into Hampshire

---

[27] Wiener, *Men of Blood* (2004) pp.41–50. Wiener's main thesis rests on a significant nineteenth-century fall in male violence under the impact of 'a deliberate civilizing offensive' by the middle classes along with changes in the attitude of the criminal justice system to crimes against the person.

[28] Anderson, 'Brief Legal History of Prize Fighting in 19c America', *Sport in History* 24, 2004, p.40. In South Wales, they fought on 'bloody spots above the valley townships': Stead and Williams, eds., *Wales and its Boxers* (2008) p.16. Jimmy Wilde (b.1892) was trained by his father-in-law Dai Davies, a so called 'mountain man' (p.64).

[29] Leading sporting houses in London in 1860 included Nat Langham's *Cambrian*, Owen Swift's *Horseshoe*, George Bryers' *Black Horse*, Harry Brunton's *George & Dragon*, and Mr. Bishop's at 170 New Bond Street.

[30] *Bell's Life*, 12 February, 15, 27 April 1860.

[31] John Hollingshead, 'The Great Pugilistic Revival', *All the Year Round*, 19 May 1860. Dickens had intended to go himself but changed his mind: Reynolds, 'Dickens and Prize Fighting', *Dickens Studies Newsletter*, June 1983, p.48.

[32] *New York Times*, 30 April 1860.

the line was free and all aboard were at liberty to get off on arrival.[33] At dawn, about 1,500 passengers got down outside Farnborough to tramp the last half mile across marshy ground to be met by twenty men with sticks and chairs who were there to decide who should see the law broken sitting down, and who should see the law broken standing up. It was rumoured that Prime Minister Palmerston and the young Prince of Wales were among the sitting-down classes.[34] Lord Lovain told parliament that he had heard of 'great names as having been present [Name!]'.[35] Hollingshead was just as discreet, letting it be known that although all classes were present, including Americans, country folk, and a 'small sprinkling of aristocracy', most of the crowd were *cogniscenti*.

Tom stepped into the ring at 7am. He was 34 years old, 5'8" tall and 11 stone in weight—just over his fighting best. Famous from a hundred sporting prints and photographs (7s 6d each on application to his manager), everyone agreed he looked dapper, 'well set up', 'hard as nails'.[36] Still believing in the skin-hardening properties of vinegar, it was remarked that he looked like 'a square brick of walnut'. The most striking thing about the American was the whiteness of his skin and a perfectly broken nose. Hollingshead said it was a nose you could hang a key on: a 'celestial', and a bad sign to physiognomists the world over.[37]

Stripping, or 'peeling', was a vital part of ring ceremonial, sometimes inviting applause, always inviting scrutiny. A boxer's build told punters how seriously he had trained and how far he intended to take it. Victory usually went to the bigger man, the greater force.[38] Sayers, though bull-necked, was not particularly muscled.[39] Heenan was five inches taller, seven years younger, two and a half stone heavier, and muscular, with a far longer reach. Only across the shoulders did the two men match. *The Times* said Sayers looked at his man long and hard, as well he might. *Bell's Life* said they were as a horse to a hen.[40]

After a quick word about the weather—'Beautiful morning' said Heenan. 'Do you want to bet on it?' said Sayers—they shook hands and tossed for corners where they planted their colours, Heenan's stars and stripes, Sayers' Royal Standard on a cream background with broad crimson border (available from Owen Swift's).[41] At 7.29am they got up and came to the middle, the Englishman squinting into the sun, his two seconds behind him ('like wicket keepers'), plus

[33] *The Times*, 24 January 1860; *Bell's Life*, 22 April 1860; Butler, *Boxing in Britain* (1972) pp.38–40.
[34] Sawyer, *Noble Art* (1989) pp.68–9.
[35] Commons Sitting, 15 May 1860, *Hansard*, series 3, vol. 158, cc.1319–21.
[36] *Bell's Life*, 22 April 1860. See Lloyd, *Great Prize Fight* (1977).
[37] 'We associate the Snub and the Celestial in nearly the same category, as they both indicate natural weakness, mean, disagreeable disposition, with petty insolence': Eden Warwick, 'Notes on Noses' (1864) in Cowling, ed., *Artist as Anthropologist* (1989) p.82. See also Sawyer, *Noble Art* (1989) pp.67–68, and *Bell's Life*, 22 April 1860.
[38] Remnick, *King of the World* (1998) p.5.   [39] Anon, *Tom Sayers* (1866) p.56.
[40] *Bell's Life*, 22 April 1860; *The Times*, 18 April 1860.
[41] Weather anecdote told to John L Sullivan by another American fighter called Yankee Sullivan who claimed to have been there: Sargent, *John L Sullivan* (1892) p.37. *Vanity Fair* mentioned Heenan's

Gideon the manager, Fuller the 'ped' (professional walker), who was his trainer, a friend named Cunningham, Heenan's former conqueror John Morrissey, a 3'6" dwarf fighter called Jimmy Holden, and someone called 'The Birdman' making queer 'haloo' sounds in a cape. Heenan's corner was hardly mentioned: trainers Madonald and Cusick were there and possibly some of the Americans who had been at Ben Caunt's sporting house the night before: Mr. Moore, Heenan's uncle, Captain Martin, and one Billy Mulligan a very determined looking fellow according to the *New York Times*. Frank Lewis Dowling, editor of *Bell's Life* and key figure in the English ring, was the referee. Both fighters struck the approved attitude before going into some quick short movements, fists low, bobbing and teasing until first blood went to Sayers square on Heenan's nose, 'nobbing' in the parlance, 'uproarious applause' in the crowd. The round ended with Sayers punching his way out of a neck hold before dropping laughing to the floor.[42]

This set the pattern which, in all honesty, Dickens' man found boring. London Rules allowed fighters to punch, wrestle, and throw but not to butt, bite, kick, gouge, slap, strangle, scratch, or hit below the waist or when a man was down. Fighters therefore aimed their punches straight at the head rather than at the body, preferably at the temple or under the ear, but not usually from the side and not as hard as one might imagine because the hand is delicate and the skull is hard. Blows were not taps because there was no points-scoring. If not aiming at the head, fighters would jab in the eyes or face, or look for an opportunity to wind a man with a 'peg' to the stomach, or grab him and throw him from the neck over the hip landing heavily on top ('cross buttock'). Grabs that didn't result in throws could deteriorate into clinches, or holds. When they were tired, fighters held on to each other. After a longer exchange, or 'rally', they might take a breather. 'Fibbing' involved short jabs at close quarters. The shorter the reach, the more powerful the punch springing from the legs. More fibbed against than fibber, Heenan used his long arms to keep Sayers at bay, but a long reach tired the arm. One special favourite was to catch your opponent in a neck lock with one arm ('suit in chancery') and fib away in the face with the other hand.[43] Hair got in the way. You could tell prize-fighters by their clean shaves and cropped heads. You could also tell them by their noses. Sala liked the Turf Tap at Tattersall's because it was the one sporting pub in town where the landlord didn't have a broken nose.

colours in a ditty but we cannot be sure whether it was so: Mott, *History of American Magazines* (1938) p.202.

[42] *Bell's Life*, 22 April 1860.
[43] Dowling, *Fistiana* (1846) pp.105–6; Dowling, *Fistiana* (1841) p.363; Belcher, *Art of Boxing* (1815) p.17. Temple, ear, and stomach had been favourite targets since the beginning: Godfrey, *Treatise* (1747) pp.46–66.

The *New York Times* man didn't fancy upstairs at Caunt's because of the 'broken mugs, battered noses and crooked eyes'.[44]

As the smaller man, Sayers liked to keep on the move, but in round three he took a hard left on the nose (applause) and in round four he dropped after one on the jaw (more applause) before going back to his corner 'blinking like a dissipated owl'. Round five saw him down and straight back up again, this time looking flushed. In round six he was driven back with a blow to his right arm doing what it was supposed to do—take the punch. His arm swelling alarmingly, the Englishman was shocked into some fancy footwork to keep the American at bay and the next two rounds lasted nearly half an hour between them. Heenan had the final say however, knocking Sayers 'clean off his pins' to finish round eight.[45]

By now, having taken a lot of jabs, one side of Heenan's face had swollen blue, while Sayers' face was beginning to look 'like a battered copper tea kettle'. Sayers would hit and take a look. Heenan would grab and make a throw. Neither decisively. At 8.30am the local constabulary turned up, but stayed on the edge of the crowd as the odds, like the fight itself, stuck on evens. An hour later, Sayers was breathing heavily, freely spitting blood, right arm out of it against his chest, left hand constantly in Heenan's eyes but knuckles too puffy for hard punching. Heenan, a 'disgusting sight', according to the *Sydney Morning Herald*, was revealing himself as a man too strong to lose and not skilled enough to win.[46] And he was having difficulty seeing.

In round thirty-seven the American got hold of his man and dragged him over to the ropes. Everyone knew what this meant. Rule 28 stated that 'where a man shall have his antagonist across the ropes . . . helpless, and endanger his life by strangulation or apoplexy . . . it shall be in the power of the referee to direct the seconds to take their man away and thus conclude the round'.[47] But the referee did not do this, nor did the umpires call foul, nor did the ringside Americans believe that that was what Heenan was trying to do. They saw it as a simple attempt at a throw resisted by Sayers. The constables thought otherwise and on witnessing attempted murder they moved in to break up a fight which, in the melee that followed, resumed with Heenan out of control dragging the Englishman back to the ropes.[48] As Sayers' face turned black under 190lb downward pressure, some of the crowd urged Heenan to 'hold him!' At this point it was claimed that John Morrissey intervened from Sayers' corner to cut the ropes followed by the police to

[44] *New York Times*, 30 April 1860; Sala, *Twice Round the Clock* (1858) p.196; *The Racing Times*, 28 December 1863.

[45] *Bell's Life*, 22 April 1860.

[46] *Sydney Morning Herald*, 18 June 1860. The *New York Times* (30 April 1860) reckoned he was hardly marked. Accounts differ.

[47] Dowling, *Fistiana* (1846) pp.105–6.

[48] Some reports say three more rounds were fought but without the referee's authority to decide the end of the old, and two exhausted men coming to scratch to decide the start of the new, it was difficult to know when one round ended and another began.

separate both men who promptly fell exhausted to the grass.[49] No one was sure what happened next because of the brawling inside and outside what was left of a ring. Heenan's camp had always suspected that too much had been wagered by the English on their man to let him lose. The two fighters were last seen scarpering for the station—Heenan led by the hand. Back in London at the sign of *The Swan*, Old Kent Road, *The Times* reported that the American had been put to bed while for his part Tom turned up next day at Owen Swift's asking for his money. *The New York Times* reported differently but no matter, a photograph was taken of his battered face and a cast of his damaged arm.[50] Sports writers on both sides of the Atlantic were already busy turning a nasty case of common assault into a heroic draw between two great sporting nations.[51]

As *Bell's* had predicted, and much against what it had originally hoped, this was effectively the beginning of the end of the old prize-ring as a national institution. *Bell's* had never liked the ring and never missed an opportunity to say so. It hoped for better however; hence its part in promoting Sayers Heenan. Right from early days *The Times* never made a secret of its disdain for the ring while still reporting it. In 1867 *Sporting Life* asked how long backers would continue to find the money for something so disgusting and fraudulent. It is worthy of note that the 1867 Dangerous Performances Act was inspired by high wire walking, not prize-fighting. The following year *Sporting Life* announced that the prize ring was 'as dead as a door nail'.[52]

It limped on to the end of the century in Britain, in parts of the Empire, and in the USA, but no longer trusted, always on the back foot and well away from what it wanted most—a mass press. Fighters and promoters wanted newspapermen on their side, within a legal businesslike framework to ensure that they stayed there.[53] The last man to call himself world champion under London Rules was another Irish American, John L Sullivan (1882–89), but on that day in Hampshire in 1860, what was billed as the championship of the world was disgraced the minute it descended into torture and farce. It cannot have gone unnoticed, even by Sayers himself, that the man *Bell's Life* celebrated for his 'bottom', the man *The Saturday Review* lauded for his valour, the man instantly recognized for his patriotic

---

[49] On strangulation: *Illustrated Times*, 21 April 1860; *Bell's Life*, 22 April 1860. On the intervention: *The Saturday Review*, 28 April 1860 corroborated by *All the Year Round*, 19 May 1860. Morrrissey denied cutting the ropes but after a bit more murder and mayhem in New York, he went on to have a successful career at the races, at the gaming tables, on Wall Street, and in the US Congress: *New York Clipper* (1879) pp.20–2.

[50] Lynch, *Prize Ring* (1925) p.xxvi.

[51] *The Times*, 18 April 1860; Anon, *Sayers* (1866) pp.182–4.

[52] *Sporting Life*, 1 January 1868. Blondin caught the Dangerous Performances mood with his 1859 high wire crossing of Niagara Falls, manager on his back while cooking a pancake. In 1862 'Madame Genevieve' was seriously injured doing high wire fireworks at Highbury: *Punch*, 22 November 1862. See also, John Johnson Collection, Bodleian, Circuses Box 4.

[53] On London, the sporting press, and the mass circulation newspapers as engines of commercial sport: Harvey, 'Modern British Sporting Culture', Oxford D Phil (1996) pp.83–93, p.113.

defence of his belt in the face of a foreign challenge, was nearly murdered in a corner of an English field while his countrymen cheered.[54]

Tom's World

It was said that Tom Sayers believed thoroughly in Captain Barclay, partially in magistrates, and not at all in anyone else's point of view.[55] This was Tom's world. Fifty years before, Barclay had trained the English champion Cribb for his fight with the American Molyneaux.[56] Sayers would have known how Cribb had stood for England, how things had gone badly for him at first, and how the ring was invaded when he got into trouble. He also would have known how Barclay got Cribb into proper shape for the second fight, which he won with ease. Old time fight heroes were shaped by the sporting houses of London. They were also shaped, in a way, at the magistrates' bench, which had the power to stop it all. But not that much. Owen Swift killed three men in prize-fights and was found guilty of manslaughter for the third, but still he managed to go on as a respected figure putting his name to books on boxing, running an important pub, and assuming a prominent position in match-making. Dowling noted that he was one of the new rules' most esteemed tutors, as well he might be.[57] The night before Farnborough, a hundred fighters and ex fighters gathered at his Soho premises.

Tom was a Camden man. He'd come there bricklaying. He'd run two pubs. He liked to trot around the place in a gig pulled by a dun cob doing as he pleased, and was known for his 'sublime indifference' to anything other than that. Once at a dinner given in his honour he cleared his plate before going straight to sleep on the sofa. When a German prince observed of Mr. Punch in 1828 that he had something of the rum, lemon, and sugar in him, being 'pretty indifferent to the confusion he causes', he might have been speaking of Tom.[58]

The prize-ring was as much part of the plebeian way of being English as fox-hunting was part of the gentry's. Pierce Egan's foundational history *Boxiana* (1812–19) was plundered again and again by newspapers and magazines, prints and drawings. Boxing had a strong sense of its own history, its own heroes, and its own place in the constitution of the country as a way of settling things that was

---

[54] *Bell's Life*, 22 April 1860; *The Saturday Review*, 25 April 1860.

[55] Lloyd, *Great Prize Fight* (1977) p.53.

[56] They fought at East Grinstead on 3 December 1810 and again in Rutland on 28 September 1811. Tom Cribb (1781–1848) won both contests to be hailed as the prime English sporting ornament of his day: *Pancratia* (1815) p.346. Cribb stayed champion to lead on the first edition of *The Fancy* in 1821, even though he had not fought for ten years.

[57] Swift's manslaughter of Brighton Bill in Essex had led to a revision of London Rules: *Fistiana* (1841) p.86. *Annual Register* 1838 (1839) p.41.

[58] For Mr. Punch: Golby and Purdue, *Civilization of the Crowd* (1984) p.14; for Tom's way: *Sporting Life*, 11 November 1865.

uniquely English, but open to others who embraced it as well, including Irish, Jews, and blacks.[59] Which is to say, on a good day, prize-fighting was seen as a representative institution that made the country what it was. Belts were handed on from champion to champion, veteran fighters acknowledged, new ones positioned in the narrative, a game where the old did not grow old but stayed on the walls in peeling prints and posters.[60] George the Barber, Stevenson the Coachman, Buckhorse the face, Pearce the Game Chicken, Randall the *Non Pareil*, Broughton versus Slack, Mendoza versus Humphreys, Jackson versus Mendoza, Cribb versus Molyneaux, Cribb versus Molyneaux, again, Gully versus Gregson, Hickman versus Neate, Spring versus Langan, Sayers versus Heenan—these men were known for their bottom, for their attitude, for the things they said and did, for their fight history and, above all, for their part in what constituted a poor man's history of national honour. 'Every man who has the honour of the British fist at heart must look with admiration on the Bottom, the Wind, the Game of the champion Slack'.[61] When the British heavyweight champion Joe Beckett fought the Frenchman Georges Carpentier in London in 1919, everyone saw that he was completely out-boxed. Arnold Bennett observed however that you could sense the deep personal involvement of the crowd on his side.[62]

On Tom Spring's accession to Cribb's championship in 1823, there was a benefit at the Fives Court with a sovereign and a dinner for every old fighter present. When Tom Hickman was killed in a drag cart accident the same year, a benefit exhibition by all the top men, including Spring, raised £136 for Hickman's wife and children.[63] With the emergence of popular theatre and music hall, there was a sense in which the fistic and the comedic, the local and heroic, benefit and testimonial, exhibition and display, all merged into one running show. Joe Elvin's 'Grand Testimonial' at the South London Hall in 1899, included 'Mohawk Minstrels', 'Nigger Buskers', and 'Leading Jockeys' as well as a 'Grand Scientific Display of Boxing' and the promise of a visit from working-class royalty Dan Leno, Marie Lloyd, and Charlie Chaplin.[64] Nearby, the Bermondsey champion Tom Causer ran a pub that treated its clientele to a gallery of belts and cups and

[59] For example, Dee, 'Boxing and British-Jewish Identity', *Sport in History* 32, 2012, p.363.

[60] On profusions of prints: Boxing Print Collection, Gen Mss 4012, Beinecke Rare Book and Ms Library, Yale.

[61] Slack celebrated in *The Connoisseur*, 22 August 1754. See also the Boxing Print Collection, Gen Mss 402: Beinecke Library, Yale, mainly by Fores of Picadilly; *The Fancy*, 21 April 1821. 'There was not such a battle since / Jack Langham tackled Spring': 'Sayers' & Heenan's Great Fight' (1860), from Hindley, *Street Literature* (1871), vol. ii, p.124.

[62] 'It was as genuine as British fundamental decency': Arnold Bennett, 'The Prize Fight' (1920) in Cox, *Boxing in Art and Literature* (1935) p.145.

[63] Miles, *Pugilistica* (1906) vol. ii, pp.135–6. Spring's dinner was Cribb's treat for The Fancy (here called 'amateurs' meaning lovers of the sport) as well as for veteran fighters: Dowling, *Fights for the Championship* (1855) p.71.

[64] Poster, John Johnson, Bodleian, Boxing Folder Large. Dan Leno (George Wild Galvin, 1860–1904), actor-comedian, clog dancer, and panto dame, was the greatest stage performer of his day.

fine wines and spirits seven days a week, and dancing, music, bagatelle, sing song, and 'judge and jury' sessions on rest days.[65] Six weeks before Heenan, it must have been common knowledge that this was going to be Tom's last fight, and he had his benefit in Southwark. When he retired, he took to the stage of *The Britannia* in Hoxton as pantomime clown and local hero in a sort of standing benefit.[66] 'The Brit' was London's largest and cheapest, sixpence to get in, big enough for live animals, shouty boys and girls, cakes and oranges and huge ham sandwiches on trays.[67] When boxing became local as well as legal, honest fighters were given money-raising benefits, originally in sporting pubs but later in small halls.

In other words, long after the old-time fighters had left the scene, their part in the story of being English, and British, and Irish, was recognized.[68] Alongside hunting scenes and populist politicians, they adorned pub parlours and home hearths, faced each other on cheap jugs and posed in gaudy breeches as Staffordshire figures. Dowling made great play of the manner in which they stood—body poised, head well back, knuckles up, left foot forward—for all the ring was a stage, fighters actors on it.[69] Down among the knuckle classes, costers loved the penny gaff and the rat pit. Serving out (knocking flat) a policeman was 'the bravest act by which a coster can distinguish himself'.[70] Popular theatre enjoyed freak sensations (a musical fish, a lion that ate with a spoon, 'Frog Man') as well as 'tableaux scenes' where audiences were invited to gaze at 'The Casual Ward', or 'The Work Girls of London', or fight heroes striking their attitudes, or showing their belts, or indulging in a bit of slap.[71] At Astley's, all in an evening, you could witness 'The Brute Tamer of Pompei' and 'Cupid in the Soot Bag' and it is hard not to see women's fights in this sense as sensational, even though reports insisted that they could be serious. In 1822 Sally and Nancy went at it in St. George's Fields. According to *The Fancy*, they each had short hair and short jackets but no shortage of 'fine science' in a 'regular mill' over eleven rounds. *Bell's Life* reported two London women throwing their bonnets into the ring in front of 2,000 people in 1824. It ended, we are told, in mud and blood and torn

[65] Shipley, 'Tom Causer', *History Workshop Journal* 15, 1983, pp.29–30.

[66] The pantomime clown? 'a glutton and a thief...always in mischief and in roguery', according to Leigh Hunt in the *Examiner* (1833) in Yeandle, ed., *Politics. performance and popular culture* (2016) p.64.

[67] Norwood, 'The Britannia Theatre', Leicester PhD (2006) p.4; *The Era*, 3 November 1888; *Britannia*, Saturday Programme, 29 April 1876. Thanks to Dr Norwood for leading me into the boxing world of popular theatre.

[68] See for example *The Sporting World's* 'History of British Boxing from Fig and Broughton to the Present Time', no 1, Saturday 15 March 1845. Magriel, 'Pugilism in English Pottery', *Antiques*, January 1948; Johnes and Taylor, 'Boxing in History', *Sport in History* 31, 2011, p.357.

[69] Dowling, *Fistiana* (1841) pp. 297–8. Famous 'attitudes' were struck in Young's mezzotint of 'Richard Humphreys' (1788) and Crozer's equally popular 'Mendoza versus Humphreys at Doncaster' (1790): *Antiques Collector*, January 1939, pp.350–52, 364.

[70] Mayhew, *London Labour* (1852) p.24.

[71] Handbills, 'Spring v Langan' (1824), 'Randall v Martin' (1824): John Johnson, Bodleian, Sport Box 8; for freaks, John Johnson, Bodleian, Animals on Show Box 1; on the ring as 'utterly self-contained', like the theatre: Berkowitz and Ungar, *Jewish and Black Boxers* (2007) p.86. Among the most famous prints were Cruikshank's and Turner's 'Fives Court' (1822 and 1825), set in the heart of London, showing famous faces of the ring and Fancy past and present.

clothes—torn clothes reminding the historian of 'smock races' where women ran against each other in various states of undress. Like women runners, or fox hunters, or bull runners, or powder monkeys aboard His Majesty's ships of the line, women prize-fighters were uncommon but acknowledged.[72]

Once fighting moved out of the fields, the darkened theatre became the model venue. In training, repetition was the grammar of actors and fighters alike, and after a career in boxing there was always a career on the stage.[73] Just like Sayers and Heenan, Sandow the strongman and Blondin the tight rope performer knew all too well what it was to wear tights and make up.[74]

Money and contacts came through a network of publicans, pugs (pugilists), gamblers, bookies, impresarios, and boxing *cogniscenti* all known together as *The Fancy* (fans). This 1858 description of an untypical sporting pub tells us what a typical one looked like:

'And yet, though the place is almost 'used' by sporting men, it has very little appearance of a 'sporting' public house. No portraits of 'coaching incidents', or famous prize-fighters, decorate its walls; no glass cases containing the stuffed anatomies of dogs of preternaturally small size, and that have killed unheard of numbers of rats in a minimum of minutes, ornament its bar-parlour, no loudly-boisterous talk about the last fight, or the next race coming off, echoes through its bar; and the landlord hasn't a broken nose. The behaviour of the company is grave and decorous, almost melancholy; and on the bench outside, wary-looking stablemen, and sober grooms converse in discreet undertone . . .'[75]

Nobody boxed for fun except a handful of aristocrats and they didn't box for real. Thomas Hughes' public schoolboy hero Tom Brown fought 'Slogger' Williams in exactly the same way that Sayers fought Heenan, but Hughes himself only sparred.[76] That the men Hughes sparred with at the London Workingman's College took it easy on him didn't prevent him from advising boys to 'fight it out: and don't give in while you can stand and see'—advice, paradoxically, observed in 1860 by the American.[77]

Any man in serious training needed assurance that the other side was going to show up and pay up. Stake monies were deposited in instalments through trusted

---

[72] *Bell's Life*, 10 October 1824; *The Fancy*,1821–22, p.475; Astley's poster (nd), Museum of London. For female powder monkeys aboard HMS Goliath at the Battle of the Nile (1798) see Taylor, *Sons of the Waves* (2020): 'One woman bore a son [son of a gun] in the heat of the action. She belonged to Edinburgh' (p.284).

[73] Dowling, *Fistiana* (1846) pp.109–11; Fitzsimmons, *Physical Culture* (1901) p.18; 'One of the Fancy', *Boxiana* (1812) pp.39–40.

[74] Litherland, 'Sporting Entertainments', *Sport in History* 35, 2015.

[75] *The Turf Tap*, mainly a racing house, Lower Grosvenor Place, near Hyde Park, London: Sala, *Twice Round the Clock* (1858) p.196.

[76] Read on for Hughes' analogy of Slogger Williams with Bill Neate, and Hazlitt's analogy of Neate with Entellus.

[77] Hughes, *Tom Brown's Schooldays* (1857) p.302. Hughes' sparring partners took good care 'not to hit the gentleman on the nose' though once a 'burly dokker' did just that: MacAloon, *Great Symbol* (2008) fn.90.

sporting public houses whatever the sport, whether boxing, or rowing, or 'ped'. If one side didn't pay, they lost their stake and the contest was off. Sporting houses were also involved in agreeing match terms, including corner men, referees and umpires, setting fees, organizing venues, tickets, publicity, security, and so on.[78] Sometimes pubs accommodated fighters and hosted their training. In 1822 there were fourteen key sporting houses in London run by former fighters, including Cribb's *Union Arms* corner of Panton and Oxendon Street, Tom Belcher's *Castle Tavern* in Holborn, and Jack Randall's *Hole in the Wall* in Chancery Lane.[79] By Tom's time, Nat Langham's and Owen Swift's had joined The Fancy.

The real problem was not with the stakes but with the betting.[80] Throwing a fight was known as a 'cross' and it was far easier to bet against yourself and throw a fight than it was to win a fight or move the odds. John Gully, one of The Fancy's old time heroes (champion of England, 1807–08), was a known organizer of race course coups against the odds.[81] Heenan, after a short and undistinguished career (loss, draw, loss, loss), went on to marry the daughter of a well-known New York gambler and it was widely rumoured that his third fight, against Tom King at Wadhurst in Sussex in 1863, was thrown. His last fight, in 1864, involved massive stakes of $10,000 and was surrendered early.[82]

Once in the ring, only the puncher and the punched could possibly know how effective a blow was. If a man went down falsely, it was impossible to prove it. If it was a fraud, far better that the puncher was in on it too, but if he wasn't, and he suspected a cross, he was more likely to give himself (and his punch) the benefit of the doubt and claim the victory. The Fancy watched closely but they could never be sure. If there was a cross it was just as likely to have originated with them. Stakes were public and bets were private but because the odds continued to be called ringside, fighters were aware of changes in the betting as they fought. Not only that, but there were frauds finer than simply win or lose. Punters could bet in multiples not just on who, but on what, and when, and how things would turn out. In 1824 there was panic at rumours of a 'cross' at Royston.[83] On the morning before, one of the fighters, Hudson, put six bets on himself to win in a number of

[78] *The Fancy, or The Sportsman's Guide* (1826) p.31.

[79] *The Fancy* (1826) vol. i, nos. 1–8, 1821–22, pp.174–5. Other houses were in Smithfields, Islington, Windmill Street, St. James Street, Bow Street, Stratford, and the at Fives Court in St. Martin's Street complete with elevated stage, the former headquarters of Regency pugilism. Next to it stood Bill Richmond's *Horse & Dolphin*, another house in the network: *Fistiana* (1841) pp. 43–8; and Samuel, *East End Underworld* (1981) p.129.

[80] For prize-fighting, cock-fighting, and racing as 'a trinity of popular sports ... linked inextricably to betting and to each other': Chinn, *Better Betting* (2004) p.18.

[81] Anon, *John Gully, Prize fighter, Great Betting Man etc* (1863) p.8. Gully was a butcher and a debtor before he became a prize-fighter, gambler, coal owner, and Radical MP for Pontefract supporting working-class causes, including universal suffrage, anti-Corn Law, anti-flogging in the army, and Church disestablishment: https://victoriancommons.wordpress.com.

[82] *The Racing Times*, 28 December 1863; Anon, *Prize Ring Heroes* (1889) p.85.

[83] *Bell's Life*, 16 May 1824.

ways, and the odds moved in his favour. This was curious. Fighters wanting to bet usually got someone else to lay the bet and it could have been that that had happened as well, only the other way. In the afternoon, when large sums (up from London) were put on Hudson's opponent, the markets were thrown into turmoil with rumours of a cross. But a cross which way? On fight day crowds gathered in Royston and it wasn't long before all bets were off. Next day leading members of The Fancy gathered at Belcher's in Holborn to try and work out what had happened. As we have seen, Sayers himself was accused of manipulating the odds in his fight against Bainge in 1858.[84] Though heavier and taller, his young opponent was a novice. Tom's preparations included a party the night before with steam fiddle and 'Hebrew Minstrels'.

'High and Heroic State'

In the end, everything that mattered in Tom's world led up to the fight itself. Cruikshank's 13-foot-long painted strip 'Going to a Fight' (1819) follows the crowd over forty-one frames as they make their way across the capital.[85] There was nothing quite like going to a fight. The peasant poet John Clare said he "caught the mania" on his third visit to London in 1824. Clare was mad about actresses. He was mad about theatres. He was mad about the shops, the streets, and all the ploughing to be done in these London fields, but he swooned at the sight of fighters. Six years later we find him fighting under the name of Jack Randall ready to take on all comers £500 a side at High Beech lunatic asylum, Epping Forest.[86] When there was going to be a fight, all London seemed up for it. Lord Byron and William Hazlitt caught the mania too, and as another way of being there learned 'Flash', the street slang of The Fancy.[87]

Boxing was unquestionably a literary taste, and Hazlitt was there and writing about it long before George Bernard Shaw's famous quip.[88] But Pierce Egan was hooked before Hazlitt. His *Boxiana* series opened up a language where nobody was really hurt or money lost. Rather, 'blunt' was exchanged so that 'conks' got flattened and 'nobs' got 'teased'. Egan's best boxing slang, like the prints and pictures, stood uneasily between gentility and the sick bucket. It was 'flash' to read that 'two better coves had never stripped in a finer display of noble British feeling'. But it was not flash to read in the small print that one cove had been carried to the

[84] *Bell's Life*, 10 January, 14 February 1858.
[85] 14 shillings plain, £1 coloured, unreeled from a mahogany box: I R Cruikshank, with P Egan, 'Going to a Fight' (YCBA 1819).
[86] Bate, *John Clare* (2003) p.263.
[87] *The Champion*, 22 November 1814; *Manchester Guardian*, 23 June 1821; 'The Great Fight', John Johnson, Bodleian, Sport Box 2; Hotten, *Modern Slang* (1860) pp.4–6, p.8, pp.251–61.
[88] *Sunday News*, 10 July 1927.

mark where the other had proceeded to beat him to death. Vile in any language, Flash not excepted, this was no better than 'Jacco Macoco' the 'Hoxton Monkey' who in his fights with dogs (including Cribb's 20 lb bitch 'Puss' at Duck Lane pit in 1821) was only ever covered in 'claret' or 'ruby', never called blood.[89] Jacco would shit and sweat in fear the night before a fight but once in the pit he went mad scratching and slitting. Later in the century, the public emergence of urban gangs—Scuttlers, Hooligans, and Peaky Blinders—showed just how violent Tom's world could be. Remarking on prints of Sayers and Heenan in English country churchyards and The Emerald Isle, Charles Dickens reflected, as no doubt Sayers and Heenan reflected, on the 'pastoral and meditative nature of their peaceful calling'.[90] Tom's violent world suited him and people like him. Some blamed poverty but such an excuse was, as The Spectator remarked, 'a very comfortable doctrine, even for prize-fighters'.[91] People wanted to be there. William Cobbett wanted to be there. Ladies wanted to be there, or so he observed:

> Belcher has, by the sons of cant, in every class of life, been held up to us as a monster, a perfect ruffian; yet there are very few persons who would not wish to see Belcher: few from whom marks of admiration have not, at some time, been extorted by his combats; and scarcely a female saint, perhaps, who would not, on her way to the conventicle, or even during the shuffling there to be heard, take a peep at him from beneath her hood.[92]

Hazlitt was there when London's Thomas Hickman, 'The Gas' (he worked in a gasworks) took on Bristol's Bill Neate, at Hungerford on 11 December 1821. 'Reader! Have you ever seen a fight?' Hazlitt asks, and he takes you there. Once there, we see how Neate and Hickman give what they have to give without let or hindrance—like Englishmen do, as Milton and Shakespeare and Cribb and Nelson did. And so does Hazlitt. And so do you. And so does the whole fraternity of the ring, including the man Hazlitt meets on the way who could very well have been Cobbett. Next morning, Hazlitt's companion calls round to say hadn't it been a full day? 'A complete thing?'.[93]

Hazlitt made heroes of Neate and Hickman for going at it like Englishmen, not tapping at it like French petits maitres. A man more used to seeing Keane and Kemble and Siddons strut their stuff on the London stage, Hazlitt saw Bill Neate

[89] On the death, handbill: 'Fight between Jack Brown and Bob Forbester', Leadgate. 22 May 1838: John Johnson, Bodleian, Boxing Folder Large; The Fancy 1826, pp.143–4. On 'Puss', Cribb's champion ratter: Northampton Herald, 9 June 1894.

[90] Boddy, Boxing (2006) pp.80–3. On gangs fighting with belt buckles and knives: Davies, 'Real Peaky Blinders', BBC History, September 2019.

[91] The Spectator, 10 February 1866.

[92] Cobbett in Political Register (1805) quoted in Sawyer, Noble Art (1989) pp.56–7.

[93] Hazlitt, 'The Fight' (1821) in Paulin and Chandler, eds., The Fight and Other Writings (2000) p.133, p.156.

go down, clench his teeth, and knit his brow against the sun. When he saw Tom Hickman go down

> ...his face was like a human skull, a death's head, spouting blood...the eyes were filled with blood, the nose streamed with blood, the mouth gaped blood...yet he fought on...This is the most astonishing thing of all, this is *the high and heroic state of man.*[94]

On that day Hazlitt said he saw other things as well. He said he saw things whole. He said he saw the English people for what they were, different from their rulers, not apt to pretend like Neate and Hickman were not apt to pretend.[95] He told them they were a nation of heroes; not debauched or cowardly like other nations. He told them that like their navy, like their army, like their boxers, they were willing to shake hands with death 'as a brother'. He told them that as Englishmen, anything less than this, anything servile, or cowardly, or unmanly, was beneath them. It was a standard defence of the ring that it had taught Englishmen to box, not stab like Italians, or fight light like Venetians. But he was wrong to suppose that women didn't box. He was also rather ahead of himself in denying in 1825 what he had deliberately made room to say in 1821—that when it came to knocking men over, as it were, women were the more effective sex, and he dedicated 'The Fight' to the ladies and 'how many more ye kill'.[96]

Cobbett told the nation a similar story. That tyrants should shake at the people's coming. That men were men. That the true strength of a State depended on the nation's bravery. Hazlitt tried to explain why a brave nation should tolerate the servility of monarchy and in answer launched a thousand constitutional theories where 'We ask only for the stage effect'. William Windham, Secretary for War, said he did not want to turn the people into politicians. He wanted far more: he wanted them to be themselves for 'courage does not arise from mere boxing, from the mere beating, or being beat; but from the sentiments excited by the contemplation and cultivation of such practices'.[97]

These were old thoughts on the relationship between popular constitutionalism and manliness. Yet in spite of Cobbett's warnings on sexual transgression, well

---

[94] ibid, p.152. John Kemble, Edmund Keane, and Sarah Siddons were the greatest actors of the age and Hazlitt had reviewed them many times with a particularly visceral approach.

[95] Hazlitt, 'What Is the People?' (1818) p.388.

[96] On foreign methods: de Blainville, *Travels* (1754) p.555; Sharpe, *Letters from Italy* (1766) p.173; Radford, 'National Sporting Hero', *Identities*, 2005, pp.253–7; Poole, 'Murder of William Claypole', paper to the University of Leicester 2012; Davis, *Public Violence in Venice* (1994). On naval courage, Hazlitt, 'Jack Tars' (1825) pp.157–8. Women boxing in *The Fancy*, 1826, p.475, and Latimer, *Annals of Bristol*, 1893, p.168, albeit as exceptions to the rule. Hazlitt predicted Walter Bagehot on the constitution in his 'Spirit of Monarchy' (1813) p.340.

[97] Cobbett and Windham as explained in Ungar, 'Boxing as a Battle Ground for Conservatives and Radicals in late Georgian London', *Sport in History* 31, 2011, pp.365–74; Hazlitt, 'Character of Cobbett' (1821) p.140.

into the twentieth century young boxers would kiss and embrace before a fight. In the 1890s, in Sunday morning battles in the Durham coalfield, Albert Shakesby saw boys shake hands and kiss before going 'raw knux' to the finish. In the 1920s, the British army was still trying to discourage kissing. In the 1980s, we find Mike Tyson kissing his trainer Cus D'Amato just before battle.[98] On racial transgression, the great black American fighters of the first half of the twentieth century preferred to avoid the best black challengers because there was more risk and less money in it.[99] But if tasteful gentlemen ever thought fighters base, or vulgar, Hazlitt advised that they 'do something to show as much pluck, or as much self-possession as this, before you assume a superiority which you have never given a similar proof of by any one action in the whole course of your lives'.[100]

After the Neate Hickman fight, England's champion essayist Hazlitt went up to England's champion fighter and asked him if he thought it was a good one? 'Yes', replied Cribb. '*Pretty well*'.

By this time Tom Cribb had evolved into a living version of John Bull, and had retired into an unassailable reputation running the *Union Arms* in Panton Street.[101] Egan's *Boxiana* had been launched (1813) on the broad shoulders of Cribb's war time reputation, and ran till nearly the end of the decade. In 1814, along with John Jackson, Bill Richmond, Tom Belcher, and others, Cribb had sparred before the Tsar of Russia, the King of Prussia, and Field Marshal Blucher. He sparred again in 1819, this time for the Archduke Maximillian. In 1821, age 40, he was chief fistic pageboy at the Coronation of George IV in Westminster Abbey, put on the door to keep the Queen out and hypocrisy in.[102]

In his famous 1817 essay on national identity ('The Character of John Bull') Hazlitt presented Bull as a sort of Cribb-like national hero ('In short John is a great blockhead' whose 'greatest delight' is to do battle), and in his 1821 essay on Cobbett, he did much the same ('feels his own strength only by resistance').[103] Bull and Cribb and Cobbett. Cobbett and Cribb and Bull. Hazlitt made them one. Their blows as hard as their characters were impenetrable, Hazlitt reckoned the people had as much an idea of the one as they had of the other and, in his 1821 essay, in a brilliant shuffle from writing about fighting to fight-writing, he is the

[98] Oates, *On Boxing* (2006) p.123. 'A gay boxer was an unimaginable phrase' and remains so: Donald McCrae, 'The terrifying night Griffith answered gay taunts', *The Guardian*, 11 September 2015; Shakesby, *Street Arab* (1910) p.46; Riedi & Mason, 'Leather', *Canadian Journal of History* 41 (2006) p.498.

[99] Remnick, *King of the World* (1999) pp.24–5.   [100] Hazlitt, 'The Fight' (1821) p.153.

[101] On John Bull as a national symbol: Taylor, 'Iconography', *Past & Present*, 134 (1992).

[102] Radford, 'British Boxers', *Identities*, 2005, p.261. George's estranged wife, Queen Caroline, was shut out of her husband's coronation. She received a surprising amount of popular sympathy at the king's hypocritical attempts to annul their marriage.

[103] Hazlitt, 'The Character of William Cobbett' (1821) p.133.

challenger stepping into the ring to do battle with William Cobbett, the great man, champion of post-1815 English Radicalism.[104]

At first, Hazlitt the lighter of the two concedes to Cobbett's great storming reputation, but he thinks that maybe this very power ('mutton fist') could be a weakness and if he is able to survive the first few attacks he might have a chance. By round three, lo and behold he finds arguing with Cobbett 'is not so difficult' after all but in round four he is forced to give ground to his opponent's ability not only to hit, but to parry. This doesn't last and in the next phase of the essay Hazlitt shows how Cobbett's dazzling individuality gives way to *ego* and *ego* to his own 'momentary, violent and irritable humours'. He can't stay focussed. He cheats. He starts head-butting friends and enemies alike. Round six sees the young challenger beginning to take heart in the thought that Cobbett's real weakness is that he cannot take criticism, and possibly lacks guile. Round seven and Hazlitt (to his own satisfaction at least) staggers the champion, a bully 'not prepared for resistance', finally dropping him with 'a few smart blows'. Huzzah. We have a new champion.

William Hazlitt died in 1830 and was buried quietly in St Anne's, Soho. Cobbett died in 1835 and was laid to rest with considerable ceremony attended by a few thousand farm labourers near his birthplace at St Andrews, Farnham. Three massive flag stones were laid across his grave and at least one mourner signed himself 'John Bull'.[105] Cribb died in 1848, nearly forgotten now, except among The Fancy. Buried near where he lived with his son (a baker) at St. Mary Magdalen, Woolwich, it took six years, another war, and 20 tonnes of Portland stone to re-remember the man once the embodiment of national identity. A British Lion was put to guard the tomb but nobody remembered. Cribb had lived too long. His old age coincided with the decline of the ring.

Bottom

Cobbett found his high and heroic state in a one-man war with OLD CORRUPTION and THE THING—his names for what came to be called in the 1950s the 'Establishment'. Cribb found his high and heroic state in a time of war with France when English boxers came to stand for *bulk*—a physical quality which, unlike liberty, was not weightless. When Hazlitt contrasted Neate's 19

---

[104] 'Radicalism was... a running battle between the people and the unreformed House of Commons within which one issue after another was thrown to the fore. Around this battle there grew up (or, perhaps one should say, Cobbett created) a radical martyrology and, more especially, a demonology, in which the Prince Regent, Castlereagh, Sidmouth, the spies... the Manchester Yeomanry, Peel and paper-money, and half-hearted or equivocal reformers like Brougham all had their ritual parts': Thompson, *Making of the English Working Class* (1963) p.604.

[105] *The Westmoreland Gazette*, 27 June 1835.

Bristolian stones with Hickman's metropolitan 'gas', he was writing in the high and heroic tradition. In the same vein Gillray depicted Napoleon as the tiny 'Corsican Fairy' (1803), or 'Little Boney', while Rowlandson, Williamson, the Cruikshanks, and others piled in with English giants. So we have, for example, Daniel Lambert, at 50 stone, England's heaviest man celebrated as a great sports-man and a 'Modern Hercules'; we have 'John Bull Tipping All Nine' at skittles; 'John Bull Peppering Boney Front and Rear' with his fists; and 'Honest Pat', big lad, giving French invaders an honest 'Irish Welcome'. Our fighters did not go in for 'pastry cook' 'fly flap' Parisian blows. London slang confirmed it. Our men had bottom.[106]

Boxing prints had long shown prize-fighters like prize bulls (major muscle groups, small heads, grassy settings). Hogarth's 1748 *The Gates of Calais*, witness to a prime side of English beef, set English plenty against French famine.[107] The French lick their lips, the English smack their lips. The English taste for beef was legendary. Cheap beverages such as 'beef cakes' for soup were popular before the rise of *Bovril* in the 1870s and *Oxo* in 1910. *Marmite* was developed in Burton on Trent from 1902 as a brewer's yeast extract that gave the impression of meatiness without being meat. In 1909 St. James' Hall, Newcastle upon Tyne, offered boxers 10s and a joint of beef if they won.[108]

British beef loaned its rump to myths of English plenty. English prize-fighters loaned their bulk to myths of English liberty. Sport confirmed that in England you could do as you pleased. Pierce Egan's *Tom and Jerry's Rambles and Sprees through the Metropolis* featured the actions of 'a brave and free people', said Egan, their liberty 'not to be acquired in the CLOSET', nor 'from tutors', but by custom, 'by free and unrestrained intercourse' with each other. After growing tired of West End fashion, Tom and Jerry and Bob Logic (the Oxonian) make their way eastwards for a bit of life and liberty which they most certainly found at 'All Max' where every cove was welcome, 'colour or country no obstacle... Lascars, blacks, jack-rats, coal-heavers, dustmen, women of colour old and young and a sprinkling

---

[106] Jon Bee's *Dictionary* of sporting slang (1823), defined 'Bottom' as 'spunk', 'lastingness', and 'a fight pertinaceously maintained'. For Bonaparte against the boxers: John Johnson, Bodleian, French Revolution Box 3, and John Johnson, Boxing Folder 6. Ireland, 'Capt Barclay', *Graphic Illustrations* (1999) p.122. The Irish prize-fighter Daniel Donnelly (1788–1820) rose to prominence on the back of three wins over mediocre English opposition, a bit of blarney, and a lot of bulk: Garnham, 'Dan Donnelly', *Irish Historical Studies* 37, 2012. Daniel Lambert (1770–1809), the Leicester giant was celebrated in posters and cartoons, especially during the war years when you could see him for 1s at 53 Piccadilly, 12noon–5pm: 'Mr Daniel Lambert' (London Fairburn, Minores 1806) and John Johnson Collection, Bodleian, Entertainments Box 6.

[107] Hogarth's painting carries 'an array of centuries-old Protestant stereotypes': Colley, *Britons* (1992) pp.33–7.

[108] For boxers depicted like cattle: John Johnson, Bodleian, Boxing Folder 6. On beef in national identity: Rogers, *Beef and Liberty* (2004) p.118. On beverages: handbills, John Johnson, Bodleian, Food Box 1. St James' Hall: Moffat, *Northern Sportsman* (1999) p.22. Mary Shelley's 'other', *Frankenstein*, is a vegetarian and so are H G Wells' *Eloi* in his *The Time Machine* (1895). See Stuart, *Bloodless Revolution* (2006) pp.372–4.

of the remnant of once fine girls and all jigging together'. Theirs was a very narrow liberty it has to be said, more mockers and joshers than everyday people. Even so, 'mechanicals' were part of Tom and Jerry's do-as-you-please and, according to Egan, the best part.[109] Egan's *Boxiana* was dedicated to British soldiers and sailors who were animated 'by a native spirit...found principally to originate from what the fastidious term vulgar sports'.[110]

From James Figg (1695–1734) onwards, prize-fighters stood in a constitutional line of 'British plebeian...honour'[111] expressed in how they settled their differences ('woe unto him who would use a weapon'),[112] took their pleasures (not always nice),[113] and enjoyed their sport (not always legal).[114] The Fancy walked their walk ('quick jerk') and talked their talk ('Flash') in white box coats (double great) like common coachmen and according to Hazlitt, every butcher and broker in Tothill Fields wanted to join them.[115] In going to the fight with Joe Toms there and Jack Pigot back the champion essayist wanted us to know that he had done *just exactly as he pleased*. Two years after Peterloo and in a period of political repression, of his own free will and while of sound mind he, William Hazlitt, had taken the Brentford stage and walked nine miles in order to watch two Englishmen break the law.[116]

Boxers' qualities were analogous to regiments of the line. Soldiers fought shoulder to shoulder, in dense formations.[117] At the critical point where the line had to resist being broke or having its flank turned, 'the man is everything'.[118] In the end the line moved forward no matter what. Wellington nurtured a view of himself and his soldiers as morbid and taciturn in the face of an enemy who was impulsive and excitable.[119] In particular, the British army was known for its 'square'—a formation that wheeled into shape when its flank had been turned. Each side of the square comprised two tiers of soldiers, one standing, one kneeling, intended to repulse cavalry attacks by giving constant fire in spite of numerous loading procedures. In point of fact, the square was a rich crimson target for all the shot and shell an enemy could pour into it.[120] Nevertheless, commentators praised

---

[109] Egan, *Life in London* (1821) p.vi, pp.24–5.   [110] Egan, *Boxiana* (1812) Preface.

[111] Anon, *Pancratia* (1815) pp.26–8.

[112] Duckershoff, *English Workman* (1899) p.67. Similarly observed in 1727 by Saussure: Malcolmson, *Popular Recreations* (1973) p.42.

[113] *Bell's Life*, 17 October 1824; 2 January, 20 February 1825.   [114] Hall, *Retrospect* (1883) p.16,

[115] Hazlitt, 'Character of Cobbett' (1821) p.141.   [116] ibid, p.156.

[117] Until 'the introduction of breech-loading rifles made such tactics suicidal': French, *Military Identities* (2009) p.24. Glover, *Peninsular Preparation* (1963) explains how infantry tactics came to favour dispersed movement (p.111).

[118] Maguire, *British Army under Wellington* (1904) p.4.

[119] Shaw, *Romantic Imagination* (2002) p.2; Pears, 'Gentleman and Hero', in Porter, ed., *Myths of the English* (1994) p.216.

[120] Anon, *New Manual* (1764) pp.3–6; Anon, *Campaign Waterloo* (1816) pp.14–16. On vulnerability and last resort: Tombs, *England and the English* (2014) p.413; Wolseley, *Soldier's Pocket Book* (1869) p.229.

Wellington's lines and squares for their steady and undemonstrative ability to take punishment and give it. *Boxiana* called all this 'bottom', or 'gluttony'. Military historians called it 'stubborn' at Talerva (1809), 'measured' at Albuera (1811), 'unwavering' at Vittoria (1812), and 'steady' at Waterloo (1815). Wellington, who had a way with words, called it 'fair bludgeon work'.[121]

Line discipline was really a matter of self possession. When it began its inexorable walk forward, a regiment of the line proved itself. But it had to be able to see and feel its own order.[122] The war in the Crimea (1854–56) was an old war in the sense that commanders used tactics that would have been familiar to Napoleon and Wellington. Battles still depended on men in lines. They may have been scum of the earth and subject to the lash, but they were high and heroic when they stood up and moved.[123] At the Battle of Alma, Colour Sergeant Mason of the 33rd Duke of Wellington's Regiment walked forward holding his brother in law's hand. As they crossed the plain they could see Russian aristocratic ladies on specially constructed viewing platforms. Ninety yards from the enemy, in the face of point blank gunnery, the regiment stopped, unfurled its colours, and fired.[124] The Victoria Cross (red ribbon) was instituted after this victory as the highest honour in the land. Awarded *For Valour* in the very face of the enemy, few would know that the real enemy in this war was dysentry.[125]

The Navy expected the same self possession and was graced with the same medal (blue ribbon). The quarterdeck was the navy's equivalent of the line.[126] Command centre of the ship, it was also a theatre of nerve in moments of mortal danger when the decks were cleared and everybody was expected to lie face down except ship's senior officers who were expected to stand and take it.[127] So that everyone else could do their duty, everyone on the quarterdeck had to be seen doing theirs. Lightly screened on three sides, but completely open and exposed on the fourth, this is what they called the 'slaughterhouse'. At Trafalgar, just so there could be no doubt about his nerve or who he was, Nelson went out in full regalia to

---

[121] At Hougoumont, so long had the squares stood their ground 'we were tempted to believe that they had taken root in the soil if these very battalions had not majestically moved forward a few minutes after sunset': Maguire, *British Army under Wellington* (1907) pp.32–8; MacFarlane, *Duke of Wellington* (1886) pp.48, 81, 107, 106, 109, 139; MacFarlane, *Great Battles* (1854) p.232.

[122] '...the most important of all formations': Palmer, *Details of the Line Movements* (1812) p.1, p.205.

[123] Wolseley, *Soldier's Pocket Book* (1869) p.229. 'Scum of the earth' comment by Wellington, 11 November 1831, in Stanhope, *Notes of Conversations* (1888).

[124] Mason, *Primitive Methodist Soldier* (1877) pp.149–56.

[125] Out of 97,864 troops sent to the Crimea, the British Army lost 4,602 in action and 17,225 to infectious diseases, particularly dysentry: Gill and Gill, 'Nightingale in Scutari: her legacy re-examined', *Clinical Infectious Diseases*, 450 (2005) pp.1799–805. The little brown cross was worth 3d in bronze but £10 a year in pension: Beeton, *Victoria Cross* (1867) pp.3–4.

[126] Rodger, *Wooden World* (1988) pp.244–9.

[127] On Nelson's flagship HMS Victory 'the stage was set for the event which, more than any other, came to identify Trafalgar in British national consciousness: the beatification of the hero in the ultimately honourable act of self sacrifice': Nicolson, *Men of Honour* (2005) p.116.

stand there and have his back broken by a French sniper at fifty feet. And if Nelson was loved for his self-possession, so was Able Seaman Richard Parker, hanged from the yardarm for mutiny in full view of the fleet at Medway, 30 June 1797.[128] *The Times* fully approved of a man who refused the cap in order to signal the moment of his own strangulation. When Hazlitt made Neate strong and silent in the face of Hickman's bully and bluster, he understood what his country had come to value (when it could be bothered to value them at all) in its soldiers and sailors. Our best men were 'civil, silent' he said. On his death, the London press likened Tom Sayers' indomitable endurance, his 'quiet stoicism', his 'sublime indifference' to punishment, to one of Wellington's squares.[129]

Gentlemen

High and heroic states called forth high and heroic gentlemen. Allied army officers appeared on the streets of Paris in 1814 carefully tailored to emphasize cavalry-man's thighs, sloping shoulders, and tight waists. The dolman showed genitalia and buttocks. The pelisse was worn a little off the shoulder. Shakos, plumes, and pom poms made men tall. Braids, plates, and chains made them shine. After twenty years of war, there could be no questioning the fighting qualities of gentlemen, just as there could be no questioning the gentlemanly qualities of prize-fighters.[130] In the Greek view of life, stoicism was as open to the slave as it was to the free man.[131] Often as not, as in the case of Hamilton Mortimer's *Broughton* (c.1767), prize-fighters were modelled from what painters found in classical figures or, as with Rysbrack's *Hercules* (1763), classical figures were modelled from what sculptors found in prize-fighters. Hogarth painted Figg (1730), Gillray painted Jackson (1788), Gericault painted Molyneaux (1811), Marshall painted Gully, Belcher, and Jackson (1803–10), and Drummond painted Gully (1808).[132]

The classical impulse was literary as well as visual. Hazlitt took his Hickman Neate essay 'The Fight' from Virgil's *Aeneid*, where Dares fights Entellus. Hickman is Dares, the young and conceited one, who in Virgil's 'lists appears / stalking he strides, his head erected . . . / And drew the wonder of the gazing throng

[128] Richard Parker, *The Times*, 3 July 1797. On the quarterdeck as a 'slaughterhouse', see: Taylor, *Sons of the Waves* (2020) p.283.

[129] *The Daily Telegraph*, 10 May, 10 November 1865; *Sporting Life*, 11 November 1865. Hazlitt thought Hickman's bluster 'not manly': Hazlitt, 'Character of Cobbett' (1821) pp.148–9.

[130] John Johnson, Bodleian, French Revolution Box 3. Conan Doyle's Brigadier Gerard enjoyed dressing up and unsheathing his sword: Doyle, *Exploits* (1899) p.89.

[131] Dickinson, *Greek View of Life* (1896) p.203, p.144.

[132] Sawyer, *Noble Art* (1989) pp.40–50. For gentlemanly portraits of Broughton, Humphreys, Jackson, Belcher, Cribb, and others: Lynch, *The Prize Ring* (1925) plates iv–xviii. 'John Broughton' by John Hamilton Mortimer: YCBA (c.1767). One of the earliest boxing paintings is Van Heemskerk's 'The Bruising Match' (c.1700): Heiny, 'Boxing in British Sporting Art', Oregon PhD (1987) fig. i.

...Presuming his force, with sparkling eyes / Already he devours the promis'd prize'.[133] Hazlitt has Hickman entering

> ...from the other side [where] there was a similar rush and an opening made, and the Gasman came forward with a conscious air of anticipated triumph, too much like the cock of the walk. He strutted out more than became a hero, sucked oranges with a supercilious air...and went up and looked at Neate, which was an act of supererogation.[134]

Neate, on the other hand, is Entellus, older and heavier in Hazlitt's essay (if in point of fact the younger man). There was no denying he had old man's knees however. As Hazlitt says:

> ...from the opposite side entered Neate...He rolled along, swathed in his loose great coat, his knock knees bending beneath his huge bulk...[135]

Or as Virgil puts it:

> ...keeping their heads up...
> They begin to spar, fist to fist
> And provoke a battle
> > The one better at moving
> His feet, relying on his youth
> > The other powerful in limb
> And bulks, but his slower legs quiver,
> > His knees are unsteady...[136]

Hogarth's early picture of a prize-fighter (Figg 1730) is of a violent man coming at you all chin and bone.[137] His 'March to Finchley' (1746) shows the shaven heads of two fighters in the thick of a mob while a drunken army gets ready to march. But twenty years later Mortimer's picture of Broughton puts the fighter in an Italianate garden. Even though Broughton himself looks like what he is—a Thames waterman about to kick off—the garden indicates finer qualities. In an era when the pointed turned-out foot in art represented superior rank and erect posture represented authority, by late century all the top fighters were every inch gentlemen.[138] Figg comes hunched, in an old coat. Ben Marshall's pictures of Gully, Belcher, and Jackson on the other hand show them well dressed, well

---

[133] Virgil, *Aeneid* (29–19 BCE) Book v, after Dryden. Hazlitt is inter-textual with Virgil just as Virgil is inter-textual with Homer. His hero Aeneus is stoical and vulnerable.
[134] Hazlitt, 'The Fight' (1822) p.150.   [135] ibid.   [136] Virgil, *Aneid*, book v, after A S Kline.
[137] Sawyer, *Noble Art* (1989) p.36.
[138] Simon, 'The Eyes Have It', *Literary Review*, October 2019.

'turned out', as the saying goes, and straight as a die. In Rowlandson's 1787 picture of Richard Humphreys fighting a butcher, the ring is the calmest place in town. All the fight lies in the crowd, not Humphreys. Hoppner's 1788 painting of Humphreys, engraved by John Young, has him striking a wild and beautiful attitude in a wild and beautiful landscape. Having performed before gentlemen, Humphreys has become a gentleman himself. Yet in the end, in his three epic contests with Mendoza, it was admitted that the Jew was the better man.[139]

Daniel Mendoza achieved the high and heroic state first by finding a patron, and then by opening a school for sparring in Capel Street—handy for young gentlemen working at the Royal Exchange. Only then did Mendoza's gentlemanly qualities begin to shine.[140] Although their feet were turned out after the fashion, Molyneaux and Cribb were never allowed to be gentlemen. Molyneaux was too dangerous and too black. In any case he was an American. Cribb, his conqueror, was a hero to his face but 'a stupid beast' behind his back.[141] Bill Richmond, another black American, in his case brought back to England as a child, was known as a wit and boxing stylist and doesn't appear to have suffered any racial or anti-American prejudice. Pictures of him show all the gentlemanly attributes. In a distinguished career, he lost narrowly to the younger and heavier Cribb in 1805 and supported Molyneaux when no one else would—though that did not prevent him taking an honoured part in London matches, portraitures, exhibitions, and generally self-styled gentlemanly sporting gatherings. Retiring to run the *Horse & Dolphin*, next to the Fives Court in St. Martin's Street, Richmond was drawn by Dighton in 1810, shared a carriage with Gully at Belcher's funeral in 1811, exhibited for European royalty in 1814, and stood doorman with Cribb at the Coronation in 1821. A benefit was held for Richmond's wife and children in 1830 and he was still affectionately remembered by *Bell's Life* eleven years after.[142] Was this black American former slave really a gentleman? *Of course* he was. Probably.

[139] Humphreys is 'the Gentleman Boxer' in his fight with Martin 'the Bath Butcher': Thomas Rowlandson, 'The Prize Fight' (YCBA 1787 Rare Books and Ms). For his 'every posture': *Whitehall Evening Post*, 10–12 January 1788; for more painterly moments: *The World*, 10 January 1788; for Mendoza the better man: *Whitehall Evening Post*, 30 September–2 October 1790, and in the *London Chronicle*, 30 September–2 October 1790. Hoppner's painting is held in the New York Metropolitan Museum.

[140] Mendoza, *Memoirs* (1808) p.225.

[141] So said Byron's friend Hobhouse: Burnett, *Regency Dandy* (1981) p.108. Byron called Cribb 'very facetious', 'he don't like his situation', 'wants to fight again': Cox, *Boxing in Art and Literature* (1935) p.92: YCBA, Beinecke Library.

[142] For the illustration, 'A Striking View of Richmond', Noble Art, YCBA Reference Library, 11 x 8, March 1810; 9 February 1830 benefit: handbill, John Johnson, Bodleian, Sport Box 2; celebrated by Egan, *Boxiana* (1812) pp.440–9, and remembered by Dowling, *Fistiana* (1841) p.46, pp.54–5. Bill Richmond and Tom Molyneaux feature in *Pancratia* (1815): 'Richmond officiated for his COLOURED brother' (p.341). In the Yale Centre for British Art in New Haven there is 'Bust of a Man' (formerly called 'Psyche'), a black limestone bust (27 x 20 inches) of a black man by Francis Harwood bought by Andrew Mellon in the 1960s. Just across the way from the YCBA, in the grounds of Yale University, there is a statue of Nathaniel Hale, Yale's first patriot hero, hanged as a spy by British armed forces on 22 September 1776. The story goes that Bill Richmond, then 13 years old, was allowed by his master

The most celebrated gentleman fighter of the Regency era was 'Gentleman' John Jackson, also known as 'The Emperor'. Son of a London builder, Jackson took great pains with his physique, his attire, his address, and the company he kept. He had beaten Mendoza (1795) for the putative championship by swinging him round by the hair but all that was forgotten amid the quiffs and combs of his 13 New Bond Street sparring rooms. Byron went there, so for that matter did Tom and Jerry. John Jackson was lucky. He only fought three times and enjoyed the best that London had to offer on the strength of it. In John Gully, who was not one 'from which an artist might model', Jackson even enjoyed the improving services of an ugly companion.[143] In 1812 he appeared centre piece in one of Smeeton's two large prints of twenty-two gentlemen fighters, most of whom looked the part, including Mendoza, Molineux (sic) and Richmond.[144]

In London, all gentlemen were sportsmen and some sportsmen were gentle-men. Pierce Egan knew his way round the metropolitan sporting world and wrote about it to great comic effect—sparring in Bond Street, fencing in St. James' Street, disporting in Drury Lane, cockfighting at Westminster, 'Blue Ruin' everywhere and 'Black Sal' to finish with. This was Egan's idea of the true metropolitan sportsman. *Blackwoods* on the other hand reckoned Keats, Shelly, Hazlitt and all

Major General Hugh Smithson (later 2nd Duke of Northumberland), to pull the lever on Hale. There is also the suggestion that 'Bust of a Man' might be a bust of Bill Richmond because a near identical 'Bust of a Man' bought by the J Paul Getty Museum in 1988 had been the property of the dukes of Northumberland and was sold by them at auction at Stanwick Hall in 1922, cited in the 1865 inventory as 'a fine bust in black marble—W. Richmond the pugilist'. It is certainly true that Smithson (later family name Percy) brought Richmond back to England and had him educated and apprenticed (*Boxiana*, 1818, vol. i, p.440), corroborated by the Duke of Northumberland's personal papers that refer to "a little black boy" being put to school at the Duke's expense in 1778 (uncatalogued scrapbook, Alnwick Castle). In addition, it was said that the Nathaniel Hale story came from Bill Richmond himself and whether that was true or not, it was certainly the case that it was published without contradiction while Richmond was still alive. However, there is no hard evidence that either the Mellon or the Getty 'Bust of a Man' is in fact Bill Richmond. The inscribed date of 1758 seems to clearly refute the suggestion, Richmond having been born in 1763. But experts brought in by Mellon variously cited the sixteenth century, or the eighteenth century, or the nineteenth century as the bust's true date. Wikipedia, of course, has no difficulty reporting all the rumours. Levenson's article 'Haptic Blackness: The Double Life of an 18th century Bust' says that black statuary was usually of servants. The bust also has a facial scar, proud mark, according to Joyce Carol Oates, of a fighter: Oates, *On Boxing* (2006) p.50.

[143] Egan, *Boxiana* (1812) vol. i, pp.287–93; Gully, *Life and Career* (1863) p.7. On the celebration of John Jackson: Turner, 'Portrait for study of Gentleman John Jackson, Pugilist' (1800), and Ben Marshall, 'Gentleman John Jackson', engraving: YCBA Rare Books and Ms; Byron, *Letters*, 1973, vol. iii, 10 April 1814, p.257; I R & G Cruikshank, 'Art of Self Defence. Tom and Jerry Receiving Instructions from Mr Jackson at his rooms in Bond Street', coloured print, Beinecke Library, Yale University nd.

[144] Fighters past and present are Gibbons, Jones, Lancaster, Belcher (T), Baldwin, Power, Gulley (sic), Fosbrook, Belcher (J) 'by permission of his widow from an Original Portrait in Her Possession', Berks, Jackson, Gregson, Slack, Humphries (sic), Mendoza, Ward, Richmond, Dutch Sam, Stevenson, Pearce, Smith (Buckhorse), and Molineux (sic): printed by G Smeeton, 139 St. Martins Lane, August and September 1812.

the radical crew were Cockney milk-sops. Only Tories could be true sportsmen, only Tories had bottom.[145]

What about in real life? On 20 April 1814, in a busy day, Lord Byron composed an ode to Napoleon, sparred for an hour, ate six biscuits, and drank four bottles of soda water before admiring himself in the mirror. 'I am here boxing in a Turkish pelisse to prevent obesity'.[146] It was in the gentlemanly era that boxing put on the rich silk dressing gown, or long coat.[147] Sparring lessons had been sold from the 1780s as the gentleman's answer to flab and 'the insults of inferiors'.[148] Jack Broughton ended his days charging 5s a lesson (but a guinea if he had to get out of his chair).[149] Cruikshank's picture 'Sparring School' shows a fit man hitting a fat man with padded gloves.[150] Nobody got hurt sparring with professionals unless they asked for it.[151] Charles Dickens' Mr. Toots, having come into money, furnishes his apartment to include a sporting enclose. On the walls there are race horse prints which he never looks at, and during the day he takes billiard lessons from a marker, fencing lessons from a life guard, and athletic lessons from a Cornishman 'who was up for anything'. Three times a week he pays 'The Game Chicken' 10s 6d to hit him about the head which he thought of, when he could think at all, as 'sparring'.[152] Sparring, reckoned Egan, 'is certainly a mock encounter', like the theatre, 'a representation'.[153]

So infused was Regency London with representations of gentlemanliness, frame twenty-six of Cruikshank's 'Going to a Fight' (1819) caricatures 'Sir Isaac (the Hereford Philosopher)' assuring his philosophy students that 'milling coves' are no more than 'out and out STOICS', 'who have brought themselves to imagine that feeling is a mere matter of opinion'.[154] A steady stream of illustrations showed the other side of bruising. Turner might have portrayed John Jackson as a gentleman, but William Locke showed 'The Pugilist Johnson' as an out and out ruffian. Gillray's 'Two Men at Fisticuffs' is brutal. Rowlandson might have given John Jackson his finest pose, but he also represented 'A Sporting Cove' as a rake

---

[145] *Blackwood's*, March 1821.

[146] Byron, *Letters* (1973), vol. ii, p.84; Lynch, *Prize Ring* (1925) p.33.

[147] On dressing gowns: 'The Art of Boxing. The J Terry Bender Collection', 22 February–1 April 1978 (Emily Lowe Gallery, Hempstead, New York 1978): YCBA Reference Library. Mike Tyson went into the ring in an old pullover and no socks. He felt 'more like a warrior this way': Oates, *On Boxing* (2006) p.122.

[148] Amateur of Eminence, *Complete Art of Boxing* (1788) p. iv.

[149] Gee, John (Jack) Broughton (1703–89), ODNB.

[150] Plaque, *Broughton's Academy*, August 1743, John Johnson, Bodleian, Boxing Folder Large; I R Cruikshank, 'Sparring School' 1817.

[151] Jackson, *Sporting Days* (1932) p.45.

[152] Charles Dickens, *Dombey & Sons* (1848) p.222. Dickens calls his fighter 'The Game Chicken' after a real fighter from a previous time. The Chicken wears a white great coat and can be found at the bar of *The Black Badger*.

[153] Egan, *Boxiana* (1812–19) p.54.   [154] I R Cruikshank, 'Going to a Fight' (1819) YCBA.

and a wreck.[155] There are precious few heroes in *Le Boxeur Blesse*, the work of a French prisoner of war.[156] The victor walks off with his backers. The vanquished sits on a stool humiliated, a woman kneeling by his side. In popular culture there was a long association of strong and violent bodies with criminal and salacious acts. The Mendoza Humphreys fights drew a flock of letters to *The Times* loathing the life of fighters as nasty, brutish, short, and fraudulent.[157] Fighters, we have to conclude, were only gentlemen when they were sparring. When they were going about their business they were bloody savages. In the same year that Marie Antionette advised her people to eat cake, Rev. Barry advised English prize-fighters to play quoits.[158]

After 1860

After Sayers fought Heenan, the Prime Minister had to calm the House of Commons. No it wasn't true that the South Eastern Railway Company had tipped 3,000 ruffians on Farnborough. No it wasn't true that there had been a riot. There had been no more of a riot with a lot of people watching two men boxing than there had been a riot with a lot of people watching two men go up in a balloon, said the Prime Minister. 'There they stand ... no injury done to anyone'.[159]

Talk of Sayers Heenan was everywhere. All the newspapers reported it. *Bell's* brought out a special same day edition. Hazlewood's comedy, 'The Champion of England; or, Tom and the Boy', appeared at Hoxton *Britannia* from 30 April.[160] Someone calling himself 'Lord Chief Baron Nicholson' at *The Cider Cellars*, Covent Garden, promised to answer the indictment taken against Mr. Thomas Sayers by Mr. John Bright of The Peace Society. Mr. Sayers to appear in person. 'There will be no humbug about this'. Otherwise, the *Cellars* were serving up satires on the recent Divorce Act, semi-nude poses, and grilled chops.[161]

---

[155] William Locke, 'Portrait of the Pugilist Johnson' (1790), rough sketch: YCBA Rare Books and Ms.; Gillray, 'Two Men at Fisticuffs': ibid; Thomas Rowlandson, 'A Sporting Cove' (c.1820): ibid.

[156] By 'Un Francais Prisonnier du Guerre': YCBA Rare Books and Ms.

[157] *The Times*, 8, 9, 12, 15 January 1788; 16 February, 9 August, 17 November 1788; 12 February 1789. On strong bodies and violent associations: John Johnson, Bodleian, Crime Box 1–2. On the power to persuade the poor and ignorant: Hume, *History of England*, in Hole, *Pulpits* (2004) p.70. On Enlightenment physical exaggerations of the poor as irrational: Porter, *Age of Reason* (2004) p.247. On good taste being a thing of the mind not the body: eighteenth and nineteenth century sages Addison, Richardson, Burke, Reynolds, Shaftesbury, Arnold et al.: in Denvir, *Art, Design and Society* (1983).

[158] Barry, *Letter on Boxing* (1789) p.8.

[159] Palmerston, Commons, 15 May 1860, *Hansard*. But there was a riot over two men in a balloon on Leicester racecourse four years later: Cynthia Brown, 'When the balloon didn't go up', *Leicester Historian* 26, 2010, pp.9–15. *Punch* decided immediately that fighting was old hat: 'A Lay of Ancient London', *Punch*, 28 April 1860.

[160] *The Era*, 29 April, 6 May 1860. Fight songs and shows were upcoming at *The Marylebone*, *The Royal Olympic*, and *Wilton's of Whitechapel*.

[161] Next door to *The Adelphi* in The Strand: *The Era*, 13 May 1860.

At first, Tom did very well. He enjoyed the love of the people. 'You *are* a naughty boy Tom!' scoffed *The Cornhill*, while *Punch* mocked Oxford University proctors for preventing 'a person named Sayers' visiting a college (invited by students presumably). Talking of incorrigible troublemakers, what about 'a person named Pusey?' it asked.[162] More helpfully, it was rumoured that parliament, the Stock Exchange, and Lloyds of London had banded together to raise £3,000 for Tom, to be put in government stocks at 4.5 per cent on condition that he never fought again.[163] In addition, he got to keep his championship belt and one of the two replicas that lay on the table of *The Alhambra Palace* Leicester Square where he and Heenan walked arm in arm round the stage (Heenan stooping) before being subjected to best man banter and a lot of puffery about the meaning of belts.[164] Dowling of *Bell's* spoke sentimentally to the American: 'take this token, cherish it', while Wilkes of the *Spirit of the Times* told the Englishman that he had fought with 'not a low word, not a coarse look'. The boxers, who only two weeks before had threatened to fight all over again when Heenan claimed Tom's original belt, didn't know what to say. Their speeches were 'models of brevity and pith'. Now they had their replicas, they were brothers in arms. Tom couldn't buckle his belt but knew what to do when asked to hold out his hand for the money.[165]

Sometime in 1862 we find him investing in his own circus, but Federal naval action put a stop to an intended money-spinning tour of the United States and our 'mighty LITTLE HERO', according to *The Times*, seems to have lost all his savings.[166] That same year he went on the boards of *The Britannia* in his championship belt with his 'TWO CELEBRATED MULES' Barney and Pete sometimes striking Grecian poses (Tom that is, not the mules), sometimes not.[167] In 1863, by now not in the best of health, he enjoyed another Britannia benefit, Heenan coming down from his seat in the wings to take a second turn at reorganizing Tom's face—now caked in make-up.[168] In 'Abou Hassan and The Sleeper of Baghdad' Tom took his place in a long line of *Brit* pantomime clowns, including 'Hickory Dickory Dock' (1863), 'Little Busy Bee' (1864), and 'Old Daddy Long Legs' (1865).[169] We may bear in mind that, in Dickens' view, like an Italian opera for the deaf, what actually happened on the stage of *The Brit*

[162] *Cornhill Magazine*, July 1860; *Punch*, 21 December 1861. In 1959 Oxford and Cambridge universities joined forces as the Pierce Egan Boxing Club to take on the Royal Navy in Oxford Town Hall. Fighting for Oxford was Kris Kristofferson: programme, John Johnson, Bodleian, Sport Box 3.

[163] Anon, *Life, Death and Funeral of Tom Sayers* (1865) pp.11–13: Beinecke Library, Yale University; Lloyd, *Great Prize Fight* (1977) pp.114–15.

[164] W W Travers' 'The Champion's Belt or, Tom and The Boy', at *The Victoria*, 6 May 1860: Norwood, 'Pugilists and Greasepaint', *Nineteenth-Century Theatre and Film* 36 (2009) pp.63–73.

[165] *The Times*, 31 May 1860.   [166] *The Era*, 12 October 1862.

[167] Tom forgot the poses five minutes after being shown them, according to Harold Furness, *Famous Fights Past and Present*, vol. i, no 7, p.110.

[168] *Famous Fights*, ibid; handbills, *New Britannia*, 27 February 1863: Hackney Archives, 43, 2–63.

[169] Norwood, 'Britannia Theatre', Leicester PhD (2008) pp.2–4; playbills, *New Britannia*, Hackney Archives; 'Tom Sayers as CLOWN' (J. Redington, printer, Hoxton 1863).

(rather than off it) was of limited interest.[170] On 10 December 1863, Sayers turned up as Heenan's second in the fight with King dressed out of the *Britannia's* clothes basket in a long yellow jumper, fur cap, and high leather jackboots.[171] A bankrupt in 1862, 'prematurely aged' by 1863, a diabetic and heavy drinker by 1864, Tom died on 9 November 1865 after doing twenty-four hours hard at the home of his bootmaker on Camden High Street. The costers told Henry Mayhew that *The Britannia* was 'staunch to melodrama' and Tom didn't let them down. He was 39, and had been suffering from a lung infection since February.[172]

It was London's funeral of the year. The King of Camden was attended by 10,000 of his subjects, a swaying band, and a banner. Led by sixteen black-plumed carriages, his dog 'Lion', and his pony and phaeton, the two-mile cortege halted at the waymarks of Tom's world as they made their way to Highgate: at *The Redcap*, at *The Bull and Last*, at *The Britannia*, and at his favourite Camden street corner.[173] Fighting broke out at the cemetery gates, but by and large the crowd was serious. Lion was sold at auction, lot 103, to a North London publican for £30.00. He stands guard over Tom's tombstone still. His old collar was inscribed: 'I am Tom Sayers' dog. Whose dog are you?' Cribb's historic pieces went for £55.10s. Tom's championship belt for £33.12s. The one remaining mule made £13.00, the mare £23.00.[174] *The Spectator* called the whole thing grotesque, brainless, loathsome, sad, disgusting: the sport of harpies and capitalists.[175]

Heenan died age 38 on 25 October 1873 in River City, Wyoming, also from TB. He too had made some unfortunate business decisions. According to one of his more diplomatic obituarists: 'it could never be said of him that he did a dishonourable act according to the code of those with whom his lines were laid'.[176]

Both men died young but the story of the fight lived on, absorbed into the stories the two nations told themselves. Schoolboys took sides—'Sayers or Heenan?' Carpentier, first of the true modern fighters, compared his methods with their methods. With all due modesty, so did George Bernard Shaw. John L Sullivan, last of the great prize-fighters, remembered how Boston Massachussetts still talked about Sayers Heenan in the 1870s, and how Heenan's replica belt had not been paid for and how he had to give it back. The Australian Kelly gang knew what a 'Heenan hug' was, and talked of putting one on a

---

[170] Dickens, *Household Words*, 13 April 1850, in Slater, ed., *Dickens' Journalism* (1998) p.201.

[171] *Racing Times*, 28 December 1863.

[172] *Sporting Life*, 11 November 1865; Anon, *Life and Death and Funeral* (1865) p.13; *Racing Times*, 28 December 1863. He went to Brighton but suffered a relapse in August returning to his sister's in London in October. On *The Brit* see letter to *The Era*, 9 December 1893 and Neuberg, ed., *Mayhew* (1985) p.21.

[173] Lynch, *Prize Ring* (1925) plate xxix.

[174] It seems Tom's father made about £500 out of the auction: British Library Theatre Cuttings 67 (1865): 1 December 1865. 'Lion' in Lynch, *Prize Ring* (1925) plate xxix.

[175] *The Spectator*, 10 February 1866   [176] Anon, *Death and Memoir* (1873) p.3.

trooper.[177] Five years after his death the *Sporting Magazine* was still talking about Tom. That he met all the burgesses of Chester sitting on a sofa until, weary of it, he sauntered out. That an actor once threw his hat from the stage and it landed on plumb on Tom's head. That he learned from a Cumberland wrestler how to throw a man. That he pinned a 30-guinea brooch to his chest for safety's sake. That his son is nice looking. That his father is nice looking. That Sarah Sayers turned up to the funeral. That the only man to ever beat him, Nat Langham, turned up too, in a Garibaldi shirt. That Tom's coffin looked small. That the band played the Dead March. And on and on. When he was dying of consumption, did you know he lived with his sister but they fell out? *The Marvel* was still writing about him in 1910.[178]

News of the death of the prize-ring had been a tad premature. After years of rumours, in 1863 *Bell's Life* called for a 'united effort on the part of all classes' to put an end to it. *The Racing Times* agreed. *Bell's* stopped reporting prize-fights, the Railway Act stopped serving them, and Lord Palmerston was forced to turn to the French press for praise of an old English 'bottom' that, it has to be said, for over a hundred years had been pointed largely at them.[179] Even so, local challenges to fight, to ped, to race, to row, to throw, to dare, all went on, as did The Fancy under other names including the Top Johnnies, the Gas Bags, the 'three card mob and all that lark'.[180] In 1913 Walter Sickert did a self portrait and called it 'The Bust of Tom Sayers'.[181] Sickert stood for the Camden Art Group and Sayers, it seems, still stood for Camden.

Old ring styles lingered on. There's a photograph of Jack Johnson fighting Tommy Burns for the World Heavyweight Championship at Rushcutter's Bay, Sydney, on 21 December 1908. Burns is in the deep crouch attitude of the sort that Mendoza and Humphreys took in 1790, while Johnson is straight backed, hands

[177] https://trove.nla.gov.au/newspaper/article/199362803?afterLoad=ShowCorrections. See also Sargent, *John L Sullivan* (1892) p.37; Carpentier, *My Methods* (nd 1920s) p.80. On schoolboys: *The Referee*, 3 February 1924. George Bernard Shaw on Carpentier: *The Nation*, 1919, p.108.

[178] 'Tom Sayers' Win', 'Tom Sayers on the Halls', *The Marvel*, 26 February, 5 March 1910.

[179] Palmerston, Commons, 15 May 1860: *Hansard*. *Bell's Life* as reported in the *Salford Weekly News*, 12 December 1863, and there was further opposition in *The Racing Times*, 28 December 1863. The less influential *Illustrated Times* (21 April 1860) also called for a ban. Dowling's *Fistiana* had reckoned the ring was drawing to 'a close' in 1841 (p.62). Jem Mace seems to have been a magnet for crooked fights in the late 1850s (*Licensed Victuallers' Mirror*, 20 September 1889). In 1847 *Sportsman's Magazine* printed reports about fight fixing by the legendary Hickman in 1822 (6 February 1847). See also Brailsford, *Sport, Time and Society* (1991) p.92.

[180] Samuel, *East End Underworld* (1981) p.12. Salford newspapers reported 400 turning up to watch a fight in a park in 1877, or £5 a side for a fight in a pub in Odsall in 1913: *Salford Weekly News*, 7 July 1877; *Salford Reporter*, 6 September 1913. In Newcastle upon Tyne, rowing challenges were more frequent, with large stakes, inter-river and intercontinental matches, and local heroes such as Bob Chambers and James Renforth: *Newcastle Daily Chronicle*, 28 September 1868; 4 June, 18 August 1869; 24 August 1871.

[181] Ashmolean Museum, Oxford.

low; the sort of stance Heenan and Sayers took in 1860.[182] Jack Johnson's illustrious boxing career, indeed, was strewn with allegations of 'crosses' as of old, and his fight against the British champion Wells was banned by the Home Secretary for fear of a breach of the peace—nothing new there.[183] Every Saturday night when the pubs came out men would strip and fight bare fisted London Rules. Long after grabbing and throwing had been banished from the ring, schoolboys continued to put each other's heads in chancery and throw cross buttock. In a fight or an invitation to fight, boys stayed silent, put up their fists and were not supposed to cry.[184] Nor did the sporting life of the theatre or fairground fade.[185]

Many aspects of the old prize-ring carried on except the gentlemanly patronage that used to hold it together. Dowling recalled how Jackson, Cribb, Gully, Tom Belcher, and other celebrated fighters, along with over a hundred gentlemen, including Byron and the Duke of Clarence, had come together in 1814 to form The Pugilistic Club. They commended a new era, he said, where 'their countenance and sanction' was sought.[186] Egan's famous 'Key to the Picture of The Fancy Going to a Fight at Moulsey Hurst' (1819) was dedicated, by permission, to Gentleman John Jackson and the Pugilistic Club. But gentlemanly patronage was always difficult to measure. The most one can say is that it worked for those who believed in it. By the 1830s, with prize-ring deaths and crosses and rumours of crosses, Dowling declared the old authority over. Gentlemen couldn't go to fights anymore without fear of intimidation and the old guard were getting too old to defend themselves. Jackson, long past swinging men by the hair, gave up his sparring rooms in 1824.

In any case, by the time of Sayers Heenan, young gents had more tasteful things to do and their social authority was not so clear.[187] At this point a most unlikely sporting hero appeared. John Sholto Douglass became 8th Marquess of Queensberry in 1858. Coming from an aristocratic sporting line—his father had been master of the Cottesmore and the Quorn—Sholto Douglas was intent on the full sporting life, but for now, in his misspent youth, he was interested in boxing and gave his name to an alternative code drawn up by his old Cambridge friend

---

[182] Photograph, *Observer Magazine*, December 2002; allegations of Johnson 'crosses' in fights with with Burns 1908, Kaufmann 1909, Jeffries 1910, Moran 1914, Willard 1915, all in Ward, *Unforgiveable Blackness* (2006) pp.269–71.

[183] Remnick, *King of the World* (1999) p.87.

[184] Johnson, *This Boy* (2014) p.226; Des Newell, 'The Plebeian Honour Fight', RHS Symposium, University of Northampton, 2015; Harry Rickards, 'Stout and Bitter' song 1868: Spellman Collection, University of Reading.

[185] 'Suffolk Prodigies', poster and handbill, *Britannia Theatre*, Hoxton; sensations, John Johnson, Bodleian, Circuses Box 4, Animals on Show Box 1.

[186] Dowling, *Fistiana* (1841) p.38, pp.60–2. The Duke of Clarence went on to become King William IV (1830–37). The favoured 'safe' fight venue of Moulsey Hurst was near his estate.

[187] Heggie, 'Bodies, Sport and Science', *Past & Present* 231, 2016, pp.172–4.

John Graham Chambers.[188] Under the 'Queensberry Rules' gentlemanly sparring was taken and written up into something that eventually replaced London Rules. Padded gloves, three and four minute rounds, one minute breaks, four weight divisions, head and body the only targets, fists the only weapon, jabbing and moving but down is down with ten seconds to stand up and fight on—the new rules had the charm of actually looking like a modern moving sport with the added attraction of clear winners and losers. Rounds didn't go on forever. Boxers scored points for clean blows. The gloves that protected the hands were made for harder hitting. Unless you got to your feet by ten, you were out, out for the count.[189]

It took a while for the new rules to settle their differences with the old.[190] Sholto Douglas had boxed something like this at Cambridge and done a bit of coaching at the London Amateur Athletic Club, founded in 1866 by Chambers. In 1867, that club, now called the Amateur Athletic Association, hosted its first 'amateur' boxing championships according to the sparring conventions practiced at Cambridge (though as yet without points scoring) drawn up by Chambers and patronized by Queensberry. The club enjoyed some aristocratic patronage as of old, and Queensberry enjoyed the compliment of giving his name to a new boxing code.

Sayers would have understood some of what went on at these amateur championships, but not much. For a start, he would not have been allowed in, because he was not an amateur, or a gentleman. Keeping fighters like Sayers out, encouraged men like Chambers in, and young bloods could rekindle their love of physical daring without being beaten up by a professional. But if by some accident Sayers had been still alive, and if by some miracle he had been allowed to compete, not only would he have expected his money at the end, he would have been baffled by the speed and manouevre with no opportunity to grab or hold, to drag or go down. Sayers, indeed, stood for everything the AAA was trying to banish. They would not have welcomed Tom's pickled face and spikey boots. They would not have welcomed the company he kept. They would not have enjoyed rumours of a

---

[188] Queensberry, *10th Marquess* (1942) p.107, p.128. Sholto Douglas (1844–1900) inherited £750,000 and left £300,000 with nothing obvious to show for it except an exceptionally hectic life. According to his biographer, his four sons found their father 'a source of ambiguity and confusion'. His third son, Alfred Douglas, or 'Bosie', was a close friend of Oscar Wilde and it was Queensberry's harrowing of the pair that led to the notorious trial of the 8th Marquess in April 1895 that led in turn to Wilde's even more notorious trial, imprisonment and death: Stratmann, *9th Marquess of Queensberry* (2011) p.137, p.145, and ch.18. Douglas was the 8th Marquess in his own day but the posthumous restoration of the 3rd Marquess made him the 9th. John Graham Chambers is often confused with the professional boxer and iron moulder Arthur Chambers (pp. 76–7).

[189] Shipley, 'Boxing', in Mason, ed., *Sport in Britain* (1989) p.81.

[190] Courts had great difficulty deciding between Prize Ring or Queensberry as to what sort of fight had actually taken place: Boddy, 'Under Queensberry Rules', *Sport in History* 31, 2011, pp.402–4. Prize-fighting was never entirely driven away. Outside the law and majority taste, it carried on, appropriately enough, among outsiders and itinerants: 'Tyson Fury: reflections of a gypsy fighter', *Independent*, 30 October 2011. Fury (b. Manchester 1988, 30 wins, 1 draw, 0 losses) won the World Heavyweight Championship first in 2015 and again in 2020.

'cross'. The Amateur Boxing Association followed in 1880, active mainly in London, founded by two Queensberry cup holders and holding its first championships in 1881. University and public school amateur boxing clubs followed. Oxford and Cambridge finally got round to punching each other in the head in 1897.[191] The army and navy were already boxing Queensberry by this time, and the police joined them in 1906.[192] By 1906 amateur boxing was settled in its rules and institutions while professional boxers and promoters were still making matches whenever and however they could in small halls and other venues—by London Rules ('practically obsolete'), or Blanchard's Fair Play Rules ('seldom used'), or Queensberry Rules, or Queensberry Endurance Rules. Meanwhile a new Fancy of sporting gentlemen and promoters had begun to gather around a new professional boxing body calling itself The National Sporting Club (NSC).[193]

The NSC was founded in 1891 in Covent Garden.[194] It had started life as a small private fight spot called The Pelican Club, but three years of scandal forced it to close its doors. Queensberry and the 5th Earl Lonsdale, both former Pelicans, gave their blessings to the new body, which went to the opposite extremes of sporting manners from the old prize-ring. Not only was it indoors not outside, there was no rowdiness or food throwing (a Pelican speciality), no talking, and strict rules of membership. Fights took place in silence broken only by the popping of corks. No different in essence from the East End's very different professional fight venue, 'Wonderland', the NSC was a business venture that aspired to a new American taste for rich young men with gardenias in their button holes lending good manners to something which looked like GBH to everybody else.[195] The NSC's adoption of Queensberry Rules along with doctors and stewards and weight divisions that mixed part-time amateurs with part-time professionals, saved the day for boxing.

Working-class families often made ends meet by working for a few shillings when they could get it. Once in the ring they also found themselves fighting for ship or regiment, local pub or hall, town or 'end'. Bermondsey alone produced six British champions.[196] On 19 October 1910, 'Bombardier' Billy Wells (Champion of India) fought 'Private' Dan Voyles (Irish Guards) at King's Hall, Southwark. Wells is a good example of the new boxing.[197] Born in 1887 at 250 Cable Street, Shadwell, deep in the East End of London, he came from a family of Thames

---

[191] Spierenburg tells us that duelling also increased among European elites in the 1860s: *Men and Violence* (1998) p.64, p.75.

[192] Mason and Riedi, *Sport and the Military* (2010) pp.18–20.

[193] Naughton, *Kings of the Queensberry Realm* (1902) pp.38–41.

[194] Daghy, *National Sporting Club* (1956).

[195] *Sala's Journal*, 24 September 1892; Harding, *Lonsdale's Belts* (1994) p.85; Shipley, 'Tom Causer', *History Workshop Journal* 15, 1983, pp.47–50.

[196] Shipley, ibid, p.35.

[197] '...sleekly groomed, comfortably off, holding moderate views, successful in business...very much a Metropolitan man, not [really] an East Ender': Shipley, *Billy Wells* (1993) p.186.

lightermen (although his father was a professional musician). He learned to box at school at a time when a progressive London School Board was expanding its sports provision. He switched to more serious fights through a boys' club attached to the school, and then moved up into the working men's clubs' London championships where he showed what he could do. *All amateur.* At 19, he joined the Royal Artillery and was posted to Rawalpindi, quickly dominating the army heavyweight division. Once out of the army, he had his first professional fight age 23 with 'Gunner' Mills and in 1911 won the British Heavyweight Championship at the NSC. When he was prevented from fighting Jack Johnson that same year, Home Secretary Winston Churchill saved the Bombardier from a thrashing from a man who had had more professional fights than Wells had had rounds.

By this time, the National Sporting Club effectively controlled professional boxing in Britain. In 1929, the British Boxing Board of Control was formed out of its ranks. In an age that still enjoyed the lustre of aristocratic patronage, by fighting according to one lord's (eponymous) rules and awarding honours by another lord's (eponymous) belts, the NSC saved the sport from shame by avoiding savagery, checking fitness, guaranteeing the money, and clinging on to the high and heroic gentlemanly myth.[198] For the rest, it offered sport as theatrical promotion.[199] In the 1860s the theatre had taken steps to control rowdy crowds and where impressarios led, boxing promotors followed. They installed seats, darkened the hall, and brightened the ring with powerful electric lamps.[200] Soon, there would be a special way of *hintro-doosing* the fighters too, which Richard Hoggart called 'big dipper'.[201] Nevertheless, inspite of the new venues and (eventually) the new rules, all the old clowning and melodrama remained. The training camps and weigh-ins continued to attract press attention, along with the silk dressing gowns and gaudy belts. The old reputation for 'bottom' carried on too, though they no longer called it that. The line of champions didn't fade except in peeling posters and the line drawn between old style champions like Sayers and new style champions like the Bombadier was understood but not broken. Promoters replaced publicans but pubs remained central, and the old benefit exhibitions and slapstick stayed. You could shake Nel Tarleton's hand on Blackpool Pier. You could hear

---

[198] Further examples of aristocratic patronage include the Currie Cup for cricket (South Africa 1889), the Sheffield Cup for cricket (Australia 1892), the Stanley Cup for ice hockey (Canada 1893), the Curzon Cresta Cup (St Moritz 1910), and the Bledisloe Cup for rugby (New Zealand 1931): Huggins, 'Sport and the Upper Classes', *Sport in History*, 2008, p.376.

[199] Hugh Lowther (1859-1944), 5th Earl Lonsdale, was another celebrated MFH who was a founding member and first president of the NSC. He awarded his famous gold and porcelain Lonsdale Belts from 1909.

[200] Davison, *Contemporary Drama* (1982) pp.11–12, p.164. The 'Wonderland' venue converted to boxing in 1894: Samuel, *East End Underworld* (1981) p.315.

[201] Hoggart, *Uses of Literacy* (1958) p.123.

Randolph Turpin beat the best pound for pound fighter in the world on the radio. You could see Terry Downes at the horror movies after he had fought six world champions and beaten three. Henry Cooper put the best heavyweight of all time on his backside. Did you see *that*? You could, again and again, now that there was television.

The stories went on. The ring was now indisputably a theatre, not a rat pit. Win or lose, the Coxhoe flyweight and light tenor Bob Bates would stand there and end his fights with a song. He knew there was more to boxing than fighting.[202]

Modern American Era

On 7 September 1892 James 'Gentleman Jim' Corbett beat John L Sullivan in New Orleans for what promoters in both the United States and the British Empire were now calling the World Heavyweight Championship. Corbett and Sullivan not only fought under glaring lights before an army of sportswriters, they self-consciously stood for modern sporting razzmatazz, including jazz, glamour, and cheap suits. Professional boxing turned American. Sullivan, 'the most celebrated American of his era', who fought under both London and Queensberry, understood that Queensberry favoured the bigger, more aggressive man.[203] In three-minute rounds which demanded constant movement and fast hitting, sometimes in combination, with no going down, it was much more difficult to fight tactically. In short, modern boxing favoured Heenan over Sayers. In a clearly demarcated, fast, well-lit canvas ring, with well-shod hands and slippered feet and referees charged to keep things open and moving, fighters could impose their size and speed.[204] The ten-second rule invented the 'knock out' as the centre piece of the modern ring. What is a knock out? It is when a blow to the head causes the brain to hit the skull causing chemical imbalance and cerebral concussion Or, as Norman Mailer put it, 'Frazier's head smote his spine and his legs came apart like falling walls'.[205] In the modern ring there is nowhere to hide against a faster man of comparative or greater weight who is out to rotate your skull. Sullivan came to England in 1887 as the 'KO specialist'. He made knocking-out tours averaging twelve minutes a fight. So did Jack Dempsey. So did Joe Louis. So did Mike Tyson. So did booth fighters at the fair when it was getting late and time to say Goodnight Cuthbert.[206]

---

[202] *Shields Gazette*, 10 March 2006.   [203] Ward, *Unforgivable Blackness* (2006) p.15, p.58.

[204] Remnick, *King of the World* (1999) p.5.

[205] Mailer, in Sugden, *Boxing and Society* (1996) p.173. On Queensberry Rules promoting a more aggressive style: Bradley, *Boxing Referee* (1910) pp.25–6; Gorn, *Manly Art* (1989) pp.204–6; Heller, *Forty World Champions* (1985), in conversation with Dempsey (p.62).

[206] 'I was the first to demonstrate under Marquess of Queensberry rules that I would knock a man out of time in less than four rounds which means, in actual fighting time, twelve minutes': Sullivan in Sargent, *John L Sullivan* (1892) p.238; Heller, *Forty World Champions*, on Dempsey (1975) p.62; Ward, *Unforgivable Blackness* (2006).

The other way to box modern was to tire your opponent with sheer aggression in the old fashioned way before the final KO (Marciano), or to move with speed and jab scoring points with the orthodox 'straight left' (Ali).[207] Dempsey beat Willard at Toledo in 1919 giving away 70 pounds. Baer beat Carnera at Madison Square Garden in 1934 giving away 54 pounds. Rocky Marciano was really a light heavyweight. Georges Carpentier was the first to catch the eye in this regard, dazzling much heavier men with his fast hands and quick feet. Every inch the modern man, nobody would have taken him for a boxer. 'He might have been a barrister, a poet, a musician, a Foreign Office attache, a Fellow of All Souls' rather than a pit boy from Lens.[208] Gene Tunney was another fighter who swapped bottom for his dancing feet, as it were, as was Jack Johnson. 'Gunboat' Smith said Billy Wells wouldn't even fight him, 'that's how clever he was'. Giving away 35 pounds, Englishman Robert Fitzsimmons defeated James Corbett for the world championship in 1897 just as Corbett had defeated Sullivan in 1892—with greater speed and harder hitting. In a way, this was the fight Sayers Heenan had wanted to be: international, modern, decisive. Fitzsimmons' book *Physical Culture & Self Defense* was written by a middle weight boxer with the overweight businessman in mind. Once upon a time, Bob had fought London Rules, but when he appeared as a self-improver in front of his neat clapperboard all-American house, it was clear the ring had started to enter modern life, the only sport to stretch from the suburb to the ghetto.[209] It had long been in print and on the stage of course, but now it was at the movies and on the radio, in kids' comics and cigarette cards, part of politics and pornography, health and fitness, offering representations ranging from how nobody (in real life) fights, as at the movies, to how everybody (in real life) talks, as in pulp fiction.[210]

---

[207] Shipley, 'Boxing', in Mason, ed., *Sport in Britain* (1989) p.84.

[208] Bennett, 'The Prize Fight' (1920) in Cox, *Boxing* (1935) p.143.

[209] Fitzsimmons, *Physical Culture* (1901) p.44. Fitzsimmons held world middle, light heavy, and heavyweight titles but he was really a middleweight at around 12 stone. Carpentier, *My Methods* (nd 1920s) p.80 and Cox, *Boxing in Art and Literature* (1935) p.143; Tunney in *The Observer*, 14 February 1954; Johnson, in Oates, *On Boxing* (2006) pp.242–3; 'Gunboat' Smith and 'Bombadier' Wells: Heller, *Forty World Champions* (1975) p.37.

[210] Boxing on film began in 1894 with Edison's six minute showing of Corbett sparring. On boxing and photography, radio, cigarette cards, etc, see: John Johnson, Bodleian, Sport Box 3. On boxing and politics Ward takes the title of his book, 'Unforgivable Blackness' from W E B Du Bois' reference to Jack Johnson in *The Crisis*, August 1914. In support of Du Bois' thesis, Joseph Goebbels in Klemperer, *Diaries* (1999) p.201. On boxing and pornography: Fay meets Curly in Hughes' *Patent Leather Kid* (1917) p.2. Very unusually, Jack London's short story *The Game* (1905) purports to consider boxing from a woman's point of view. On boxing as nobody really fights it, see almost any fight scene at the movies, or reflect on Ernest Hemingway's pugilistic obsessions: Norman Mailer, 'Punching Papa', *New York Review of Books*, 1 February 1963. On boxing as everybody speaks it: Robert McCrum, 'Alpha Mailer', *The Observer*, 4 February 2007, or, as an example, Joe Williams in the *New York World Telegram* reporting 'Seaman' Tommy Watson versus 'Kid' Chocolate at Madison Square Garden, 19 May 1933, in Jarrett, *Byker to Broadway* (1997) p.151. On the semiotics: Scott, 'Boxing and Masculine Identity', in Dine and Crosson, eds., *Sport, Representation, and Evolving Identities* (2010).

Soon, the psychologists would come to take a look. Boxing is not an easy subject to explain but whatever it was, the 'Bass-Durkee Hostility Inventory' was never going to do it.[211] A J Liebling spent thirty years at *The New Yorker* reporting on the 'fight game' like a Manhattan Pierce Egan. For him, this was a modern science, but he took you there by talking the way you talked and writing about guys who looked the way you looked. This fighter had a face 'like a well worn coin'. That one had a head 'like a sick music box'. The other one didn't know the rules 'Cos you got a guy knocking over set ups, you don't know what you got'.[212] Carlo Rotella writes about working-class America's embrace of boxing in the 1940s. They didn't talk about it much, he says, because being 'good with your hands' was enough.[213]

We started this chapter asking what made people want to inflict beatings and what made other people want to watch? And the answer, in Sayers and Heenan's case at least, is obvious—backers made the match and newspapers and other networks, including popular theatre and The Fancy, stoked the interest. Once it was game on, it was hard to pull out. That there was some money to be made is clear, and the more brutal the encounter the less chance of a cross. All true and obvious. But the real reason Sayers and Heenan did what they did was because they were good at it. They had a talent for violence that entertained other men who only had a taste for it. That is the deep play of boxing. Nothing else compares. Nothing else counts. In a violent world, it was not the fighters who glorified the violence but the violence that glorified them.

---

[211] Goldstein, *Why We Watch* (1998) pp.17–23. A British university psychologist tried to understand the violence by trying to understand the men who inflicted it. His research methods involved the old gentlemanly sparring performance: Beattie, *Shadows of Boxing* (2003) pp.38–40.

[212] Liebling, *Sweet Science* (1951) p.20, p.28, p.34.

[213] C Rotella, *Good with their Hands* (2002).

4

Custom

The poor, having little else, keep their culture intact as part of their
vitality...

(Paul Theroux, *Deep South*, 2015)

'A Free and Happy People'

Among the historic seals, charters, and other civic regalia held in the mayor's
parlour in Stamford Town Hall, there are two silver-plated bull's horns presented
to Brother Haycock by his fellow townsmen in 1836. Fashioned to commemorate
his part in the annual bull-running, something which many in the town believed
had been observed since 1228, the presentation marked not just his part in a local
English sporting custom, but, in Stamford's eyes 'the RIGHT OF FREE WILL in
the BRITISH SUBJECT to follow his pleasures or his inclinations' in order to
render them all 'a Free and Happy People'.[1]

Every 13th November Stamford ran the bull and slaughtered it. While the more
genteel or elderly residents would take their seats on carts or carriages, or look
down from upstairs windows, or pull the curtains, the 'Bullards' would take their
'sport' in the sense that most concerns this chapter, in the wide sense according to
what gave them pleasure.[2] When it came to sport, the gentry did as they pleased.
The Bullards, on the other hand, had to fight for the right. They were
Stamfordians, and they claimed the same privileges as their forebears.[3]

It is fair to say that on this special day the Stamford Bullards broke just about
every notion of civility in the book. They ran and screamed. They swore and went
where they willed. They taxed innocent passers-by. They obstructed her majesty's
highway and performed acts of wanton cruelty. According to their opponents,
they were stupid and rustic, vulgar and ignorant, and lumpish and provincial too.

---

[1] Poster, 'Stamford Bull Running' (Stamford 1837): S[tamford] T[own] H[all] A[rchives], P[hillips]
C[ollection] vol. 183, folio 28; 'To the Worthy Independent Electors of the Town & Borough of
Stamford' (Stamford 24 July 1796): STHA, PC 183, folio 7.

[2] 'Sweet smiling village, loveliest of the lawn / Thy sports are fled, and all thy charms withdrawn...':
Oliver Goldsmith, 'The Deserted Village' (1770). A few defenders of custom pointed out that bull-
running was personally courageous too: Drakard, *History* (1822) p.416.

[3] John Leland in 1543, William Camden in 1586, and Daniel Defoe in 1724, all reported on the
town's privileges, or 'liberties': Grigson, 'Stamford 1461-1961', *Geographical Magazine*, May 1961,
pp.42–54. 13th November was bull-running day except when it fell on a Sunday.

Worst of all, they would not do what they were told. We can be sure that on that day at least they were more than willing to offer some of the 'recognized weapons' of plebeian resistance which, according to Keith Thomas at least, included 'winking, pointing, yawning, nudging, mimicking, spitting, sniggering, "mooning", and farting'.[4]

At 11am with the church bells pealing, the hapless bull was led into St. Leonard's Street where he was left to trot about. At noon, with a little judicious shifting of the barricades, he was given the freedom of the town and the Bullards with him. Now was the time to disport. If he showed his mettle, so did they, and 'he was what the bullards term a good one'.[5] If he did not show his mettle, the dogs were unleashed and his tormentors ran him 'hivee, skivie, tag and rag' in scenes of cruelty, breach of the peace, obstruction, intimidation, and riot.[6] Even if he did show sport, the dogs might be allowed theirs anyway.

It didn't finish in some bloody corner. Sometime in the afternoon, the bull would be tipped off the town bridge into the River Welland where he struggled for life before losing it on the town meadows. Later he would be served up in Stamford's more patriotic hostelries. No public house could afford to be against the Bullards on that day. Traumatized bull meant tenderized beef. According to custom.

Then there were those (it is impossible to tell how many) who saw bull-running as disgusting and wanted it stopped. They had friends in London and one or two in Stamford, including Richard Newcomb, proprietor of one of the country's leading provincial newspapers, the *Stamford Mercury*.[7] Others, probably the majority, did not want bull-running stopped because the custom was old, popular, and had nothing to do with outsiders. When in 1837 a Collyweston farmer provided a bull to take on the 'Liberal principles' of the abolitionists—particularly Newcomb, and his 'spies from London'—the farmer's friends asked for subscriptions 'however small' to buy him a silver snuff box (monies to Mr. Lowson of the *Boat Inn* or to Mr. Prout of the *Sun Inn*).[8]

'However small' tells us something about popular support for the Bullards—a problem not only for Newcomb, but also for the Cecils across the river at Burghley House. The Cecils' 'Red' party had successfully managed the parliamentary seat in uncontested elections since 1734 and their domination of the town involved long-standing attempts to manage the running. Newcomb had never been happy with

    [4]   Thomas, *Pursuit of Civility* (2018) p.107.
    [5]   *Essex Standard*, 24 November 1837. Bullard headquarters was The Olive Branch, 3 St. Leonard's Street, and the bull was customarily stabled in The Royal Oak at 6 St. Leonard's Street: Smith, *Stamford* (1992) pp. 83–4.
    [6]   Butcher, *Survey* (1646) pp.24–5.
    [7]   Richard Newcomb (1798–1851) newspaperman, bookseller, businessman, supporter of enclosure, justice of the peace, Mayor of Stamford (1847), who emerged late in the day as the Cecil family's foremost local opponent, turning Whig Reformer at the 1830 election.
    [8]   Poster, 'Stamford Bull Running' (Stamford, November 1837): STHA, PC 183, folio 30.

the Bullards, or the Cecils, and in 1826 he broke cover. 'Originally of the Tory School' he turned against the running even though 'the populace was in favour'.[9] As Rosemary Sweet makes clear, Stamford borough traditions were complex but the point was simple: bull-running was never just about bull-running. It was part of a much wider political question over the extent to which boroughs could retain their liberty.[10]

Stamford's metropolitan opponents couldn't give a fig about scot-and-lot and custom, but they did care about cruel and disgusting scenes in the street. Grouped in and around the National Society for the Prevention of Cruelty to Animals, with six earls, one duke, one duchess, three countesses, five MPs, six lords, and a young Queen on its side, a powerful combination of Evangelicals and humanitarians were gathering.[11] These were the sort of people who could go to see the Home Secretary, petition Her Majesty, lobby members of parliament, talk with influential insiders or even ride up the Great North Road with her 14th Dragoon Guards if she so wished. They were not the sort of people who were used to being beaten or contradicted by the likes of Mr. Lowson or Mr. Prout. At first it was their intention to shame the bull runners. But it proved difficult to shame those whose constitution told them to be proud. Political economy had long found plebeian festivals a waste of time, money, and the patience of political economists, but even they and their new humanitarian friends could not budge these ignorant folk who had long made it clear that even if 'The Silken Sons of Luxury' *'may deride'* their sport/'Hardy Bullards' would 'Hail the Day / Dear to Stamford's loyal sons, the Games / Your early Fathers fought...'[12]

By 1830 the last and most notorious bull-baitings had been put down: Aylesbury in 1822, Beverley in 1823, Lincoln and Thame in 1826, and Birmingham in 1830. Tutbury had finished running bulls as long ago as 1778, leaving Stamford infamous and alone. In 1726, Howgrave's history of the town had condemned the sport as 'cruel and barbarous'. In 1741 Stamford churchwardens had been denied their pay for fear they spent it at the running. More serious attempts by the Cecils to stop it in 1788 and 1789 were met with effigies, painted faces, execrable noises, and a 600-strong running mob led by 'a corpulent female in a smock frock' called Ann Blades. Further excitements followed in 1792, 1802, 1809, 1813, 1819, and 1822. In 1802, in the teeth of parliamentary opposition, the town petitioned parliament to retain the running and William Windham, former Secretary of State for War (interested in the Stamford seat) spoke in its defence as

---

[9] Obituary, *Stamford Mercury*, 26 March 1851.

[10] 'There was "still considerable value in appealing to the civic ideology of independence, chartered rights, and freemen's privileges which derived their meaning from a sense of local urban identity and tradition': Sweet, 'Freemen and Independence', *Past & Present* 161, 1998, p.85.

[11] Harrison, 'Animals and the State', *English Historical Review* 88, 1973, p.788. N[ational] S[ociety] for the P[revention] of C[ruelty] to A[nimals], Horsham, *4th Annual Report* (1836). Victoria became the Society's patron on becoming Queen in 1837.

[12] Handbill, 'The Bullards' Frolicks. A New Song' (1802): STHA, PC 183, folio 8. On popular custom and the political economists: Hatcher, 'Labour, Leisure and Economic Thought', *Past & Present* 160, 1998, p.77.

part of that great antiquity that underpinned the constitution. In 1819, John Drakard's Tory Radical *Stamford News* defended the running against that 'bastard humanity which froths and foams at one yearly indulgence of the lower orders and sympathizes with the daily and destructive enjoyments of the high and wealthy'.[13] Did game birds not bleed? Were fine horses not run to death? Were foxes not eaten alive?

Stamford had been dominated since 1561 by the Cecils. Between 1734 and 1885, when the constituency was absorbed into Lincolnshire Eastern Division, except on two occasions, all members of parliament were nominated by them.[14] Town politics was increasingly tied up with the town's economic prospects, but the bull-running overshadowed every parliamentary contest. In 1796, an independent candidate promised to respect 'The Ancient Rights' of the borough and the ancient 'Rights and Privileges of the Plebeians'. In the 1809 election, Mr. Joshua Jepson Oddy, a rich merchant based in London but probably from Stamford, fought the Cecils partly on the grounds of opening up the town to trade but equally, as it turned out, on the grounds of defending the running. 'Oddy for EVER', and 'For ODDY and a BULL'. He lost but the battle went on. In 1829 an itinerant Baptist preacher, having spent 14 November up to his waist in the same cold waters in which the bull had bled the day before, invoked Psalm cxix: 'I Beheld the Transgressors and was Grieved'. He was joined the following year by another anti-Bullard who felt so confident of his support in the town that he chose not to give his name and address.[15] A further spate of invective against the sporting lower orders followed in 1833 ('detestable, disgraceful, dreadful'), and again in 1837, but by now the war on Stamford had gone all the way up to the laws of England.[16]

In his famous *Commentaries on the Laws of England* (1765–69), Judge Blackstone described two kinds of custom. One, 'customs in general', appertaining

---

[13] Drakard, in Smith, *Stamford* (1994), p.76; Windham spoke in the House of Commons, 24 May 1802: NSPCA Records, vol. i, 1800–1822. For bull-running handbills see: STHA, PC 183 folios 2, 3, 4, 6, 7, 8, 9,10, 11, 12, 13, 14, 16, 17. On bull-baiting: Malcolmson, *Popular Recreations* (1973), pp.124–6; Hailstone, *Buckinghamshire* (1957) p.2; on bull-running: Gardiner, *Wisbech* (1898), p.52; Howgrave, *Essay* (1726) p.54. On running misreported as baiting: *Gentleman's Magazine*, December 1802. Prints concentrated on baiting by dogs with most sympathy for the dogs: see for example two watercolours by Samuel Howitt (YCBA, Rare Books and Ms) 'Bull Attacking Mastiff' and 'Bull Attacking Dog' (nd).

[14] Rogers, *Making of Stamford* (1965) p.96.

[15] Poster, *Humanitas*, 'Stamford Bull Running', 10 November 1830 (1830): STHA, PC 183, folio 20; tract, Winks, 'Sermon in General Baptist Meeting House, Stamford' (15 November 1829). Winks went on to play a leading part in the suppression of Leicester's 'Whipping Toms' in 1836, as explained in Thomas Cook's 'Personal Reminiscences': *Leicester Chronicle and Leicestershire Mercury*, 21 February 1880. See poster, *Fairplay*, 'Stamford Bull Running', 6 November 1830: STHA, PC 183, folio 19. See also, handbill, Roger Burton, 'To the worthy independent Electors of the Town & Borough of Stamford', 24 July 1796: STHA, PC 183, folio 7; and address, 'Free Election. Bull Running', 'Oddy for Ever' (1809) and 'Address to The Independent Electors of Stamford', 'A New Song': STHA, PC 183, folio 9.

[16] Handbills, 'Bull Running' (1833): STHA, PC 183, folios 17, 18, 24; ibid, 'Stamford Bull Running' (1837) folio 25.

to the welfare of all, for example keeping the peace; and two, 'customs in particular', appertaining to a particular practice whose binding power lay not in statute or judicial opinion, but in 'long and immemorial usage' universally recognized.[17] Clearly the Stamford Bullards came under the laws of England as a 'custom in particular', even though, less clearly, evidence as to its immemorial use and universal recognition was patchy. Butcher's *Survey* of 1646 claimed thirteenth-century antecedents, without evidence.[18] Peck's *History* of 1726 looked to an oral tradition, as legally validated by Blackstone. Stamford bull-running, Peck said, was verified by an 'accumulated wisdom' 'insensibly incorporated' into the town's constitution. Not in a document. Not in a charter. Not in a magistrate. Not in a law. Certainly not in an opinion, but incorporated into a custom turned into an annual plebiscite. On that day at least, when the constitution was upheld, everyone was freeborn:

> At length the happy Day, the Day of Joy and Gladness, this Day of Mirth and Pastime is once more return'd. On this Day there is no King in Stamford; we are every one of us High and Mighty Lords of the united Parishes in a General Bull-running... everyone of us a Lord... of Rule and Misrule, a King in Stamford, and a Heroe everywhere else.[19]

Few in Stamford doubted the argument from immemorial use and common practice. They saw the running as not only entirely popular, but entirely lawful, for 'when a reasonable Act once done is found to be good, and beneficial to the People, and agreeable to their nature and disposition, then do they use it and practice it again and again and so by often iteration and multiplication of the Act, it becomes a Custom; and being continued without interruption time out of mind, it obtaineth the force of a law', so said Carter in 1696.[20] Six years after it had been put down, Burton got carried away with himself. The bull-running had been the 'idol of the people of Stamford', he said, and 'it was to them what the Olympic games were to the ancients of Rome'. Metropolitan observers hated the cruelty, but time and again they were forced to admit that 'the population in general appear to regard this day as a season of high festivity. All seemed in high spirits... and there were many women' casting off 'all appearance of decency and order and plung[ing] into every excess of riot... without shame'. You could buy lustreware jugs depicting the scene. 'Oddy and a Bull'. 'A Bull for Ever'. 'Ann Blades Stamford 1792'. Ann was known as the 'Bull Woman' and wore a costume of blue, together with a heavy blue bullstick and a fancy for taxing passers by.[21]

[17] Blackstone, *Commentaries* 1765–69 (1788) vol. i, pp.45–6.
[18] Butcher, *Survey* (1646) pp.24–5; Peck, *Academia Tertia Anglicana* (1727).
[19] Tract in Peck, *History of the Stamford Bull Runnings* (1726).
[20] Carter, *Lex Customaria* (1696) quoted in Thompson, *Customs in Common* (1993) p.97.
[21] Anon, 'Stamford Bull Running' (1830): STHA, PC 183, folio 51, pp.12–15; Burton, *Chronology of Stamford* (1846) p.52.

The harder part of the argument involved Blackstone's clause on whether or not a peculiar custom was universally recognized because this meant that Stamford's business was somebody else's business as well. Without documentary evidence, persuading outsiders that the running was or had been a peculiar custom universally recognized was always going to be difficult. Nevertheless, by the time battle recommenced in 1833 the first question was not whether bull-running was old, or whether it was legal, but whether it was decent.[22]

The NSPCA's first move was tentative and came in November 1833 when it offered rewards of up to £10 for any information leading to the prevention of cruelty to animals at what it called Stamford's 'annual fair'. On the day itself the reward went up to £20 but no information was forthcoming.[23] The following year, housed now in 3 Exeter Hall, home of good causes, the Society took a more sophisticated view. In a letter to Stamford magistrates the NSPCA's solicitor John Gilbert Meymott expressed his earnest hope that they could act in unison under an interpretation of Richard Martin's 1822 Cruel Treatment of Cattle Act (copy kindly provided) that included 'bulls' under the category of 'oxen'. Still looking for documentary evidence as to its antiquity, Meymott wondered 'whether the Tenure of some estates, property or rights does not depend on the keeping up?'. The 1834 running went ahead all the same. Charles Dickens reckoned that all society would be best served by always travelling in the opposite direction to Exeter Hall, but he and the Bullards were not comrades either. Dickens didn't like cant, wherever it came from.[24]

In 1835, the Cruelty to Animals Act entered the statute book, adding vital generalizations to Martin's original statute.[25] Martin had tried to extend the application of his Act at the time of its passing but failed to counter the Home Secretary's rebuke that if an extension went ahead 'there was scarce an animal ... that would not be protected'. Too true. The passing of the 1835 Act proved Peel right. With a law now against cruelty to animals in general, and with a

---

[22] 'A few stupid brutal amateurs' according to the *Morning Herald*, 8 November 1833, whose higher principles included the 'progress of human intelligence' and the voice of 'law, humanity or religion'. Another way of judging the running might have been by Bentham's utility principle where what mattered were the relative amounts of pain and pleasure afforded the bull and the Bullards respectively: Bentham, *Fragment* (1776) p.25, pp.126–8, pp.151–63. Bentham stated that 'the welfare of mankind' was 'inseparably connected with the downfall of his [Blackstone's] works' (p.4).

[23] NSPCA minutes, vol. i, 5 November 1833; handbill, A Bullard, 'To the Inhabitants of Stamford' (1833), STHA, PC 183, folio 28, and 'Bull Running' 'utterly incompatible with Christianity', ibid, folio 17.

[24] 'It might be laid down as a very good general rule ... that whatever Exeter Hall champions is the thing by no means to be done': Dickens, *The Examiner*, 19 August 1848, in Slater, ed., *Dickens' Journalism* (1998) p.110; NSCPA minutes, vol. i, 5 May, 2 June 1834.

[25] Malcolmson says the Act 'unequivocally established the illegality of all blood sports' (*Popular Recreations*, 1973, p.124) but it did not include wild animals and therefore field sports remained untouched.

metropolitan elite ready to promote it, and the tormentation of bulls all but over anyway, the Bullards were on notice.[26]

With many more reasons to be cheerful in 1835 than in 1834, solicitor Meymott increased pressure on Stamford magistrates by offering rewards of up to £1,000—a staggering amount. He sent the Mayor a copy of the new Act, and, so that he could have some hard evidence of what actually went on, he despatched a former Metropolitan police officer to the town in order to gauge the size and intensity of the running. He soon had his answer: a shrieking mob ('many very respectable'), twenty-eight running Bullards, torchlight gatherings at the homes 'of those known to be averse', and, hardest to bear, no action whatsoever from the magistrates.[27]

The next year Meymott sent two former constables to observe proceedings (the Bullards called it spying) while the Society embarked on a vigorous lobbying campaign at the Home Office. NSPCA Secretary Henry Thomas told Lord John Russell that which no Home Secretary ever wanted to hear: that the town's middle class had lost its nerve.[28] In the event, the Home Office stayed out, the Society went in, and the bull-running went ahead. The spies thought they witnessed a riot and Mr. William Haycock, Town Surveyor of Highways, was presented with his silver horns.

In 1837 the NSPCA changed tack. Instead of trying to prise Stamford open from the inside by offering rewards and prodding magistrates, Meynott and Thomas decided to come down heavily from the outside. Indictments were issued against seven men on 2 March 1837 and warrants for four on the 8th, including Haycock. The Stamford response was to call the prosecution 'Malicious, Base, Wicked and Vexatious',[29] but this was not the view of the judge who, in the case of *Rex v Richardson* at Lincoln Assizes on 18 July 1837, found all four men guilty of riot on 13 November last. The traditional legal view was that 'assembling at wakes, or other festival times, or meetings for exercise of common sports or diversions, such as bull baiting etc' was *not* riotous, but in this case the judge took a different view.[30] He was not, he said, in the least interested in how old or how particular the custom was. It meant nothing to him what Earl Warenne did or did not do that ancient day when he looked from the castle walls and saw two bulls fighting and gave chase and called on the butchers of Stamford to keep the custom &c &c. Even

[26] *Hansard*: House of Commons debate, 21 February 1826, vol. 14, cc.647–52.

[27] NSPCA minutes, vol. ii, 3, 14, 31 October, 4 November 1835. There is a 'Public Caution' notice in the Phillips' Collection that raises the possibility that troops may have been present in 1835. But from the absence of any corroborating evidence and the March date, this handbill may have been sent to magistrates as an example of what they *could* do if required: 'Public Caution' 'in the event of the Troops being ordered to fire, their Fire will be effective' (Horse Guards, 27 March 1835) STHA, PC 183, folio 22. There never was any question of troops using firearms in Stamford. Poster, 'Stamford Bull Running' 'designated by certain Fanatics as Brutal' (1835), STHA, PC 183, folio 23.

[28] NSPCA minutes, 11 November 1836.

[29] Handbill, 'Stamford Bull Running' (Stamford, 14 March 1837): STHA, PC 183, folio 25.

[30] As in Burn's *Justice of the Peace* handbook (1762. 1830 ed.): Harvey, 'British Sporting Culture', Oxford DPhil (1996) p.131.

if the custom was 800 years old, he said, 'the court could know nothing of it'. As for documentary evidence, what did it matter to him that an 'old book said that an old Lord looked over a wall and saw a bull?' The point was to keep the peace, not the custom.[31] Pending good behaviour, sentences were withheld until 13 November next.

Everything went ahead for the 1837 running. Early in the morning NSPCA men Rogerson and Smith tried the Town Hall door only to find it locked. Along with Mr. Thomas, they had already been to an extraordinary Sunday meeting of magistrates the day before where they had been met with considerable hostility. Pointedly asked how the NSPCA would deploy Stamford's 243 Special Constables if it was up to him, Mr. Thomas offered a strategy (of the kind that would soon be deployed against Chartists) only for the magistrates to opine that their Special Constables were useless anyway. Trying to be helpful, Thomas offered a strategy for the best fifty. The magistrates responded that all of them were useless, so useless indeed that Chief Constable Reed, who was in drink, was allowed to threaten and abuse his guests: 'Three pretty fellows you are! I shall know you tomorrow!'.[32] When tomorrow came, in spite of (or because of) last minute reminders from the magistrates that Lincoln Assizes had ruled against the running, the landlord of *The Boat Inn* released a bull and the town ran riot through its own streets contrary to law but according to custom.[33] The bench claimed to be horrified, but Richard Newcomb, the NSPCA's best informant, reported that this was all a deception, that the town magistrates believed in the custom 'by Charter and by Law', and loathed outside interference as specious, hypocritical, and unwarranted. What did it have to do with people '100 miles off?' 'An Englishman is not an animal to be driven'. As the defence had argued at Lincoln—

> What had the NSPCA to do with the stopping up of the streets in Stamford by waggons? They came here to try and protect bulls, and they ended in protecting waggons ... God knows whether there was any society for preventing waggons placed at the ends of streets—there were societies for nearly all purposes now-a-days.[34]

After two nights at the *Carpenters' Arms*, Messrs Thomas, Rogerson, and Smith made their excuses and left. Thomas had been advised by Newcomb to leave

---

[31] NSPCA minutes, vol. ii, 2 January, 6 February, 2, 8, March, 18 July 1837; chapbook, Anon, *Stamford Bull Running. Report of a Criminal Prosecution (Rex v Richardson and others), Lincoln Summer Assizes 18 July 1837* (Stamford 1837): STHA, PC 183, folio 5; handbills, STHA, PC 183, folios 25, 27, 28; *Morning Herald*, 16 November 1838. Story of Earl Warenne: Nevinson, *History of Stanford* (sic) (1879) p.20.

[32] NSPCA minutes, 4 December 1837.

[33] 'Bull Running in Stamford' (Stamford, 9 November 1837), signed by mayor and magistrates, describing the Lincoln judgement as 'disgraceful and contrary to law': STHA, PC 183, folio 29.

[34] Chapbook, *Stamford Bull Running* (1837) ibid, folio 41.

shortly after his brush with Reed, and Rogerson and Smith were glad to go soon after being forced to share the streets with, in their own words, 'the lowest vagabonds' along with the 'apparently more respectable'. They had come to prevent a riot. They left having been an incitement to it. Good intentions in ruins, they collected their £3 fee and 10s a day expenses and moved out. 'The shouting and yelling was terrific', they reported.[35]

Almost at once, and against the Attorney General's clear advice (given 30 December 1837), Meymott took Stamford magistrates to the higher Court of Queen's Bench. Founded in 1215, Queen's Bench was as old as the bull-running itself and as a mark of its clear impartiality it bore the name of the NSPCA's most senior patron.[36] With special jurisdiction for the actions of public authorities, Queen's Bench ruled in February 1838 that the Lincoln judgment was correct and that what Stamford did, and what its magistrates condoned, was most certainly unlawful. The defendants had been misled by so much talk of custom and old books and other nonsense. The Lincoln judgment should be respected at all times; not just year to year. 'It was not a proper practice to be continued' and 'for the future it must be considered as an illegal practice'. Stamford's justices of the peace were bound over to keep their own peace.[37]

Hugely encouraged, Meymott went into overdrive. He called upon sympathetic MPs to send a signed letter to Lord John Russell at the Home Office. He pressed Russell to come down hard upon the Stamford magistrates for not doing their duty. He called for placards and posters to be put up, and a capable superintendent of the Metropolitan Police with a dozen constables to be sent, reassuring the Home Secretary that the NSPCA would reimburse the Home Office for its trouble.[38]

Meymott then wrote to his key informant Newcomb asking him 'how the matter stands' with the town magistrates and was told, completely against the odds and stopping him in his tracks, that since being put on notice by a higher court there had been 'a wonderful change' of feelings among them, and that they were going to put it down, but that it was extremely important that Meymott kept well out of it. Meymott then wrote to the Stamford bench on 3 November threatening them to do their duty. Three days before the running, the Home Office started studding all Stamford's flash points: 14th Dragoons at St. Martin's, the *Three Tuns*, Scotgate, and *O'Brien's Arms*, and a special squad of twenty Metropolitan police posted near the Town Hall. The whole town was fly-posted with cautions: 'Notice of the above is hereby given pursuant to the Orders of the

---

[35] NSPCA minutes, vol. ii, 4 December 1837.

[36] 'Stamford Bull Running 1209-1839', unidentified newspaper cutting: STHA, PC 183, folio 41.

[37] NSPCA, minutes, vol. ii, 30 December 1837, 5 February 1838.

[38] Legal costs for Lincoln Assizes and Queen's Bench were £102 9 6d plus £16 1s 8d shorthand reporting: ibid. Wiener draws attention to the 'sheer size of the police intervention' in such disputes from the 1830s: *Men of Blood* (2004) p.19.

Secretary of State' signed by Jackson the Mayor and magistrates Hunt, Rodew, and Newcomb. A bull was sneaked out at 11am on the day, then another, but both animals were taken in hand by the constables. A few heifers and a third bull followed, as if from nowhere, but the Dragoons chased the heifers and collared the bull. The Chief Constable, with soldiers and constables in attendance, then made three token arrests—all labourers. As the day darkened, the whole town stood tense in a constitutional stand-off between the rights of the people and the authority of a court but at 7.30 in the evening victory over the Bullards was finally declared. The NSPCA minute read: 'the spell is broken'.[39]

Only the spell was not broken. In 1839 more troops and police were sent in, with yet more warnings, pickets, and sentries. In spite of which, a bull was kept the night before at the *Royal Oak*, farm waggons moved in at dawn, St Mary's tolled its bells, and a crowd of about 300, including a noticeable number of women, ran the beast, tipped it, slaughtered it, and served it, all in the customary way. Magistrates made a few desultory arrests but otherwise stood off. In the NSPCA's view, there was not much chance of a prosecution because this time it had kept its distance. Fair warned by Newcomb early in October that it was the intention of 'certain persons' to run the bull again, Meymott had roused the whole influence of the Society in London, only to fail in Stamford. Spirits at Exeter Hall fell very low indeed. You can imagine the National Association for the Prevention of Cruelty to Animals asking its next door neighbour, The Association for Promoting Rational Humanity, where had it all gone wrong?[40]

Then, in 1840, just at the point when Meymott was being told that another running was in the offing and that they were in an 'almost hopeless state here', Secretary Thomas heard from other friends of the Society (3–4 November), including Newcomb, that all was not lost and there had been another change of mind. Even though they had heard such things before, and even though the Mayor was a Bullard and Home Secretary Normanby had taken to speaking laconically on the matter, it would appear that the principal inhabitants of Stamford had met privately at the Town Hall where they had resolved for a second time to take the matter in hand ('to seize the issue and address it') and settle the Bullards once and for all ('to save the expense and discredit'). Outsiders must keep out. It was imperative that 'the whole of the inhabitants…come forward of themselves

---

[39] NSPCA minutes, 1 October, 5, 19 November 1838; poster, 'Stamford Bull Running', 7 November 1838, 'troops to enforce obedience': STHA, PC 183, folio 31. On the arrests of labourers Woodall, Snarey, and Kisbee, deposition, 17 November 1838: STHA, PC 183, folio 48. Richard Lowe-Lauri's Royal Historical Society prize-winning essay 'Bull by the Horns' (*History Today* 62, 2012) argued that compared with public order, animal welfare came low on the NSPCA's hierarchy of Stamford objectives. This misreads what the Society had on its hands. It was battling to enforce the courts' rulings, and the courts' rulings were entirely to do with public order.

[40] NSPCA, minutes, vol. iii, 7 October, 2 December 1839, 6 January 1840; poster, 'Bull Running Stamford', 'absolute directions' to suppress (4 November 1839): STHA, PC 183, folio 32; handbill, 'Instructions to Special Constables' (Town Hall, 12 November 1839): STHA, PC 183, folio 33; poster, 'Bull Running Prosecutions' (27 December 1839): STHA, PC 183, folio 35.

without foreigners'. Principal inhabitants Holland, Pilkinton, Brackenbury and Woodroffe told Mr. Secretary Thomas that they recommended that 'the Society will stand aloof this year with the express understanding that the authorities of the Borough in conjunction with the inhabitants will prevent the outrage'. Newcomb assured Meynott that the town could do it provided 'no foreign force' was introduced'.[41] And this time, Meymott did stay out. And the town did do it. And the bull was not run. After standing around calling 'A Bull!' 'A Bull!' some youths tried to run a steer which was quickly caught and so were they: two month's hard labour or a fine they could not pay. The following year there was not so much as a cat call.

Clearly there had been negotiations including the town's principal inhabitants beforehand. Clearly some sort of agreement had been reached. Clearly the NSPCA's seven-year part in the matter was downplayed. As Newcomb told Thomas, 'It is not the fashion to attribute this happy circumstance to the Society... but I *know* that the merit is wholly theirs'.[42] Men like Richard Newcomb, after Lord Burghley the most important man in Stamford, emerge as a new kind of civic leader, someone committed to a completely different sense of who, or what, happens on the streets of their town.[43]

Even so, it's hard to know why those guardians of the freedom of the streets, 'the principal inhabitants', decided to take the matter in hand so decisively only ten days before the running.[44] They might have caught wind of the Lord Lieutenant's £450 bill for police and military; *The Morning Post* thought so.[45] They might have had had enough of the Cecils and their 'Tory Burlesque' across the river.[46] They might have run out of patience with the age old custom of publicans making money and ratepayers picking up the tab. Or it might have been that a century of middle-class reform had done its work and Stamford took on, not before time, what historians used to call the Spirit of the Age.[47] Whatever it was, it wasn't long (1850) before 'ci-devant' Bullards were having jolly suppers in their own memory, and town theatre audiences were calling for 'A Bull' at the close of performances. And it wasn't that much longer (1856) before bull-running ceased to be vile and started to be heritage. 'Up came Bill Christian, his whip he did crack'. Indeed it was only a matter of time before memorialists would start getting

---

[41] NSPCA, minutes, vol. iv, 2, 3 November 1840; poster, 'Borough of Stamford' meeting, 3 November 1840, and poster, 'Memorial of Inhabitants' asking for contribution towards costs of suppression: STHA, PC 183, folio 36.

[42] NSPCA, minutes, 14 November 1841, 6 December 1841.

[43] Newton & Smith, *The Stamford Mercury* (1999) pp.83–101, pp.280–1.

[44] Joyce, *Rule of Freedom* (2003) ch. 5.

[45] 'Saddled with an enormous expense': *Morning Post*, 19 November 1840; poster, 'H Gilchrist, Mayor, 14 November 1840': STHA, PC 183, folio 37.

[46] At one point, town Tories even took to parodying themselves, in their apparent support for ancient rights and customs: *Leicester Chronicle*, 9 December 1837.

[47] Morgan, *Manners, Morals, and Class in England* (1994) pp.12–20.

their facts wrong.[48] In 1891 Rev. Carroll of Tallington presented the Corporation with a portrait of the running. At its centre stands an unruly Ann Blades. Another painting shows an unruly Fan Plowright, town prostitute. At some point Mr. Haycock donated his 608th bull's horns to the Town Hall.

Finer Feelings

For the bull runners, custom was who they were, the common life, the constitution in its most literal form, what the Scottish philosopher David Hume called 'a peculiar set of manners [made] habitual [by] the nature of government'. For the reformers, custom, or this custom at any rate, was hateful and immoral. Bull-running, like bull-baiting, or prize-fighting, or cock-fighting, or slavery, 'steels the heart against every tender, amiable and generous impression' said a pamphlet of 1802, and when in 1814 Hazlitt said the public taste was vitiated in proportion to its popularity ('lowered with every infusion...of common opinion'), he was thinking of the vulgar classes, not the finer feelings.[49] Public displays of violence were less and less acceptable.[50] Strutt's encyclopaedic review of *The Sports and Pastimes of the People of England*, published in 1801, was very clear that bull-baiting, 'which rarely happens', 'is attended only by the lowest and most despicable'.[51]

The trouble was, what was considered despicable depended on what side of the rope you stood. Throwing a 2 pound whinstone across Newcastle Town Moor was sport to the bowlers and danger for the passers-by. 'Backsword' by villagers looked like assault to visitors. After playing pitch and toss in Oliver's Ale House in 1785, the 5s won by Thomas Johnson was the same 5s stolen from Mark Lawson.[52] And

---

[48] Walcott, *Memorials* (1867) referred to bull-*baiting* in Stamford as part of the bad old past (pp.26–7). *The Era*, 12 November 1850; Hodgkinson and Tebbutt, *Stamford in 1850* (1954) p.11; handbill, 'Song: The Luffenham Bull' (Stamford, 1856) based on the 1816 version: STHA, PC 183, folio 21. Hume is quoted in Tombs, *The English and their History* (2014) p.300.

[49] Hazlitt, 'Whether the Fine Arts Are Promoted by Academies", *The Champion*, 11 September 1814, in Howe, ed., *Complete Works* (1933) vol. xviii, p.46. Hazlitt seems to have changed his mind by the time of 'The Fight'. On matters of the heart: Stockdale, *Remonstrance* (1802) p.24; Johnson, *Sportsmen's Cyclopedia* (1831): John Johnson, Bodleian, Sport Box 3. On the closeness of prize-fighting to cock-fighting: Anon, *Directions for Breeding Game Cocks* (1780).

[50] This seemingly modest sentence connects to a much wider debate on what can go wrong when scholars apply abstract theories to changing meanings over long periods of time. Note Hanlon's scathing review of Robert Pinker's book on the modern decline of violence, *The Better Angels of Our Nature* (2011) in *English Historical Review*, 128, 2013. Pinker is a psychologist. Historians of sport have been equally unhappy with the measuring of meaning of 'violence' in Norbert Elias' theory of *The Civilizing Process* (1939). Elias was a sociologist. See Collins, 'History, Theory and the Civilizing Process', *Sport in History* 25, 2005, and Vamplew, 'Some comments on the Civilizing Process', *Sport in History* 27, 2007. For a single empirical example of a complete repudiation of the Elias thesis, see: Stedman Jones, 'The Redemptive Power of Violence?', *History Workshop Journal* 65, 2008.

[51] Strutt, *Sports and Pastimes* (1801) p.349.

[52] Pitch and Toss, deposition of Thomas Johnson, 21 July 1785, North East Circuit, National Archives, ASSI/45/35; bowling, depositions George Humble and Andrew Murdue, 15 July 1785, ibid; backsword, Charles Turner, 'Backswords' (*c*.1810): 8 x 11 inches, ink and watercolour: Rare Books and Ms, YCBA.

so on. Nearly all English popular taste had a propensity to stray beyond what was considered boisterous into what was considered shameful. Strutt allowed for the 'misrule' element in all English custom—its 'facetious spirit', its 'mock dignities', its ability to turn the world upside down.[53] When sport was legible as custom, those who didn't like it generally accepted it. When it was illegible, finer feelings came to the fore. Sport became a problem.[54]

Village cricket was the great exception because it was played by gentlemen and villagers alike. Both sides knew the script. A parish sport taken up by the gentry and played originally in the southern counties but linking up with county ties and country houses, by the end of the eighteenth century cricket was both rustic *and* fashionable. Out of the village cricket match, a minor school of English topographical painters emerged.[55] Out of the village cricket match, a minor school of English jurists emerged. Mary Mitford's umpires sound remarkably like umpires in our own day, humming and hawing, looking round and trying to look wise.[56] Out of the village cricket match, a minor school of satirists emerged, sketching a game that foreigners could never understand only as a way of showing just how well the English could—beautifully caught by A G Macdonell's *England, Their England* in 1933 and Alistair Cooke's letter from America in 1954.[57] When cricket was played at Lord's, for money, 'hard money', it was open to hard men. When it was played in a country park as an afternoon fete, it was open to ladies and gentlemen alike. When it was played as part of natural parish rhythms—'ever the source whence the great supply of cricketers must come'—everyone understood it. Thomas Turner found space for cricket in his everyday life in the same way that he found space for gossip. Mary Russell Mitford, writing stories from Three Mile Cross near Reading, stressed how much the cricket team meant to village life.

But customs where the point of the custom was lost, or elusive, or involved spasms of drunkenness, noise, begging, bragging, cursing, over-familiarity and otherwise blatant disregard for others, put those in authority in a difficult personal position. Arm's length was the preferred distance. Poor people knew each other by their nick names—'Bodger' Johnson, 'Gogle' Gotheridge, 'Mucky' Billinge,

---

[53] Strutt, *Sports and Pastimes* (1801) p.446, p.484.

[54] Wilson, *Sense of the People* (1995) p.4; Storch, 'Introduction', *Popular Culture* (1982) p.3.

[55] YCBA: Francis Cotes (1776–70), 'Charles Collyer as a Boy, with a Cricket Bat' (1776) oil on canvas, 36 × 28 inches; Henry Alken (1785–1851), 'Scenes of Cricket' (1827) oil on canvas, 6 × 70 inches; Anon, 'A Game of Cricket. The Royal Academy Club in Marylebone Fields, now Regent's Park' (1790), pencil and oil, 10 × 11 inches; Anon, 'First Grand Match of Cricket played by members of the Royal Academy Society on Hampstead Court Green' (1836) oil on canvas, 22 × 32 inches. See also Strutt, *Sports and Pastimes* (1801) p.175, and Underdown, *Start of Play* (2000) p.72.

[56] Mitford, *Our Village* (1824–32) p.175.

[57] Where Cooke tells the story of the American funny man Will Rogers who on being asked by the Prince of Wales if he could think of any improvements to cricket, replied that the players could eat less. Finding breaks for 'lunch' and 'tea' thoroughly unacceptable while spectators waited patiently for play to resume, Rogers said he would advise: 'Now listen fellers, no food till you're through': *Manchester Guardian*, 26 July 1954.

'Dipper' Millington, and so on. In domestic service, therefore, in order to keep the distance right, servants were commonly addressed with the utmost formality.[58] The more public the stage, the more formal the exchange. In these circumstances, challenging custom could be ill advised.[59] Any effective rebuke by a notable ran the risk of inviting a response, and whether that came silently by night or aggressively by day or anonymously by satire or by squib, that would require another response and so on and so forth to turn it into the labour of Sisyphus. All very tiresome. There were people in the parish best avoided. Custom involved reciprocal gestures and reciprocal gestures, in small circles at least, tended to follow you around.[60] It was unwise for a gentleman to get involved with certain people.

Then there were gentlemen who didn't bother at all. In 1767 Rev. Cole spent Shrove Tuesday in front of the fire drinking tea and mulling over land sales. It was a stormy day in Bletchley and he did that rather than what he was obliged to do, which was watch the annual football match on the village green. Two weeks before, he'd spent Valentine's Day morning in bed while village children hallooed beneath his window. The year before that, he'd given thirty of his parishioners a harvest supper in the kitchen ('Jem dressed out with Ribbands & Tom Herne dancing') but went to bed early leaving them to it. Monday 5 May was the town's beating of the bounds and Cole was supposed to go and meet the party at the corner of Rickby Wood but 'it being so Windy & the Roads so bad for a Chaise I did not care to go the whole way'.[61] Like the Radnorshire curate Francis Kilvert, Cole liked to keep on the right side of his feelings. Kilvert liked to keep the score in village cricket matches but lay in bed on fair nights listening to the men making their way home 'talking at once loud and fast and angry, humming and huzzing... blood... on fire... a sudden blaze... a retort, a word, a blow'.[62] It was no secret that village sport could involve ruction.[63]

Custom was valued by those who had fewer ways of managing change or opposing it.[64] Poachers claimed their liberty from the land, the same liberty as the gentry. Prize-fighters stood in a national tradition of being violent and

---

[58] Arthur, 'Church Broughton Ts' (1974): see Arthur, "Church Broughton Parish, Derbyshire: an oral history 1900-1940', DMU PhD (2020).

[59] Wade, Introduction to Dicey, *Introduction to the study of the Law of the Constitution* (1885) p.cxcvii.

[60] 'The unreciprocated gift...makes the person who has accepted it inferior': Mauss, *The Gift* (1950) p.83.

[61] Stokes, ed., *Bletchley Diary Rev William Cole* (1931) p.191, p.181, p.46.

[62] Plomer, ed., *Kilvert's Diary* (1938) p.239. The *Labour League Examiner* (4 July 1874) could not resist 'the beardless curate' who, thrust upon a parish, 'fresh from wines and bump suppers at Oxford', 'finds himself at once a leader'.

[63] For example, see: Witts, *Diary* (1979) p.108, or North East Circuit Depositions 1784–86, Thomas Johnson, 21 July 1785 or Andrew Mordue, 15 July 1785: NRO, ASSI/45/35. Maxwell, *Border Sketches* (1847) vol. i, p.158.

[64] Joyce, *Visions* (1991) p.150.

gentlemanly at the same time. Bullards took their place as small upholders of a vast constitutional edifice built on precedent. Paradoxically, the *idea* of country and constitution seems to have mattered most to those who had so little of country and constitution in the first place. What else could give so much meaning to their difficult lives? Many years later, a great sports journalist would remark of football that it was 'inherent in the people' and in Stamford at least, so was the bull running. These were established performances, not spontaneous actions or something got up for the day.[65]

And because custom was one of the ways in which all communities held together, and learnt their part, it was never going to be surrendered lightly. The great northern hiring fairs were the most important custom in the rural calendar, and remained important long after the introduction of labour exchanges.[66] Girls learned how to cook and care for their babies from their mothers and grandmothers.[67] Most land tenures were held by custom.[68] Thompson and others showed how what was often called the mob was far more likely to have been the enforcers of what was customarily considered reasonable. In the case of bread riots or attacks on machinery, mob action usually involved the redistribution of food or work according to notions of what had been done before.[69] All trades worked by custom and practice. English free miners defined themselves and their living by it—from Cornish tin to Pennine lead.[70] 'Working habits were intrinsically irregular', says Sir Keith. But working habits were intrinsically regular too, even the irregularities, says Dr Reid, who has shown how long it took the regular (but irregular) custom of 'St Monday' holiday to die in Birmingham.[71] Harrison has shown regular but customary work patterns in Bristol well before the factory system arrived.[72] Workshop culture was patriarchal, held together by practice, incorporating craft divisions of labour according to skill and age: 'its initiation rituals and rites of passage, its treats and forfeits, its banter and repartee, and its heavy practical jokes'.[73] This sort of workshop tomfoolery, or 'sport', extended to parody and subversion and did not stop at the work bench. It could extend to weddings (another day off).[74] It could extend to public house banter and

---

[65] Hopcraft, *Football Man* (1968) Introduction.

[66] 'a truly popular and vital cultural form': Caunce, 'Hiring Fairs', *Past & Present* 217, 2012, p.246.

[67] 'well meaning creatures follow implicitly the example and transmitted customs of their great grand mothers': Baillie, *Advice to Mothers* (1812) p.vi.

[68] Daunton, *Progress and Poverty* (1995) p.107 and ch.4 'Open Fields and Enclosure'; see Searle, 'Cumbrian Customary Economy in 18c', *Past & Present*, 110, 1986.

[69] The classic work remains: Thompson, 'Moral Economy', *Past & Present* 50, 1971, p.76. He traces the influence of the Book of Orders (1630) on markets in much the same way that the next chapter traces the influence of the Book of Sports (1618) on play.

[70] Wood, 'English Free Miners and the Law', in Griffiths et al., *Experience of Authority in Early Modern England* (1996) p.277.

[71] Thomas, *Ends of Life* (2009) p.99. Reid, 'St Monday', *Past & Present* 71, 1976, p.76: 'It is axiomatic that the long-neglected historical study of leisure must proceed from a firm understanding of work'.

[72] Harrison, 'Ordering of the Urban Environment', *Past & Present* 110, 1986, p.166.   [73] ibid.

[74] Reid, 'Weddings, Weekdays', *Past & Present* 153, 1996.

roistering. It could extend to street frolics. In 1783 we find the Abingdon 'pot-wallopers' (householders enfranchised by custom) electing their own Mayor complete with fool, morris dancers, and motley jacket. Bamford remembered Ashton and Middleton dignifying their Mayor with a tipple. According to custom. Rowlandson's 'Two Girls Tippling' suggests there was no shame in it.[75]

For magistrates (although clearly not the Stamford ones), the difference between a pushy crowd and a breach of the peace was always going to be tight.[76] Urban jostling unsettled hierarchies, and in the crush of a great fair, St. Barts for instance, it wasn't only your feelings that could be squeezed.[77] Plough Monday, Shrove Tuesday, All Souls, Whitsun Ales, Whitsun Games, Whitsun Walks, May Day, Church Ales, Midsummer Eve, Harvest, Gleaning, St. Thomas Day, Hallow'een, Guy Fawkes, Christmas Eve, New Year's Eve—every season involved some form of 'misrule', with 'collecting' or 'treating', where passers-by would be entreated to give, with consequences if they didn't.[78] A little less than robbery, a little more than begging, the election of both the Abingdon and Middleton street mayors involved collecting. England's most famous sporting hero had been a collector.[79] Robin collected from the rich to give to the poor it is true, while English custom, on the other hand authorized the poor to collect from the rich in order to give to themselves. In Derbyshire, Ben Kirkland used to stand on his head for half a crown while Teddy Orme had his chimney bagged by local kids who had their reasons. In Cumberland, a 'bidden' wedding invited guests to put money on the bride's lap. A 'brideswain' did it all over again, without the wedding. Female harvesters would run across fields asking for money from passing travellers.[80] Sometimes it could be difficult to understand what you were being asked for, but as long as the meaning held, so did the possibility of consent. Church Broughton guyers may have been terrifying but they were welcome. As the vicar's daughter remembered:

---

[75] Thomas Rowlandson, 'Two Girls Tippling' (nd): YCBA Rare Books and Ms; Townsend, *Jackson's Oxford Journal* (1914) 5, 26 September 1855; mock mayors usually paraded about: Deacon, *Liskeard* (1989) pp.80–1; Bamford, *Passages* (1848) vol. i, p.126; *Abingdon Herald*, 25 June 1870; Leach, *Morris Dancing* (1987) pp.6–11.

[76] The 1714 Riot Act tried to clear up common law confusion on the difference between an illegal assembly and a riot but given that magistrates were not always in a position to see or be heard, the point at which force of arms was lawful was unclear, and all parties, including the authorities, were liable for prosecution should things go wrong: Hayter, *Army and the Crowd* (1978) pp.9–11.

[77] Visits to the theatre or the pleasure garden were more discrete, with separate zones for the polite and impolite classes: Heller, 'The individual and the crowd at 18c London Fairs', *Past & Present* 208, 2010, pp.132–8.

[78] Strutt, *Sports and Pastimes* (1801) Book iv, 'Pastimes Appropriated to Particular Seasons'.

[79] First recorded in William Langland's *Piers Plowman* (1377), Robin Hood was the consummate English sporting hero: Dobson and Taylor, *Robin Hood* (1996) pp.57–8. For local versions of the great sportsman, see for example, 'Tom Hickathrift' in Gardiner, *Wisbech* (1898) p.390.

[80] Askew, *Cockermouth* (1872) p.84. An 'upshot' was a social dance similarly arranged: Jollie, *Cumberland Manners* (1796) p.iii. Hardy, *Harvest Customs* (1844) p.4, and Messrs Kirkland and Orme in Arthur, 'Church Broughton Ts' (1974).

They were quite famous. They did it to the Duke of Devonshire. For weeks beforehand the mothers would be sewing—of course the coats inside out, and then rows of frills of bright paper frills; just handed on and on. They would always begin at the Vicarage on Christmas Eve and we were all beautifully cleaned up and in they came. We cleared the kitchen and they tramped round and round. The great idea was to tramp round and round in a circle. And of course my sister was terrified of all these black faces. She would look at them; she'd hide her face. Oh it was a great joke. We knew a lot of it by heart. Gotheridge was one, Harold Gotheridge's father was one. Oh, Brother Wagstaff [was one]! They were all in the Oddfellows together. They used to meet in the club room at *The Holly Bush*.[81]

In Cornwall, on May Day, principal inhabitants could find themselves taxed by day and mocked by night if they didn't meet the customary rate. Billy-Buck, Blather-Dick, Tosspot, Fool, Tom Fool, Dick Fool, and Hub Bub were all customary clowns who could hurt with the truth. Branks, Whirligigs, Ceffyl Pren, Skimmington, Charivari, Rattening, Pelting, Donkeying, Rough Music, and Riding the Stang all hurt in more physical ways.[82] In Cambridgeshire, Molly Dancers cadged on Plough Monday, girls chanted for penny buns on St. Valentine's Day, children begged and Morris men danced for money on May Day, sang carols for treats at Christmas, while at Harvest you might open your door to blackened faces and stumpy sticks asking for reward: 'Mump, Mump... I'll give you a Thump'.[83]

Mumping, mumming, maying, marling, mollying, dolling, first footing, fooling, gooding, shutting, lifting, heaving, and guying were all forms of collecting. 'Plough Bullocks' ploughed up your door way if you didn't oblige. 'Crockers' showered you with crockery. 'Lifters' lifted you up (not in a nice way). 'Bullards' caught you in a passage. 'Soulers' whined, 'Toms' whipped, and 'First Footers' demanded the right to step inside. Whitsun Ales, Harvest Suppers, penny for the Guy, money for the Mummers, doles for the Dolers, pittance for the Bullards, coins for the well-wishers, a kiss for the First Footers—it was the custom to be charitable, even though, in Chester, 'lifting, or rather assembling in a riotous manner of a considerable number (I am sorry to say) of females at all the gates and other thoroughfares of this city, extorts money from every man whose business may oblige him to pass

---

[81] Ruth Auden, on Church Broughton *guyers* in the 1920s as told to Janet Arthur, 'Church Broughton Ts' (1974). See the *Derby Daily Express*, 27 January 1931.

[82] Thompson, 'Moral Economy', *Past & Present* 50, 1971; Behagg, 'Folk Violence', in Storch, ed., *Popular Culture* (1982) ch. 7; Brown, 'Riding the Stang', *Antiquities*, 1910, pp.33–4; Jones, 'Women, Community' in John, ed., *Our Mother's Land* (1991) p.34.

[83] S Widnall, *Grantchester* (1875) p.135; J Rowe, *Cornwall* (1953) p.261; S Baring Gould, *Cornwall* (1899) p.170.

this way'.[84] In times of moral panic, there were calls for the reformation of manners *tout court*.[85]

This was all sport. Even if it was regular, the use of slang, or what Jonathan Bee called 'Slang Whangery', could hide it from outsiders.[86] Many sports happened in quiet corners where risks were taken and bets laid—in a covert to catch a bird, in a close to wager at bowls, in a sheep track to play marbles, in a pub back yard to throw quoits, on a corner or gable end to pitch and toss. Cocks fought behind closed doors, or in the deepest countryside. At Deeping St James, Lincolnshire, they fought cocks on Shrove Tuesday. The landlord of The George and Dragon and twenty others, apparently, 'did not know they were doing wrong . . . it had been the custom'.[87] Most fields had names known only to parishioners. Unidentified fields were harder to place and enclosure reassigned them.[88] Cecil Sharp noted how befriending a peasant stopped short of telling you his songs.[89] John Clare noted how it stopped short of his places to play.[90] Early antiquarians didn't bother looking for peasants *or* their songs. County histories were often written as if poor people lived somewhere else. 'Many ancient customs prevail . . . the familiarity or outward significance of which occasion them to pass without much attention'.[91] Farmers were keen on having servants, but they were less keen on what they liked them to do when not serving. 'I never let them [go to fairs], particularly the girls', said Farmer Tuckett down in Devon.[92] Few outsiders were clear what happened on 'Well Sunday'. Few outsiders knew why Abingdon Corporation threw buns. John Wesley didn't know what to make of 'span farthing' but he knew more than Cobbett for even William Cobbett, man of the people, thought coalminers lived underground and 'sometimes it is said seldom see the surface at all though they live to a considerable age'. This was not true, though Henry Perlee Parker's 'Pitmen at Play' (1830) makes them look like it might have been. They look like brigands, deep in their country.[93] In the face of an early nineteenth-century glut of finer feelings from those who had plenty of everything already, Cobbett spent his life arguing that 'something must be left' for those who had so little.[94]

---

[84] Barber and Ditchfield, *Old Cheshire* (1910) pp.242–3. See also: Green, *Knutsford* (1859) pp.81–5; Chambers, *Book of Days* (1869) p.95, p.741; Bushaway, *By Rite* (1982) pp.180–8; Bryan, *Matlock* (1903) p.111; Jones-Baker, *Old Hertfordshire* (1974) p.9; Porter, *Cambridgeshire* (1969) p.123.

[85] Shoemaker, 'Worrying about Crime', *Past & Present* 234, 2017, p.74.

[86] Bee, *Slang* (1823) pp.158–9. And for 'reasons hard to find' for the custom: Blackstone, *Commentaries* (1820) p.8.

[87] SPCA 14th Annual Report 1840, p.87; *Northampton Mercury*, 7 February 1785.

[88] Fraser, *Field Names* (1947) p.8, p.28.   [89] Sharp, *English Folk Song* (1907) p.171.

[90] Clare, 'Childish Recollections': *Village Minstrel* (1821) pp.14–15.

[91] Hutchinson, *View of Northumberland* (1778) vol. ii, App. p.3; Lysons, *Magna Britannia* (1808) makes no mention of village customs.

[92] Tuckett of Dunsford, in 1843, in Hoskins, *Old Devon* (1966) pp.198–201.

[93] Parker, 'Pitmen at Play', *Arts Council GB Exhibition* (1982) p.18. Cobbett, *Tour* (1832) p.38; 'Ewanian', *Penrith* (1894) on 'Well Sunday' (p.188); Abingdon Local Studies Library Leaflet AB 392; Wesley in Bruce, *Hand Book* (1863) p.96.

[94] *Political Register*, 29 January 1803, in Dyck, *Cobbett* (1992) p.143. Dyck explains how Cobbett worked to revive village sport. In 1805, he held a single stick contest at his Botley Farm with an astonishing 30 guineas prize money.

The truth was, if you wanted the people to be free of their customs it was better that they had no customs at all. The good doctor William Penny Brookes started his own 'Olympian Games' in Much Wenlock in 1851 free from any precedent. His games stemmed out of the reading group he had founded, and represented a bid for the moral improvement of the village against all those other games that otherwise put authority off limits.[95]

All Human Life

What went round came round. The church year was cyclical and life affirming, spirit to flesh. *Candlemas*, 2 February, for Mary, half way between Winter and Spring. *Lady Day*, 25 March, nine months before Christmas and seeding. *Easter*, and the coming of new life. *Rogationtide*, early May, and prayers ('rogationes') for the crops. *Midsummer*, 24 June, six months after Christmas, longest day and Feast of St. John the Baptist. *Lammas*, or 'Loaf Mass', 1 August, first harvest. *Bartlemas*, 24 August, pigs ringed for the patron saint of butchers. *Michaelmas*, 29 September, animals off the common. *St. Lukes Day*, 18 October, lambs counted in. *St. Martin's Feast*, 11 November, grazing over. *Christmas*, 25 December.[96]

Custom hosted the natural cycle. *Bell's Life* reckoned that every northern village, 'almost without exception', enjoyed at least 'one great day' in the year. Emma Griffin reckoned this applied everywhere.[97] At Helpston, John Clare looked forward to how weeks scarcely came 'without promise of some fresh delight': love secrets on Valentine's Day, pigeon milk on April Fool's, gingerbreads (horse shaped) at Easter, midnight romps on St. Martin's Eve, dancing on May Day, frumenty pudding at sheep shearing, carts bedizened at harvest, girls dreaming on St. Thomas Eve, mummers scheming at Christmas and back rackapelting with the boys again on Plough Monday.[98] D H Lawrence's *Sons and Lovers* recalled the annual Eastwood wakes:

> Her husband was a miner. They had only been in their new home three weeks when the wakes, a fair, began. Morel, she knew, was sure to make a holiday of it. He went off early...
>
> ... [and] when the light was fading and Mrs Morel could see no more to sew, she rose and went to the door. Everywhere was the sound of excitement, the restlessness of the holiday... women coming home from the wakes, the children

[95] Polley, 'Olimpick Games', ICSHC, 21 November 2017.
[96] Nicolson, *Earls of Paradise* (2008) pp.42–5.
[97] Griffin, *England's Revelry* (2005) p.27; *Bell's Life*, 15 November 1846.
[98] Bate, *John Clare* (2003) p.62.

hugging a white lamb with green legs, or a wooden horse. Occasionally a man lurched past, almost as full as he could carry ... The stay at home mothers stood gossiping at the corners of the alley as the twilight sank.

'Here an' I browt thee a bit o' brandysnap, an' a coconut for th' children'. He laid the gingerbread and the coconut, a hairy object, on the table. 'Nay, tha niver said thankyer for nowt i' thy life, did ter?'[99]

What came round went round. The aristocratic 'season'—part-politics, part-fashion, part-sport—lasted from November to June coinciding in the capital from the 1690s with annual parliaments.[100] Every village sport and festival not involved in betting (and some that were, like village cricket) happened according to the time of the year.[101] Children learned seasonal rhythms from their games and their games from the seasonal rhythms. Not only how, but where, and *when*: when to play tipit, when to play marbles, or peg tops, skips, dibs, hop scotch, froggy, kingy, bobbing, gurning, two ball and chuck ball. Any time or summer time? When to play and *where* to play: in old devotional places once purged of religion now half remembered in child lore; and in everyday places too, in the street, up the lane, on the beach, by the stream, at the park, against the wall, in the gutter: whip and top in Spring; cricket and kites in Summer; marbles in Autumn; football and cloggy boggies in Winter. Mr. Hoyle of Failsworth told the *Oldham Weekly Chronicle* in 1963 what it was like playing out at the turn of the century:

... there was always a kind of unwritten law amongst us and that was everyone had to 'play the game' and anyone who continually or peevishly would not play fair, he or she was told to clear off somewhere else, because you see we had to make our games with our own rules, which though not writen down were understood by all.[102]

Girls still whipped the longrope in 1957 to a seventeenth-century chant: 'Bluebells Cockleshells' leading into 'Charlie Chaplin went to France, to teach the ladies how to *dance*'. The rhyme changed pace on the beat.[103] Local custom could be elusive for outsiders, particularly when it was child lore, but for insiders custom was understood by all to beat an invisible rhythm that formed strong feelings of

[99] Lawrence, *Sons and Lovers* (1913) p.14.   [100] Greig, *The Beau Monde* (2013) pp.3–10.
[101] Village cricket, where 'all the fun of a race day is embodied': Box, *English Game of Cricket* (1877) p.44; Vaisey, ed., *Diary of Thomas Turner* (1994) p.45.
[102] Mr. E Hoyle, born 1896: LaRO, Preston, DDX 978/1/20; and Thompson, *Lark Rise* (1945) p.134, p.281. See Alexandra Walsham, *Reformation of the Landscape* (2011), for 16c 17c Protestant attempts to secularize the landscape.
[103] https://www.bl.uk/playtimes/articles/skipping-games: Julia Bishop, British Library (2016). 'Charlie Chaplin went to France' was filmed by the Opies in Edinburgh in 1957. King, M and R, *Street Games* (1926) vol. i, p.6. See also Gomme, *Traditional Games* (1894–98) Introduction.

attachment, part of what Robert Chambers called 'those feelings beyond self', what William King called the 'peculiar secrets' of a place, and what John Sullivan called that 'almanac of social existence' that 'hovers about'.[104]

For those who knew where to find it, custom was free and near to hand. William and Dorothy Wordsworth walked the same paths over and over. Lucy Newlyn thinks it was 'fundamentally therapeutic' to their 'collaborative processes'. William called for the rediscovery of the 'old songs'—'a few strong instincts and a few plain rules'. Until the coming of the railway, nearly all of the people walked nearly all of the time. Thomas Jones, framework knitter, opened the Leicester Footpaths Preservation Society (1850) with his ode 'Hurrah for Our Ancient Pathways!'. John Clare remembered criss-crossing open fields or playing with what was to hand, whether it was marbles as a boy or having 'a heedless Fuck' at Stamford Fair as a youth. They bowled ('booled') on Sunderland Town Moor with the heavy smooth blue pebbles they found on the beach. They played cricket at Whitburn with a large sycamore in the way. They played football at Chester le Street up and down le street. Footballers' 'goals' were nothing more than natural markers denoting their 'goal', or destination. They 'camped' in Norfolk on fields of any size with footballs of any shape. They went 'goal running' in Suffolk without a ball. At East Hoathley they danced without music. At Sutton they skated on thin ice. In Westmorland they chased each other with only an old Norse name ('tig') for a reason. Welsh drovers raced their ponies. Thames watermen raced their boats. Durham miners competed with pick and shovel for the title 'Big Hewer'. May day wild flowers were plucked from the hedgerows. 'Mischeef Neet' invited pranks. Chasing and catching a girl ('which necessitates a pretty close hold') wasn't illegal, cost nothing, and seemed to organize itself. They were all out to play, whatever it was they played. In Brittany, name-calling was an organized sport: 'Short-Range Pissers' versus the 'Yellow Assed Dogs'.[105] Tilford Green Fair offered single stick for a hat, wrestling for a cheese, and a sack race for a 'Belcher handkerchief'——Jem the celebrated prize-fighter, the handkerchief blue and white spotted. Dressing up and looking good were important. On Marlborough Common at Whit, women raced in their bare feet for a linen smock. Wakes were parish church saints' feast days, falling once a year usually in summer. Royston

---

[104] Chambers, *Book of Days* (1869) Preface; King to Braintree Overseers, 18 October 1832, in Sokoll, *Pauper Letters* (2001); Sullivan, *Cumberland and Westmorland* (1857) p.171.

[105] Helias, *Horse of Pride* (1975) p.286, p.26; on the walks, Newlyn, *William and Dorothy Wordsworth* (2013) p.311; on the songs, *Manchester Guardian* 25 June 1924; more on walking, Thomas Jones, *Leicester Mercury*, 22 June 1850; Bate, *John Clare* (2003) p.135; Mitchell, *Sunderland* (1919) p.117; cricket, *Shields Gazette*, 9 May 2012; M[onthly] C[hronicle] of N[ort]h C[ountry] L[ore] and L[egend], February 1889, vol. iii; Dymond, 'Lost Social Institution', *Rural History* 1, 1990; Vaisey, *Diary Thomas Turner* (1754–65) p.65, and party at Jeremiah French's house, 22 February 1758, p.178; 'tig' perhaps from Old Norse 'tegia' to touch according to Ferguson, *Northmen* (1856) pp.150–1; Jones-Baker, *Old Herts* (1974) p.184, and unbending authority in Oliver, *New Picture* (1831) p.216; MCNCLL, April 1887, vol. i, p.iii; Bamford, *Passages* (1848) p.138.

races were held every 14 May. Cheshire races were held at Barthomley. Shrove football was played everywhere. Ash Wednesday followed Shrove Tuesday and Shrove Tuesday fell so many days before Easter. Hock Day fell in the week following the second Tuesday after Easter. Grasmere Sports falls on the third Thursday after the first Monday in August, Ambleside on the Thursday before the first Monday in August. In the northern English counties and in Scotland, New Year's Eve was a night wake, involving the same parading round and 'first foots', another form of collecting, only this time in the dark, and never for money. Black Fell in County Durham was the recognized site for colliers' sports (and union meetings), White Horse Hill in Berkshire for farm labourers' sports, Barrowfields in Lancashire for weavers' 'Hitch Hatch' and 'Sheppey', London Bridge to Chelsea for Doggett's Coat and Badge raced every August with a splendid silver badge on a bright red coat for the winner. Sports were seasonal just like agriculture, or religion, or courting, and tied to specific times and places, just like charitable bequests.[106]

It wasn't just in the villages and it wasn't just in the nineteenth century. In 1911 we find Birmingham City Council prosecuting 132 boys for playing street football. We find Melanie Tebbutt's father, in his own words, 'walking out' and 'messing about' in the same places, night after night, in 1930s Northampton. We find Arsenal supporters finding their way back to old haunts, old manors, old mates, according to invisible boundaries.[107]

Sport was usually tied to 'pastimes' and pastimes to virtually anything you thought was playful or fun. In Church Broughton they thought Mrs. Sharratt throwing darts from out of her mouth was fun. In the Fens, they thought a May Day garland tied to a girl's door was playful. Then they attended 'to our domestic concerns till after part of the day our sports then began ... dancing, playing at ball and every thing of sport we could devize ...'.[108] Gentlemen enclosers called Horton Heath a 'waste' but its 150 acres provided livings for thirty cottages and sport for 100 children. 'Wastes indeed!' taunted Cobbett.[109] The village inn, inside

---

[106] Doggett's, Strutt, *Sports and Pastimes* (1801) p.156 and F Burney, 'View at Chelsea' (nd) watercolour 11 x 16 inches, YCBA Rare Books and Ms; Tilford Green Fair 29 July 1814 in Nevill, *Sporting Days* (1910) p.163; that special costumes 'of considerable intricacy' might be made: Rattenbury, 'Tatterdemalions', in Yeos, eds., *Popular Culture and Class Conflict* (1981) p.44; Whitsun Revels on Marlborough Common: Porter, *Cambridgeshire* (1969) p.240; John Johnson, Bodleian, *Fairs and Festivals* Box 2; Poole, 'Wakes Holidays', Lancaster PhD (1985) pp.84–5; Axon, *Bygone Lancashire* (1892) pp.175–7; Grasmere in Davies, *Walk Around the Lakes* (1979) p.286; Metcalfe, *Northumberland* (1982) p.487; *Jackson's Oxford Journal* 29 April 1780, reported 40,000 people on White Horse Hill (Townsend); Barrowfields in Bamford, *Passages* (1848) vol. i, p.13; Charities, Brown, *Municipal Charities of Chester* (1875) pp.8–9.

[107] Robbins and Cohen, *Knuckle Sandwich* (1978) p.147—who refer to beating the bounds as the 'symbolic interdict' of youth territoriality (p.74); Tebbutt, *Being Boys* (2012) p.233; on Birmingham streets: Daunton, *Working Class Housing* (1983) p.269.

[108] Denson, *Peasant's Voice* (1830) p.10. On Mrs. Sharratt: Arthur, 'Church Broughton Ts' (1974).

[109] Cobbett, in Williamson and Bellamy, *Property and Landscape* (1987) p.115.

and out, was a sporting venue all year round, and a standard scene in English watercolour painting.[110]

Pierce Egan may have laughed at rustic sports as a lot of old 'Johnny Rawnobs' ('nothing like ceremony about it') but looked at objectively, for all its simplicity, it was not unorganized and involved people reminding themselves who they were over and over again.[111] Custom included everyone, and kept the range of human life broad. As part of a natural and divine cycle, the York medieval Mystery Plays mixed the Folk with the whole of Creation up to the Ascension. Ordinary tradesmen ('mystery' 'mestier', 'metier') performed their 'plays', mixing everything into one great paradigm of change and redemption that included everybody by going right back to the beginning.[112]

York was a great religious festival but Thomas Rowbottom's Lancashire diary addressed all human life too, mixing everything up by means of wondrous punctuation and a taste for anything that caught his fancy. His entries for 1792 indicate a lot of foot racing and quoits and 'a great deal of commotion in consequence of a certain pamphlet called Paine's "Rights of Man"'.[113] The Nottingham stockinger Joseph Woolley threw everything into his diary from anecdotes and digressions to legal judgments and his own vagrant opinions. In the time he wasn't sitting at his frame, he enjoyed a 'spoart' that was as unruly as his spelling and his grammar, from 'fine spoart among the wimmen' with Ruddington Volunteers, to 'Some Swagering fellowes' at the prize fight, to the two Clifton lads who went to the Races where 'fop like they strutted about' 'hats in Stile', neckerchiefs tucked in bosoms making them 'look like a fan tail pidgeon'.[114] This was to 'disport'. This was to frolic, to amuse. This was everything that pleased. Woolley particularly liked putting in his diary things 'that had never happened before'.[115] It wasn't only the prize-fighters who gave benefits. Being for the benefit of Mr. Kite on 14 February 1843 on Rochdale Town Meadows, Pablo Fanque's Circus Royale ('Last Night but Three!') featured Zanthus the dancing horse and Mr. Henderson the celebrated somerset (somersault) thrower. 'Over Men & Horses, through Hoops, over Garters, and lastly through a Hogshead of REAL FIRE! In this branch of the profession Mr. Henderson challenges THE WORLD'.[116]

---

[110] See for instance, M Rooker (1743–1801) 'Game of Bowls on the Bowling Green outside the Bunch of Grapes Inn, Hurst, Berkshire' (nd): YCBA Rare Books and Ms.

[111] Egan, Book of Sports (1832) pp.258–64. It was commonly observed that the sports of the country gentry were not the sports of the agricultural labourer: Heath, Peasant Life (1872) pp.344–5.

[112] 'the story is vast': Max Jones, designer, York Minster Mystery Plays (2016) p.40.

[113] Rowbottom, Diary (1996) 3 December 1792.

[114] After paying board, frame rent, and materials, 'all of Woolley's expenditure was on himself, and that on pleasure, or "taking his amusement" ...' (p.194): Steedman, An Everyday Life (2013) p.82, p.113.

[115] ibid, p.251.

[116] John Lennon bought this poster in Sevenoaks and made it into a song for the Beatles' Sergeant Pepper album (1967), a work of all musical life mixed with English popular culture. Pablo Fanque (1810–71) was born William Darby in Norwich, later changing his name for professional purposes.

The *Badminton Library of Sport* published a volume on dancing before it published a volume on cycling.[117] There was no strong sense as yet of sport as a single all-encompassing noun applied to codified elite competition. It was a verb as well, and could mean many things across many customs. Swalwell Hopping in 1758 included dancing and foot racing and a man eating a cock alive 'feathers, entrails &c'. Wylam Hopping in 1828 dispensed with the cock but kept the foot-racing and offered a prize for the best whistler. Barrowfields Sports included dancing and singing.[118] Mayhew's London costers loved the same things: 'Flash dancing? Lots! Show their legs an' all. Prime!'.[119] Costers walked with a quick little swagger, just like The Fancy.[120] Church Ales were beer festivals organized to raise parochial funds, with games. Keith Wrightson quotes a bishop saying they were for 'the civilizing of people...lawful recreation...making friends...feats of charity...open house'.[121] In Cumberland and Lancashire, sports and festivals were hard to tell apart while John Timbs' *Curiosities of London* teemed with chancers from every part of the world. People's 'sport', in other words, defied definition. Just as the old recipe books (1573) mixed cures for deafness with recipes for spinach pudding, just as the old carnivals mixed flower carts and big shiny buttons, just as Woolley's diary mixed fighting and fucking with at least six different forms of 'spoart', just as the old punch bowls were cupped in everyone's hands for all sorts of conviviality, so the new nineteenth-century mass circulation newspapers included everything sporting that could be reported to as many people as possible—from murders and love potions to who won the 2 o'clock at Wincanton. In the *News of the World*, as in the York Mystery Plays, all human life was there.[122]

The first black English Circus owner, he was acknowledged as a great equestrian, showman, and performer. Lennon knew a great line when he saw one.

[117] Watson, 'The Badminton Library', in Peek, ed., *Poetry of Sport* (1896) p. xxvii.

[118] Rowlandson's 'The Ballad Singers' leaves us in no doubt that rustic singers could be charming: YCBA Rare Books and Ms (nd), watercolour, 5 × 4 inches. Compare these two girls with his two divas, also in the YCBA: 'The Opera Singers' (1790–95) watercolour 6 × 5 inches and the inelegant 'Elegant Company Dancing' (nd) watercolour 4 × 7 inches.

[119] Quennell, *Mayhew's London* (1851) pp.82–3; Bourn, *Whickham* (1902) p.63; 'Wylam Hopping', Wilson Collection, NCL; Bamford, *Passages* (1893) p.138.

[120] 'The Lambeth Walk' was made popular on the London stage by Mecca Ballrooms: Abra, 'Novelty Dances', *20c British History* 20, 2009.

[121] Quoted in Collinson, *Birthpangs* (1991) p.142. See also Aspin, *Ancient Customs* (1832) p.189.

[122] 'All human life is there' was the motto of the *News of the World* (1843–2011), a major British Sunday newspaper that specialized in sensation and amusement. Scott, *Bygone Cumberland* (1899) p.188 and Axon, *Bygone Lancashire* (1892) pp.175–7; John Partridge's *The Treasurie of Commodious Conceits and Hidden Secretes* (1573) in Adam Smyth, *London Review of Books*, 5 January 2017; memoirs of Mr. Hoyle of Failsworth, born 1896, in LaRO, Preston, DO X978/1/20; *Ashton Register*, 23 August 1856; the stockinger in Steedman's *Everyday Life* (2013) p.104; Harvey, 'Punch Parties and Masculinity in the 18c', *Past & Present* 214, 2012; McWilliam on *Reynold's News* in Chase and Dyck, eds., *Living and Learning* (1996) p.183. Wolfreys sees Victorian taste for Gothic 'heterogeneity of subjects' in the same terms: *Victorian Hauntings* (2001) p.13.

Being the People

What came round went round. Custom was the way in which the poor physically constituted and reconstituted themselves in order to remind their betters (and themselves) that they were there, that they had a history, that it was their country too, and that there were more ways of being represented in an unrepresentative system than through a Member of Parliament.[123] Cobbett drew great inspiration from this. Taking John Chamberlayne's 1718 *Magna Britannia Notitia* as his historical marker, he told a story which began when once upon a time there lived a free people 'much given to Prodigality, Sports and Pastimes'.[124] Cobbett can hardly mention the people without mentioning their bounty and he can hardly mention their bounty without warning what would befall the country without it.[125]

Thomas Paine claimed there was no constitution if there was no written constitution. Walter Bagehot called the constitution a middle class secret and wanted it to stay that way in the face of one million working men voters—'hard hands', he called them.[126] But for all its obscurities, the constitution's final authority lay in the people, not Members of Parliament. The judges agreed that 'as by law established' final authority derived from common law, and common law was not something handed down from above—from a court or a king say, or from a single document—but something handed-up from below, case on case, shaped out of the unwitting will and experience of the community.[127] There was some doubt that this was entirely true in practice, but it was hammered out for good reason in seventeenth-century arguments over where authority finally lay in the struggle between king and parliament, and it was hammered out all over again in the wars with revolutionary France. When English people, therefore, said they did something because 'they' (meaning they and their forbears) had always done it, and it was their liberty to do it, they were reflecting not only their history but a

---

[123] Joyce on democracy as 'ordinary and heroic' (*Visions of the People*, 1991, p.318), and on the constitution as the 'master narrative' (*Democratic Subjects*, 1994, p.87, p.101, p.119). The great constitutional lawyer Dicey recognized the force of custom and convention in cabinet government 'and indeed [across] the whole administrative machine': *Introduction to the study of the Law of the Constitution* (1885) p.cxcvii. E P Thompson thought popular amusements 'defied analysis' (*The Making of the English Working Class*, 1968, p.411), but found an 'ambience' of constitutionalism in them in his *Customs in Common* (1991) p.478, p.6, p.2. Thompson stressed oral transmission.

[124] Cobbett, *Political Register*, 21 August 1824, 3 August 1833; Dyck, *Cobbett* (1992) pp.20–1; Chamberlayne, *Magna Britannia* (1718) pp.185–6.

[125] From the *Political Register* February, March, April, July 1809, in Cobbett, J M, and Cobbett, J P, *Selections* (1835) vol. ii, pp.71, 119, 214, 374–5.

[126] Colls, 'After Bagehot', *Political Quarterly*, 2007, pp.518–26, and Colls, 'Constitution of the English', *History Workshop Journal*, 1998, pp.97–100. Epstein, 'Our real consitution', in Vernon, ed., *Re-reading the Constitution* (1996) p.24.

[127] 'an imposing social fact' that made it English: Amos, *English Constitution* (1934) p.8; Postema, *Bentham and the Common Law Tradition* (1986) pp.8–9.

constitution which Judge Blackstone ('the great teacher of our laws') himself described as nothing more than a set of 'unwritten customs'.[128]

It was the common view therefore that the people embodied their laws and their constitution in their practices.[129] This is what they meant when the said they were freeborn. This is what Strutt meant when he turned to the people's sports and pastimes as an indication of their 'true state' and 'natural disposition'.[130] This is what Paine missed when he said there was no constitution. This is what Carlyle missed when he said the people had nothing to say.[131] This is what unreformed parliaments could not bear to hear at a time when they, and other experts, particularly educational experts, were convinced of the people's inherent psychological instabilites.[132] Yet, as James Vernon points out, the constitution was the 'most potent symbol of Englishness' in the nineteenth century, well observed by all, and 'although few could agree on its nature and meaning', it was not, and was not intended to be, anything invisible, hidden, or specious, and not representative of anything other than the nation as a whole which most certainly did exist as an historic and emotional unity. When the people manifested themselves in customary ways, therefore, they were making the constitution real.[133] That is why the language of popular constitutionalism could be spoken on both sides of the political divide, radical *or* loyalist, or radical *as* loyalist, in a long line of patriot radicals going back to Pitt the Elder in the 1750s, Burke and Paine and the Foxite Whigs in the 1790s, and Pitt and Cobbett and Henry Hunt and the Chartists thereafter, up to populist Gladstonian Liberals and 'One Nation' Disraelian Tories up to Churchillian Labour, 'Nationalization' and Orwell in the 1940s.[134] That is why it was wrong to think that just because there was no document the English people did not have a constitution or think they were not constituted.[135] That is

---

[128] Blackstone, in Arnheim, ed., *Common Law* (1994) p.xix.

[129] Fulcher, 'The English people and their constitution', in Vernon, ed., *Re-reading the Constitution* (1996) p.62. Cobbett looked to Blackstone as his teacher as did all major radical and popular movements up to and including the Chartists.

[130] On continuity as 'the dominant characteristic in the development of English government': Keir, *Constitutional History* (1938) pp.1–2, p.7. For the qualifying argument that English common law was touched by the 'silent transfer' of Roman civil law through the king's courts, see Quincey of Harvard in Stein, *Roman Civil Law* (1988) p.151.

[131] Stedman Jones, 'Redemptive Power', *History Workshop Journal* 65, 2008, pp.10–12; and Strutt, *Sports and Pastimes* (1801) p.2.

[132] Colls, 'Coal, Class and Education', *Past & Present* 73, 1976, pp. 86–91, and Colls, *Pitmen* (1987) pp.41–3.

[133] Vernon, 'Narrating the constitution', in Vernon, ed., *Re-reading the Constitution* (1996) pp. 1–9. Rogers confirms this in his *Crowds, Cultures and Politics in Georgian Britain* (1998) p.195. 'There is no doubt that living for centuries under the common law must have produced many Anglo-Saxon attitudes': Jennings, *Queen's Government* (1934) p.87.

[134] Dickinson, ed., *Britain and the French Revolution* (1989) pp.105–7; Taylor, 'John Bull', *Past & Present* 134, 1992, p.126; and Colls, *Orwell* (2013).

[135] Colls, *Identity of England* (2002) ch. 1, 'The Law Becomes You', ch. 2, 'Uniting the Kingdoms', ch. 3, 'Constituting the Modern Nation'.

why, in a country that said it did not need a written constitution, being the people was a vital performance and remained so until the 1920s when the middle classes finally 'identified themselves as the constitutional classes' thus removing this great national prize from the rest of the population.[136] Later, when experts went in search of the constitution they couldn't find it. They found themselves looking instead at that broad swathe of sensible middle-class feeling called public opinion.[137]

Nobody idealized it better than Sir Matthew Hale in his *History of the Common Law of England* (1713). Common law had grown, he said, 'insensibly', 'upon the People', by a coalition of 'successive Exigencies' that had made the 'Frame of English Government' match the 'Disposition of the English Nation'. The frame matched the disposition. The disposition matched the frame. The constitution matched the people. Freeman's *Growth of the English Constitution* (1872) and Dicey's *Laws of the Constitution* (1885) said the same—that the constitution rested case by case upon a legal tradition which had developed whole and unbroken since the fourteenth century.[138]

In short, the theory was that English common law had no theory, and was nothing more than experience approved by practice. In point of fact case law needed the mind of a judicial bench to organize it and an executive to apply it, but the idea still prevailed that this was the constitution in its most visceral sense so that when custom clashed with the courts, winning the case was not necessarily the same thing as winning the argument.[139] Like the temper of the men it was supposed to represent, in the real world the English constitution was seen as prosaic, practical, unwitting, case-hardened, not wordy or legalistic. How the people had ended up with so little constitution inside parliament but so much outside it is another question, but bottom-up common law Englishness found its perfect foil during the French Wars when the revolutionaries took it upon themselves to rebuild France top down, edict upon edict, starting from scratch. Horrified, Burke reflected on the anarchy of France. Horrified, Paine reflected on

---

[136] 'Defence of the middle classes, therefore, became defence of the constitution': McKibbin, *Classes and Cultures* (1998) p.58. See Neuheiser, *Crown, Church and Constitution* (2016) for the rise of a popular Conservatism between 1815 and 1867 that drew on popular constitutionalism, and Jon Lawrence, *Speaking for the People 1867–1914* (1998) for subtle probing of what sort of representative-ness this actually offered.

[137] Johnson, *In Search of the Constitution* (1977) p.45; and Mount, *British Constitution Now* (1992) and Hennessy, *Hidden Wiring* (1995).

[138] Hale, *History of the Common Law* (1713) p.41; Freeman, *Growth of the English Constitution* (1872) p.100, p.109, p.113; Dicey, *Laws of the Constitution* (1885) p.3.

[139] See Jenks' revision of Blackstone's *Stephen's Commentaries* (1922) pp.488–532. What do you do with parliamentary sovereignty when parliament itself fails to respect it? Gibson answers that argu-ments from common law and custom were rhetorically bolstered by arguments from Natural Law and Scripture as (further, or higher) sources of authority: Gibson, 'Chartists and the Constitution', *Journal of British Studies* 56, 2017, pp.70–4.

the dead hand of England. For him, human rights did not exist by custom, but in reason. For Burke, when it came to free peoples, custom *was* reason.[140]

Being the People was not when popular custom mirrored the constitution, or when there was no need for politics because everyday life was enshrined in common law. Far from it. England was a country of grotesque inequalities which the law confirmed, and as we have seen there were plenty people with finer feelings who thought the labouring poor should have as little presence as possible. It is worth remembering that all this rhetoric of old English custom did not prevent the people wearing old English cast-offs.[141] No one supposed that in their customs they could see the entire edifice of the constitution.[142] Common law was too technically obscure for that. But neither the law nor the constitution could afford to be seen as separate from the people, and their wishes, and custom allowed them, once a year at least, to stand in its glory and rattle the cage. When organized politically, they were capable of remembering their ancient liberty in free Saxon moots and Magna Carta (1215), in Simon De Montfort's parliament (1265), and in a Bill of Rights (1689) that vigorously asserted the rights of the subject against the Crown and the liberties of the people against all non-consenting legal, fiscal, military, and political force. Occasionally, one Chartist wing would call for 'physical force' over constitutional ('moral') force but, in fact, once on the streets, the actual difference between the two was slight. When Chartists presented their 1842 petition—six miles long with three million signatures—they said they could prove their case by reference to custom.[143]

At the heart of post-1815 radical politics was a platform that saw universal suffrage as the realization of a constitution that had been won by history but now was under threat and needed the protection that only the people could give it.[144] Cobbett the Tory Radical 'wished to see no innovation in England'. O'Connor the Irish Chartist asked 'that we may live to see the restoration of old English times'. 'Patriot' gained special radical resonance. The use of the phrase 'from time immemorial' became ubiquitous. Common law was raised.[145] Norman Yoke torn down.[146] In the shadow of mill chimneys and colliery winding engines,

---

[140] Burke, 'Appeal to the Old Whigs' (1791) p.41; Paine, *Rights of Man* (1791–92) pp.63–4. Burke won the argument, in England at least.

[141] Heath, *Peasant Life* (1872) p.295.

[142] On ethnological fantasies about totally 'closed' societies: Auge, *Non-Places* (2008) p.36.

[143] Thompson stressed 'the essential precondition' of the constitution was 'that it shall display an independence from gross manipulation and shall seem to be just': *Whigs and Hunters* (1975) p.263. See also Hay, Linebaugh, and others: *Albion's Fatal Tree* (1975).

[144] Colls, *Identity of England* (2002) ch. 1; Belchem, 'Republicanism, Popular Constitutionalism and the Radical Platform', *Social History* 6, 1981, p.9.

[145] as 'the sedimentation of…daily practice': Pond, 'English Radicalism', *Quarterly Review* 2008, pp.28–9.

[146] On the 'Norman Yoke': Hill, *Puritanism and Revolution* (1965) pp.60–77.

radicals talked about the theft of old English liberty, not about the labour theory of value.[147]

Twentieth-century historians would come to write the history of the period as a history of class struggle. In fact, Chartism was a constitutional struggle before it was a class struggle, a political movement before it was an economic one.[148] All through the 1830s and 1840s, populist politicians attacked a system that had taken the land, monopolized the constitution, and made itself rich.[149] Cobbett called it OLD CORRUPTION.[150] No wonder the Game Laws, which encompassed all these things, were so detested. Again and again, the people re-enacted the constitution. Chartism in that sense might be seen as a festival of inclusion—all the people against all the monopolists. After the Chartists came the popular constitutionalism of the John Bright Liberals, strong in the North. After them came the popular constitutionalism of Labour, strong in the arm. At about the same time, working-class Unionism went on the march in Ulster. It's possible to see the Durham Miners' Gala and Northern Ireland's Orange Parades as two of the century's most long lasting popular constitutional performances.[151]

Peterloo, 16 August 1819

One week before Middleton's annual Rushbearing holiday (third Saturday in August), people gathered on the weavers' sports ground of Barrowfields. Two rows of the most 'comely and decent looking youths', with laurel in their hands, were put at the front, with men in ranks of five behind, followed by the band, followed by colours of silk, followed by a crimson cap on a tall pole and the people performing the people behind. At the very head of the march were 'our handsomest' girls, garlanded, and ready to dance and sing. The Lancashire handloom weaver Samuel Bamford, who was present, estimated that there were 6,000 people

---

[147] The constitution remained 'central to the way the people imagined themselves': Vernon, Introduction, *Re-Reading the Constitution* (1996) pp.1–2, p.13; Epstein, 'Our Real Constitution', in Vernon, ibid, p.25. For the argument that there were no law books in Normandy, and England was different: Keeton, *Norman Conquest and Common Law* (1966), and van Caenegem, *Birth of English Common Law* (1973).

[148] Mary Povey talks about the creeping language of the 'social body' and the 'body politic' from the 1770s. Peter Yeandle and others talk about how this 'body' made itself known, from political platforms and theatre sets to in the streets and fields and festive meetings: Povey, *Making a Social Body* (1995) pp.7–8, p.24; Yeandle et al., eds., *Politics, performance and popular culture* (2016).

[149] Stedman Jones, *Languages of Class* (1983) ch. 3 'Rethinking Chartism', p.91, p.95, p.104.

[150] Cobbett, *Advice to Young Men* (1830) p.318.

[151] Temple, *Big Meeting* (2011) p.4, and Bryan, *Orange Parades* (2007) p.24. Ernest Jones in 1848 pictured Chartists charging down from the hills into Downing Street and the corrupt of every class sinking with the rise of the 'brave and bold' of every class: Weisser, Chartism', *Albion* 13, 1981, p.23. Bagehot referred to 'our freedom' as 'the result of centuries of resistance...to the executive government': *English Constitution* (1867) p.262. The popular historian and Liberal, J R Green took it upon himself to give words to an otherwise unlettered and unwordy people: Brundage, *People's Historian* (1994) p.91.

assembled that morning, including stewards, and they were arrayed like this not, as one might think, to rehearse their annual Rushbearing, but to march the seven miles to Manchester in order to gather at a meeting organized by the Manchester Patriotic Union and hear the famous patriot politician Henry 'Orator' Hunt. A green banner declared 'Annual Parliaments and Universal Suffrage' in gilded letters. 'Libertas' was embroidered on the crimson cap. Before they set off, 3,000 of the company formed a hollow square to be reminded by their captain that this was not a festival but a march. 'Accompanied by our friends and our dearest and most tender connections', said Bamford, they went slowly forward to Manchester where they met other contingents from other manufacturing towns and villages, who did the same.

The 'manufacturing districts', as these straggling places were called, were seen by the government as trouble spots. All through the 1820s and 1830s, nervous magistrates were writing to the Home Office asking for military assistance. In addition to a general post-war depression in trade, a law to enact dearer bread had been passed in 1815, *Habeas Corpus*, keystone to the constitution, had been suspended in 1817, and two new Acts commonly referred to as the 'Gagging Acts', had been introduced in 1818 to keep people off the streets. In other words, working-class Lancashire knew what a constitutional crisis felt like but in spite of all, on reaching Manchester in their finest clothes and best behaviour, everyone who saw them agreed that this was clearly 'a gala day', a family day out. Next week it would be the Rushbearing.[152]

Then, to their utter astonishment, this crowd of some 60,000 men, women, and children were trampled and cut at by the Yeomanry and charged down by the Hussars. Having started the day in a customary sporting place, Barrowfields, the people of Middleton found themselves under the hooves in another customary sporting place, St. Peter's Fields. It would become normal for Radicals and Chartists and trade unionists to gather in their thousands at places such as these—Kersal Moor outside Manchester, Hartshead Moor outside Bradford, the Forth and Town Moor outside Newcastle—but the St. Peter's Fields incident was unusual in that by attacking the people in their honourable and most good spirited performance as the people, a political class had soiled their own constitution.

In only a matter of minutes, eighteen were dying from their wounds and hundreds more were lying crushed and injured. We can only make sense of the shock if we acknowledge that these men and women had a strong sense of their part in the constitution in the first place. Property belonged to others, and for that the propertied classes got the vote. But liberty, and the native entitlement that went with it, belonged to the people. By taking to the streets or gathering in the

---

[152] See the independent evidences of witnesses Rev. Edward Stanley, Rector of Alderley, William Jollife, lieutenant 15th Hussars, and John Benjamin Smith, a young Manchester businessman: Bruton, *Three Accounts of Peterloo* (1919) p.50.

fields, they made it real according to custom. Now, when it and they were under attack from parliament they were defending their old liberties by asking for new ones.[153] After the bravery of the Hussars at Waterloo four years before, Radicals called it 'Peterloo' in contempt.

The Lancashire weavers had dared bring their constitutional rights to town, but according to custom, trades and towns were usually the same thing. Before 1835, companies and corporations processed in honour of both. In 1823, the glass-makers of Newcastle (unincorporated) processed each with a glass star round his neck and a glass feather in his hat. The newspaper tells us that 'the rays of the sun' fell upon 'the glittering column [with] a richness and grandeur that defy description'. Clearly they weren't there for a fight. In 1825, Yorkshire woolcombers (incorporated) marched for their patron saint, Bishop Blaize. A mile long, the Bradford procession was led by the Masters, followed by their Sons and Apprentices on horseback, with colours; followed by the woolcombers' King and Queen and Royals, Jason and his Fleece, Bishop Blaize and his entourage, the Shepherd and Shepherdess with swains followed by foremen and woolsorters, combers two by two in cap and wigs of wool, all with colours.[154] Masters and men moving forward as one, this was a vital part of civic ceremonial. There were hundreds of others.

Met by Manchester female reformers in white dresses holding silk flags, Hunt, the main speaker noticed the festival atmosphere at once. White was best. Aprons and shirts, tablecloths and petticoats, Hunt's top hat, the Fancy's great coat, the worker's Sunday best, all aspired to be white. Bands and rush carts were other marks. Filled with rushes, ornamented in flowers and ribbons, and drawn by young men, each cart stood for its parish and each parish for its people. At the trials following the massacre, Mr. Justice Bayley asked what a 'rush cart' was. It was patiently explained to him that processions were the custom in Lancashire. Friendly societies, trade societies, trade unions, Sunday schools, Wakes, Orangemen, Radicals, Owenites, Chartists—all processed with bands and banners and symbols, usually in good humour.[155] In 'Scotch Cattle', cross dressing Welsh

[153] Bamford, *Passages* (1848) vol. i, p.180; vol. ii, pp.150–2. Bamford tried to stress the political innocence of the occasion by featuring the gaiety and good order. But in 1817 he had been arrested for serious offences and brought before the Privy Council with six other men who, we are told, were 'brimful of Lancashire humour'. Bamford was clearly not to be cowed by the great men who included Castlereagh and Sidmouth. 'He was rather fond of seeing himself as a "freeborn Englishman" and of magnifying the prerogatives that belonged to him in that capacity': ibid, Introduction by Henry Dunckley, vol. i, p.11.

[154] Walker, *Costume of Yorkshire* (1814), pp.78–80; glassmakers in Newcastle, in Lancaster, Colls, and Lancaster, eds., *Newcastle* (2001) p.325, as reported in the *Newcastle Courant*, 2 September 1823.

[155] Poole, 'March to Peterloo', *Past & Present* 192, 2006: 'the reformers played out the role of unenfranchised citizens, presenting the government with the unanswerable physical presence of vast bodies of freeborn English men and women assembled to proclaim their lost rights' (p.112).

ironworkers wearing bulls' horns visited blacklegs.[156] During the Preston cotton operatives' strike of 1853, Dickens spotted the giant crown of a maypole raised behind the chairman of delegates. 'There was no other symbol'.[157] Chartists called for a *holiday* when they meant a strike. Cooke Taylor remarked how stopping the mills 'had much more an aspect of a holiday than a riot'.[158]

In 1840 the Manchester dyers, dressers, and boilermakers gathered to meet Chartists McDouall and Collins on their release from gaol. Lined up six abreast and led by two marshals on horseback with green scarves and green and white favours carrying a large portrait of McDouall, the operatives went the two miles to Salford in full marching order: twenty committee men with staves, scarves and favours, 'THREE NATIONAL FLAGS', eight young women in white, with favours and 'MAGNIFICENT BANNER' of the Dyers and Dressers, followed by 'LARGE BANNER' showing 'The Massacre of Peterloo', and 'SPLENDID BANNER' of the Wigan Charter Association with various icons including banner of 'British Lion Rampant' trampling 'Aristocracy, Shopocracy, White Slavery and State Paupers', followed by 'BANNER OF THE MANCHESTER BOILERMAKERS'. We should not forget the music. Popular constitutionalism loved to sing and it sang everything, from choral hymns to songs of labour and nation, to songs more mischievous and light.[159]

It wasn't until rural depopulation suddenly became a national question that intellectuals started to fret about the draining away of custom.[160] Soon, every antiquarian in the land was convinced that there was no time to lose in reviving customs which, not so long back, had been characterized as lost. The Oxford professor of Jurisprudence rediscovered the uses of custom in old craft privileges. London County Council rediscovered the uses of custom in commemoration schemes. The National Playing Fields Association rediscovered the importance of places of play. Folk revivalists rediscovered the idea of an unwritten constitution as a model for the transmission of unwritten (but cherished) folk song. The Arts and Crafts movement too, struggled to bring art and craft and custom together as a movement of national regeneration. Ralph Vaughan Williams and Percy Dearmer compiled their *English Hymnal* (1906) in order to revive church

---

[156] 'stressing the transient and liminal': Jones, 'Symbol, Ritual and Popular Protest', *Welsh History Review* 26, 2012, p.51.

[157] The meeting was held down a lane in a former cock pit: Dickens, *Household Words*, 11 February 1854, in Slater, ed., *Dickens' Journalism* (1998) p.205. On festive mass meetings: Hovell, *Chartist Movement* (1918) p.119. Hunt, *Memoirs* (1820) p.611.

[158] Cooke Taylor, *Notes of a Tour* (1841) p.321; Prothero, 'William Benbow and the concept of the General Strike', *Past & Present* 63, 1974, pp.132–4.

[159] For commemorative gatherings of choirs to sing Chartist songs, see blackstoneedgegathering.org. uk and Scheckner, *Anthology of Chartist Poetry* (1989). On the march: Williams, Introduction, in Gorman, *Banner Bright* (1976) pp.1–2. On popular song as self-celebration: Colls, *Collier's Rant* (1977).

[160] Gail Marshall identified 1859 as a key moment for custom: Darwin very firmly against it but Eliot, Mill, Dickens, Samuel Smiles, and Mrs. Beeton all more or less in favour: inaugural professorial lecture, University of Leicester, 22 March 2011.

congregations through customary melodies.[161] Having lost so many folk to migration, the folklorists went in search of the one, eternal peasant.[162] Unfortunately, by this time, customary meanings had become so unintelligible to intellectuals that scholars were being driven to explain why survivals in culture had no meaning to anybody.[163] George Bourne reckoned it was as easy to write of the Chinese as it was to write of his Surrey peasant neighbours.[164]

Popular customs have so often been depicted as reactionary and, as in the Stamford case, pitiful. Yet there was more to popular custom than that.[165] What happened at St. Peter's Fields in 1819 was not defensive so much as assertive, a clear bid by people to reinstate their place as true patriots in what they thought was, or should be, theirs already. Scattered across the country but tied to specific landscapes, trivial and elusive in one place, jolly and perambulatory in another, serious and politically aware in another yet all sharing the same intention to constitute and be the constituted, no wonder historians have been baffled about what to make of custom.[166] It was easy when it was meant to be difficult, political when it was supposed to be dumb, female when it was meant to be male, and lingered on when it should have got out of the way.

[161] On Arts and Crafts regeneration: Palmer-Heathman, 'Lift Up a Living Nation', *Cultural and Social History* online 25 February 2017. On craft privileges and customs: Pollock, *Genius of the Common Law* (1912) pp.95–100. On reviving folklore: Wright, *English Folklore* (1928) where folklore exists 'in its unconscious way' 'to decipher the unwritten' (pp.6–7). On LCC custom as tutored by Gomme, the County Clerk: Ito, 'Municipalization', *London Journal*, 2017, p.3. On playing fields: NPFA *Jubilee Handbook* (1953), founded in 1925 by local authorities, the Carnegie Trust, and the Ministry of Health.

[162] 'In gossiping about his own life Bettesworth is unawares telling of similar lives, as lived for ages, of a type of Englishman that may perhaps be hard to meet with in time to come': Bourne, *Bettesworth Book* (1901) p.11.

[163] Edmund Tylor called old and half forgotten customs 'survivals in culture' in his influential *Primitive Culture* (1871), i, p.21. For broader ramifications of this subject see: Colls, *Identity of England* (2002) ch. 15 'Natives'.

[164] Bourne, *Change in the Village* (1912) p.x. For various theories of not understanding the folk, see Sumner, *Folkways* (1906) p.55; Gomme, *Traditional Games* (1894) vol. ii, p.475; Metcalfe, 'Shameful Conquest', Bath Spa MA (2013) p.3, p.19; Henderson, *Folk-lore of the Northern Counties* (1866) p.xvii; Eggar, *Remembrances* (1970) pp. 184–6; Barber and Ditchfield, *Old Cheshire* (1910) p.263; Scott, *Bygone Cumberland* (1899) p.188, p.194; Dixon, *Old Wedding Customs* (1888) p.4, and *Upper Coquetdale* (1903) p.59.

[165] "Cultural change' is a polite euphemism for the process by which some cultural forms and practices are driven out of the centre of popular life': Hall, 'Notes on Deconstructing 'The Popular', in Samuel, ed., *People's History* (1981) pp.227–8.

[166] Hutton warned that history of custom 'is not a book which works up to any obvious conclusions': *Stations of the Sun* (1996) pp.414–18. Griffin was reluctant to offer any general theory: *England's Revelry* (2005) pp.212–14.

5

Home

In the past, economic life had been constrained by the need to maintain social cohesion. It was conducted in social markets— markets that were embedded in society and subject to many kinds of regulation and restraint. The goal of the experiment that was conducted in mid-Victorian England was to demolish these social markets...

(John Gray, *False Dawn*, 1998)

'I'm an Englishman ain't I?' rejoined the Dodger. 'Where are my privileges?'.

(The Artful Dodger, in Dickens' *Oliver Twist*, 1837)

Butterworth's Lancashire 1831–36

Writing about the great American urban upheaval of the 1950s, Kevin Lynch reported 'evidence of widespread, almost pathological attachment to anything that had survived'.[1] This chapter is about the part played by sport in attachment to a sense of home after the world's first industrial upheaval.

Writing in 1810, the antiquarian John Brand invoked the antiquarian Henry Bourne writing in 1725 about parish festivals in the north of England. The parishioners 'deck themselves out', he said, and hold 'open doors', and other entertainments, and in the morning they go to church, and in the afternoon and evening they eat and drink 'with all sorts of Rural Pastimes and Exercises'. Taking Henry Bourne as the high time of parish custom in 1725, John Brand wrote in 1810 as if he was writing in the time of its decline, a view which was confirmed in the 1840s by the antiquary F R Raines and the memorialist Samuel Bamford who dated the beginning of the end of Lancashire parish festivals as around 1810. All this was endorsed a generation later by a mass circulation local and regional press which started looking back to the 1810s as the last of the 'olden times' and spoke to people who, all things considered, knew about such things.[2]

---

[1] Lynch, *Image of the City* (1960) p.42.
[2] For Brand, Bourne and Raines, in Snape, *Church of England in an Industrializing Society* (2003) p.23, p.30; *Manchester Gazette*, 11, 26 December 1885 and *Daily Telegraph*, 15 October 1888, 15

In this context, Edwin Butterworth's researches are revealing. Researching in what was seen as the final phase of the old culture (1831–35),[3] he was the researcher for Edward Baines' monumental *History of Lancashire*, published in 1836. Baines, who had been in St. Peter's Fields on 16 August 1819, was Radical MP for Leeds and proprietor of the *Leeds Mercury*. On Baines' behalf, Butterworth tramped sixty-nine parishes as well as the borough of Clitheroe, the township of Bowland with Leagram, and the parochial chapelries of Colne, Burnley, New Church, and Padiham in Whalley where he asked parishioners questions under nine heads of enquiry, one of which addressed 'Customs, Habits &c'.[4] Neither man doubted that Lancashire could be known through its parishes.

Butterworth travelled round taking in people and their sense of place. He preferred staying in temperance hotels to village inns, and he preferred talking to literate men rather than 'clodpoles', as he called them. At St. Helens, he found the schoolmaster talkative, but his 'love of trifles and pedantry' frustrating. When he wanted good information, he went to the parish clerk. When he needed more information, he went to the railway office, if there was one. Not all parish clerks were equally helpful. At Bolton, the clerk blundered and Butterworth told him so. At Warrington it was Butterworth who blundered (got the date wrong). At Leigh, the parish clerk thought the church was called St. Peter's because it had a weathercock. At Brindle, Mr. Fowler was 'wretched looking' but Butterworth classed him as a good informant. At Warrington, the sexton refused to talk to him because he was working for a well-known radical. 'I denied that I was a Radical in the sense he took it', said Butterworth. 'I loved the church'.[5] With painstaking patience, and intelligence, Butterworth took his question about 'Customs, Habits &c' up and down the county.

John Walton is clear that nineteenth-century Lancashire suffered widespread industrialization and significant environmental damage.[6] And it is clear from Butterworth that the old parish life was in decline, if not right across the county. Many parishes retained at least one major annual custom, something he calls a

---

January 1897. Bamford is inexact on his dates but generally speaking he recalls a rich seasonal *prior* culture lasting into the 1820s—Christmas, Shrove-tide, Easter, Whitsuntide, and May Day especially noted: *Early Days* (1843) ch. xv.

[3] 'The recording of folklore was always an eleventh hour mission': Ó Giollàin, 'Celebrations and Rituals', in Biagini and Daly, eds., *Modern Ireland* (2017) p.299.

[4] Instructions to Mr. Butterworth, November 1834: Butterworth Papers, Harris Library, Preston, BAI/B/59. The great conurbations of Manchester, Liverpool, and Preston Butterworth did not cover. Baines' published *History* however gives them major attention *except* for their parish 'Custom Habits &c'. Manchester carried a population at this time of 182,812, while Liverpool was loaded with 'the processes of future greatness'. In Preston, Baines remarked how the young needed saving from the mass congestion of the factory system. In these intensely urban places the parish meant far less: Baines, *History of Lancashire* (1836), vol. ii, p.212; vol. iv, p.149, p.367.

[5] 'Journal of Excursions in Lancashire to collect historical information for Mr. Baines' History of Lancashire 1831–36', vol. ii, October 1833 to September 1834: Harris Library, Preston.

[6] Walton, *Lancashire 1558–1939* (1987) p.196.

number of things because they were a number of things. In and around Colne for example, he talks about 'a wake, drinking, rushbearing, or rural feast' that prevails annually 'at almost every village', and names five. By contrast, Bowland, he was told, enjoyed no 'peculiar festivities', 'no peculiar sports', 'no remarkable sayings', 'not a dissenters' chapel', 'no steam engines', 'no improvements'. Was nothing really happening in Bowland (an isolated parish) when he visited, or was it just a bad day? There's a primness in Butterworth that would be reflected in later folklorists, and it is hard to show an absence, but one has the feeling that certain things, physical things perhaps, are not being reported.[7]

All round, Butterworth found Lancashire in the midst of an upheaval that apart from the great conurbations, did not mean that some of the old world could not survive some of the new. Mike Winstanley calls it 'a county on the verge'. Eighteenth-century upland Whalley, for instance, shows an early breakdown in parish discipline and custom. Whalley was in the first phase of industrialization (limestone, coal, cotton, woollens) and, in a parish with woeful church attendance, fewer clerical appointments, and a rapidly rising industrial population, there is evidence of a decline in church courts and calendars as well as the annual Rushbearing.[8] At Middleton, Baines noted how expansions in coal, cotton, and silk manufacture were 'the signal for the gentry withdrawing', and in the factory towns of Bolton, Preston, Blackburn, Oldham, Ashton, and Wigan he conceded that children were over-worked. But we cannot conclude that all this meant fewer sports and customs. Dean (seventy-five steam engines) and Oldham (one hundred mills) still did six wakes a-piece, Bolton le Moors still fought up and down old style ('purring'), Pendleton and Pendlebury still danced around the maypole, Lancaster still enjoyed three Rushbearings 'with fantastical head dresses', and Leigh and Bolton le Moors brought out their 'Jannock' (festival bread) and Leigh its 'Braggot' (spiced ale) on festival days, and Bury its 'Simblin' cakes during mid-Lent.[9] It is true that Warrington was full of power looms and the Rushbearing had been dead there for twenty years and the parish festival for eight. On the other hand, Wigan, 'one of the greatest manufacturing towns' with 'extensive schooling' and fifteen dissenting chapels, continued to bear rushes, host a Whit fair, and hold two parish wakes just

---

[7] Butterworth Papers, Harris Library, Preston: Colne, BAI/B/64; Bowland, BAI/B/64. On things said and not said, Jean-Marie Deguignet's *Memoirs of a Breton Peasant* (2002), written between 1897 and 1904 but discovered much later, are extremely suggestive: 'When I read accounts of Breton lore, I am more and more convinced that they have seen none of what they report, and that they have been fooled and taken in by the old rascals and drunken biddies about everything and anywhere' (p.73).

[8] On Whalley: Snape, *Church of England* (2003) pp.29–43. Winstanley notes that Baines and Butterworth mixed traditional genealogical and parochial approaches with new economic and social realities. Winstanley is confident that Baines deliberately omitted many old habits and customs: 'Researching a County History', *Northern History* xxxii, (1996) pp.153–54, p.168, p.172.

[9] Baines, *History* (1836): Preston, vol. ii, p.606; Eccles, vol. iii, p.124; Middleton, vol. ii, p.606; factory towns, vol. ii, p.520; Bolton, vol. iii, pp.75–6; Oldham, vol. iii, pp.123–6; Pendleton and Pendlebury, vol. iii, pp.123–4; Butterworth Papers: Dean, BAI/B/63; Bolton le Moors, BAI/B/63); Lancaster BAI/B/67; and Leigh BAI/B/67.

like Oldham which, in spite of its 100 cotton mills, 133 steam engines, and 600 strong Primitive Methodist Sunday School, still held wakes ('modern feasts') which, according to the parish clerk at least, were founded by the Druids.

That Wigan still spoke in the dialect (a sure sign of stagnation in Butterworth's eyes) and had steam engines by the dozen (a sure sign of progress) might suggest that Wigan was in transition from traditional to modern. Not so. The town's flourishing fairs and wakes show how progress in 1830s Lancashire, if progress it was, was not linear. Clitheroe wove calicos on power looms but continued to enjoy three Rushbearings, a Shrove Tuesday perambulation, a bit of Easter lifting, and five fairs. At Hesketh (after Christmas), at Lytham (on the beach), at Melling (Trinity Sunday), at Padiham (Easter), and at Rochdale (May Day) the young continued to gather for sport which included a bit of collecting. Pendle Forest and Downham Liberty were no longer perambulated and summer horse racing was on the wane, Ashton and Winwick had dropped their festivals, Blackburn was hanging on to its wakes, and Bury, we are told, was 'less primitive' since the introduction of a 'manufacturing system'. Cartmel was 'dull and quiet', as was Bowland, while Preston, county town but full of factories, had recently abandoned its customary guild procession. Rochdale seems to have had the best and worst of worlds. On the modern side it had two great factories, eleven dissenting chapels, and an industrial dispute which had led to a loss of life. On the traditional side boys in white posy jackets still pushed Rushbearing carts on 19 August.[10]

Just over a third of Lancashire parishes reported to Butterworth that they had stopped perambulating the parish ('beating the bounds') or did so only irregularly: 'sometimes' at Aldingham, 'occasionally' at Altcar, in 'desuetude' at Halton, 'neglected' at Lytham, 'not often' at Tunstall. At Urwick, inhabitants complained 'that for want of regular perambulation...600 acres have been unjustly detached from the original limits'. Ulverston had ceased doing it 'half a century ago', Pennington in 1820, Heysham in 1821, Chorley in 1822, Ribchester over four years ago, and Chipping over fifty. Hawkshead still perambulated up on the fell, but it was a long time since Tunstall had gone traipsing, preferring to follow parish boundaries in the parish book instead.[11]

A dozen out of seventy-four Lancashire parishes reported no sports at all, or no sports 'of a special nature', as the question asked. At Brindle, apart from the annual Whitsun wake, 'the ancient customary diversions...are no longer

[10] Butterworth Papers, Harris Library, Preston: Warrington, BAI/B/69; Wigan, BAI/B/69; Oldham, BAI/B/61; Clitheroe, BAI/B/64; Hesketh, BAI/B/65; Lytham, BAI/B/68; Melling, BAI/B/69; Padiham, BAI/B/64; Ashton, BAI/B/60; Winwick, BAI/B/66; Blackburn, BAI/B/63; Eccleston, BAI/B/63; Bury, BAI/B/63; Cartmel, BAI/B/67; Bowland, BAI/B/64; Preston, Baines, *History*, vol. ii, p.606; Rochdale, BAI/B/62.

[11] Butterworth Papers, Harris Library, Preston: Aldingham, BAI/B/69; Altcar, BAI/B/67; Halton, BAI/B/67; Lytham, BAI/B/68; Tunstall, BAI/B/69; Urwick, BAI/B/69; Ulverston, BAI/B/68; Pennington, BAI/B/67; Heysham, BAI/B/69; Chorley, BAI/B/63; Ribchester, BAI/B/65; Chipping, BAI/B/63; Hawkshead, BAI/B/66.

observed'. At Bury, there were 'no sports', at Childwall 'no peculiar sports', at Croston and Ormskirk 'no characteristic sports', at Eccleston 'no singular sports', at Ulverston 'few sports', and at Lytham 'no uncommon sports'. But to say no uncommon sports does not rule out the possibility of sports in common. Kirkham, Kirkby Ireleth, and Heysham still rolled eggs at Easter. Altcar still elected a mayor whose 'duties are not very onerous except in pugnacious strife'. Ashton, it seems, went on 'Riding the Black Lad' regardless of the Industrial Revolution.[12]

In short, everywhere Butterworth looked there were indications of a customary life sometimes suffering direct assault from the new, but flourishing (and adapting) in other places on the back of more work and wages.[13] In a way, some of these industrial villages resembled the 'close' villages of landed estates whose great owners were able to ration settlement and dominate what happened there. The mill-owning Ashworths, for instance, were as powerful in Bolton as the land-owning Cecils were in Stamford. Cooke Taylor admitted Turton Mill to be pleasant enough, but drew special attention to the 'great moral power' of the Ashworths in keeping people 'in concert'. At Quarry Bank, out of four day's holiday per year, Samuel Greg asked his factory workers to choose between Christmas Day or New Year's Day. They chose Christmas. Other mill towns more resembled uncontrolled or 'open' agricultural parishes where people herded in looking for housing.[14] Marx's description (taken from the medical officers of health) of these open parishes as 'penal settlements for the English agricultural proletariat' is not unlike Engels' descriptions of Salford as a penal settlement for the industrial proletariat.[15] Whatever the insanitary state of the open industrial village, it is there that we can expect more license and less control. Whatever the

[12] Butterworth Papers: Brindle, BAI/B/63; Bury, BAI/B/63; Childwall, BAI/B/67; Croston, BAI/B/63; Ormskirk, BAI/B/66; Eccleston, BAI/B/66; Ulverston, BAI/B/68; Lytham, BAI/B/68; Kirkham, BAI/B/68; Kirkby Ireleth, BAI/B/66; Heysham, BAI/B/69; Altcar, BAI/B/67; 'Riding the Black Lad' involved parading an effigy of a horseman, possibly Sir Ralph de Assheton: Ashton, BAI/B/60.

[13] In the Yeos' *Popular Culture and Class Conflict* (1981) Vic Gammon tried to estimate the decline of popular church music (ch. 3), Anthony Delves the decline of Shrove football (ch. 4), Alun Howkins the 'Taming of Whitsun' (ch. 7), and Eileen Yeo the rehabilitation of a failing seasonal calendar by Radicals. In Storch's *Popular Culture* (1981) David Vincent tried to estimate the decline of the oral tradition (ch. 2), John Rule the decline of popular belief in Cornwall (ch. 3), Robert Storch the survival of Guy Fawkes Night (ch. 4), Walton and Poole the Lancashire Wakes, and Doug Reid the festival calendar (ch. 6). In all cases, it is difficult to be sure about the rate and nature of decline.

[14] Greg's choice: 3rd Report SC on Mills and Factories (1840) x. p.4. Ashworth's consent: Cooke Taylor, *Notes of a Tour* (1841) p.288, p.124, p.121. Taylor remarked that the 'most striking phenomenon of the Factory system is the amount of population which it has suddenly accumulated on certain points' (p.7), and those population points are at the core of the 'open' 'closed' village debate for agriculture: Mills, 'The Poor Laws and the redistribution of population', *Trans Inst British Geographers* 26, 1959; Spencer, 'Reformulating the closed parish thesis', *Journal of Historical Geography* 26, 2000; Holderness, 'Open and Close Parishes', *Agricultural History Review* 70, 1972; Banks, '19c scandal or 20c model?', *Economic History Review* xli,1988. Cooke Taylor claims he visited almost every cottage at Turton Mill (p.31). For arguments over relative levels of cultural independence in open and close villages: Mills & Short, 'Open Close Village Model', in Reed and Wells, eds., *Class Conflict* (1990) pp.91–6.

[15] Marx, *Capital* (1867) fn. 2, p. 840.

level of control of the close industrial village, it is there we can expect less license and more sanitation.

Religious Dissent, as we shall see, was generally hostile to the parish and its customs. If the dominant employers were dissenters themselves, we can expect much putting down. But not always. When the people believed themselves to be at liberty, popular culture could spin its own life regardless of authority. Colne parochial chapelry, for instance, was a centre for cotton spinning and worsted weaving with no fewer than sixteen dissenters' chapels. Even so, 'a wake, drinking, rushbearing, or rural feast prevails annually at almost every village and country public house'. Butterworth managed to name five. At Rochdale, he managed to completely omit the Rushbearing but include a strike, while for the same town Baines managed to omit the strike but include the Rushbearing. 'The annual festival of the RUSH-BEARING is celebrated here', he said, 'and in many of the other parishes of Lancashire'. But like so much else in the old sense of place, we are told, it isn't what it was. Now down from twelve to three or four decorated carts, the parish church is 'the last place thought of' in what had degenerated into 'a mere rustic saturnalia'. The trend was reasonably clear. Even if some customs were hanging on and a few were doing well, old Lancashire was in overall decline. Blackburn used to be famous for football, but that was a century ago. Chorley no longer had a wake or a Rushbearing and had put a stop to bull-baiting, 'if sport it was'. Brindle's 'ancient customary diversions' were no longer observed. Burnley still played cricket, but nothing else, its wakes 'scarcely observed'. Whittington was 'not benefitted by any annual festival', Hoole had lost the Rushbearing, Eccleston's was in decline, Leigh and Clitheroe still went in for a bit of 'pinning' and 'lifting' but the one 'nearly obliterated' and the other generally considered 'barbarous'.[16] 'In most parishes of Lancashire . . . the old sports and festivities of the people are on the decline'. Eccles could keep on baking cakes but it was high time it stopped torturing bulls: 'a sport which, though formerly a past-time for princes, is now scarcely tolerated by the lowest of the vulgar'.[17] In 1843, Bamford recalled how Middleton's old sports and customs were no longer practised, or even known, by the young: 'a great change' in Lancashire working-class taste, he reckoned.[18] In the 1890s, 'folklorists' were seeking out those who had been young in the 1830s in order to identify the chain of transmission. In 1895, Ben Brierley remembered the old Failsworth pole, erected in the 1790s and once considered the pre-eminent symbol of the place, now consigned to times past:

---

[16] Butterworth Papers, Harris Library, Preston: Colne, BAI/B/64; Rochdale, BAI/B/62 and Baines, *History*, vol. ii, pp.635–6; Blackburn, BAI/B/63; Chorley, BAI/B/63; Brindle, BAI/B/63; Burnley, BAI/B/64; Whittington, BAI/B/69; Hoole, BAI/B/65; Eccleston, BAI/B/63; Leigh, BAI/B/67; Clitheroe, BAI/B/64.

[17] Baines, *History*, vol. iii, p.124; Butterworth Papers: Lancaster, BAI/B/67; Eccles, BAI/B/63.

[18] Bamford, *Early Days* (1843) p.119.

This spot was known as the 'rallying point . . . Here the annual rushcart was built; the fair held . . . Here cocks were fought and badgers drawn. Here effigies of Tom Paine and the first Napoloeon were burnt. Here the last of the Jacobins was tried in the saddle of a Dragoon's horse whilst the mad and bigotted populace stuck pins into his legs. Here the coronation ox was roasted, and the gifts of the charitable doled out to the starving hundreds in the good Old Times. Here the bonfire was made, the Maypole erected. Here was once a mock king crowned, whilst the shouts of idolatrous loyalty rang out on every hand. Here the procession to Peterloo halted to refresh.[19]

Parish Privileges

The church was at the heart of the parish. Until churchyards began to spill over with graves, parishioners roamed there more or less at will. It was their privilege, just as it was their privilege to be parochially christened, parochially registered, parochially settled, parochially married, parochially supported, and parochially buried.[20]

Parish was home, and there was a time when England's 15,000 parishes gave the country its molecular structure. When parishioners maintained a parish custom therefore, they were maintaining their little bit of the kingdom.[21] Black's close study of Farningham, one of Kent's 414 parishes, concluded that by operating through the church's open vestry, which set the rate, and its civil vestry, which spent it, local government was effective into the 1830s.[22] In two significant works, Keith Snell took the subject further. Affirming that nearly all English parishes were established by 1200, even if varying wildly in size and shape, he showed how they offered a fundamental reason for belonging through mortal rites in the first place and legal rights of settlement (by birth, marriage, paternity, office, rate, rent, service, apprenticeship, and residence) in the second.[23] And although they did not operate without friction (bickering between parishes over charges was

---

[19] Ben Brierley, *Failsworth. My Native Village* (1895), in Poole, 'March to Peterloo', *Past & Present* 192, 2006, p.129. On nineteenth-century tastes for things past, Peter Mandler, 'Revisiting the Olden Time', String & Bull, eds., *Tudorism* (2011), and chapters by Sweet, Wrightson, and Colls in Colls, ed., *Northumbria* (2007).

[20] Pounds, *The Parish* (2000) pp.420–3; Bettey, *Church and Community* (1979) pp.116–17. In Allworthy and Partridge on the good side and Square and Thwakum on the other, Henry Fielding's *Tom Jones* (1749) presented two sides of parish government.

[21] On the building of the state through the parish: Hindle, *State and Social Change* (2000) p.13, pp.27–31; and Morrill, in Coffey and Lim, eds., *Puritans* (2008) p.67.

[22] Black, *Local Government in a Pre-Reform English Parish* (1992) pp.380–1.

[23] Snell's close study of poor law and parish settlement papers found home and belonging 'an absolutely key concept of self and identity' across the social scale: *Spirits of Community* (2016) p.38.

common), these so-called 'heads of settlement' offered the people a material platform for belonging based on parish privileges which included housing and poor relief, some local taxation and, through the vestries, some say in how money was spent on local rights of way, roads and bridges, law and order and charitable giving, as well as the registration of births, marriages, and deaths. With the exception of parish officers (surveyor, constable, clerk, and overseer), all this was carried out voluntarily under the law by local notables, and marked in a calendar of customary events checked every so often as to extent and jurisdiction by the beating of the parish bounds.[24] Everyone was subject to the laws of parish settlement it seems, even moles. Ab Kettleby's parochial molecatchers were paid only for moles caught within the parish.[25] Which is to say: parish settlement was a kind of freehold. As a cottager you enjoyed somewhere to have and to hold. Charity taken from any other source was distasteful.[26] And if this was home, one of the ways in which it knew itself in addition to these customary rights was through its sports and customs, which were rights of a kind.

Thiselton Dyer counted about 142 customary events in the parochial calendar.[27] A wheel of 'repeated experience', they served as the means by which parishes saw themselves in concert in ways that were face to face and socially engaged. All over the country, parishes played football on Shrove Tuesday. That parts of Lincolnshire played it with a leather tube, made it different but the same.[28]

Keeper of the keys of the largest and usually the only public building, the parish clergyman, along with the magistrate, was the chief representative of the state while his church was the site of great language and music, the place where people stood and kneeled, sang and prayed and lived and died together. Contrary to appearances, the church was not entirely a top-down institution. Hymn singing was never authorized. Like a lot of customs, it just happened.[29] Church Ales, a sort of party to raise parish funds, was 'the fundamental event from which almost all parish activity grew'. Rushbearing, or *The Old Custom of Strewing Rushes; carrying Rushes to Church; the Rush Cart; Garlands in Churches; Morris Dancers; the Wakes; the Rush*, provided churches with a good clean dry earthen floor in

---

[24] 'In England and Wales we therefore had a system of belonging that put great stress on it as a concept, attaching crucial importance to it in legal terms and in matters of welfare entitlement': Snell, *Parish and Belonging* (2006)p.109. He goes on: "The very remarkable fact is that for a century across about 15,000 parishes, countless thousands, perhaps half a million people, did so...testimony to the on-going strength of personal reputation and local community sentiment...' (p.363).

[25] Snell catches the moley parishioners of Leicestershire on p.41 (ibid).

[26] Ashby, *Joseph Ashby* (1961) pp.49–50. England still had a peasant class only they were called cottagers: Neeson, *Common Right* (1996) p.298.

[27] Thiselton Dyer, *British Popular Customs* (1900) p.31.

[28] Bushaway, *By Rite* (1982) p.34. On the power of print and literacy levels in the exercise of national imagining: Anderson, *Imagined Communities* (1983). Parochial and church customs were practices and rituals as well as words.

[29] Temperley, *Music of the English Parish Church* (1983) p.3.

order to accommodate all that happened there, including revels and carols.[30] Rushbearing was observed far beyond Lancashire into Cumberland, the Midlands, and the West country, but it was the biggest event in the Lancashire festive calendar, the 'great feast of the year' according to Bamford, the life and soul of the county.[31] Decorated carts carried rushes and rushbearers to church on their patron saint's day. Usually there was inter-village rivalry for the most bedizened cart, with sports, dancing, open house, and pubs doing their best trade. Some Rushbearings could last a week. Some were quite fantastical. At Bunbury wake in Cheshire, Richard Coddingtoun was dressed as a woman by Elizabeth Symme and her lover, who then led a crowd up Church Hill with 'Cheryes' for the said Elizabeth, who sat ready to receive them.[32]

Parishes had to be small enough to be managed and large enough to be sustained. Claybrooke in Leicestershire spread across two counties, three townships, and two chapelries.[33] Perambulation established and re-established parochial limits, and therefore settlement, and therefore belonging. All who perambulated were witnesses to what Wrightson called that 'messy skein' of social networks that was home.[34] After a gap of some years, Sunderland's 1811 perambulation was led by Mr. Paxton the Rector and a joiner who remembered the way. Parish officers went along scattering gingerbread and nuts for the children and painting 'SP' at focal points. Bodmin did figs and biscuits. Cockermouth started in the middle of a stream, Chipping Wycombe in a pond, Wooler and Berwick at the same markers that served for football matches. Perambulators liked to keep their eyes on the church. Some had a 40 foot maypole to fix their radius. Some got lost and blundered into streams and hedges.[35]

The parish, then, was the force field of rural belonging, appealing, according to E P Thompson, 'to solidarities . . . almost nameless'.[36] John Stuart Mill wanted modern principles applied to most things but not to parish privileges, which he saw as protectors of the market weak against the market strong.[37] All through the nineteenth century, political economists called for the end of parish settlement in order to facilitate the free movement of labour and the destruction of the social market. To this end, the Poor Law Amendment Act of 1834 can be seen as an attack on the parish led by experts. Political economists and utilitarians

---

[30] Burton, *Old Custom* (1891) title page; Johnston et al. ed., *English Parish Drama* (1996) p.12; Pounds describes church festivals as short-lived, intense experiences: *English Parish* (2000) p.258.

[31] Bamford, *Early Days* (1843) p.130; Burton, *Rushbearing* (1891).

[32] In 1620: Baldwin, Johnston, ed., *English Parish Drama* (1996) ch. 2, p.37.

[33] Phythian-Adams, *Fields* (1978) p.28; Pounds, *English Parish* (2000) pp.75–6.

[34] Wrightson, 'Power of the Parish', in Griffiths, Fox, and Hindle, eds., *Experience of Authority* (1996) p.372.

[35] On maypoles: Chambers, *Book of Days* (1869) p.572; on perambulations: Mitchell, *Sunderland* (1919) pp.106–7; Maclean, *Bodmin* (1870) p.129; Bolton, *Cockermouth* (1912) pp.14–15; Jenkins, *Penn* (1938) p.159; Iredale, *Bondagers* (2008) p.157; on hedgerows: Fox, 'Bocage Landscapes' (1976) p.58.

[36] Thompson, *Customs* (1993) p.350, p.122.

[37] Bushaway, *By Rite* (1982) p.9.

dominated its thinking. Edwin Chadwick and Nassau Senior drafted the report that led to the Act which, in principle at least, abolished all out relief. Future recipients had to enter the workhouse as paupers and subject themselves to the 'first and most essential of all conditions...that [the pauper's] situation on the whole shall not be made...so eligible as the situation of the independent labourer of the lowest class'.[38] From now on, the poor would be relieved by Poor Law Unions in brick-built workhouses according to central regulation. Not by people they knew. From now on, parochial housing retained for pauper families would be sold off to fund new workhouses.[39] Unlike Chartist or Anti-Corn Law League demonstrators, or Suffragette marchers, or for that matter the Stamford Bullards, there were no rallies in favour of Poor Law Unions, no demonstrations in favour of workhouses, no popular demand for the end of parochial privileges.

The state was beginning to transfer old parochial functions over to new national bodies, notably to the Poor Law Unions from 1834, the local government boards from 1835, the Registrar of Births, Marriages and Deaths from 1836, the Charity Commissioners from 1853, the county and borough constabularies from 1856, the highway districts from 1865, and the school boards from 1870. Responsibility for hospitals and paupers would pass eventually to outside bodies. Even parochial unrest moved outside the parish.[40] As the old sense of place shrank, all these new central bodies took on a size and scale hitherto unknown. In addition, by 1851, there were over 20,000 Nonconformist chapels which by definition operated outside the parochial system, and only three and a half million church-goers, or half the eligible number. Tithes had been commuted in 1836 and church rates would be abolished in 1868.[41] The Church of England shrank back from its social networks. The clergy came to think God was for Sundays.[42] Sabbatarianism was much older than the Victorians, but they were the ones who made it anti-social. 'God how I hate Sundays'.[43]

Beginning in the late sixteenth century with the onset of an all-graduate ministry, the Church of England found itself fundamentally different from the

---

[38] Checklands, *Poor Law Report* (1834) p.355.

[39] About 37 per cent of housing stock in Warwickshire was owned by the parish and used for the poor, with 27 per cent in Bedfordshire, 24 per cent in Buckinghamshire, 11 per cent in Northants, and 5 per cent in Dorset: Broad, 'Housing the rural poor', *Agricultural History Review* 48, 1974.

[40] Scriven, 'Swing's aftermath', *History Workshop Journal*, 2016, accessed online 1 August 2016, http://hwj.oxfordjournals.org.

[41] Pounds, *English Parish* (2000) p.327; Snell, *Parish and Belonging* (2006) pp.471–81; Bettey, *Church and Community* (1979) p.128. On the Evangelical trans-parochial 'County Unions' from 1797, and the non-parochial home and city missions soon after, including Baptist (1792), Wesleyan (1795), Bible Society (1804), Evangelical (1809), National Society (1811), British & Foreign (1814), Lord's Day Observance (1831), YMCA (1844), and UK Teetotal Alliance (1853): all in Ward, *Religion and Society* (1972) p.45, and Kent, *Holding the Fort* (1978) pp.101–3.

[42] Obelkevich, *Religion and Rural Society* (1976) pp.127–61.

[43] Jimmy Porter in John Osborne's *Look Back in Anger* (1956).

England it purported to serve—an anomaly that remained.[44] Victorian worship was restored in the best possible taste. Old pews were ripped out, new pews ripped in, collection plates replaced pew rents, composed music replaced country music, the mighty organ replaced the mildly anarchic slightly wheezy village band. Even as they tried to get closer, the clergy moved further away. They halted the trend to baptism as a private rite and were spectacularly successful in their reinvention of 'Harvest Thanksgiving' as a stand-in for more rorty village customs. But their attempts to revive public catechism were a total failure, confirmation was rendered respectable but with far fewer takers, and the number of communicants remained miniscule. While Sunday services became more dignified, some would say brittle, the clergy struggled against the Methodist society down the road. An established church keen to reconstitute itself as a living tradition turned itself into a profession.[45]

'Every man and woman and child', said Cobbett in 1834, 'looks upon his parish as being partly his'. 'The parochial system is, no doubt, a beautiful thing in theory', amended Shaftesbury in 1855, but in the towns it 'is a mere shadow and a name'.[46] Out-migration weakened the parish. Gainsborough and Morland start painting out-migrants, and we begin to hear widespread reports about the breakdown of custom soon after.[47] Many rural churches were left to rot, and when they were eventually restored, as at Okeford Fitzpaine in 1866, it was a huge act of confidence in a parochial system trying to find its feet again in restored churches, vicarage teas, parish rooms, and garden fetes.[48] Parish magazines reached out to parishioners all over the world and rare indeed was the magazine that did not ask emigres about old forgotten customs. But after nearly half a century of extra-parochial legislation and out-migration, by the 1870s the parish's social role was all but over even if some pride and affection remained. As its historian remarked:

> 'The next few years immediately following the New Poor Law saw high proportions of gravestones proudly announcing "of this parish", sometimes even in capital letters. I have yet to see a gravestone proclaiming "of this poor law union" and I do not expect that I ever will'.[49]

---

[44] Collinson, *Birthpangs* (1991) p.95. He estimates that between 1559 and 1625 the Church of England became 'a graduate ministry, recruited from the colleges of Oxford and Cambridge: *Religion of Protestants* (1982) p.94.

[45] Obelkevich, *Religion and Rural Society* (1976) pp.127–60. On church bands, Gammon, 'Popular Church Music 1660-1870', in Yeos, eds., *Popular Culture and Class Conflict* (1981) ch. 3.

[46] Shaftesbury in 1855 in Inglis, *Churches and the Working Class* (1974) p.25; Cobbett, *Political Register*, 20 February 1834. In 1839, thirty-one Lancashire churches were subject to acts of popular repossession by Chartists: Yeo, 'Christianity in Chartist Struggle', *Past & Present* 91 (1981) p.109. On changes to church interiors: Temperley, *Music of the English Parish Church* (1983) p.5, p.323.

[47] Snell, *Spirits of Community* (2016) p.94.

[48] 'nothing tended more to the amelioration of the people': Bishop of Salisbury, at Okeford Fitzpaine's reopening, *Dorset County Chronicle & Somersetshire Gazette*, 2 August 1866.

[49] Snell, *Parish and Belonging* (2006) p.481.

Losing Land

In 1612 Cambridge Corporation acquired twenty-five acres of land near the centre of town as a place for sport and things in common. Two hundred years later the enclosure of this land exempted a portion of it known locally as 'Parker's Piece'. Exemption did not mean no development. In 1825 the Corporation allowed the building of a church at East Road. In 1827 it filled a pond and ceded more land for a new town gaol. In 1831 it sold a bit more for Park Terrace, a new cricket pitch, a brick-wall and a pathway. In 1841 the Corporation asserted its right to further acts of improvement but was successfully warded off at a public meeting for being 'at variance with ancient customs'. It tried again in 1859, also unsuccessfully. From the point of view of what the colleges liked to call Cambridge's 'chief place of recreation', what followed was patchy. University footballers played their part in inventing the modern game on Parker's Piece, schoolgirls from The Perse did their exercises, cricketers batted and bowled, locals strolled, and fatstock grazed while trees were planted and new paths laid. In 1894 electric lights were installed under the supervision of a new figure in the landscape, the 'Curator of Parker's Piece', who came with an armband (CPP). By the end of the century, piece by Parker's piece and without any great rupture, what had once been common was now municipal.[50] This was not a momentous event, even by Cambridge's standards. But it was typical of the urge to regulate.

At the beginning of the eighteenth century almost every English town had its common fields and outside the towns most arable land lay open. For most of the people most of the time, a rough and ready space was always to hand. But as the towns grew the fields were lost and there was nothing to remember except perhaps in a name. In 1831, Horatio Smith reported that Londoners had lost their sports and games because every 'green spot' was now a street and every field a building site.[51] The London festival year was in steep decline: New Year's Day 'not observed', Twelfth Night 'in desuetude', Candlemas 'lost', Palm Sunday a 'remnant', Easter Day past tense, May Day a 'faint shadow', Guy Fawkes 'falling fast', Lord Mayor's Day only 'dimly', Christmas, Morris, Hobby Horse, Misrule, and all the rest 'soon to follow into oblivion'.[52] Chambers' *Book of Days* roll-called a similar list of 'lingering', 'failing', or 'degenerated' festivals.[53] In the Midlands, the traditional Morris was in decline.[54] London's greatest fair, St. Bartholomew's, was abolished in 1855. For over fifty years, the Metropolitan Police sought to abolish

---

[50] Mitchell, *Parker's Piece* (1985) pp.30–5; Conybeare, *Cambridgeshire* (1897) p.256. Perse girls exercised on Parker's Piece until they moved into new premises that included a gym in Hills Road in 1888: Mitchell, *Perse* (1976) p.57.

[51] Smith, *Festivals* (1831)p.122.   [52] ibid, pp.132–57.

[53] Chambers, *Book of Days* (1869) p.263, p.239.

[54] Simons, 'English Pilgrimages. Morris dancing in England and beyond 1921-39', De Montfort University PhD (2019) pp.6–7; Chandler, *Ribbons, Bells & Squeaking Fiddles* (1993) p.208.

the capital's numerous unchartered suburban fairs. It wasn't until 1885 that the Home Secretary ordered the police not to interfere with steam roundabouts.[55]

Loss of common land was nearly always followed by a falling-off in custom.[56] Neeson has estimated that 20.9 per cent England was enclosed between 1750 and 1820. Carter has explored widespread loss of common rights by enclosure in Middlesex between 1656 and 1889. Griffin has argued that enclosure drastically diminished places to play in over half of Cambridgeshire between 1790 and 1837.[57] By 1900, in the southern counties of England, nearly all open land had gone and most commons, according to Chapman and Seeliger, had been 'drastically reduced'.[58] In the great northern industrial conurbations, such as Birkenhead, the transformation was complete. In other places, the transformation was incremental. In Sunderland, for instance, they still had the beach to enjoy and, on what had once been the town moor, an even square called 'The Flat'.[59] Before enclosure, Manchester's Newton Heath had actually been a heath and Bradford's Fairweather Green had actually been a green. Macclesfield's Town Field and Cuckstool Pit Green were turned into public places, Gateshead's Windmill Hills into Saltwell Park, Penrith's Barbara Plains into Edenhall Cottages and Tysoe's townlands into a registered charity adminstered by the vicar.[60] At Batsford in Nottinghamshire the Hammonds told the story of how local cricketers bickered with the man who enclosed their pitch.[61]

Every area had its lost land story to tell—trivial in one sense, fundamental in another. Although there were efforts to provide for alternative recreation in various land acts, at first results were meagre. All across the country, fairs were being turned into markets, village wakes into parish rooms, and so on. Kicking back, Northamptonshire footballers burst the fence of their local enclosure in 1765 and Thomas Willingale and sons would block the enclosure of Epping Forest a hundred years later. But victories were few and far between. Waterbeach parishioners expressed disgust at the loss of their May Day field after enclosure in 1830.[62] Workington footballers lost their field to a railway track. Great Crosby anglers lost their foreshore to a landlord. Matlock parishioners lost their wake. Whitchurch

[55] Cunningham, 'Metropolitan Fairs', in Donajgrodzki, ed., *Social Control* (1977) p.163.

[56] Laslett, *World We Have Lost* (1971) p.62.

[57] Griffin, *England's Revels* (2005) p.193; Neeson, *Commoners* (1996) p.82, pp.158–70; Carter, 'Enclosure Resistance', Middlesex PhD (1998). See also: Bushaway, *By Rite* (1982) p.242.

[58] Chapman and Seeliger, *Enclosure, Environment* (2001) p.9.

[59] East End History Project, 'Life in Sunderland's East End' (1985) p.60. For total physical transformation: Sulley, *Birkenhead* (1907).

[60] Ashby, *Joseph Ashby* (1974) p.48; Earles, *Macclesfield* (1915) pp.159–60; Manders, *Gateshead* (1973) p.240; Walker, *Penrith* (1858) p.202.

[61] Hammonds, *Bleak Age* (1947) p.78—and on how traditional playgrounds were 'checked and repressed in a drastic manner' (p.75). The King George Playing Fields Foundation was launched in 1936.

[62] *Northamptonshire Mercury*, 5 August 1765; Denson, *Peasant's Voice* (1830) pp.18–19. Willingale and lopping rights: Thompson, *Customs in Common* (1993) pp.142–3.

feasters lost their street.[63] Many a fine Georgian rectory was made out of enclosed parish lands.[64] Rev. Maine was glad to be rid of the old sports on White Horse Hill. The Vicar of Botisham gained from the 1801 enclosure along with the Rector of Trinity College Cambridge, but in Teversham, parishioners turned to their Rector for advice on how to save their village green. No use asking the Vicar of Olney (if his parish history is anything to go by), while the Vicar of West Wycombe managed to write his parish history without a single mention of the people who lived there.[65] People were expected to keep their heads down. Manchester's repository of improvement books called itself 'the Counteraction'.[66]

And as so much in the old culture was counter-acted, the sense of place waned. Cambridge Antiquarian Society went in two brakes to Melbourne in order to locate a large furze that was said to indicate the corner of an ancient Roman camp. But after much searching they concluded that it had been lost to a recent enclosure. They went home having lost a little of themselves.[67]

'In parish after parish the labourer could not get at the land', said the agricultural trade unionist Joseph Arch.[68] With enclosure 'the keystone was knocked out of the arch' of parish life. No longer peasants, but dependent now on 'demand', somebody else's demand, for 'labour', *their* labour, 'a grade had been assigned to them'.[69] After the Industrial Revolution, most people no longer occupied even their occupation.[70] All round the kingdom folk were losing the places where they had worked and played together since, well, according to custom, time immemorial. Robert Dover's 240-year-old Chipping Camden 'Olympian Games' was itself a gentry take-over of a traditional Church Ales, surrendered in 1852 not because the vicar objected to drinking but because the land was enclosed for farming.[71]

John Clare worked on local enclosure only to suffer the indignity of losing his own world by digging an extension to someone else's. When finally he left his parish he 'felt as though I was walking out of my own language'.[72] Clare's world

[63] Wilson, *Whitchurch* (1909) p.63; Scott, *Cumberland* (1899) p.200; Ince Blundell Estate Papers 1891–98: LaRO, Preston, DDWW 3/3/1, and Hunter, *Preservation of Open Spaces* (1896) pp.319–20; Bryan, *Matlock* (1903) p.110.

[64] Ward, *Religion and Society* (1972) pp.9–11.

[65] 'A Late Vicar', *West Wycombe* (1925); Maine, *Stanford* (1866) p.88; Rogers, *Botisham* (1992) p.44; Patrick, *Teversham* (1996) pp.20–1; Langley, *Olney* (1892) pp.39–40.

[66] 'A Plan…' (1885): NRO, HO 42/34. George Stephenson's Derbyshire engineering works banned all sport and recreation at work and in the vicinity of work in favour of a Friendly Society (1843), a Mechanics Institute (1845), a Garden Society (1852), company schools (1854), and a brass band: Chapman, *Clay Cross* (1987) pp.8–9.

[67] Palmer and McNeice, *Cambridgeshire* (1925) p.3.   [68] Arch in *Joseph Arch* (1898) p.44.

[69] Bourne, *Change in the Village* (1912) p.111.

[70] Good point made by Snell in *Parish and Belonging* (2006) p.492.

[71] Polley, 'Olimpick Games', 21 November 2017.

[72] Clare quoted in Forster, *Boundaries* (2019) p.1. 'Particular resentment was caused by the infringement of ancient customs. Festival days and their attendant rituals marked the high points of a labourer's year': Bate, *John Clare* (2003), p.49. Bate saw the role of the pre-enclosed landscape in the making of what he calls a 'walking poet' able to move in multiple directions.

comprised seven parishes: Helpston, Maxey, Etton, Ufford, Bainton, Northborough, and Castor. He recalled football on the village green. On Whit Sunday the young would gather at Eastwell Fountain. On Plough Monday they'd go looking for mischief. Once upon a time all these parishes were open field one to the other. In 1809 the Act for their enclosure was passed, and by 1820 it was effected. Only the parish of Castor remained open (until 1898). Before enclosure, Clare had lived in a circle of open fields where the ploughman

> Will often stoop inquisitive to trace,
> The opening beauties of a daisy's face;
> Oft will he witness, with admiring eyes,
> The brook's sweet dimples o'er the pebbles rise;
> And often, bent as o'er some magic spell,
> He'll pause, and pick his shaped stone and shell ...
>
> Thus pausing wild on all he saunters by,
> He feels enraptur'd though he knows not why,
> And hums and mutters o'er his joys in vain,
> And dwells on something which he can't explain.[73]

Although the old parochial system showed more fight perhaps than expected—for example it carried on administering ad hoc poor relief long past 1834—it reached the end of the century as a relic.[74] In the 1880s the Ordnance Survey took responsibility for surveying that which parishioners couldn't do for themselves. Cartographers walked round accompanied by elderly parishioners who advised them what to write in their 'Remark Books'. All Bingley's 'Old Characters' in 1899 were associated with a parish life redolent of times past, the same year that the Victoria County History was founded as an attempt to revive the old parochial sense of place. That people now needed to read a book in order to know their *terroir* rather spoke for itself.[75] Living traditions were rare and getting rarer. The loss of belonging was nearly complete. 'Parish pump' entered the vocabulary as to do with matters of limited scope or tedious interest. 'Semi-detached' was about to enter the vocabulary as a new form of housing defined by separation.

---

[73] Barrell, *The Dark Side of the Landscape* (1985) p.155.
[74] Snell, *Parish and Belonging* (2006) p.17; on survivals: Gomme, *Folk-Lore Relics of Early Village Life* (1883) pp.13–14.
[75] Cox's *How to Write the History of a Parish* (1879) went to four editions by 1909; Speight, *Chronicles and Stories of Old Bingley* (1899) p.257.

War on the Parish

Butterworth and Baines were progressives in the sense that they believed that everything they believed in was going to happen anyway. This included the rise of industry and the decline of custom. It also included the progress of religious Dissent with its roots in seventeenth-century Puritanism.

Of all the various Methodist groupings, it was the second largest, the Primitive Methodists, who were the most Puritan.[76] Primitive Methodists were moralizers but they were not moralizers in the liberal metropolitan sense of the NSPCA. Rather they were against everything which did not stem from the Scriptures or from their own impulses. You could become a Primitive Methodist no matter how wicked your life. But you could not be a Primitive Methodist without renouncing that life in its entirety and, among many other things, that meant war on parish sport and custom as a source of sin, reserving a particular scorn for the sort of men, usually upper class men, who called themselves 'sportsmen'. Like the Puritans of old, Primitive Methodists closed ranks, memorized texts, bandied catch-phrases, combed their hair straight, and were known as 'Ranters'.[77] That they opposed some customary notions of being English did not mean that they were against others. On the contrary, they claimed their Protestant truth out of English liberty, and had their own Protestant view of English history and language to prove it, including a special and spontaneous relationship to God which they termed being 'at liberty'. With them, the presence of God was as free and near to hand as you could get. When we consider the Puritan tradition we are in other lines of custom and belonging, but in order to understand Primitive Methodism's war on the parish, we have to understand the parish's war on Primitive Methodism.

Methodism found itself in the same legal crucible that had shaped Puritanism and its successors. With the restoration of the Church of England and monarchy in 1660, parliament had to deal with a Puritan movement which, until relatively recently (1570–1620), had taken control of the Church of England and come out against the king.[78] Between the 1662 Act of Uniformity that re-established the Church, and the Acts of 1664 (Conventicle), 1672 (Indulgence), and 1673 (Test),

---

[76] Baines was a Congregationalist. On religious census Sunday 31 March 1851, there were 1,137,102 total Wesleyan Methodist attendances against 327,647 total Primitive Methodist attendances. The Church of England drew 3,174,873 attendances: British Protestant Churches, *Religious Worship*. England and Wales. *Parliamentary Papers* 1852–53.

[77] Christopher Hill, the great historian of Puritanism, was brought up a Methodist and used the old Ranter greeting 'My One Flesh': Corfield, 'Marxism and Methodism', *Historian* 87, 2005, p.22. On straight-combed Quaker hair: Ritson, *Romance of Primitive Methodism* (1909) p.114. On despised sportsmen: Rosman, *Evangelicals* (1984) p.74.

[78] Hempton, *Methodism* (2005) p.52; Collinson, in *Birthpangs of Protestant England* (1991) says that after 1660 Puritans were driven by law into what he calls an 'alienated nonconformity' (p.155); and Collinson, *Religion of Protestants* (1982) pp.94–8.

that permitted, licensed, and kept at bay those who would not conform to it, English Puritanism in all its shapes and sizes was shepherded into an alternative legal field that permitted it, or versions of it now increasingly called 'Dissent', to co-exist, albeit with loss of some civil liberties.[79] In 1689 the Toleration Act brought these three sanctions together into a single piece of legislation which, along with the Bill of Rights, helped define a new Englishness built on the supremacy of the Church but the legal toleration of dissident minorities. When in the 1740s John Wesley found himself inside the Church but with a *de facto* new Puritanism on his hands, what was beginning to be called 'Methodism' found itself sheltering inside the Law but shuffling out of the Church.

Wesley's emphasis on personal salvation put him closer to Puritan theology too, and soon he was out and about telling the people what they must do in order to be saved. At Oxford, he and George Whitefield belonged to a tiny sect that screened itself from the outside world.[80] Even as a movement numbering hundreds of thousands (well over a million by the 1850s) Methodism continued to see itself in that very sectarian image. Robert Southey saw them as a 'distinct people', a state within a state, an 'imperium in imperio'.[81]

Wesley died in 1791, having tried to keep his mission and his movement within the Church and its legal privileges, but he left behind a highly energized network of 60,000 mainly English adherents who quickly put themselves outside the Church. 'Primitive Methodism' was a secession from this original (Wesleyan) secession. Sparked into life in May 1807 at an American style 'Camp Meeting' in Joseph Pointon's field at Mow Cop, Staffordshire, Methodists had gone there to counter-act the parish wake. In scenes described as fanatical, certainly incommunicable, converts came to believe that after a personal encounter with God they had been saved from their sins—an entirely self-diagnosed condition it has to be said, governed largely by the emotions, nameless and unique. By 1812, along with William Clowes, a potter, Hugh Bourne, a local colliery carpenter, was leading a self-declared 'Primitive' Methodist sect committed to the aggressive missioning of local parishes. They put themselves apart. Their first membership tickets proclaimed Acts 28: 'for as concerning this sect we know that everywhere it is spoken against'.[82]

Seventeenth-century Puritans had always rejoiced at being apart. Loathed as 'Intolerants', 'Precisians', and 'Porklings' (Intolerants and Precisians we can

[79] Underdown, *Fire from Heaven* (1992) p.240; Bebb, *Nonconformity* (1935) p.45; Davies, *Richard Baxter* (1887) p.293.
[80] Kent, *Holding the Fort* (1978) p.41; Davies, *Methodism* (1964) pp.51–69; Hattersley, *Brand from the Burning* (2002) pp.137–55.
[81] Southey, *Life of Wesley* (1820) vol. i, p.1.
[82] Kendall, *Origin and History of the Primitive Methodist Church* (1905) vol. i, p.97; and Anderson, 'Origins of Primitive Methodism in North Staffordshire', *PWHS*, 2007, p.36. Calder makes a great deal of the movement's desire to see itself as an outsider: *Origins of Primitive Methodism* (2016) ch. 2 'The Historiography Problem'.

understand), they sought to use the Church of England as God's purifying instrument.[83] For a generation or more Puritan clergy operated deep within the parochial system and the culture wars that were fought in places like Dorchester, Banbury, and Kidderminster saw wide flanking attacks on customary revels of every kind including music, dancing, and sport.[84] Puritan Richard Baxter imposed a moral regime on his own Kidderminster parish dividing it into 800 families at twelve moral levels from serious endeavour at the top to Papist at the bottom. Richard Culmer, vicar of Goodstone, Kent, was against everything and everyone, including Christmas. When he took an axe to his own maypole, parishioners locked him out. After the restoration of the monarchy in 1660, Puritan clergy were locked out of their church *en masse* and, over a century later, some of their dark disruptive energy found its way into Methodism.[85]

Primitive Methodists would gather outside a village and 'enter the place of their attack' singing and exhorting. Not surprisingly, this produced great excitement but, as one missioner put it, 'having been raised up from among the working classes, and not having received an academical education, and [our] appearance and dialect being correspondent to those of the disaffected, [we] generally gained a patient hearing'.[86]

First incision made, confrontation began the moment parishioners fought back or tried to go about their normal business. Soon there would be commotions at the ale house, or shoutings at the village band, or at the Rush carts, or at the wake, or at the Sabbath football match, or with the magistrate or clergyman, or indeed with virtually any parishioner who was deemed offensive to God. Watts' *Songs Divine & Moral for the use of children* put praying up against playing:

> Why should I love my sport so well,
> So content at my play,
> And lose the thoughts of heaven and hell,
> And then forget to pray?

As brothers and sisters in Christ, Primitive Methodists' first loyalty was to each other, not the parish. Brother Bourne confronted Wrekin wakes. Bro. Wedgwood confronted Barrow wakes. Bro. Lister confronted Newcastle hoppings. Bro.

[83] On the mysteries of being a 'Porkling': Coffey and Lim, 'Introduction', *Puritanism* (2008) p.20; Walsham, 'Godly and Popular Culture', ibid, p.290.

[84] Capp, *Culture Wars* (2012)p.188, pp.204–16.

[85] ibid, pp.1–2. E P Thompson understood that disruptive energy and in some ways exuded it: Thompson, *The Making* (1968) pp.404–9. Hempton thought Thompson had 'penetrated somehow to the heart of something': *Methodism. Empire of the Spirit* (2005) p.6. On Puritan moral regimes: Underdown, *Fire from Heaven* (1992) p.173; Collinson, *Birthpangs of Protestant England* (1991) p.137 and ch. 2 'The Protestant Town'; Powicke, *Richard Baxter* (1924) p.53, p.305.

[86] Kendall, *Origin and History of the Primitive Methodist Church* (1905) vol. i, pp.222–3. Networks would begin almost immediately with the nearest 'societies': Patterson, *Northern Primitive Methodism* (1909) pp.268–9.

Lockwood confronted the parish fire engine (dripping wet). Bro. Benton confronted the Duke of Rutland. Bro. Hepburn confronted Lord Londonderry (and asked him to pray). Bro. Charles confronted the Merry Andrews. Bro. Gibson refused strong drink. Bro. Fenton refused field sport ('nursery of sin'). Bro. Hindhaugh refused cards, Bro. Wall bowling, Bro. Edward Thompson football, Bro. Milner cricket, Bro. Durrant pitch and toss, Bro. Wyndham Easter revels, Sister Cosens 'carnal companions', Sister Hetherington sceptical companions, Sister McCree gay attire, Sister Temperance Frost curly hair, Sister Munday her own bonnet, Sister Spittle somebody else's bonnet, Weardale girls' their fashionable 'Ranter caps', Sister Fletcher dancing and Sister Oakden the same.[87] The list goes on for over a century. All these people mattered in thousands of stories of small local redemptions based on a hat removed, a drink refused, a bet called off, a custom faced-down, a sport surrendered. In the village of Hambridge, the place where Cecil Sharp first heard John England sing, Lucy White and Louisa Hooper gave up the very songs that launched the English Folk Revival. 'Nowadays [they] sing them at home only as they are accounted wicked by some of the village's "Methodies"'.[88]

Up in Lancashire, Butterworth counted Dissenters parish by parish.[89] The vast majority of parishes (61 out of 74) had dissenting chapels, including various types of Methodist chapel, some clustered together (15 in Wigan, 20 in Bury), others in ones and twos. Ulverston had a very distinguished seventeenth-century Quaker Meeting House. The vast majority of dissenting chapels (50 out of 61) though, were Methodist, about twenty-three of them Primitive. There were very few parishes (11 out of 74) where the parish church was the only place of worship. Roman Catholics constituted a distinct minority (17 out of 74) but in Sefton

---

[87] Fanny Oakden, P[rimitive] M[ethodist] M[agazine] 1826, p.138, and the rest: Petty, *Primitive Methodist Connexion* (1860): Bros. Lockwood and Benton (p.54), Bros. Wedgwood and Lister (pp.143–6), and others against 'bowling . . . foot races . . . cock fighting . . . pugilistic practices and other vicious practices'. Thomas Hepburn was a Durham miner and sometime Primitive lay preacher who led his trade union to victory over the most powerful energy combine in the world: *Durham Chronicle*, 14 May 1831, and Colls, *Pitmen* (1987) pp.64–100. Wearmouth cites five Primitive Methodist miners transported for 'conspiracy' (trade union meetings) who were visited by Hon. R Richardson, member of the Victoria State Legislature in 1855: *Methodism and the Working Class Movements* (1937) pp.229–30. See also: Ben Gibson, *PMM* 1840, p.278; George Fenton, *PMM* 1842, p.292; William Hindhaugh, *PMM* 1870, p.322; John Wall, *PMM* 1853, p.634; Edward Thompson, *PMM* 1834, p.32; John Milner, *PMM* 1841, p.182; Billy Durrant in Thain, *Nenthead* (1988) pp.31–7; John Wyndham in Shaw, *John Wyndham* (1878) p.99. For the sisters: Mary Cosens, *PMM* 1832, p.45; Jane Hetherington, *PMM* 1832, p.27; Margaret McCree, *PMM* 1852, p.439; Temperance Frost, *PMM* 1822, p.78; Mrs. Munday, *PMM* 1833, p.188; Sister Spittle, *PMM* 1823, p.44; Weardale girls, *PMM* 1824, p.61; Elizabeth Fletcher, *PMM* 1823, p.92.

[88] Schofield, 'Cecil Sharp and Charles Marson in Somerset 1903', *Folk Music Journal* 8, 2004, p.498.

[89] Butterworth was a well-informed correspondent and we have no reason to doubt the authenticity of his interviews. He was an inconsistent note-taker however, and does not always name or number his denominations. I have included only those Primitive Methodist chapels he designated as such. The number is almost certainly an underestimate. On Butterworth's close regional connections: Winstanley, 'Butterworth and the Manchester Press 1829-48', *Manchester Region History Review* 14, 1990.

(4 chapels) there were dissenters only. There were Israelites in Ashton, Swedenborgians in Halsall, Anabaptists in Lytham, and Ingamites in Whalley New Church, but right across Lancashire Methodist sisters and brothers of all types undermined the parochial structure by organizing across it.[90]

In the parish priest's eyes they must have looked like a band of religious paupers from the last village on. Infact they comprised 'an artful and well-linked chain of dependence... [that] the parish minister now stands single against'.[91]

Methodists saw themselves exactly the other way: standing alone against the combined power of church and state. That twenty out of twenty-three Lancashire Primitive Methodist chapels stood alone against the church would have pleased them. As they saw it, the solitary chapel ('square, red-tiled, brick') faced off the pub and sports field and any other part of village life that got between God and his people. Joseph Arch, who stood alone with his Methodist mother in her war on parish and parson and parson's wife, peeped through the church door and witnessed something he never forgot:

> In the parish church the poor were apportioned their lowly places, and taught that they must sit in them Sunday after Sunday all their lives long... the squire and the other local magnates used to sit in state in the centre of the aisle. They did not, if you please, like the look of the agricultural labourers. 'Hodge' [the archetypal agricultural labourer] sat too near them, and even in his Sunday best he was an offence to their eyes. They also objected to Hodge looking at them, so they had curtains put up...

> First, up walked the squire to the communion rails; the farmers went up next; then up went the tradesmen, the shopkeepers, the wheelwrights, and the black-smith; and then, the very last of all, went the poor agricultural labourers in their smock frocks. They walked up by themselves; nobody else knelt with them; it was as if they were unclean—and at that sight the iron entered into my poor little heart and remained fast embedded there.[92]

Arch (age 7) stood alone. Daniel (in the den) stood alone. Bunyan's *Pilgrim* (who gave up Vanity Fair) stood alone. William Clowes, founder of Primitive Methodism (who gave up dancing) stood alone. James Kirk (who gave up the pub) stood alone. John Wilson (who gave up gambling) stood alone. John Durham (who gave up bad company) stood alone. Sam Drury (who gave up cards) stood alone. George Handford (who gave up Plough Monday) stood alone. James Baker (who gave up backsword) stood alone. John Pearcy (who gave up

---

[90] On Methodist undermining of parochial structure: Pocock, 'Origins, Develoment and significance of the Circuit', Nottingham PhD (2015).

[91] Whitaker (1813), quoted in Davies and Rupp, *Methodist Church* (1965) p.312.

[92] Arch, *Joseph Arch* (1898) p.17, p.20. On the face off between chapel and pub: Parkinson, *True Stories* (1912) p.13.

cricket) stood alone. Joseph Simcock and William Hatten (who gave up church choir) stood alone. William Stokes (who gave up rural sports) stood alone. Richard Baxter who said he 'could never from my first studies endure confusion', stood alone. Those who gave up drink and Sabbath sports are too numerous to mention but Eric Liddell (who gave up the chance of running in the Olympic 100 metres) most famously stood alone.[93]

Methodists dreamed a new Zion and lived in the Bible as much as they lived in the village. In the ceaseless round of hymns and sermons, prayers and Bible readings, a new England emerged out of the old one. No cathedrals mattered here, only what was scriptural, local, near to hand and made real by word and faith not custom or superstition. At Watton 'I took my stand in the market place'. At Polstead 'I took my stand on the green'.[94] 'King Charles', 'Gypsy Smith', 'Little Willie', 'The Coloured Evangelist', 'The Street Arab', 'The Fisherman Evangelist', 'The Converted Collier', 'The Converted Athlete', 'The Converted Pugilist', and a string of other colourful sinners stood up in obscure places to stand alone, draw the crowd and save the soul. Folk Protestantism made heroes out of everyone and, in a way, standing alone against Satan without so much as a stick or a stone, was neither unsporting nor unphysical.[95] The clapping and the singing, the meltings and quickenings, the burden of sin, the wrestling like Jacob, the rush to salvation, the last wave of the hand before death, resurrection and the life to come, were all exercises of the body as well as the soul. God was a strong physical presence in life and if he wasn't the sinner had to try harder to be saved. Barnett the Burslem miner calculated whether or not he could afford to surrender two bets on the Lincoln Handicap. William Hickingbotham of Belper, a man 'devoted to rough and cruel sports', weighed up the glory (some would disagree) of being Champion Bag Racer of All England. 'Owd Roger' Haydock of Blackburn faced down fighting dogs. Robert Key faced down Sunday footballers. He had to take on 'a lad, a sort of Merry Andrew', who presented himself 'in such unnatural postures and positions' that the crowd died laughing rather than saved. So many found redemption on the edge to remember the exact time and place that became the central fact of their life. Albert Shakesby, town rough, lost his strength in confrontation with Mrs. Harrison, female missioner, Hull Third Circuit, 14 January 1904. Brother Jersey was remembered for his powerful preaching on a bright starry night in the dales. So was Brother Batty, another 'Apostle of Weardale'. Sam Edwards 'The Coloured Evangelist' was converted on the deck of a ship. 'Gypsy' Smith was born in a

---

[93] Richard Baxter in Rose, in Collinson, ed., *Puritan Character* (1989) p.vi; William Clowes in Kendall, *Origins and History* (1905) p.54. Other examples: *PMM* 1849, p.641; *PMM* 1915, p.385; *PMM* 1832, p.329; *PMM* 1819, p.49; *PMM* 1823, p.179; *PMM* 1842, p.284; *PMM* 1842, p.7; *PMM* 1869, p.96; *PMM* 1842, p.303; *PMM* 1869, p.44. An estimated 14,000 attended the May 1822 Oldham camp meeting against the parish wakes: *PMM* 1822, p.209. Liddell was a 22 year old Edinburgh University Scottish Congregationalist who refused to run in his most favoured event at the 1924 Paris Olympics because it was held on a Sunday. Nothing, not even the British Olympic Association and a relentless press could make him change his mind: Hamilton, *For The Glory* (2016) p.72. The story has a happy ending.

[94] Key, *Gospel* (1872) p.83, p.95.

[95] Folk Protestantism: Green, *Passing of Protestant England* (2011) p.149.

tent. Thomas Lidgett wanted it to be known that he writes 'not grammatical or to appear a fine fellow'. Robert Howarth's hair grew straight up. When the barber made his professional observation, Robert riposted that his soul was going the same way. Brunskill told of the Northumbrian pulpit preacher who, in a heavenly moment, placed his palm on a smooth wooden knob. '"Haud thee hand, mon", said the owner, "that's ma heed an" I shall want it aifter thae day'".[96]

Other eschatological moments were less droll. Speaking at Frodsham in 1806, Lorenzo Dow, American holy man, was suddenly drawn to a young woman who was wearing a rose in her bosom. When he picked it, it shed its leaves. Dow prophesied that she would be dead within the year and of course she was or it would never have become a parable of the movement.[97]

Methodist theology, if it had one, was based on parables of personal distress. The power of the preacher to bring on the initial crisis was key. Methodists expected more than liturgy from their services. They expected transformation. Richard Howton was a former prize-fighter turned prize-preacher who in his time had wrecked the odd pulpit or two. Advising on how to preach something which was essentially beyond words, he beseeched Prims to remember that powder is not shot, best things first, no scolding, no promises, no long bits, appeal to the children and save souls, not face.[98] It was vital that you died 'saved'. Nothing else mattered. All obituarists stressed the supreme moment.[99] Wesley wrote it into his movement through his control of the publishing house, and Hugh Bourne did the same. Another feature of seventeenth-century English (and Dutch) pietism, sudden conversion did not need a liturgy. It did not even need a church. It was entirely between convert and converter, although there was disputation over the rightful place of women converters.[100]

The whole of Methodist England was strewn with little stories of great faith and in ordinary places. Bourne opened his first Cheshire campaign 'to counteract the bad effect of the Wake or annual parish feast' at Norton in the Moors. People

---

[96] Brunskill, *Williamson* (1923) p.9. Then from the Lincoln Handicap down: Barnett, *Life Story* (1910) pp.26–7; Barfoot, *Diamond in the Rough* (1874) p.5; Whittle, *'Owd Roger'* (1912) p.85; Key, *Gospel Among the Masses* (1872) p.19; Shakesby, *Street Arab to Evangelist* (1910) pp.139–40; Jersey and Batty, in Kendall, *Origin and History* (1905) p.147; J.Y., *Sam Edwards* (1884); Smith, *Life and Work* (1910); Lidgett, *Life* (1908) p.50; Howarth, *PMM* 1842, pp.379–81. For other assorted characters and sinners who made sudden changes of heart: Kendall, *Sanderson* (1875) p.53; Mahomet, *Street Arab* (1894) p.iii; Middleton, *Fisherman Evangelist* (1950)
p.62; Morgan, *Richard Weaver* (1860s); Kendall, *Origin and History* (1905) p.209; Richard Hall, Bamford's uncle, in Samuel Bamford, *Passages* (1848) vol. i, p.156; 'Bendigo', or William Thompson of Nottingham: Allen, 'Fighting', *Expository Times*, 2007, p.178.
[97] Kent, *Holding the Fort* (1978) p.49.   [98] Grimshaw, *Prize Ring to Pulpit* (1893) pp.37–9.
[99] 98 per cent of Primitive Methodist and 88 of Wesleyan Methodist obituaries refer to the conversion experience: Wilson, 'Obituaries', *PWHS* (1998) p.218.
[100] Philotheos, 'A Letter to the People called Methodists on their unscriptural mode of addressing God at their Prayer Meetings, with brief remarks on females speaking and praying in public' (1826); Hurd, 'An Address to Women' (1842); Rees, 'Reasons for not cooperating in the alleged Sunderland Revivals' (1859).

poured in. The second camp meeting at Mow Cop attracted a magistrate who spoke 'warm' with him. At the fourth camp meeting, on 23 August 1807, Bourne was pleased to report that if there were no gains there were no losses either: 'not one member being drawn away by the vanities of the wake'. When the campaign finally faded after seven years, it was out of exhaustion, not loss of heart.[101]

They were difficult people to make civil. In 1824 Middle Rainton pit exploded killing sixty. Primitive Methodists told the orphans and widows they were hard hearted and ought to prepare themselves for the life to come. Cholera in Sunderland was regarded as 'a work of sanctification', no less, by Petty, one of the Connexion's rising stars. Village cricket in Leicestershire was howled down by praying bands. One man's heart attack was punishment for playing cricket on a Sunday, they said, while others suffered similar retribution for Sabbath sliding on the ice, Sabbath playing fives, Sabbath going hunting. Thomas Curry 'The Pious Keelman' was stabbed by somebody who didn't like the way he prayed, but parishioners usually showed their opposition in more imaginative ways. At Filey parish pigs were herded into the service while at Whitehaven the congregation was herded out. At other times fighting dogs, bleating sheep, stinking fish, bucking asses, rolling casks, and screaming children were all thrown in (and out) of Primitive prayer meetings. Charged as Ranters, Bedlamites, Fanatics, and 'disturbers of established customs' they were hosed down and shouted down.[102] Every Sabbath was a culture war, every confrontation a clash of loyalties, every convert a pearl of great price. Methodists turned New Year celebrations into 'Watchnight Services' where they watched over themselves while keeping a wary eye on the door.[103]

War on the parish stood in a long line of Puritan wars of belief. From Tyndale's Bible (1536), to Cromwell's Ironsides (1642), to Milton's *Areopagitica* (1644), to Bunyan's *Pilgrim's Progress* (1678), Puritan Englishness was tied up with God's special dispensation to his people. The Puritan Richard Baxter, who declared war on his parishioners as 'ignorant, rude and revelling', was required reading. Primitive Methodist preachers were expected to carry his *Saint's Everlasting Rest*

---

[101] Bourne, *History of the Primitive Methodists* (1823) pp.8–22, pp.56–7.

[102] 'Bedlamites' and other disturbers of custom: Parrott, *Primitive Methodists* (1866) p.63. The rest in order from the 'Hard Hearted Colliers' down: PMM 1824, pp.43–4; on cholera: Patterson, *Northern Primitive Methodism* (1909) p.250; on cricket and other Sunday sportsmen: PMM 1819, p.7; PMM 1821, p.41; PMM 1824, p.113; PMM 1826, p.47; on the stabbing: Wawn, *Thomas Curry* (1822) p.14. For pigs and fish: Shaw, *Filey Fishermen* (1867); for Whitehaven invasion: PMM 1852, p.169; for fighting dogs and other interventions: PMM 1824, p.166; PMM 1825, p.273; Petty, *History of Primitive Methodist Connexion* (1860) p.215; for cider casks and other interventions: Maynard, *Prison to Pulpit* (1896) p.28, p.48, p.90.

[103] For example: Pryce, *Bristol* (1861) p.421; Hodgson, *Shields* (1903) p.44. Despite John Wesley's comment that every man of war was a floating hell, Methodists appear to have formed a flourishing sect inside the Royal Navy during the Revolutionary and Napoleonic Wars. Above deck and below, they took their services and said their prayers. Given how they undermined the parish, it seems the Navy was not afraid they would undermine the quarter deck: Pickering, 'Methodism and the Royal Navy', EHS conference, DMU, 6 November 2019.

(1652), a discourse on death, in their knapsacks.[104] John White was famous for turning seventeenth-century Dorchester into a Puritan republic, with a ban on all sports and games. Banbury went the same way. Striving for that which was not worth having, Bunyan's Vanity Fair stood for all these sins of the flesh, a place where there is 'at all times...juggling, cheats, games, plays, fools, apes, knaves and rogues'.[105] When James I ordered his *Book of Sports* to be read from every pulpit in the land, he did so after a call from Lancashire magistrates to do the opposite and enforce the Sabbath. After that, the road to Civil War was straight. In 1618 and 1633, flying in the face of Puritanism's war on the parish, King James' *Book of Sports* deliberately endorsed Sunday as a day of sport:

> Our Good People [should] be not disturbed, letted, or discouraged from any lawful Recreation, such as Dancing, either Men or Women, Archery for Men, Leaping, Vaulting...nor from having May Games, whitsun Ales and Morris dances, and the setting up of May Poles and other Sports...and that Women shall have leave to carry Rushes to the church for the Decoring of it...[106]

In 1643 parliament hanged *The Book of Sports* in public.

Puritanism fought on after 1660 as a powerful underground Englishness. In the nineteenth century, their traditions rose again, serving to threaten to flood a parochial culture that was already under strain as Methodists of all types went about filling their own 'circuits' and 'Connexion', holding forth to teeming Sunday schools, creating their own missions, societies, prayer groups, preachers' plans and so on, including a new class of female exhorters in the steps of Miriam, Deborah, Hannah, and other Biblical women. In *Adam Bede* (1859), Dinah Morris is banned from preaching so that her readers can note the injustice of it. George Eliot's Methodists lift each other up to see over the parish boundary, not inside it. In his great work *The Making of the English Working Class*, Edward Thompson saw Methodism as a reactionary movement working against the best interests of the industrial working class and in their war on the parish one can see what he meant.[107] On the other hand, Thompson missed the simple truth that Methodism was also at war with church and state on the ground. Where they could get a hold, Methodists replaced parish custom and belonging with their own solidarities.

---

[104] As well as Bible and hymn book, and Baxter, John Fletcher's *Checks to Antinomianism* (1829), Isaac Watts' *Improvement of the Mind* (1751), and Wesley's *Sermons* were required Primitive preacher reading: Ritson, *Romance* (1909) pp.191–215.

[105] Bunyan, *Pilgrim's Progress* (1678) p.125. He based it on Stourbridge Fair, held on Stourbridge Common, Cambridge, one of the biggest in England and customary until 1933: Underdown, *Fire over Heaven* (1992) p.173, and Collinson, *Birthpangs* (1991) p.137.

[106] Anon, *The Book of Sports set forth by King James I and King Charles I* (1721). See also: Dougall, *Devil's Book* (2011) p.73, p.150, p.166.

[107] Thompson, *English Working Class* (1963) ch. xi, 'The Transforming Power of the Cross'.

The English Civil War was a sporting as well as a religious war and it did not end in 1660. Methodists of all types inherited the Puritan tradition and shut the door on Sabbath sport to produce their own heroes. At the same time, they preached a new manliness and womanliness which looked for self control over mind and body ('flesh'). In 1846 Nelson Street Sunday School Anniversary in Newcastle praised a children's performance that 'contained nothing to amuse'.[108] There wasn't much room here for childish games, or lumping about in muddy fields, or swinging by the arm on the dance floor. Chapel 'sport' was other people, self-improvement, afternoon teas, gossip, daring sermons. Chapel stewards banned drinking and gambling on the premises. In the 1880s Methodists lined up with other socially minded bodies in crusades to purge sport of publicans and bookies.[109]

Puritans were against sport in 1618, Primitive Methodists were against it in 1918, and 'War Puritans' were still against it in 1939.[110] By then however, a newly cleansed modern team version of sport had won the Protestant community over. Some still saw sport as ungodly and a step towards the secular life. Others however, like Rev. William Glaister at the Liverpool Church Congress, obviously a cricketing man, saw it as a way of attracting the young:

The best local Board of Health is a cricket ground, and the best moral club a Cricket Club, ten times better than all those clubs which call themselves YMCAs and the like which are not very invigorating... [Cricket provided] good morals, good manners and every manly virtue... I fully believe that the county to which I belong—Nottinghamshire—is largely indebted for its high standard of morality to its numerous cricket clubs'.[111]

Henry Drummond's *Baxter's Second Innings* (1892) tells the story of young Baxter's second chance at the wicket after he had been clean bowled by Sin in his first. Seventy years on, the book was still being given as a prize in Methodist

---

[108] *PMM*, 1846, p.504.

[109] 'middle-class puritans retained both their hostility to the aristocracy and revulsion at their way of life': Chinn, *Better Betting* (2004) p.13.

[110] According to the Mass Observation social research unit they included Sir John Anderson, Lord Privy Seal (Presbyterian), Sir Samuel Hoare, Home Office (Quaker), Ernest Brown, Minister of Labour (Baptist), Neville Chamberlain, Prime Minister (Unitarian) and Sir John Simon, Chancellor of the Exchequer, and Kingsley Wood, Minister of Air: 'Sport in Wartime' by 'HJN', 13 December 1939: MO file 13.

[111] Erdozain, *Problem of Pleasure* (2009) p.139. Erdozain makes much of the move by Evangelicals in favour of 'leisure' and away from what he calls the 'salvation economy'—a move which defines his core subject as that 'permanent battle with the traditional customs and pastimes [which] started to dominate the theology and mentality of the Evangelical movement. Secular pleasure seemed to be at the heart of all that evangelicals opposed [yet] increasingly it defined them' (p.68). Which is to say, he sees the pursuit of secular pleasure, or sociability, including sport, in chapel life, as a step towards the secularization of the chapels by the chapels themselves. In doing so, he seriously underestimates the draw of 'secular' activity, or sociability, in the Evangelical movement right from the start, just as he overstates the difference between what was clearly social and godly and what was clearly godly and social. It was a Methodist gift to mix the two.

companies of the Boys' Brigade.[112] By the 1920s, all Primitive Methodism's old dark destructiveness was beginning to be forgotten in a modern wave of sport and sociability with plenty of athletic metaphors about the spititual life. But it could never forget its heroic past when it had faced the old sport down:

> It was the Ranters, as the Primitive Methodists were called even in official reports, who continued the real work of Methodism, the uplifting of the lowest ranks in society. They fought the evils of drunkenness, gambling and improvidence. They took away from the pitman his gun, his dog, and his fighting cock. They gave him a frock coat for his posy jacket, hymns for his public house ditties, prayer meetings for his public house frolics. They drove into the minds of a naturally improvident race the idea that extravagance was in itself a sin... With Psalms the Roundheads and Covenanters marched into battle. Under banners embroidered with texts the pitmen assembled, lodge by lodge, at their meetings. 'He that oppresseth the poor, reproacheth his maker'.[113]

Banks of the Tyne

People migrated to the towns and took their sports with them. Love of the countryside, Chase tells us, emerged as an urban movement against urban confinement.[114] And Chartism, the Hammonds told us, emerged as a movement as much against the loss of playgrounds as against the loss of rights. The National Society for the Prevention of Cruelty to Animals, as we have seen, attacked the old sporting life from the outside. The Primitive Methodists, as we have seen, attacked it from the inside. But the biggest attack of all came from the break up of the environment that sustained it. As the *Pioneer* put in 1833, 'all our sports [have been] converted into crimes'.

In 1870, notice of yet another Newcastle Town Improvement Act brought forth a song, 'The Toon Improvement Bill', by music hall favourite Ned Corvan. Corvan subtitled his song 'Nee Pleyce Noo to Play'. Acting the child, with no place now to play, and driven from the stream filled 'wi clairts', and anxious in a world that 'cannit dee wivoot a pollis', with magistrates 'tellin us ti gan to the boardin schuel', Corvan invited audiences to sympathize with a child's loss of play in the face of a town bent on development. Down by the Quayside, or up at the Spital, or all along the Forth, people were losing their canny old toon. When Corvan told them

---

[112] Drummond, *Baxter's Second Innings* (1892). Christ, who is the captain of the team, gives Baxter his second chance with the bat.

[113] Welbourne, *Miners' Unions* (1923) pp.57–8, a point of view endorsed by Sidney Webb, MP for Seaham Harbour, in his *Durham Miners* (1921) pp.23–4. For Primitive Methodists still against the *Book of Sports* and modern sports: *PMM* 1886, p.747, and *PMM* 1894, pp.358–60.

[114] He calls it 'popular agrarianism': Chase, *'People's Farm'* (1988) pp.179–80.

that he was 'broken-hearted when aw think aboot wor canny Forth', [where] 'aw used to fullick man, (an' what a fullocker aw was)', we can presume there was a time when they had fullicked a bit themselves.[115]

Between 1840 and 1852 there were twenty-seven Acts designed to develop the canny old toon. In 1807 the Forth was described as a square plot above the river bank flanked by a double row of trees, nice for views, nice for walks, nice for playing bowls or drying your linen. In 1804 local lads played football there against the Wiltshire Militia. Parish perambulators walked from Newcastle Guildhall down to the blue stone on the bridge (with scattering of cakes and raisins) taking in the Forth, ten miles all round. In 1735 Bourne described the Forth as a 'mighty pretty place much frequented by the townspeople for its pleasing walk and rural entertainments'. In 1827 Mackenzie described it as a 'most convenient and delightful promenade'. But already there were glass works and engine works on nearby Forth Banks, including Stephenson's and Hawthorn's, and by 1842 the area had degenerated into what one observer called 'a neglected swamp'.[116]

Oliver's 1831 engraving depicted the Forth beginning to be pressed from the east by new building developments.[117] When in 1836 the Newcastle & Carlisle Railway Company announced its intention to drive from the west into the heart of the town, the price of leaseholds went through the roof and the Forth was doomed.[118] The railway company bought nearby Spital ('Hospital') land at first, but switched its interest back to the Forth soon after. In spite of rumours of insider dealing, with opposition from some councillors, more land was acquired from the corporation along with Thomas Anderson's property on Forth Banks. A poster went up. 'Encroachment on the Land. Enclosure of the Ropery Banks': 'To the Mayor and Aldermen' on behalf of the 'health and welfare of the Working Classes'. 'Your Memorialists' condemn the loss of Ropery Banks and the loss of 'a great part of the Forth which was intended for the recreation of the inhabitants', including water, fresh air, 'reclining', and children's 'sports'.[119] No matter. After some complex financial dealing between the Newcastle & Carlisle Railway to the west and the York-Newcastle-Berwick railway companies to the east, the western

---

[115] To translate the Geordie, 'a stream filled with wet mud and earth'; 'cannot do without a police officer'; 'imploring us to go to the Board School': *Corvan's Songs* (1870) 'Fullicking' was to do with playing marbles.

[116] *Monthly Chronicle of North Country Lore and Legend*, June 1887, p.172; Improvement Acts, Seymour Bell Portfolio 10; Anon, *Picture of Newcastle upon Tyne* (1807) p.19; Baillie, *Impartial History* (1801) pp.158–60; Mackenzie, *Newcastle upon Tyne* (1827) p.714, p.196; and for the engine works, Hawthorn, *Sketch* (1921).

[117] Oliver, *New Picture* (1831). Bourne provides a precise description of the old Forth by perambulation: *History* (1736) p.145.

[118] The company was founded in 1825 by the cream of Newcastle business after some previous talk of building a Newcastle-Carlisle canal: NCL, Chapman, 'Report on the Cost '(October 1824); *Tyne Mercury*, 17 August 1824. Addyman and Fawcett's work carries good maps and illustrations of what was involved: *The High Level Bridge and Newcastle Central Station* (1999).

[119] Poster, 'Encroachment...' (Newcastle, Matthew Dodds, 12 July 1844): NCL, Thos Wilson Collection, vol. x, 1842–5.

1.1 Algernon and Minna Burnaby, with 'Relic' and 'Lady', Testerton Hall, Norfolk, summer 1915. Minna takes a fence on 'Jock' at Baggrave Hall, Leicestershire, 1920. 'Algy' was joint master of The Quorn Hunt. Leicestershire Record Office DG/15/20

2.1 George Stubbs, 'Turf with Jockey Up, at Newmarket' (1765) Yale Centre for British Art B.1981.25. Equestrian art celebrated the Whig ascendancy

3.1 Gravestone: Tom Sayers and his dog 'Lion', Highgate Cemetery West (1865)

3.2 Black Limestone Bust: 'Bust of a Man', formerly known as 'Psyche', reputedly by Francis Harwood (1726–83) Yale Centre for British Art B.2006.14.11

4.1 Stamford Bull Running, Broad Street, with Ann Blades, late eighteenth-century (1792?), presented to the town by Rev F Carroll of Tallington, May 1891: Stamford Town Hall, 5.39, STC

5.1 Roger Mayne, 'Little girl turns a cartwheel, Southam Street, Kensal Town, London W 10' (1956)

6.2 Worksop College Dining Hall (1910), Worksop College Archive

7.1 'Royal Holloway College Rowing Crew' (1892), Box 4, London Metropolitan Women's Library 204.169

7.2 George Clausen, 'Schoolgirls, Haverstock Hill' (1880), Yale Centre for British Art B.1985.10.1

7.3 'Hockey on Field' (1898), Cheltenham Ladies' College

7.4 'Roderic House Lacrosse Team' (1919), Cheltenham Ladies' College

8.1 Women's Football Match between aircraft manufacturers Fairey and A V Roe (Avro), Fallowfield, Manchester, Lancashire, England, Photograph: 1944, © IWM (D 23522)

8.2 FA Cup Tie, Arsenal v Preston, Highbury (1922), TWITTER © Old Football

8.3 L S Lowry's Coming from the Mill, © The Lowry Collection, Salford

8.4 Wilf Archer, RAF India 1943: 'To my dear father for his wallet—hoping some day you can come and watch me again. I am in tip top form and playing better than ever. Your loving son, Wilf'

line eventually drove into town over forty-four arches and a lot of medieval rubble to reach Central Station in 1850, where it linked up with Robert Stephenson's High Level Bridge (1849) and George Hudson's eastern line on the other side of the river.[120] That done, Newcastle changed forever. In 1875, on the 50th anniversary of his Stockton Darlington line, George Stephenson was said to have transformed the world.[121] He had certainly transformed the Forth, which now no longer existed. The reporter for *The Graphic*, having sidled past the old Forth, now a goods yard, noted that he had to go two miles out of town in order to find some grass. Joe Wilson, Newcastle's lightest heart, was born between a fever hospital and a lead works and died next to a brick field facing an engine shed.[122] When in 1845 Newcastle Town Council debated the railway scheme, in the face of such intense and serious money-making, to roars of laughter from his fellow councillors, Mr. Robinson said that he thought the loss of a view was a serious matter.[123]

That same year Dr. Reid reported on the state of Newcastle's public health. Concluding that 'no measure would be of more importance', 'particularly to the junior population', than access to fresh air and exercise, Reid speculated on the disaster of the Forth, threats by speculative builders to the Town Moor and Castle Leazes, the recent loss of popular access to the River Tyne, and the erosion of common walks, including local 'denes' (narrow ravines with small streams). The year before, the chairman of the Town Improvement Committee was accused of personal interest in the destruction of Ropery Banks, a favourite walk. There had long been designs upon the Town Moor—1,100 acres originally bought by the burgesses in the 1650s with rights ceded to freemen in 1774—but apart from some nibbling of Castle Leazes in 1870 for parks and an infirmary (10 acres), and more nibbling for organized sport (35 acres), the Moor was broad enough to look after itself, and escaped enclosure although it didn't escape regulation. Bowling was banned in 1881.[124]

---

[120] Grainger, *Proposal* (1836); Alderman Dunn in *Proceedings of the Town Council for 1840–41*. Railway speculation prompted a land grab. Thomas Bell the surveyor called a grocer's valuation of his own land near the Forth as 'a complete farce'. They agreed on £990, not £3,000: NCL, Seymour Bell Portfolio 10. For rumours of corruption: *Tyne Mercury*, 3, 5 April, 1, 29 May 1838.

[121] *Stockton Darlington Times*, 4 September 1875 and *The Graphic*, 4 June 1881.

[122] Joe Wilson (1841–75), music hall star, singer, and songwriter: Newcastle Ordnance Survey 1879, xcvii.ii (Tyne Wear Museums). For Joe Wilson, see Colls: ODNB, https://doi.org/10.1093/ref:odnb/51480.

[123] Town Council debate on Newcastle Berwick Railway Company (1845) p.18: NCL. On the station, opened by Queen Victoria: HS, *Handbook* (1851). On surveyors and how 'John Bull, with open mouth' was 'ready to swallow any quantity of Railroad': *Illustrated London News*, 25 October 1845.

[124] Thirty-five acres were put aside for modern sports and team games including football: NCL Report, Borough of Newcastle upon Tyne, Town Moor Management Committee, 21 March 1881. Old style sporting events such as bowling were repeatedly criticized by ratepayers, town improvers, temperance bodies, and the like, but common land the Moor remained: see for example 'Peter Putright' in *Tyne Mercury*, 14 December 1841, and Temperance Society Committee, *Newcastle as It*

Little patches of land were harder to defend than a great moor. In 1819 a letter to the *Monthly Magazine* could think of nothing nicer for the town than the cultivation of small gardens.[125] By mid century, this was impossible to contemplate. Pandon Dene was lost early and by the 1850s, with the coming of Armstrong's massive engineering factories out to the west, Maiden's Walk ('commanding the vales of Tyne and Ravensworth') had been lost, and found again, now called the Scotswood Road, main artery of industrial Newcastle. Jesmond Dene, a 'romantic glen' in 1838, was sold to developers in 1872, only to be handed back to the public again as a park in 1895 by Armstrong, the man who had buried Maiden's Walk in the first place.[126]

In the midst of all this demolition of old toon belonging, you could spend 6d in the gallery for a whole evening devoted to old toon songs. Tyneside melodies included 'The Keel Row' and 'Hey Away Maw Bonny Bairn'.[127]

What Newcastle lost in open spaces it gained in public parks. Only, the sort of liberty permitted in a public park was not the sort that was free to rove. Sections 13 and 14 of the 1870 Town Improvement Act allowed for two new parks, but under the powers of the 1875 Public Health Act, nobody intent on doing more than walking upright in one of them was allowed in. An 1879 bye-law made it an offence to do anything that a child might normally want to do.[128] Local kiddars found their own space and the best novel to come out of Newcastle, Jack Common's *Kiddar's Luck* (1951), is about finding it. Not the sort of space defended by park keepers it is true, but bits of waste possessed and repossessed against the claims of other kiddars, who did the same. Street kids knew every hole and corner. Back lanes they knew intimately and, in time, it was there that boys learned to hit sixes in spaces barely wide enough to swing a horse and cart. The girls, befitting their role in life, learned to make do and mend, learning from each other how to hop and skip and hang upside down like bats. Trees and flowers they did not know. By the time the state got round to worrying about where to play, children had found their own corners. Manchester's Dr. Ashby said he hoped for airy walks where mothers could wheel their prams. Dublin's leading surgeon said he hoped

---

Is (1854). Castle Leazes was developed with the best possible intentions: two public parks, the Royal Victoria Infirmary and, in 1905, a professional football club which took the land but kept members off the pitch. Reid, *Health of Towns* (1845) pp.16–17, pp.94–6. Councillor Joseph Crawhall was accused of securing public rights of way 'where both old and young have wander'd': broadside, 'The Ropery Banks' (1844) and *Newcastle Advertiser & Commercial Herald*, 14 January 1845.

[125] *Northumberland and Newcastle Monthly Magazine*, February 1819.

[126] Maiden's Walk's scenes of 'luxuriance and beauty equalled by few other spots either in England or Wales' now covered in 'bricks and mortar': Collingwood Bruce, *Newcastle* (1863) p.87; Sopwith, *Pocket Guide* (1838) p.99; *Newcastle Weekly Chronicle*, 31 August 1872, letter from 'Rambler' on 'the last bit of landscape … free to the inhabitants except the treeless moor'; Johnson, *Making of the Tyne* (1895) p.281.

[127] handbill: 'Topliff's Merry Night' (1844): NCL, Wilson Collection vol. x, 1842–5.

[128] NCL, Newcastle Town Improvement Act (1870) sections 13 and 14; Bye Laws, Borough of Newcastle (1881).

for squares where children could 'gambol about': but not in his square they couldn't.[129]

In 1845 South Shields' beaches were praised by Dr. Reid for their fresh air and sea bathing.[130] But in 1879 the Shields, Marsden, and Whitburn Colliery Railway was opened. Barely three miles long and serving the town's rapidly expanding network of staithes and collieries, the SMWCR emerged as the most significant force in the shaping of modern Shields. If you wanted to get to the beach in order to bathe, you had to negotiate streets pierced by two major railway lines running in from the outside (the Pontop Pike & South Shields Railway and the North East Railway) and the SMWCR (aka 'The Marsden Rattler') looping round the inside. And if you did make it to the beach, the smallest beach, Herd Sands, flanked by Herd Groyne (1882) and a mighty new pier (1895), remained more or less untouched, although it was close to a very dirty river and, as the 1924 Ordnance Survey motor map shows, a commercial railway ran along its edge. If you didn't want to go there and preferred to play south of the pier instead, you were met by giant hills of ballast and refuse heaped upon open sand dunes known as The Bents, the Rattler running south barely a quarter of a mile away.[131] And if you gave up on The Bents, and the two beaches, and turned and headed for the river instead, you came upon a waterfront chock full of ships. The chances were that you couldn't get down to it and even if you could, swimming would be mad and rowing would be risky, although there were plenty who tried.

St. Hilda's parish church sat in Shields market place, hard by the Tyne.[132] It was rebuilt in 1812 due to population pressure and saw many changes after the town's first Improvement Act in 1829, but by 1879 the church itself—squat black from the smoke of its eponymous colliery and coiled round by three railway systems—had ceded most of its civil powers to the borough and other agencies.[133] If St. Hilda's wanted to celebrate May Day or Church Ales, first it would have had

---

[129] Which was Merrion Square, even though 'every class should have a recreation ground for themselves': Sir Lambert Ormsby, Inter-departmental Committee on Physical Deterioration (1904) vol. i, cmnd 2175, p.465, and Dr. Ashby (p.327). See also: Sleight, *Public Space in Melbourne 1870–1914* (2013).

[130] Reid, *Health of Towns* (1845) pp.112–15. Sea bathing in Sunderland was spoiled by factory smoke and the 'bad state of approaches' to the river. He thought few places in the country were more in need of 'public walks or vacant ground' than Gateshead (p.101).

[131] Ayton and Daniell noted a unique range of hills of Thames gravel used for collier ballast, refuse from the glass works, and cinders from the salt pans giving an 'appearance much disfigured' to the town's natural resources: *Voyage Round Great Britain* (1820) p.57. In 1896 the borough was finally moved to save its beach and foreshore with an Improvement Act that granted the leaseholders, the Harton Coal Company, further rail development along the front in return for the recreational redevelopment of the Bents, which was levelled and opened as a public park in 1901.

[132] South Shields Public Library: Ordnance Survey Tyneside Sheet 9, South Shields (1894–96); OS Tyneside Sheet 3, second edition, Mouth of the Tyne (1898); Tyne Wear Museums: Ordnance Survey, Ministry of Transport, Newcastle Road Map showing South Shields (1924–5).

[133] Hodgson, *History of South Shields* (1924) pp.100–9.

to find the room and second it would have had to find parishioners (many of whom had fled to the higher part of town).

Coal was the energy of the Industrial Revolution and the Durham coalfield was one of the great suppliers. Shields was ringed by three collieries (Harton 1844, Boldon 1869, and Marsden/Whitburn 1874), with another one in the middle (St. Hilda's 1810), and another one near the beach (Westoe 1909). Apart from local sales, all five ran coal straight to the river or the railway. While the waterfront was jamming up with docks and railways, the river moved awkwardly by. The Tyne had been a coaling port since the seventeenth century. In 1688, 612,839 tons left for English and foreign ports.[134] Defoe remarked on 'prodigious fleets' of colliers making their way to London.[135]

These were shallow-draught sailing vessels loaded by flat-bottomed keels. Larger vessels required a deeper river. Fordyce's 1846 Maritime Chart identified major navigable problems above bridge at Newcastle, and below bridge, particularly at the river mouth at Herd Sands on the south side and at the rocky outcropping 'Black Middings' on the north side.[136] At Hebburn Shoal, upstream, the river was a mere 2 inches deep at low tide. At Gateshead, further up, you could wade across. At Blaydon island, horses were led across at low water and a modest horse race was turned into the region's most famous sporting event through its most famous sporting song—George Ridley's *The Blaydon Races* (1862).[137] King's Meadow island enjoyed a sporting pub and (it was said) a sporting landlady. Herd Sands was the venue for an annual race meeting, with beer tents. Lazy bends and shoals in the river made for easy access and rowing.

By the 1850s keels had given way to spouts and steam tugs, shipwrights were about to give way to iron angle smiths, and wide canvas sails to steam boilers. An 1848 river audit counted sixty-five collieries feeding the staithes, plus riverside stacks of chemical works, glass works, engine works, docks, shipyards, ship and rail connections. The Tyne Improvement Commission took responsibility for the river in 1850.[138]

---

[134] A peak year, 'not normally surpassed until the 1720s': Levine and Wrightson, *Industrial Society* (1991) p.68.

[135] Defoe, *A Tour* (1724–26) p.535. Carrying 'coals to Newcastle' was, after all, the height of pointlessness. 'We are not all Colliers' protested *The Newcastle Magazine* in 1822 (vol. i, no vi, pp.339–42).

[136] Fordyce's *Maritime Chart of the River Tyne* (1846): NCL, Bell Collection, vol. iv. See also in the same collection 1845 prospectuses for the *Jarrow Docks and Railway Company* and the *Northumberland Dock and Percy Railway*. In 1859, the North East Railway opened Tyne Dock at South Shields, the biggest coaling dock in the world.

[137] Tune 'Brighton': 'O lads, ye shud only seen us gannin/We pass'd the foaks upon the road just as they wor stannin'/Thor wes lots i' lads an' lasses there, all wi' smilin' faces/Gawn alang the Scotswood Road, to see the Blaydon races': George Ridley Ms., 1862, *Allans Illustrated* (1862) p.451. See: advert *Racing Times* 18 May 1863.

[138] *Report of the Engineer* (1848): NCL, Bell Collection vol. iv; Bell, *Plan of the River Tyne* (1849): NCL; Metcalfe, 'Working Class Free Time', Wisconsin PhD (1968) pp.75–7. On keelmen's early battles with spouts: 'Address of the Keelmen', four, 9 October to 25 November 1822: NCL, Bell Coll, vol. ii.

The Commission's main objective was to turn a sailing and rowing river into an industrial waterway, and to do so it had to turn it into an open channel with free tidal ingress and egress. A River Police force was chartered in 1845, followed by much dredging and straightening, a river engineer in 1859, more bye-laws in 1868, a deputy harbour master (gold braid) in 1872, a Swing Bridge in 1876, Blaydon island obliterated 1865, King's Meadow island obliterated 1885 and, after nearly forty years of improvement, the completion of two major piers with lighthouses at Tynemouth and South Shields. The sea lived as it had always lived, but the Tyne Improvement Commission took away the old river and gave back the new to iron hulls and oil slicks. Boys made a living scavenging an intensely polluted river. Even the fish cleared off, and none but the most determined anglers with them. Once so plentiful it was said that Newcastle apprentices had clauses in their indentures stating that masters should not feed them salmon everyday, by the 1950s there were no salmon left. Only the most determined (or the most drunk) leapt in the river now.[139]

The old Tyne had been farmed under the conservatorship of Newcastle Corporation. A 'Water Bailiff' took the royalties and the Corporation spent them.[140] Every Ascension Day the Lord Mayor and his friends perambulated their 'parish' boundaries downstream from Hedwin Streams to Spar Hawk (various spellings) where they proclaimed their lordship of the river at Shields Bar before hauling back upstream for more sport and speeches. The barge he sat in looked like it had come out of another time, as indeed it had, but 'Barge Day' was a big day in the sporting calendar with flotillas of small craft enjoying the breeze and 'crack gigs' enjoying the racing.[141] 'Hedwyn Streams' to 'Sparhawk', fourteen miles round trip, was a customary perambulation going back at least to the seventeenth century, ratified by King's Bench. Conservatorship ended with the coming of the Tyne Improvement Commission, although that in turn was quick to reinvent the custom as a survey and the survey as a ritual, painted in oils.[142]

Tynesiders used to know their river. Keelmen and sailors laboured on it and their aquatic skills were valuable, not least to the Royal Navy. An 1822 'Address to Keelmen' made it clear how important those skills were to the Tyne's

[139] *Tidal Harbour Commission* (1849) pp.13–27; *Bill for Conservancy* (1849): NCL, Bell Collection vol. iv. The River Police was formed to regulate and watch at a rate of farthing per ton shipped: NCL, *Moorings and River Police* (29 August 1844). The deputy harbour master's hat cost 9s 6d: NCL, invoice, Tyne Hat Manufactory, Gateshead, 18 May 1872. For river business and dredging: Lendrum, 'Integrated Elite', in Colls and Lancaster, eds., *Newcastle upon Tyne* (2001) p.30.

[140] Mackenzie, *Newcastle* (1827) vol. i, p.624.

[141] Poster, 'Ascension Day Sports', 23 May 1811: NCL, Bell Collection, vol. ii; Brand, *History* (1789) p.26; *Illustrated London News*, 25 May 1844; *Newcastle Weekly Chronicle*, 12 May 1906; Milne, *North East England* (2006) pp.104–5.

[142] Until it ended as it began, in dispute between rival authorities: *Newcastle Weekly Chronicle*, 12 May 1906. The Tyneside painter Ralph Hedley did a very stately 'Barge Day' in 1891.

prosperity.[143] Thomas Wilson (1792–1860), also known as 'Cuckoo Jack', specialized in the river's lost and found. An expert oarsman, his hooks and scoops opened stagnant corners and found lost items. Newcastle quay used to host the river's old sporting fancy although by 1838, we are told, its 'saunterers' and 'loiterers' preferred the Town Moor.[144]

Professional and amateur rowing races remained popular in spite of all the hammering and drilling. When the Amateur Rowing Association banned workmen rowers in 1878, it only did so because there were so many not because there were so few. It was impossible to imagine a fox-hunting mechanic. On Tyneside, it was all too likely to find a rowing mechanic.[145] Just like the hunting, crowded fields required good manners. River sporting contests raced down protected channels.[146] Section 50 of the Tyne Improvement Act of 1865 required river users to properly position themselves on race days, and a TIC public notice of 1868 laid down right and wrong ways to conduct oneself in river crowds. None of these regulations seem to have hindered Tyneside's champion rowers who competed for large wagers before immense numbers of spectators according to the same rigmarole as prize-fighters.[147] Bob Chambers died in 1868 and a memorial service held in Walker parish church was attended by 'almost the whole of the working class . . . [of] the neighbouring factories with their wives and children . . . a pin might have been heard drop'. When they all trooped out, to the surprise of a lot of finer feelings, not a churchyard flower or shrub went with them. Harry Clasper, cokeburner and 'hero of so many fights' was 'laid in state' (1870) at Whickham parish church by sixty-five rowers slow marching three abreast led by James Renforth, 28-year-old Tyne blacksmith's striker, professional sculler and All England Champion.[148] Renforth himself died the following year in the arms of a comrade while racing for the world championship on the Kennebeccasis in Canada. 'Our Special Reporter'. 'Atlantic Cable'. 'Poor Renforth'. 'Gallant fellow'. 'Dear comrade'. 'Kelley took Renforth's head between his hands and cried bitterly'.[149]

While professional rowers raced down marked channels, the rest of the river was filling up with iron men and sailors from all over the world. In 1880, the Tyne

---

[143] Posters, addresses to keelmen up to 25 November 1822: NCL, Bell Collection, vol. ii.

[144] *Tyne Mercury*, 2 July 1838; *Monthly Chronicle of North Country Lore and Legend*, March 1890.

[145] Allison, *Amateurism in Sport* (2001) p.20. Later, it would be impossible to imagine a gentleman rower racing driver mechanic, although Graham Hill managed it. The world driving champion went to a technical college but drove in his rowing club colours: Hill, *Graham* (1977) pp.14–15.

[146] *Monthly Chronicle of North Country Lore and Legend*, June 1891; posters for regattas and rowing races 1841–48: NCL, Bell Collection, vol. iv.

[147] NCL: TIC *Public Notices* 1865 and *Bye Laws* 1868, vol. i. On Clasper's races with Thames champions see: *Illustrated London News*, 29 November 1845 and *Durham Chronicle*, 26 June 1846.

[148] *Newcastle Daily Chronicle*, 9 June 1868, 18 July 1870. Clasper spoke in honour of Chambers and 'a great rowing river' at the memorial dinner: *Newcastle Daily Chronicle*, 18 August 1869.

[149] There were rumours that he had been poisoned or drugged: *Newcastle Daily Chronicle*, 24 August 1871. Hero stories about these men were still being told on Tyneside in the 1880s: *The Graphic*, 4 June 1881. Holt and Physick see these rowers as 'the first regional sporting heroes with which the people could identify': 'Sport on Tyneside' in Colls and Lancaster, eds., *Newcastle* (2001) p.195.

Improvement Commission published its notices in eight foreign languages and got angry when the local press showed more interest in the rowing than the Russian. Every Friday and Saturday night, Tyneside music hall performed 'The People' in their own voice in their favourite role of sporting hero. Wilson's songbook contained thirty sporting songs while Monday's *Evening Chronicle* bristled with the weekend's sporting results—from proletarian 'aquatics' to quoits, foot-racing, and dogs.[150] In 1880, just before the take-off of modern football, the *Newcastle Journal* was still able to refer to rowing as 'inured in the people'.[151]

It wasn't getting any easier though. Weekend rowing matches continued above bridge where there was less traffic, but what had once been a river with 'wide pastures' and 'high revelry' was turning into a river known only for its smoke and noise.[152] The Armstrong Mitchell Elswick-Walker shipbuilding and engineering works ran along a mile of riverbank. In 1885, W J Palmer only managed to walk that riverbank by relying on 'patches of ground not built upon'. Ten years later R W Johnson supposed 'from Shields to Scotswood, there is not its like in any thirteen miles of river the world over. Ashore, afloat, from end to end...there is everywhere activity, everywhere production'.[153] Harold Mess reckoned that the riverside contained the worst property on Tyneside, even though kids still played there.[154]

In the end the local authorities took a hand in restoring the sporting life to Tynesiders. It is true Shields was a back-breaking town, whatever the weather. And it stayed dirty with an oily river running by, but the ballast hills were eventually levelled, the beaches eventually cleaned, and new parks eventually planted. The *marine* parks, so called, North and South, were especially decorous. Here you could stroll with the pram, play football or bowls, feed the swans, fish for tiddlers, catch the sun, lick an ice cream and listen to the music if not necessarily all at once then at least all in a summer afternoon.

It took the historians a long time before they saw the loss of playgrounds as an historical issue. It took them even longer to see the municipal provision of public

---

[150] 'Wor Geordy's Accoont o' The Great Boat Races Wiv Electrick Tallygraff': NCL, Hayler Cuttings, vol. ii, 16 June 1863; *Newcastle Weekly Leader*, 3 November 1906, and *Newcastle Daily Chronicle*, 29 October 1890; Joe Wilson, *Tyneside Songs* (1873).
[151] *Newcastle Daily Journal*, 10 February 1880. On the river's masts, though soon it would be funnels: Gibson, *Historical Memoir* (1862) p.111. On eight languages: NCL, TIC *Public Notices*, 18 September 1880 'Notice to Sea Captains'. On 'important meetings [that] were crowded out in order that the boat race might be included': NCL, TIC *Proceedings* 14 September 1876 and *Newcastle Daily Chronicle*, 9 June, 28 September 1868. Riverine London sustained a similar plebeian rowing culture and contests between Tyne and Thames were eagerly anticipated. For the full glory of Doggett's Coat and Badge, an annual championship race for Thames watermen, which goes on: Strutt, *Sports and Pastimes* (1801) Book ii, p.156. There is a fine if somewhat refined view of this race at Chelsea by Burney, in YCBA Rare Books and Ms: watercolour, nd, 11 x 16 inches, B2001.2.695.
[152] *The Graphic*, 4 June 1881.
[153] Palmer, *Tyne* (1882) p.271; Johnson, *Making of the Tyne* (1895) p.43.
[154] Mess, *Industrial Tyneside* (1928) p.96.

parks as an historical necessity. It's difficult to say why. It might have been that most academics lived in suburban networks that were not short of places to play or reasons to belong. It might have been to do with a traditional intellectual bias against sport, or a disinclination to see the working class for what it was rather than what it should be.[155] Or it might have been to do with a view of the body as lower than things of the mind. Late in the day, John and Barbara Hammond took the matter up in their *Age of the Chartists* (1930) as 'The Loss of Playgrounds'—praised by G M Trevelyan for laying down 'another layer of truth' about the Industrial Revolution. Later, the leading historian of English landscape would spare no adjectives in his description of defiled and poisoned land. It had been a bleak age indeed when members of parliament could find the loss of sport something to laugh at. 'On the commons, the sports of the village took place (Laughter)', Roebuck told the House. 'They might laugh if they liked; he considered this to be a point of much importance. He liked that the poor should have the right of going on the commons with their wives and families; he liked to go himself... and he did not wish to take away what he enjoyed himself.'[156]

Pointillism

Up in the Pennines, where North and South Tyne joined, the gentry continued to shoot and poor men continued to poach: all in a land of liberty.[157] Down in Leicestershire, ladies and gentlemen continued to ride where they pleased: *fay ce que voudras*. In London and other hard places, men continued to fight for money. In every parish, ways of belonging that involved custom and sport, it is fair to say, were sustained by a popular affection struggling to survive.

Not everything we feel is written down, not everything we know is said, yet nobody could be in any doubt about the Stamford Bullards' point of view. They embodied it in what they did because, like the constitution itself, what they did had to function in order to be recognized and it had to be recognized in order to function.[158] They said it over and over again, in a variety of ways, that the bull-

---

[155] 'Those who are pent up for 10 months a year in a crowd of three million Cockneys, love our remaining playgrounds of fresh air and unenclosed pasture': Leslie Stephen on climbing in the Alps: *Playground of Europe* (1872), quoted in Holt, 'An Englishman in the Alps', *IJHS*, 1992, p.423.

[156] John Arthur Roebuck was MP for Shefield (1859-68, 1874-79), in Hammonds, *Bleak Age* (1947) p.86; Trevelyan, in Lubenow: 'Eminent Victorians', in Taylor and Wolf, eds., *The Victorians* (2004) p.40. *Bleak Age* was a revised version of *Age of the Chartists*. Collini points out that intellectuals were alerted to the problem of sport and liberty not so much by what they found in front of their eyes but by their love of the Ancient World: *Common Writing* (2016) p.188. Hoskins called St Helen's 'the landscape from Hell': *Making of the English Landscape* (1955) p.222.

[157] 'The use of the country for purposes of recreation should not be left to depend entirely upon the good will of a limited class': Hunter, *Open Spaces* (1896) p.vii.

[158] This was Dicey's description of a constitution which he described as 'the fruit not of abstract theory but of that instinct which (it is supposed) has enabled Englishmen... to build up sound and

running honoured them. Had not bulls and bulldogs been national emblems from time immemorial? Had not John Bull's blood and guts won the day a thousand times? Was it not an Englishman's liberty to eat roast beef while the French ate nothing at all?[159]

Patriotism for these people was not something imposed on them from above. On the contrary. Like Marx's 'opium of the people', it was what they had largely created for themselves to meet real needs and desires—the 'soul of a soulless world'. Even nationalist Irishmen understood this trait in the English, just as they above all people understood the deep ties of 'home' that bound it together. When they finally broke with the English in 1918, sport was one of the ways they broke, and parish sport was one of the ways they continued to belong. In 'the greatest single act of defiance outside the purely political sphere', Irishmen gathered on 4 August 1918 to play and watch Gaelic Games without a licence. In 1887 the Gaelic Athletic Association ruled that the clubs of the GAA should be denoted by their parish boundaries.[160]

People understood the annual festive cycle in the here and now, all alive in the mind at once, affirming the lives of those who went before. Landscape affirmed the cycle in time and place. Church and state affirmed the cycle in liturgy and law. Nature and religion affirmed the cycle in resurrection and new life. Had not the Ancients affirmed that we are not here to be forgotten? That we live on? That places matter? That people have distinctive qualities? That the many are not always wrong and that the few (the faction) are not always right? When David Hume talked in favour of 'a regular system of liberty' he was not talking about politics, but precedents.[161] True, the Bullards' rhyming schemes were not of the best. True, sport and animal cruelty often ran together and the Stamford running might have been a shabby example of it. But it was thought wrong to break the circle. Perambulation went round and came round. Place mattered. Not just any place, but the same place. In 2018 Kerry Hudson went back to the town where she'd had a troubled childhood. She walked over to the single rusting goalpost she'd swung from, and touched the cold metal to say thank you for helping her to survive.[162]

Thomas Paine and Karl Marx thought the working class would be the first to see themselves as citizens of the world, not any place in particular.[163] In this they were mistaken. The English idea of liberty fitted not universal principles, but that which counted as custom or, just to be absolutely clear, that which counted, in Sir

---

lasting institutions much as bees construct a honeycomb without undergoing the degradation of understanding the principles on which they raise' it: Dicey, *Law of the Constitution* (1885) p.3.

[159] 'No man can look back on British history without feeling proud . . .', 'Englishmen were never to be slaves': Daniel O'Connell dressed in a suit of green: broadside, 'Visit to Newcastle' (14 September 1835).
[160] Cronin et al, *The GAA* (2009) p.40; De Burca, *GAA* (1999) p.112. It was seen as 'a major act of defiance which linked the GAA to the gathering momentum of radical nationalism': Cronin, ibid p.152.
[161] Burrow, *History of Histories* (2009) p.33, p.94.
[162] Hudson, *Lowborn* (2019) p.114.   [163] Snell, *Parish and Belonging* (2006) p.78.

Edward Coke's definition, as a felony—taking in 'the time, the place, the manner, and the intent'. There could be no custom without the time, the place, the manner, and the intent, and there could be no sport without liberty, something which Blackstone defined as 'the power of locomotion'.[164] Stamford was defeated by outsiders whose feelings did not stretch to see all this as a crucial part of who these people thought they were. Patrick Joyce called this insider-ness *dúchas*—Irish for the attribution of innate environmental qualities in a people.[165] In the old sporting life, every sport carried *dúchas*.[166]

Many came to see that something had been lost. They did not agree on what it was or what to call it, but something was missing and Cobbett and Clare, Disraeli and Marx, Eliot and the Brontes, Dickens, Hardy and D H Lawrence, and many others recognized the change. Thomas Hardy's first novel, *Under the Greenwood Tree* (1872) depicted 'Mellstock' as a place still inhabited by those whose 'long acquaintance with each other's ways...rendered words between them almost superfluous'. Jude's village of 'Marygreen' in *Jude the Obscure* (1895), by contrast, is a place dismembered and thrown to the railway.[167] Jude dies alone in the town.

Joining up fifteen thousand parish dots, all different but the same, is tricky. But it should be clear. Whether running a bull, or kicking a ball, or dancing and singing, or bearing rushes, or marching from Barrowfields to St. Peter's Fields, or sculling down river or *fullicking* on the Forth, there was a time when all these things reminded the people who they were and where they belonged and were part of what Paul Theroux called their vitality. It took a while for them to accept the loss and another while to try to repair it. Sport and custom brought people together and helped them belong.[168] If there was a sense of place, they were it. If custom meant anything, it meant them.

---

[164] Blackstone, *Commentaries* (1820) pp. 33–74. See also: Lobban, *Common Law* (1991) pp.3–4.

[165] Joyce translates dúchas in his essay 'The Journey West', *Field Day Review* (2014) p.16. But the quality was understood in English as well: Jefferies, *Hodge* (1880) on the agricultural labourer 'built up like an oak' p.368, and Holdenby, *Folk* (1913) 'absorbed...quite unwittingly' p.19.

[166] For a fine English example, see the celebration of Joseph Allison, leadminer, local hero, and champion wrestler in Lee, *Wrestling in the North Country* (1953) p.88.

[167] Snell, *Spirits of Community* (2016) p.117–18. In *Jude the Obscure* the chapters come like stations: 'At Marygreen', 'At Christminster', 'At Melchester', 'At Shaston', 'At Aldbrickham and Elsewhere'. Gatrell calls *Jude* a railway novel: 'Wessex', in Kramer ed., *Cambridge Companion* (2005) p.29.

[168] 'The parish, it seems, is the perfect size for a successful moral community': Giles Fraser, *The Guardian*, 26 May 2017.

6

New Moral Worlds

...let no one write Latin Humbug or English either over my bones.

(Diary of Edward Thring, 1859)

Cricketers

Consider how the boys in the photograph shown in Figure 6.1 stand.[1] They do not present themselves as a team. They do not look like cricketers. They do not look like cricket teams will come to look—all grinning to camera.[2] On the contrary, they line up more or less as they please and although it will be another thirty years before cricketers dress in whites, these boys are dedicated followers of fashion nevertheless: straw hat or peaked cap, bow tie or 'Eton collar', tail coat buttoned at the top to show waistcoat beneath. One boy sports a bold cavalry stripe down his trousers. Towards the end of the nineteenth century, public schools such as Uppingham, and team games such as cricket, became part of the new moral world of the British Empire.[3] But this photograph shows a moment just before that world began. These are young gentlemen at play rather than imperialists on a mission. Boys are the masters here.

From left to right we have: Edward Solbe (it says 'Selby' on the back of the photograph), 16 years old, cross-over single fastening jacket and bow tie, cap in hand, son of a local clergyman. He went on to join the diplomatic corps in China. Next to him is Horace Stafford O'Brien, gentleman's son, of Tixover Grange, also local, also 16, also single fastening and bow, wearing the German blue-peaked cap recently introduced into the School by the headmaster and his wife. Next to him, Marmaduke Athorpe, son of J C Athorpe of Dinnington Hall, Rotherham, 15,

---

[1] Uppingham School Archive & Library [USAL] photograph album.

[2] Arms folded, front row seated, all beaming to camera became the standard pose for teams including professionals, but for early signs of the shift from loungers to grinners compare, for example, the Uppingham School 1st cricket XI in 1877 with the School 1st football XI in 1897: USAL photograph album. For the revolution in presenting oneself for portraiture, see Colin Jones, *The Smile Revolution* (2014) pp.178–80.

[3] 'Heroes of the Cricket Field', *The Young Men*, December 1900. How to welcome African students to a garden party: poster, Colwyn Bay, 31 July 1899: John Johnson, Bodleian, Sport Box 6. The first Indian cricket tour to England was in 1911. Some historians have called cricket 'a hegemonic cultural form': Bateman, 'Cricket, Literature and Empire', *International Journal of Regional and Local Studies* 2, 2005, p.63. The first Australian cricket tour to England in 1868 was 'Aboriginal': Mallett, *The Cricketer*, December 1997.

Fig. 6.1 Uppingham School Cricketers (1858): Uppingham School Archive and Library

a School praeposter (or prefect), wearing a straw 'boater' redolent of that other sport of rowing as most famously celebrated at Eton. Eton College, in fact, is one of the schools these cricketers would most love to emulate.

Next to Athorpe is Thomas Frederick Fowler, 17, of Huntingdon, cap pulled low, eyes straight down, quality coat, flash waistcoat, trousers tight, hands thrust defiantly in pockets. Soon, all English schoolboys would be told to keep their hands out of their pockets and Uppingham would instruct that trouser pockets be sewn up. But Thomas Fowler, we learn, is not only a cricketer, he's a 'blood', also known to his peers as 'The Man', someone who is pre-eminent in sport and fashion. As an Uppingham 'Satire on Bloods' for 1907 had it: 'Your coat, alas! Must be of sombre black/Yet let it have a slit up the back'.[4]

There were sartorial bloods and there were sporting bloods and usually it was the sporting bloods ('before whom the lesser fry burnt incense') who came top dog.[5] Mr. Fowler would go on to get his blue at Cambridge but before that he distinguished himself at Uppingham by getting expelled.

---

[4] On coats, Uppingham School Magazine, 335, xiv, July 1907: USAL. On pockets, House Rule 3, Uppingham School Guide Book (1870) p.20: USAL. One boy remembered how boys in the 1860s would modify the School cap's 'oppressively Teutonic aspect' with a stitch or two: Patterson, *Sixty Years* (1909) pp.18–19.

[5] Rome, History (Ts 1950) p.132: USAL.

Headmaster Rev. Edward Thring (sitting, front) described the reason for Fowler's expulsion as his part in a system of 'organized hypocrisy and profligacy' with written instructions on how to deceive masters. But Thring did not elaborate on what this boy, together with another boy, Williams, had got up to. 'Bloods' like them were in the habit of going down Uppingham High Street linking arms and one thing you could be sure of, they never went quietly.[6] Fowler's parents fought the expulsions with 'baffled malice', said Thring. Either way, in or out, hard luck or poor judgement, the Head raised his index finger and young Fowler, the blood, The Man, had to walk.[7]

Next to him stands John Henry Green, at 19, oldest boy in the School and captain of cricket. This Green is not to be confused with C E Green, only 12, recently arrived, and destined to become one of Uppingham's all-time sporting heroes after pulverizing the Rossall bowling in 1863.[8] 'J H', on the other hand, 'a very good looking boy' according to Patterson, went on to be the founding Captain and President of Uppingham Rovers, one of the best amateur touring sides in the country. And here he is, in all his pomp, blood brother to Fowler on his right and head boy to Thring on his left. After a 3rd in History at Wadham, he went on to become Rector of Knaptoft and Mowsley.

Next to Thring stands Rev. Walter Earle, cap in hand looking like a servant but otherwise dressed the same as the Head and recently persuaded by him to build a school house out on the London Road. Earle looks out of place: as if he has been told to 'stand there'.

Peering over Earle's shoulder is Theodore Bell, age 18, captain of football and the man with that year's best bowling average. 'Untiring and cheerful' according to our memorialist, 'Dory' Bell went on to be a solicitor in Epsom and kept in touch with his old school. Five years later he would be one of the founders of the Football Association.[9]

Theodore Wicks sits in front of Bell seemingly impervious to Earle standing in front of him. Son of Mr. C Wicks of Cherry Hinton, Cambridge, young Wicks left later that year, as did Edward Moore standing next to him. Moore came from Spalding, he was 14 years old, and it says on the back that the photograph belongs to him. On the end of the line in Eton collar and short cut jacket is Edward Willis, 15, leaning easily on his friend, the impervious Mr. Wicks. Son of Rev. T Willis of Cuckfield in Sussex, after an Uppingham Exhibition and Mods at Balliol, he went on to join the Oxford University Mission in Calcutta.

---

[6] School Guide Book for 1870 ruled that boys must walk no more than two abreast (p.21): USAL.

[7] Thring's Diary, 30 May, 1 June 1859: USAL. On Fowler and all the boys mentioned here: Uppingham School Roll 1853–1947: USAL.

[8] Details of match and innings ('tall Vividar' in 'An Antient Legende') given in School Magazine, June 1863. Charles Ernest Green was a founding member of the Uppingham cricket cult.

[9] Bell attended the first meeting of the FA on 26 October 1863 in Lincoln's Inn Fields, on behalf of Surbiton Football Club. Twelve years on, we find him playing fives with Thring against the School. They lost: Parkin, *Thring: Life, Diary, Letters* (1900) p.187; Patterson, *Sixty Years* (1909) p.19.

Did these boys see themselves as English sporting heroes? Not like they saw Tom Sayers as an English sporting hero, or the master of the Cottesmore. But the time would come when public schools would so expand in numbers and significance that many would come to see public school cricket as synonymous with an English golden age.[10] John Graham went to Uppingham in the 1880s and learned its sporting myths by heart, including the story of the Cambridge University XI that once fielded five Uppingham OBs. In 1950 *The Times* wondered how long the cricketing myths could last—the one they had in mind was the incomparable 1902 MCC Test team to Australia ('to us in this country no names even sound so sweet') now long gone. John Wolfenden, former headmaster, normally very level, swore that it was at Uppingham that he saw one of the finest games of rugby 'ever seen by man'. *By man!* Organized sport at Uppingham became so important that exclusion from games was a punishment, not a privilege.[11]

Whatever this is, it is not a photograph of imperial mastery. The boys are unsmiling because in 1858 camera exposure took too long to hold a smile, and anyway who would they smile for? Not a mere photographer. This is a picture of boys together in the knowledge that they are men of a similar caste, blood and captain at their heart. Thring looks genial enough, even if he knows by now that dealing with boys like these can be wearing.

Thring of Uppingham

He had arrived at Uppingham in 1853 on a paltry £150 a year, plus house and servants. His job was to run a school containing twenty-five scholars who sat on wooden forms while two masters sat in chairs at either end of the hall instructing them in Latin and Greek. Founded in 1584 jointly with Oakham School, the hall was the school. When they were not in it, the boys played games and roamed around.

The new headmaster had a few ideas but no real teaching experience. Cambridge followed Eton followed by a curacy in Gloucester in 1847 where, after five months and a bit of school mastering, he suffered some sort of nervous breakdown.[12] Returning to occasional private tutoring in 1849, he took up light church duties in 1851 relieved by a grand European tour in 1852 where he met his future wife, Marie, in Bonn.[13] The following year, age 32, he took up his post in a

---

[10] See for instance sermons by the bishops of Oxford, Carlisle, Manchester and Bedford at Uppingham's 300th anniversary, Uppingham Tercentenary (1884): USAL.

[11] School Guide Book (1870) p.23. Graham, *Forty Years* (1932) p.28, p.13; *The Times*, 14 September 1950; Wolfenden, *Turning Points* (1976) p.84.

[12] Parkin is vague about how much teaching Thring did in Gloucester. Thring himself says 'almost daily', and later talks about teaching 'a class' of 'little labourers' sons': Parkin, *Thring* (1900) p.48.

[13] Matthews, *By God's Grace* (1984) pp.74–8.

market town of 2,000 people in England's smallest county. Uppingham Grammar School was just off the market square. The railway had recently arrived a couple of miles away at Manton, raising Thring's hopes for an expansion in numbers even though the school trustees had other ideas. He walked prospective parents back to the station with his dog.

Thring's first diary entry, 11 April 1854, expresses modest hopes in a neat hand. Although his household servants remain 'infamous', he says, and the house is still in need of repair, he has just scored fifteen runs with the boys and we find him

> A most happy husband just ending the first quarter of the first school term of our married life . . . somewhat settled after the bustle of furnishing and the still greater annoyances of a disorganized household. Engaged in honourable work and prospering in it, may God give us strength to do his will gallantly . . . What great work Education is, how one ought to look carefully to the result of all one does especially the punishment inflicted, and not merely to consider what is deserved but what is good.'If all got their deserts who'd escape whipping?' May God keep our hearts fresh and childlike and not let them be hardened by the vexations which must happen. Boys mean well on the whole . . . [14]

After that, entries suddenly cease. When he returns to the brass locked volume the entry is wrongly dated '1859', the handwriting has collapsed into a wide-eyed scrawl, and there is a warning as if from the grave that

> If any of this is ever published let it not be by any child of mine but by some good impartial man who will understand the general impression, without doing injustice by producing the crude and often mistaken ideas that go to form that impression. Neither Nettleship nore Skrine must do it. From different reasons they do not understand.

> Let no one write Latin Humbug or English either over my bones. No word of praise or blame if they love me.

Here began Edward Thring's record of all who did not love him: 'this cross' he had to bear; this 'heavy burden', this 'care, care' against all the 'attacks' of 'venomous' and 'sordid' enemies.[15] After his death, all but two of his diaries were burned by his biographer Parkin at the behest of Mrs. Thring, but the two volumes that did survive, the first and the last, testify to a deeply neurotic man.[16] One day he could feel 'deeply the peace of . . . divine aid' and be happy. The next day he could 'hate

---

[14] Diary, 11 April 1854.

[15] Comments recorded in diary entries December 1858 to December 1859.

[16] The 20 December 1858 diary entry is a long and impassioned retrospective where Thring claims he came to the School in 1853 with clear and principled plans for a completely new vision only to be confronted by bigotry. Information about the burning of the diaries was provided by Mr. Jerry

this life' for the most trifling reason ('Hodgkinson having taken offence at my thinking of another man as secretary of our Committee').[17] In 1858 Thring says he does not want to be a great headmaster. In 1862 he shows he isn't by flogging two boys for having a pea-shooter.[18] In the cricket photograph he may look like one of the boys—favourite hat and huge bow tie—but we know that he had boy rebellions on his hands in 1853 and 1855 which were followed by conflicts on all fronts in 1858 and 1859, with more parental battles in 1861–62, and sniping, tittle tattle and mounting debt well into the 1870s even though he thought he had finally cleared his debts in 1866 except for £600 he owed his father. In 1859 we find him in total 'despair'. In 1860 he thinks the School has had a 'wonderful' year. In 1861 he is 'utterly crippled' by worry. In 1865 he is at war with all the boys, or thinks he is. In 1872 all the masters are for him. In 1873 they are all against him. In 1874 after a parental meeting in the town hotel about typhoid, one parent tells Thring's favourite housemaster Hodgkinson that both he and the headmaster are 'murderers'. Only the year before, with the vanquishing of Haileybury at cricket, Thring thought he had a triumph on his hands but woe of woes he found the team toasting their victory with claret. This immensely small breach of rules took the headmaster to the brink: 'one of the most utter acts of treason', 'betrayal of trust by leaders', 'deliberate lying', 'very grievous', 'I really don't know what to do'.[19]

The truth is, although Thring was buried (1887) with full school honours and a statue (1892) depicting him as a deeply loved man, he never stopped battling with the boys against what he saw as their disobedient and impure lives. When he tried to fit latches to the outside of seniors' study doors, they called it a 'loss of privilege' and a 'degradation'.[20] What can we make of that? Whether a battle over privacy or secrecy, it was certainly a power struggle between him and them. In 1855 Thring lost almost everything by 'degrading' his praeposters after they had failed to put down card playing—a poisonous little tussle which left him trying to cane a senior boy who refused to kneel.

I told him to kneel, he hesitated. I took out my watch [and] gave him two minutes and if before that time he had not knelt he would return to his father's with my servant by the next train. Down he went and was flogged.[21]

Rudman, School Archivist, 24 July 2017. The two volumes that survived are for 1854–62 and 1886–87. Parkin's *Life* (1900) chooses selectively from these and dates in between.

[17] Diary, 3 October 1861.   [18] Diary, 18 February 1862; 20 December 1858.
[19] In 1872 the masters signed a manifesto celebrating Uppingham as 'virtually a new foundation and Mr Thring the founder': Tozer, 'Physical Education', Leicester MEd (1974) p.141. The other quotations are all from Parkin's *Diary* entries (1900) year on year.
[20] Old Boy, *Early Days* (1904) p.79.   [21] Diary, 20 December 1858.

Without the support of the older boys, Thring could not be the great man he wanted to be: the man who made you tremble, the man who stunned you to silence, the man who gave you his all.[22] As Uppingham's cricket improved and with it the School's prestige as a 'great' (his favourite adjective) 'School' (he dropped 'Grammar' from the name in 1866), he came to fear the emergence of young cricketing bloods as rivals to his authority. Young Green should have been captain of cricket long before 1864. He had played for the First XI age 13 in 1859 and went on to captain Cambridge, play for various England teams, and preside over the MCC, but at Uppingham, a school of 235 boys, Thring blocked his captaincy because at the time he was at war with the cricket seniors. Later, when the England professional Heathfield Harman Stephenson came to the School on Green's advice, and Uppingham quickly moved to the top of the Lillywhite rankings, and the captain of cricket got his blue jacket to go with his silk scarf, Thring was still ever watchful and his cane ever bent.[23] It took him nine years to accept Stephenson, and even then he refused to put him on the books. Boys paid instead.[24]

Early in his tenure the School Trustees had kept Thring waiting at the door 'dangling like a servant' and he never forgave them for that.[25] In his very last diary entry, they seem to be the only people in England who did not realize they had a national hero on their hands:

> ...nice bit of Trusteedom today. I had sent in a bill of £60 which I have already paid myself for repairs done in the School House. They have returned it to me by their Clerk with a note [saying]...that it is rejected as some of the items are private. I believe on looking it over that there is 6 to 8 pounds private [and] of course this was wrong. But to think of the blackguard way in which they dealt with the oversight—I only wish I had half the money I have spent on the House.[26]

In order to drive up school numbers (in order to drive down financial reliance on the Trust), Thring recruited masters who were willing to sink their own money into a school that could earn its keep by board and lodging. Surrendering his sole right to take boarders, he saw the appointment of Robert Hodgkinson, Old Etonian friend and fellow investor, as a key strategic move—lifting the 'crushing weight' of another master, Blakiston, 'a canker' who along with a lot of other

[22] Old Boy, *Early Days* (1904) pp.149–51.
[23] Patterson, *Sixty Years* (1909) pp.21–2. Stephenson captained the first England tour of Australia December 1861 to March 1862.
[24] Tozer, *Magnetism of Thring* (2016) pp.20–2.
[25] Uppingham was a joint foundation. The Trustees adminstered Robert Johnson's 1584 charity to the tune, in Thring's time, of over £3,000 per year.
[26] Diary, 15 October 1887; and 20 December 1858, 5 November, 22 December 1859, and Tozer, 'Physical Education', MEd (1974) pp.130–41.

people had 'reduced me and our system to the brink of ruin'.[27] Thring acquired
Lorne House in 1856 and refurbished it as a model investment. Baverstock,
another old Etonian pal, built West Deyne in 1859. Hodgkinson built Old
Constables in the same year, and The Lodge in 1868. Walter Earle, the man in
the photograph, built Brooklands on London Road in 1860. School rolls hit the
300 mark by the early 1870s, by which time housemasters owned over 90 per cent
of school assets.[28]

During these years Thring seems to have been everywhere all at once. Recalling
his own dismal experience as a boy at Ilminster ('prison morality'), and Eton
('great, bare, dirty'), he walked Uppingham every evening bidding goodnight to
every chamber.[29] His day started when first bell rang at 6, second bell at 6.30, and
address to the assembled School at 7am. Once, when he was a few seconds late for
assembly, he told the praeposters on the door to shut it in his face so that he
should wait along with other malingerers.[30] In 1861, Mr. Mrs. Thring were so
preoccupied by their heavy duties that they failed to notice that their maid was
pregnant. She gave birth in the kitchen during the night and Thring made it his
business in the morning to pack the father ('a little lad of seventeen') off on the
train and take mother and baby round to the workhouse. He thought it was a
terrible affliction for them both. But by God's grace he and his wife would see it
through.[31]

In 1876 Thring took the whole school away for a year to save it from a local
typhoid epidemic. This was a decisive action both for the boys' health and the
school's reputation. Three hundred beds left Uppingham for Borth on the Welsh
coast and, such was his growing authority, 297 boys turned up to sleep in them.[32]

He got more and more of his own way but never all of it. He knew from his Eton
days that 'boys' side'—that is, the boys' liberty to give and gather consent, to levy
resources, and make sport—was a far more real experience of a school than
anything the masters could know or make happen. He praised Eton for its
freedom, but at the same time knew that 'a mob of boys cannot be educated'
and blamed Thomas Arnold at Rugby for weakness in the face of them. He
thought, for instance, that Arnold had not been a great headmaster because his
historic compromise with the senior boys was based on their personal devotion to
him rather than to the school itself. 'A school may enshrine [an] individual in their

[27] Diary, 20 December 1858.
[28] Tozer, 'Physical Education', MEd (1974) p.48; Matthews, *By God's Grace* (1984) p.96; Metcalfe,
Uppingham (1995) pp.23–9; Oliver Hill File, notes by Belk: USAL. Parkin estimated that Thring had
raised school income from £1,000 pa to £10,000 and feared that the Public School Act of 1868 would
interfere: *Thring* (1900) p.149.
[29] Parkin, *Thring* (1900) pp.23–4.
[30] '...go on, go on and shut the door': letter of Arthur Hawley to Mr. Bothamley, 1 November
1948: USAL.
[31] Diary, 21 November 1861.   [32] Shipton, History Notes (2001): USAL.

hearts' Thring told himself, but 'there are times when a man must build his ship as well as be able to command her'.[33] Before any cult of the personality, he wanted 'a good strong system set on foot'. In the event, he made his own relationship with the older boys and was not averse to a bit of hero worship, but, right up until his final years, it was always touch and go and no one, least of all him, doubted that he would be the first to go if his venture failed. He said he felt 'banged about' by the demands of creating an institution that he wanted to use to reshape human nature. As well he might. His diary comment of 1865 was directed at his own unhappiness but it might just as easily have been directed at the boys'. Note the factory analogy.

I get quite puzzled as to the moral effect of all this...how far the unconscious character is shaped for good whilst one thinks one is simply being banged about is as unknown to the man himself as the same sort of thing must be to the wool which is flung in at one end of a machine, carded, torn, worried, washed, entangled, disentangled, pulled, squeezed, thumped in the darkness, and comes out cloth at the other end. I hope this is so.[34]

When he died in 1887, Thring's Uppingham comprised over three hundred boys, a corps of committed masters, nine boarding houses, two workshops, one sanatorium, one laboratory, one indoor pool (heated), one big field, some small rented fields, a School Magazine, a School Song 'Ho, boys ho!' (lyrics by the Headmaster), lots of braid and a neo-Gothic campus with more dead-weight buildings in the offing.[35] That he came to raise the standing of the School is not in doubt. But the point is that Edward Thring, a man of no real experience, was powered to do this by a broad Church culture interested in reconfiguring public schools as new moral worlds.[36]

Tom Brown

Thomas Hughes' *Tom Brown's Schooldays*, published in 1857, was a product of that culture, and exercised an immense influence on the middle-class public imagination. Hughes had attended Rugby under Thomas Arnold's headship. Tom Brown, who does the same, arrives as 'the commonest type of English boy' and leaves as a new type of English hero.

---

[33] Diary, 20 December 1858. On liberty and the mob: Parkin, *Thring* (1900) p.18, p.23.
[34] Parkin, ibid, p.131.
[35] A later headmaster would come to reflect on how the School 'dangerously underrated' the psychological impact of its architecture 'within and without the system': J P W M, 'A New Campus' (June 1967); 'Songs of Uppingham School' (nd): USAL.
[36] Chandler, 'Emergent Athleticism', *IJHS*, 1988, p.312.

Brought up in the Vale of the White Horse, young Tom comes from a land of heroes. Was not this where Alfred won the Battle of Ashdown? Are not its parish 'veasts' (wakes) the oldest in the land? It doesn't matter that Tom is gentry, and it doesn't matter that he casts off an old England in order to find a young one—these native things can never be forgotten. Village boys teach Tom how to wrestle.

Hughes thought parish life was breaking up in his native Berkshire just as Butterworth thought it was breaking up in his native Lancashire. Farmers were going off to be gentlemen and gentlemen were going off to be 'cosmopolites'. The wakes were dying out and, without the protection of their customs and liberties, the people were being ground down. Very early in the story, Tom's narrator ('An Old Boy') says industrial England needs a new 'spirit'—'some *bona fide* equivalent for the games of the old country, something spirited to put in place of the back-swording and wrestling and racing'. 'In all the new fangled comprehensive plans which I see, this is all left out'.[37]

After a rip-roaring ride through hunting country, Tom arrives for his first day at Rugby. He has hardly got down from the coach when he is pressed into a football match where he finds himself in the House's thin front line against the rest of the School.[38] Suddenly, Rugby is Thermopylae and Tom is a Spartan. Greatness is about to engulf him: great fields, great captains, great elms, great hall, great fires, great beef-joints, great beards, and above all, the great Dr. Arnold, who sees all.

Except he doesn't. For all his gifts, the great headmaster cannot see into the boys' side of school life. He cannot see, for example, how Tom and his friend East have been thrown into a large and disgruntled lower 4th who are being unlawfully exploited (that is, 'fagged', or made to do an older boy's bidding) by a renegade 5th form led by weak bloods and the venal Flashman. A timid ruling class (masters and 6th form) are turning a blind eye. With the departure of Brooke, strong man of the House, School House in 1834 is deprived, like the English people are deprived, of their 'lawful masters and protectors'.[39]

Here is one class struggle that Karl Marx missed. Tom and East move from the role of Greek hoplites in a football match to English trade unionists in a labour dispute and end up leading a strike against the unlawful exploiters, which they win, and beat up Flashman, which they enjoy. After a moment of hubris involving a second class struggle, this time with an overbearing local landowner, Tom and East learn the non-Marxist but entirely Christian Socialist lesson that sometimes the best victories are over yourself.

At this point, having fought for his liberty like all Englishmen must, Tom finds a pretty young wife called Arthur and retires to the suburbs. Which is to say, he

---

[37] Hughes, *Tom Brown's Schooldays* (1857) pp.41–2.
[38] Tom sits up top of the coach and endures, like Englishmen do, and eats at an old hunting inn, sporting prints everywhere, where the tables can hardly bear the weight of the roasts: Hughes, *Tom Brown's Schooldays* (1857) p.76. Football match (p.123).
[39] ibid, p.167.

finds the nearest Hughes could find for womanly influence in a story about boys, and settles down to regular meals and friendship in the boys' side of school life. Arthur is a 'slightly pale boy with blue eyes and light fair hair'. During the day, Tom goes round the school 'blowing off steam' while Arthur (the Little Eva of English literature) appears to stay at home preparing the food. They share supper time together. Please note: there is no sex in this book just as there was no sex in the English public school.[40] Always a blood at heart, but much steadier now, Tom begins a deep transformation. He starts saying his prayers. He stops using cribs. He joins the headmaster's supporters. East, who is boys' side to the last is not impressed ('My sympathies are all the other way'), but he and Tom remain friends.[41]

Now the novel moves to dramatic crisis. Hughes has to show how an old blood can become a new blood but not lose his liberty, his courage, his love of custom, or his sense of belonging. This is the moral heart of the story, which Hughes shows not by having Tom go over to something high-minded and spiritual, but by putting him (of all places) in the prize ring. Tom has led the boys to victory, only to go over to the suburban life with Arthur. He must remain, however, a true Englishman willing 'to box and run and row'.[42]

Enter 'Slogger' Williams. Williams reckoned himself 'King of the form'. This includes a bit of bullying and when it is Arthur who is being bullied, Tom steps in. Fight? *Fight*. '"Fight!" Fight!"' 'The news ran like wildfire'. 'Huzza there's going to be a fight between Slogger Williams and Tom Brown!' And so there was.

Slogger is keen to get on with it. Off with jacket, waistcoat, braces. Handkerchief for a sash, shirtsleeves rolled up, East for a handler, Martin for a knee, ready steady heart pounding time to listen to your corner. 'Now old boy, don't you open your mouth to say a word...we'll do all that...keep all your breath and strength'. Slogger, it must be said, is much bigger, a year older, and peels well in the old *Bell's Life* parlance (all arms and shoulders). But lo and behold he is 'shipwrecky about the knees' and we are reminded not only of Entellus' dodgy knees but Bill Neate's dodgy knees. We are reminded, indeed, that boxing is a literary taste.[43]

Not just Williams' knees, the prize ring itself in 1857 was in very bad shape. No longer acknowledged as the nursery of English heroes and three years before Sayers Heenan, why does Hughes put Tom in there? Because he is taking old English fighting qualities and pitting them in defence of the innocent. Gentlemen

---

[40] Hughes voiced his opposition to what he called 'small friend systems' in boarding schools, and appeared to blame those boys, 'the worst sort we breed', who get 'petted' and spoilt for 'everything in this world and the next': ibid, pp.235–6, p.233. 'Little Eva', or Evangeline St. Clare, was an angelic character in Harriet Beecher Stowe's best-selling novel of 1852, *Uncle Tom's Cabin*.

[41] Hughes, *Tom Brown's Schooldays* (1857) p.338.

[42] And in so doing launched 10,000 school sports stories: ibid, p,42. Hughes had no doubt they were living in times of 'the advent to power of the great body of the people' (p.xxiv).

[43] Attributed to George Bernard Shaw. For classical and neo-classical ring references, see chapter 3 'Bottom'.

still need their liberty and bottom of course, but the new moral world of the public school gives them virtue as well.

Thirty minutes into the fight, Williams is blowing hard and taking hits while Tom is running away with it. He throws Slogger with a trick he learned in the Vale. Then the fight stops as quickly as it started because word is out that the rozzers are on their way. Enter Dr Arnold. This is fair, if not quite *que voudrais faire*. It's not cricket either, the true character-sport of the new moral world.[44] But it *is* fought out, with rules, and reason, not a penny changing hands and with a handshake at the end. Slogger is a man and a brother after all. When Tom leaves Rugby for Oxford and nearly gets thrashed by town roughs, he is frightened not because he is afraid but because he is appalled.[45]

His heroism was not all the school's doing. Hughes' message is that Arnold's Rugby kept boys' side open while bringing it onside for truth. And because Tom feels personally responsible for this new moral gentlemanliness, it is a far keener thing than anything a blood could sport, though a blood he remains. Whatever Thring was going through at Uppingham in 1857, in Tom Brown and Thomas Arnold he had the new model boy and the new model master. The life of schools, no less than the life of individuals, is lived largely in the imagination.[46]

Clarendon and Taunton

Four years after publication of *Tom Brown's Schooldays*, a Royal Commission was set up to investigate the revenues and management of Eton College, probably the most prestigious school in the country.[47] The Commission asked Eton 9,621 questions but broadened its remit to investigate nine hand-picked named 'public schools' and the education of rich young men in general.[48]

W E Gladstone, a Clarendon commissioner, made their problem plain:

We are all in danger of timidity in dealing with the work of reform, because the abuses that exist are so bound up with private interests, and because...it is our habit in this country to treat private interests with an extravagant tenderness...

---

[44] Cricket is 'more than a game', it is a boy's 'birthright', and something that 'merges the individual'. The novel ends with Tom, age 19, Captain of the First XI playing 'Lords men', hard hitters straight out of *Bell's* who win narrowly. They invite Tom to join them and his transformation is assured: ibid, p.346, p.354.

[45] Holt, 'Public School Literature', Oxford DPhil (2006) p.70, p.106.

[46] A remark about the life of nations made by the British politician Enoch Powell: quoted in Nairn, *Break-Up of Britain* (1981) p.266.

[47] In response to an anonymous article in the *Edinburgh Review* 230, April 1861.

[48] Clarendon schools (not their foundational names) were Winchester (1382), Eton (1440), Charterhouse (1611), St. Paul's (1509), Shrewsbury (1552), Westminster (1560), Merchant Taylors' (1561), Rugby (1567), and Harrow (1572). The 1868 Public Schools Act applied to boarding schools only, thus excluding St. Paul's and Merchant Taylors'.

[but] the truth is that all laxity in dealing with what in a large sense is certainly public property approximates more or less to dishonesty... the amount of work we get out of the boys at our public schools, speaking of the mass of them, is scandalously small.[49]

Boys were under-taught and under-supervised. At Radley, they were under-fed.[50] Having usurped their original charters, the schools had grown just as they wished. Winchester's Warden and Fellows for instance, titular appointments mainly, took half College income.[51] All schools suffered periodic outbreaks of disorder. In 1845, Eton abandoned its annual river riot, 'Montem' (the year after Thring had been its Captain), and in 1855, it abandoned its annual triangular Lords match with Harrow and Winchester. A rowdy week of cricket in London was more than the schools could stand.[52] Mesmerized by its 'two fold cult of sport and soldiership', Henry Salt remembered life at Eton as life *Among the Savages* (1921), while William Golding's *Lord of the Flies* (1954) probed how far the savagery could go.[53]

The Clarendon Commission reported in 1864, and the Taunton Commission followed in 1868 with a report into 782 other fee-paying 'endowed schools'. The joint result of these two commissions—the Public School Act of 1868 and the Endowed School Act of 1869—gave schools the liberty to build again. Key features included new governing bodies, new powers of admission in order to boost boarding and fee income, and new executive authority granted to a new generation of headmasters and headmistresses.

Thus, for example, Rev. Dr. Robert Poole (Rugby, University College Oxford, formerly master at Clifton) was appointed headmaster of Bedford Modern in 1877. To the boys, he was 'Guvvie', 'the Chief', 'the Old Man', 'the Doctor'—the man who promised change while at the same time, in his own words, promising them the right 'to carry on the School among themselves as their own commonwealth and republic'. To the governors, he was committed to making Bedford in the image of better and older schools—his own experiences at Arnold's Rugby and Percival's Clifton College Bristol figured strongly. To the parents, he represented the best a modern school could be. 'Big School' was opened in 1881with great chair, gallery, and organ. To the wider civil society, Poole promised an

---

[49] Clarendon Commission, Appendix ii, PP 1864, vol. xx, p.42.

[50] Boyd, *Radley* (1948) p.87. Boys sat in forms. Prefects kept order. Shocking revelations at Bowes Academy in 1823 showed how schools could keep their secrets—a Court of Common Pleas case which Dickens used for his indictment of nasty boys' schools in *Nicholas Nickleby* (1838).

[51] Custance, ed., *Winchester* (1982) p.353. See also: Moody, *Winchester College* (1820) pp.18–20.

[52] Clarendon Commission, PP 1864, xx, p.68. Lords cricket: Leach, *Winchester College* (1899) p.444. See also Leach for examples of riots (pp.396–425). 1797 was a lively year right across schools: Hilton, *Mad Bad* (2006) p.466. Thring's Montem excesses cost his father a small fortune, £640: Parkin, *Thring* (1900) pp.29–39.

[53] Golding taught at two ancient grammar schools and, having 'lived for many years with small boys', reckoned he knew them with 'awful precision': Sandbrook, *Dream Factory* (2016) p.344. Salt, *Seventy Years Among the Savages* (1921) p.16.

experiment in human development, for 'those things which were thrown open to the whole of the English nation ought not to be confined to any special or privileged classes'.[54]

Clarendon made thirty-two recommendations designed to turn a small set of in-grown institutions into an elite network of largely boarding establishments popularly known as public schools, each charged with educating a rising number of privileged young men destined to hold key positions in government, the civil service, the military, the empire, the church, the universities, and all the usual institutions, though less so in business.[55] By the turn of the century, a number of pioneering girls' schools had joined them, though their prospectuses, like their fee income, were generally more modest. As Cardwell did with the army, Clarendon and Taunton did with the schools: they removed an inherent propensity for failure.

In his final report, Clarendon gently thanked the schools for 'the obligations which England owes them', asked that they should 'be treated with the utmost tenderness', and promptly dismissed them as effective makers of men.[56] The commissioners did not stint in their criticisms of the *ancien regime*, even though they thanked it for keeping faith with the classical languages, and for serving the national character by leaving the boys free to follow their 'love of healthy sports and exercises'.[57] Stone throwing not included.[58] And as well as the enabling Acts of 1868 and 1869, reforming headmasters had at their disposal the towering reputation of Arnold, his former pupils and those who imagined they had been his former pupils, plus the entrepreneurial opportunities afforded by a rapidly expanding market in middle-class manners. Acting on all this supply and demand, and driven by a desire to emulate as much as to innovate, headmasters and headmistresses (both soon to emerge as key social figures) reinvented the idea of 'the school' for the world.

[54] Underwood, *Bedford Modern* (1981) pp.50–1.

[55] Not least the key position of First Lord of the Treasury. Out of fifty-five Prime Ministers up to 2019, thirty-eight were educated at public school, thirty-three at Eton, Harrow, or Westminster. See report from the Social Mobility Commission reported in *The Guardian* 31 October 2017. By 1916, 60 per cent of cabinet ministers had been to public school, 34.7 per cent of them to Eton. By 1914 only 18 per cent top businessmen had been to public school, and only 3.6 per cent to one of the Clarendon nine: Berghoff, 'Public Schools and the Decline of the British Economy', *Past & Present* 129, 1990, pp.148–9, pp.156–8.

[56] Clarendon Commission, PP 1864, xx, p.56.   [57] ibid.

[58] Harrow schoolboys had stone fights with navvies working on the London and North-Western Railway. Preston Grammar schoolboys had stone fights with neighbouring factory children: Mangan, *Athleticism* (2000) p.31, and Recollections of Samuel Leach, P160/2: LaRO. Organized sport is hardly mentioned in school prospectuses. Eton in 1796 had Mr. Angelo for fencing and Mr. Slingsby for dancing, but no mention of anyone, or anything, for games: John Johnson, Bodleian, Education Box 1. See also Harvey, 'Evolution', Oxford DPhil (1996) who says public schools were 'almost without… effect' in their impact on sport until the second half of the nineteenth century (p.415).

Building 'The Wall'

According to their flowery crests and latin tags, the schools had been there forever. There's a photograph of Worksop College dining hall, taken about 1910, that looks like it was built for a strange masculine cult. The ceiling is so high you expect the cawing of crows. The walls fall away from a great height. The tables are heavy with plate.[59] On the edge of Clumber Park, it's hard not to think of ancient warriors eating here.[60] Taunton had criticized the siting of so many ancient foundations as 'ugly without and dingy within'.[61] In the second half of the century, huge efforts went into the rebuilding of schools, usually in neo-Gothic.[62] William Whyte described Victorian and Edwardian school-building as a 'case of conspicuous construction'.[63] Equally huge efforts went into appointing heads who favoured sport. At Bedford it was said that while the bad old headmaster Fanshawe chose to view the School Regatta from his house, the good new headmaster Phillpotts joined the boys on the rugger field.[64] At Winchester, Ridding drained a sports field: 'an event . . . which perhaps did more than any other . . . to restore Winchester to its old position'.[65] In 1900 Marlborough had 68 acres and Uppingham 49 acres of playing fields compared to the two they each had in 1845. Harrow had thirty-four football pitches. Thirty-three years into her headship, Dorothea Beale at Cheltenham finally agreed to have a field leased in 1891, bought in 1894. By 1911, and now in the hands of a headmistress who had donated her hockey stick to what the College called 'cock-house', studded with silver plate inscriptions, Cheltenham Girls' had twenty-six tennis courts, two fives courts, two gyms, a swimming pool, and 12 acres of playing fields. Merchant Taylors' girls got a hockey field and a science lab at the eighth time of asking. The field cost £2 per year.[66] Roedean on the other hand had a strong female sporting ethos right from the start.[67]

All the 'new scheme' schools under the Acts copied the Clarendon nine in their basic look and organization. Playing fields swept up to the gate where the Gothic cast its shadows. At the heart of the school was usually the bed, the cubicle, and the house—a way of living together replicated across the Empire. In house,

---

[59] Postcard, Worksop College Dining Hall (Buchanan, Croydon, nd): WCA. The Great Hall was modelled on Westminster Hall.

[60] Cocks, 'Sodomy, Class and Moral Reform', *Past & Present* 190, 2006, p.123.

[61] Taunton Commission, PP1868, pp.278–80.

[62] On neo-Gothic longings: Malekow, *Gothic Images* (1996) pp.124–5; Lewis, 'Feminine Presence', in Roper and Tosh, eds., *Manful Assertions* (1991) pp.180–1. Colin Matthew described Gothic as 'indiscriminate nostalgia': *Nineteenth Century* (2000) p.265.

[63] Whyte, *Oxford Jackson* (2006) p.148.   [64] Sargeaunt, *Bedford* (1925) p.146.

[65] In 1868, Leach, *Winchester* (1899) p.501.

[66] Harrop, *Merchant Taylors'* (1988) p.36; Steadman, *Days of Miss Beale* (1931) p.82, and Anon, 'History of games in College'. Lilian Faithfull, headmistress of Cheltenham (1907–22) was President of the All England Women's Hockey Federation.

[67] de Zouche, *Roedean School* (1955) ch. 8.

boys and girls learned the pecking order.[68] On the sports field they learned it all over again.

The worst that could happen to a boarding school was the death of a pupil on the premises. School prospectuses began to include sporting facilities and health provision.[69] New scheme schools drew attention, for instance, to the sanatorium at Bradfield, the drains at Coventry High, the hygiene at Keswick, the food at Bedales, and the 'integral' physical education at Edgbaston Girls. Temple Grove told you it was safely situated on 'the outskirts of town'. Bedford measured your chest. Blackheath Holland House gave you a silver spoon, of all things. At Frensham High, joy of joys, you had Miss Wildblood for dance.[70]

Thring called all this estate The Wall, 'the dead, unfeeling ever-lasting pressure of the permanent structure'. 'Never rest until you have got the almighty wall on your side' he said, and rejected Classicists for Gothicists in his choice of architects.[71] It was not just a matter of physical assets. 'School' only happened when it was assembled and for that it needed not only the right facilities but a way of looking at itself regularly and completely. Whether this was done in chapel, or in the dining hall, or in the big hall, all great schools had a stage and all great heads an exit and entrance strategy. Flanked by senior staff and prefects, gown flapping, papers shuffling, this was the head's daily show. He looked upon them while they looked upon him, and upon themselves being looked upon. In Bedford Great Hall the boys faced him in his chair of state raised on a dias under a balustrade. Looking up to the rafters, junior boys had never seen anything so lofty. Looking down on the heavy oak chairs, senior boys had never seen anything so immovable. When Bedford Great Hall burned down in 1979, people were surprised how recent it was.[72] As they were supposed to do. That was true of nearly all the schools and school halls except the genuinely ancient. Eton, for instance, had its chapel stone laid by Henry VI in 1641.[73]

Sherborne and Bristol got their hall, or 'Big School' in 1879, Cheltenham Ladies' in 1883, made to resemble a theatre on the site of a theatre, Oundle in 1908, and so on, chapter after chapter of architectural accretion.[74] Kate Westaway at Bedford High wanted not some canting 'academy' but a place with its great hall (1882) where governesses were now called mistresses and sport was played even if at first

---

[68] 'I say, Betty, come into my cubicle after lights out tonight': *Every Girl's Annual*, pp.72–3. On the school house as an imperial system of living together: Joyce, *State of Freedom* (2013) p.287.

[69] Boyd, *Radley* (1948) p.282.

[70] All examples except Bedford (Sargeaunt, p.144) are from John Johnson, Bodleian, Education Box 1, 2, 5, 6, 7, 8.

[71] G E Street got the commission and thanked him for the opportunity to build his Wall: Parkin, *Thring* (1900) p.106, pp.217–18. See also Seaborne, *The English School* (1971) for nineteenth-century architectural elaboration of the simple schoolroom.

[72] Barlen, ed., *Bedford School and the Great Fire* (1984) p.35, p.19.

[73] Eton was clearly less good at history than being old: Chattock, *Eton* (1874) p.25.

[74] Gourley, *Sherborne* (1951) p.163; Hill, *Bristol* (1961) pp.108–10; Clarke, *Cheltenham* (1953) pp.67; Anon, *Sanderson of Oundle* (1923) pp.42–51.

the girls had to play hockey with walking sticks and netball into a waste paper basket. Bedford High finally got its mighty chair and organ in 1898 and we can be sure that 'Kate', as she was known, made the most of both. Now 'the School was complete, its traditions established', she said.[75] Bedford Modern got its platform, chair, organ, panels, and mouldings in 1881. Bedford School Great Hall (1891) hosted lectures on Nansen, Shackleton, and Selous while remembering its own heroes in gilded letters. In the cricket pavilion there was a plaque to Henry Cross MA, Exhibitioner, Scholar, Rower, Master: died Atbara, Sudan, September 1898.[76]

To some, architecture *was* the school. Architects arrived promising historicity. Headmasters left marking their words with what they'd built. At Cheltenham, Beale built a small gothic kingdom. Heppenstall arrived at The Perse in 1864 to swear he had a school to lead but, as he put it, 'no school anything' to stand by. He wanted school things. He wanted school meanings. He wanted what Leach at Winchester called 'the spell' or what Newton at Uppingham called 'inherited forms'.[77] As Sellar and Yeatman observed in 1930, history is not what happened but what you are able to remember happened, and Thring's Gothic Wall was intended to help you do that.[78]

Ghosts in the Machine

After his death in 1842 age 47, Thomas Arnold was mythologized as the model headmaster. Arthur Stanley's landmark *Life and Correspondence* (1846) painted a picture of the great headmaster who had arrived fully formed at Rugby in 1828 intending to impose a new moral order.[79] Rugby made him known and, as we have seen, *Tom Brown's Schooldays* made him famous.

Only, this was not how it was. Arnold's headship contained little that was genuinely reforming. There were no moves to protect the young or integrate the sporting life. Fagging remained. Flogging remained. Boys' side remained. He introduced some useful subjects, but ancient grammar stayed dominant. The highpoint of the school week was his Sunday sermon.[80] Arnold himself was said to be moody, got up late, and was, it seems, not easy to know.[81]

---

[75] Dr. K M Westaway MA (Cantab), headmistress 1924–49, author of *Bedford High School* (1932) p.60, p.208. Muriel Madden added to the daily drama by playing the organ with one arm missing: Weston, *Organ and Organists* (1998) pp.3–5.

[76] Sargeaunt, *Bedford School* (1925) pp.170. Connisbee, *Bedford Modern* (1964) pp.57–8; Godber and Hutchins, eds., *Bedford High* (1982) pp.27–8.

[77] Newton, *Newton* (1925) p.16; Leach, *Winchester* (1899) p.538; Gray, *Perse* (1921) p.128. John Ruskin and Dorothea Beale enjoyed a close correspondence.

[78] 'All other history defeats itself': *1066 And All That* (1930) p.5—the satirical textbook of grammar and public school history teaching. Sellar was a housemaster at Charterhouse.

[79] Stanley, *Life and Correspondence* (1846) pp. 76–82, p.93.   [80] ibid, pp.259–60.

[81] According to Strachey, who was not a supporter: *Eminent Victorians* (1918) p.164.

Nevertheless, his ghost grew.[82] An indefatiguable self-publicist with influential friends, Arnold's personal relationship with some of his senior boys created a mythology that continued long after he died—a narrative that was open to Uppingham and all the other new and reforming schools.[83] Old Rugbeians like Thomas Hughes and Arnold's son Matthew became eminent Victorians. Other Old Rugbeians, including Arnold's biographer Arthur Stanley, were behind moves to reform Oxford University in the 1850s and the public schools in the 1860s.[84] The Clarendon Commission devoted no special section to Arnold but it was clear that he was their *eminence grise*, their 'great man', the man who had built a 'great school'. It was also the case that he seems to have laid his emotions on every boy with his 'deep, ringing searching voice', or perhaps it was in 'his look' as Tom thought, or in his administration of the sacraments, or how he hovered about. Arnold made a fetish of his own holy spirit it has to be said, something that *Tom Brown's Schooldays* did not try to avoid.[85] This is Hughes talking of Arnold in 1857. But it could have been C S Lewis talking of Aslan in 1950:

> . . . the great grim man whom I've feared more than anybody on earth . . . he lifted me up just as if I'd been a little child . . . he seemed to bear all I'd felt . . . he sat down by me and stroked my head . . . I told him all . . . he seemed to spread round me like a healing . . . and light . . . and plant me on a rock.[86]

Generations of public school histories conjured their own ghosts in the machine. Most went from head to head, starting with the first great reformer, or with one or two hopeless cases that went before in order to show how great he or she really was.[87]

But charisma is something given, not owned, and because the giving had to be entire, the circumstances had to be larger than life, like classical statues, or Thring's Wall, or death. Ada McDowall had been headmistress of Bedford High

---

[82] Allison and Maclean called it a 'Deathless Myth': 'There's a Deathless Myth in the Close Tonight', *IJHS*, 2012.

[83] Including Cheltenham (1840), Marlborough (1843), Radley (1847), Lancing (1848), Bradfield (1850), Wellington (1859), and all the Bedford schools.

[84] Bill, *University Reform* (1973) p.112.

[85] On Rugby as Clarendon's model school and headmaster, HM Comms, 1864, xx, p.298, 260; and 'greatness', and 'trembling voice', and 'glistening eye', in Stanley, *Life and Correspondence* (1846) p.86, p.125; voice and look in Hughes, *Tom Brown's Schooldays* (1857) p.142, p.199. In 1970 the out-going captain of Worksop College wrote to his successor advising that while he should act boys' side he must stay morally 'pledged and loyal' to the headmaster: Captain's School Report, Christmas 1970: WCA.

[86] Hughes, ibid, p.340. Aslan appears in C S Lewis' *Narnia Chronicles* (1950–56). Lewis did a year at Malvern College (1913–14) and was privately educated by a former headmaster of Lurgan College. See Kelman on six kinds of hero and note how model headmasters fulfilled all requirements: *Prophets* (1924) p.103, p.89, p.103, pp.113–16.

[87] Darwin's classic work, *The English Public School* (1929), devoted chapter xi to the great headmasters of the first division: Arnold of Rugby, Thring of Uppingham, Keate of Eton, Butler of Shrewsbury, Sanderson of Oundle, and Almond of Loretto. He thought English public schoolboys formed a 'typical' body of men: *English Public School* (1929) p.19, p.29.

for only a few months when she died in childbirth. The girls were made to sit in the dark while Tennyson's *In Memoriam* was read over them.[88]

The morning *tableau* in the great hall was as near as most schools got to everyday charisma. Loukes of Abingdon remembered large men in large buildings (they shrank as he grew older). Jones of Eton remembered headship as a totem. In India, Thring was rated 'omniscient'. At the same time, the school in full array was obliged to bear witness not only to the headmaster or mistress but to itself. This involved a certain theatricality. Moberly of Winchester thought a head should give the school the 'stamp' of his personality. So did Beale of Cheltenham. Her marble bust was placed for all to see alongside Queen Victoria's, so they looked like sisters. Long after her death, old girls remembered 'that look' and Cheltenham Ladies' College could only think of itself as an expression of the personality behind it. Warre of Eton was remembered for the 'vibrant bass' and 'sudden tenor' of his voice, Havilland for his 'wizard's charms', Luxmore for the 'eye that quelled you'. At Bedford, Frost's 'leonine roar' kept you alert. At Bristol, it was Caldicott's deep resonance. At Notting Hill and Ealing, it was Miss Jones' ('Jonah') deep resonance. At St. Swithun's Winchester, it was Miss Finlay's 'light and clear' intonation. At Kingswood, Osborne could turn on the 'devastating power' of his voice, Kaye of Bedford Modern ('whose daily walk from School House to school became a legend') could bring the school to silence in a moment, while West of Brentwood could calm 'the storm with a long quiet look of feigned astonishment followed by a few sharp whispered words'. All this 'awed the school', and Hilliard the senior prefect concluded that the secret of school mastering lay in a master's first call for quiet. At King Edward Girls', Birmingham, Miss Jacques (Gymnastics and Games), remembered the names of 398 out of 400 girls at her retirement party. Pity the two she forgot. Waiting for Carter to march into Bedford Great Hall, all eyes on the door and then a quick step, broad chest, flowing beard and 'what a roar!' 'After a very long minute he would extend his hand for silence'. At Edgbaston, Miss Young would sweep in smelling of lavender water, an acolyte in her wake carrying a Bible on a cushion. Waiting for Kate Westaway to flow into Bedford High Great Hall, you could almost hear the drumming of shields. Not that she needed great voice in a school where the girls were not allowed to speak. At North London Collegiate, they were not allowed to feel sick. Spotting a woozing girl, Miss Buss shot across the row and shook her fist in the girl's face. 'You dare faint!' she said. And of course she didn't.[89] Headmistresses could match

---

[88] Westaway, *Bedford High* (1932) p.42; Godber and Hutchins, *Bedford High* (1982) pp.111–12.

[89] Francis Mary Buss, in Kamm, *How Different* (1958) p.227. School and headmaster references to be found in the following works: Loukes, Abingdon, *The Griffin* (1963) p.77; Jones, Eton, *Victorian Boyhood* (1955) p.224, p.178; Wren, *Indian Teachers* (1910) pp.89–91; Moberly of Winchester, HM Comms 1864, xxi, p.354; Beale of Cheltenham, Steadman, *Miss Beale* (1931) p.xiii, p.100; Warre et al. of Eton, Jones, *Victorian Boyhood* (1955) p.152; Frost and Kaye of Bedford Modern, Underwood, *Bedford Modern* (1981) p.153, pp.67–9; Caldicott of Bristol, Hill, *Bristol Grammar* (1951) p.111; Jones of Notting Hill, Sayers, *Fountain Unsealed* (1973) p.19; Finlay of St. Swithun's, Winchester, Bain,

headmasters in all things except income.[90] The Girls' Public Day School Company encouraged its headmistresses to learn from each other and helped spread their methods.[91] Once in the private system, masters and mistresses rarely left it. Heads arrived having been groomed.

All great teachers had their own song and dance acts. At Dover College, W L Dyson sported a canary coloured waistcoat, J E B Roberts leapt onto tables, L W Chubb knotted his rope, 'Dutchy' Holland ordained his 'Order of Tough Guys' while Mr. Lee, who must have been eligible, wore the bullet that nearly killed him in his tie.[92] All performers had their stage names—'Basher', 'Betty', 'Charlie', 'Jugger', 'Kate', 'Kipper', 'Pan', 'Polly', '*RAS*'. In girls' schools, the more serious the school, generally the more feminist its intentions. Chelmsford County High dared speak of the New Woman. At South Hampstead High, Mary Benton, fond of wearing shirt, tie, and Homburg, wrote a leave of absence for one of her suffragette staff who was unexpectedly detained in Holloway Gaol. At Leeds High, Miss Kennedy now terrified her staff like once she had terrified her Cambridge tutors. At Manchester High, houses were named after women— none of them sporting. Some girls' schools took to gilding their academic high achievers' names on the walls. Dorothea Beale never stopped telling her girls to read and read, but not the sort of story where they lived happily ever after. Other schools, like Roedean, founded by the Lawrence sisters, succeeded above all because they were serious. Ursula Brangwen went to Nottingham Grammar and 'trembled like a postulant' on first writing Ancient Greek. Or so Lawrence imagined she would.[93]

So much awe, but in closed communities studying young love in a sacred language, the silence was deafening. Alec Waugh's *The Loom of Youth* (1917) attracted a lot of attention for mentioning it at Sherborne, and Cyril Connolly recalled that character plus prettiness was the winning combination at Eton, but in

St Swithun's (1984) p.45; West of Brentwood School, Lewis, *Brentwood* (1981) p.134; Osborne and Hilliard of Kingswood, Ives, *Kingswood* (1920) p.134, p.176; Jacques of Birmingham, Candler & Jacques, *King Edward VI High School for Girls* (1971) p.110; Carter of Bedford, Sargeaunt, *Bedford School* (1925) p.201; Westaway of Bedford High, Westaway, *Bedford High* (1932) p.198. In spite of her ban on girls talking, not uncommon, Westaway was a feminist who saw her school as a miniature of the women's movement (p.173). The Inspector General of schools in the Transvaal said they liked their stories moral: *Some Suggestions* (1916) p.22.

   [90] Headmasters' ability 'cannot be over-estimated' reckoned Taunton, pricing it at £1000 per annum for first class schools and £500 pa for second class: *Taunton Comm*, PP1868, p.147. In 1875 Watford endowed schools merged, the headmistress on £50 per annum, £2 maximum per pupil capitation; the headmaster on £200 per annum, £3 capitation: Hughes & Sweeney, *Watford GSBG* (1954) p.30.
   [91] Sondheimer and Bodington, eds., *GPDST* (1972) p.29.
   [92] Whitney, *Dover College* (1982) pp.33–6.
   [93] Ursula in D H Lawrence's *The Rainbow* (1915) p.269. For the rest: Kenyon, *Chelmsford County High* (1982) p.26; Benton in Bodington, *South Hampstead High* (1976) p.13; Jewell, *Leeds Girls' High* (1976) p.109; France, *Central High School for Girls* (1970); Candler and Jacques, *King Edward VI, Birmingham* (1971); Steadman, *Days of Miss Beale* (1931) p.103; de Zouche, *Roedean School* (1955).

fact, both accounts were matter of fact. Waugh's is full of what was by then the standard schoolboy stuff—rotten luck, good form, cracking show, best friend. Only on page 242 does he venture to say that 'Gordon began to take an interest in Morcombe', a move which, he admits, led to 'a certain side' of school life.[94] Soon after, Alec's brother Evelyn would introduce the nation to Capt. Grimes, the first unrepentant sexual abuser of little boys in English literature.[95]

The bloodier side of school life—'no refinement, no sentiment, no passion'— was put to paper by John Addington Symonds in his unpublished memoir of Harrow in the 1850s. What one particular boy 'did to deserve his punishment' he never heard,

> but after they had rolled upon the floor with him and exposed his person in public—they took to trampling on him, whenever he appeared in that mean dining room, about those dirty passages, upon the sordid court through which we entered from the road into our barracks, Currey and Clayton and Barber ['playing ostentatiously with a prodigiously developed phallus'] and the rest of the brood squirted saliva and what they called 'gobs' upon their bitch, cuffed and kicked him ... shied books at him and drove him with obscene curses whimpering to his den.[96]

As a young man, Symonds was very clear in private about the scale and seriousness of sexual abuse by boys on boys (but including Vaughan, the headmaster). His image of boys in bed together in a culture where 'every boy of good looks had a female name and was recognized either as a public prostitute or some bigger fellow's bitch', to say the least, widens our appreciation of the meaning of sport in the public school.

After all, 'Come here!' could bring sixteen boys double quick to your door. Fags did not 'fag'. They were *fagged*.[97] Sending a son to boarding school was a major decision for parents, many of whom were keen to stress family life and all the morals which they supposed the school was there to promote. But they must have known that boarding involved liberties that could test a boy sexually, and it

---

[94] Waugh, *Loom of Youth* (1917) p.242, p.245. Connolly remarked that homosexual boys were stimulated by the classical curriculum but the nearest he and his Oxford circle got to sport was running up bills: *Enemies of Promise* (1938) p.235.

[95] In *Decline and Fall* (1928).

[96] Symonds (1840–93) was at Harrow between 1854 and 1858. His manuscript was deposited in the London Library on the death of his friend and biographer Horatio Brown in 1926. Brown had been given the memoir and published a heavily expurgated biography of Symonds in 1893. Grosskurth published an abridged version of the memoir in 1984. Chandos used the most revealing sexual aspects to effect in his *Boys Together* (1985) pp.310–15. The full and unabridged memoir was edited and published by Regis: *The Memoirs of John Addington Symonds* (2016), pp.137–52. See also: Symonds, *Studies of the Greek Poets* (1873): 'The best minds of our youth are exposed to the influences of paederastic literature' (p.134).

[97] HM Comms (1864) xx, pp.95–6.

remains difficult to understand why they exposed their sons to it. Perhaps they reasoned that whatever else it was, this was his peer group and sooner or later he was going to have to face the bloods so better do it now in a school they knew, rather than in a barracks or a wardroom or a brothel. It took a long time before psychological theories began to appear on the consequences of child abuse in closed institutions. Duffell called it the making of the 'strategic survival personality'. Renton talked about 'attachment patterns' and 'emotional transfer'.[98] 'Testing' was as near as the British ruling class got to an educational methodology.[99] You went to school in order to be tested. You learned your verbs in order to be tested. You played sport in order to be tested. You might as well go to bed in order to be tested. On 25 January 1860, Harrow new boy Edward Parker wrote to his mother saying he liked it better every day. 'You can't think what fun we have', he told her. 'Every night we play at Highcock & in the day racquets and football'. Three days later in a letter to his father he said 'I want to tell you a great many things which I can't'.[100]

There is just too much *sotto voce*. Either this was a more innocent age than our own, or there was a code. One historian thinks that kissing girls goodnight came from the domestic ambience many girls' schools (and some boys' schools) were keen to promote.[101] At Heathfield, Miss Wyatt's lavender water was the fragrance of a thousand goodnight confidences. In Eastbourne, night time kissing was finally replaced by 'hearty handshakes'.[102] We are told that Corbin of Taunton liked to pour his soul into chosen boys, that Arnold at Rugby had a reputation for being 'suffocatingly personal' and would sit young ones on his knee, that Bampton at Beaumont spooned them honey before bed, that Wilson at Radley hosted sleepovers, that Norman was simply 'unfitted' and didn't last long while Sewell, the founder, would hand out memory rings to the chosen ones. If a boy didn't shrink from Sewell's first light touch, 'he knew the direct emotional approach was easy'. So many silent kisses and secret crushes. So many 'cracks' and longings and sudden flights in the night. The bonds that brought schools together when boys were boys seem to have been the same bonds that kept their secrets when they were men. Beale of Cheltenham forbade all infatuations. It was said John Le Carre first learned loyalty and betrayal at Sherborne.[103]

---

[98] Duffell, *The Making of Them* (2000) p.71; Renton, *Stiff Upper* (2014) p.98. p.286.

[99] The first official 'test match' in cricket was Australia versus England at Melbourne in 1877.

[100] In Rothery's study of landed families from the seventeenth to the twentieth centuries, the language of 'honour', 'pride', and 'independence' stayed constant over 300 hundred years, but the reformed public schools intensified and internalized its meaning: *Man's Estate* (2012) pp.73–4, pp.93–5, p.180, and *passim*.

[101] De Bellaigue, *Educating Women* (2007) p.20, p.105.

[102] Queenwood, Eastbourne, Petrie Carew, *Many Years* (1967) p.76; Dyhouse, *Girls Growing Up* (1981) p.71.

[103] According to Lewis, in Roper and Tosh, eds., *Manful Assertions* (1991) p.182. John Le Carre's real name is David Cornwell (b.1931). Renton argues that *The Perfect Spy* (1986) based espionage on public school survival techniques. The rest: Spooner, *Taunton* (1968) p.60; Arnold, Custance, ed.,

Only very rarely were the great heads remembered as great teachers. Mary Buss was remembered as such in a memorial window at North London Collegiate, but most of them were remembered for building the machine. Caldicott at Bristol Grammar, a 'masterful personality', introduced heating, lighting, scholarships, prizes, bells, clocks, caps, a timetable, a disciplinary code, a wider curriculum, rising rolls, new school buildings, and a serious sporting ethos—although he felt games had nothing to do with him personally. In all this he may be taken as Alpha minus high-achieving typical.[104] Cook took Wantage from sixteen boys and one boarder to forty boys and eighty boarders. Robinson and Swallow at Chigwell, Morris at Lady Berkeley's, Heppenstall at The Perse, Thompson at Radley, Phillpotts at Bedford, and scores more (virtually all of them after 1869) built their walls and filled their houses.[105] Poulter of High Wycombe Grammar gave up his garden for a sports field ('at last a schoolmaster indeed'). Newbold reorganized St. Bees in order to farm fees, so did Jones at Notting Hill, Nelligan at Croydon, and Stephenson at Felsted (in spite of the sugar beet factory next door). At Sherborne, Harper built a new school inside the old one. At Charterhouse, Haig Brown moved the whole school lock stock and goal posts to Godalming. Lidbetter swelled Wigton by going co-educational. Grundy grew Abingdon and kept it on the direct grant list, while Layng got himself (and the school) readmitted to Headmasters' Conference. What was said of Abingdon School in 1889 can be taken as public school cliché:

A spick and span school built in a fashionable part of the town, has now superseded the old one beside the abbey gateway. One looks in vain for Master Bennett's 'poore schollars' and Roysse's 'Free school...'[106]

Winchester (1982) p.387, and Stanley, *Life and Correspondence* (1846) pp.132–8; Levi, *Beaumont* (1901) p.53; Boyd, *Radley* (1948) p.205, p.155, p.97. Hornung (ex Uppingham) tells a strange story about necks, and falling on them, in *Fathers of Men* (1902) pp.vi–vii; Sunday evenings at Radley allowed fellows to entertain boys in their rooms: Raikes, *Fifty Years* (1897), pp.63–7; Cheltenham Ladies: Kamm, *How Different* (1958) p.178; on sudden flights, most famously by Dr. Vaughan, headmaster of Harrow, long obscured for reasons explained by Symonds. The first art of history is not to mistake the present for the past, but it would be negligent not to note the flow of contemporary revelations of sexual abuse at boarding schools. One of many: 'Head may have burnt evidence of sexual abuse': Downside Abbey, Somerset, *The Times*, 16 December 2017. See Renton, *Stiff Upper* (2017).

[104] He did all this between 1860 and 1883: Hill, *Bristol* (1951) pp.86–107. For the Frances Mary Buss memorial window and bust: John Johnson, Bodleian, Memorials Box.

[105] Sugden, *Wantage* (1924) p.56; Stott, *Chigwell* (1960) p.125; Hornsby and Griffin, *Lady Berkeley's* (1984) p.105; Mitchell, *Perse* (1976) pp.54–5; Raikes, *Radley* (1897) p.145; Sargeaunt, *Bedford* (1925) pp.123–43.

[106] Davis, 'Abingdon', *English Illustrated Magazine* 1888–89, p,592. Ashford and Haworth, *Royal Grammar* (1962) p.33; Old Beghians, *St Bees* (1939) p.48; Magnus, *Jubilee* (1923) p.87; Craze, *Felsted* (1955) p.298; Gourlay, *Sherborne* (1951) p.104, p.127; Old Scholars, *Wigton* (1916) pp.50–1; Cobban, *Abingdon* (1970) Introduction, and Townsend, *Abingdon* (1910) p.73.

Sometimes fame was fortuitous. Bampton of Beaumont established a Roman Catholic public school that just happened to be next door to Windsor Castle. Winkfield of Ely was fortunate enough to be headmaster when Roberson ran 100 yards in 10.5 and young Holman bowled Ranjitsinhji for twenty-seven. Eton, naturally, never had anything to prove.[107] Sometimes fame was richly deserved. Beale at Cheltenham resisted a sports field almost to the end, but built a school of great beauty in the meantime and not only schooling, but teacher training, extra mural, an Oxford College (St Hilda's), an East End Mission (St Hilda's in the East), and free porridge breakfasts for poor children. When the Bethnal Green girls played the College girls on the asphalt, they called them the 'Old Cheltenham Ladies'—which did not go down well.[108]

If headmasters and headmistresses were the new lords of the realm, the schools were their great houses—forming not so much a feudal pyramid as a constellation of planets, companies of men and women, knights and retainers, founders and fellows and all who had been before and were yet to come. Once you had been, you had been. Like your class of degree, you could never change your school or your head. But as Thring found out at Uppingham, 'fellowship' is a difficult thing to read in a boys' side school. At Radley, Warden Sewell tried to cane the Senior Prefect and found out the hard way that 'to cane the Senior Prefect was like caning the King'. His successor Warden Thomas was forced to hire three farm labourers to hold boys down. They came in spitting on their hands. Dreadful misjudgements such as this were the stuff boy rebellions were made of.[109] Wykehamists could tell the severity of their flogging by the status of their flogger: 'bibling' by the headmaster (in the small of the back), 'tunding' by the boys (over the shoulder), and 'spanking' by the Sixth (bare buttocks).[110]

According to a ranking that was hard to explain and never made clear, masters were paid a proportion of fees and emoluments according to whether they were classicists or athletes, Oxbridge graduates or housemasters, and so on. Marlborough's 'brave young masters who came among us', we can assume, were high status.[111] Then there were the fencers and dancers and science tutors, brought in and paid *pro rata*. Filling your boarding houses and making them nice made you money. Thring was particularly proud of his taste in curtains.[112]

[107] Chattock, *Sketches of Eton* (1874) p.20; Anon, *Beaumont* (1911) p.31; Saunders, *King's School, Ely* (1970) pp.18–20;

[108] Cheltenham Ladies' College Magazine, no. 2, 1922; porridge at 1d per head in Magazine Jan 1880.

[109] Boyd, *Radley* (1948) p.151.

[110] Custance, ed., *Winchester* (1982) p.452; Leach, *Winchester* (1899) pp.458–61.

[111] *Recollections of Marlborough College by an Old Boy* (1869) quoted in Honey, 'Victorian Public School', Oxford DPhil (1970) p.134.

[112] HM Comms (1864) xxi, Evidences 1, where 'profit on the boarders is the greatest item' (p.80), and Evidences 2 on differences between masters (pp. 246–50, p.275); Whyte, 'Building a public school community 1860-1910', *History of Education*, 32, 6, 2003, p.619. In the 1860s Eton boys were paying a total of £1,300 per year between them for sports clubs: HM Comms (1864) p.97. Once the fee system

Many fell short. Again, not always for reasons easy to explain. It would appear that nobody fitted the bill at Radley and even then, the last and the best, Ferguson (1925–37), wasn't that great for reasons not given. Stevens of Bradfield suffered sudden multiple resignations of his staff. Bedford Modern proved hard to please: Moore (1831–60) was not sophisticated enough, Finlinson (1860–77) not clever enough, Poole (1877–1900) not religious enough, and Kaye (1901–16) not humble enough. Bradfield enjoyed a run of lax heads ranging from the pompous to the swishing. Sanderson at Oundle may have built the finest school in the country; pity for him that he was not and never had been an athlete. Warre of Eton had a First from Balliol and a reputation as the finest rowing coach in England. 'No headmaster was ever more honoured' said Clutton-Brock. But he too fell short. Gillespy at Gloucester was found short of a degree, and had to go. Felsted's back-to-back headmasters Mr. Squire and Mr. Surridge, between them, had no foundationers, no boarders, and no pupils. At least they had their pensions.[113]

School history books taught that Danish invaders came in waves upon the Saxon unready. According to *The Carthusian* for June 1931, they came in the form of a 'wave of 'ellish 'eadmasters . . . '[114]

Alma Mater

Working-class men needed to work, but upper-class men needed to play. This was a fact of life.[115] In the public school world, playing sport for wages wasn't done. Whatever agonies the administrators of the Amateur Athletic Association or the Rugby Football Union may have had with professional players, public schoolboys didn't much care that you could win a fiver for running a race in Hackney or how much a Yorkshireman might get paid for playing rugby on a Saturday afternoon in Castleford. The main thing was not to break the personal bonds forged at school and carried on into college, club, and suburb—a state of mind, a spirit, a 'subtle, elusive and all but vanished' world of sporting endeavour.[116] Thring's brother John called football 'the simplest game' because of the feelings of 'courtesy

---

was reformed, public school masters and mistresses were better able to see that their salaries were no better than state teachers on the Burnham scale: Underwood, *Bedford Modern* (1981) ch.11. For a variety of school accounts and accounting practices, including tariffs for libraries and carpeting and fees for fencing and modern language tuition: John Johnson, Bodleian, Education Box 1, 2, 5, 6, 7, 8.

[113] Craze, *Felsted* (1955) p.150; Boyd, *Radley* (1948) p.350; Leach, *Bradfield* (1900) p.152; Conisbee, *Bedford Modern* (1964) p.32; Leach, *Bradfield* (1900) p.97, p.140; Anon, *Oundle* (1923) pp.78–9; Jones, *Victorian Boyhood* (1955) p.178; Clutton-Brock, *Eton* (1900) p.168, p.173; Robertson, *King's School, Gloucester* (1974) pp.178–81; Lewis, *Brentwood* (1981) ch.19.

[114] W C Sellar, in *The Carthusian*, June 1931.

[115] Strachey, *Eminent Victorians* (1918) p.188; *Bell's Life*, 3 January 1874.

[116] Taylor, *On the Corinthian Spirit* (2006) pp.3–4.

and good feeling' he hoped it would engender.[117] He remarked that the 'power is gentle', born out of brotherly feelings, all part of a new moral world sometimes called 'Amateur'.[118] In the same year (1863) that John Thring published effectively the rules of modern football, Uppingham boys took complete control of sport in the School and the young men of the London football clubs formed what they called the 'Football Association' as a mutual, something quite different from other ways of playing whether landed (Burnaby), professional (Sayers), local (Stamford), or commercial.[119] The FA Cup Final, which went on to overtake The Derby as the high point in English sporting life, was at first a sort of school challenge for a silver cup.

Clarendon and Taunton set the elite standard. For the rest of the population, the Newcastle Commission (1858–61) led to Forster's Education Act of 1870 which extended state-funded schooling for all through locally elected School Boards—an example of serious state intervention in a supposedly *laissez faire* century. In 1902, Balfour disbanded the School Boards and, working through the new local education authorities (LEAs), encouraged 'secondary', or 'grammar', or 'high' schools (the names got as complicated as the funding) in order to mimic the endowed schools at a fraction of the cost. Professors and inspectors of schools wanted grammar schools with playing fields. So did teachers.[120] So did parents. So did pupils, who were there because they had passed an entrance exam and left having spent five years studying a neo-classical curriculum in the company of men in gowns. Alan Johnson went to Sloane Grammar. Their playing field was a bus ride away but he loved the fresh air and freedom. He also loved sharing it with the girls of Carlyle Grammar next door.[121]

By the 1930s, three quarters of all British children were educated to elementary level at least, nearly all in state schools, up to the age of 14. There were huge variations, but as a general rule, 350,000 thousand other children were privately educated, and over 40,000 of them enjoyed a public school education up to the age of 18.[122] After 1944 all British children received a secondary education but

---

[117] Thring, *The Winter Game* (1863) pp.9–10 and Preface to first edition. Sporting bonds between like-minded men? Nowhere more so than in the Gaelic Athletic Association: Rouse, *Sport and Ireland* (2015) pp.141–4.

[118] 'A central tenet of amateurism was the regulation of violent play': Holt, 'Amateur Body', *Sport in History* 25 (2006) p.358, p.362. On 'Athletic Festivals' for medals and prizes but not cash or wagers: *Sporting Chronicle*, 13 August 1875.

[119] Minutes of the FA, vol. i, 1863–75: 1 December 1863, 20 July 1871: FA HQ. Suburban London was the heart of amateurism. All founder members of the FA represented London suburban clubs made up of former pupils of public and endowed schools.

[120] Sir Robert Morant, Chief Inspector of Schools, was an ardent Wykhemist. Sir Michael Sadler, Professor of Educational Administration at Manchester, urged a games ethic in state schools and pupil teachers' centres: *Report* (1905) p.92. For a provocative piece on how the 1902 Act was designed to halt the progressive direction of the London School Board: Simon, 'Reeder's Alternative System', in Colls and Rodger, eds., *Cities of Ideas* (2004) p.181.

[121] Johnson, *This Boy* (2014) p.149.

[122] McKibbin, *Classes and Cultures* (1998) p.249. See *The Guardian's* report (31 October 2017) 'Enduring power of the old boys' network' for research on how the Clarendon schools accounted for 10

only a minority of working-class children went to grammar schools. For the majority there were rarely any playing fields and 'exercises' were the order of the day. Johnson Street Stepney and Camden Street Camden might have plated their school doors in order to save them from the daily kicking, but the buildings had fine touches too, and the desks had flap seats to allow stand-up exercises, ten minutes a day, raise the head, trunk straight, heels together now for 'Greeting the Big Toe'.[123] What competitive sport there was, was usually supplied by keen teachers out of hours.[124]

Laygate Lane elementary school opened in 1870. Downwind from a brewery, next to a piggery, and situated on a busy hill leading down to a busy river, the foundation stone read 'Board School' not 'Boarding School'. Laygate had no boarders or playing fields. Its two storey architecture bore a passing resemblance to a factory—raw materials going in downstairs right, refined products going out upstairs left graded according to quality 'A' 'B' 'C' and 'D' classes. Children had to wait until 1938 for Laygate's first sports day, held in a local park. They did, however, do indoor physical exercises in their 'plimmies' and went into the school yard twice a day for 'play' time—swarms of girls and boys in separate yards with climbing frames ('monkey bars') for those who preferred hanging to running. Sport in the yard, however, was strictly unofficial and usually out of order: three strokes of the cane for playing football, two for climbing the spouts, and five on Walter Youl (4 December 1883) for a spot of prize-fighting. Only the head and certificated teachers could use the cane, about five beatings a week all told: 'strokes' on the bottom, 'stripes' on the back, 'palmies' on the hand. Playing for the school football team was the greatest achievement a boy could imagine, but only a boy. Until the onset of school netball in the 1930s, girls were usually denied the power of representing anyone or anything but themselves.[125]

Clarendon and Taunton showed what could be done when supply met demand in a rising market. Forster's working-class board schools were not open to market forces but that is not to say they were free from emulation. Laygate played in

per cent of *Who's Who* entries but only 0.15 per cent of British pupils. In 1897 they comprised 20 per cent of entries.

[123] Exercise without movement, 'for use in London Board Schools': Bergman-Osterberg, *Ling's Swedish System* (1887) and Knudsen, *Gymnastics* (1920) figs 16–26. On Boarding school environments: Robson, *School Architecture* (1874) p.297, pp.213–18, p.172; Koven, *Slummimg* (2005) pp.228–33; Kynaston, *Austerity Britain* (2007) p.367.

[124] Often through outside amateur bodies such as the English Schools' Football Association (1904): Kerrigan, 'Teachers and the origins of elementary school football', *History of Education* 29, 2000, p.5. Starting with the London Schools Football Association (1885), other schools' FAs followed. Mangan calls these keen teachers the 'missing men' of football history in *Soccer & Society*, 2008, p.184.

[125] Laygate Lane School, South Shields: School Log Book 1883–1906, and Punishment Book 1901: school archive, head teacher's office.

Oxford and Cambridge blue quarters. Many schools, and not only public schools, lived by their sporting reputations.[126]

Modern schooling moralized sport and nationalized it. The new moralism lay not in notions of fairness because sporting contests had always involved notions of fairness. It lay in the high esteem attached to a physical mastery left largely in the hands of the pupils themselves but not outside the notice of teachers. After that, esteem could be attached to anything that that mastery could be said to represent, the hall, the school, the college, the club, the county, the country.[127] School sport remained the subject of a thousand homilies for in the game of life as in the game of cricket, Baxter always had a second innings.[128] In the middle-class imagination, the moralization of school sport was not about pious analogies rather than friendships forged every day shoulder to shoulder and arm in arm. At Cambridge, Quiller Couch advised that manly verbs should be played straight bat.[129]

Sherborne wouldn't name its best players because being Sherborne was sufficient.[130] Bell's Life opined that amateur sport had made the English public schoolboy 'one of the finest fellows in the world'. Social psychology emerged too late to catch boarding schools' part in the making of what academics called 'normative' or 'group behaviour'. But after three generations of cricketers plastered on everything from cigarette cards to ceramics, and ten or more school generations having embedded themselves in places of great scenic beauty and apparent historical significance, elite schools could be mistaken for the soul of English cricket just as they could be mistaken for the soul of English identity. In the 1950s, John Arlott and E W (Jim) Swanton took all this meaning and broadcast it to the nation.

BBC sport recruited almost exclusively from the public school camp. Swanton and Arlott spoke cricket unto the masses. Their summer commentaries lasted all day long and took the same high moral tone adopted by the public schools mixed

---

[126] Superbly defied when Colin Smith willfully loses a race in Alan Sillitoe's borstal novel *The Loneliness of the Long Distance Runner* (1959).

[127] On representative cricket: *Encyclopaedia of Sport and Games* (1911) vol. i, pp.439–40. Rugby Union allowed a player to choose his country (vol. ii, p.274) but Association Football did not (p.275).

[128] But first you must take the long walk back. *The Long Walk Back* by Dougie Blaxland is a play about the England cricketer Chris Lewis who made some wrong choices and ended up doing six years in prison, performed at Grace Road, Leicestershire County Cricket Club, 20 April 2019: for an account of its premier at Portland HMP, see Matthew Engel, Guardian, 2 April 2019; Drummond, *Baxter's Second Innings* (1892) with a cover in fine cricketing colours. Henry Drummond (1851–1897) was a Free Church of Scotland minister, biologist, lecturer, and missionary.

[129] So 'you can tell a man's style': Dodd, 'Englishness and the National Culture', in Colls and Dodd, eds., *Englishness 1880–1920* (1986) p.30. In the 1920s, McDougall (*The Group Mind*) and Allport, 'Influence of the Group on Association and Thought' (*Journal of Experimental Psychology*) began to ask to what extent social institutions could create new values: Thomson, *History of Psychology* (1968) pp.370–2.

[130] Gourley, *Sherborne* (1951) p.214. On sport 'slotting' the gentlemanly code into an otherwise busy commercial middle-class life: Matthew, *Nineteenth Century* (2000) p.89.

with asides about the landscape and literature. Arlott (Queen Mary Grammar, Basingstoke) tended to take the professionals' side, Swanton (Cranleigh) the gentlemen's, but both men were flexible about what that could mean. Swanton sounded like a headmaster in earnest. Arlott sounded like the village smithie. For these two 'voices of cricket', as the sun set over Lords, Hegel's Owl of Minerva was always ready to spread her wings.[131]

Except, that is, when the West Indies turned up. In 1950 they beat England for the first time at Lords in front of a home crowd. On that day, 30 June, there was no room for setting suns as another new moral world showed up, beautifully caught in C L R James' *Beyond a Boundary*:

> West Indians crowding to Tests bring with them the whole past history and future hopes of the islands...We of the West Indies have no [identity] at all, none that we know of. To such people the three Ws [Weekes, Walcott, Worrell], Ram [Ramadhin], and Val [Valentine] wrecking the English batting help fill a huge gap in their consciousness and their needs.[132]

> Across this sacred sward of cricket, when the last English wickets had fallen to the West Indies, swept wild rejoicing crowds. Leading them was the gleaming black-faced calypso singer 'Lord Kitchener'. Right around the ground he went on an African war dance, all in slow time. Kitch, with a khaki sash over a bright blue short (sic) carried an outsized guitar which he strummed wildly. (*Trinidad Guardian* 30 June 1950)[133]

> The point about cricket and watching it was the reconnection with home... Cricket was front and centre of Caribbean life. It was the best way of celebrating being Caribbean, watching with all of the other West Indians, whether it was in Old Trafford, the Oval, Edgbaston—all places with substantial West Indian populations...It was, you know, a case of, we're catching hell here but cricket can be a respite—and a chance to show our flair, style...We invented the pitch invasion. (Colin Babb 2019)[134]

Virtually all who testified to the Clarendon Commission saw the classics as a living tradition, the very finest the schools had to offer. Classics dominated all other

---

[131] Swanton was a public school man through and through. Millions of BBC listeners and *Guardian* and *Telegraph* readers were treated every summer to random explorations of the main themes of this book: Fay and Kynaston, *Soul of English Cricket* (2019) p.304, pp.339–40. Neville Cardus, cricket correspondent of the *Manchester Guardian* from 1919, is generally regarded as the man who brought the 'golden age' into cricket writing: Hamilton, *The Great Romantic* (2019). The elegaic cricketing mood continues in Mike Henderson's stroll round the county grounds *That Will Be England Gone* (2020).
[132] James, *Beyond a Boundary* (1963) p.225.   [133] Grant, *Homecoming* (2019)p.238.
[134] Colin Babb, ibid, p.240.

subjects at Eton well into the 1930s.[135] But very few boys preferred Latin and Greek to sport.[136] It was the heroic connotations of the body that defined the ancients, not the languages.[137] And because it was the bloods who really counted, not the Greeks, West Indian fast bowlers found their place in the sun. 'The Putney Flappers' idol' for 1929 was Sir James Croft, Oxford cox and 'devastating' driver of fast cars.[138]

[135] HM Commission, 1864, xx, p.247, p.271; Byrne and Churchill, *Eton* (1940) p.41. For Classicism in worker education: Collini, 'Literary Critic', *TRHS*, 2004, pp.101–4; and Goldman, *Dons and Workers* (1995) pp.24–5, 292–4.

[136] Fearon at Winchester experienced the full horror of Wordsworth's Greco-Latin primer *Graecae Grammaticae Rudimenta*, 'the slaughter house' of learning according to Wren. Virginia Woolf, who was taught at home, associated sport with paederasty: 'On Not Knowing Greek', in Evangelista, 'Colony', 2006, p.61; Stray, 'Wordsworth's Graecae Grammaticae Rudimenta (1834) ', *De Philologis Et Philogia* ii (2016) p.98, p.110; Wren, *Indian Teachers* (1910), pp.89–91. In an earlier period, long orations in Greek or Latin served more to keep order than lend enlightenment: 'Short Account' (1845) and Chitty, *Medal Speaking at Winchester 1761–1815* (1905) p.24: John Johnson, Bodleian, Education Box 1, 2, 5, 6, 7, 8.

[137] Hornblower and Spawforth, *Classical Civilization* (2004) p.295.

[138] Hill, Boat Race 'Official Centenary Souvenir' (1929): John Johnson, Bodleian, Sport Box 13.

7

Bloods

'This is being young,
        Assumption of the startled century'
                        (Philip Larkin, 'How Distant' 1965)

As a student at Cambridge, Edward Thring had mixed with the Christian Socialists—friends of F D Maurice and Thomas Hughes, supporters of Lord Shaftesbury—in their Trinity Street circle. In 1861 he was glad to appoint one of their number, William Witts, founder of the Cambridge Working Men's College, to teach at Uppingham. In 1862 he spent the day with Maurice and some of his circle at Kibworth. There was substantial overlap between what Christian Socialists said they wanted to achieve in a theocracy, and what public school reformers said they wanted to achieve in a school. They wanted to build a new kind of man.

New Moral Bloods

Thring was aware of the Anglican school network. Although not particularly interested in cricket or football themselves, Cotton at Marlborough and Vaughan at Harrow had shown how to accommodate sport within existing rubrics and in 1857, as we have seen, Hughes caught the mood with his *Tom Brown's Schooldays*, an exaltation of Arnold's headship and, in a way, all headships.[1]

In this sense, the reformed public schools were innovative rather than reactionary institutions, and Thring found his path increasingly lit by other heads so that after ten years at Uppingham he felt he could see 'a new world rolling into sight'. As an outsider he was committed to emulating the Clarendon nine (one of

---

[1] Thring and the Christian Socialists: Tozer, 'Magnetism of Edward Thring' (2016) p.10. He met Maurice at nearby Kibworth on 20 September 1862. By now Tozer reckons there was a Christian community at Uppingham being taught carpentry, metalwork, and gardening as well as Classics and Maths. On the sporting vanguard at Marlborough, Harrow, Lancing, Uppingham, and Loretto, see: Mangan, *Athleticism* (1981), where he argues that the headmasters worked to change the culture not by forward planning but by 'parallel innovation' (p.42). For a small but intellectually formidable resistance to the growing sporting cult, particularly at Eton, see: Dewey, 'Socratic Teachers', *International Journal* 1, 2, 1995.

which he attended) and, as we have seen, the 1868 Public School Act gave them the legal means to start re-inventing themselves. In 1869 the Endowed Schools Act allowed the same powers to a far greater number of other foundations, including Thring's, with a Commission to spread those powers across the country. Also in 1869, Thring founded the Headmasters' Conference, a bold move on his part that brought together, eventually, not only the Clarendon schools but all the drive and ambition of the lesser endowments.[2] Thring sat in state knowing that great men were converging on his school. He prayed that convergence might mean parity:

> Now the masters' meeting is close at hand. I am well satisfied at the men who are coming... I think the school is in very sound heart. This cheers me. The masters coming are: Harper-Sherborne; Pears-Repton; Welldon-Tunbridge; G Butler-Liverpool; Wratislaw-Bury; Stokoe-Richmond; Blore-Bromsgrove; Wood-Oakham; Mitchinson-Canterbury; Grignon-Felsted; Sanderson-(sic); Dyne-Highgate; Jessopp-Norwich; Carver-Dulwich... May God keep us all and give us wisdom.[3]

Although Uppingham boys' lives were full of ad hoc games with masters and locals joining in, Thring made one of his early bids for authority by trying to align what the boys did off their own bat with what he wanted them to do under his mastership.[4] A boys' Committee of Games and Court of Appeal was established in 1857; a gym in 1859. Soon, mortar boards and tassels were dropped for peaked sports caps, rambling and marbles, hop scotch and peg hop were dropped for football and cricket, with bans on boxing in 1860 (the year of Sayers), rounders in 1868, quoits in 1869, and bowls in 1870. The building of a quasi-independent boarding-house system based on inter-house rivalry introduced a new dynamic to School sport.

Few things in Thring's diary make him happy, but when he plays football or cricket with the boys, he is happy. 'I could not help thinking with some pride [he is 41] what Headmaster of a great school ever played a match at football before. Would either dignity or shins suffer it? I think not'.[5] Liberty made the difference between a great public school and a pinched private one and Thring, who had once preached a sermon on 'he that hath no pleasure in the strength of a horse or legs of a man', now called on the boys to play for life itself.[6] Marbles was pointless.

[2] The other Royal Commission, chaired by the Duke of Newcastle (1858–61), reported on 'sound and cheap' 'Popular Education'.

[3] Parkin, *Thring* (1900) p.176, p.175.

[4] For informal 'Games and Pastimes' at Uppingham before Thring: memoir in An Old Boy, *Early Days* (1904) ch. 10.

[5] Diary, 14 February 1862.

[6] Psalm cxlvii 10, quoted in Patterson, *Sixty Years* (1909) pp.53–4.

Cricket on the other hand, according to the School Magazine, could be 'full liberty':

> It is no good to have erratic geniuses only, who can occasionally get great scores or make astounding catches, *all* should be safe men up to a certain point, working steadily together; when that point is reached, there is full liberty for any one who can go beyond.[7]

It was boasted that Uppingham never admitted to having a 'games master' for what true blood would want such a person when they could do it for themselves?[8] But liberty for the pike is death to the minnow, and generations of boys who were not sporty suffered at the hands of those who were, or thought they were, a distinction the School Magazine wished to make clear.[9]

> The first of those who the position proud
> Have gain'd by one consent of all the crowd,
> Who bow to them as servant bows to lord,
> And worship them by ev'ry deed and word.
>
> The other class, of those whose honour dim
> Rest as with themselves (and on a paltry trim),
> These are the more o'er weening of the two,
> Although the others lead the senseless crew.

Walker remembered the custom of throwing boys over Hill House railings.[10] Turner remembered coming to school only to be crowded, lied to, mocked, humiliated, wrongly advised, wheedled into a fight, and invited to perform ridiculous tasks. He must sing. He must drink salt water. He must have rancid grease in his hair, jalap in his tea, ink in his mouth, mud on his 'inexpressibles'. They want to carry him into tea on two fingers, but first he must stretch out his arms and inflate his belly to make himself light. At which point he is punched in the pit of it.[11] No tea for him. There was also unwanted sexual attention. Thring was aware of this, and recruited married housemasters only, no more than thirty boys to a house, and made it known that he wanted his charges to know domestic comforts, not the bare board life he had known at Eton.[12]

---

[7] Editorial, School Magazine, May 1864.
[8] '...letters addressed to the Games Master are sent back with 'Not known at Uppingham School': letter of J Lomax-Simpson from 49 Rutland Gate, Kensington, to Headmaster, 26 May 1965: USAL.
[9] School Magazine, July 1907.   [10] Memoirs II 1886–96 (Ts Jan 1957): USAL.
[11] In 1864, Turner, Memoir (Ts 31 July 1933): USAL.   [12] Parkin, *Thring* (1900) pp.250–2.

Publication of a boys' monthly School Magazine from 1863 carried Thring's revolution forward by institutionalizing what had once been casual play into organized sport. Issue number 8 asked whether Uppingham was going to be a school for *Mr. Agonistes* and his five sons, or *Mr. Scholastes* and his two sons? The five sporting sons were Cricket, Football, Fives, Hockey, and Cross Country. The two scholarly sons were Classicus and Mathematicus. There was no doubt what the editor thought. He was overrun with sport in any case, page after page of it, crammed with match reports, seniors' suppers, captains' toasts, sports days and field days, trout fishing in America, Lancers in Bengal, cricket at Lords. And lots of questions. What do we mean by modern sport? How do we keep fit? When will the new cricket pavilion be ready? What are the paper chasers? *'Sublimely happy'*. Who are the rowers? *'Noblest set on earth'*. Footballers? *'Ne'er saw a finer sight'*. Praeposters? *'Demi-gods'* and so on. Houses played each other almost every day. All this boyish emulation was repeated and remembered right across the country, school upon school, day after day, year after year, blood on blood, until the moral world of English public school life entered the national soul:

> It is curious, or it seems curious at first sight, how many anniversaries occur in our School year, how often we feel inclined to say 'This time last year such and such a thing happened' etc and how nothing of importance is allowed to be forgotten owing to its echoes, as it were, which are forever recurring at fixed intervals. Old Boys' Matches, Praeposters' suppers, the leaving of Captains, the Eleven, and the Games, the leaving of Editors and Committeemen...give each year something characteristic, and vary, while they do not unsettle, the round of our school life.   (Uppingham School Magazine, 1863)[13]

> With all [these popular comics], the supposed 'glamour' of public-school life is played for all it is worth. There is all the usual paraphernalia—lock-up, roll-call, house matches, fagging, prefects, cosy teas round the study fire etc etc—and constant reference to the 'old school', the 'old grey stones'...the 'team spirit' of the 'Greyfriars men'. As for the snob-appeal, it is completely shameless...nearly all the time the boy who reads these papers—in nine cases out of ten a boy who is going to spend his life working in a shop, in a factory or in some subordinate job in an office—is led to identify with people in positions of command...
> (George Orwell, 'Boys' Weeklies', 1940)[14]

In a school of 300 boys where every boy knew his circle—'Bim' and 'Bear', 'Jeppy' and 'Jumbo'—reputations mattered. Gentlemen must not be vulgar. Gentlemen must not sham. Gentlemen must not soil their hands. Gentlemen must not part

---

[13] School Magazine, July, December 1863.
[14] Orwell, 'Boys' Weeklies' (1940) in Orwell and Angus, eds., *Collected Essays* (1970) vol. i, p.526.

their hair in the middle ('for by doing so he forfeits the manliness of his look'). Gentlemen must get in the first team.[15] 'First team colours are permanent; other trims are not'. 'Cave wore a Zingarie ribbon and a Quiduunc tie with every hope of seeing the Cambridge sash round his lithe waist later'.[16] Thring understood that a little bit of ribbon was the way to a reputation. School colours meant parity with boys greater than you. School fixtures meant parity with schools greater than yours. When Green led Uppingham to victory over Rossall by nine wickets, we can only assume the boys saw what Thring saw:

> The importance of this should be estimated not merely from the cricketing side of the question . . . The school has at last got what has been its uppermost desire for many years, the opportunity of playing another school, and that a great one.[17]

Even so, headmasters had to be watchful. Uppingham School Magazine did not see itself as a receptacle for 'incipient authors'. It said it wanted 'active power'.[18]

Bloods already ran the Magazine, the Games Committee, all the teams and all the caps and captaincies, coats and customs, rules and reputations that went into a sporting life that was itself written into the School constitution—a copy of which was furnished to every pupil.[19] In 1888, Century Magazine ran a front page story asking how Uppingham had attained a name far greater than any American equivalent. It concluded that Thring had built on boyish passions that were already in play, giving them a 'structural completeness' in the School's official life which expressed itself in turn as an 'ideal completeness' in the School's official philosophy.[20] Which was another way of saying that he had built a community of believers. When he died he was the second most famous headmaster in the world after Arnold.[21] On that cold wet day in October 1887, the new bloods were allowed to march eight abreast through the town in his name, which was more than the old bloods ever managed.[22]

---

[15] 'Is He a Gentleman?' School Magazine, December 1864. Nicknames in 'Last train back', Old Uppinghamians FC, Records (nd 1913?) p.55: USAL.
[16] On Zingarie ribbons: Hornung, himself an old boy of the School, in Fathers of Men (1919) p.135; Committee of Games, 1893: USAL. See also: Breward and Tosh, Manful Assertions (1998) p.4, and Davidoff, Best Circles (1973) p.43.
[17] School Magazine, June 1863.   [18] School Magazine, November 1863.
[19] General Rules (1877). There are photographs of the nine boy members of the Committee of Games, top of the School hierarchy, for 1888 and 1891, in the USAL photograph albums.
[20] '. . . the accepted function of the English public school is as much to mould character as to train intellect': Century Magazine, xxxvi, 1888, p.653. The piece was written by George Parkin, the man who would be Thring's hagiographer.
[21] 'One can hardly imagine a school attaining such a pinnacle of greatness in so comparatively short a period': Ludgate Monthly, April 1894.
[22] Walker, Memoirs II 1886–96 (Ts January 1957). It took some time before Thring and Parkin were unpicked: Willison, Parkin (1929) p.134.

Culture or Anarchy?

In the year of the Endowed School Act, a series of essays appeared in *Cornhill Magazine* which were later published as *Culture and Anarchy*, one of the most influential texts in nineteenth-century English letters. The author was Matthew Arnold, son of Thomas, Inspector of Schools, poet, and cultural critic. Now that they had put their hands on power, he asked the middle classes to choose. Did they want 'anarchy', the old English upper class notion of doing what you want, also known as liberty? Or did they want 'culture', a tenderized, Anglicized version of the old classical curriculum?

Arnold was writing against a trend in the teaching of classics that favoured Rome over Greece and Imperial Rome over Republican Rome.[23] As the British Empire grew, so did comparisons with the Roman Empire. But Matthew Arnold was not interested in Empire. He was interested in England and its future leaders. He called the aristocracy 'Barbarians'—and Minna and Algy spring to mind in a sporting life characterized in *Culture and Anarchy* as 'consist[ing] principally in outward gifts and graces, looks, manners, accomplishments, prowess...and all the manly exercises'.[24] He called the middle-classes 'Philistines', not the first one to do so, certainly not the last and, in his case, something to do with a personal aversion to northern chapel-going which we might associate with Methodism. The vulgar masses (Tom Sayers and his Camden friends?) he called the 'Populace'. Arnold dismissed each of these classes as forces for good in themselves, and put his hopes on educating the best of each to a condition he called 'Culture', or 'Hellenism'—a new classical principle that would replace the old (and failing) aristocratic principle. Edward Thring's brother John called for a sort of football where the power is gentle. Matthew Arnold called for a sort of classics where the power is tempered. It was the sign of an 'untempered nature', Arnold thought,

> ...to give yourself up to things which relate to the body; to make...a great fuss about exercise, a great fuss about eating...drinking...walking, a great fuss about riding. All these things ought to be done merely by the way...*spirit and character must be our real concern.*

At the very moment, then, when elite schools were off the leash and ready to grow, England's chief inspector of cultural health was calling not for the end of the aristocracy but new versions of it, not for more sport but for less.[25] Temple of

---

[23] Butler, *Britain and its Empire* (2014) p.85.

[24] Arnold, *Culture and Anarchy* (1869) pp.106–5.

[25] ibid, p.66, pp.91–6. Nathaniel Woodard's public school building programme started as a mission to raise the middle classes intellectually: Heaney, *Mission to the Middle Classes* (1969) p.72. At about this time, in matters of government, Walter Bagehot was also calling on the middle classes to take on a new mission. At the heart of both was a desire to hide middle-class dullness beneath aristocratic brio:

Rugby and Moberly of Winchester had testified to how the ancient languages left 'behind a certain residuum of power'. It was this residual power that Arnold, Thring, and a gallery of other new moral heads, were working to revive.[26]

It is true that Matthew Arnold never understood how men like Thring worked day in day out to make sport a key part of their (not yet) culturally significant institutions. But he did understand that schools had to mean something more than a boy's liberty to do as he pleased and his family's ability to pay for it. In that sense Arnold and Thring were working to the same middle from different ends— Thring practical, by trial and error in a small market town beset by jealousy and bickering; Arnold inspectorial, lofty, Francophile, driven by the idea.[27]

Once upon a time English public school boys went out to sport and left civilization behind in the schoolroom. By the end of the century, they were a new moral force flaring up in the world. Whatever else contributed to the making of modern sport, its origins in the reformed public school network was crucial. Physical striving was offered as spiritual striving. Matthew Arnold may have called for culture over anarchy, but sport is what he got.

Boys' Side

The boys' side of school life was never in the headmasters' hands. Schools were supposed to be in *loco parentis* but when it came to real life bloods ran the show.[28] '"If a prefect himself was a bully, would others stop him?" "They could not prevent him"'.[29] Right from their first day, new boys were initiated into layers of custom and practice—some from the school itself, some from out of a dark cupboard of boy custom—not to piss in the courtyard, not to undo your coat, not to sleep with your arms out, not to sleep with your arms in, or go beyond the shops, or not know 'notions', or wear a coloured tie. Nor, without entitlement, were you supposed to throw a snowball, walk more than three abreast, abuse the library key, wear a badge, pet small boys, or sit in front of a certain tree unless you were a member of the first team.[30] Boys, certain boys that is, were expected to sing in hall

English Constitution (1867) p.248; Colls, 'Constitution', *History Workshop Journal*, 2000, p.100; Colls, 'After Bagehot', *Political Quarterly* 4, 2007, pp.520–2.

[26] Dilke, *Mint Mark* (1965) p.7.
[27] Knowledge he described as 'drudgery': Collini, *Arnold* (1988) p.21.
[28] Boddice, 'Public School Authority', *Gender and Education*, 2009, p.169.
[29] Fearon (New College Oxford): Clarendon Commision PP 1864, xxi, Evidences 1, p.380, p.369.
[30] Acccording to which school you went to: Stott, *Chigwell* (1960) pp.94–5; Firth, *Winchester* (1949) p.216, pp.37–8; Furley, *Winchester in 1867* (nd) p.216; Harrow Monitors' Duties and Privileges (1948): John Johnson, Bodleian, Education Box 1, 2, 5, 6, 7, 8; Guide Book, Uppingham (1870) p.23: USAL; Leach, *Bradfield* (1900) p.91; the Lord's Tree was a Winchester privilege restricted to 'men' who were members of the First Cricket XI: McDonald, *England* (1933) p.279.

at Rugby, carve their name at Harrow, ask for the 'book' at Eton, stand in a cupboard at Winchester, sit at special table at Beaumont (except Sunday), sport a walking stick, wear a button hole, lie in a deck chair, carry a crop, pass sentence, do 'Hills', and hundreds of other minor privileges and forfeits running round a school life that was boys' side first and school side second.[31] A mountain of petty custom indicated who you were as you went through both halves of the school—the headmaster's half and the boys' half. Few boys' customs carried official sanction but there again, few were censured either. In *Tom Brown's Schooldays*, boys' side is the first thing Tom learns. When hero Brooke appeals to School House to support the Head, he appeals to boys' side first: 'come now, any of you, name a custom that he has put down'.

Boy custom at Winchester was written into manuscript books called 'Notions'. Itself a notion of English common law, every 'notion' was a previous practice or privilege definitively fixed but at the same time deliberately obscured. Here is a true story of Wykehamists. McPherson the house senior resisted taking a beating from Pollock the assistant prefect because contrary to notions Pollock had come in unannounced. Whyte the full prefect intervened and consulted the relevant manuscript book before taking the case to Ridding the headmaster who, at the time, was concerned about College order and, not wishing to provoke resentment or rebellion, referred the matter to the previous headmaster Moberly, who also happened to be his father-in-law. Moberly appeared to support the notion that house senior McPherson should be 'tunded' (one of three sorts of customary beating) by assistant prefect Pollock but no more than the conventional ten strokes even though the book said thirty (as in 2 *Corinthians* II). There were further notions to do with prefectorial and sub-prefectorial powers and, just to clarify matters, notions in transcript liked to drop the definite article and replace the 'y' and the 'i' with the 'o' sound, and all 'ations' with the 'a' sound.[32] After this, other public school jargon seems straightforward by comparison.[33] After this, mass floggings seem reasonable. After this, the idea that a prefect could get a fag to field for him while he sat in a chair seems more than sporting.

There are thousands of examples of boys' side knowledge. It didn't matter that the knowledge was arcane. So was half the curriculum to most boys. While the heads were busy gathering up their executive powers from the outside, schools remained boys' side in all the things that mattered to boys on the inside. In 1912, the report of the 40th Headmasters' Conference representing 115 schools made no mention of games not because there were no games—on the contrary—but because games were not strictly to do with them. At Bristol Grammar, the head

---

[31] *Strand Magazine*, xii, 1896; Dilke, *Moberly's* (1965) p.102, and Firth, *Winchester* (1949) pp.16–18; Levi, *Beaumont* (1961) p.66; Guide Book, Uppingham (1870) p.23.
[32] Gwyn, in Custance, ed., *Winchester* (1982) ch.13.   [33] Boyd, *Radley* (1948) pp.194–6.

asked what business games were of his. At Rugby, boys ran the School Close. At Uppingham, they ran the Upper Field. (In 1917 J P Graham dreamed he saw Christ appear with all the company of boys above it.) At Charterhouse, young Mr. Trevor-Roper hunted on a horse. At Eton, cricket was 'a sort of profession' and paid for, while the captain of boats was the greatest man in the college. At Harrow, Mr. Boucher paid £13.15.9 for one term's optional extras that included fencing and drawing. Sherborne boys only played if they fancied playing. If they didn't like a decision, they packed in. At Chigwell, boys agreed 13 to 1 on blue and white caps for football. At Bedford Modern, it was caps in Winter and bashers in Summer.[34] Team games remained in boy hands in 1912 like they had in 1864.[35] For Wykehamists, mixing with the First XI was said to be 'like eating and drinking new life'. Warner at Rugby liked to be fagged because it gave him an opportunity of 'talking to the swells'.[36] Public schools inscribed sport in their magazines and annals, in their match reports and games committee minute books.[37] Chigwell's 'Curator' wrote the Games Book in a heavy hand. For the 1890–91 football season, the 'power and go' of Moody was put against the 'apparently nervous' disposition of Hindley. Poor old Hindley. Poor old Frost, standing 6 stone wet through, we are told 'he has shown too much fear to be of any great service'.[38] Season after season house performances were reported as if the house was a living thing with a mind and a memory of its own (which of course it was). At Winchester, 'Budge' Firth was a prize-winner in English and Latin, but for house and college he was ever the man who took ten wickets for forty-one against Eton. J B Wentworth-Smith was Worksop College's supreme sporting hero for 1933, but only until the next one came along.[39] Staff room conversations never tired of wondering whether the rugger XV of 1910 surpassed the rugger XV of 1921, or 1932, or what-do-you-think 1949? Which of the Wallings brothers was best? Could the four Wallingses have got the better of the four Pickwoads? There were men in the dining room who had stayed long enough to remember such things. Staff photographs on the

---

[34] Underwood, *Bedford Modern* (1981) p.171; Report Headmasters' Conference (1912); Hill, *Bristol* (1951) p.115, pp.155–66; Clarendon Commission PP 1864, xxi, Evidences 2, p.274, p.293; ibid, xx, p.257; Patterson, *Uppingham Cricket* (1909) p.ix; Graham, *Forty Years* (1932) p.31; Sisman, *Trevor Roper* (2010) p.28; Johnson, *Eton Reform* (1861) p.28, and Clarendon Commission PP 1864, xx, p.35; An Account Midsummer 1857 of Mr. Boucher: John Johnson, Bodleian, Education Box; Gourley, *Sherborne* (1951) fn.11, p.208; Chigwell School Levee Minute Book 1903–17, 4 October 1904: Chigwell School Archive (CSA).

[35] Clarendon Commission PP 1864, xxi, Evidences 2, p.288, p.295.

[36] ibid, p.289; on fags fielding, Evidences 1, p.388, p.358, and Evidences 2, p.269.

[37] For sports kit and annals: WCA. At Rugby, boys ran the library too: Clarendon Commission PP 1864, xxi, Evidences 2, pp.294–5; Dolling, *Ten Years* (1896) p.192.

[38] Chigwell Games Book 1890–91 where Smyth (major) forgot to enter the 1909 cricket results as reported in the Levee Minute Book, 28 October 1909: CSA.

[39] 'Budge' in 1917, in Dilke, *Moberly* (1965) p.140; house reports 1933, *Talbot Annals*, May 1933–April 1936: WCA.

walls showed young men growing into old ones. Masters got old, but boys were forever young.

Thring was very clear: boys' side formed 'a complete society', 'a definite world', 'a small republic'.[40] At some schools it was called a boys' *levee*, or 'levy', because of its power to raise resources. Its remit was wider in the boarding schools than in the day schools because only there could the bloods dominate from last lights out to first morning call. Boys' side was entitled to levy itself, teach itself, select itself, play itself, judge itself, name itself, dress itself, feed itself, fag itself, and even flog itself, after its own notions. Almost the only thing it couldn't do was abscond. At Eton, white tie was school custom. All the other sartorial touches, swallow coats, collars, button holes and silks, top hats and straw boaters, were up to the boys. 'Each big boy decided for himself when he had attained a sufficiently prominent position' but, make no mistake, 'he would be advised soon enough should he have got it wrong'.[41] Boaters signified public school. No street kid would be seen dead in one. There's a remarkable overhead photograph of thousands of bashers cramming and craning to see C B Fry bat against the South Africans in 1907.[42]

Strong bonding was a mark of the blood. In the 1950s, Marsden and Jackson found that 'the critical point of conflict' in grammar schools was the degree to which boys felt that nothing less than total loyalty was demanded from the team.[43] Looking like a gentleman was equally important.[44] It paired you with the bloods and segregated you from the swots and the plebs.[45] The working class played in vest and drawers or with their sleeves rolled up. They were used to working that way. Bloods covered themselves in jerseys and long sleeves, college scarves wound and round.[46] Harold Larwood the England fast bowler knew all about vests and drawers. Born one of five sons in Nuncargate in 1904, he worked as a putter and a filler down the pit before signing for Nottinghamshire in 1922. He had seen a mate lose his arm underground, but on signing professionally he took on the cap, blazer, scarf, and photographic lustre of a public school man. He was no blood however, fast as he was. That role was reserved for his captain, Jardine, who was taller and richer and had more jerseys. Between them, Larwood sweating with the

---

[40]   Thring in 1873 according to Honey, 'Victorian Public School', Oxford DPhil (1970) p.166. 'Small republic' quoted in *Century Magazine*, September 1888, pp.653–5.

[41]   Byrne and Churchill, *Eton* (1940) pp.212–14.

[42]   At Lords: 'The Worship of C B Fry', *Daily Express*, 21 August 1907; in Levett: 'Degenerate Days', *Sport in History* 38, 2018, p.47.

[43]   Jackson and Marsden, *Education and the Working Class* (1962) pp.107–8.

[44]   In Leiden it still is: 'Leon Klaver, Kleermakers', 'van het Britse Traditional Tailoring ontwikkeld' (2019).

[45]   'Union and segregation are the two fundamental functions of fashion': Simmel, 'Fashion', *American Journal of Sociology*, 1957, p.544.

[46]   For example, D Coy 2nd Battalion Leicestershire Regt., Khartoum, 1924, gymnastics team: Army sports photos, LCRO, DE 6007/172. Unusually for a gentleman, Gladstone appears in his shirtsleeves felling trees at Hawarden in 1877: McCormack, ed., *Public Men* (2007) p.113.

ball, Jardine imperious in the field, they showed what one-nation Conservatism looked like in whites.[47]

How you looked had to do with how you signed up to the sporting life. Caps with or without tassells? Long scarves or very long scarves? Strong colours or plain white? Stripes or hoops? Quarters or halves? Dark blue or light blue? Collar up or down? Pads or no pads? Gloves or no gloves and where? (on the hand or jauntily in the back pocket?) On 31 March 1914 Mr. E H Stewart Walde proposed a white blazer for the Chigwell First XI but Moore (major) proposed dark blue instead (with light blue ribbon) and the headmaster was beaten by a single vote.[48] Hugh Thomas said you could tell a public school man at Oxford by the great heap of sports kit slumped in the corner of his room.[49]

Whites were a particular gesture. Not to be seen much around factory or pit, they had been fashionable on high days and holidays in nineteenth-century Lancashire and were now the mark of the modern man of leisure. In Huxley's *Crome Yellow*, Denis, every inch a gent, chooses white flannels.[50] Riders might get their hard hat from Lincoln & Bennett's and wear Oxford mixture cutaway, but all modern cricketers wore whites from top to toe even their boots. Rationalists said white reflected the sun's rays, but Tom Brown's School House wore whites to show they weren't scared of hackers. Truth was, modern sport was accumulating an astonishing ecology of signs.[51]

Sporting colours and badges, ribbons and trims, medals and shields, caps and scarfs, ways of playing and not playing, 'cricket' and 'not cricket' were doled out by the boys. Clutton-Brock said Eton's rules as to colours were 'too elaborate to be given in full'. Darwin called school colours 'a vast and complicated edifice'.[52] At Cheltenham it was team captains who chose the teams and got their colours. Representative sportsmen wore jerseys trimmed with ribbon, and those in the Upper Sixth who had colours were permitted to stand in the top line at football matches. At Clifton, Henry Newbolt learnt the true value of a ribboned coat. Every school suffered interminable negotiations over change or half change? colours or half colours? (permanent or minor?) ribbon or braid? (gold or green?), medal or shield? (silver or plate?), cap or blazer? (cream or blue?). Every house wanted a 'pot' on the shelf. Every boy who hadn't given up on this sporting life wanted something in his lapel. Just to remind us that not all boys adhered, Chigwell

---

[47] '... a real leader of men' according to Larwood, who took his orders to great effect in intimidating the Australians: Keating, *The Guardian*, 21 May 2014. For Larwood in sepia: *The Observer*, photograph, 5 July 2009. See also: Hamilton, *Larwood* (2009) and Douglas, *Jardine* (2002).
[48] Chigwell School Levee Minute Book, 31 March 1914: CSA.
[49] Thomas, *Establishment* (1959) p.33.   [50] Huxley, *Crome Yellow* (1921) p.15.
[51] Surtees dresses Mr. Sponge in *Sporting Tour* (1853), and shows how Sponge understood all the meanings of his apparel (p.3).
[52] Darwin, *English Public School* (1929) p.91; Clutton-Brock, *Eton* (1900) p.180. Ways of playing? 'This was the work of boys...': Allison and Maclean, 'Deathless Myth', *IJHS*, 2012, p.1881.

School Levee Minute Book for 1 March 1913 saw a proposal to replace the school sports day obstacle and sack race with a throwing the cricket ball competition. The response? 'That the Obstacle and Sack races formed an attraction to the spectators and were the only source of interest in the Sports to non-athletic boys'.[53]

Everywhere middle-class girls looked they were confronted by chin-up boys who insisted that cricket pads were second nature and that 'guts' is what you wanted. Sport certainly provided the cliché. If you couldn't play like a hero then at least you could talk like one.[54] There were sportsmen and 'slackers'.[55] There were men and boys, blues and badgers, 'ding dong battles', 'text book tries', balls 'in the box', and balls 'in the back of the net'.[56] Of course there were always those who preferred to go blackberrying or read a book or be left alone with their feelings ('All English training is a system of deadening feeling'), and there were words for them too, just as there were words for all those on the outside: so many 'boms' (abominations) and 'swipes' (servants). Cheltenham boys used to tell each other to 'Jewoff', presumably back to the Jew House. At Trinity Hall, Thornely was only 3rd XV so he was obliged, or so he felt, to 'fall back on my mind'.[57] Looking back on his schooldays at Eton, Aldous Huxley dwelled on the deficiencies of a system which could do nothing better for his body than football.[58] On the other hand, public schoolboys knew how to fit in at university.

Girls' Side

The Taunton Commission asked Mary Buss whether she thought a girl's education should be different from a boy's. She thought not, providing they were 'in the same rank of life'. She also thought it was 'rather difficult to ascertain what is the proper education for a boy' anyway.[59]

For Buss' generation of headmistresses it was important to catch up on the boys and if that meant buying a field, or lugging everything out to a field, in order to have a sports day, so be it.[60] This is not to say that girls wanted to be boys any

---

[53] The Chigwellian, no 1, 1882–83, p.2: CSA; Morgan, Cheltenham (1968) pp.113–14; Clifton College, Bristol: 'And it's not for the sake of a ribboned coat/Or the selfish hope of a season's fame' (Henry Newbolt, Vitaï Lampada 1892).

[54] Simon Raven on the importance of 'guts' at public school and as sometime captain in the King's Shropshire Light Infantry: Thomas, Establishment (1959) p.52.

[55] Turner, Boys Will Be Boys (1948) p.278.

[56] All to be found in school magazines of the period but in this case: Talbot Annals vol. iv: WCA.

[57] Turner, Memoirs (1936) p.22; 'Jewoff', Morgan, Cheltenham College (1968) p. 184, p.106; Blackberry pickers in Sargeaunt, Bedford School (1925) p.137. 'Boms' at The Leys; 'Swipes' at Stonyhurst: Farmer, Public School Word Book (1900). On 'English training' for deadening feelings: Tarr, in Wyndham Lewis, Tarr (1918) p.29.

[58] Murray, Aldous Huxley (2002) p.23.   [59] Ridley, Buss (1896) p.7, p.9.

[60] Kamm, How Different (1958) p.222.

more than Mary Buss wanted to be Edward Thring. Not every girl wanted to be a suburban tennis star. Eve Colpus shows how during the 1920s and 1930s, a lot of well-educated young women wanted more from life than fun. They wanted to be stretched, and not just at the net.[61]

Taunton called for the reform and expansion of middle-class schooling. It also called for justice. In the wake of revelations about original foundations, Dorothea Beale's short report to the Commissioners on the misappropriation of girls' endowments asked in effect for the original monies to be shared out again.[62] The richest school in the country, for example, Christ's Hospital with £56,000 per year, had been founded in 1552 for the London fatherless poor but by the 1860s it was no longer for them and it was no longer equally for girls. Along with other great endowments, it had neglected its charges. When the educational reformer Emily Davies argued that where an original foundation made no mention of sex, commissioners should assume that that meant girls had been originally included as of right, not all commissioners agreed. They did agree however that 'It cannot be denied that the picture brought before us of the state of Middle Class Female Education is, on the whole, unfavourable'. Taunton advised that foundations be changed regardless of the donor's original intentions.[63]

In 1871 the Women's Education Union was founded to press their case. In 1872 the Girls' Public Day School Company was founded with £12,000 capital and 24,000 shares to build quality schools for girls. George Eliot's *Middlemarch* was published the same year. Basing her story on two young women who have not been properly educated and have no idea what a proper education would look like, Eliot joined the debate. Dorothea Brooke decides that a proper education is an academic education or, to put it George Eliot's way, a proper education is 'a labrynth of petty causes, a walled-in maze of small paths'. Rosamond Vincy, by contrast, had not given the question much thought. Why should she? She had been 'the flower of Mrs Lemon's school', one of the best in the country, where she was 'taught all that was demanded in the accomplished female, even to extras, such as getting in and out of a carriage'? Both women are good riders it has to be said, but Dorothea thinks riding is childish and Rosamond never thinks of it at all: it's just another accomplishment, like playing the piano, or flirting. Such is the unique experience of education, Eliot seems to be saying in answer to the question

---

[61] As they 'explored connections between ideas of goodness, social purpose and personal happiness [alongside] expanding educational, professional and public opportunities': Colpus, 'Women, Service and Self-Actualization', *Past & Present* 238, 2018, p.204.

[62] Beale: Schools Enquiry Commission, *Report*, 1867–68 (1970), p.5, p.17.

[63] *Taunton Commission Report*, PP1868, p.548. It also concluded that reformed schools needed to be able to charge higher fees because seventeenth-century levels of fee income would not be sustainable, and schools should have the right 'to amend or change the original charitable foundation' in order to be so.

put by Taunton to Miss Buss, neither Dorothea or Rosamund are able to know what sort of education they should have had without having had it.[64]

The Girls' Public Day School Company opened its first school in Chelsea in 1873 and its first provincial school in Norwich in 1875. By the time the Company was wound up to form an equally successful Trust in 1905, it was responsible for thirty-seven schools with around 8,000 pupils.[65] In its centenary year, the GPDST estimated that all told it had taught over 135,000 girls up to standard, 'not ... in isolation', but by grooming female teachers, by serving as a model and a rallying point for allied schools, and by winning legal battles regarding trust monies at Bedford for example, tax exemptions at Wimbledon, and direct grants from the state in 1922.[66]

If headmistresses were good their reputations went before them. Buss of North London Collegiate was a particular GPDSC favourite, but there were others including Beale at Cheltenham, Shirreff at Chelsea, Nicol at Bath, Nelligan at Croydon, and Harriet Morant Jones at Notting Hill & Ealing. Other heads followed in their wake, especially with the coming of the 1902 (Balfour) Education Act that encouraged the expansion of local education authority secondary schools for girls under Board of Education inspection. They too soon had their histories, their walls, their gilt names and Latin tags.[67]

What they did not have were playing fields. At Birmingham the girls hardly dared step out of doors for the dirt and traffic. When they wanted a gym they relied on the one good arm of Mr. Twist the school porter to push 300 chairs against the hall wall.[68] Brighton girls may have started a school football club in 1884, but most schoolgirls, if they played football at all, like the girls of Notting Hill & Ealing, kicked at each other in a tiny backyard while Capt. Norgrave gave callisthenic lessons in his more spacious rooms next door.[69]

Before the 1869 reforms, Carol Dyhouse estimates there were over 500 girls' schools quartered in private houses—unranked, unsporting, and, for the most part, unacademic.[70] Right into the 1960s, women teachers could speak in defence of 'an intrinsic feminine need' to be taught in domestic surroundings.[71] Mary Neal

---

[64] Along the same lines, Wyndham Lewis' character Tarr 'had viewed everything in terms of sport for so long that he had no other machinery to work with and sport might perhaps, for the fun of the thing, be induced to cast out sport': *Tarr* (1918) p.32. Eliot, *Middlemarch* (1872) p.29, p.96.

[65] Magnus, *Jubilee Book* (1923) p.173.

[66] On re-appropriation of trust funds in the Bedford new scheme: Godber, *The Harpur Trust* (1973) p.110. 'Direct Grant' rewarded endowed schools in 1922 for opening a proportion of places to scholarship pupils. Wimbledon High fought the tax battle in 1925: Sondheimer & Bodington, *GPDST* (1972) p.106, p.17.

[67] See for example Kenyon, *Chelmsford Girls' High School* (1982) and Lloyd, *Story of a School* (Manchester High) (1895). On private educational entrepreneurs, another major source of private schooling, see for example, Rachel Lowe, *Adcote School* (1987).

[68] Candler and Jacques, *King Edward VI School* (1921) p.175.

[69] Sayers, *Fountain Unsealed* (1923) p.23.   [70] Dyhouse, *Girls Growing Up* (1981) p.47.

[71] Petrie Carew, *Many Years* (1967) p.xiii; McCrone, *Physical Emancipation* (1988) p.7.

called it an education in 'cliché, taboos, conventionalities and prohibitions' and Christina de Bellaigue thinks that about half middle-class girls were receiving it by the 1850s.[72] Taunton listed all the things girls' schools did not have compared to boys': not the numbers, not the buildings, not the traditions, not the discipline, not the 6th form, not the exams, not the sense of entitlement, and certainly not the fields.[73]

Locked-in for most of the day, pre-reform schools had to get their girls out and make them walk. If they couldn't walk, they might be drilled. Bergman-Osterberg recommended ten minutes per day in light clothing. Unfortunately, her instructions—'Tiles cover! Distance forward, place! Two! Position! Open files, march, two! To the right (or left), face!'—were unintelligible.[74] Cheltenham Ladies' walked every afternoon. Queenswood girls walked three times round the square every day. Enid Blyth remembered crocodiling along Eastbourne seafront while wounded soldiers sat on benches calling 'Left', 'Right', 'Left', 'Left', to put them off their step. Frances Power remembered 'dismal walks' with twenty-five girls age 9 to 19 from 32 Brunswick Terrace Brighton, and 'dreary hours' reciting verbs afterwards.[75] Almost any kind of physical activity made life more bearable. Marching to music at Hampstead High made Tuesday afternoons 'something to remember'. Miss Johnson's eurythmic classes at Manchester Central High were a joy, far nicer than ring drill. Miss Bedding's Swedish Drill at Leeds High was better than the German version. Altrincham Girls' School broke with inhibition by building bike sheds in 1912 but went back to inhibition in 1913 by introducing 'The Graceful Bicycle Riding and Posture Contest'.[76]

Because as a rule state schools did not have playing fields, elementary schools drilled according to Army Field Exercise Book 1870. The new municipal secondary (high) schools maintained the drill tradition for the same reason. On those rare occasions when playing fields were available, section 36 of the 1904 Inter Departmental Committee Report on Physical Deterioration recommended games, and under article 90 of the New Code of 1903, permitted heads and headmistresses to buy footballs and skipping ropes. 'But see Article 12 (f)'. Deep breathing, drill and dumb bells were often the best state schools could manage.[77] The Board

---

[72] De Bellaigue, *Educating Women* (2007) pp.13–14, p.139; Neal Ts, 'As a Tale that is Told' (1937): Mary Neal Archive, Vaughan Williams Memorial Library, Cecil Sharp House. I am grateful to Dr. Matt Simons for this reference.

[73] *Taunton Commission Report*, PP1868, pp.558–60.

[74] Osterberg, *Ling's Swedish System* (1887).

[75] Petrie Carew, *Many Years* (1967) p.124; Steadman, *Miss Beale* (1931) p.92; 'Everything was taught to us in inverse importance': Power quoted in Gosden, *How They Were Taught* (1969). To see them walking, see George Clausen's painting, *Schoolgirls. Haverstock Hill* (1880): Figure 7.2.

[76] Kendrick, *Altrincham Girls'* (1974) p.8; Bodington, *South Hampstead High* (1976) p.10; France, *Central High School for Girls* (1920) p.28, p.20; Jewell, *Leeds GHS* (1976) p.75. Ariel Cycles advertised a specially designed ladies' bicycle for Christmas: *Manchester Guardian*, 11 December 1899.

[77] Yoxall and Gray, *New Code* (1903) p.30; Knudsen, *Text Book of Gymnastics* (1920) pp.20–1.

of Education Syllabus of Physical Exercises for 1909 included country dancing, but then schools had to find someone to teach it.

It was in the endowed sector that girls' side pressure for sport was strongest. Beale at Cheltenham saw team sport as a male problem rather than a female opportunity but even she, in the end, had to give way. *'Then buy a field!'* she told them.[78] Trouble was, finding it. Cheltenham hockey players first had to make their way down the Malvern Road in mackintoshes to hide their legs before going through a little gate and crossing a furrowed field along a row of elms to a shed where the corner flags and ashplant walking sticks were kept. Captain for the day was the girl who had learned the rules from her brother. Sides were chosen from the keen and the stray. Play ended at 4pm. Then all the way back across the fields and back down the Malvern Road with muddy knees and wet shoes. Cheltenham once had a hockey teacher who would stand on the line and shout 'Shoot yourself!'.[79] At times they must have felt like it.

Experimental co-educational public schools such as Bedales (1893) and Summerhill (1921) saw competitive sport as part of the male capitalist agenda. They preferred the older meaning of sport as 'play' and reckoned Pacifism, Communism, and Bicyclism, made pupils feel more free.[80] All the same, where it was done well, girls' school sport was one of the great women's emancipatory movements. Adolescent girls knew the language of the body in one sense. Sport taught them it in another. Every other emancipation was just words. The Women's Social and Political Union (WSPU) encouraged marches and processions where women walked tall. An estimated 40,000 marched in the Women's Coronation Procession in 1911, including the Gymnastic Teachers' Suffrage Society. Five thousand followed Emily Wilding Davison's bedecked coffin in 1913.[81] For real feminine beauty, the WSPU went classical with flowing robes. No corset. When they really wanted a male idiot, they went sporting. 'WEEDY YOUTH', fag in mouth, 'give us a copper old sport'.[82]

---

[78] Kamm, *How Different* (1958) p.222. On Beale's principled stand against masculine combativeness: Holt, 'Public School Life', Oxford DPhil (2000) p.98, p.68. There were only two sentences on 'bodily exercise' in Buss' report to the Taunton Commission.

[79] Steadman, *Miss Beale* (1931) pp.83–5.

[80] Bedales was described in 1978 as '...a school free from the defects of the traditional English Public School' (Henderson, *Bedales School*, p.11) where, according to Iris Murdoch, 'Jesus often had to share the stage with Lenin': Watkins, 'Inventing International Citizenship. Badminton School', *History of Education*, 36, 2007, p.329. Unlike its progressive peers, Badminton (Bristol) was girls only.

[81] Davison had thrown herself under the King's horse at Epsom: John Johnson, Bodleian, Women's Suffrage Box 4, and WSPU Official Programme for Coronation, 17 June 1913: ibid, Box 3.

[82] Women's Beauty & Health magazine called for 'superb womanhood' based on sport and play in 1902, and the London Ladies Amateur Swimming Club held its first Annual Water Galas from 1909: poster, City of London ASC, 27 September 1912, and *Women's Beauty & Health* (April 1902): John Johnson, Bodleian, Sport Box 6. For feminist take-up of classical models: *The Suffragette* 23, I, 21 March 1913; and weedy youth: *Votes for Women* vi, 287, 5 September 1913. Corsets held you in, flowing robes made you free: Summers, *Bound to Please* (2001) pp. 151–4.

If not self-consciously feminist, girls' schools were objectively women-centred. Kathleen McCrone thinks school sport was double edged in that it offered girls the liberty of the playing field on the one hand but 'a repressive and containing mechanism' on the other by offering a sporting life that idealized what it was to be a man.[83] And yet it wasn't the sport that repressed and contained, only malicious contrasts with boys' and that, we can suppose, girls' schools were more able to resist.

Hockey quickly started making its way into the new female sporting life. The All England Women's Hockey Association was founded in 1896, although without the support of the men's Hockey Association (1886).[84] Lacrosse too made its way into girls' side, led by the most prestigious schools. The All England Ladies Lacrosse Association was founded in 1912, this time with the support of the men's English Lacrosse Union (1892). Cricket never ceased to be popular with privately educated young women; school loyalties just made it more serious. The 28-year-old woman who told Mass Observation that she loved 'the exquisiteness of a Hutton off drive or the incredible fineness of a Hardstaff leg glance' clearly knew about the game even though she said she didn't play it.[85] In the end, whatever modifications were made on behalf of 'the ladies', the cut and thrust of competitive sport has to be compared with what it replaced. Sport and exercise challenged unrealistic ideas about what was natural in women. Tunbridge Wells girls' gym display was open only to those fathers who were doctors. Croydon Girls' High idea of fitness training involved elegantly picking up ribbons from the floor. Ipswich Girls' kept an iron maypole for legs. Edgbaston kept an iron collar for chins.[86]

By the turn of the century, girls' schools were vying to show their commitment to playing fields, sanatoria, and plenty to eat. Innisfree School for Girls, Gerrard's Cross, put physical health to the fore. They had tennis, cricket, and netball. They were going to get hockey and lacrosse. Sanitation was good. Rooms were airy.[87] Cups and shields for sport led to cups and shields for academic achievement. Boys' schools were the model here, but there were age old differences in how girls and boys were seen which proved hard to shift. 'Character' weighed heavy on both sides and 'sport' as well, but girls were clearly more suited to dance and deportment in the same way that they were clearly more suited to home and family. Swimming was considered especially suitable. Roedean built a secret tunnel to the sea.[88] But the main difference was that girls' schools started out with no great traditions of their own. Whether boys lived out, or boarded in, they enjoyed

[83] McCrone, *Physical Emancipation* (1988) p.2.
[84] Watson, 'England Women's Hockey Tour', *IJHS*, 2016, p.2078.
[85] Report on Sport for National Panel July 1949: University of Sussex MO Archive file 3141.
[86] Macrae, *Female Life Cycle* (2016) ch 3.
[87] Prospectuses (nd 1920s): John Johnson: Bodleian, Education Box.
[88] Parker, 'Swimming', *IJHS*, 2010, p.686.

historic entitlements. The Taunton Commission Report was shy in talking about these things, although buried towards the end it did talk about 'impalpable' influences, 'entirely subject' to boys' side attitudes, that 'often form the main consideration'. As far as we can tell, there was no girls' side equivalent.[89]

Small groups of girls in private homes were a world away from what Thring found on his arrival at Uppingham, let alone what he saw as a boy at Eton. Many girls' schools forbade pupils even to speak.[90] This could have consequences. At Eastbourne, one girl indicated on a country walk that she had swallowed some glass. They rushed her back to find she had said she had swallowed some grass. At Notting Hill and Ealing, they joked about Rule 8 as enforced by 'Prefect-Girles light ... tinne medals bright':

> One calls 'No talking on ye stair,
> Lest mischief ye befall!
> One single fyle! One double fyle!
> No talking in ye Hall'[91]

Katherine Mansfield once said of her time at Queen's College that she 'lived in the girls' as well as the buildings, and here we can find the clue.[92] Those girls who wanted sport and liberty had to scratch their own traditions from poor soil. South Hampstead's first society was a games society started by the girls themselves. They had a ledger, but no facilities. Roedean girls went riding and running from the earliest days in Kemptown, but no fields yet.[93] Bedford Girls' Modern founded their own cricket club but had to be screened from the boys next door. Bedford Girls' High magazine 'Aqulia' helped girls chose their own captains—but only helped.[94] Edgbaston, Cheltenham, and North Oxford Girls also enjoyed their own in-house magazines although sport did not dominate and at Cheltenham it hardly featured at all in a crushingly academic journal that dealt with sport like it dealt with hygiene: 'For girls and women the varieties of exercise are somewhat restricted but a ride or a good walk, provided it be not on a level road, or a game at Lawn Tennis, are not to be surpassed'. That the Magazine should appeal for contributions that were not 'touched up' by teachers, and that girls should be given as free a hand 'as possible' rather speaks for itself. St. Swithun's Winchester

[89] *Taunton Commission Report*, PP1868, pp.200–1.

[90] For examples: at Cheltenham, Steadman (1931) p.113; at Roedean, de Zouche (1955) p.84; at South Hampstead, Bodington (1976) p.8.

[91] Sayers, *Fountain Unsealed* (1973), rhyme by Emma Salter, School Magazine, p.44; Eastbourne, in Petrie Carew, *Many Years* (1967) p.123.

[92] Grylls, *Queen's College* (1948) p.69.   [93] de Zouche, *Roedean* (1955) pp.32–6.

[94] Godber and Hutchins, *Bedford High* (1982) chs 7, 8, 9; Broadway and Buss, *Bedford Girls' Modern* (1982) pp.156–7.

ran their own house matches and Miss Ottley of Worcester allowed cricket only on the understanding that she 'totally detested' it.[95]

Cheltenham Ladies' founded their 'Captains' Club' in 1903. It is not unreasonable to suppose that the Club was the result of pressure from the girls and perhaps staff—the first games mistress having been appointed in 1896, and the first hockey match having been played in 1895. Whoever pushed for sport hardest, there is no doubt that there was a side to Cheltenham young ladies that was girls' side first. They defended their majority representation in the Captains' Club (by one), they insisted on the election of President, Secretary, and Treasurer, on team captains and their selection of teams. We can get a feel of girls' exuberance for the sporting life simply by noting the College's repeated calls for order: for less bad behaviour, less rough play, less cheering, no cheek, no climbing over the railings and, in lacrosse, no tackling across, no banging up, no shooting hard, and no body pivoting. In other words, no lacrosse.[96] Even in Miss Beale's day, girls knew how to report a match in the jargon, with 'sharp struggles' in mid field, 'sweeping past' on the wing, 'baffling' the backs and greatest sporting question of all: 'But what may not happen in five minutes?'[97] In 1920 the headmistress, herself a top ranked hockey player, warned that girls who did not play games should not be looked down upon, that 'College came always before games', and that games 'were not the beginning and end of everything'.[98] The Cheltenham Old Girls' Guild was yet another Beale innovation. Its members were eligible to play for and serve the Captains' Club, and we should not underestimate its growing influence on 'the bond of sympathy formed only in youth' that it encouraged. When one Old Girl went to the US on an England Ladies hockey tour she reported to her bullies back home that when it came to sport, American girls didn't have a clue. They embraced. They ate suet pudding. They had a half-time lie down. *On rugs.*[99]

Like the boys, Cheltenham ladies enjoyed a bewildering mosaic of signs and symbols in hats and hat bands, scarfs and colours, brooches (1905), ties (1907), and badges (1913). Cheltenham seems to have had its own version of the bloods and all these things mattered, to them at least.[100] Captains' Club decided in 1907

---

[95] Dyhouse, *Girls Growing* (1981) pp.67–8; Cheltenham Ladies' College (CLC) Magazine, 1883, 4, 8, p.23, 1931, 52, 20, p.66; lecture by E T Wilson MD; Bain, *St Swithun's* (1984) p.9.

[96] Cheltenham Ladies' College Captains' Club (CLCCC) Minute Book (1921–39), 4 February 1932; CLCCC Minute Book (1917–20) October 1917: 'At the same time it was felt by the Club that the Selection Committee ought primarily to represent the opinions of the girls themselves'; example of repeated calls for better manners, ibid, September 1917.

[97] Match report for 7 December 1895: Collegians v Old Girls, written up in Constitution of the CLCCC, December 1921.

[98] CLCCC Minute Book (1917–20), 17 December 1920, Miss Faithfull in the chair leading Captains' Club discussion on what to do with 'carelessness' and 'refusals'.

[99] Kate Lidderdale, 'The English Hockey Team in America', CLC Magazine, 1922, 2; bonds and belonging, CLC Magazine, XXII, Autumn 1890.

[100] C. Downie, St. Helen's champion house, Secretary Captains' Club (1908–10), Cricket Select Committee (1910), Cricket XI (1906–08), Cricket Captain (1907–08), Hockey XI (1906–10), Captain

that ties should be knitted, with white stripes of differing breadth according to 1st or 2nd team, and in 1922 it decided

> That each College or House team in which a girl figures shall be indicated by a different coloured star in the corners of her College or House CLC badge. In the case of girls in College teams, and House teams for different games, House stars shall go outside the College badge, on the tunic. That House colours should be indicated by a strip of House ribbon placed above the CLC badge, that green tunics shall be worn by the College 1st teams for matches.[101]
>
> (Constitution, 1922)

> Why all this fuss about a little ball?
> Almost before I ask myself, I know;
> It is man's greatest wish to conquer all,
> To reach the goal where he has aimed to go.
> And yet, on holiday, I have no itch
> To go and stand upon a hockey pitch.[102]
>
> (Rosalind Franey, 1964)

At the same time, it is clear that the College was not willing to give girls' side full rein. All Captains' Club meetings were chaired by a member of staff, another staff member was always present as President of the Field Committee but had no vote, and another member was not present but had the right of veto as President of the Games Committee. Team captains could call a meeting at any time, but so could the chair.[103] In the 1920s, chairs started using captains to do their business for them. Miss Smith used the Captains' Club as a conduit for order. Girls were not to enter cubicles before the bell. Girls were not to talk at the pool edge, or stand there, or go above the five-foot water mark, or not wear regulation bathing caps.[104] Miss Nicholls did not approve of girls cheering the College versus Staff match 'without restraint [and] using nicknames for the members of the staff who were playing'.[105] Message from head: 'cheering not to go on indiscriminately the whole time'. Message from Miss Bickmore: captains not to be shy about asking questions after Mr. White's lecture, but only the right questions.[106] All wicket keepers

---

Hockey (1910), 2nd Hockey XI (1907–08), Captains' Club representative, Playground Committee (1908–11): CLCCC Members (1907–29).

[101] Constitution of CLCCC, 1922.   [102] Rosalind Franey, CLCCC Magazine, 1964, 85.
[103] Constitution of the CLCCC, December 1921.
[104] Miss Hilda Hursthouse Smith, PE teacher (1922-33), CLCCC Minute Book (1921–39) 15 May 1925.
[105] Miss Nicholls, CLCCC Minute Book (1917–20) March 1918.
[106] ibid, Miss Bickmore, 14 October 1920; Miss Faithfull, November 1919.

were to wear gloves, at least on the left hand.[107] All captains to ensure that skirts for hockey were not less than 6 inches from the ground.[108] A 'refusal', or a 'ref', was work handed in so late the teacher refused to mark it. A 'careless' was a mistake. So many carelessnesses made a ref, so many refs made a disqualification from games.

How you looked was as important for girls' side as for boys'. It hadn't been long since young women had been liberated from wasp waist corsets into the glorious freedoms of the liberty bodice, the sexless shirt, and the gymslip. There had been a time when crinolines came with a cord to lift the skirt. Now Newnham College played tennis in dresses full of pockets (for the balls) and in 1922 the Boat Club turned out in shorts.[109] Scullers in collars and ties did not look like rowers and were not going to be able to give of their best.[110] Brims (up or down?) Hats (on or off?) Shirts (in or out?) Ties (tight or slack?) Hair (bunched or loose?) Skirts (above or below?) Cardigans (buttoned up or vee?) Shoes (heels or flatties?) It's the details that make a culture and culture that interprets the details. At one extreme, these were skirmishes over the limits of school authority. At the other, these were massive battles over the female image. At King Edward VI Birmingham, the move to change blouses 'aroused an extraordinary amount of discussion and excitement'. At St. Helen's & St. Katherine's Abingdon, the right to wear 'posture girdles' was decided by gym staff. The girdle, infact, was only a piece of tape in house colours hanging from the waist. Central High Manchester suffered 'constant guerilla warfare about hat brims'. Miss Beale banned corsets at Cheltenham. Edgbaston High tried to introduce a sort of romper suit for the gym. In an inspired moment, Roedean introduced North African *djibahs*. Girls loved them. Parents took another view.[111]

During the 1920s the gymslip (with or without girdle) drove all before it. Said to have been invented by Mary Tait, a student of Madame Bergman-Osterberg, but then adopted across the country as basic school uniform, the black or navy gym slip—short, loose, pleated, square collar, and sash—changed everything about how modern girls looked and moved.[112] Eventually it morphed into the pinafore and the pinafore into the mini dress, but in essence it neutralized the female figure

[107] CLCCC Minute Book, 15 June 1903.   [108] ibid, 17 November 1903.

[109] Collection box 4, TWL 2004.169, 2004.192, TWL 2004.170: Women's Library, London Metropolitan University; Smalley, 'Newnham and Girton', Leicester MA 2010, pp.21–2.

[110] Team photographs TWL 2004.169 and170: Women's Library, London Metropolitan University.

[111] De Zouche, *Roedean* (1955) p.73, and Candler and Jacques, *King Edward VI* (1971) p.113; Groves, *Nuns, Buns* (2003) p.129; France, *Central High* (1970) p.31; Steadman, *Miss Beale* (1931) p.49; Whitcut, *Edgbaston HS* (1976) p.71.

[112] Martina Bergman-Osterberg (1849–1915) was influential in various physical education teacher training initiatives, including the founding of Dartford College where Mary Tait attended in 1897. She served as Superintendant of the London School Board Physical Education for girls and infant schools from 1881–85, after PE had been made compulsory in 1876. See May, *Bergman-Osterberg* (1969), and Godber and Hutchins, *Bedford High* (1982) pp.162–3.

while allowing free movement. All arms and legs now, girls lifted the hem above and below the knee as fashion demanded. Mary Quant added style and daring.[113] Accessories mattered just as much. Helen Taylor's greatest sporting moment at Eastbourne (1908–13) was her first pair of sunglasses.[114]

That not everybody liked team games did not mean that they did not like to sport. At Edgehill, Bideford, the girls called it 'escapades' and had them by night. Nude swimming and shinning down the drainpipes were more perhaps than one might expect from a Methodist girls' boarding school.[115] At Sherborne, boys and girls 'trundled'. At Bedales they 'corridored'. At Queenwood, they danced with torches and on one occasion stood entranced while the girl with red hair danced the *ballets Russes*. At Cheltenham the girls went mad with joy at the announcement that the war was over. They yelled themselves black in the face, went dancing dressed as divas and demons, couldn't move for the crush, couldn't hear for the noise, and couldn't not end the evening flat out on their beds eating chocolate.[116] At [S]notting Hill High, Kathryn Flett was 'rubbish at hockey' but as the girl with the peroxide hair she found her own sporting life elsewhere.[117]

All this, along with the boys' side traditions, fed into that new student ethos that developed with the expansion of civic universities from the 1930s and especially with the spurt in new universities from the 1960s. No one, least of all university authorities, doubted that the undergrad experience they were so keen to impart depended on a collegiate life that gave the impression that students could and must do as they pleased.[118] No lecture or laboratory could match the emotions associated with that life, and 'sport' in both the narrow and wide sense was an inevitable part. Having completed nine terms, students got their BA. But there had to be more to university life than this and so there was, including 'debating, singing, acting, sport and talking until 3 in the morning about everything under the sun'.[119] From all the paraphernalia of obeying the rules to all the magic of breaking them, university students invented the modern university and something of what it was to be young.[120]

Alice Smalley's account of student life at Newnham and Girton noted that rule-breaking grew in direct proportion to rule-making. If there was Sunday Lunch,

[113] Mary Quant (1934–): English fashion designer. 'K stands for KNEES which are much in evidence': Principal's report, Cheltenham Ladies' College Magazine, 1968, 89. 'Mini skirts are powerful' (but not as powerful as sports kit): Amelia Tait, *New Statesman* 25 October 2019.

[114] Petrie Carew, *Many Years* (1967) p.117.   [115] Shaw, *Edgehill* (1988) p.23, p.30.

[116] Diary of 13 year-old Margery Hunter Woods, Cheltenham Ladies' College Magazine, 89, 68, pp.57–8.

[117] Flett, 'Please Miss I'm back', *The Observer*, 25 August 2001; Petrie Carew, *Many Years* (1967) p.122. I am grateful to Tim and Izzie Beazley for Sherborne trundling; Bedale corridoring is to be found in Henderson, *Bedales* (1978) p.46.

[118] 'Learning is not the sole function of a university. It is also a mileu, a place where a spell is cast over the student': Annan, *The Dons* (2000) p.54.

[119] R J White, 'Cambridge Life' (1960) in Gosden, ed., *How They Were Taught* (1969) p.273.

[120] Pedersen, 'Enchanting Modernity', *History of Universities*, 2002, pp.166–8.

there was the Leaving Sunday Dinner Society, once a term, up to London on the train. If there was No Smoking, there was The Clough Hall Smoking Society, Blue Room, Saturdays: 'smokes provided'. There was (and for all I know still is) The Drinking Society, Library, after 10pm. There was also night climbing.[121] No one could claim for a moment that climbing up and over Girton College in the dark was not a sport. Cambridge girls claimed their liberty no less than Edward Whymper or Minna Burnaby. They certainly had no need of *The Roof-Climber's Guide to Trinity* (1899) or *Night Climbers of Cambridge* (1937) in order to learn how to do it, any more than they required boots or ice picks. Rebecca Wetten threw off her shoes to free climb her way over the Cambridge History Faculty in a pink May Ball gown.[122] There seems to have been something of the blood in this taste for danger, whether in the Alps or half way across the college roof.

On 26 July 1895 Mrs Henry Sidgwick, Principal of Newnham College ('Nora' to her friends) laid Roedean's new school foundation stone. In her speech to a school that fronted the sea, she acknowledged the role of the sporting life in expanding the lives of girls. What 'used to be the monopoly of boys', was girls' side now, she said. This meant swimming. This meant cricket and lacrosse. This meant taking possession. This meant having, as Virginia Woolf was not to say a generation later, a mind of one's own.[123]

Nobody's Fault?

It was suggested to the young Charles Dickens that his first book should be about a club of stupid sportsmen. He refused. The idea was not new, he said. For Jane Austen, dogs and guns equalled stupidity and, by and large, she avoids stupidity. For George Eliot, those who are fond of horses are not the most interesting people, while Dickens—the most famous man in England and its most powerful commentator—went on to leave a trail of flattened sportsmen in his wake: Dorrit, or 'Tip' to his friends, a nonentity; Sparkler the same; Gowan, never without his dog (sure sign); Wobbler, circumlocutor; Sir Leicester Dedlock, reactionary; Lord Tite Barnacle, parasite; Sir Mulberry Hawk, predator; Mr. Hamilton Veneering, shallow; Mr. Toots, not right in the head; Dumpkins and Podder, *cricketers*, and so forth. Surtees' sporting types ranged from Sir Harry Scattercash ('always ready for a drink') to Mr. Waffles ('who like many men with nothing to do, was unpunctual'). Rawdon Crawley and

---

[121] Smalley, 'Newnham and Girton', Leicester MA 2010, pp.166–7.

[122] As told in 'The shadowy climbers scaling Cambridge's college rooftops': BBC News, 11 April 2019. Whymper (1840–1911) made the first sporting ascent of the Matterhorn in 1865.

[123] *A Room of One's Own* (1929) published after Woolf had delivered two lectures at Girton and Newnham; 'Address by Mrs Sidgwick', opening Roedean School (1895): John Johnson, Bodleian, Education Box.

George Osborne in Trollope's *Vanity Fair* (1848) sport but do not impress. Half the frauds Mayhew found on the streets of London pretended to be gentlemen: so many *swells* and *geezers* always short of *rhino*. In 1852 one army officer's idea of sport was to pay someone to knock over a drunk, or cartwheel across a pastry shop. Even the best sportsmen need a helping hand. Rochester crashes past Jane on a mighty hunter led by a bounding hound. He falls off. She rushes up. Is there anything she can do? Too much, it turns out.[124]

The blood's desire to live dangerously won few friends outside the clique.[125] Mad sporting squires like Osbaldeston, or Waterford, or Mytton, or Baird, lost fortunes gambling and became celebrities of a sort (the wrong sort) in the process. When the 5th Earl Lonsdale claimed he had beaten John L Sullivan in a private fight in New York, we are reminded that the same man claimed the North Pole was pink.[126] The provincial press was full of foolish goings on, from *battues* in the park to accidents in the wood. Dickens' Mr. Winkler carries his gun wrong and Mr. Pickwick, for reasons we cannot go into here, objects to the indignity of being shot in a wheelbarrow.[127] There had been a time when young gentlemen did not know or care about manners. Life was lived through the body—the hunt, the ball, and the dinner, the bloods, the bucks, and the blades. But as private life became more private and finely tuned, the difference between what was vulgar and not vulgar became more noticed.[128]

George Osbaldestone's *Autobiography* (1856) is astonishingly frank in its list of vulgar exploits. As a *non pareil*, an out and outer, a plunger, a thruster, and master of nine hunts, this man, this top sporting squire of his day, played everything and grouse were not the only thing he bagged in pairs.[129] He did as he pleased, or said

---

[124] Rochester dominates Charlotte Bronte's *Jane Eyre* (1847), except when Jane does. He loves to hunt, drink, smoke, and escort French actresses but 'Quaker' Jane beats him every time, and gives him new sight. My Dickens examples come from *Bleak House* (1852), *Dombey & Son* (1846–48), and *Little Dorrit* (1857). On Pickwick, see Pierce and Wheeler, *Dickens Dictionary* (1878) p.19. Mayhew's gentlemen pimps and beggars are to be found in his *London Labour* (1850–52) pp.335, 390–4. 'Rhino' is sporting slang for money. Willoughby and Middleton are sportsmen at odds with each other in Austen's *Sense and Sensibility* (1811) and there are other sporting dullards in her *Mansfield Park* (1814) and *Persuasion* (1817).

[125] D'Cruze, *Everyday Violence* (2000) pp.5–6.

[126] Sutherland, *Mad Hatters* (1987) p.29, p.63, p.138; Onslow, *The Squire* (1980) p.112. The Marquis of Waterford organized private cat killings when hunting in Leicestershire: CPSA, vol. ii, minutes, 5 December 1836.

[127] From voluminous examples of shooting accidents across all counties: *Durham County Advertiser*, 16 January 1819 and 'Veritas', *Dangerous Sportsmen* (1861). On needless and pointless massacre of game birds (*battues*): *Sportsman's Magazine*, 16 January 1847.

[128] Collins, *Sport in Capitalist Society* (2013) p.42. On representations of the male body in art: Schehr, *Andrology* (1997) pp. 114–19. On the new etiquette: Morgan, *Manners, Morals and Class* (1994) p.62 and Bucknall, *LRB*, 15 June 2017. On fine taste and commodity choice: Humphreys, *Tate* (2001) pp. 58–64. On the old visual culture of the beau and demi-monde: Hilton, *Mad Bad* (2006) p.36, p.133.

[129] He recounts bedding two cousins at once in a Nottingham hotel: Osbaldestone, *Autobiography* (1856) pp.18–25, p.41.

he did. Frith's famous painting 'Derby Day' (1858) shows Osbaldestone types doing the same. The Derby was England's greatest sporting event, a 'fusion of the people and the peerage' according to the *Daily Telegraph*, who 'mobbed and nobbed together'.[130] Betting on the horses, the dogs, and later the football results were working-class hobbies too, involving a fair amount of skill ('form'). In this great national liking for a flutter, everybody knew the Derby winner, the jockey, and maybe the trainer if not the owner. For the vast majority of working-class bettors, it is safe to say that betting was part of their small change economy, not a social problem except insofar as off-course betting was made illegal in 1853.[131] But as the aristocratic set refused to mend their ways, more serious mid Victorians started picturing them as degenerate.[132] After the Derby, Hippolyte Taine went to a little brothel in Cremorne Gardens with his sporting pals. There he found the classes dancing with each other, rather miserably, he had to admit.[133]

Racing men were advised to 'avoid looking into the mirror' for fear of vanity, but racing's real problem was on course betting.[134] Trollope warned against corruption. Nimrod pleaded for true aristocrats to save their sport. So did *The Racing Times*. So did *Punch*. So did the *Sporting Magazine*. *Punch's History* (1922), included a chapter on 'Recreation, Sport and Pastime' as a tale of aristocratic futility.[135]

Surtees' Mr. 'Soapy' Sponge is represented as a fraud in all things to do with horses except his horsemanship. Espied on his usual predatory circuit round Piccadilly, we find him taking 'long checks' on women and horses both, his two favourite subjects.[136] You can tell Soapy by his horsey gait and tight trousers. *The Illustrated Sporting News & Theatrical & Musical Review* for 1863 captures the flavour of his life. That Maccaroni won The Derby and the 2000 Guineas in fine style goes without saying, but the adverts at the back for brisker whiskers and erectile dysfunction tell us more.[137] Soapy's was a world where gentlemen would suddenly bolt, odds suddenly shorten, and bookies suddenly disappear. By the 1850s, this sporting world, led by racing and boxing, once so popular,

---

[130] *Daily Telegraph*, 26 May 1864.

[131] And driven into illegal corners until 1960 when it was made legal again. Chinn leads you into this sporting underground in *Better Betting* (2004): pp.72–133.

[132] According to the painters. Cowling's *Artist as Anthropologist* (1989) picks out the pathological side (p.139). On degeneration as a 'European disorder' applied to lower as well as upper classes: Pick, *Faces of Degeneration* (1989) p.198, p.253. Deuchar, *Sporting Art* (1988) pp.88–102, and for champagne picnics on carriage roofs: *The Graphic*, 18 June 1869.

[133] Taine, *Notes* (1860–70) p.46.   [134] Anon, *English Gentleman* (1849) pp.103–4.

[135] *Sporting Magazine*, 1863, p.44; Trollope, *British Sports* (1868) p.1; Nimrod, *The Chace* (1837) pp.99–100; *The Racing Times* periodically campaigned to clean up the turf: for example, 5 January, 9, 16 March, 21 December 1863. There were criminal syndicates in racing in the 1920s: Shore, 'Racecourse Wars', *20c British History* 22, 2011.

[136] On which 'he had voted himself a consummate judge': Surtees, *Mr Sponge's* (1853) p.126.

[137] *Illustrated Sporting News*, 30 May 1863.

once so English, was falling into low regard.[138] Cribb died in 1848 without hardly a mention. Caunt was declared champion in 1850 with a belly too big to take the great man's belt.[139]

Long indulged, the sporting gent joke was beginning to wear a bit thin. Lord Dundreary (an upper class twit) appeared in Tom Taylor's hit *Our American Cousin* (1861) and everyone recognized the type. 'Little Tich' too, the music hall comedian, was named after a scandal—the Tichborne Case—that challenged the aristocratic principle at base. Thackeray's 'snobs' inhabited every sphere of polite society, but the 'big shots', the ones who blasted away on the moors, or the fox-hunters who rode so expansively through meagre villages, were particularly prominent. Chartists never stopped defending the true constitution and attacking a *faux* aristocracy. A mid-century moral alliance of Gladstonian Liberals and Evangelical Christians brought aristocratic misdemeanours into the moral spotlight. John Bright thundered, Oxbridge found it increasingly difficult to defend its hide-bound curriculum, clergymen found it increasingly difficult to join the hunt. So did respectable women. Peel repealed the Corn Laws in 1846 and with it price subsidies for landowners: a huge emotional shift. Sir Stafford Northcote, who went on to sit on the Taunton Commission, reported on the Civil Service in 1854 recommending promotion by merit, not birth: another huge emotional shift.[140]

In the past, there had always had been some old boy to wheel out of the shires to cry 'balderdash' at any talk of reform. By the 1860s however the whole class was on the defensive. Criticized on the usual grounds as reactionary and monopolistic, the most telling criticism was emotional.[141] In 1858, Thomas Assheton Smith, the great hunter, found himself the hunted when a letter to *The Times* likened him to 'an insulated fragment of some former period'—and the same criticism was being made fifty years later when another great landowning MFH, Sir Willoughby de Broke, was the man to mock after he had led opposition to reform of the the House of Lords.[142] The civil service, the professions, the church, the monarchy,

---

[138] See for example *Leicester Mercury*, 8 October 1842; *Leicester Chronicle*, 27 June 1863. For comments on a truer sporting manliness: Capt. Blenkinsopp-Coulson in his address to RSPCA: 10th Annual Report 1883, p.22.

[139] Harvey, 'Evolution', Oxford DPhil (1996) pp. 271–85.

[140] On the big shots: *The Medusa*, 6 March 1819; on Gladstonian Liberals: Morley, *Fortnightly Review*, 10 October 1869; on Oxbridge curriculum: Evangelista, 'Colony of Hellas', *British Studies*, 2006, pp.53–7; on depravity: Anon, *The English Gentleman* (1849) pp.2–4; on social criticism: Donajgrodzki, ed., *Social Control* (1977) p.55, and Diamond, *Victorian Sensation* (2004) pp.137–47, p.283. Cannadine devoted a whole book to the spotlight on aristocratic degeneration: *Decline and Fall* (1990), and see for example shooting plutocrats, pp.355–70. 'Little Tich' was the comedian and dancer Harry Relph (1867–1928), nicknamed after the notoriously false claim to the Tichborne estates (1873–74). Relph was 4 foot 6 inches tall and 'tich' came to mean small.

[141] Taylor, *Lords of Misrule* (2004) p.15 and ch 3, pp.79–83.

[142] The *Hunting and Polo Journal* for October 1925 could still see de Broke as a hero (p.213) but George Dangerfield's classic account of pre-war England portrayed him and his friends, the 'Ditchers', as out and out do or die reactionaries and that is what they remained: 'Their Lordships Die in the Dark', *The Strange Death of Liberal England* 1910–1914 (1935) pp.52–68. For an example of the old

the army, the landed gentry, the schools and universities, the pensioners of the system, and all the old centres of masculine prestige, field sports especially, were beginning to creak at the top while the Industrial Revolution was busy churning everything up below. We can call this as a crisis of elite masculinity if we like and if we did, the new headmaster cult from the 1860s could be seen as one response to it.[143] Coleridge had lodged the principle and practice of Permanence in the constitution firmly with the landed class. He looked to them for the fundamentals—the discipline, cohesion and durability—that all societies must have. But it was all going wrong. The aristocratic principle, still strong in closed institutions like the army but collapsing everywhere else, was failing in its duty, as John Stuart Mill put it, to provide the state with that 'something', that 'fixed point', that 'something settled', 'not to be called into question', which all successful states require.[144]

Little Dorrit (1857) was Dickens' most ambitious attack on this failure of fundamentals. Little Dorrit's father is a debtor of the Marshalsea Prison in Southwark. Though a pauper completely without means, or any fixed point other than his place of incarceration, for all that he sees himself as an aristocrat. He calls himself 'Father' of the Prison as if it was the House of Commons. He goes round cadging calling it 'a kindness' as if it was an honour. Written during the middle 1850s in an age of hegemonic muddle and failure, Dickens' working title for the novel was 'Nobody's Fault'.[145]

Somebody's Fault

Whose fault it was became all too clear in the winter of 1854 when the British army found itself in Russia freezing to death. By the close of the Crimean War, in 1856, some 11,000 soldiers, or nearly a quarter of the expeditionary force, had died, the overwhelming majority from cold, cholera, and dysentry. William Russell of *The Times* invited ladies back home to gaze into a mass grave of British soldiers staring at the sky 'covered with scarlet and blue cloth with lace and broidery and blood'.[146] *The Times*' 1854 Christmas message was that the British army, along with their French and Turkish allies, was conducting a

---

'Balderdash', see Sir David Baird in *Tom Spring's Life*, 29 May 1842. About Assheton Smith: letter to *The Times* in Itzkowitz, *Peculiar Privilege* (1977) p.138.

[143] Protherough, 'Shaping the Image of the Great Headmaster', *Educational Studies*, 1984, p.240.
[144] Mill, 'Coleridge' (1840), in Robson, ed., *Collected Works* (1969) vol. x, pp.133–4, p.163.
[145] Dickens finished it the year after the Crimean Board of Enquiry and remarked that 'The power of Nobody is becoming...enormous in England': Dickens in *Household Words*: Slater, ed., *Dickens' Journalism*, vol. 3, 1851–59 (1998) p.396.
[146] Russell, *British Expedition* (1858) pp.216–17.

campaign of incredible ineptitude.[147] Supplies were insufficient, water contaminated, clothing inadequate, trenches flooded, tents fragile, battles inconclusive (only one clear victory, Alma), and Raglan, the Commander in Chief, hardly to be seen. The army was the largest single item of public expenditure, greater even than the navy. In January 1855, Prime Minister Aberdeen resigned. His government had been contemplating a brilliant plan whereby remaining home forces were sent to Russia while foreign mercenaries were brought in to keep order at home.[148]

The Crimean War found its way into popular myth long before the war was over. Girls were named Alma and woolen hats Balaclavas.[149] The disasters were sensed before they happened because after a British force had been swallowed whole at Kabul in 1842, there had been a decade of failed attempts to reform the army.[150] Wellington was Commander-in-Chief and that was enough to douse the reformers. No one dared take him on. But after his death, blame could be laid personally for the debacle in The Crimea. It was not just that the Duke of Cambridge, 35 years old and in charge of the First Infantry Division, was the Queen's cousin, or that Estcourt, the Adjutant General, most unfortunately had his photograph taken sleeping in a deckchair in the middle of the gravest crisis in British military history, or that Lord Raglan the Commander-in-Chief had last seen active service against Napoleon, or that Lords Cardigan and Lucan all but destroyed the cavalry between them.[151] It was that these men had failed to live up to their own reasons for being there. This was killing after all, and that, anciently and traditionally, was aristocratic business.[152] British cavalry officers' early morning races at Kamara may well have caught the Cossack pickets' attention, but not only did these free British spirits not win the war, they lost the argument.[153] The army his chosen profession, the horse his chosen instrument, 'This is *the* Man', Wellington had assured Raglan—the man to whom the country looks 'in moments of difficulty and danger'.[154]

Soon after the Duke's death in 1852, Lord Hardinge had tried to renew the reform campaign but the outbreak of war in 1853 caught him out and the charge of the Light Brigade on 25 October 1854 caught them all out. Someone, a lot of

---

[147] *The Times*, 23 December 1854. Out of the eleven generals, only one, Scarlett of the Heavy Brigade, proved competent: Hibbert, *Raglan* (1961) pp.13–16, p.41.

[148] Coates, 'How *The Times* went to war with a government', *The Times*, 31 October 2009.

[149] Markovits, *Crimean War in the British Imagination* (2009).

[150] 'The British army, as is well known, is the dernier resort of the idle, the deprived, and the destitute': 'Staff Sergeant', 'British Army' (1846) p.270. For a full account of the 1840s reform campaign, and its failure: Strachan, *Reform of British Army* (1984).

[151] Photograph of Estcourt by Roger Fenton from his Crimean War Collection: Tom Crewe, *LRB*, 16 November 2017.

[152] Anderson, *Liberal State* (1967) p.108.

[153] Russell, *British Expedition* (1858) p.584. As well as the racing, there were Eton Harrow cricket matches: Markovits, *Crimean War* (2009) fn.26, p.233.

[154] Wellington to Lord Fitzroy Somerset, Baron Raglan, 8 December 1845, cited in Strachan, *Reform* (1984) p.14.

people in fact, had blundered. Six hundred and seventy-three officers and men of what was reckoned to be the best cavalry corps in the world charged the Russian lines in the best sporting spirit. Riding at a good clip, Cardigan holding the line like a master of hounds ('Hold hard sir!'),[155] their final full cry into Russian ranks brought them to bear on nothing they could take or break and they could do no other than to turn and make the long way back. In utterly humiliating circumstances, about 270 men and over half the horses were killed or died from their wounds. Four weeks into the campaign, this was the most exciting run in British hunt history. But what were they hunting? Given the futility, one is tempted to think only the excitement. Above all, this was the most high-handed failure in the most aristocratic of British institutions. Wellington's 'Man' was dying in a heap of lace.[156]

By March 1855 over half the Crimean expeditionary force was unfit to fight and that effectively put it in the hands of a woman because to save it from defeat was to save it from itself. With the help of Sir Sidney Herbert, Secretary for War, Florence Nightingale's nursing corps ('one great organized whole' as she described it) showed the way. While the nurses scrubbed, Sutherland and Rawlinson, doctor and engineer, managed to provide clean water. By 1856 the death rate had dropped tenfold. There were further examples of gross military incompetence in India (1857), Bengal (1861), and Jamaica (1865), with a sudden scare over home defence in 1859. A Royal Commission into the army's sanitary condition was set up under Sir Sidney Herbert in 1857. Nightingale pressed her case for efficient administration undergirded by proper statistical information. She likened current annual mortality rates to the Commander-in-Chief taking 1,100 men out onto Salisbury Plain once a year in order to shoot them.

After Nightingale and Herbert, army mortality fell rates lower than the national average. In 1862 the Peel Commission report on army organizational reform, set up in 1858, was met with die-hard resistance from inside the army. But learning from reforms to other elite masculine institutions, including the civil service and the public schools, and bearing in mind Prussia's quick military victories over Austria in 1866 and France in 1870, Cardwell's army reforms between 1868 and 1874 gradually expelled the aristocratic principle by looking at the evidence, by abolishing purchase of commissions, by bringing regulation to bear, and by investing in regiments rather than lords as schools of war. Cardwell effectively established the modern army. Col. Wolseley called on officers to live as much like their men as possible, to know 'that the feudal system has passed away', and to encourage 'manly sports' in all ranks. By 1918, this was a sporting army.[157] In

---

[155] 'Hold hard...': Surtees, *Mr Sponge's* (1853) p.123.
[156] Markovits, *Crimean War* (2009) p.189.
[157] Mason, Tony, and E Riedi, *Sport and the Military* (2010)p.110. Pollock, *Nightingale* (1910) pp.384–86; *Nightingale, Notes* (1858) vol. i, p.5, vol. ii, p.xxxvii; *Nightingale, Hospitals* (1880) vol. i, p.3,

India, British soldiering was probably the most comprehensively sporting life in the world.[158] There was nothing new in this. Military failure had led to sporting revolutions before.[159]

In a life of boredom interspersed with danger, sporting *esprit de corps* was all important. In 1916 Capt. F E Breacher led the Royal Leicesters at Guedecourt with a blast of the Quorn Tally Ho. Right into the 1960s, being commissioned into a cavalry regiment was the most a young blood could wish for.[160] Thomas Hughes once told his old school that his generation had grown up believing that a 'big fight' was coming, a fight that would 'try all our powers'.[161]

Tests and Heroes

After the military shocks of the 1850s, newspapers increasingly told a tale of soldiers, explorers, missionaries and sportsmen out on the edge being tested in all their powers. Empire was critical. The Duke of Wellington made his name fighting Tipu Sultan before he turned to Napoleon. Indian police exams required a pass in shooting and horsemanship. 'Gym-Khana' was Anglo-*Hindi*. There was racing in Nairobi and Lusaka, polo in Delhi and Dublin, and game wherever you looked. In 1906 the Viceroy's 'Big Game' party shot 3,999 grouse, 2,827 wild fowl, 50 bears, and 2 tigers. What was a sporting life in Britain and Ireland was offered now as an exotic holiday in India. No longer was the British Empire just somewhere out there. It was back here too, and in so-called test matches where the British and Irish went out to test themselves against the colonies and the dominions, in cricket or in rugby, they played their part in forging a new identity which we might call imperial.[162] It worked the other way as well. The first official Indian cricket tour, in

vol. ii, pp.47–90; Bostridge, Nightingale (2009) p.314; Biddulph, Cardwell (1904) p.116. See also Sweetman, War and Administration. Wolseley, Soldier–s Pocket Book (1869) pp.1–10. (1984).

[158] ibid, ch 2. For sporting resistance to army reform see 'Uncle Scribbler' on 'Our Next Military Examination' in *Sportsman's Magazine*, 1860, p.405. For India, where officers were criticized for too much sport, too little soldiering, see the correspondence of Lt. Col. D L Weir, 2nd Leicester Regiment, 1909–14: LRO, DE 2913/1/2; First army gym 1860, first army athletics 1876, first army football 1888, first army boxing 1911: Riedi and Mason, 'Leather', *Canadian Journal*, 2006, pp.489–97.

[159] Not least in Germany, Sweden, and France: Heggie, 'Bodies, Sport and Science', *Past & Present*, 2016, pp.174–9.

[160] Jan Morris, 'Patriotism', *Encounter*, January 1962; Capt. Breacher rallied A Coy on 25 September 1916: LRO, DE 6007/376 llied. On *esprit de corps*: David French tells a story from the Norfolk Regiment at base camp Etaples in 1917. A sergeant is instructed to lecture his men on *esprit de corps*. He marches them across the beach and orders them to sit down. '*Sprit de corpse*', he explained, 'is like this 'ere. If you was in the canteen and I come in and you said, "what you going t'ave, sergeant?" that's *sprit de corpse*. Now you can smoke'": French, *Military Identities* (2009) p.1.

[161] Hughes, *Address* (1891) in Saunders, ed., Introduction, *Tom Brown's* (1999) p.x. Not that stoicism was new. Knox refers to Regency gamblers who held onto their feelings when misfortune struck: *Winter Evenings* (1805) p.89.

[162] 'The British Empire of the 1890s resembled nothing more than an enormous sports complex': Ferguson, *Empire* (2004) p.260. In 1869 the *Sportsman's Magazine* was telling the joys of tracking bears

1911, brought together a team for Great Britain and Ireland that could hardly dare gather in India. The die was cast. Prince and Untouchable, Hindu and Sikh, Muslim and Farsi: if India was to be a nation, it was going to look something like this cricket team.[163]

When the British were shocked in the field—as they were against the Boers in 1899–1902 for instance, or against the All Blacks in 1905—there were calls for more men, more sport, more testing.[164] Kipling's *The Islanders* (1905) referred to how the British army in South Africa had been forced to find its hardened riders from out of the colonies, out of Australia and Canada: 'And ye vaunted your fathomless powers, and ye vaunted your iron pride / Ere – ye fawned on the Younger Nations for the men who could shoot and ride / Then ye returned to your trinkets, then ye contented your souls / With the flannelled fools at the wicket, or the muddied oafs at the goals.'

The Great War started in a bloodbath. The first battle of Ypres (19 October to 30 November 1914) saw the British Expeditionary Force, that is, the regular British army, decimated.[165] The rush to the colours was mainly to fill this hole by men who knew it wasn't going to be a picnic. The public schools, meanwhile, played their part by marching their boys up and down the playing fields and likening the fighting to every known sport.

By the winter of 1914, the trenches were just about as far from a school playing field as it was possible to get. Capt. Nevill was killed the moment he led his East Surreys over the top with his famous football kick into enemy lines. British losses were highest among junior officers. Bedford School lost 454 old boys and inscribed their names in a great hall English Valhalla.[166] Over half casualties were caused by artillery and another third by small arms and machine gun fire. For those who didn't die but lost their limbs, or their looks, or their minds, war pensions were scaled from two limbs lost (any type), to an arm or an eye, to blindness, paralysis, lunacy, incontinence, or a combination of disabilities. Face, mouth and stomach injuries caused by flying shrapnel were particularly feared.[167]

Out of the 627 Victoria Crosses awarded during the War, 163 of them, or 26 per cent of the total, were awarded to former public schoolboys, many of them athletes.[168] Given 'For Valour' and open to all ranks, the VC was a medal, as Lord Hardinge carefully explained to Prince Albert, 'which even Crowned Heads

in the Himalayas, spearing boars in Bengal, and shooting quail in Ceylon: p.236, p.466, p.413. See also MacKenzie, *Empire of Nature* (1988).

[163] 'Team India' is now a potent national symbol with an unparalleled popular appeal'; Kidambi, *Cricket Country* (2019) p.330.
[164] 'Has the Public School Boy Deteriorated?', *Strand Magazine*, February 1905.
[165] Tombs, *English and their History* (2014) p.608.   [166] Barlen, ed., *Bedford School* (1984) p.15.
[167] Bourke, *Dismembering the Male* (1996) p.33. By 1918, 41,000 limbs had been amputated.
[168] Seldon and Walsh, *Public Schools and the Great War* (2013) pp.235–43.

cannot wear'. The value attached by soldiers to a little bit of ribbon, he went on, was 'inestimable'.[169]

Wilfred Owen called dying for your country the 'old lie', but one of the big questions of the War is how what military strategists call 'combat motivation' remained so strong. Between 1914 and 1918 the front line moved significantly only once, and yet the 'normative power', and 'unit cohesion', of British forces stayed intact. Why did they decide to stick and fight? Various reasons have been offered by military historians.[170] Most importantly, perhaps, it is argued that the British army saw itself as a citizens' army, there because it wanted to be, with no time for 'bull' but plenty of time for the common decencies. Connected to this was an abiding sense of some of the common values we have seen expressed in this volume. Patriotism for the Tommies, it would seem, was far less a matter of King and Country and far more a matter of home and belonging, being of good heart, being with your pals. 'Pals' battalions and the Territorial regiments were deliberately founded on local ties.[171] John Keegan tells how it came about, during the first two years of the war, 'one of the most curious social confrontations in British history and, in its long term implications, one of the most significant':

> 'It was almost always a meeting of strangers. It was sometimes a meeting of near foreigners...the mutual incomprehension, good humoured but absolute, which took hold of a platoon and its new officer, fresh from England, when first they met...when nicely raised young men from West Country vicarages or South Coast watering places came face to face with 40 Durham miners, Yorkshire furnacemen, Clydeside riveters, and the two sides found that they could scarcely understand each other's speech'.[172]

Well, except not quite. One language they did understand was the sporting life, sharing some of the same fetishes and snobberies it is true, but also the same rules and rubric. After a thirty-year football craze (not to mention forty years of army drilling in the schools) officers and men recognized they were the same side after all. Not just in football and cricket, but in racing and boxing (the old sports), and athletics and cycling (the new), the sporting life had emblazoned common custom and practice, new ways of having friends and being free, that war now raised to the highest levels of importance. That was behind the lines. At the front, the sporting life did not go away. First there was trench sport, for the junior officers at any rate,

---

[169] Seldon and Walsh, ibid, p.243. Eton alone won thirteen, Harrow nine, and Uppingham four. 'The links between boyish play and soldiering were apparent in every variety of responses to the war which I have concerned myself with in this book': Markovits, *Crimean War* (2009) p.189. Crook, *Evolution of the VC* (1975) p.13; Correspondence Papers for the Victoria Cross: W.O. 98/2.

[170] See Watson, *Enduring the Great War* (2009).   [171] Ibid, p.64.

[172] Keegan, *Face of Battle* (1976) p.221. For trench sport: Lewis-Stempel, Six Weeks (2011) pp. 44–5, p.118. Junior officer casualties were often double that of other ranks (p.7, p.183). Owen calls it 'the old lie' in his astonishing Dulce et Decorum Est (1920).

dressed to kill rather than die in uniforms they had assembled for themselves boys' side. Harrods or Burberry? Trench coat or Yelta? Scarves and jumpers or British Warm? The Wipers' Times carried all the latest fashions. Then there was trench warfare, night raids not dorm raids, all ranks, with knives and knuckledusters and knobkerries, the most palpitating sport of their short and getting shorter lives. Finally there was trench survival, prizes for the better hole, the hottest meal or the warmest billet—for former public schoolboys at least, a bit like school and a bit like hell. War was the ultimate test. Duty had to be done to the things one knew. 'Now God be thanked', wrote Rupert Brooke, 'who has matched us with this hour'.[173]

In 1815 there were only two British heroes, Nelson and Wellington. By 1918 there was nearly a million dead and well over a million more sick and disabled.[174] The Great War ran across the new moral worlds like a river of blood. Everything before it came to be seen as in a dream, long summer days playing cricket. Everything after it came to be seen as not so much a victory as a tragedy. University College Leicester was founded as a war memorial: *ut vitam habeant*. But everyone knew they didn't really.[175] Public school men wrote the poetry that changed how the Great War, and all war, came to be seen. At first it was warrior poetry, full of Christian knights with a sporting chance. Then there were immense blasts, barbed wire, and gas. 'Gas!'[176]

---

[173] Strachan, *To Arms* (2003) p.137.

[174] On the role of the public schools in the slaughter, Robert Tombs notes that the phrase 'Lions led by Donkeys' was not contemporary but invented in the 1960s as a book title: *English and their History* (2014) pp.620–1.

[175] 'Patriotism was...fit only for civilians or prisoners': Graves, *Goodbye to All That* (1929) p.157. See also: Fussell, *Great War and Modern Memory* (1977).

[176] 'Gas! GAS! Quick boys! - / An ecstasy of fumbling...' The first gas attack on British troops happened with 88 tonnes of chlorine phosgene at Wieltje, Ypres, 19 December 1915. The first had taken place eight months before, on two French colonial divisions, also at Ypres, 22 April 1915. See Parker, *The Old Lie* (1987) p.250.

8

Moderns

Big football blooms at its most beautiful where the soil is stoniest, the air dirtiest, the people most congested. His career begins in the streets, where they play a kind of football uninhibited by rules or touchlines, a swaying, yelling storm...

(*The Observer*, 27 April 1952)

Jim Baxter said he spent every spare minute of his boyhood kicking a ball. Brought up in a large family, four in a bed, he needed no excuses because football was a given, a law of nature. Baxter said he was 'normal enough to dislike school and love football'. Bobby Lennox thought nothing was more normal yet more important. He never played for his primary school because he could never get over big match nerves.[1] This is not the only chapter in the history of our sporting life where English, Scottish, Welsh, and Irish lives were not so very different. Football was a working-class language every boy understood. Steve Heighway remarked that professional players rarely talked about their backgrounds because they were all so similar.[2]

Back Lane Football

Football conquered the world because, like all popular customs, it was simple, cheap, and near to hand. As with hunting, it involved a kind of roving liberty with intent to kill.[3] As with boxing, it required heart. As with the parish, it fostered belonging and as with the schools and universities it was capable of providing new models of what it was to be young.

The Football Association laid down the laws of the game in the 1860s, and after that it was available and adaptable. Martin's 1857 *Book of Sports* explained 'Football' as a game for young children along with 'Stay' and 'Prisoner's Base'. But everyone who learnt how to play football in the century that followed learned

---

[1] Bobby Lennox, b. Saltcoats 1943, Celtic (1961–78), Scotland × 10: Lennox, *Million Miles* (2007) p.15; Jim Baxter, b. Hill of Beath, Fifeshire 1939, Raith Rovers (1957–60), Glasgow Rangers (1960–65), Sunderland (1965–67), Scotland × 34: Baxter, *Baxter* (1984) p.7.

[2] *Liverpool. My Team* (1977) p.181.

[3] Most of the kids who feature in this chapter called Association Football 'futta', or 'footie', or 'futball'. None of them called it 'soccer', which was public school slang for 'Association'.

not from a book but by watching and doing. Bill Pickford, who played amateur for Hampshire in the 1880s, never read a football rule book until he was 21 and when he did, he couldn't understand it.[4]

First you needed, or thought you needed, a pair of football boots. Boots had studs and although most football matches happened in the sort of streets where studs were useless, every boy remembered his first pair. Alex James got his age 10. Now 'the snag was finding a ball'. Ron Burgess and Bob Paisley had neither boots nor ball, making do with a pig's bladder (for the ball). Billy Liddell's first boots came on Christmas Day 1929. He wore them till after dark. Jackie Milburn played in his Christmas Day boots by torchlight until the dawn came up. He had to borrow boots for his first club trial. He got them from a friend who got them from a friend who worked for the Co-op. Peter Doherty never owned a pair in his life. At Coleraine, he found his from a great pile dumped on the floor. Two made a pair.[5]

Training was just as improvised. Doherty and Burgess never stopped kicking the ball back and forth against the wall. Graeme Souness kicked a ball against the wall two hours a day, five days a week, all weathers.[6] Bobby Charlton did the same, hammering his wall into an obsession, his 'purest pleasure', his 'greatest love'.[7] Dixie Dean called his first trainer 'Wes Hall' because Birkenhead Methodist Wesleyan Hall was the perfect height and slope for him to run its length heading the ball back and forth. Stan Mortensen's heading practice was against a backyard wall, Nat Lofthouse's against a stable block.[8]

Stewart Imlach was brought up in Lossiemouth, on The Square, a concrete area crossed by diagonal paths that made the cross of St. Andrew.[9] Ian Callaghan

[4] Pickford, *Recollections* (1939) pp.11–12; Martin, *Book of Sports* (1857) p.32. At first, cyclists were advised to learn how to ride by finding a book rather than a friend: Albemarle and Hillier, *Cycling* (1889) p.34.

[5] Peter Doherty, b. Magherafelt, Co Derry, 1914, Manchester City (1936–45), Huddersfield Town (1949–53), Ireland × 16: Doherty, *Spotlight on Football* (1947) pp.15–16; Alex James, b. Bellshill, Lanarks, 1901, Arsenal (1929–37), Scotland × 8: Harding, *Alex James* (1988) p.12; Ron Burgess, b. Cwm, Rhondda 1918, Tottenham Hotspur (1938–54), Wales × 32: Burgess, *My Life* (1952) pp.9–10; Bob Paisley, b. Hetton le Hole, Co Durham, 1919, Liverpool (1939–54): Paisley, *Lifetime in Football* (1983) p.2; Billy Liddell, b. Townhill, Dunfermline, 1922, Liverpool (1938–61), Scotland × 37: Liddell, *My Success* (1960) pp.7–9; Jackie Milburn, b. Ashington, Northumberland, 1924, Newcastle United (1943–57), England × 13; Milburn, *Golden Goals* (1957) p.11, Gibson, *Wor Jackie* (1990) p.110. Baxter, Burgess, James, Paisley, Liddell, and Milburn were all sons of miners and, for a time, miners themselves. It wasn't just footballers who played with what was near to hand. Harold Larwood, first a Nottinghamshire miner, then England's fastest bowler, learned cricket with his four brothers with bats made by their father out of scraps of wood: Hamilton, *Larwood* (2009) p.40.

[6] Graeme Souness, b. Edinburgh, 1953, Middlesbrough (1972–78), Liverpool (1978–84), Scotland × 54: Souness, *No Half Measures* (1988) pp.29–31.

[7] Bobby Charlton, b. Ashington, 1937, Manchester United (1956–73), England × 106: Charlton, *My Manchester United Years* (2007) p.47.

[8] Nat Lofthouse, b. Bolton, 1925, Bolton Wanderers (1946–60), England × 33: Lofthouse, *Goals Galore* (1954) p.14; Stan Mortensen, b. South Shields, 1921, Blackpool (1941–55), England × 25: Mortensen, *Football is My Game* (1949) pp. 8–9; William Ralph 'Dixie' Dean, b. Birkenhead, 1907, Everton (1925–37), England × 16: Walsh, *Dixie Dean* (1977) p.21.

[9] Stewart Imlach, b. Lossiemouth, 1952, Nottingham Forest (1955–60), Scotland × 4: Gary Imlach, *My Father* (2006) p.30.

played in Carlyl Gardens, Toxteth, another concrete square. Steve Perryman played on Bancroft Court *cul de sac*, Northolt, Middlesex. *The Observer*'s notion that street footballers played 'uninhibited by rules or touchlines' in 'a swaying, yelling storm' could not have been more wrong. In all these tight urban corners the game was played according to rules determined by old heads and how many players. On your own? Play against the wall, or 'keepy up'. Two of you? Head tennis, or 'doors' where each man defended his own back door and attacked the rest. Odd numbers? One in goal and two sides even. Or doors. Even numbers? Proper sides. But how to choose? Captains were chosen by popular consent and then it was their turn to choose—best players first, best friends second, then the constant ones, then the drifters and no hopers, finally the younger kids should both captains agree to tolerate them. He doesn't know the rules! He's too little! She's a girl! *You* have her then. When the sides were picked and the match was on, newcomers had to hang around until there were even numbers and they were invited to go 'cock or hen'. Captains picked cock or hen but didn't know who was what. Nobody had a shirt or shorts. If there happened to be a lot of players and a proper ball, everybody went to the park, if it allowed ball games. But it didn't really matter where you played. All you needed was a ball. Streets and back lanes, passageways and alleyways, low ground, high ground, housing squares, scraps of land, lamp posts in a line, passes across the street, headers over a rope - 'we didn't know what grass was' says Callaghan.[10] NO BALL GAMES notices had to get used to the constant beat of the ball.[11] All games were serious, but proper games demanded equal numbers, a common code, and a quick look round by old pros, veterans of a thousand street battles. These boys had been running these streets since, well, since they could run.

Imlach and friends played up and down Lossiemouth fish market.[12] Callaghan and friends kicked off with workers from Toxteth bottling plant. Tommy Smith took on the bay windows in Liverpool's busy Commercial Road. Denis Compton left lamp posts standing in Hendon. Raich Carter left them for dead in Sunderland.[13] If there was no ball, Nat Lofthouse made do with what he could find. Jackie Milburn kicked the same stone to school and back every day for three years. If there was no stone, things were really bad.[14]

---

[10] Ian Callaghan, b. Liverpool, 1942, Liverpool (1959–78), England × 4: Keith, *Cally* (1977) pp.13–18; Steve Perryman, b. Northolt, 1951, Tottenham Hotspur (1969–86), England × 1: Perryman, *Man for All Seasons* (1985) pp.16–19. *The Observer* showed how little it knew about street football on 27 April 1952.

[11] Robins and Cohen, *Knuckle Sandwich* (1978) p.145, p.126.

[12] Imlach, *My Father* (2006) pp.38–9.

[13] Raich Carter, b. Sunderland, 1913, Sunderland (1931–39), Hull City (1948–52), England × 13: Carter, *Footballer's Progress* (1950) p.168; Tommy Smith, b. Liverpool 1945, Liverpool (1968–72), England × 1: Smith, *I did it the hard way* (1980) p.9; Denis Compton, b. Hendon 1918, Arsenal (1936–50): Heald, *Denis Compton* (2006) p.9.

[14] Milburn, *Jackie Milburn* (2003) p.15; Lofthouse, *Goals Galore*, p.13.

Repetition made the 'touch' of the ball instinctual and close-packed housing kept players close. The 1858 Housing Act stipulated a minimum space of 10 by 15 feet at the back of a dwelling free from any other building. Local bye-laws laid down minimum spaces between rows. At 20 Bell Street, Middlebrough, Don Revie played in a back lane 10-feet wide. In Grenville Street, Jarrow, Arthur Barton played in a back lane 15-feet wide. At Charterhouse School, boys played in a cloister 12-feet wide. In Berlin the British ambassador liked to play in the Embassy passage. George Best learned his slippery skills on 'The Chicken Run' on the Cregagh Estate, Belfast—a narrow strip that was supposed to have grass but which was otherwise well named.[15]

Most British people were used to living in crowds. It defined part of who they were. Crowded inside the house and out of it, in the street or on the bus, hard at work or on the beach, nowhere was more crowded than the football stadium. Archibald Leitch, inventor of the British football stadium, allowed a standing width of 16 inches per person.[16] Books about spectators are rare, but clearly the density of the crowd made for survival strategies: somewhere you could see, somewhere you could pee, somewhere familiar, somewhere safe, somewhere not next to a moron and not in front of a child. Above all, you had to be able to see at least two corners of the pitch on your toes and get out safely at the end. Football crowds could be difficult places for women, and few went.[17]

Some village customs migrated to the towns. Guy Fawkes' night bonfires might have scorched and blistered back doors, but generally speaking urban customs were made to suit close-packed living. Girls played to rhymes and rhythms that involved two quick feet and almost no space. Playing football with uneven sides in tight spaces might mean a running keeper who could get back in time to use his hands in a zone that was visible only to those who played in it. The wall pass was invented in back lanes too narrow for wingers, using the wall as an extra man. Too narrow for passing and too hard for tackling, streets did not encourage rugby. Tag rugby was possible, but it wasn't the same. Back lane cricketers on the other hand developed a very fine sense of the quick nick because the boundary (the wall) was

---

[15] George Best, b. Belfast 1946, Manchester United (1963–74), various clubs (1976–81), Northern Ireland × 37: Collins, *Blessed* (2001) p.23; Don Revie, b. Middlesbrough 1928, Leicester City (1944–49), Manchester City (1951–56): Revie, *Soccer's Happy Wanderer* (1955) p.16; Barton, *Penny World* (1969) p.181. British Ambassador played 1908–14: Bruce, *Silken Dalliance* (1946) p.95. On bye-laws: Muthesius, *English Terraced House* (1982) p.137. The Housing Acts were influenced by Chadwick's *Report on the Sanitary Condition of the Labouring Population* (HL 1842) xxvi: 'on comparing the proportion of deaths amongst all classes…the general influence of the locality becomes strikingly apparent' (p.164).

[16] Inglis, *Engineering Archie* (2007) p.194.

[17] John Williams writes a rare account of watching the game, in his case from block 207, Kop End, Anfield, one third of the way up, just to the right of the goal: 'fellahs' in front, moaners to the rear, one nutter, and Steve, who makes speeches standing up (is there any other way to make speeches?): *Into the Red* (2001) pp.18–19. For spectator survival strategies: Ward and Williams, *Football Nation* (2009) p.23.

so close. If you smashed the ball over it the game could well be over. If the back door was locked and the folks were known to be nasty, you might as well take a chance and climb over. If the folks were known to be nice, you might do the same and test their niceness. Or, if you could be bothered, you could go round to the front door and ask politely. Either way you were out: six and out if you got the ball back.

Stanley Matthews remembered honing his football skills—the hint, the feint, the move—in and out of a line of chairs in his Hanley back yard. When he poisoned his foot he practiced with a tea cosy on it.[18] Tom Finney learnt the same skills on Holmeslack Back Fields—not fields as such but ash covered waste. When he was 7 he was taken to Deepdale, home of Preston North End. 'You could have fitted half a dozen of our backyard pitches into one half'. Finney was not the first town kid to love the wide green space of the football stadium made glorious summer with the coming of flood lights (1950). Like all these boys, he played to his heroes. Baggy shorts, cuffs over wrists, immaculate hair, inside left and a 'perky trot', Tom Finney didn't dream of being Alex James. He *was* Alex James.[19]

Up in Orbiston, near Bellshill where James was born, Matt Busby was someone else doing the perky trot. They called Orbiston's thirty-two cottages 'Cannibal Island' but half the village boys wanted their hair as slick as their football.[20]

Bobby Robson was brought up in Langley Park. His father, a Durham miner, was rewarded by the National Coal Board with football tickets for fifty-one years unstinting service. Bobby's street team called themselves 'The Netty Boys', an unlovely name for a particular way of building lavatories like sentry boxes. Playing between walls, the street may have looked like prison but 'we thought it was Utopia'. Robson broke his arm getting the ball off the coal house roof—not quite in the backyard, but not quite over the wall either.[21]

Some league clubs such as Leicester Fosse and Preston North End originated as street sides. South Shields Adelaide FC was founded in Adelaide Street in the Laygate area of the town before progressing through junior leagues into the Northern Alliance, before joining the Football League in 1919.[22] As a child, Stanley Matthews never went anywhere in the street without the ball at his feet. Nor did Len Shackleton. It was the thing to do in Bradford. 'Nine out of ten kids did it'. 'Shack' knew all the tricks: the spin, the one-two, the back-heel penalty.

---

[18] Stanley Matthews, b.1915, Hanley, Stoke City (1932–47, 1966–65), Blackpool (1947–61), England × 83: Matthews, *Feet First* (1948) p.13. See the *Manchester Guardian*, 2 May 1953 on Matthews' tight corner skills in the FA Cup Final, Blackpool 4, Bolton Wanderers 3.

[19] Tom Finney, b. Preston, 1921, Preston North End (1946–60), England × 76: Finney, *Football Round the World* (1953) pp.11–12.

[20] Matt Busby, b. Orbiston, Lanarkshire, 1910, Manchester City (1928–36), Liverpool (1936–41), Scotland × 1, manager of Manchester United (1945–69): Busby, *My Story* (1957) p.35, p.199.

[21] Bobby Robson, b. Sacriston, Co Durham, 1935, Fulham (1950–56, 1962–67), West Bromwich Albion (1956–62) England × 20: Robson, *Time on the Grass* (1982) pp.15–16.

[22] *Shields Gazette*, 13 December 2012.

And when they couldn't play out, they played in, furniture pushed to one side, headers against the sitting room wall and diving over the settee.[23] You were 'born into it'.[24] Anywhere. Everywhere. In Dagenham's last remaining meadow (with Alf Ramsey and his brothers), or on a flattened Pelaw slag heap (with Bryan Robson), or just two minutes over the way in Sheffield (with Gordon Banks), or close enough in Birmingham to nip back home to listen to 'Dick Barton' on the wireless before heading back for the second half (with Ron Atkinson). Tony Collins makes the point that public school rugger men tended to prefer the freemasonry of itinerant clubs rather than deep local connection. We note the taste in names: 'Wanderers', 'Rovers', 'Nomads', and 'Gypsies' versus 'Cities', 'Towns' and 'Uniteds'.[25]

Asked when he first started playing football, Willie Johnston said he couldn't remember. It had always been there.[26] Playing football was a seasonal obsession and children claimed customary rights.[27] They might get chased from one place to the next but the next place was only down the road and if it was held by other kids then it was time for some street diplomacy. Most residents were tolerant. Some men joined in on their way to the pub, putting their caps and jackets down as a kind of deposit that said they were boys at heart. There were few cars or lorries on the streets in the 1950s, and none in the back lanes except for the coalman and his wagon—a demon pair who could wreck ten lines of washing in one filthy surge. When the cars and lorries did begin to arrive they made the streets dangerous. Street play defined the inner parochial boundaries of working-class community, and the women of Hardwick Street for one, built their barricades out of prams and dustbins in order to defend it.[28] By the 1950s, photographers were going in search of back lane children as emblems of the organic community.[29] In the 1960s, street play was seen as the key to progressive teacher training and at the heart of

---

[23] Len Shackleton, b. Bradford 1923, Newcastle United (1946–48), Sunderland (1948–57), England × 5: Shackleton, *Clown Prince* (1955) p.31.

[24] Walvin, *Different Times* (2014) p.150.

[25] Collins, *English Rugby Union* (2009) p.107. There are exceptions of course, notably Wolverhampton Wanderers and Blackburn Rovers. Alf Ramsey, b. Dagenham, 1922, Southampton (1943–49), Tottenham Hotspur (1949–55), England × 32, Ipswich manager 1955–63, England manager 1963–74: Ramsey, *Talking Football* (1952) p.12; Bryan Robson, b. Witton Gilbert, Co Durham, 1957, West Bromwich Albion (1975–81), Manchester United (1981–94), Middlesbrough (1994–97), England × 90: Robson, *United I Stand* (1984) p.15; Gordon Banks, b. Tinsley, Sheffield, 1937, Leicester City (1959–67), Stoke City (1967–73), England × 73: Banks, *Banks of England* (1980) p.7; Ron Atkinson, b. Liverpool, 1939, Oxford United (1958–71): Atkinson, *United to Win* (1984) p.15.

[26] Willie Johnston, b. Cardenden, Fife, 1946, Glasgow Rangers (1964–72), West Bromwich Albion (1972–79), Scotland × 22: Johnston, *On the Wing* (1983) p.1.

[27] Connecting 'daily life to fundamental patterns': Binkley, 'Kitsch', *Journal of Material Culture* 5 (2000) p.133.

[28] 'Battle of Hardwick Street', 11–16 October 1956: Cowman, 'Play Streets', *Social History*, 2017, pp.234–7. There were 2 million cars on the road in Great Britain in 1938, 11 million in 1969. See: Gunn, 'People and the Car', *Social History*, 2013, and Colls, 'When We Lived in Communities', in Colls and Rodger, eds., *Cities of Ideas* (2004).

[29] Including Roger Mayne in Notting Hill, Jimmy Forsyth in Newcastle's West End, and Nigel Anderson in London's East End.

attempts to rebuild what the planners had torn down. According to one town plan that clearly wasn't going to work, child play ought to be 'an integral part of senior management structures'.[30]

Bill Shankly once said that all you needed to play football was the sky, a ball, and some grass. But who had grass?[31] Cobbled streets absorbed a winter game originally intended for grass. It didn't matter where you went, it was always the same sort of street, the same sort of rules, the same sort of boys. 'We are the Lambeth Boys / We are expected wherever we go.'[32] Up to the park was playing away. Outside your door was playing at home. Muzzy Izzet played in Vallance Road, E2. Johan Cruyff played on the corner of Tuinbouwstraat and Akkerstraat. Ferenc Puskas played on the suburban wastes of Kispest. On the pustyrs of Moscow, the barrios of Buenos Airies, and the grunds of Budapest the world taught itself to play.[33] Football was unquestionably part of Britain's informal empire, especially in Europe and Latin America. Local elites wanted closer ties with British dynamism, and playing football was a sign.[34]

Football crowds could look like the masses incarnate in a sea of caps and knobbly faces. But in themselves, crowds were a standing conference of local historians, very serious and focussed most of the time, madly excited some of the time. 'Home' and 'away' were the two most important words in football, making everyone belong. Every Saturday afternoon the BBC intoned the football league results with special changes of voice for home wins, draws, and away wins. On gala days, home crowds dressed up as if for a parish wake. At Grimsby they had a Lucky Cod. At Barnsley they had Amos the Donkey. At Leicester they had Filbert the Fox. Black Cat suits at Southampton, Lion suits at Milwall, Sailor suits at Plymouth, Welsh Woman's hat and shawl at Swansea, Guyers at Blackpool, rattles and rosettes everywhere, it took the people a long time to surrender their parochial right to be ridiculous.[35] Clarke and Williams are right to observe that there is nothing as *operatic* as 50,000 bedecked supporters singing they favourite anthem.[36] They might stand in the same place for thirty years. They might stand where their fathers have stood. Even if they did not know a single player ('your heroes are invariably people you haven't met')[37] they knew someone who did.

---

[30] Tony Chilton, 'Child's Play in Newcastle upon Tyne' (1985) p.7, and Peter Malpass, 'Rebuilding Byker', *Architectural Review*, 1974. See Ken Worpole, 'The Child in the Street', *The Guardian*, 6 May 2008.

[31] Clarke and Williams, *Game Revisited* (2019) p.7.

[32] Karel Reisz, dir., *We Are the Lambeth Boys* (Free Cinema Movement, Look at Britain 1959).

[33] Goldblatt, *Ball is Round* (2006) p.196; Taylor and Jamrich, *Puskas* (1997) pp.16–17; Izzet, *My Story* (2015) p.19. 'When I was young to play outside was really normal. We wouldn't think about it...': Cruyff quoted in *The Guardian*, 12 May 2018. Johann Cruyff, b. Amsterdam, 1947, Ajax (1964–73), Barcelona (1973–8), Netherlands x 48; Ferenc Puskas, b. Budapest, 1927, Honved Budapest (1943–55), Real Madrid (1958–66), Hungary x 85: Taylor & Jamrich, *Puskas* (1997) pp.16–17.

[34] Robinson and Gallagher, *Africa and the Victorians* (1961) pp.3–4.

[35] Featherstone-Dawes, *Football: Those Were The Days* (2011).

[36] *Game Revisited* (2019) p.90.   [37] Brian Clough, *Cloughie* (2002) p.17.

Journeymen who had been taught by custom and belonging loathed being shown what they knew already. While the rest of a team looked on in amazement, Milburn recalled Bobby Mitchell ('the most educated left foot I ever saw') having a chalk mark inscribed on his boot to demonstrate how to side-foot the ball.[38] Bill Shankly thought the natural ability of a player was 'far too precious tae be messed about wi".[39] Walter Winterbottom's 1952 FA coaching manual said that the best coaching took place in 'settings closely resembling the game itself'. Yet for players who had learned their trade in all the cannibal islands of the land, Winterbottom's chapter on 'Kicking' was more designed for a fracture than a pass. Fig. 7 described 'The Oblique Approach':

> The standing foot is still placed parallel to the line of the kick by moving it outwards. This enables the right hip to swing round. If the run-up is fast, the player will check the oblique impetus by leaning slightly to the left as the standing foot goes down alongside the ball.[40]

Girls' Play

Why didn't girls play and if they did why don't we know about it? [41] In the first place we have to admit that as soon as they were old enough to be useful at home, many working-class girls moved into a life of 'spasmodic servitude' 'with no hours of recognized leisure [and] no direct remuneration . . . under the authority of one who, commonly overworked herself, considers that she has a claim on her daughter's whole time and energy'. Working-class girls were caught up early in the labour process of turning wages into nutrition. Working-class boys, on the other hand, grew up knowing that one day they'd be obliged to roam, learning on the job, in squads and teams.[42] In other words, at the very time that boys took it as their right to go as they pleased, girls had to be at home watching out for their mothers just as their mothers were at home watching out for them. This was the prime reason why football wasn't as customary or as near for daughters. Mothers passed their needs onto their daughters and their daughters onto their daughters.

Yet street and back lane belonged to the girls just as much as to the boys.[43] Everything else that happened there, from 'tig' and 'two ball' to the ragman, the

---

[38] 'I says, "Hey that's me finished with him"': quoted in Hutchinson, *The Toon* (1997) p.163. And that was him finished with Milburn, who was dropped. On players' hostility to coaching: Wagg, *Football World* (1984) ch. 7.

[39] *The Guardian*, 17 December 1968.

[40] Winterbottom, *Soccer Coaching* (1952) p.20. Walter Winterbottom, b. Oldham, 1913, Manchester United (1936–38), first England manager (1946–62). Half the humour of Featherstone-Dawes' collection of old football photographs relates to absurd training methods. See the cover: *Football* (2011).

[41] It seems they did in Sir Philip Sidney's *Arcadia* (1580) where 'A time there is for all, my mother often says / When she, with skirt tucked very high / With girls at football plays'.

[42] Griffin, *Bread Winner. An Intimate History of the Victorian Economy* (2020). Working-class women's lives in Middlesbrough, as described by Lady Florence Bell, *At The Works* (1907) p.219.

[43] Beautifully caricatured from the boys' side in James, *Unreliable Memoirs* (1980) ch. 3.

binman, and the coalman, was part of their world as well. So why not girls kicking-in? Why not girls asking if their little sister could play? Why not girls obsessed with ball against the wall? Melanie Tebbutt says boys had greater 'spatial confidence' but that was only true in their own spheres of competence and even there, women were beginning to show. Darts leagues in the 1930s only wanted them out because they were knocking so hard to be let in, while on the dance floor it was the boys who lacked the confidence and the girls who exuded it.[44] In working-class sport, the main idea was to win. Except for larking around (a sporting life never to be underestimated)[45] there were no nicely 'social' games such as tennis where, like dancing or skippies, you could join in more or less regardless. No boy joined the skipping line in order to win, although they left it often enough in order to save face. On the other hand, Fred Trueman didn't take any prisoners fast bowling his sisters. And to be fair to them, they didn't ask that he should.[46]

So, to rephrase the question, why didn't the girls play to win? They were more than capable of learning the skill set and once in motion they would have learned the taste of victory. Neighbourhoods, after all, were more female territory than male.[47] Women's labour dominated. What they said was lore. Minding and watching, borrowing and sharing, sweeping and scrubbing and gossiping and the endless hanging out to dry—there was little fear of men casting their baleful influence here. And men shared the domestic life too. Being interested in football can be included along with gambling ('a flutter') as an example of the domestic craft hobby described by McKibbin as something 'freely chosen', 'demand[ing] knowledge and sustained interest'.[48] Women had their craft hobbies, and it would be a mistake to think they knew nothing about football from the other side of the newspaper. One Mass Observer out and about met a young woman in a pub in Blackpool who kept crossing her leg over his leg while talking football 'about chaps he had never heard of'.[49] The Kings saw street play in 1926 as trans-generational, geographically savvy, constantly moving, and frequently mischievous. Street football could have been a girls' part of this too, at least until adolescence when the culture began pulling energies elsewhere.[50]

[44] Tebbutt, *Making Youth* (2016) p.79; Tebbutt, *Being Boys* (2012) p.214; Chaplin, *Darts in England* (2009) pp.174–81.

[45] Logan, 'Blackpool 1930', *North West Labour History*, 2013.

[46] Waters, *Trueman* (2011) pp.41–4. On middle-class social sports '...where the participation of women was not only permissible but necessary': McKibbin, *Classes and Cultures* (1998) p.369.

[47] 'a closed system', 'a moral arena'; Tebbutt, *Women's Talk* (1995) pp.2–9, p.149.

[48] McKibbin, 'Work and Hobbies in Britain 1880-1950', in Winter, ed., *Working Class* (1983) p.129. Also: McKibbin, 'Working-class Gambling', *Past & Present* 82, 1979, pp.154–6.

[49] Cross, ed., *Worktowners at Blackpool* (1990) p.165.

[50] '...creating a human environment which was both pleasurable to make and pleasurable to consume': Joanna Bourke, 'Housewifery in Working Class England 1860–1914', *Past & Present* 143, 1994, p.180. Olsen thinks fathers were revived as domestic authority figures in this period: *Juvenile Nation 1880–1914* (2014) pp.19–20. On street play: Madge and Robert King, *Street Games* (1926).

Yet blaming the absence of women's football on culture doesn't take us very far either. Of course it was 'the culture'. But that only kicks the question, as it were, down the road, while blaming it on the 'comparative advantage' of males over females fails to deal with comparative advantage between males as the whole point of the game. Catching and juggling and skipping is what girls did, occasionally letting boys into the line. They played with what was near to hand— skipping ropes made out of cotton spindles, handstands against the wall, hopscotch on the chalky pavement, babies in the pram, kittens on the step, cartwheels through the air. But they didn't want to play football and weren't invited to.[51]

Why then that extraordinary outburst of women's football during the First World War? There were women's teams in just about every major industrial centre, including the Gretna munitions factory nine miles long served by two new townships of young women, the National Projectile Factory teams on Hackney Marshes, the National Shell Filling Factory in Swansea, unbeaten in all of 1918, while in Barrow in Furness, there was the West Cumbrian Women's Cup, and in the North East, the Munitionettes' Challenge Cup.[52] From the first match on 3 February 1917 between the women of the Wallsend Slipway and Engineering and the women of the North East Marine Engineering, Brennan estimates that North East women played at least 268 organized football matches up to the end of the war. Apart from Wheatley Hill Rosy Rapids FC, who were formed in 1909, most of these women's teams were wartime. One look at Mary Dorrian or Mary Lynes would question theories of female lack of confidence.[53]

'Dick, Kerr Ladies' was the most famous, working at Dick, Kerr's factory in Preston. Their first match was against another factory team, Arundel Coulthard, at the Deepdale ground, on Christmas Day 1917. They won 4–0 in front of 10,000 people. Their best and most outspoken player, Lily Parr, went on to turn professional and play against men as well as women. Up to 1921 it has been estimated that this club played sixty-seven charity and exhibition matches to a total of

[51] As far as we can tell. Osborne and Skillen say there's not enough research: 'State of Play', *Sport in History* 2010, p.190. Back lanes looked less interesting to outsiders: Redmayne, *Men, Mines, and Memories* (1942) p.8. For inside accounts: Owen, *Two Rooms* (2005) p.120, p.223, and Woodruff, *Nab End* (2003) pp.169–70.

[52] Brader notes teams ranging from Glasgow to London: 'Timbertown Girls', Warwick PhD (2001) pp.213–15.

[53] Some of the games were for charity—for instance the match between the women of Armstrong-Whitworth No 43 Shop (Elswick) and the soldiers of the Jane Cowen Rehabilitation Home, Benwell, at Stanley 24 November 1917. Eight of the male players were one legged. Most games were serious and/or cup games: Brennan, *Munitionettes* (2007) p.9.

around 900,000 spectators.[54] There were many more women's teams during this period, and at least 150 clubs we know about.[55] Carlisle Record Office has plates of women's teams kitted out just like the men's, and other record offices have similar.[56] Some say that girls didn't play football until they went into the factories. But young women had always worked in factories.[57] Some say it all started with dinner-time kickabouts with the lads. But why did they play with the lads at dinner times and not at other times? Some say that it was the factory welfare officers who formed women's clubs.[58] But a lot of women's factory teams were unofficial with no welfare involved. It is also said, somewhat against the evidence, that girls played anyway and factory teams merely organized what was already in existence.[59]

There had been a touring exhibition of women's football in 1895 led by the strangely elusive (to historians) Miss Nettie Honeyball.[60] There were definitely working-class women in this side, including the mixed race Clarke sisters Emma and Florence from Plumstead, but it petered out after a year.[61] An English Ladies Football Association was founded at Blackburn on 10 December 1921, five days after the Football Association declared a ground ban on female players. There were contemporary comic strip stories of girls like Meg Foster 'the popular mill girl captain', who showed the boys how and there were real young women like Meggie Scott of Jarrow, boxer, swimmer and goalkeeper, and Bella Reay of Blyth Spartans who scored 100 goals in a season.

Inspite of the exceptions—and the Great War is quite a big exception—it's hard to know for sure but it would seem that the leisure life of working-class women was short and sweet and, judging from the evidence, included football only rarely.[62] The 1930 Lancashire 'Cotton Queen' did not play, neither did Gracie Fields though she was an avid Rochdale supporter and recorded 'Pass. Shoot. Goal' in 1931.[63] Scissors Cigarettes were intended for women,

[54] Lily Parr, b. St Helen's 1905, Dick, Kerr's Ladies (1919–21), Preston Ladies (1921–51), included by BBC History Magazine as one of '100 Women Who Changed the World', May 2018. See Gail Newsham, In a League of Their Own. The Dick, Kerr Ladies 1917–65 (2014).

[55] Russell, Football and the English (2007) pp.95–8; Williams, Rough Girls (2008) p.29, p.46; Lopez, Women on the Ball (1997) p.1.

[56] See zinc block engravings, Carlisle Munitions Workers XI, 1917: CRO, DB 20/521/10.

[57] Williamson, Belles of the Ball (1991) p.35.   [58] Jacobs, Dick, Kerr Ladies (2004) p.56.

[59] 'women in the north of the country had always played football...': ibid, p.31. See Melling, 'Pea Soup and Politics', IJHS 16, 1999.

[60] Lee, 'Introduction', 'Crouch End', and 'National Game', IJHS 24, 2007.

[61] Andy Mitchell, http://www.scottishsporthistory.com/sports-history-news-and-blog/archives/09-2019.

[62] Selina Todd's investigation finds inter-war leisure on a scale and with an opportunity 'previously unknown', but makes no mention of sport: 'Young Women, Work and Leisure', Historical Journal 48, 2005, p.795; Meg in Riches, Comic Book Heroes (2009) p.46; Meggie in Moffat, Northern Sportsman (1999) np; Bella in Brader, 'Timbertown' (2001) p.213; and more in Melling, 'Ray of the Rovers', IJHS 15, 1998, p.99.

[63] See Conway, 'Making the Mill Girl Modern?' 20c British History 24, 2013.

but their cards featured women playing every sport *but* football.[64] The 1933 Women's Health Enquiry Committee found seriously low levels of fitness among working-class mothers, with high incidences of anaemia, rheumatism, swollen legs, varicose veins, constipation, and headache. Out of 250 testimonies, only two said they went to fitness classes. Girls and young women did other things of course. They danced and skated and, if they could afford it, they cycled and hiked at weekends. The bicycle was a great liberator for women if they could afford one. Janet Ashbee, down in the Cotswolds, called for more exercise for women as part of a balanced and healthy community.[65] But there was no shortage of exercise on display Saturday nights at the Streatham Locarno in 1939 when Mass Observation noted that three young women and three young men danced with no fewer than fifty-eight partners between them in a single evening. Middle and upper-class women might find modernity in slim bodies and Egyptian cigarettes.[66] Working-class girls found it in dancing and cinema and, for an increasing number, the sort of job that demanded clean clothes and nice manners. The most succinct fitness story from the 1933 enquiry was the most typical: the Birmingham mother of five who sat on the step if it was sunny.[67]

Not all working-class wives and daughters lived the life of property-less servitude described by Lady Bell in Middlesbrough. But most did.[68] When men became football heroes, if they remembered the women at all, they remembered them as the ones who made the sporting life possible, not the ones who lived it. Cissie Charlton remembered being treated at the World Cup Final: 'This can't be real. I was such an ordinary Mam, the wife of a miner...'. Of family life at 11 Valley Road, Middlesbrough, Brian Clough, one of nine, recalled how his mother 'ran the show'. Alex James' wife Peggy came straight to the point: 'Alex was a great lover of his home, when he was in it.'[69]

---

[64] Cigarette Card volumes for Scissors and Ogden's: John Johnson Collection, Bodleian.

[65] 'One only has to look at the anaemic & sickly women (I could cite a score) & girls here to grasp how their physical development has been neglected'. She was calling for swimming lessons: Polley, 'The Ashbees, the Guild of Handicraft, and Sport in the Cotswolds 1902-07', Ts (2019) p.15.
'Once they had tried the sport, the taste for it seized them with full force... through all the terrible drawbacks with which feminine cycling was handicapped in its initial stages': Albemarle and Hillier, *Cycling* (1889) p.187; Taylor, *The Leaguers* (2005) p.250.

[66] 'Actually, the best thing in Cairo is the Ghezira Club where they have polo, racing, tennis, golf, and everyone who is anyone goes there for tea': McKibbin, *Classes and Cultures* (1998) p.29. Cigarettes were seen as emancipatory: Elliot, *Women and Smoking* (2009). See also Skillen, *Women, Sport and Modernity in Interwar Britain* (2013).

[67] Spring Rice, *Working-Class Wives* (1939) p.34, p.90, p.115. McKibbin sums up: *Classes and Cultures* (1998) pp.339-41.

[68] Janes Yeo observes how the new 'Social Science' put motherhood firmly inside the home: *Contest for Social Science* (1996) p.21.

[69] Harding, *James* (1988) p.74; Brian Clough, b. Middlesbrough, 1935, Middlesbrough (1955-61), Sunderland (1961-64), England × 2, manager Hartlepools United (1965-67), Derby County (1967-73), Nottingham Forest (1975-93), twice winner of the European Cup with Forest, best manager England never had: Clough, *Cloughie* (2002) p.31. Jackie Charlton, b. Ashington, 1935, Leeds United (1952-73), England × 35: Charlton, *Leeds and England* (1967) p.10.

Worlds of Labour

In his *News from Nowhere* (1890) William Morris' New Man is not 'our friend' the protagonist but a minor character, Dick, the waterman, who rows for sport as well as for work. Dick takes our friend up river for the haymaking. When offered some reward for his trouble, Dick refuses. What on earth would he do with money? He did it for fun, for play, for sport. Not for labour.[70]

Professional footballers were new men too, but they never doubted the value of their labour. This is not to say they were wealthy. Penny Watson's husband Dave was an England player. With a new home, a couple of cars, family holidays in Spain, and some random press attention, their lives were comfortable, not glamorous.[71] Just a generation before, Stewart Imlach had been a Scottish International and FA Cup winner with Nottingham Forest. He went off to training on his bike in the morning and mended broken seats in the stand in the afternoon. He never doubted he would go back to making and mending when he retired.[72]

Given the men who played and the men who paid them to play, football took on industrial habits. John Fletcher's short film, *The Saturday Men*, shows the world of labour inhabited by West Bromwich Albion players in the 1960s. Sly smokes and heavy ale, plenty grime and kidding, whatever local attention these men found on the field, there can be no doubt that everything else in their working lives—from chipped tea mugs to worry about work and wages—was strictly ordinary. Infact it was not all that different from the millions of their contemporaries also moving into new estates and saving up for family holidays. British Pathe News went into the Manchester United dressing room after their victory over Leicester City in the 1963 FA Cup Final. They found one of the most famous sides in the world celebrating victory by drinking and champagne out of a tea cup.[73]

In 1963, professional footballers were earning a little bit more than skilled manual workers (about £10 to £20 per week), with fewer contractual rights and less chance of overtime. By 1972, a first team player at Tottenham Hotspur was earning a great deal more, about £200 per week as opposed to average skilled wage of £30, but in every other respect Spurs players were from a working-class background and took a broadly working-class view of life. They were hired and fired. They showed no interest in the directors. They were mostly London lads. Only one read a broadsheet. One still lived with his parents in a council flat in

---

[70] Morris, *News from Nowhere* (1890) p.9.

[71] 'piddling wages, modest homes and modest lifestyles': Davies, *Glory Game* (1972) p.15. Dave Watson, b. Stapleford, Notts, 1946, Rotherham United (1967–70), Sunderland (1970–75), Manchester City (1975–79), England x 65: Penny Watson, *My Dear Watson* (1981).

[72] Imlach, *My Father* (2006) p.83, pp.56–8. Worlds of labour did not necessarily mean that most players for most top clubs were local, but they all came from similar backgrounds: Hearty, 'Liverpool and Everton and community ties', DMU MA (2020) p.33.

[73] 1963 Wembly Cup: www.youtube.com; Fletcher, dir., *Saturday Men* (1962).

Shoreditch. One still didn't have a phone. Out of eighteen first team players, ten saw professional football as just a job. Those who saw it as a career thought enjoying it meant it couldn't be a job. No one saw it as particularly glamorous. 'You go out the same time every day...I'm given orders' (Alan Mullery). 'I get paid so it's a job.' (Ralph Coates). 'It's not relaxing. I never say I'm going to *play* football' (Mike England). 'It's work, that's what I always call it. It's the job I do. What else can you call it?' (Phil Beal).[74]

Most professional footballers up to the 1960s accepted this world of labour because their expectations of work and wages, like their expectations of life, were close to home. All Newcastle United's star players in the 1940s for instance, including the exotically named Robledo brothers, came from northern colliery villages.[75] When they signed for the club they expected little more (a little more) than their friends. A boy's football career could take many paths, nearly all of them, whether amateur or professional, to nowhere very different. George Stobart Watson was a well-known local sportsman in the years after the war. He signed as an amateur for Darlington in the English Third Division but never played in the Football League. The nearest he got to it was as a reserve against Accrington Stanley in 1948. Previously he'd played for the Fleet Air Arm (without going to sea), then for Cockfield, a mining village, and later for Evenwood Town who won the Northern League in 1950. At about this time, George was offered professional terms with Newcastle United but reckoned he was better off playing amateur and working on the railway. But note: amateur did not mean he did not get paid. Because it was difficult to track gate receipts, clubs were earning more than their accounts showed. In other words, it was commonly believed that successful amateur clubs made illicit payments to themselves in order to be able to make illicit payments to their players, usually, as in George's case, tucked into his boot. After Evenwood, he moved to Bishop Auckland which, along with Crook Town, was the most illustrious northern amateur side.[76]

There were three levels of playing football seriously—junior, non-league, and league—each one capable of a full sporting life, but which one a player took was mostly down to chance and very little to do with whether he was paid or not. Some 'amateurs' were paid. Some 'professionals' were not paid, or they were paid very little, according to what the club was prepared to risk on a young talent or an old one.

Many boys were already at work before they signed for a club and what they signed depended on how old they were, how good they were, how local they were,

---

[74] Davies, *Glory Game* (1972) pp.313–14.

[75] Charlie Wayman (Chilton Colliery), Tommy Walker (Esh Winning), Ernie Taylor (Hylton Colliery), Bobby Cowell (Trimdon Colliery), Charlie Crowe (Walker Colliery), Jackie Milburn and Len Shackleton (Hazelrigg Colliery): Gibson, *Wor Jackie* (1990) p.21. Ted and Geroge Robledo, whose father was Chilean, were brought up by their English mother in West Melton, near Barnsley.

[76] Correspondence and conversations with Robin Watson, April 2018.

and club ways of doing business. A boy could insure himself against an uncertain professional future by signing for the club as an amateur and as a craft apprentice with a local firm. Dixie Dean left school at 14 and signed for Everton as an amateur, and for The Wirral Railway as an apprentice boilermaker. It's not clear how many boilers he made but night shift saw him in the engine shed sprinting out to kick rats against the wall.[77] At 14, Raich Carter went as an apprentice electrician at Sunderland Forge Company while playing for Whitburn St Mary's. At 18, he signed for Sunderland FC as an amateur, ostensibly without payment, but once Sunderland had a second look they took him as an apprentice professional on £3 per week, which was considerably more than he got at the forge. Raich kept 10 shillings and gave the rest to his mother.[78] Ian Callaghan was apprenticed to a French polisher for three years before signing professional for Liverpool FC age 18. Ian St. John signed for Motherwell FC at 17 while working in a steel works. One evening he was playing for Scotland at Hampden Park; next morning he was back at work. Tom Finney served his time as a plumber while playing as an amateur. When he retired from the game he went back to being a plumber.[79] Don Revie left school at 14 to be an apprentice bricklayer. The day he signed for Leicester City he had worked a shift the day before, catching the night train down. Arriving early, he wandered round with his boots under his arm wrapped in brown paper. Finally let into the ground, the 16 year old found he had swapped one trade for another. Septimus Smith, club trainer (trainers were nearly always former players) became Revie's journeyman.[80] Tommy Lawton was a Burnley office boy at 15 before signing professional for Everton at 17. Billy Liddell signed amateur for Liverpool at 16 on the understanding, initiated by his parents, that he had 'homely lodgings' and an accountancy traineeship, which he completed.[81] Ron Burgess went down the pit at 14 before signing for Tottenham Hotspur as an amateur at 17, paying his own way with an apprenticeship at a local metal works. White Hart Lane's idea of a football apprenticeship was no coaching and not allowed on the pitch. After a couple of years playing junior football, the club 'released' Burgess. But from what?[82] Stan Mortensen went straight from school to work in the dockside timberyards while playing for St. Andrew's local side.[83] George Raynor played for a string of professional clubs who paid no wages out of season. Told by the labour exchange that footballers were seasonal workers only, he went bagging coal instead. At 18, while playing in a local league and working as a milkman, Eddie Hapgood was offered a summer job on one of the

[77] Walsh, *Dixie Dean* (1977) p.23.   [78] Carter, *Footballer's Progress* (1950) pp.19–20.

[79] Finney, *Football* (1953) p.18; Keith, *Cally* (1977) p.18; Ward and Williams, *Football Nation* (2009) p.112.

[80] Septimus Smith, b. Whitburn, Co. Durham, 1912, 7th son, Leicester City (1929–49), England × 1, in Revie, *Happy Wanderer* (1955) chapter 'What I Owe to Sep Smith', pp.23–4.

[81] Liddell, *Soccer Story* (1960) p.28; Lawton, *Football's My Business* (1946) pp.1–5.

[82] Burgess, *Football* (1952) p.19.   [83] Mortensen, *Football is My Game* (1949) pp.9–10.

director's coal wagons. No chance. Young Eddie preferred lifting milk crates. Between dairy floats and coal wagons 'I figured there was a social distinction'.[84] Gordon Banks left school at 15 also to go summer coal bagging before turning to bricklaying, before being conscripted for the Royal Signals where, we can be sure, he played football without end.[85] Bob Paisley saw war service with the Royal Artillery through North Africa and Italy in all kinds of sporting encounters, some of them explosive. Before the war he had signed professional at Liverpool, before that he had been an apprentice bricklayer, before that he'd worked down Hetton colliery. Paisley, whose father had been seriously injured in the same pit, had seen a thing or two before his football career started. He did not believe in trying to make football more important than life, and the Liverpool manager who said it was, was only kidding.[86]

Films of miners always showed them scuttling in the dark, as if they lived there. But it was the light and the space that they loved and they enjoyed a rich sporting culture that included racing pigeons and whippets. The Durham miners fought the 1926 General Strike with every community weapon to hand, including cricket and football. It was a warm summer. Men went back to work rested and sunburnt, the women freed from the muck and the shifts, but Bowburn FC barred any members who went back early. Chopwell FC tried to register with the county FA as 'Chopwell Soviets' but settled for 'Reds'. Langley Park FC had to leave the league because they couldn't afford the ball.[87] Billy Meredith, one of a family of eight, worked at Chirk colliery before moving to Manchester City at 20, on amateur terms. 'My heart was full of it' he told *Athletic News*. Unusually for sportsmen, the Meredith family were Primitive Methodist teetotalers.[88] Jimmy Seed signed professional at 17 having just come up from a shift at Whitburn Colliery. They gave him five sovereigns though it should have been £10 ('football speaks only one language').[89] Jim Baxter left cabinet making for coal mining because his pals were earning five times more down the pit. Most club signings were preceded with a trial, and nine stone Jim had to get the under-manager's permission to change his shift in order to attend. 'A trial for Raith Rovers? It's a plate of porridge you need'. When he did eventually sign he was on £7 per week at the pit and £3 per week basic from the Rovers, plus 5s expenses,

[84] Eddie Hapgood, b. Bristol, 1908, Arsenal (1927–44), England × 30, in Hapgood, *Football Ambassador* (1945) p.12; Raynor, *Football Ambassador at Large* (1960) p.13.

[85] Banks, *Banks* (1980) pp.5–7.

[86] Paisley, *Lifetime in Football* (1983) p.168. Bill Shankly famously remarked that although some people said they thought football was a matter of life and death he thought it was more important than that.

[87] Barron, *The 1926 Miners' Lockout* (2010) p.77, p.112, p.56, p.236.

[88] Billy Meredith, b. Chirk, Denbighshire, 1886, played Manchester City (1894–1906), Manchester United (1906–21), Manchester City (1921–24), Wales × 48: Harding, *Football Wizard* (1998) p.19.

[89] Jimmy Seed, b. Blackhill, 1896, played Sunderland (1913–19), Tottenham Hotspur (1920–27), Sheffield Wednesday (1926–31), England × 5: Seed, *Soccer from the Inside* (1947) p.23.

plus £9 for each first team appearance. 'So it all added up very nicely'.[90] Nat Lofthouse signed professional for Bolton Wanderers age 15 on a pay as you go £1 10s per match plus £20 signing on fee, all done and dusted in the club office, young Nat with an orangeade in his hand and his Dad with a whisky and soda in his. Lofthouse was called up in 1943 to work at Mossley Colliery. His match day began after work on Fridays: home from work and a meal at 4pm, bed by 6.30pm, up at 3.30am, coal face by 5.30am, full shift, out and away to catch the club bus at 12.30pm. Here was a player who showered *before* matches, and he wasn't the only one.[91] Len Shackleton was another Bevin Boy, working at Fryston colliery, Castleford, before moving to Gosforth colliery, Newcastle, where he got the chance to work and play with an apprentice fitter called John Edward Thompson Milburn. Shackleton, who had first signed professional for Arsenal at 15 before getting his marching orders at 16 (too small) and moving back home to sign for Bradford Park Avenue at 17, worked for GEC radios before finally signing for Newcastle United age 23. 'Shack' went to matches on JET's motorbike: 'Shack on the back, both with wor pit gear on'.[92]

Some lads signed on as club 'apprentices' in the hope that they might learn something while dogsbodying around the ground. Stanley Matthews signed amateur forms for Stoke at 15, ostensibly as an office boy, but there was a whip-round for him every time he played for the first team if they had a win. Bobby Moore signed for West Ham, also at 15, where he swept the terraces, cleaned the toilets, and spruced up the paintwork.[93] Mick Rathbone started his day washing six pairs of Birmingham City boots and ended it cleaning the manager's car. The dressing room was completely out of bounds. At least he got a free pint of milk. Another London boy, Denis Compton, was double talented so he had a double dose, signing for Lords ground staff in the summer and Highbury ground staff in the winter where he too did his share of sweeping, not with the ball. When Steve Perryman first saw Spurs' owners, he wondered who they were.[94] In Budapest, Ferenc Puskas had his debut at 16 for Kispest who paid him in money and sausages. Harry Hall was paid with a Harris Tweed coat.[95] Ron Atkinson joined the Molineux ground staff as an apprentice and like the rest did all the sweeping and the scrubbing only at Wolves you did it before you trained. At 17, he decided to take an engineering apprenticeship, reducing him to amateur status. At 21, he

[90] Baxter, *Baxter* (1984) p.12.   [91] Lofthouse, *Goals Galore* (1954) p.21, p.23.

[92] Kirkup, *Milburn* (1990) p.24; Milburn, *Man of Two Halves* (2003) pp.28–38. Milburn was a powerful sprinter and his nickname 'JET' came from his initials. 'Bevin Boys' were conscripted coalminers named after wartime the Minister of Labour.

[93] Bobby Moore, b. Barking, Essex, 1941, West Ham United (1958–74), Fulham (1974–77), England × 108: Powell, *Moore* (1976) p.133; Matthews, *Feet First* (1948) pp.13–15.

[94] Perryman, *All Seasons* (1986) p.49; Rathbone, *Smell of Football* (2011) ch.1; Heald, *Compton* (2006) p.21.

[95] Poole, *Tyneside Memories* (1988) p.60; Taylor and Jamrich, eds., *Puskas* (1997) p.26.

moved to Headington United, a non League club, where he earned £25 per week, far more than at Molineaux.[96]

Just as the public schoolmen had their *alma mater* so these boys had their craft apprenticeships, understood as an ordinary part of being a man and making a living. Manchester United built their ground on the biggest industrial estate in the country. In the 1950s, 54,000 people worked at Trafford Park—as many as watched the football. West Ham, 'The Hammers', were made out of an iron works. Arsenal, 'The Gunners', came out of a gun. Reading were 'The Biscuitmen', Stoke 'The Potters', Luton 'The Hatters', Northampton 'The Cobblers', Walsall 'The Saddlers', Sheffield United 'The Blades', Grimsby Town 'The Mariners', and so on. The Football League reflected the topography of the Industrial Revolution. Players gained satisfaction and meaning from their craft, and learned from other craftsmen. The man reputed to be the first modern football manager had formerly managed a munitions factory. 'Footballers must work', he said, but it was a strange set of employers they worked for.[97] For this was a business dominated by hard-headed local businessmen (and solicitors) who had a few bob and yet whose propensity to make money out of the game was severely limited. They kept the professional game local, but made far less out of it than the gambling syndicates who had no local connections whatsoever.[98] There were severe restrictions on what they could do with their capital, on how much they could pay their shareholders, and to what extent they could vary or promote their product. Football clubs wanted to dominate the opposition but the attractiveness of their product (if it was a product) depended on the opposition *not* being dominated, and leagues were graded accordingly.

After 1895, once registered with a club, players needed permission in order to move to another one. This was called 'retention'. When players wanted to be released, 'transfer' fees were sweeteners paid by the buying club to the selling club. The player got nothing out of this other than his reason for moving in the first place. But if his employers did not want him to move, they could retain. This allowed poorer clubs to hold onto better players but even if they did not want him to play, they could still retain him. Part of 'retention' was the maximum wage, set by the League in 1901 at £4 per week or about double the regular earnings of a skilled worker, though in both cases earnings were irregular. As far as the account

[96] Headington became Oxford United in 1960 and joined the Football League in 1962: Atkinson, *United* (1984) p.17.

[97] Chapman, *Herbert Chapman on Football* (1934) p.111. On the industrial relations model: Carter, *Football Manager* (2006) p.32. On football economics: Sloane, 'Economics of Professional Football', *Scottish Journal of Political Economy*, June 1971; 'If football were a proper business', *Management Today*, January 2003. See also Korr, *West Ham United* (1986) p.27, and Taylor, *Association Game* (2013) pp.192–8.

[98] The Football Pools avoided the Gaming Act by claiming that betting was not a matter of chance: They were said to have taken £40 million in the 1935–36 season: Graves and Hodge, *Long Weekend* (1940) p.384. On Tottenham Hotspur as not a normal commercial operation: Davies, *Glory Game* (1972) p.105, and Alan Sugar, *The Times*, 8 October 2010.

books show, West Ham were keeping well below this maximum in 1906, paying players about £2 10s per week on average.[99] The maximum wage went up by the odd pound or two as time went by. By 1947 it stood at £12 per week and by 1961 at about £20—in both cases roughly representative of best working-class wages for those years, including overtime and bonuses.

Professional footballers may have seen themselves as workers but in truth their conditions of employment were inferior. Unlike footballers, workers were not 'registered' to their employers and they were not, at least to their knowledge, bound by wage caps. Workers were free to move and work elsewhere. Footballers were not. Having bound themselves to their employer and normally not expecting anything more than training and a bit of skivvying, most professional footballers were the apprentices who never grew up. As Matt Taylor points out, 'no other industry exhibited such tight and strictly regulated restrictions on an employee's freedom of contract'.[100]

Having been legally advised that professional footballers did not come under the Employers' Liability (for accidents at work) Act of 1880, or the Workmen's Compensation Acts of 1897–1900, and representing men half of whose careers ended in injury at work, the Professional Footballers' Association was founded in 1907 in order to challenge these conditions of employment. Under the Employer's Liability Act, they wanted their members to be defined as workmen.[101] In 1909, two years after the founding of the PFA, and led by Billy Meredith who had learned the lessons of solidarity in the Welsh coalfield, Manchester United players went on strike in order to win trade union recognition. In fact, the 1906 Workmen's Compensation Act had already recognized footballers as workmen, and the National Insurance commissioners would do the same in 1912. So, by that date there was no question under the law that professional footballers were workmen doing a job, but retain and transfer and wage capping continued to keep them outside the real world of labour. It took another fifty years, in 1961, that under pressure from the PFA again, the Football League agreed to abolish wage capping—a move ratified by Mr. Justice Wilberforce two years later, along with remarks on retention as 'an unreasonable restraint of trade'.[102] Players did not get

[99] Korr, *West Ham United* (1986) pp.15–16.   [100] Taylor, *The Leaguers 1900–39* (2005) p.101.
[101] The injury figures come from the 1950s (24 per cent knees, 10 per cent heads, 10 per cent legs). It is a reasonable supposition that figures were at least as bad in 1907: Ward and Williams, *Football Nation* (2009) p.66. Then there were injuries at the other place of work: 'Alec Hall has unfortunately suffered a foot injury at work which will prevent him turning out tomorrow': *Grimsby Evening Telegraph*, 28 August 1942.
[102] Meredith in Harding, *Football Wizard* (1998) and in *The Guardian*, 21 October 2009. On the history of the PFA: Harding, *Behind the Glory* (2009). The most complete account of football as a business and footballers as workers is to be found in Taylor, *The Leaguers 1900–39* (2005), chs. 3, 4, and in Taylor, 'Work and Play: the professional footballer in England 1900–50', *The Sports Historian* 22, 2002. Like the working class more generally, footballers were expected to bring energy to the national life: Levi, *Our Workmen* (1868) p.8.

unrestrained trading until 1978 and, even then, with full freedom of contract, still they had to wait until 1995 with the Bosman ruling (European Court of Justice) before they could move, out of contract, without transfer fees.

The apprentice–journeyman relationship was the invisible thread that held the male side of working-class community together, and football was no exception.[103] If girls were the great excluded from football, they were the great excluded from apprenticeship. The best football autobiographies recognize these worlds of labour. Shankly at Liverpool made the 'boot room' his centre of operations where the journeymen met to talk craft and solidarity.[104] Shackleton at Sunderland was the perennial sorcerer's apprentice, full of pranks, but like all time-served tradesmen, he knew what he was worth. If he did not like being sold, he did not like being undersold.[105] Hunter Davies' *Glory Game* understands this world very well. Alan Gowling's *Football Inside Out* is a journeyman's manual.[106] Eamon Dunphy's *Diary of a Professional Footballer* is dedicated to the true pro. Time-served, and faithful to the guild, there is no place in Dunphy's sporting life for 'cowboys', or know-alls who live off the labour of others.[107]

Billy Wright signed professional for Wolverhampton Wanderers at 14 in 1937 for £2 per week. In 1950, at the height of his powers, he still lived at Mrs. Colley's boarding house, and he still joined her of an evening for a bit of rug making by the fireside. One day, he hoped to have enough money to settle down with a house of his own and a car in the drive. His favourite clothes were sports jacket and flannels (same as Nat Lofthouse) and in the evenings he was learning to be a book-keeper at the local technical college (same as Billy Liddell).[108] When Wright married the popular singer Joy Beverley of the Beverley Sisters, they were earning £1,000 per week for singing 'I Saw Mommy Kissing Santa Claus' and he was earning £24 per week captaining Wolves and England.[109] It was a man's world alright, and a world we have lost.

---

[103] '... transmitted in the codes of apprenticeship and inheritance which operate in the interior, shaping its narrative, its dispositions of mental and manual skill': Cohen, 'Public sociology and the ethnographic stake in community studies', paper given at the 'Michael Young at 100' conference, ICS, Barbican, 11 September 2015.

[104] Williams, *Into the Red* (2001) p.68. Taylor takes the industrial analogy further: 'Football's Engineers?' *Sport in History*, 2010, p.138.

[105] Jack, *Shackleton* (1955) pp.18–19. The journeyman–apprentice banter continues, especially in the lower leagues where players' wages are modest and they are more likely to share the same background.

[106] Gowling, *Football Inside Out* (1977).

[107] Dunphy, *Only a Game?* (1976). On flash managers, as usual Brian Clough was the exception: 'Directors hate him' (p.123).

[108] Wright, *Captain of England* (1950) pp.124–7.

[109] *Daily Telegraph*, 1 September 2015. It was generally supposed that he was gaining from her glamour rather than she from his. Compare the marriage of David and Victoria Beckham in 1999.

A Local Life

Football talk quickly became as important as football itself—a sort of second life. The Footballers' Arms in Burnley was the 'Home of Football Chat'. George Haworth, former captain of Accrington Stanley and proprietor of The Swan in Accrington, called on friends old and new to 'hear the latest football gossip'. Publicans continued to act as stakeholders and matchmakers as they did in days of Sayers Heenan, and they continued to tolerate what the law did not see, including for example one Joseph Ludwicke who was arrested at Bilston in 1886 charged with deserting his wife and family. 'The prisoner had been known in the district for some months as "the male barmaid" accepting engagements in various public houses, and serving the customers in female attire, his feminine voice and general get up as a fast young woman proving very attractive and a source of profit to his employers. It now turns out he is a Lancashire weaver'.[110]

In 1908 around 40 per cent of professional footballers in England and Wales played for their local club. Perhaps an inch or two taller and a pound or two heavier at around 5 feet 7 inches and over 11 stone, but not particularly different in build or outlook from other young manual workers of their age and class, footballers were local celebrities on the crest of the new Saturday night economy.[111] When they lost, the town lost. When they won, the town noticed.[112] Sunderland won the FA Cup in 1937. They left Kings Cross the locomotive draped in red and white to be met by cheering crowds at every station on their way north. Back on Wearside, there was bunting everywhere and the team was met by a brass band and a civic reception. No royal visitor to the town could have expected more. But this was not the best of it. Carter the captain remembered that

---

[110] *Football Field & Sports Telegram*, iii, 68, 2 January 1886.

[111] Preceded by the weekend summer domestic economy that included garden games and lawn mowers: Lunn & Co Annual catalogue (1887) Telegram 'Muscular, London': John Johnson, Bodelian, Sports Box 15. In 1908, out of 392 leading footballers of all codes amateur and professional, average age was 27, average height was 5 feet 7 inches, and average weight was 11 stone 7 pounds. Out of 251 professional players, average age was 24 and 40 per cent played for local clubs. Lightest player was William Winstanley, Wigan collier and professional player for Leigh Northern Rugby Football Union (later Rugby League) at 5 feet 9 inches and 9 stone. Full-time professionals were so rare as to be specifically mentioned: eg Thomas Broad, West Bromwich Albion, b. Stalybridge, 21 years old, 5 feet 9 inches, 12 stone: all from Ross Brown ed., *Football Who's Who* (1908). Based on army samples, Bailey and others estimate the average height of young men in 1914 at 5 feet 6 inches: 'Health, height and household', *Economic History Review* 69, 2016, p.41. Floud estimates 5 feet 7 inches and 10 stone: 'Height, weight and body mass since 1820', *National Bureau* (1998) tables 3 and 4. For 'household names' and 'heroes in their own sphere' see Glanville, ed., *Footballers' Who's Who* (1956) p.2. Day estimated that the average Manchester working-class young man at the time of William Winstanley of Wigan was about 5 feet 6 inches and 9 stone 9 pounds, which he compares to the ideal type public school sportsman at 5 feet 10 inches and 12 stone: 'The Athletic Body', paper to ICSHC, DMU, 27 April 2012.

[112] Walley, *Accrington Stanley* (2006) p.50. For the role of the Northern League in giving self respect to hard-pressed towns and villages: Hunt, *Northumbrian Goalfields* (1989) p.1.

...stepping outside [the town hall] was like stepping into an alarm signal. Suddenly everything went off. The tugs and ships in the river were hooting and blowing their sirens, railway engines shrilled their whistles, bells rang and rattles clacked, there was shouting and cheering...a thick concrete wall of deafening din ... 'Ha-way, Ha-way, Ha-way!' cried half a million throats.[113]

Boys born in the 1860s joined a football craze that lasted over a hundred years. Wilfred George Archer, born 1920, like so many footballers of his generation, remembered his first pair of boots: 3s 6d with two pairs of laces and a dozen studs. 'They threw in a calendar of hunting scenes as well'.[114] The passion never left him, playing for various colliery teams well into middle age, including Seaham Harbour in their pomp, and for the forces in India during the war where he won a front room full of cups including the All India Cup—twice as big as the FA Cup—with an RAF Cawnpore side all leading aircraftsmen except for the manager who was a flight lieutenant. When Wilf was demobbed in 1946, he signed for his home town side South Shields FC promising to play in an efficient manner, to the best of his ability, according to the rules of the Football Association, for £2.10s per match. When he ceased being paid to play, in 1954, he became an FA 'Permit Player' which allowed him 'to continue the game without remuneration' although still a professional and disallowed from all amateur competition.[115] At school, Wilf was friends with Stan Mortensen, one day to become a great star. As a young war-time itinerant professional at Grimsby, he played wing to Peter Doherty's centre forward, another great star. When he was older, he played against Hughie Gallacher, once Newcastle United's finest, perhaps their greatest. Like George Watson, that Wilf didn't become a league player was down to time and chance and preference. He knew his worth, a role he could handle and enjoy in the place he belonged. These things ran in families. Wilf signed for Harton Colliery Welfare in 1954 but his father, another Wilf, had won the Tyneside Munitions Workers' League, one of the toughest in the country, with Harton in 1917. When his son was asked what he would do if he had his time again, he said he saw kids playing in the park and wanted to pinch their ball.[116] Which, at 73, was answer enough.

The game that this generation came to love had nothing to do with the old 'folk' football that their grandfathers might have heard of but almost certainly never played, and everything to do with those public school correspondents to Bell's Life and The Sporting Gazette—Thring at Uppingham, Alcock of the Football

---

[113] Carter, Footballer's Progress (1950) p.136. The town historian thought the club's FA Cup wins of 1937 and 1973 were Sunderland's proudest moments in a history going back to Bede: Corfe, Sunderland (1973) p.93.
[114] Shields Gazette, 2 July 1993.
[115] Football Association, Permit, 2 September 1954; The Burt, Lahore All India De Montmorency Football Tournament, April 1945 programme: B&A Railway (IFA Champions 1944) v RAF Cawnpore; Photo All India Victory 1945: memorabilia and conversations with Lynda Archer, September 2018.
[116] 'I would train and train and train': Shields Gazette, 2 July 1993.

Association, 'Etoniensis' and 'Rugbiensis'—who stumbled upon ways of reaching the people through football far more effectually than Matthew Arnold did through something he called culture.[117] In 1863 'Etoniensis' wrote to *The Times* calling on the leading public schools, London clubs, and universities to convene a meeting to inaugurate a national game for the winter.[118] On the day chosen, Monday 26 October 1863, the leading schools did not turn up but eleven London clubs and schools did, to sit down, call themselves the Football Association, and draw up a new set of laws of the game.[119]

News of this association of footballers spread. In 1864 the *Leeds Mercury* reported the strange case of a hundred boys turning up at dawn in response to an advert to start a football team. In 1865 *The Sportsman* reported that football had 'ceased to be the property of the public schools' and was 'now making its way into the suburbs'. In 1866 the FA improved its laws, making the game more open. In 1871 they inaugurated the FA Challenge Cup, open to all associates. In 1884, the *Salford Reporter* reported crowds of two to three thousand 'in little more than a dozen year's growth'. In 1901, *Football Who's Who* could report that Association Football retained its 'powerful sway' in spite of war in South Africa (from which football fans borrowed Afrikaans 'Spioenkop' to name the steeply banked terracing behind the goals). In 1861, a letter to *The Field* had mused on the possible impact of football migrating from the college quadrangle to the village green. In 1909 they had their answer, of sorts, when Bere Regis beat Blandford Forum amidst sensational scenes.[120] The *Football Almanac* had already declared football to be without question the country's most popular sport.[121] Everyone wanted a go—including a player with a wooden leg according to minute 21 of the FA Council meeting of 1907. In 1858, *Bell's Life* gave more coverage to pigeon shooting.[122] Now football was *habitus*, and went without saying. Matches were reported in the newspapers as if readers knew the game already, which of course they did.

---

[117] Kitching, 'A Winter Game for the People?', unpublished paper, ICSHC, DMU, 2015, p.5. Peter Swain has found evidence of a revived form of folk football played for money wagers in Lancashire in the 1820s. Key to this revival was finding places to play. Masters finds similar stirrings in York after the city's 1825 Improvement Act, which named football as a nuisance. In both cases the matches were intermittent. Compared to this, Neil Tranter refers to football leagues and national governing bodies as 'the new dispensation' and he is surely right. See Swain, 'Cultural Continuity', *Sport in History* 28, 2008, pp.567–8, and 'The Grander Design', *Sport in History* 34, 2014, p.538; Masters, 'Rugby, Football and the Working Classes in York', *Borthwick Papers* 123 and 124, 2014, p.7; and Tranter, *Sport, Society and Economy* (1998) p.141.

[118] *The Times*, 5 October 1863.

[119] Collins, 'Football before 1871', Ts, ICSHC, DMU, August 2018.

[120] According to Bere Regis Parish Magazine, 1909. Other references from *The Field*, 12 October 1861; *Leeds Mercury*, 7 March, 30 April 1864; *The Sportsman*, 18 November 1865; *Salford Reporter*, 25 October 1884; *Football Who's Who* (1901). Battle of Spion Kop involved heavy losses by Lancashire regiments, 23–24 January 1900.

[121] Gibson and Pickford, *Association Football* (1906). See reporting across mixed football codes in the *Sporting Chronicle*, 2 February 1875.

[122] *Bell's Life*, 21 February 1858.

While intellectuals found urban life morally repugnant, workers took a more pragmatic, view. Children's stories went on depicting football in the old public school way as kick and rush 'raining in red hot shots', but in fact football was now a game for moderns—a fast passing game in a world of cigarettes and slipper baths, cheap suits, embrocation, beer and brilliantine, and you can get a good idea of it from match day programmes.[123] Dave Russell stresses that strong sense of northern brio that accompanied all this shine.[124] William Woodruff remembered Saturday nights and Sunday mornings in Blackburn: Griffin Street FC, going to the pictures, or hops at St. Philip's Church hall, tight suits, the long lie in.[125]

Public school men last won the FA Challenge Cup in 1882 when upper-class Old Etonians beat working-class Blackburn Rovers 1-0 at Kennington Oval—a close run thing for those who saw the game as public school property.[126] The following year however, it was Blackburn Olympic who beat Old Etonians to take the cup north where it stayed until 1901 when a team of London professionals took it back south. The *Manchester Guardian* referred to the Blackburn victory as the 'Waterloo' moment for public school football. The FA investigated Olympic for illegal payments soon after their famous victory but nothing came of it. They legalized payments from 1885. Professionalism was clearly the way up and amateurism was clearly the way out.

In 1888 the Football League was formed out of twelve nominally professional clubs, all northern or midland, Lancashire at the core, each one rooted in the local life. By 1900 there was a total of eighteen clubs in the First and Second Divisions of the Football League, and in 1921 Third Division 'South' and Third Division 'North' were established to join them.[127] Gentlemen may have administered the thousands of clubs that made up the Football Association, but businessmen ran the eighty-six clubs of the Football League. Between them they wiped the platter clean by coming to a deal that allowed Association Football to spread based on mass participatory amateurism at the bottom, elite professionalism at the top and, as we have seen, a mix of each in all the various transitions in and out of the game in between. It is worth pointing out that cricket, like football, managed to mix

---

[123] A 'system of passing' as reported in the *Manchester Guardian*, 21 March 1892. Historians can find an early consumer culture for young men in, for example, The *Official Programme of the Manchester Clubs* [Manchester City Football Club, Newton Heath FC, Broughton Rangers FC, and Salford Northern Rugby Union FC] 3 September 1898. See also *Oriental Notes*, Official Organ of Clapton Orient FC, 2 September 1907, 1d. In 1938 Justin Evans commended using football's 'unrivalled appeal' in attracting boys to boys' clubs: *First Steps* (1938) p.30.

[124] Russell, *Football and the English* (1997) p.66, *Looking North* (2004) p.237, and his talk about football and popular music, including brass bands, to a conference of sports historians: ICSHC, DMU, 25 October 2015.

[125] Woodruff, *Road to Nab End* (1993) pp.177–9.

[126] Corinthians were founded that same year, seen by Bolsmann and Porter as a deliberate bid to uphold the amateur ethos (including plenty fun and late nights) in the face of the new, more serious professional game: *English Gentlemen and World Soccer* (London, Routledge 2018).

[127] Taylor, 'Football League', *IJRLS* 2, 2005, pp.23–4.

players of varying contractual standing in spite of huge differences in social class. A big working-class game in spite of its public school image, the cricket authorities nevertheless kept a tight grip on their codes and conventions.[128] A lad might play hard ball league cricket on a Friday night, no quarter given. He might play grammar school cricket next morning, pats on the back, clapping each other off the field. Even though the MCC's 7,000 members in 1945 'were as unrepresentative of the national polity as any society could be', it was still the same game and the same governing body.[129] Other modern sports, rugby say, or athletics, or rowing, were unable to come to such an arrangement. Rugby League and Rugby Union split not only the game but the country.[130]

A correspondent to the *Sunderland Post* in 1881 thought that Association Football needed only to be known in order to be popular.[131] Although at first some clubs continued to mix and match codes according to the fixture list, after the astonishing popularity of the FA Cup from 1871, and the regular rhythm of the Football League after 1888, no one was in any doubt that 'football' was the people's game and in 1914 they couldn't go to war without it.[132]

An Associational Life

People were showing an appetite for providing things for themselves. In 1938, York had sixty five football and rugby clubs, sixty-one cricket clubs, fifty-two rowing clubs, fifty-one bowling clubs, and eighteen tennis clubs.[133] In the 1890s the Cooperative Wholesale Society's Lancashire strongholds showed every sign of

[128] Boitard's painting of a cricket match in 1740 looks recognizably modern. A common cricketing code was drawn up by the MCC at Lord's in the 1780s. Cricket's gentlemen governors did not mind paying players to play just as they did not mind paying servants to serve. Nor did they mind that women played. There was a revival of the game in girls' private schools and colleges in the 1890s. Nor did gentlemen mind mixing with professionals on and off the field as long as they didn't have to change and travel with them. The painting is in Altham, *History of Cricket* (1926) p.32. Cricket was Ireland's most popular game until the nationalists pilloried it: Rouse, *Sport in Ireland* (2015) p.123. Girls' school cricket in Sandiford, *Cricket and the Victorians* (1994) pp. 45–7.

[129] McKibbin, *Classes and Cultures* (1998) p.339. Local league and grammar school cricket as my brother played it. See Harry Pearson's slow turn through the little northern clubs who in the 1890s opted, like their football cousins, to play in leagues: *Slipless in Settle* (2012). Pearson understands how sport makes the stories people live by.

[130] Northern Rugby Union (later Rugby League) broke away in 1895 to be 'confined to a comparatively narrow strip of northern England with Liverpool at one end and Hull at the other...the heartland of much of the historic industrial working class': McKibbin, ibid, p.352. Rugby Union took most of the rest, including working-class South Wales and bits of middle-class public school Scotland and Ireland.

[131] *Sunderland Daily Post*, 16 November 1881. *The Sporting Chronicle*, 2 February 1875, reported on fourteen football matches of various codes. *The Sporting Gazette* berated the Burton men for all choosing the 'prerogatives of a goalkeeper': 25 November 1876.

[132] The equivalent of a £250,000 dedicated campaign for national morale every week, according to Mass Observation at the outbreak of war in 1939: 'HJN', 'Sport in Wartime', 13 December 1939: File 13, MO. See Lane Jackson, *Sporting Days* (1932) p.23.

[133] Clark, *British Clubs* (2001) p.476.

growing as fast in groceries as their football clubs were growing in football. Whereas members of the CWS ran their own show as part of a gigantic theatre of cooperative and mutual enterprise numbering millions of members, members of professional football clubs, so called, ran nothing. They were the people who paid to watch a game organized by somebody else.[134]

No late nineteenth-century social activity spread the name of 'association' more widely than Association Football and of course the Football Association started life as just that, an association of fellows intent on producing football for themselves. By the 1890s however, with the entry of private capital into the game, no association meant 'association' less than the clubs of the Football League. The League had replaced the old gentlemanly model of fixtures based on old school networks, with a business model based on selling 'sport' as a finely graded competition. Unlike the cooperatives, or the guilds, or the friendly societies, or the trade unions, or the club and institute unions, or the Workers' Educational Association, or the churches and chapels, or indeed the old folk football or the thousands of little new clubs sprouting up on every street corner, League capitalists were not interested in turning football into something local people did for themselves. They were interested in. Well what were they interested in? It is here that David Storey's original *This Sporting Life* has some interesting things to say.[135]

Founded at a public meeting in 1871 with all the usual rigmarole of club life including members and subscriptions, Reading Football Club narrowly voted to stay a club in the associational sense at a heated general meeting in September 1894. The case for going professional was simple: make more money, pay more money, get more money, and trophies. It rarely worked out that way of course, but the men with the money seemed to get something personal out of it and civic belonging was good for business. The case *against* going professional, which incidentally was supported by some of Reading's leading businessmen, was about keeping Reading Football Club local and genuinely associational. The following year the club voted to pay its players, or some of them, some of the time, and in 1897 it turned itself into a limited liability company with shareholders and directors and the battle for the associational life was over.[136]

This is not to suppose that paying to watch football or being paid to play it was seen in any way as alien or unprincipled by those who did. Paying and being paid for sport in nineteenth-century England was far more significant than late-century

---

[134] On the peak moment of 'associationism' in the CWS: Stephen Yeo, *Who Was J T W Mitchell?* (1995). For associationism as an alternative to capitalism and communism, see Yeo's *History of Association, Cooperation, and un-Statist Socialism in 19c and 20c Britain* (2018).

[135] 'It's only a game old sport', He caught hold of my sleeve in a confidential way. 'It's all a game', he said. 'For Weaver's benefit': Storey, *This Sporting Life* (1960) pp.55-6; Collins, *Sport in Capitalist Society* (2013) p.79.

[136] At Reading FC 'a working-class organization, in some senses, had been created, but made possible by being within a specifically business mould': Yeo, *Voluntary Organizations* (1976) p.194.

amateurs liked to suppose. Like the time-served coachmaker and professional cricketer Thomas Hunt, who made £20 a game plus expenses, a good few hundred sportsmen made a living according to the season.[137] Private coaching, exhibitions, and personal security widened their services but whatever these men did in order to make a living, it is difficult to imagine them refusing to take money in the name of an amateur ideal foisted on them by those who, by and large, had plenty of money already. Some players might have refused payment based on strict religious or moral principles, but it would not have occurred to most of them to hand back that which was fairly earned. It would not have occurred to men like Tommy Brownlow of 3 Margaret Street, Coalville, for instance, not to be paid for playing for Whitwick Imperial on Saturdays any more than it would have occurred to him not to be paid for hewing at Snibstone Colliery the rest of the week.[138] That was how households made ends meet: main wage Friday, bits and bobs anywhere else. Along with his brother Walter (South Leicester Colliery, Hugglescote FC), Tommy had lost three brothers in the war and did not need reminding that life was uncertain. The big amateur clubs were awash with gate money anyway, and nobody begrudged the lads. At a certain level of competition, payments were normative. Given that many apprentices and juniors played as part-time amateurs for professional clubs, and given that many seniors played as part-time professionals for amateur clubs, the difference between them could never be one of principle. To pay or not to play was up to those who had the money and made the rules. Nothing to do with Tommy Brownlow. Of course, what was a gain for an individual could be a loss for society.[139]

Below the few dozen elite clubs of the League (Reading joined in 1920) it was a different story for all the other thousands of little clubs signed up to FA governance and replicating Football League competition but otherwise running their own affairs.[140] Leicester had its own league side (1894) made out of a school side (1884) but it also enjoyed, for example, its own Leicester & District Mutual Sunday School Football League, five divisions, from Anstey Primitive Methodists at the top (black and white, change in the Sunday School) to Emmanuel Sunday School XI at the bottom (no colours, change 'On Ground').[141] The Prims may have lost their old hostility to sport, but not their energy and drive.

---

[137] Report on the death of the 'remarkably good looking' Thomas Hunt in a railway accident at Rochdale. He was 39 and had played professional cricket since he was 25: *Manchester Guardian*, 13 September 1858. I am grateful to my colleague, Mr. R L Greenall for this reference. Adrian Harvey stresses longstanding professional and commercial markets for sport: 'Evolution', Oxford DPhil (1998) p.441.

[138] *Leicester Football Mail*, 3 January 1920.

[139] For arguments over payments: Kitching, 'The Sunderland Split of 1888', paper to ICSHC, DMU, 5 May 2017, and 'Crook Town FC and the Durham FA 1927-31', Ms, ICSHC, DMU, February 2018.

[140] Not *quite* a business. 'Billingham Synthonia have the unique distinction of being the only club in Britain named after a fertiliser': Pearson, *The Far Corner* (1994) p.49.

[141] *Sport Mercury*, ed. H E Adcock, *Football Annual* (1925).

An expanding market in football depended on an expanding market in local newspapers, and *vice versa*. First sign of this revolution in the nation's sporting life came with the local football 'specials', selling on the streets same day late afternoon and early evening. Printed on coloured paper—*'Per-hink Hun!'* "*Guhuhree-ee-un Fi-nuul!*" as the street vendors had it—football specials quickly established themselves along with bottled beer and the *palais de danse* as part of a young man's Saturday night out. At first, the huge demand for rapid results was met by pigeon post (newspapers had their own lofts), followed by telegrams and then telephone calls to editors, who spoke to compositors, who set the linotype ('line of type') ready for the printers whose rotary press made copy double quick. By 1913, forty-eight towns had their football specials. Birmingham was first with *Saturday Night*, perfectly named, selling at half a penny. By 1889, the *Blackburn Evening Express* was hitting the streets with four editions in two hours. In 1894, Barnsley had fresh sporting news at 8am, 4pm, 6pm, and 7pm. The old gentlemanly scrawl was over. Fast and factual was the mark of the new journalism.[142] Football results joined racing results at the heart of this sporting life. Horse racing still dominated the front page of Manchester's *Sporting Chronicle* but football now filled the back. Monday night was round-up night.[143]

Newsreels followed the specials into football's local roots. 'Actuality' reels showed local people *to* local people—a winning formula. A certain cinematic trope developed: the crowd, the captains, the handshake, the spin, a jerky kick off, rattles, and happy faces direct to camera. The first BBC radio football commentary was Arsenal versus Sheffield United at Highbury on 22 January 1927. The first FA Cup Final BBC radio commentary was Arsenal versus Cardiff, Wembley, same year. The BBC swiftly corrected a natural northern bias in the game just as it set about building a new metropolitan-centred sporting calendar for other sports ranging from the Boat Race and the Derby to Wembley, Wimbledon, and Lords. The Grand National happened somewhere up north.[144]

It took a while for the BBC and other official bodies to understand that Association Football was England's greatest sport. People could be killed in a football stadium without (it would appear) hardly anyone outside Bolton noticing, as when thirty-three were killed in a crush at Burnden Park in 1946.[145] It took the state a long time to include organized sport in the school day and even then it was up to the teachers. School football depended almost entirely on their goodwill.[146]

[142] *Saturday Night* came out in 1887: Domeneghetti, *Back Page* (2014) pp.29–34, p.65; *Barnsley Sporting News*, 11 July 1894. See Wiener, *Papers for the Millions* (1988) p.xviii. Frank Keating remembered the specials: 'Last Days of the Pinks and Greens', *Guardian* 24 January 2006.

[143] *Barnsley Sporting News*, 20 October 1894 and Manchester's *Sporting Chronicle*, 6 January, 5 September 1908.

[144] Whannel, *Fields in Vision* (1992) p.17.

[145] McKibbin, *Democracy and Political Culture* (2019) p.133.

[146] Mason, *Sport in Britain* (1989) p.2.

The Festival of Britain in 1951 included sport, but not as a key event.[147] International football matches remained low key until England won the World Cup in a decade when England became a byword for talent. Arthur Hopcraft finally caught the breeze in 1968 with his masterpiece *The Football Man*. He knew fans were wealth and if he freely admitted the vulgarity of the game, he also understood its intensity. Football was 'inherent in the people', he said.[148] Nothing got so close. In a match against Grays in 1894, the Southend crowd got so close to their keeper that one of them saved the ball.[149]

When Saturday Came

Emma Griffin says that '... freed from the meanest subsistence' the Industrial Revolution brought more jobs, more money, and more liberty.[150] In the first football outbreak, somewhere between 1880 and 1913, average earnings went up by 41 per cent.[151] Just at this point where children were growing taller and child mortality rates were falling faster, football took off.[152] Once children were free from 'tender lungs, cramped bowels and aching bones', they could get out more. Once they were less likely to get tuberculosis, they could grow more. Once they had enough calories, they found the energy.[153]

At first, expectations of life at birth in England's largest industrial cities had fallen catastrophically. Between 1851 and 1870, Manchester, Leeds, Bradford, Sheffield, and Liverpool all experienced environmental collapse and serious deteriorations in living standards just up to the point, in the 1880s, when they also started to enjoy a serious hike in real earnings. This was an odd situation but not inexplicable. People could find more work and make more money if not in

---

[147] Wilton, 'Galaxy of sporting events', *Sport in History*, 2016, p.473.

[148] Hopcraft, *Football Man* (1968) Introduction. On the 1960s: Savage, *1966* (2015) p.286.

[149] *Southend Echo & Prittlewell, Leigh, Shoebury and Rochford Argus*, 21 November 1894.

[150] Griffin, *Liberty's Dawn* (2013) p.17; Feinstein, 'New Estimates', *EcHR* xliii, 1990, p.602; Allen, *Industrial Revolution* (2009) p.25, p.140. Beaven sees male workers as the major beneficiaries of the new surplus, and major consumers of the new entertainment: *Leisure, Citizenship and Working Class Men* (2005) pp.43–5.

[151] Jerram sees football as part of an urban sexual revolution too: *Streetlife* (2011) p.187.

[152] Griffin stresses the role of a dynamic urban economy in raising standards of living: 'Diets, Hunger and Living Standards', *Past & Present* 239, 2018, p.111. Gazely and Newell stress the freedom from absolute poverty of skilled working-class families (23 per cent) over unskilled (50 per cent): 'Poverty in Edwardian Britain', *EcHR* 64, 2011, p.69. Bailey and others show how stature rose as family size fell 1890–1940: 'Health, height and Household', *EcHR* 69, 2016, p.51. Hatton shows how infant mortality fell from 155 deaths per 1,000 live births in 1871–1875, to 40 per 1000 live births in 1950, with child mortality rates substantially lower and falling: 'Infant mortality and the health of survivors, Britain 1910-50', *EcHR* 64, 2011, pp.960–1.

[153] On tender lungs, Sharpe, 'Explaining short stature', *Economic History Review* 65, 2012, p.1491; on calories, Gazeley and Newell, 'Urban working-class food consumption', *EcHR* 68, 2015, p.121.

conditions of their own choosing.[154] In 1858, although the *Manchester Guardian* could ridicule Prince Albert's idea of reviving the ancient Olympics, it did think that workers shut up for ten hours a day in factories deserved to get out more.[155]

The case against factories was very specific and very consistent. Everywhere they looked factory inspectors found problems with children's lungs, eyes, feet, and pelvis. In the 1840s, Lord Ashley had drawn on the findings of eighty surgeons and physicians in order to ratify widespread rumours of physical exhaustion, dehydration, irritation, and amputation.[156] Bolton mill children were walking on average twenty-five miles a day while their hands swelled and their lungs struggled to cope with the heat.[157] In Oldham, the new Surat cotton fibre filled the air with particles.[158] In Sheffield, their full weight bearing down on heavy files, grinders and sharpeners were found 'spitting steel'.[159] In London, young shop assistants were on their feet seventy-four hours a week. In Manchester, female shop assistants faced the same pelvic deformities as mill girls, plus defective eyesight, digestion, and circulation.[160] The 1840 Select Committee on Mills and Factories tried very hard to get Dr. Fox of Derby Infirmary to say that a ten-hour day was injurious to the health of 9 year olds, but he would not say it. He had seen them time after time coming out of the factory ready to play. He admired their pluck. He could not deny what his own eyes had seen.[161] Plenty of expert witnesses testified that children came out of the mills looking happy, 'the boys...as merry as crickets', 'not one girl who looked as if she would refuse an invitation to dance'.[162]

Richard Oastler told the Factory Commissioners straight. 'Any old washerwoman could tell you that 10 hours a day is too long for any child', and suggested that the children might be given little seats to ease their legs and feet. But not too many washerwomen were invited to give evidence to the Factory Commissioners and the little seats (called 'Oastlers') were never taken seriously. A great deal of the

---

[154] In Manchester and Liverpool, environmental deterioration persisted well into the 1900s: Szreter and Mooney, 'Urbanization, mortality...', *EcHR*, li, 1998, p.88, p.110, and the Inter-Departmental Committee *Report on Physical Deterioration* (1904) pp.4–5. Allen shows how eighteenth-century British workers once had been considered the tallest in Europe but their average height fell in the first half the nineteenth century: *Industrial Revolution* (2017) p.78. On environmental pollution, see *Report* from the Poor Law Commissioners into Sanitary Condition of Labouring Population: House of Lords, PP1842, vol. xxvi.

[155] *Manchester Guardian*, 30 September 1858. Get out more and live a better life certainly than that described by Charles Dickens in his portrait of 'Coketown' (Preston), in *Hard Times* (1854): 'Exactly in the ratio as they worked long and monotonously, the craving grew within them for some physical relief—some relaxation encouraging good humour and good spirits' (p.67).

[156] Ashley Cooper, *Ten Hours* (1844) p.10; Ure, *Philosophy of Manufactures* (1835) p.16.

[157] Fielden, *Curse of the Factory System* (1836) pp.xl–xliii, p.32. The Association of Mill Owners responded to the twenty-five-mile charge by saying that fewer young children and women worked in factories than before, and piecers were nowadays walking only eight not fifteen miles a day: *Factory Legislation* (1845) pp.8–11.

[158] Inspectors of Factories, PP1863, p.63.

[159] Children's Employment Commission, 4th Report, PP1865, p.viii.

[160] Select Committee Shop Regulation Bill, PP1886, p.15, p.101, pp.67–9.

[161] Select Committee on Mills and Factories, 6th Report, PP 1840, pp.67–8.

[162] Cooke-Taylor, *Notes of a Tour* (1841) p.36.

most exploited labour was shut away from view in last phase, small scale, domestic production where child labour surged to finish what machines could not.[163] London print shops? 'Slaughter houses'. Luton brickfields? 'Purgatory'. Birmingham metal works? 'Loathsome'. Rural straw plaiting? 'The straw cuts their mouths'.[164]

Hippolyte Taine looked at Manchester factories in the 1860s and saw prisons. Ruggles Brise looked at prisons in the 1920s and saw factories.[165] The 1904 Inter Departmental Report on Physical Deterioration recommended public health tests on young people's height, chest size, weight, head, shoulders, hips, and eyes.[166] Slowly the answer dawned that just as with prisons, the state could at least control the amount of time spent there.

The first effective movement against factory hours came from the shop floor, the so-called 'Short Time' committees, supported by radicals and Tories alike, but staffed by workers across a Leeds–Manchester axis.[167] The 1833 Factory Act made it illegal to employ children under 9 in textile factories but rejected the call, made by the Committees on grounds of family life and recreation, for an early finish on Saturday. With one eye on organized schooling as a new form of class control, factory reformers introduced a 'half-time system' for children age 9 to 13, restricting their working day to six and a half hours, morning or afternoon, with schooling in the half they did not work.[168] Young people (14 to 18 years) and women continued to work long hours (twelve and ten per day), but not nights. Such was their old English liberty to do as they pleased, adult males were left unregulated.

This 1844 Factory Act stipulated how long children might work, but not exactly *when*, and the 1847 Factory Act, although finally delivering the iconic ten-hour day, still failed to plug loopholes in just how much time children were legally permitted to spend on site. A standardized working day had to be legislated for, and the 1850 and 1853 Acts delivered it as 6am to 6pm, with ninety minutes for meals, no work on Sundays, and Saturday half day starting at 2pm. When did Saturday come?[169] 'Saturday', the idea of the Short Time Committees since 1833, finally came to pass in 1853.[170]

---

[163] Humphries, *Child Labour* (2011) p.366; *The Daily News* 1906 Exhibition of Sweated Industries showed what was otherwise hidden from public view: Mudie-Smith, *Sweated Industries* (1906). On Oastler: Ward, *The Factory Movement 1830–55* (1962) p.44, and on 'Oastlers': Dodd, *Factory System Illustrated* (1842) p.45. Mess supported the idea of seats for children as perfectly reasonable: *Factory Legislation 1891–1924* (1926) p.15.

[164] Cooke-Taylor, *Factory System* (1894) p.92.

[165] Taine, *Notes from England* (1860–70) p.219; Ruggles-Brise for a definition of 'imprisonment' as a modern system not unlike a factory: *English Prison System* (1921) p.205.

[166] *Report*, cd 2i75, vol. xxxii, PP1904, pp.11–19.

[167] Short Time Committees, *Address…from the Meeting of Delegates* (1833).

[168] 'Thus began the long history of the 'half-time system': Ward, *Factory Movement* (1962) p.300.

[169] *When Saturday Comes* (WSC) is a British football magazine founded in 1986.

[170] The 1853 Act corrected a loophole in the 1850 Act which was intended to correct a loophole in the 1847 Act. On the standard day: Hutchins and Harrison, *History of Factory Legislation* (1903) p.107; Mess, *Factory Legislation* (1926) p.15. Marx identified the 1847 Ten Hours Act as 'the first time that in

Afternoon finish meant afternoon time to play. Other workplaces followed the 1853 pattern but the Lancashire cotton districts led the way. Because they knew the infrastructure of modern industry first, they knew the infrastructure of modern sport first: regulation, transportation, association, civic pride, and a sharp differentiation between work and play. Saturday came to include not only the pleasures of an afternoon out, but some of the wider treats that working-class Lancashire was pioneering as well, including fish and chips and bed and breakfast. Noting the changes since Engels' observations in *The Condition of the Working Class* in 1845, Stedman Jones called this surplus of spare time and loose change 'the re-making of a working class'. In 1883, James Kerr, Vice President of the Lancashire FA, concurred that there had been a great improvement. Once seen as a relief from factory work, football was seen now as a means of enduring it. 'They might be the best spinners and the best weavers in the world but if they have not the bone and muscle...'. We can guess the rest. In any case, factories were becoming better places to work and, even, identify.[171]

It was always possible for superior people to see Saturday football as a lower form of life. Surely the working class should have better things to do?[172] A good deal of contemporary debate over Amateurism was dipped in the notion that watching certain sports was vulgar and watching certain other sports was refined. This remained the case until the 1990s when having a favourite football club became the middle-class fun thing to have. Before that, the game was an irritant to finer feelings.

The old folk football was essentially a slow-moving melee for any number of players usually between different parts of town. In Ashbourne, first documented 1683, 'up' towners played 'down' towners on Shrove Tuesdays and Ash Wednesdays. Scrums were called 'hugs' and you 'goaled' the ball into your own 'goal' (so to speak). The game was so rough and disorderly it was moved out of town in 1862.[173] Charles Booth's 'Sporting Set' of the 1890s hardly went near a

---

broad daylight the political economy of the middle class succumbed to the political economy of the working class': Fernbach, ed., *First International and After* (1864. 1974) p.79.

[171] Late nineteenth-century improvements in factory life, with elements of custom and belonging, are described in Joyce, *Work, Society, & Politics* (1982) chs. 4 and 5. Kerr is quoted in Mason, *Association Football* (1980) p.225. Stedman Jones' remade working class is in 'Working-Class Culture 1870–1900', in Stedman Jones, ed., *Languages of Class* (1983). For Lancashire leisure, a field John Walton has made his own, see his *The Blackpool Landlady* (1986), *Fish and Chips* (1994), and *The British Seaside* (2000). Manchester Football Association was founded in 1884, even if its clubs were older: James and Day, 'Association Football Culture in Manchester 1840–84', *Sport in History* 34, 2014, p.53. See also Russell, 'Rugby and Soccer Zones in Yorkshire and Lancashire 1860–1914', *IJHS* 5, 1988; and Lewis, 'Professional Football in Lancashire 1870–1914', Lancaster PhD (1993).

[172] Perhaps like planning the revolution? Collins, *Sport in Capitalist Society* (2013) p.51.

[173] Collins, in Collins et al., eds., *Traditional British Rural Sports* (2005) p.34.

ball, yet still they represented that 'great mass of rough, immoral and uneducated physical force' that so threatened the suburbs.[174]

In the modern football crowd, intellectuals saw everything they feared in 'the inert mass', including drinking and betting, gullibility, ignorance, grossness, and, much later, as with the 'CHAVs', council housing and violence.[175] Nineteenth-century social science congresses went out in search of cooperatives and properly regulated factories, but they didn't visit football matches.[176] In a classic work, Gustave Le Bon's *The Crowd* (1896) declared crowds as 'everywhere distinguished by feminine characteristics', hysteria in particular. The founder of the Boy Scout movement saw football fans as degenerate.[177] Sociologists (Hobson, Hobhouse, Masterman) saw them as jingos, or anarchists, or weak-willed. Some socialists saw them as sport dope fiends and lined up with Methodists and Teetotallers to show the road to salvation.[178] Charles Booth noted how cricket and football were offered by youth organizations 'to take the taste away' of organized religion.[179] Other socialists, the Ashbees' Guild of Handicrafts for instance, well understood what had been lost over the previous hundred years and sought to replace it with 'indigenous materials and native traditions' that included football. Way down in Chipping Campden, there were no crowds or professionals, only guildsmen and guildswomen searching for the simple life. When one of them, a silversmith, decided to go and play for Milwall Reserves, the chief utopian could not quite hide his feelings:

> Had our Milwall George—George Colverd of the beefy brawny Eating House down by the Docks not been a person of real character, hooligan and all, I should not have minded, but to lose him just because he was a fine athlete—one of the very things one wants to encourage wisely, was too bad.[180]

---

[174] Rev. Folly talking to the Social Science Association, 1868, in Janes Yeo, *Contest for Social Science* (1996) p.175; Booth, in Mark Clapson, 'Gambling', in England and Day, eds., *Retrieved Riches* (1998) p.369.

[175] 'inert mass' of the 'football crowd that form 90% of the electorate': Cheltenham Ladies' College Magazine, 'Where College Girls Are Needed', 1922, no 2. On Chavs and Hillsborough: Jones, *Chavs* (2012) p.69. Ninety-four people were killed in a fatal forward crush in the crowd at the Leppings Lane end of the Hillsborough Stadium in Sheffield in 1989.

[176] Yeo, *Contest for Social Science* (1996) p.154.

[177] Baden Powell in *Scouting for Boys* as quoted in Featherstone, *Englishness* (2009) p.29; Le Bon, *The Crowd* (1896) p.57, p.21, and, along similar lines in Urwick's *Studies of Boy Life* (1904), Hall's *Adolescence* (1911) and Trotter's *Instincts of the Herd* (1916).

[178] Masterman, *Condition of England* (1909) pp.108–14; Hobson, *Imperialism* (1902) pp.186–9; Hobhouse, *Democracy and Reaction* (1905) pp.76–8. Socialist journal *Gateway* saw football supporters as 'doped with sports news': Yeo, *New Life* (2018) p.176.

[179] Booth, *Life and Labour* (1903) p.79.

[180] Letter of C R Ashbee, quoted in Polley, 'The Ashbees, the Guild of Handicraft, and Sport in the Cotswolds 1902–07', Ts (2019) p.10. The Guildsmen and women of Ditchling also seem to have embraced sport as part of their arts and crafts Utopia: see posters in Ditchling Museum of Art & Craft.

It was as if there were no juvenile delinquents before football.[181] There were certainly no football pitches in Ebenezer Howard's workers' paradise.[182] The National Council of Labour Colleges had no idea what sort of men played it.[183] The BBC had no notion that they might want to talk about it.[184] Richard Hoggart's *The Uses of Literacy* (1957) is the masterpiece of twentieth-century northern working-class life, but it is a life without football. 'Faulkner' and 'Freud' feature in the index, but not Football or Rugby. In Hoggart's Hunslet, 'the body got little direct verbal attention', apparently.[185] Young and Willmott's classic anthropological study of *Family and Kinship in East London* (1957) was based on the mothers so FAKINEL no football there, although we are told that Mr. Aves saw his brother at the match on Saturdays. Adolescent studies noted that boys liked football but not the more significant fact that they organized it as well. The Central Advisory Council for Education reported in 1948 that most boys appeared to be devoted. 'They played football on weekdays; on Saturdays they played or watched football; they said that they preferred football and when asked what they would like to do more out of school they did not hesitate to put football'.[186]

On Saturday 30 July 1966, Mr. Tony Benn, leading Labour politician and man of the people, must have been the only adult male of sound mind in England who did not know. Or if he did know, he didn't put it in his diary.[187]

It is of course true that the professional clubs were businesses. It was equally true that modern football was part of the new economy. But whatever else it was, football was not a capitalist plot. Reyrolle's made switchgear for the world's electricity suppliers. Employing 12,000 workers and taking 500 apprentices a year, they offered football and seventeen other sports. Boys wanted to work there for good wages and the sporting life. False consciousness didn't come into it.[188]

Nor was it just a question of health and welfare. Long before Alphonse Reyrolle, Blackstone thought English liberty consisted of 'the powers of loco-motion', of 'changing situation' and of 'removing one's person to one's own inclination

---

[181] Not true: King, 'Juvenile Delinquency in England', *Past & Present* 160, 1998, p.116.

[182] Howard, *Garden Cities* (1898) and Hunt, *Building Jerusalem* (2005) p.430. Howard had no place for football pitches in his garden city but Cadbury did: *Bourneville Village Trust* (1924).

[183] NALC, *Labour and Leisure* (1944) p.4.

[184] Popular music was similarly underplayed—hence the success of Radio Luxembourg, almost another national institution: Tebbutt, 'Listening to Youth', *History Workshop Journal* 84, 2017.

[185] Hoggart, *Uses of Literacy* (1957) and *A Local Habitation* (1986) vol. i, p.58.

[186] Clearly the CACE needed better sampling techniques: Mason, 'Football', in Mason, ed., *Sport in Britain* (1989) p.146. Willmott and Young, *Family and Kinship* (1957) p.103; Willmott, *Adolescent Boys in East London* (1966) p.30.

[187] 'All day doing nothing on Saturday': Benn, *Out of the Wilderness. Diaries 1963–67* (1988) pp.462–3. Thanks to my colleague Dilwyn Porter for this reference.

[188] Owen, *Reyrolle Story* (2007) p.67. Correspondence and conversation with George Smith, June 2017.

without restraint'.[189] Leigh Rose, the Sunderland goalkeeper, may have taken this to extremes in the quieter moments of the game with his cross bar acrobatics, but every football crowd that has ever been moved has been moved by the beauty of locomotion.[190] Kop Ends can keep moving and chanting for impossibly long shifts. Contrary to the 1853 Factory Act, they won't sit down and they won't shut up. They are the parish on a war footing.[191]

Harry Pearson thought he could tell whether a player was amateur or professional by the size of his thighs. But the truth was you could tell whose game it really was simply by looking at the crowd—a mountain of flat caps living an incrementally better life.[192] Brian Clough retired in 1993 after a remarkable career as a manager and a player. A little lost in his later years, as if TV punditry and a beautiful garden weren't enough, he kept a flat cap in the drawer.[193]

Flowing Line of Liberty

Arthur Hopcraft once described the 'flowing line' of Bobby Charlton's running. It was a line, he said, with 'no disfiguring barbs in it' and 'a heavy and razor sharp arrow at its end'.[194] All the great forwards, and Charlton was the greatest English forward, were great because they could move quickly and dangerously out of deep positions. Scoring was the heavy arrow. Wingers on the other hand lived off three feet of cliff edge. Stanley Matthews didn't so much flow as dart. Tom Finney loved Hampden Park because it gave him a bit more room. Various formations, particularly Herbert Chapman's famous 'W' 'M' shape, were designed to discipline positional play and, as the saying goes, encourage teams 'to keep their shape'. But all the great teams knew that football was a simple game about changing shape by flowing into spaces ahead of the ball. Matt Busby's Manchester United always wanted to keep running off the ball.[195] Alf Ramsey's England was what he called 'a moving team'. Kevin Keegan's Newcastle United wanted all lines flowing, all of the time, whatever the odds.[196]

---

[189] Blackstone, *Commentaries* (1820) p.33.

[190] Leigh Rose's antics (1907–10): *Shields Gazette*, 10 March 2006. Goalkeepers evolved with goal posts (1866), crossbars (1875), and a law for one particular player allowed to use his hands (1871), to be the last man back (1887), in his own 'box' (1912): Wilson, *The Outsider* (2012) p.13.

[191] Commonly called 'havin a laff'. Follow the lads Big Sid, Nobby, Dave, Brother Dave, Father Steve, Geordie, Kev, and Big Mickey in Brian Hall's *Life of Brian in Black and White* (2007). ~Not havin a laff was Simon Barnes, 'Baffling Culture of Vileness', *The Times*, 6 January 2006.

[192] Pearson, *Far Corner* (1994) p.62.   [193] Hamilton, *Provided You Don't Kiss Me* (2007) p.221.

[194] Hopcraft, *Football Man* (1968) p.82.

[195] With 'none of this "W" formation business': Busby, *My Story* (1957) p.160.

[196] 'You wouldn't believe the space': Steve McManaman, on Liverpool v Newcastle United, 3 April 1996: *Sunday Telegraph*, 20 January 2008. Kevin Keegan, b. 1951, Armthorpe, Liverpool (1971–77), Hamburg SV (1977–80), Newcastle United (1982–84), England x 63, European Footballer of the Year 1978, 1979, manager Newcastle United (1992–97).

England's supreme sporting moment came in 1966 when they won the World Cup and every one of them became a hero, a team that everyone (but Tony Benn) could name. But England's decisive moment had come thirteen years before when they lost 3–6 to Hungary, also at Wembley. The Hungarians arrived as the first footballing moderns. Their deep-lying centre forward Hidegkuti was not doing anything the English hadn't done before. Lawton had played deep in the 1930s, and Revie would play it in the 1950s. Tottenham had played it first in 1925 after changes to the off-side law had made coming out of deep positions more effective.[197] The difference with the Hungarians was that their centre forward, there to drag defences out before splitting them with incisive passes in, operated at the heart of a fluid system where positions flowed one into the other.[198] Pressing is the most important feature of the modern game but it still remains uncertain where best to press because when everything is moving, contestation can turn everything round in a second. Charlton's flowing line, in other words, was an expression of liberty from out of any number of contestations.

Much like the laws of the game as approved by the FA in 1863, John Stuart Mill's *On Liberty* (1859) stressed liberty as an associational condition based on laws that allowed free expression in an open society. Mill went on to question the limits of contestation that could be applied to what was otherwise 'free voluntary and undeceived'. Without liberty, he argued, all philosophies were pointless. Without contestation, he argued, all philosophies were 'enfeebled'.[199] Liberty might be free and voluntary in the first place but how much liberty you were allowed depended on contestation in the second, based on laws whose ultimate sanction was the will of the wider society (the association) who made them up. All of this, Mill contended, depended in turn on transparency, on the survey of all by all so that the final free expression (the flowing line if you like) could be fairly judged.

Those former public schoolboys representing eleven London football clubs and schools who first met to call themselves the FA may or may not have had John Stuart Mill in mind.[200] Their minute book makes no mention of him attending the meeting, and he for one thought physical activity was inferior to mental. But most of them did manage to agree on a game that allowed players to enjoy their liberty, while allowing others to challenge it, while others looked on to see whether the challenge was lawful.

---

[197] Wolstenholme, *Sports Special* (1956) pp.50–1; Seed, *Soccer from the Inside* (1947) p.17.

[198] Taylor and Jamovich, *Puskas* (1997) p.70. In the 1953 match, Stan Cullis counted ninety-four Hungarian long balls, sixty of them in the air. The great Hungarian ball playing myth, he contended, happened only in the last half hour when England were tired and dispirited: *All for The Wolves* (1960) ch.3. But how did they get tired and dispirited?

[199] Collini, ed., *On Liberty and Other Writings* (1989) p.153; Mill, *On Liberty* (1859) p.70.

[200] They were: Barnes, Civil Service, Crusaders, Forest Club (Leytonstone), No Name Club (Kilburn), Crystal Palace, Blackheath, Kensington School, Percival House (Blackheath), Surbiton, and Blackheath Proprietary School. Charterhouse sent a delegate.

Having agreed what to call themselves, the men of 1863 invited six leading public schools, including Rugby, to join them.[201] Charterhouse, having already sent its captain, decided not to bother. At their second meeting, on 10 November, the FA discussed all that was allowed to break the flowing line under the various codes of the various schools that played the game. 'Hacking', 'Mauling', 'Tripping', 'Holding', 'Running with the Ball', 'Charging', and 'Knocking On' were all scrutinized. At their third meeting, a week later, tripping was the only contestation that had been taken off the table while all the others remained.

It was at their fourth meeting on 24 November that Charles William Alcock of the Forest Club Leytonstone made the crucial proposal that the FA move to adopt Cambridge University rules that embraced the game 'with the greatest simplicity'. His own club had adopted Cambridge rules in 1862. At their fifth meeting on 1 December two opposing points of view had emerged.[202] Morley of the Barnes Club spoke in support of Alcock, making the case on behalf of all those footballers who did not wish their liberty to be lawfully contested with a kick (or 'hack') below the knee. More support for this position came from the Sheffield Association (founded 1857) in a letter criticizing current FA laws 9 and 10 as 'directly opposed' to the free flowing principles of how they thought football should be played. Law 9 allowed running holding the ball. Law 10 allowed 'any player on the opposite side [to] be at liberty to charge, hold, trap or hack' the running player 'or to wrest the ball from him'. Law 10 narrowly avoided the charge of GBH by stating that 'no player shall be held and hacked at the same time'. Against the libertarians, or Millians, if we can call them that, Mr. Campbell of the Blackheath Club said that in his view, and in the opinion of many other London clubs, hacking *was* football and getting rid of it spoke more of 'pipes and grog' than real football. For

> ... if you do away with all the courage and pluck of the game ... I will be bound to bring a lot of Frenchmen who would beat you on a week's practice (loud laughter). I think that Mr Alcock ought not to have put such a resolution and I think it does not denote the opinion of the London clubs.[203]

In spite of the obvious good humour that prevailed between these very young men (a total of forty three attended the meetings, average age 21 years 5 months)[204] who saw themselves as bloods first and committee members second, modern

[201] The following discussion on the laws of the game is drawn from the minutes of the Football Association, vol. i, 1863–75: FA, formerly in Soho Square, London. Booth's description of the state of club football before the FA will not go unrecognized to thousands of Saturday afternoon and Sunday morning players: 'fixtures *ad hoc*, starting times erratic, playing conditions variable, organization frequently very casual ...': Booth, *Father of Modern Sport* (2002)p.40.

[202] Booth, ibid, pp.95–120.   [203] Minutes of the FA, vol. i: Football Association.

[204] Andy Mitchell has made a study of all who contributed to the first six meetings: http://www.scottishsporthistory.com/sports-history-news-and-blog/found-the-founders-of-the-football-association.

football staggered over the line at the FA's sixth meeting on 8 December 1863 with agreement on eleven players and thirteen laws, the most important of which was law 9 which stated that 'No player shall carry the ball', and an amended version of law 10 which stated that 'Neither tripping nor hacking shall be allowed and no player shall use his hands to hold or push an adversary'.

This was nearly the birth of modern football but not quite because there was also law 6, the so-called 'offside law'. Here, except for kicks from behind the goal line, a player was deemed 'Out of Play immediately he is in front of the ball'—a stipulation that made Association Football look not like modern football but the old public school slow charge, albeit without the carrying, hacking, or holding. As long as players were not allowed to get in front of the ball, incisive passing and nearly all aspects of what came to be the modern game, including positional play and varieties of forward movement into space, were unlawful. It was the Scots, who had no offside law, who connected the flowing line to other flowing lines by developing a forward passing game. It didn't take the FA long to realize their mistake and they liberalized their code in 1866. From then until 1925 when it was reduced to two, a player was deemed onside if three opposition players including the goalkeeper were between him and the ball.[205]

Now the modern game could begin. Having finally arrived at a practical philosophy of play, the FA stuck by it. In 1871 they refused to play a match with the Sheffield FA according to Sheffield laws even though the match was due to be played in Sheffield and even though Sheffield had been staunch for the FA from the outset. Also in 1871, and wanting to spread the game, the FA 'resolved unanimously that it is desirable that a Challenge Cup should be established... for which all clubs belonging to the Association should be invited'. It was Leytonstone's Alcock again who made this crucial proposal.[206] An Old Harrovian, he remembered strenuous inter-house competitions for silver cups. Sixteen clubs paid their subs and entered the first round. Alcock's club Wanderers, (formerly Forest) won it 1–0 playing flamboyantly in red and black with orange hoops. The venue was Kennington Oval, home of Surrey County Cricket Club. Built in the 1840s on a customary London sporting venue and scene of the great Chartist demonstration of 1848, the Oval stood in the tradition of popular

[205] Harvey, 'Playing by the Rules', *Sport in History* 31, 2011, p.336. For offside apologetics: Jonathan Wilson: 'Why is the modern offside law a work of genius?', *The Guardian*, 13 April 2010. Laws 9 and 10 are currently embodied in FIFA law 12 that defends Millian principles by stating the unlawfulness of handling, charging, jumping, kicking, pushing, striking, tripping, and all careless, reckless, obstructive, and excessively forceful play or abuse. However, in recent times, contrary to law 12 and the philosophy of the game in general, holding, holding off, and pulling have evolved as largely accepted forms of play.

[206] C W Alcock (1842–1907) born Sunderland, Harrow School (1855–59), founder member of Forest Club (1859), and Wanderers (1863), an influential figure in the FA from 1863, FA Committee member from 1866, FA general secretary from 1870, the man behind the first international match with Scotland (1–0) in 1870 and the First FA Challenge Cup (Wanderers 1 Royal Engineers 0) in 1872. He was 'the most important figure of his time in the shaping of modern football': Holt, *ODNB* 2004.

constitutionalism. The FA Challenge Cup proved enormously popular and in a way constitutional, eventually replacing The Derby as the greatest event in the English sporting calendar. In 1872, with £1-13s-5d in the bank, the Football Association was ready to conquer the world.

There are many ways to foot a ball. Other codes flourished as well as Association. Gaelic Football was invented in Ireland in 1887 as a counter to the English. Australian Rules preceded all modern codes, first presented in Melbourne in 1859. American Football was developed at Yale in the 1860s where Walter Camp's ideas about performance measurement proved influential.[207] American 'gridiron' was intended to solve the problem of English scrummaging. Named after the famous public school who claimed ownership of the rival code, Rugby football stayed with the catching and holding, the carrying and rucking. While Association Football emphasized the liberty to move, rugby football emphasized the liberty to contest. Ever since the foundation of the Rugby Football Union in 1871, and in spite of the efforts of the Northern Rugby Football Union, or 'League', to open up the flowing line, rugby football remained bedevilled by the complexity of not being caught in front of the ball under conditions of over-whelming physical contestation.[208] In a grossly prejudiced observation, the *Salford Reporter* commented in 1905 that 'people will not waste an hour and a half watching men spend their strength in pushing each other in a scrimmage'.[209] Although they do.

Modern Sport

Even though many Suffragettes including the Pankhursts were sporty, the Women's Social and Political Union targeted what it saw, quite correctly, as male sporting bastions.[210] In 1914, in a daring attack, the Prime Minister was kidnapped at his golf club by a team of elite feminists disguised as Boy Scouts. Taken off and tortured before promising to force a female franchise reform bill through the Commons, Mr. Asquith's failure to keep his promise led to more outrages. Lords' cricket ground and Epsom races were attacked and Henley

---

[207] Oriard, 'In the beginning', in Pope, ed., *New American Sports History* (1997) pp.89–116; Rouse, *Sport and Ireland* (2015) pp.123–33. See also Cronin, Duncan, and Rouse, *The GAA* (2009) for photographs and documents on the political invention of modern Irish sport.

[208] Collins, 'Rugby League World' Website February 2011. On 1886 moves to open up the field, abolish hack and trip, and thin the scrum by increasing the number of three quarters to four: Arthur Budd, *Football* (1899): John Johnson, Bodleian, Sports Box 8. In World Cup competitions 1930–2002, teams usually do better with ten players rather than eleven: Caliendo, 'Ten Do It Better', *12A Discussion* no 2158 (June 2008) p.13.

[209] *Salford Reporter*, 1 July 1905.

[210] Kay, 'Sport, Suffrage and Society', *IJHS* 25, 2008, pp.1343–8. The Pankhursts were Clarion (bicycling) Club members. Annie Kenney and Sylvia Pankhurst employed boxers as bodyguards. In *The Women's Who's Who of 1913*, 178 out of 650 women mentioned sport as a hobby.

Regatta was penetrated from below by young women in a submarine. Parliament finally saw sense however, and in 1914 a reforming Liberal administration passed the Women's Franchise Act. The WSPU held a banquet for the Metropolitan Police and Dr. Garrett Anderson was called to attend to the editors of the *Pall Mall Gazette* who had fainted from the shock.

It was the torture that did it. No man, not even the Prime Minister, could endure three days force feeding of modern feminist poetry.[211]

Modern sport helped bring women out of the shadows of their own shyness. Sheet music illustrations in the 1860s liked to show women's eyes as very large, larger than any other part of the face.[212] The girl might have shoulders, she might have a bosom and long fingers, but rarely did she have any arms and never any legs or feet, the corset serving as a kind of hard border to all that moved below.[213] 'I am So Very Shy', a musical hit from the 1860s, would not have done for Madame Bergman-Osterberg whose gymslip offered no border and plenty of free movement.[214] *Illustrated Chips* liked to draw sporting girls as 'Modern Types'.[215] As early as 1879, *Good Words* magazine was dreaming of girls with muscles, 'well strung' and 'polished'. As late as 2002, *Bend It Like Beckham* was looking forward to the liberty of Jesminder Bhamra and other footballers like her. Lacrosse, introduced at St. Leonard's School, St Andrews, in 1890, first caught the idea of sporting girls as fleet, strong, and free: 'a beautiful sight'.[216]

The same could be said of all those sports eventually introduced into schools and clubs—tennis and table tennis, hockey and netball, mixed doubles and golf, but also, a little later, for young workers and university students, cycling and hiking. Long skirts were useless. Knickerbockers (same as for men) were prime.[217] As we have noted, going dancing remained a working-class girl's most important physical expression. According to the *Dancing Times* of 1927, it was 'a compelling impulse', 'a channel for emotions', while *Picture Post* in 1943, in a neat

---

[211] A tale told by Cicely Hamilton on a thin cream paper frieze in Arts & Crafts blue and plum: *A Matter of Sport* (nd, no publisher): London Metropolitan University Women's Archive. *Chuckles* featured a story of Suffragettes sneaking into men's sporting venues: 10, 17 January 1914.

[212] Sheet music covers: John Johnson, Bodleian, Box 5. Some Victorians claimed the eye as 'window of the soul'. For one civil servant's taste for the hidden female parts, arms and legs especially: Hudson, *Munby* (1974) p.113.

[213] Colls, 'Girls Just Wanna Have Fun', Bodleian Archive; 'Corsets for 1910' (PP Press Liverpool 1910), 'We don't want to cramp your style' (Berlei 1935), and Simpsons of Piccadilly (Lastex 1938): John Johnson, Bodleian, Women's Clothing and Millinery Box 1.

[214] *Illustrated Sporting and Dramatic News*, 15 March 1884; Westmann, *Sport* (1939) p.49; McCrone, *Playing the Game* (1988); May, *Mde Bergman-Osterberg* (1969).

[215] *Illustrated Chips*, 21 February 1891.

[216] Boyd, *Lacrosse* (1969) p.17; Hamilton Fletcher, *Good Words*, August 1879, p.534: John Johnson, Bodleian, Sport Box 1; 'I'd bent it just like Beckham. It was my best shot ever': Dhami, *Bend It* (2002) p.149, and movie by Gurinder Chadha starring Parminder Nagra.

[217] Albermarle and Hillier, *Guide to Cycling* (c.1900) pp.179–85. For a women's history of tennis see *A People's History* of Tennis (2020) by David Berry.

comparison which underestimated both parties, opined that 'dancing is to the coloured people what sport is to the British'.[218]

Modern Dance, self-consciously free form, was influenced by jazz and art.[219] Modern ballroom dancing, strictly controlled in step and hold and eagerly performed every Saturday night, was just as American, just as jazzy, and just as eager to explore the floor. Modern sport and modern dance each stressed whole body action or, as according to Professor Buckland, 'spatial and rhythmic freedoms' that changed modern notions of civility.[220] In Hobsbawm's description of jazz as 'a marvellous combination of solo creation and collective exhilaration', Count Basie might have been a footballer, Pele might have been a musician, and George Best might have been a dancer, which, in a way he was. Isadore Minsky's observation that 'It don't mean a thing (if it ain't got that swing)', music by Duke Ellington, is Brazilian football at its best.[221] Down in the Black Country, Duncan Edwards, destined to be seen as one of the all-time football greats, was disappointed to miss a dance competition because he had been picked for England.[222]

Sport and dance were the two greatest influences on modern fashion, but fashion is never open to simple interpretation. The wasp corset, for instance, coincided with the rise of the Women's Social and Political Union, while the Mod look for girls in the 1960s affected the dazzled (big) eye look of children while claiming full freedoms of the adult. Given that clothes are notoriously hard to interpret, it's not difficult to know what to make of Mr. Potter's 1875 defence of his decision to play against Sale FC without his socks on. He said he did it because other sportsmen were doing it. It was the fashion. And at around this time Greenburg the tailor was promising to rig out his customers in all the 'toggery' of sporting fashion—from 'Flash' to 'Yiddish'.[223] The working man's passion for the flat cap was a sporting fashion, this time taken from the gentry.[224] The representative **sporting** 'cap', with tassells, awarded after special matches, came straight out of the public school wardrobe.[225] So did blazers with badges, sports

[218] Nott, *Going to the Palais* (2015) p.162.
[219] 'an art form at the centre of the modernist impulse': Christiansen, 'Dance to the Music of Time', *Literary Review*, December 2018.
[220] Buckland, 'Dancing Out of Time' in Dodds and Cook, eds., *Bodies of Sound* (2012) pp.100–2.
[221] Best 'had resolved to be completely free', like a dancer: Burn, *Best and Edwards* (2006) p.158. 'Pele', Edson Arantes Nascimento, b. Minas Gerais, Brazil, 1940, Santo (1956–74), Brazil x 92, blessed with perfect balance and flow, with a kick like a donkey, commonly considered the greatest player of all time. Hobsbawm on jazz: *Uncommon People* (1998) p.338.
[222] Leighton, *Duncan Edwards* (2012) p.33. He was a schoolboy Morris dancer.
[223] Poster, C Greenburg, 'Working Men's Tailor . . . for Flash Toggery', 5, White Lion Street, Chelsea: John Johnson, Bodleian, Men's Clothes Box 2. Chris Breward finds the poster a mix of 'backslang, coster, Yiddish, theatrical, criminal and nautical argot': *Hidden Comsumer* (1999) p.156. Potter is without his socks in *Sporting Chronicle*, 13 January 1875. Carol Dyhouse referred to the difficulty of interpreting fashion in a paper given to DMU, 28 November 2012.
[224] Calthorp, *English Dress* (1934) p.116.
[225] Russell, et al., *Encyclopedia of British Football* (2002).

jackets and flannels, and gorgeous football shirts. Lytton Strachey saw a beautiful modern boy on the London Underground. He was wearing a dark blue shirt with yellow edging and straw coloured lacing. Strachey followed him off the train only to lose him (and his heart) to a bunch of other boys on their way to play football for Express Dairies.[226]

One Sunday afternoon in the Potteries, it was dark blue neckerchiefs ('Belchers') that caught the eye. Charles Shaw's memoir of Tunstall Primitive Methodist Sunday School Anniversary avoids all the salvation cliché about lost souls and broken sportsmen. The boys who turned up that afternoon were local prize-fighters. Smart, very welcome, and pleased to be there,

> ... they came in quietly without any air of swagger, and yet with assurance. They knew they were expected and welcome. They were mostly young men, strong, active, and with an exceptionally virile look ... They all wore neckerchiefs about three inches deep with the ends tied in little bows at the front ... all dark blue silk with small white spots. You saw no other class but the class these men represented with these neck ties on.[227]

During the 1920s and 1930s women joined what Orwell called the 'naked democracy of the swimming pools'.[228] The big-eye so-shy past was finally blacked out with sunglasses, never out of fashion since. On top of this there were short shorts and skirts, brogues and 'tennis shoes' (later to become 'trainers'), slips and slacks, much searching for the sunlight in *Aertex* and *Burberry*, *Dunlop* and *Daks*, and much searching for the 'New Man' and the 'He Man' at Hector Powe and Austin Reed. Fred Perry was the dominant English sportsman of the 1930s, three times Wimbledon champion.[229] When he retired he founded a clothing brand based on the short sleeved 'sports shirt' (1952), complete with laurel wreath symbol. So we have white for Wimbledon, dark blue for fighters and sailors, whipcords for golfers, rough stuff for the fells, flannels for the courts, shorts for football and boxing, cavalry twill for everybody and linens back on the beach. Corduroy? 'The navvy gave us the idea. We're rather proud of it. Wears for ever, almost, and the rougher you treat it, the better it looks'.[230] Scott Fitzgerald's *The Great Gatsby* (1925) might have been kitted out by these people.

---

[226] Strachey to Henry Lamb, 20 February 1914: *Sunday Telegraph*, 13 March 2005.

[227] Known as 'Belcher' neckerchiefs after the legendary prize-fighter Jem Belcher (1781–1811): Charles Shaw, 'An Old Potter', *When I was a Child* (1903) p.214. I am grateful to Jeremy Crump for this reference.

[228] Orwell, 'Lion and the Unicorn' (1940), *Collected Works*, vol. xii, pp.408–9, p.393.

[229] Fred Perry, b. Stockport 1909, d. Melbourne 1995, Australian Open champion 1934, French 1935, US 1933, 1934, 1936, Wimbledon 1934, 1935, 1936.

[230] Brochures, posters, and price lists include Daks for men and Simpson's Lastex for ladies: John Johnson, Bodleian, Men's Clothes Box 5.

Sport was the mark of being modern.[231] Badge and colours in clear modernist design mattered to football fans, even to those who had no chance of sporting them. At Anfield, Ibrox, Roker, Ewood, Hampden, Ayresome, Deepdale, Hillsbrough, Craven Cottage, Goodison, and elsewhere the Scottish engineer Archibald Leitch turned the football stadium into something minimal, rational, angular—and cheap.[232] In the 1920s, 'New Art' and 'Contructivism' influenced the design of continental stadia.[233] Italian avant gardeists and Fascists found in football the flow and colour they cherished in art. Gerado Dottori's dynamic 'Football Match' (1928) is to be compared with L S Lowry's altogether more pastoral 'Going to the Match' (1928).[234] Soon, all in white—'sleeker...strolling... effortless...easy...simple'—Real Madrid were the coolest footballers in Europe.[235] 'Football is the game modernity plays'.[236]

Ends of Life

The first copy of the *Daily Mail* came out on 1 September 1896. Soon, *The Mail* had football correspondents 'in all the great centres' inundating its editorial offices with new sporting cliché.[237] There had been a time when parish sports were being driven out.[238] Now the people had a whole new sporting life. Sport could even be seen as one of the ends of life.[239]

Right into the 1960s, along with work, over-time, trade unions, the pub, and the internal combustion engine, popular music, cigarettes, and horse racing, football was integral to the life of 'men' as many men chose to define it, which was almost entirely local.[240] To what extent modern football changed society it is impossible to say. Some have argued that its rule-based competitiveness made society more fair minded and therefore more coherent.[241] It is just as possible (and just as tedious) to argue the other way.

---

[231] On the sporting life as the modern life, see Ralph Hedley's painting 'Pitman's Pay Old Style and New Style' showing one man a drunk, the other an athlete: *Monthly Chronicle of North Country Lore and Legend*, September 1891.

[232] Inglis, *Engineering Archie* (2007) ch. 3.

[233] Including Gropius, Bauhaus and Meyer: Strozek, 'Sport and Modernity', CESH, ICSHC, DMU, 5 September 2016; Bale, *Landscape and Modern Sport* (1994) p.75.

[234] Haxall and Physick, *Picturing the Beautiful Game* (2018) figs 5.2 and 12.1.

[235] Walvin, *Different Times* (2014) p.154.   [236] Goldblatt, *Ball is Round* (2006) p.4,

[237] Football cliché as identified by one of *The Observer's* lesser known football correspondents: Porter, 'B S Johnson: experimental writer and football correspondent', paper to ICSHC, DMU, 20 January 2016. On early football reportage, see for instance, *Barnsley Sports News*, 20 October 1894.

[238] Reduced to a choice between pub or chapel, according to Jospeh Arch, *Autobiography* (1899) p.103.

[239] And if it wasn't an end of life it was certainly something men could talk about as if it was. Physical pleasure is not included in Keith Thomas' ground-breaking history, *Ends of Life* (2009) p.2.

[240] Mellor on the 'intense parochialism' of one-club support: 'Football Crowds in NW England', *Sports Historian*, 19, 1999, p.38.

[241] Lever, *Soccer Madness* (1984) p.3, p.14.

In 1992, after 104 years, First Division clubs resigned from the Football League in order to create their own 'Premier League', along with Sky Sports, an international media corporation. This is not the place to account for what happened next—globalization and the role played by English football as its lead signifier— suffice to say that on 26 December 1999 Chelsea kicked off without a single English player. The English Premier League the most free floating commodity offered to the least free floating consumers,. For all its hype as a 'new theatre of being', it is equally true that there is no being without belonging. At this point, football had already started to become so detached from real life that a privately educated Oxford undergraduate, son of a distinguished football journalist, could pass himself off, on London day returns, as a Manchester United hard man or, as he put it, 'a nauseating wanker'.[242] And yet, genuine club traditions went on all the same—on the terraces if not in the board room. They said what they always said: we are the club and this is our history, which is local, not global, which is personal, not corporate. Systemic football violence after 1960 is harder to explain. For the historian it's easier to come up with reasons than answers—other than to say that the collapse of industrial forms of labour and apprenticeship from the 1970s was the biggest single social change to the lives of working-class young men. The Hooligans ran free, whereas not so long before older men would have intervened with all the authority of time-served journeymen who decided whether you worked or not. Sport has always carried a violent charge: violence can be a sport in itself.[243]

Saturday comes less and less. Or, to put it another way, Saturday comes every day as part of the Premier League package. Television decides the schedules, smaller clubs can't afford the wages, less affluent spectators can't afford the tickets, players can't afford to stop moving and managers can't afford to keep shopping. If it was a proper business it would be dead.[244]

But this is also the period when other people have started to show that football, with all its freedoms and belongings, can apply to them just as it can apply to everybody else. None of this could have happened without what went before in other sports, in the schools and universities, in the amateur clubs and youth groups, on the cinder tracks, and at the net. Women wanted to be moderns too. In 1950, Susan Noel thought that what had got to be achieved in women's sport had been achieved. Along with Frances Stephen the golfer, Fanny Blankers-Koen the sprinter, and Joyce Gardiner and Thelma Carpenter, billiards professionals, she cited (she *had* to cite) 'Miss Eyre', the hockey player. 'So here we are. We have come to stay'.[245]

[242] *The Guardian*, 7 December 2002.
[243] 'One of the things people missed about football hooliganism, he thought, was that it was *fun*': Sandbrook, *Who Dares Wins* (2019) p.219. He is referring to Bill Buford, another Oxbridge pretend hard man, who wrote the most influential account of 1980s English football violence, *Among the Thugs* (1990).
[244] Goldblatt, *Age of Football* (2019) pp.3–4 and *passim*. See Jonathan Liew, 'Left Field', *New Statesman*, 8–14 May 2020.
[245] Noel, ed., *Sportswoman's Manual* (1950), Introduction.

Conclusion

> One of my principal aims in the *Excursion* has been to put the
> commonplace truths of the human affections especially, in an
> interesting point of view; & rather to remind men of their knowledge
> as it lurks inoperative and unvalued in their own minds, than to attempt
> to convey recondite or refined truth.
>
> (Wordsworth to Coleridge, 22 May 1815)

When news of Nelson's great victory at the Nile reached London in 1798, *The
Times* reported on 'the mob' gathering 'as usual' at the Admiralty Office to insist
'on every person of genteel appearance pulling off their hats'. When Nelson was
killed at the Battle of Trafalgar he was buried in St. Paul's Cathedral in a funeral
that lasted five days.[1]

In 1805 Nelson was the nation's only real hero. After him, popular heroes
started to appear from further afield. In 1840, Thomas Carlyle lectured on heroes
for the London season. It cost one guinea for six, not one of them a lord or a
warrior. In 1856, the Victoria Cross was struck and made open to all ranks,
followed by its civilian equivalent, the Albert Medal, whose first recipient was a
Devon farmer. In 1859, Samuel Smiles' best-selling book *Self Help* celebrated
provincial self-made men, and made them heroes too. By the end of the century,
tales of manly devotion were staples of popular literature and commemoration.
True, many like Gordon of Khartoum and Scott of the Antarctic were gentlemen
martyrs, but the defenders of Rorke's Drift were ordinary soldiers, Mrs. Pankhurst
eventually found her place in the national hall of fame, and an increasing number
of domestic heroes were sportsmen—W G Grace the most celebrated, but plenty
local heroes too, including sporting squires and poaching kings, school captains,
club captains, champion jockeys, cup winners and all the rest.[2]

The Great War widened the killing field. Over a quarter of the British male
population served, but apart from what sport they could muster, in the face of battle
it was more a war of numbing bombardment than heroic combat. Rather than men
dying in battle, lads fell in fields, as if they had been playing there.[3] The Wimbledon
Men's Singles Champion fell at Neuve Chapelle on 9 May 1915. The England rugby

---

[1] *The Times*, 3 October 1798.
[2] William George Grace (1848–1915), cricketer, captain of England, MCC and Gloucestershire, was
the most famous sportsman of his generation.
[3] 'lad', 'a beautiful brave doomed boy': Fussell, *Great War and Modern Memory* (1975) pp.282–3.

captain fell in Ploegsteert Wood on 5 August 1915. The second black player in the Football League (and first black officer in the British Army) fell at Pas-de-Calais on 25 March 1918.[4] In history, there was nothing new about heroes falling on behalf of a grateful state. The British were not alone in this although, all things considered, their anti-militarist traditions meant they were never the most convinced.[5]

In the Second World War it was difficult to talk seriously about warrior heroes anymore. Fighter pilots were the last because their killing seemed all the more sporting. They scrambled out of deckchairs in cricket jumpers, fought hand to hand in the sky, and came back, if they came back at all, with scores.

At 11.30 am on 29 May 1953, when a New Zealand beekeeper said that he and Tenzing Norgay had 'knocked the bastard off', everybody in the British Empire knew what he was talking about. A year later, on 6 May 1954, when a young doctor clocked 3.59.4 on the Iffley Road track in Oxford, again, everybody knew what that meant. Warriors were out, beekeepers and doctors were in. By the time of the Rome Olympics in 1960, British sporting heroes were almost entirely everyday people. Soon, they would be called 'celebrities'. Nowadays, with digital media, anybody can be famous for anything.

The Vatican turned to sport and modernism after 1945.[6] Soviet Communism harboured all sorts of hopes about the capacity of sport to produce a new type of human being.[7] Typically, and ridiculously, it did so at the expense of everyday health (*fizkul'tura*).[8] Same for Fascism. Same for China. As the humble but ubiquitous baseball cap attests, modern sport is a form of gigantic cultural power.[9] In recent times, almost every country on earth has embraced the sporting hero as model citizen.[10]

If it is true that people invest something of their heroes in themselves, it is also true that they invest something of themselves in their heroes. In the England football team, the eleven men or women in white with three lions on their shirt stand for the rest, just as the rest, quite wondrously, believe that somehow they stand for them. Patriotism in the English tradition is more a belief in each other than in greatness. As the pre-eminent national institution, the National Health Service stands for exactly that. When the Coronavirus was at its most virulent, on

---

[4] Anthony Frederick Wilding was the tennis champion (1883–1915); Ronnie William Poulton was the rugby captain (1889–1915); Walter Tull was the black footballer (1888–1918). The *Weekly Dispatch* for 13 April 1913 saw in Mrs. Pankhurst a leader capable of heroism although that rather begs the question of whether she was a hero.

[5] Barczewski, *Heroic Failure* (2016) p.4.

[6] Serapiglia, 'Muscular Catholicism', *Lustopie* 18 (2019).

[7] Schiller, 'Communism, Youth, and Sport', in Tomlinson, ed., *Sport and the Transformation of Modern Europe* (2011) p.50, p.64.

[8] Katzer, 'Soviet Physical Culture', in Tomlinson, ed., ibid, pp.29–30.

[9] Riess, *Sport in Industrial America* (1995) p.4, p.180.

[10] Dine and Crosson, Introduction, *Sport, Representation and Evolving Identities* (2010) pp.2–4; Introduction, Tomlinson, ed., ibid, p.2, Martin, *Sport Italia* (2011) p.85; Holt, *Sport and Society in Modern France* (1981) p.4.

VE Day 2020, people draped the NHS badge and rainbow with the Union Flag in their windows.

By the 1930s, organized sport in England was big enough and modern enough to feature in Aldous Huxley's *Brave New World* as a state-run industry. From eighteenth-century landed gentlemen to twentieth-century utopian fantasists, sport has been a vital part of English civil life for over 200 years. Of course a lot has changed since 1960. The sporting life, like life in general, has become more global and money-centred. Whether it has become more content is another question. To address these questions would take another book in itself. At the heart of this book is an historical sense of liberty mixed with an everyday sense of belonging. It is not exactly Isaiah Berlin's notion of 'positive' liberty free from restraint. Nor is it his 'negative' liberty either, something that depends on others. It was what it was, it is what it is, people wanting to be free and secure at the same time.[11]

I set out to write this book in order to show that sport has existed at every level in every corner of the national life—always to hand, never without meaning. Across eight chapters and a wide range of sporting experiences—from sport that cost a fortune to play that cost nothing at all—I have demonstrated the depth and breadth of one of England's great civil cultures. I began thinking that sport was a minor subject, a national story no doubt, but not the only one or the most important one. Now at the end of the book I think it is a major subject not in itself perhaps, but in the way it is woven in to almost everything else we do. Everything that appears in this history has been part of the ordinary life of English men and women. It might be that sport makes us happier. It might be that play makes us more sane. It might be that the Lego Professor of Play at Cambridge is a more important appointment than the Regius Professor of History.

In F Scott Fitzgerald's *The Great Gatsby*, Jay Gatsby calls people 'Old Sport' as a mark of endearment, as a recognition that they, like him, play the game. Playing the game, enjoying the land, sensing the liberty, respecting contestation, valuing home, showing a bit of heart, recognizing it in others, knowing that not everyone is political, or has to be, that not everyone knows what they think or (whichever comes first) how to say it, and understanding above all that sport is an enduring part of our liberty just as the 'we' who play it is an enduring mark of our sovereignty—writing this book has made me think our history over again. Sport has always been its own reward and for the vast majority who have ever played it, nothing more. I see sport now as all the more extraordinary for its ordinariness, for how it has reached into every part of our imagination. London opened its 2012 Olympic Games by calling the place we live 'The Isles of Wonder'. This sporting life still stood for something wondrous.

---

[11] See Jon Lawrence's conclusions to his search for community in post-war England: *Me, Me, Me* (2019) pp.228–9.

Bibliography

1. Printed Works

Abbott, P E, and J Tamplin, *British Gallantry Awards* (London, Nimrod Dix 1981)

Abingdon Local Studies, 'Origins of Bun Throwing' (AB 392)

Abler, T S, *Hinterland Warriors and Military Dress* (Oxford, Berg 1999)

Abra, Allison, 'Doing The Lambeth Walk. Novelty Dances and the British Nation', *20c British History*, 20, 3 2009: https://doi.org/10.1093/tcbh/hwp035, accessed 20 January 2019

Act, for granting further powers for establishing and maintaining an efficient River Police and for regulating the said Port [of Newcastle upon Tyne], 9 Victoria 1845

Act, for Improvement of Newcastle upon Tyne, 33 & 34 Victoria 1870

Act, for regulating and improving the Borough of Newcastle upon Tyne, 30 June 1837

Adam, Clive, ed., *Love, Labour and Loss. 300 Years of British Livestock Farming in Art* (Carlisle, Tullie House 2002)

Adams, George Burton, *Constitutional History of England* (London, Cape 1920)

Addyman, John, and B Fawcett, *The High Level Bridge and Newcastle Central Station* (Newcastle, NE Railway Association 1999)

Albemarle, Lord, and L Hillier, *The Classic Guide to Cycling* (1889. Stroud, Amberley 2015)

Alken, Henry, *The National Sports of Great Britain* (London, Thos McLean 1821–3)

Alken, Henry, *Master of British Sporting Art* (Lincoln, Usher Art Gallery 1948)

Alken, Henry, *Exhibition of Original Drawings* (London, Ellis & Smith 1949)

Allan's Illustrated Edition of Tyneside Songs (1862. Newcastle, Frank Graham 1972)

Allen, David, 'Fighting the Good Fight', *Expository Times* 119, 2007

Allen, Dean, 'National Heroes: Sport and the Creation of Icons', *Sport in History* 33, 2013

Allen, Richard, 'Quakers, Morals and popular Culture in the Long 18th Century', in H Berry and J Gregory, eds., *Creating and Consuming Culture in NE England 1660–1830* (Aldershot, Ashgate 2004)

Allen, Robert C, 'Agriculture during the Industrial Revolution 1700-1850', in Floud and Johnson, eds., *Cambridge Economic History* (Cambridge, Cambridge University Press 2004) vol i

Allen, Robert C, *The British Industrial Revolution in Global Perspective* (Cambridge, Cambridge University Press 2009)

Allen, Robert C, *The Industrial Revolution. VSI* (Oxford, Oxford University Press 2017)

Allison, Lincoln, *Amateurism in Sport* (London, Routledge 2001)

Allison, L, and R Maclean, 'There's a Deathless Myth in the Close Tonight. Rugby's Place', *International Journal Sports History* 29, 13, 2012

Altham, H S, *A History of Cricket* (London, Geo Allen & Unwin 1926)

Amis, Martin, *Lionel Asbo. State of England* (London, Jonathan Cape 2012)

Amos, Sir Maurice, *The English Constitution* (London, Longmans Green 1934)

'An Amateur of Eminence', *The Complete Art of Boxing according to the Modern Method ... to which is added The General History of Boxing* (London, M Follingsby 1788)

'An Operator', *The Fancy; or True Sportsman's Guide* (London, McGowan 1826)

Anderson, Benedict, *Imagined Communities. Reflections on the Origin and Spread of Nationalism* (London, Verso 1983)

Anderson, Jack, 'Pugilstic Prosecutions. Prize fighting and the courts in 19c Britain', *Sports Historian* 21, 2, 2001

Anderson, Jack, 'A Brief Legal History of Prize Fighting in 19c America', *Sport in History* 24, I, 2004

Anderson, John H, 'Sidelights on the Origins of Primitive Methodism in N Staffs', *Proceedings Wesley Historical Society* 56, May 2007

Anderson, Misty G, 'Whitefield, Foote and the Theatricality of Methodism', *Studies in 18C Culture* 34, 2005

Anderson, Olive, *A Liberal State at War* (New York, St. Martins 1967)

Anderson, Patricia, *The Printed Image and the Transformation of Popular Culture 1790–1860* (Oxford, Clarendon Press 1991)

Andrews, Anthony, and Robert Leach, eds., *A Scrapbook of Victorian Entertainment* (Blackie 1976)

Andrews, C Bruyn, *The Torrington Diaries containing the tours through England and Wales of the Hon John Byng 1781–94* (1936. London, Methuen 1970) vol. iii

Annan, Noel, *The Dons* (London, Harper Collins 2000)

Anon, *Book of Sports set forth by K. James I and K. Charles with Remarks upon the same in Vindication of King Charles I . . . by a Gentleman* (London, issued by King James 1721)

Anon, or 'The Town Spy', *A View of London and Westminster: Or, The Town Spy* (London, Warner 1728), two parts

Anon, *Some Considerations on the Game Laws* (London, A Dodd 1753)

Anon, *A New Manual and Platoon Exercise, published by Authority* (Dublin, Boulter Grierson 1764)

Anon, *Concise Table of the Game Laws, respecting Hares, Partridges & Pheasants, Shewing at One View the Several Offences, the Acts Creating (sic) the Penalties; the persons to whom such Penalties are given, the manner of recovering them, the Costs a Plaintiff is intitled to, and the time when the Information or Action ought to be brought* (London, Uriel, Wilkie & Debret *c.*1773)

Anon, *Elements of Opposition* (London, J Hatchard 1803)

Anon, *Picture of Newcastle upon Tyne* (Newcastle, Akenhead 1807)

Anon, *Pancratia; or a History of Pugilism; containing a full account of every battle from the time of Broughton and Slack, down to the Present, interspersed with anecdotes of all the celebrated Pugilists of this country . . . embellished with a correct and elegantly engraved Portrait of the Champion, Cribb* (London, Chapple 1815)

Anon, *The Campaign of Waterloo illustrated with Engravings of Les Quatre Bras, La Belle Alliance, Hougomont, La Haye Sainte* (London, Binsley & Son 1816)

Anon, *Letter on the subject of Female Poachers* (Knaresbrough, Wilson 1827)

Anon, *Stamford Bull Running* (Stamford, Robert Johnson November 1837) handbill

Anon, *The Life of a Fox, written by himself with illustrations by Thos Smith* (London, Whittaker 1843)

Anon, *The Book of Sports, British and Foreign* (London, Walter Spiers 1843) vol. i

Anon, *The English Gentleman* (London, Geo Bell 1849)

Anon, *Scene in a School exhibiting certain . . . occurrences* (Newcastle, Barkas 1850)

Anon, *Florence Nightingale* (London, Houlston & Wright, nd, 1856?)

Anon, Lady, *Life Amongst the Colliers* (London, Saunders, Otley 1862)

Anon, *Life and Extraordinary Career of John Gulley. Butcher Boy. Prize Fighter. Great Betting Man. Publican & MP for Pontefract* (London at Eight Shops, nd, 1863?)

Anon, *Skittles. A Biography of a Fascinating Woman. Never Before Published* (London, George Vickers 1864)

Anon, *Annals of London* (London, 1865)

Anon, *The Life, Death & Funeral of Tom Sayers* (London, Illustrated Police News 1865)

Anon, author of 'Pugilistica', *Tom Sayers, sometime Champion of England, His Life and Pugilistic Career* (London, Beeton 1866)

Anon, *Just Out Price One Penny, Death and Memoir of J C Heenan and Tom Sayers* (London, Elliot, nd, 1873)

Anon, *Historical Account of Newcastle upon Tyne 100 Years Ago ... shewing The Right of the Town to the Fore Shore of the whole of the River, from Sparrow Hawk to Hedwin Streams* (Newcastle, Fordyce 1885)

Anon, Vicar, 'A Late', *A Short History with Description of the Parish of West Wycombe, County of Bucks, Diocese of Oxford* (High Wycombe, Bucks Free Press 1925)

Anon, *Old English Sporting Books* (New York, Scribner's 1928)

Anon (Lilias Haggard), *I Walked by Night. Being the Life & History of the King of the Norfolk Poachers written by Himself*, Lilias Rider Haggard, ed. (London, Nicholson & Watson 1935)

Anon, *Inn Signs. Their History and Meaning* (London, Brewers' Society 1939)

Anti-Game Law League, *The Game Laws* (London, AGLL 1880)

Arch, Joseph, *Joseph Arch. The Story of his Life* (London, Hutchinson 1898)

Arch, Joseph, *From Ploughtail to Parliament. An Autobiography* (1898. London, Cresset 1986)

Armstrong, Karen, *The Bible* (London, Atlantic Books 2007)

Arnheim, Michael, ed., *Common Law* (Aldershot, Dartmouth 1994)

Arnold, Arthur, *The Land and the People* (Manchester, CWS 1888)

Arnold, Matthew, *The Study of Celtic Literature* (1867. London Smith, Elder 1905)

Arnold, Matthew, *Culture and Anarchy*, ed., Stefan Collini (1867–9. Cambridge, Cambridge University Press 1993)

Arthur, Theo, 'Old Time Football', in William Andrews, *Bygone Derbyshire* (Derby, Frank Murray 1892)

Arts Council, *Coal. British Mining in Art 1680–1980* (London, ACGB 1982)

Asbury, Herbert, *The Gangs of New York* (1927. New York, Avalon 1998)

Ashby, M K, *Joseph Ashby of Tysoe 1859–1919* (1961. London, Merlin 1974)

Ashley, Lord Anthony Ashley Cooper, 'Ten Hours Factory Bill. Speech in House of Commons, 15 March 1844' (1844. New York, Amo Press 1972)

Ashton, Rosemary, *Little Germany. Exile and Asylum in Victorian England* (Oxford, Oxford University Press 1986)

Askew, John, *A Guide to the interesting places in and around Cockermouth* (Cockermouth, Isaac Evening 1872)

Aspin, Jehosaphat, *Ancient Customs, Sports and Pastimes of the English, with 12 engravings* (London, John Harris St. Paul's Churchyard 1832)

Association of Mill Owners, 'Factory Legislation. Report of the Central Committee ... engaged in the cotton trade, 1844' (1845. New York, Amo Press 1972)

Atkinson, J A, *Out Door Shows* (London, Rowney and Foster 1821)

Auge, Marc, *Non-Places. An Introduction to Supermodernity* (1995. London, Verso 2008)

Austen, Rev. F W, *Rectors of Two Essex Parishes and Their Times* (Colchester, Benham 1943)

Axon, Ernest, *Bygone Lancashire* (Manchester, Brook & Chrystal 1892)

Ayton, Richard, and William Daniell, *A Voyage Round Great Britain Undertaken in the Summer of the Year 1813* (London, Longman 1820) vol vi, p.57.

Baden Powell, Robert, *Rovering to Success* (London, Herbert Jenkins 1922)

Bagehot, Walter, *The English Constitution* (1867. London, Fontana 1963)

Bailey, A R, et al., 'Disciplining Youthful Methodist Bodies in 19C Cornwall', *Annals Association American Geographers* 97, 2007

Bailey, Peter, *Leisure and Class in Victorian England* (London, RKP 1978)

Bailey, Peter, 'Ally Sloper's Half Holiday', *History Workshop* 16, 1983

Bailey, R E, T J Hatton, and K Inwood, 'Health, height and household at the turn 20c', *Economic History Review* 69, i, 2016

Baillie, J, *An Impartial History of the Town and County of Newcastle upon Tyne and its vicinity* (Newcastle, Anderson 1801)

Baillie, J, *Advice to Mothers, on the best means of promoting the health . . . of their offspring* (Newcastle, Mackenzie & Dent 1812)

Baines, Edward, *History of the County Palatine and Duchy of Lancaster* (London, Fisher 1836) vols. i, ii, iii, iv

Baker, W J, 'The Leisure Revolution in Victorian England. Review of Recent Literature', *Journal of Sport History* 6, 77, 1979

Bale, John, *Landscapes of Modern Sport* (Leicester, Leicester University Press 1994)

Bale, John, 'How Much of a Hero? The Fractured Image of Roger Bannister', *Sport in History* 26, 2, 2006

Ball, Stuart, *Portrait of a Party. The Conservative Party in Britain 1918–45* (Oxford, Oxford University Press 2013)

Bamford, Samuel, *Bamford's Passages in the Life of a Radical and Early Days* (1848. London, T Fisher 1893) 2 vols., Introduction by Henry Dunckley

Banks, Sarah, 'Nineteenth-Century scandal or Twentieth-Century model? A new look at 'open' and 'close' parishes', *Economic History Review*, 2nd series, xli, 1988

Barber, Ven Edward, and Rev. P H Ditchfield, eds., *Memorials of Old Cheshire* (London, Geo Allen 1910)

Barbour, Ralph Henry, *The Book of School and College Sports* (New York, D Appleton 1904)

Barczewski, Stephanie, *Heroic Failure and the British* (London, Yale University Press 2016)

Barfoot, Rev. John, *A Diamond in the Rough or Christian Heroism in Humble Life being jottings concerning that remarkable peasant preacher William Hickingbotham of Belper, Derbyshire* (London, James Clarke 1874)

Baring-Gould, Sabine, *Book of Cornwall* (London, Methuen 1899)

Barnes, Simon, *The Meaning of Sport* (London, Short Books 2006)

Barnett, W O, *The Life Story of W O Barnett* (Congleton 1910)

Barrell, J, *The Dark Side of the Landscape. The Rural Poor in English Painting 1730–1840* (Cambridge, Cambridge University Press 1985)

Barron, Hester, *The 1926 Miners' Lockout. Meanings of Community in the Durham Coalfield* (Oxford, Oxford University Press 2010)

Barry, Rev. Edward, *A Letter on the Practice of Boxing* (London, Bew 1789)

Barton, Arthur, *The Penny World. A Boyhood Recalled* (London, Hutchinson 1969)

Bass, D, *A List of Sporting Ladies for 1804* (Newcastle, Bass, 1804) handbill

Bate, Jonathan, *John Clare. A Biography* (London, Picador 2003)

Bateman, Anthony, 'Cricket, Literature and Empire', *International Journal of Regional & Local Studies* 2, i, 2005

Bateman, Anthony, 'Cricket Writing. Heritage and Ideology', in Jeffrey Hill, et al., eds., *Sport, History, and Heritage. Studies in Public Representation* (Woodbridge, Boydell Press 2012)

Baudrillard, Jean, *The Illusion of the End* (Stanford, Stanford University Press 1994) trans. Chris Turner

Bauman, R, and Sherzer, J, eds., *Explorations in the Ethnography of Speaking* (Cambridge, Cambridge University Press 1974)

Baxter, Richard, *The Saints Everlasting Rest* (1651. Liverpool, Nuttall 1809)

Bayliss, D, 'Altrincham in 1841', Altrincham History Society paper no 5, 1994

Beale, Dorothea, *Report from Schools Inquiry Commission on the Education of Girls (1867–68)* (London, David Nutt 1870)

Beattie, Geoffrey, *The Shadows of Boxing. Prince Naseem and Those he Left Behind* (London, Orion 2003)

Beaven, Brad, *Leisure, Citizenship and Working-Class Men in Britain 1850–1945* (Manchester, Manchester University Press 2005)

Bebb, E D, *Nonconformity and Social and Economic Life 1660–1800* (London, Epworth 1935)

Beckford, Peter, *Thoughts on Hunting* (London, Bremner 1798)

Bee, Jon, *Slang. A Dictionary of The Turf, The Ring, The Chase, The Pit, of Bon-Ton and the Varieties of Life... Words and Phrases That are Necessarily, or Purposely, Cramp, Mutative, and Unintelligible Outside Their Respective Spheres* (London, T Hughes 1823)

Beeton, S O, *Our Soldiers and the Victoria Cross* (London, Ward, Lock & Tyler 1867)

Behagg, Clive, 'Secrecy, Ritual and Folk Violence: the opacity of the workplace in the first half of the 19th century', in R Storch ed., *Popular Culture and Custom in 19th Century England* (London, Croom Helm 1982)

Belchem, John, "Republicanism, Popular Constitutionalism and the Radical Platform', *Social History* 6, 1, 1981.

Belcher, Thomas, *The Art of Boxing; or Science of Manual defence clearly displayed on rational principles whereby Every Person may easily make themselves of that Manly Acquirement* (London, Mason 1815?)

Bell, I T W, *Plan of the River Tyne between Hedwin Streams above Newcastle on Tyne and the Place Called Spar Hawke in the Sea, Shewing Towns, Villages, Manufactories & Coal Staithes on the River Banks with an alphabetical list of the collieries shipping in the Tyne* (Newcastle 4 inches: 1 mile, c.1849)

Bell, Julian, *What is Painting?* (London, Thames & Hudson 2004)

Bell, Lady Florence, *At the Works. A Study of a Manufacturing Town* (London, E Arnold 1907)

Bellaigue, Christina de, *Educating Women. Schooling and Identity in England and France 1800–67* (Oxford, Oxford University Press 2007)

Belsey, H, 'A newly discovered work by Francesco Harwood', *The Burlington Magazine* cxxii, 1980

Benn, Tony, *Out of the Wilderness, Diaries 1963–67* (London, Arrow 1988)

Bentham, Jeremy, *A Fragment on Government* (1776. Oxford, Basil Blackwell 1948)

Berg, Maxine, 'Consumption in Britain', in Floud and Johnson, eds., *Cambridge Economic History* (Cambridge, Cambridge University Press 2004) vol i

Berg, Maxine, *Luxury and Pleasure in 18c Britain* (Oxford, Oxford University Press 2005)

Berg, Maxine, 'Fashion Markets of Early Modern Europe', *Journal for the Study of British Cultures* 13/1, 2006

Berghoff, Hartmut, 'Public Schools and the Decline of the British Economy 1870-1914', *Past & Present* 129, November 1990

Bergman-Osterberg, Martina, *Ling's Swedish System. Gymnastic Tables published for use in London Board Schools* (London, J Martin & Son 1887)

Berkeley, George, Bishop of Cloyne, 'The Fox Hunters', in Quiller-Couch, Sir Arthur, ed., *The Oxford Book of English Prose* (Oxford, Oxford University Press 1925)

Berkowitz, Michael, and Ruti Ungar, *Fighting Back? Jewish and Black Boxers in Britain* (London, UCL 2007)

Bettey, J H, *Church and Community. The Parish Church in English Life* (Bradford on Avon, Moonraker Press 1979)

Betting Man, A, *Out of the Ring. Scenes of Sporting Life* (London, Ward, Lock & Tyler, nd, 1870s?)

Biagini, Eugenio, and Mary Daly, eds., *Cambridge Social History of Modern Ireland* (Cambridge, Cambridge University Press 2017)

Biddulph, Gen Sir Robert, *Lord Cardwell at the War Office 1868–74* (London, John Murray 1904)

Bill, E G W, *University Reform in 19c Oxford* (Oxford, Oxford University Press 1973)

Bindman, David, *Ape to Apollo. Aesthetics and the Idea of Race in the 18th c* (Ithaca, Cornell University Press 2002)

Binfield, Clyde, 'Victorian Values and Industrious Connexions', *Proceedings WHS* 55, 2006

Binkley, Sam, 'Kitsch as a Repetitive System', *Journal of Material Culture* 5, 2, 2000

Black, Shirley Burgoyne, *Local Government, Law and Order in a Pre-Reform English Parish 1790–1834* (Mellen Research Press, Lampeter 1992)

Blackstone's Commentaries on the Laws and Constitution of England abridged for the use of students and adapted to modern statutes and decisions, ed., John Gifford (London, Sir Richard Phillips 1820)

Blackstone, Sir William, *The Sovereignty of the Law. Selections from Blackstone's Commentaries on the Laws of England*, ed., Gareth Jones (London, Macmillan 1973)

Blainville de, M, *Travels Through Holland, Germany, Switzerland and other parts of Europe but especially Italy* (London 1734) vol. i

Blair, Richard S, *Memoir of Billy Durrant* (London, Fenwick 1884)

Blaxland, Dougie, *The Long Walk Back* (Playdead Press 2019)

Blok, Anton, *Honour and Violence* (Cambridge, Polity 2001)

Blyth, Henry, *Skittles. The Last Victorian Courtesan. The Life and Times of Catherine Walters* (London, Rupert Hart Davis 1970)

Boddy, Kasia, *Boxing. A Cultural History* (London, Reaktion 2008)

Boddy, Kasia, 'Some Competing Analogies for Sport', *Journal of Sport History* 37, i, Spring 2010

Boddy, Kasia, 'Under Queensberry Rules, so to Speak', *Sport in History* 31, 4, 2011

Bodington, Prunella R, *The Kindling and the Flame. A Centenary Review of the History of South Hampstead High School* (Hampstead, Bodington 1976)

Bolsmann, Chris, and Dilwyn Porter, *English Gentlemen and World Soccer* (London, Routledge 2018)

Bolton, John, *Wordsworth's Birthplace. Being the parochial history and local government of the ancient borough of Cockermouth* (Cockermouth, John Fletcher 1912)

Book of Sports set forth by K. James I and K. Charles with Remarks upon the same in Vindication of King Charles I ... by a Gentleman (London, issued by King James 1721)

Booth, Charles, *Life and Labour of the People of London. Notes on Social Influences* (London, Macmillan 1903)

Booth, Keith, *The Father of Modern Sport. Charles W Alcock* (Manchester, Parris Wood 2002)

Borough of Newcastle upon Tyne, *Bye Laws for Armstrong and Elswick Parks* (1881)

Borsay, Peter, *History of Leisure* (Basingstoke, Palgrave Macmillan 2006)

Bostridge, Mark, *Florence Nightingale* (London, Penguin 2009)

Bourdieu, Pierre, *Outline of a Theory of Practice* (New York, Cambridge University Press 1977)

Bourdieu, Pierre, *Distinction. A Social Critique of the Judgement of Taste* (1984. Abingdon, Routledge 2010)

Bourke, Joanna, *Dismembering the Male. Men's Bodies, Britain and the Great War* (London, Reaktion 1996)

Bourke, Joanna, 'Housewifery in Working-Class England 1860–1914', *Past & Present* 143, May 1994

Bourn, William, *Annals of the Parish of Whickham* (Consett, Guardian Office 1902)

Bourne, George, (George Sturt) *The Bettesworth Book. Talks with a Surrey Peasant* (1901. London, Duckworth 1911)

Bourne, George, *Change in the Village* (1912. London, Duckworth 1966)

Bourne, Henry, *History of Newcastle upon Tyne* (Newcastle, John White 1736)

Bourne, Hugh, *History of the Primitive Methodists* (Bemersley, PM Connexion 1823)

Bournville Village Trust, *Bournville 1924* (Birmingham, BVT 1924)

Bournville Village Trust 1900–1955 (Birmingham, BVT 1955)

Bower, Alan, *Work & Play, from a collection of old postcards of Derbyshire* (Derby, Hall & Sons 1986)

Box, Charles, *The English Game of Cricket* (London, The Field Office 1877)

Boyd, Margaret, *Lacrosse. Playing and Coaching* (London, Kaye & Ward 1969)

Boys' Own Library, *The Cup Tie Mystery* (BOL 1921)

Bradley, Cuthbert, *Fox-Hunting from Shire to Shire; With Many Noted Packs* (London, Geo Routledge 1912)

Bradley, J Frank, *The Boxing Referee* (London, Queenhithe 1910)

Brailsford, *Sport and Society. Elizabeth to Anne* (London, Routledge 1969)

Brailsford, Dennis, *Sport, Time and Society. The British at Play* (London, Routledge 1991)

Brailsford, Dennis, *A Taste for Diversions. Sport in Georgian England* (Cambridge, Lutterworth Press 1998)

Brailsford, Dennis, 'Pierce Egan', *Oxford Dictionary of National Biography* (Oxford, Oxford University Press 2004)

Bramwell, William, *Account of the Life and Death of Ann Cutler to which are added, The Conversion of Cramby, an American Negro, Conversion of a Deist, Also an account of some Martyrs of Popery* (Bemersley, J Bourne 1824)

Brand, John, *Observations on the Popular Antiquities of Great Britain* (1777. London H G Bohn 1849) 3rd edn.

Brand, John, *History & Antiquities of the Town and County of Newcastle upon Tyne* (London, White & Son 1789) vol. i

Brandt, Francis Frederick, *Habet! A short treatise on The Law of the Land as it affects Pugilism* (London, Robert Hardwicke 1857)

Bratton, J, *The Making of the West End Stage. Marriage, Management and the Mapping of Gender in London 1830–1870* (Cambridge, Cambridge University Press 2011)

Brennan, Patrick, *The Munitionettes. A History of Women's Football in NE England during the Great War* (Rowlands Gill, Donmouth 2007)

Breward, Christopher, *The Hidden Consumer. Masculinities, Fashion, and City Life 1860–1914* (Manchester, Manchester University Press 1999)

Briggs, Asa, 'Cholera and Society', *Past & Present* 19, April 1961

Bright, John, *Game Laws*. Speeches of Rt. Hon John Bright, MP Birmingham, and P A Taylor, MP Leicester, in House of Commons, 10 & 27 August 1880 (London, Anti Game Law League 1880)

Brigstocke, Hugh, ed., *The Oxford Companion to Western Art* (Oxford, Oxford University Press 2001)

Broad, John, 'Housing the rural poor in Southern England', *Agricultural History Review* 48 (1974)

Brockie, William, *Sunderland Notables* (Sunderland, Hills 1894)

Brody, Alan, *The English Mummers and Their Plays* (London, RKP 1971)

Broke de, Lord Willoughby, *The Sport of Our Ancestors, Being a collection of prose and verse setting forth The Sport of Fox Hunting As they knew it* (London, Constable 1921)

Bronte, Charlotte, *Jane Eyre* (1847. Oxford, Oxford University Press 2000)

Brooks, Mike, *Wrestling for God* (Belfast, Christian Journals 1976)

Brooks, W A, *Report of the Engineer on the state of the River Tyne* (Newcastle, 14 March 1848)

Brown, Cynthia, 'When the Balloon didn't go up' *Leicester Historian*, 26, 2010

Brown, G T, 'Riding the Stang', *Antiquities of Sunderland* xi, 1910

Brown, Paul, *The Friday Book* (Newcastle, Bealls 1934)—articles fom Friday's Newcastle Journal

Brown, Paul, *The Second Friday Book of North Country Sketches* (Newcastle, Bealls 1935)

Brown, William, *A History of The Municipal Charities of Chester 1837–75* (Chester, Trustees 1875)

Brown, Rev. William, *Centenary of Primitive Methodism in Hetton Circuit* (Durham 1923)

Browne, Capt. T H, *History of the English Turf 1904–30* (London, Virtue & Co 1931)

Bruce, H J, *Silken Dalliance* (London, Constable 1946)

Bruce, Rev. J Collingwood, *Handbook of Newcastle On Tyne* (London, Longman Green 1863)

Brundage, A, *The People's Historian. John Richard Green and the Writing of History in Victorian England* (Westport, Conn, Greenwood Press 1994)

Brunskill, Rev. F R, *Life of John Williamson* (Willington, Paxton 1923)

Bruton, F A, *Three Accounts of Peterloo and The Story of Peterloo* (1919. Manchester, folkcustoms 2014)

Bryan, Benjamin, *Matlock. Manor and Parish* (London, Bemrose 1903)

Bryan, Dominic, *Orange Parades. The Politics of Ritual, Tradition and Control* (London, Pluto Press 2000)

Buckland, Teresa, 'Dancing Out of Time: the forgotten Boston of Edwardian England', in S Dodds and S C Cook, eds., *Bodies of Sound. Studies Across Popular Music and Dance* (Farnham, Ashgate 2012)

Bucknell, Clare, 'I can scarce hold my pen', *London Review of Books*, 15 June 2017

Buford, Bill, *Among the Thugs. The Experience and Seduction of Crowd Violence* (London, Secker & Warburg 1990)

'Bullards' Frolicks; or, all Alive at Stamford' (Stamford, J Drakard 1802)

Bunyan, John, *The Pilgrim's Progress* (1678. Nathaniel Ponder 'at the Peacock in the Poultrey', part two, 1684)

Bunyan, John, *The Pilgrim's Progress* (1678. Penguin, Harmondsworth 1968)

Burca, Marcus de, *The Gaelic Athletic Association. A History* (Dublin, Gill 1999)

Burke, Edmund, 'Appeal to the Old Whigs from the New' (1791) in, *Works* (London, C&J Rivington 1826) vol vi

Burke, Peter, 'Viewpoint. The Invention of Leisure in early Modern Europe', *Past & Present* 146, February 1995

Burn, Gordon, *Best and Edwards. Football, Fame and Oblivion* (London, Faber & Faber 2006)

Burnett, T A J, *Rise and Fall of a Regency Dandy* (London, John Murray 1981)

Burnette, Joyce, *Gender, work and wages in the Industrial Revolution in Britain* (Cambridge, Cambridge University Press 2008)

Burrow, John, *A History of Histories* (London, Penguin 2009)

Burton, Alfred, *Rush-Bearing: An Account of the Old Custom of Strewing Rushes; Carrying Rushes to Church; The Rush-Cart; Garlands in Churches; Morris Dancers; The Wakes; The Rush* (Manchester, Brook & Chrystal 1891)

Burton, George, *Chronolgy of Stamford* (Stamford, Robert Bagley 1846)

Burton, William, *The Description of Leicestershire* (Leicester, J Gregory 1777)

Bushaway, Bob, *By Rite. Custom, Ceremony and Community in England 1700–1880* (London, Junction Books 1982)

Butcher, Richard, *The Survey and Antiquities of the Towne of Stamford, with its Antient Foundation, Grants, Privileges & Several Donations* (London, Forcet 1646)

Butler, Frank, *A History of Boxing in Britain* (London, Arthur Barker 1972)

Butler, Lise, 'Michael Young, the ICS, and the Politics of Kinship', *20c British History*, 2015, http:/tcbh.oxfordjournals.org, accessed February 2015

Butler, Sarah, *Britain and its Empire in the Shadow of Rome* (London, Bloomsbury 2014)

Butterfield, Herbert, *The Whig Interpretation of History* (1931. New York, W W Norton 1965)

Cahill, Kevin, *Who Owns Britain?* (Edinburgh, Canongate 2001)

Caine, Caesar, *Cleator and Cleator Moor: Past and Present* (1916. Beckernet Bookshop 1973)

Calder, Sandy, *The Origins of Primitive Methodism* (Woodbridge, Boydell, 2016)

Caliendo, Marco, 'Ten Do It better? An Empirical Analysis of an Old Football Myth', *12A Discussion paper* no.2158, June 2006

Calthrop, Dion Clayton, *English Dress from Victoria to George V* (London, Chapman & Hall 1934)

Calvocoressi, Rupert and Seymour, Susan, 'Landscape Parks and the Memorialization of Empire', *Rural History* 18, 2007, pp.95–118

Cannadine, David, *The Decline and Fall of the British Aristocracy* (New Haven, Yale University Press 1990)

Cannam, Helen, 'The Battle of Stanhope – Myth and Reality', *Journal of Weardale Field Study Society* 9, 1997

Cantor, G, 'Humphrey Davy: A Study in Nacrisissm?' *Notes and Records. The Royal Society Journal of the History of Science* 72, 3, (September 2018)

Capp, Bernard, *England's Culture Wars. Puritan Reformation and its Enemies in the Interregnum 1649–1660* (Oxford, Oxford University Press 2012)

Carey, Brycchan, 'John Wesley's Thoughts upon Slavery', *Bulletin of the John Rylands University Library* 85, 2–3, 2003

Carlyle, Thomas, *On Heroes* (1841. Lincoln, University of Nebraska Press 1966)

Carlyle, T, *Reminiscences* (1881. Oxford, Oxford University Press 1997)

Carpentier, Georges, *My Methods, or Boxing as a Fine Art* (London, Athletic publications, nd, 1920s)

Carr, Raymond, *English Fox Hunting. A History* (London, Weidenfeld & Nicolson 1976)

Carter, Neil, *The Football Manager* (Abingdon, Routledge 2006)

Carter, Neil, *Medicine, Sport and the Body. A Historical Perspective* (London, Bloomsbury 2012)

Carter, Thomas and W H Long, *War Medals of the British Army 1650-1891* (London, Novic & Wilson 1893)

Cassell's Book of Sports and Pastimes (London, Cassell 1893)

Caunce, S A, 'The Hiring Fairs of Northern England 1890-1930', *Past & Present* 217, November 2012

'Cecil' [Cornelius Tongue], *Records of the Chase and Memoirs of Celebrated Sportsmen* (London, Longman, Brown, Green & Longman 1854)

Chadwick, Edwin, Secretary to the Board of Poor Law Commissioners, *Report* on the Sanitary Condition of the Labouring Population of Great Britain, (HL) xxvi, 1842

Challenor, Bromley, ed., *Selections from the Municipal Chronicles of the Borough of Abingdon 1555-1897* (Abingdon, Wm Hooke 1898)

Chamberlayne, John, *Magna Britannia Notitia: or, the Perfect State of Great Britain with divers Remarks upon the Ancient State thereof* (London, for Timothy Goodwin et al. 1718)

Chambers, Robert, ed., *The Book of Days. A miscellany of Popular Antiquities in connection with The Calendar including Anecdote, Biography & History, Curiosities of Literature and Oddities of Human Life and Character* (London & Edinburgh, W & R Chambers 1869) vol. ii

Chandler, Keith, *Ribbons, Bells and Squeaking Fiddles. Social History of the Morris in the English South Midlands* (London, Hisarlik 1993)

Chandler, T J L, 'Emergent Athleticism. Games in two English Public Schools 1800-60', *International Journal History of Sport* 5, 3, 1988.

Chandos, John, *Boys Together. English Public Schools 1800-64* (Oxford, Oxford University Press 1985)

Chaplin, Patrick, *Darts in England 1900-39* (Manchester, Manchester University Press 2009)

Chapman, John, and Sylvia Seeliger, *Enclosure, Environment and Landscape in Southern England* (Stroud, Tempus 2001)

Chapman, Stanley, *The Clay Cross Company 1837-1987* (Clay Cross, Biwater 1987)

Charlton, Edward, *Memorials of North Tyndale and its Four Surnames* (Newcastle 1871)

Charlton, Edward, *Society in Northumberland in the Last Century*. Lecture to the Literary & Philosophical Society, Newcastle upon Tyne, 18 January 1874 (Newcastle, A Reid 1874)

Chase, Malcolm, *'The People's Farm'. English Radical Agrarianism 1775-1840* (Oxford, Clarendon Press 1988)

Chase, Malcolm, and Ian Dyck, eds., *Living and Learning. Essays in Honour of J F C Harrison* (Aldershot, Scolar Press 1996)

Checkland, S G & E O A, eds., *The Poor Law Report of 1834* (Harmondsworth, Penguin 1974)

Cheshire Federation Women's Institutes, *Cheshire Village Memories* (Malpas, CFWI 1951?)

Chilton, Tony, 'Children's Play in Newcastle upon Tyne', Association for Children's Play & National Playing Fields Association, 1985

Chinn, Carl, *Better Betting with a Decent Feller. A Social History of Bookmaking* (London, Arum 2004)

Christie, Rev. J, *Northumberland* (Newcastle, Mawson, Swan, Morgan 1893)

Clapham, Richard, *Foxhunting on the Lakeland Fells* (London, Longman's Green 1920)

Clapson, Mark, 'Gambling, the 'fancy' and Booth's role and reputation', in David Englander and Rosemary O' Day, eds., *Retrieved Riches: Social Investigation in Britain 1840-1914* (Aldershot, Ashgate 1998)

Clare, John, 'Childish Recollections', 'Village Minstrel', 'Helpston Green', and others in *The Village Minstrel and Other Poems* (London, Taylor & Drury Stamford 1821) 2 vols.

Clark, JCD, *English Society 1688-1932* (Cambridge, Cambridge University Press 1987)

Clark, Peter, *British Clubs and Societies 1580-1800. The Origins of an Associational World* (Oxford, Oxford University Press 2001)

Clark, Stuart, 'Inversion, Misrule and the Meaning of Witchcraft', *Past & Present* 87, May 1980

Clarke, J, with C Crichter and R Johnson, eds., *Working Class Culture. Studies in history and theory* (London, Hutchinson & CCCS 1979)

Clarke, J. Stirling, *The Ladies Equestrian Guide; or, the habit of the horse: A treatise on Female Equitation* (London, Day & Son 1857)

Clarke, Stuart Roy, with John Williams, *The Game Revisited* (Liverpool, Bluecoat Press 2019)

Clayden, Paul, *Our Common Land* (Henley, Open Spaces Society 2003)

Clayton, Rev. R, 'Dissuasives from Frequenting the Race Course' (Newcastle 1841)

Clee, Nicholas, 'Who's the Daddy of them All?', *Observer Sports Magazine*, March 2007

Cleveland, Harry, *Fisticuffs and Personalities of the Prize Ring* (London, Sampson Low 1923)

Clough, Brian, with John Sadler, *Cloughie: Walking on Water* (London, Headline 2002)

Clowes, William, *The Journals of William Clowes* (London, Hallam and Holiday 1844)

Coates, Tim, 'How The Times went to war with a Government', *The Times*, 31 October 2009.

Cobbett, J M, and J P Cobbett, eds., *Selections from Cobbett's Poltical Works* (London, Ann Cobbett nd 1835?) vol. i

Cobbett, William, *Rural Rides* (1830. London, Dent 1912) two vols.

Cobbett, William, *Advice to Young Men* (1830. Oxford, Oxford University Press 1981)

Cobbett, William, *Cobbett's Tour in Scotland; and in the four Northern Counties of England in the autumn of the year 1832* (London, 11 Bolt Court, Fleet St. 1833)

Cocks, H G, 'Safeguarding Civility: Sodomy, Class and Moral Reform in early 19c England', *Past & Present* 190, February 2006

Coffey, John and P C H Lim, 'Introduction', *The Cambridge Companion to Puritanism* (Cambridge, Cambridge University Press 2008)

Colley, Linda, *Britons. Forging the Nation 1707-1837* (London, Pimlico 1992)

Collini, Stefan, *Arnold* (Oxford, Oxford University Press 1988)

Collini, Stefan, ed., *On Liberty and other Writings* (Cambridge, Cambridge University Press 1998)

Collini, Stefan, 'The Literary Critic and the Village Labourer', *Trans RHS* 6, xiv, 2004

Collini, Stefan, Common Reading (Oxford,Oxford University Press 2008)

Collini, Stefan, 'A tale of two critics', *The Guardian*, 17 August 2013

Collini, Stefan, Common Writing (Oxford, Oxford University Press 2016)

Collins, Marcus, 'The fall of the English gentleman', *Historical Review* 75, February 2002

Collins, Roy, with George Best, *Blessed. The Autobiography* (London, Ebury Press 2001)

Collins, Tony, 'Review article: History, Theory and the Civilizing Process', *Sport in History* 25, 2, 2005

Collins, Tony, 'Wembley, the Rugby League Cup Final and Northern English Identity', *International Journal of Regional & Local Studies* 2, i, 2005

Collins, Tony, *Sport in Capitalist Society* (Abingdon, Routledge 2013)

Collins, Tony, J Martin, and W Vamplew, eds., *Encyclopaedia of Traditional British Rural Sports* (Abingdon, Routledge 2005)

Collinson, Patrick, *The Religion of Protestants. The Church in English Society 1559–1625* (Oxford, Clarendon Press 1982)

Collinson, Patrick, *The Puritan Character. Polemics and Polarities in early 17c English Culture* (Berkeley, University California Press 1989)

Collinson, Patrick, *The Birthpangs of Protestant England* (Basingstoke, Macmillan 1991)

Colls, Robert, *The Collier's Rant. Song and Culture in the Industrial Village* (London, Croom Helm 1977)

Colls, Robert, *The Pitmen of the Northern Coalfield. Work, Culture and Protest 1790–1850* (Manchester, Manchester University Press 1987)

Colls, Robert, 'The Constitution of the English', *History Workshop Journal* 46, 1998

Colls, Robert, *Identity of England* (Oxford, Oxford University Press 2002)

Colls, Robert, 'When We Lived in Communities', in R Colls and R Rodger, eds., *Cities of Ideas. Civil Society and Urban Governance in Britain 1800–2000* (Aldershot, Ashgate 2004)

Colls, Robert, 'After Bagehot: Re-thinking the Constitution', *Political Quarterly* 4, 2007

Colls, Robert, 'The New Northumbrians', in Colls, ed., *Northumbria. History and Identity 547–2000* (Chichester, Phillimore 2007)

Colls, Robert, *George Orwell. English Rebel* (Oxford, Oxford University Press 2013)

Colls, Robert and Bill Lancaster, eds., *Newcastle upon Tyne. A Modern History* (Chichester, Phillimore 2001)

Colls, Robert and Dodd, Philip, eds., *Englishness. Politics and Letters 1880–1920* (1986. London, Bloomsbury 2014)

Colpus, Eve, 'Women, Service and Self-actualization in Inter-War Britain', *Past & Present* 238, February 2018

Committee of Enquiry, *Juvenile Delinquency* (Leics. Schoolmasters' Assoc. 1938)

Connolly, Cyril, *Enemies of Promise* (1938. London, Routledge, Kegan Paul 1949)

Consolidated Minutes of the Primitive Methodist Connexion approved 1849 (London, Thos Holliday 1850)

Conway, Rebecca, 'Making the Mill Girl Modern? Beauty, Industry and the Popular Newspaper in 1930s England', *20c British History* 24, 4, December 2013

Conybeare, Rev. Edward, *A History of Cambridgeshire* (London, Elliot Stock 1897)

Cooke-Taylor, R W, *The Factory System and the Factory Acts* (1894. London, Methuen 1912)

Cooke-Taylor, W, *Notes of a Tour in the Manufacturing Districts of Lancashire* (1841. London, Frank Cass 1968)

Cooper, Anthony Ashley, 7th Earl Shaftesbury, *Speech on 10 Hours Factory Bill* (1844. New York, Carpenter 1972)

Corfe, Tom, *Sunderland* (Newcastle, Frank Graham 1973)

Corfield, Penny, 'Christopher Hill. Marxism and Methodism', *Historian* 87, 2005

Corvan, Ned, *Corvan's Songs* (Newcastle On Tyne, W Stewart, News Agent, The Side, nd, 1870?)

Couch, Sir Arthur Quiller, ed., *Oxford Book of English Prose* (Oxford, Oxford University Press 1925)

Country Gentleman (A), 'A Proprietor of Game'. *A Letter on the Game Laws* (London, Baldwin, Cradock, Joy 1815)

Country Gentleman (A), *Thoughts on the expediency of legalizing the Sale of Game* (London, John Murray 1823)

Countryside Alliance and Council of Hunting Associations, *How to Keep Hunting Handbook* (Countryside Alliance, 2006)

Cowling, Mary, *The Artist as Anthropologist. The Representation of Type and Character in Victorian Art* (Cambridge, Cambridge University Press 1989)

Cowman, Krista, 'Play streets, women, children and the problem of urban traffic', *Social History* 42, 2, 2017

Cox, J C, *How to Write the History of a Parish* (1879. London, Allen & Unwin 1909)

Cox, William D, *Boxing in Art and Literature* (New York, William D Cox 1935)

Crewe, Tom, 'Roger Fenton', *London Review of Books*, 16 November 2017

Cronin, Mike, *Sport and Nationalism in Ireland* (Dublin, Four Courts 1999)

Cronin, Mike, with Mark Duncan and Paul Rouse, *The GAA. A People's History* (Cork, Collins Press 2009)

Cronin, Mike, with Roisin Higgins, *Places We Play* (Cork, Collins Press 2011)

Cronin, *Sport. A Very Short Introduction* (Oxford, Oxford University Press 2014)

Crook, M J, *The Evolution of the Victoria Cross* (Tunbridge Wells, Midas 1975)

Cross, Gary, ed., *Worktowners at Blackpool. Mass Observation and Popular Leisure in the 1930s* (London, Routledge 1990)

Crump, Jeremy, 'Horse-racing and liberal governance in 19th century Leicester', *Sport in History* 36 (2) 2016

Cruze, Shani D', ed., *Everyday Violence in Britain 1850–1950* (Harlow, Pearson 2000)

Cunningham, Hugh, 'The Metropolitan Fairs: a case study in the social control of leisure', in A J Donajgrodzki, ed., *Social Control in Nineteenth Century Britain* (London, Croom Helm, 1977)

Cunningham, Hugh, *Leisure and the Industrial Revolution* (London, Croom Helm 1980)

Currie, Robert, *Methodism Divided* (London, Faber & Faber 1968)

Currie, Robert, and Alan Gilbert and Lee Horsley, *Churches and Churchgoers. Patterns of Church Growth in the British Isles since 1700* (Oxford, Oxford University Press 1977)

Dabhoiwala, Faramerz. 'Lust and Liberty', *Past & Present* 207, May 2010

Daghy, Guy, *Noble and Manly. The History of the National Sporting Club* (London, Hutchinson 1956)

Dangerfield, George, *The Strange Death of Liberal England 1910–1914* (1935. New York, Capricorn Books, 1961)

Daniels, Bruce C, *Puritans at Play. Leisure and Recreation in Colonial New England* (Basingstoke, Macmillan 1996)

Darbon, Sebastien, *Les fondaments du systeme sportif: essai d'anthropologie historique* (Paris, L'Harmattan 2014)

Darwin, Bernard, *The English Public School* (London, Longman's Green 1929)

Daunton, M J, *House and Home in the Victorian City* (London, Edward Arnold 1983)

Daunton, M J, *Progress and Poverty. An Economic and Social History of Britain 1700–1850* (Oxford, Oxford University Press 1995)

Davidoff, Leonore, *The Best Circles. Society, Etiquette and the Season* (London, Croom Helm 1973)

Davies, Andrew, 'The Real Peaky Blinders', *BBC History Magazine*, September 2019

Davies, Hunter, *The Glory Game* (1972. Edinburgh, Mainstream 2007)

Davies, Hunter, *A Walk Around the Lakes* (London, Weidenfeld & Nicolson 1979)

Davies, Ian Hamilton, *The Life of Richard Baxter of Kidderminster* (London, W Kent 1887)

Davies, J C, *Fear, Myth and History. The Ranters and their Historians* (Cambridge, Cambridge University Press 2002)

Davies, Rupert, *Methodism* (Harmondsworth, Penguin 1964)

Davies, Rupert and Gordon Rupp, eds., *A History of the Methodist Church in Great Britain* (London, Epworth Press 1965) vol. i

Davis, L, 'Abingdon', in *English Illustrated Magazine*, 1888–89

Davis, Philip, *The Victorians* (Oxford, Oxford University Press 2002)

Davis, Robert C, *Popular Culture and Public Violence in Late Renaissance Venice* (Oxford, Oxford University Press 1994)

Davison, A W, *Derby. Its Rise and Progress* (London, Bemrose & Sons 1906)

Davison, Peter, *Contemporary Drama and the Popular Dramatic Tradition in England* (London, Macmillan 1982)

Davison, Peter, *Popular Appeal in English Drama to 1850* (London, Macmillan 1982)

Dawson, Rev. Joseph, *Peter Mackenzie. His Life and Labours* (London, Charles H Kelly 1896)

Deacon, Bernard, *Liskeard and its People* (Redruth, Deacon 1989)

Dee, Dave, 'The Hefty Hebrew. Boxing and British-Jewish Identity', *Sport in History* 32, 3, 2012

Dee, Dave, *Sport and British Jewry 1890–1960* (Manchester, Manchester University Press 2013)

Defoe, Daniel, *A Tour through the Whole Island of Great Britain* (1724–26. Harmondsworth, Penguin 1978)

Deguignet, Jean-Marie, *Memoirs of a Breton Peasant* (1998. New York, Seven Stories Press, English translation 2002)

Delluc, Brigitte and Gilles, *Lascaux* (Editions SuOuest 2015)

Denson, John, of Waterbeach, *A Peasant's Voice to Landowners* (1830. Cambridge, Cambs Record Society 1991)

Denvir, Bernard, *Art Design and Society 1689–1789* (Harlow, Longmans 1983)

Deuchar, Stephen, *Sporting Art in 18c England* (New Haven, Yale University Press 1988)

Devey, T V, *Records of Wolsingham* (Newcastle, 1926)

Dewey, C, 'Socratic Teachers' part 1, 'Opposition to the Cult of Athletics at Eton 1870–1914', *International Journal of the History of Sport* 12, i, April 1995; and part 2, 'The Counter Attack', ibid, 12, iii, December 1995.

Dhami, Narinder, *Bend It Like Beckham* (2002. London, Hodder & Stoughton 2018)

Dicey, A V, *Introduction to the Study of the Law of the Constitution* (1885. London, Macmillan 1964) with an Introduction by E C S Wade, Downing Professor of the Laws of England in the University of Cambridge

Dickens, Charles, *Dombey & Sons* (London, Bradbury & Evans 1848)

Dickens, Charles, *Hard Times. For These Times* (1854. Penguin, Harmondsworth 1978)

Dickens, Charles, *Dickens' Journalism*, Michael Slater, ed., vol. 2 (London, Dent 1996), vol. 3, (London, Dent 1998)

Dickens, Charles, *Little Dorrit* (1857. Ware, Wordsworth 2002)

Dickenson, Rev. John, 'The Distinctive Characteristics of Primitive Methodism', in *Heroic Men: the Death Roll of the Primitive Methodist Ministry 1888–1889* (London, Joseph Toulson 1889)

Dickinson, G, *Allendale and Whitfield* (Newcastle 1903)

Dickinson, H T, ed., *Britain and the French Revolution 1789–1815* (Basingstoke, Macmillan 1989)

Dickinson, W, A *Glossary of the Words and Phrases, Pertaining to the Dialect of Cumberland* (London, Bemrose 1899)

Dine, Philip, *French Rugby Football. A Cultural History* (Oxford, Berg 2001)

Dine, Philip, and Sean Crosson, eds., 'Introduction', *Sport, Representation and Evolving Identities in Europe* (Bern, Peter Lang 2010)

Directions for Breeding Game Cocks ... with Calculations for Betting (London, MacGowan 1780)

Disney, John, *The Laws of Gaming. Wagers, Horse-Racing and Gaming-Houses* (London, Butterworth 1806)

Dixon, D D, 'Old Coquetdale Customs: Salmon Poaching', *Archaeologia Aeliana* xv, new series 1892

Dixon, D D, *Upper Coquetdale, Northumberland. Its history, traditions, folk-lore and scenery* (Newcastle, R Redpath 1903)

Dixon, DD, *Old Wedding Customs in Upper Coquetdale and Alndale* (Newcastle Courant, December 1888)

Dixon, William Scarth, *In the North Countree: annals and anecdotes of horse, hound, and herd* (London, Grant Richards 1900)

Dixon, William Scarth, *The Quorn Hunt* (London, Hunt Clubs 1921)

Dobson, R B, and J Taylor, *Rymes of Robyn Hood* (London, Heinemann 1976)

Dodd, William, 'A Factory Cripple', *The Factory System in a series of letters to Rt. Hon. Lord Ashley* (1842. London, Frank Cass 1968) with an Introduction by W H Chaloner

Doherty, Gillian M, *The Irish Ordnance Survey* (Dublin, Four Courts Press 2006)

Dolling, R, *Ten Years in a Portsmouth Slum* (London, Swan Sonnenschein 1896)

Domeneghetti, Roger, *From the Back Page to the Front Room. Football's Journey through the English Media* (Huddersfield, Ockley Boooks 2014)

Donajgrodzki, A P, ed., *Social Control in Nineteenth Century Britain* (London, Croom Helm 1977)

O' Donnell, *Visit to Newcastle, Monday 14 September* 1835

Doran, John, *'Mann' and Manners at the Court of Florence 1740–86* (London, Bentley 1876) 2 vols.

Dorre, G M, *Victorian Fiction and the Cult of the Horse* (Aldershot, Ashgate 2006)

Dougall, Alistair, *The Devil's Book. Charles I, the Book of Sports and Puritanism in Tudor and early Stuart England* (Exeter, University Exeter Press 2011)

Douglas, Christopher, *Douglas Jardine. Spartan Cricketer* (London, Methuen 2002)

Dowling, Frank Lewis [Editor Bell's Life in London], *Fistiana; or, the Oracle of the Ring* (London, Wm Clement 1841 & 1846)

Dowling, Frank Lewis, *The Championship of England* (London, Bell's Life 1860) and *Fights for the Championship* (London, Bell's Life 1860)

Doyle, A Conan, *The Exploits of Brigadier Gerard* (London, George Newnes 1899)

Drakard, John, *The History of Stamford* (Stamford, Drakard 1822)

'Druid' (The), (Henry Hall Dixon), *The Post and the Paddock: with recollections of George IV, Sam Chifney, and other Turf Celebrities* (London, Piper, Stephenson 1856)

Drummond, Henry, *Baxter's Second Innings* (London, Hodder & Stoughton 1892)

Duckershoff, Ernst, 'A German Coal Miner', *How the English Workman Lives* (London, P S King, 1899)

Duffell, Nick, *The Making of Them. The British Attitude to Children and the Boarding School System* (London, Lone Arrow 2000)

Dunning, Eric, with Patrick Murphy and John Williams, *The Roots of Football Hooliganism* (London, RKP 1988)

Dunning, Eric, 'Sport in the Civilizing Process', in Dunning et al., eds., *The Sports Process* (Leeds 1993)

Durham County Playing Fields Association, *Jubilee Handbook* (1952)

Dyck, Ian, *William Cobbett and Rural Popular Culture* (Cambridge, Cambridge University Press 1992)

Dyhouse, Carol, *Girls Growing Up in Late Victorian and Edwardian England* (London, RKP 1981)

Dymond, David, 'A Lost Social Institution. The Camping Close', *Rural History* 1, 2, 1990

Earles, John, *Streets and Houses of Old Macclesfield* (Macclesfield, Robert Brown 1915)

East End History Project, 'Life in Sunderland's East End in the 1930s' (Sunderland, Community Arts 1985)

Edelman, Robert, and Wayne Wilson, eds., *Oxford Handbook of Sports History* (New York, Oxford University Press 2017) and Introduction

Edgerton, David, *The Rise and Fall of the British Nation* (London, Allen Lane 2018)

Edwards, Joseph, *Brief History of Landholding in England* (London, Land Values Publications 1909)

Edwards, Roger, *The Game Laws, and their effects on the Rural Population and Society in general* (London, Pitman 1862)

Egan, Pierce ('One of the Fancy'), *Boxiana; or Sketches of Ancient and Modern Pugilism from the days of the renowned Broughton and Slack to The Heroes of the Present Milling Era dedicated to that distinguished patron of Old English Sports Captain Barclay* (London, G. Smeeton 1812) vol. i

Egan, Pierce, *Boxiana; or, Sketches of Modern Pugilism from the Championship of Crib to the Present Time dedicated to the Rt Hon Earl of Yarmouth* (London, Sherwood, Neeley, Jones 1818) vols. i & ii

Egan, Pierce, *Key to the Picture of the Fancy Going to a Fight at Moulsey Hurst dedicated, by Permission, to Mr Jackson and the Pugilistic Club designed and etched by I R Cruikshank under the direction of P Egan* (London, Jones 1819)

Egan, Pierce, *Life in London; or the Day and Night Scenes of Jerry Hawkins Esq, and his elegant friend Corinthian Tom accompanied by Bob Logic, the Oxonian in their Rambles and Sprees through the Metropolis dedicated to his most gracious Majesty King George the Fourth with love and patronage* (London, Sherwood, Neely 19 July 1821)

Egan, Pierce, *Book of Sports, and Mirror of Life: embracing The Turf, The Chase, The Ring, and The Stage interspersed with Original Memoirs of Sporting Men* (London, Tegg 1832)

Egan, Pierce, Introduction by John Ford, *Boxiana; or Sketches of Ancient and Modern Pugilism from the days of the renowned James Figg and Jack Broughton to the heroes of the later Milling Era, Jack Scroggins and Tom Hickman* (1812–19 weekly; London, Folio Society 1976)

Egerton, Judy, ed., *British Sporting and Animal Paintings 1655–1867* (Tate gallery, YCBA 1978)

Egerton, Judy, and Dudley Snelgrove, eds., *British Sporting and Animal Drawings 1500–1850* (Tate Gallery, YCBA 1978)

Eggar, J Alfred, *Remembrances of Life and Customs in Gilbert White's, Cobbett's, and Charles Kingsley's Country* (London, Simpkin, nd, 1920s?)

Egglestone, W. M, *Stanhope Memorials of Bishop Butler* (London, Simpkin Marshall 1878)

Egglestone, W. M, *The Bonny Moor Hen, or The Battle of Stanhope with ballad* (Stanhope, Eggleston, nd, 1882?)

Egglestone, W. M, *Stanhope and its Neighbourhood* (Stanhope, Egglestone 1882)

Eichberg, Henning, 'The Enclosure of the Body', *Journal of Contemporary History* 21, January 1986

Elias, Norbert, *The Civilizing Process. The History of Manners* (1939. Oxford, Blackwell 1969) and *State Formation and Civilization* (Oxford, Blackwell 1982)

Elias, Norbert, and Eric Dunning, *Quest for Excitement. Sport and Leisure in the Civilizing Process* (1986. Dublin, UCD Press 2008)

Eliot, George, *Middlemarch* (1871–72. London, Penguin 1994)

Ellenberger, Nancy W, *Balfour's World. Aristocracy and Political Culture at the Fin de Siecle* (Woodbridge, Boydell Press 2015)

Elliot, Rosemary, *Women and Smoking since* 1890 (London, Routledge 2009)

Ellis, Julie-Ann, 'Methodism and the Labour Movement in S Australia', *Labor History* 64, May 1993

Emmison, F G, *Elizabethan Life: Morals and The Church Courts* (Chelmsford, Essex County Council 1973)

Epstein, James, 'Our real constitution', in Vernon, ed., *Re-reading the Constitution* (Cambridge, Cambridge University Press 1996)

Erdozain, Dominic, *The Problem of Pleasure. Sport, Recreation and the Crisis of Victorian Religion* (Woodbridge, Boydell Press 2010)

Erdozain, Dominic, review of books on secularism, *English Historical Review* cxxvii, 2012

Erickson, Joyce, 'Perfect Love'. Achieving Sanctification...in the Life Writings of Early Methodist Women', *Prose Studies* 20 (2), 1997

Evangelista, Stefano, 'A Colony of Hellas. 19c England and the Legacy of Ancient Greece', *Journal for Study of British Cultures* 13, i, 2006

Evans, E, *Howel Harris. Evangelist 1714–1773* (Cardiff, University Wales Press 1974)

Evans, H, *First Steps in Club Leadership* (London, National Assoc Boys' Clubs 1938)

Every Girl's Annual (London, Pilgrim Press 1929)

'Ewanian', *History of Penrith* (Penrith, William Furness 1894)

Farmer, John S, *The Public School Word Book* (London, Hirschfeld 1900) privately printed

Fawcett, J W, *Memorials of Early Primitive Methodism in County Durham 1820–29* (Durham, Fawcett 1908)

Fawcett, William, *Saddle Room sayings, with topics, anecdotes and stories of the Hunter, in Paddock, in Stable and Hunting Field by Wm Fawcett, author of Hill Hunting in the North, Hunting Days in Northumbria, Sporting Days in Tynedale-land* (London, Constable, nd, 1920s)

Fay, Stephen, and David Kynaston, *Arlott, Swanton and the Soul of English Cricket* (London, Bloomsbury 2019)

Featherston, J R, *Weardale Men and Manners* (Durham, Humble 1840)

Featherstone, Simon, *Englishness. Twentieth Century Popular Culture and the Forming of English Identity* (Edinburgh, Edinburgh University Press 2009)

Featherstone-Dawes, W, *Football: Those Were The Days* (London, Portico 2011)

Feinstein, Charles, 'New Estimates of Average Earnings in the UK 1880–1913', *Economic History Review*, 2nd series, xliii, 4, 1990

Ferguson, Niall, *Empire. How Britain Made the Modern World* (London, Penguin 2004)

Ferguson, Robert, *The Northmen in Cumberland and Westmoreland* (London, Longman; Carlisle, R & J Steel 1856)

Fetherstonhaugh, Col T, *Our Cumberland Villages* (Carlisle, Thurnam 1925)

Field, Clive D, 'The social structure of English Methodism', *British Journal of Sociology* 28, 1977

Fielding, Henry, *The Humorous and Diverting History of Tom Jones, A Foundling* (London, R Snagg, printer 1775)

Fielding, John, *The Curse of the Factory System* (1836. London, Frank Cass 1969)

Finch, Jonathan, 'The Extreme Sport of Hedge-laying', *British Archaeology*, March/April 2005

Finney, Isaac, *Macklesfelde in ye Olden Time* (Macclesfield, Advertiser Office 1873)

Fisher, D R, ed., *History of Parliament 1820–32* (Cambridge, Cambridge University Press 2009)

Fitzsimmons, Robert, *Physical Culture and Self Defense* (London, Author's Syndicate 1901)

Fleischer, Nat, *Black Dynamite. The Story of the Negro in the Prize Ring from 1782–1938* (The Ring, New York City 1938)

Fletcher, Alfred, *Centenary Souvenir. Carville Chapel, Wallsend 1812–1912* (Newcastle, Doig Bros 1912)

Floud, R, 'Height, weight and body mass of the British population since 1820', National Bureau of Economic Research (Cambridge MA) October 1998

Floud, R, and Johnson, P, eds., *Cambridge Economic History of Modern Britain* (Cambridge, Cambridge University Press 2004) vol. I, 1700–1860

Football Association, *Rules of Association Football* (1863. Bodleian Library Oxford 2006) Introduction by Melvyn Bragg

Forrest, Susanna, *If Wishes Were Horses: an equine obsession* (London, Atlantic Books 2012)

Forster, Bill, *Boundaries. A survey of the parish boundary of Empingham in Rutland* (Empingham 2019)

Fort, Tom, *Casting Shadows. Fish and Fishing in Britain* (London, William Collins 2020)

Foster, William, *Praying Billy The Street Preacher; or remarkable answers to prayer* (Rochdale, WMSSU 1910)

Fothergill, G A, *Twenty Sporting Designs* (Edinburgh, Fothergill 1911)

Foucault, Michel, *Discipline and Punish. The Birth of the Prison* (London, Allen Lane 1977)

Fox, H S A, 'The functioning of bocage landscapes in Devon and Cornwall 1500-1800', in *Les Bocages* (Rennes, CNRS 1976)

Fraser, William, *Field-Names in South Derbyshire* (Ipswich, Norman Adlard 1947)

Freeman, A E, 'The Morality of Field Sports', in John Morley, ed., *Fortnightly Review* xxxiv, October 1869

Freeman, E M, *The Growth of the English Constitution from earliest Times* (1872. London, Macmillan 1890)

French, David, *Military Identities. The Regimental System, the British Army and the British People c.1870–2000* (Oxford, Oxford University Press 2009)

French, Henry and Mark Rothery, *Man's Estate. Landed Gentry Masculinities 1660–1900* (Oxford, Oxford University Press 2012)

Fulcher, Jonathan, 'The English People and their constitution after Waterloo', in Vernon, ed., *Re-reading the Constitution* (Cambridge, Cambridge University Press 1996)

Furness, Harold, *Famous Fights Past & Present* (Police Budget Edition, nd or location)

Furness, William, 'Ewanian', *History of Penrith* (Penrith, Furness 1894)

Fussell, Paul, *The Great War and Modern Memory* (Oxford, Oxford University Press 1977)

Fussell, Paul, *The Boys' Crusade. American GIs in Europe* (London, Weidenfeld & Nicolson 2004)

Game Laws, Report from Select Committee; together with the Proceedings of the Committee, Minutes of Evidence and Appendix, House of Commons 1872

Gammon, Vic, 'The Rise and Suppression of Popular Church Music 1660–1870', in Yeos, eds., *Popular Culture and Class Conflict 1590–1914* (Brighton, Harvester 1981)

Garbutt, Thomas, *Substance of an address delivered on 1 April 1834 at a Social Meeting of the teachers and friends of the Methodist Sabbath School Howden* (Howden, W F Pratt printer 1834)

Gardiner, F J, *History of Wisbech and Neighbourhood 1848–1898* (Wisbech, Gardiner 1898)

Garnham, Neal, 'Dan Donnelly as an Irish Sporting Hero', *Irish Historical Studies* 37, 148, Nov 2011

Garrido, F & A, trans. Laura Suffield, *Il Centenario de la plaza de toros de la Real Maestranza de Caballeria de Ronda* (Ronda 1988)

Gash, Norman, 'Charles James Apperley', *Oxford Dictionary of National Biography* (Oxford, Oxford University Press 2004)

Gaskell, P, *Artisans and Machinery: the moral and physical condition of the Manufacturing population considered with reference to Mechanical Substitutes for Human Labour* (1836. London, Frank Cass 1968)

Gattrell, Simon, 'Wessex', in D Kramer, ed., *The Cambridge Companion to Thomas Hardy* (Cambridge, Cambridge University Press 2005)

Gazeley, Ian, and Andrew Newell, 'Poverty in Edwardian Britain', *Economic History Review* 64, i, 2011

Gazeley, Ian, and Andrew Newell, 'Urban working-class food consumption and nutrition in Britain in 1904', *Economic History Review* 68, i, 2015

Gee, Tony, 'Jack Broughton', *Oxford Dictionary of National Biography* (Oxford, Oxford University Press 2004)

Geertz, Clifford, 'Thick Description: Toward an Interpretive Theory of Culture', ch 1, and 'Deep Play: Notes on the Balinese Cockfight', ch 15, in *The Interpretation of Cultures* (London, Fontana 1993)

George, Henry, *The Land Question: selected essays* (1881. New York, Schalkenbach Foundation 1982)

George, Henry, *Progress and Poverty* (London, Kegan Paul 1883)

Gibson, Josh, 'The Chartists and the Constitution: Revisiting the British Popular Constitution', *Journal of British Studies* 56 (Jan 2017)

Gibson, W S, *An Historical Memoir on Northumberland* (Newcastle, Longman Green 1862)

Gilbert, Alan D, 'Methodism, dissent and political stability in early industrial England', *Journal of Religious History* 10, 1978–79

Gilbert, P K, *The Citizen's Body* (Columbus, Ohio SUP 2007)

Gilbert, P K, *Cholera and Nation* (New York, SUNYP 2009)

Gilbey, Sir Walter, *Animal Painters* (London, Vinton & Co, 1905)

Gilchrist, Paul, 'Manliness and Post-War Recovery: C E Montague's "Action"', *Sport in History* 33, 3, 2013

Gillespie, Charles, 'The Work of Elie Halevy', *Journal of Modern History* 22, 3, 1950

Gilpin, William, *Observations on Picturesque Beauty* (London, Blamire, The Strand 1786)

Ginswick, J, ed., *Labour and the Poor. Letters to The Morning Chronicle* (1849–51. London, Frank Cass 1983) vol. ii

Giollain, Diarmuid O, 'Celebrations and Rituals', in Biagini and Daly, eds., *Cambridge Social History of Modern Ireland* (Cambridge, Cambridge University Press 2017)

Girouard, Mark, *Return to Camelot. Chivalry and the English Gentleman* (New Haven, Yale University Press 1981)

Glanfield, John, *Bravest of the Brave. The Story of the Victoria* Cross (Stroud, Sutton 2005)

Glanville, Brian, ed., *Footballers' Who Who* (Manchester Empire News 1955–56)

Glover, Richard, *Peninsular Preparation. The reform of the British Army 1795–1809* (Cambridge, Cambridge University Press 1963)

Godfrey, Capt John, *Treatise upon the useful Science of Defence connecting the Small and Backsword and showing the Affinity between them with some observations upon Boxing, and the Characters of the most noble Boxers within the Auth*or's Time (London, Robinson 1747)

Golby, J M, and A W Purdue, *The Civilization of the Crowd. Popular Culture in England 1750–1900* (1984. Stroud, Sutton 1999)

Goldblatt, David, *The Ball is Round. A Global History of Football* (London, Viking 2006)

Goldblatt, David, *The Age of Football: The Global Game in the Twenty-First Century* (Basingstoke, Macmillan 2019)

Goldman, Lawrence, *Dons and Workers. Oxford Adult Education Since 1850* (Oxford, Clarendon Press 1995)

Goldstein, Jeffrey, *Why We Watch. The Attractions of Violent Entertainment* (New York, Oxford University Press 1998)

Gomme, Alice Bertha, *The Traditional Games of England, Scotland and Ireland* (1894. 1898. London, Thames & Hudson 1984)

Gomme, George Laurence, *Folk-Lore Relics of Early Village Life* (London, Elliot Stock 1883)

Goodfellow, David M, *Tyneside. The Social Facts* (1940. Newcastle, CWS 1942)

Gorn, Elliott J, *The Manly Art* (London, Robson Books 1989)

Gorn, Elliott J, 'The Meanings of Prize Fighting', in Steve Pope, ed., *The New American Sport History* (Urbana, UIP 1997)

Gosden, P H J H, ed., *How They Were Taught* (Oxford, Basil Blackwell 1969)

Gosse, Edmund, *Father and Son* (1907. London, Penguin 1986)

Graham, Dorothy, 'Chosen by God. The Female Travelling Preachers of early Primitive Methodism', *Proceedings WHS* 49, 1993

Graham, John P, *Forty Years of Uppingham* (London, Macmillan 1932)

Grainger, Richard, *Proposal for Concentrating the Termini of the Newcastle and Carlisle, the Great North of England, and the proposed Edinburgh Railways; and for providing spacious and eligible depots, with convenient access, from these several Railways to the Town of Newcastle* (Newcastle, Hodgson printer, 1836)

Grant, Colin, *Homecoming. Voices of the Windrush Generation* (London, Jonathan Cape 2019)

Graves, Charles, *Mr Punch's History of Modern England* (London, Cassell 1922) vol. iii, 1874–92

Graves, Robert, *Goodbye to All That* (1929. Harmondsworth, Penguin 1966)

Graves, Robert, and Alan Hodge, *The Long Weekend. A Social History of Great Britain 1918–1939* (1940. London, Hutchinson 1985)

Gray, John, *False Dawn. The Delusions of Global Capitalism* (London, Granta Books 1998)

Gray, William, *Chorographia, or A survey of Newcastle upon Tyne* (1649. Newcastle, Frank Graham 1970)

Green, Benny, *Shaw's Characters* (London, Elm Tree Books 1978)

Green, Brian, *To Read and Sew: James Allen's Girls' School 1741–1991* (Dulwich, The Governors 1991)

Green, Henry, *Knutsford. Its Traditions and History, with Reminiscences, Anecdotes and Notices of the Neighbourhood* (London, Smith Elder 1859)

Green, Henry, [Henry Yorke] *Pack My Bag. A Self-Portrait* (London, Hogarth Press 1952)

Green, S J D, *The Passing of Protestant England. Secularization and Social Change c. 1920-1960* (Cambridge, Cambridge University Press 2011)

Greg, Samuel, *Two Letters to Leonard Horner Esq on the capabilities of the factory system* (London, Taylor & Walton 1840)

Greig, Andrew, *Preferred Lies. A Journey to the Heart of Golf* (London, Phoenix 2007)

Greig, Hannah, *The Beau Monde. Fashionable Society in Georgian London* (Oxford, Oxford University Press 2013)

Greville, Lady, ed., *Ladies in the Field. Sketches of Sport* (London, Ward & Downey 1894)

Griffin, Emma, *England's Revelry. A History of Popular Sports and Pastimes 1660-1830* (Oxford, Oxford University Press British Academy 2005)

Griffin, Emma, *Blood Sport. Hunting in Britain since 1066* (New Haven, Yale University Press 2007)

Griffin, Emma, *Liberty's Dawn. A People's History of the Industrial Revolution* (New Haven, Yale University Press 2013)

Griffin, Emma, 'Diets, Hunger and Living Standards during the British Industrial Revolution', *Past & Present* 239, May 2018

Griffin, Emma, Bread Winner. *An Intimate History of the Victorian Economy* (New Haven, Yale University Press 2020)

Griffiths, Paul, et al., *The Experience of Authority in Early Modern England* (Basingstoke, Macmillan 1996)

Grigson, Geoffrey, 'Stamford 1461-1961', *The Geographical Magazine* xxxiv, May 1961

Grimshaw, Allen, *From the Prize Ring to the Pulpit or, Richard Howton, the Converted Pugilist (with portrait). Biographical Sketch* (Keighley, T Wells 1898)

Grindrod, Ralph Barnes, *The Slaves of the Needle; an exposure of the distressed condition, moral and physical, of dress-makers, milliners, embroiderers, slop workers &c* (1844. New York, Amo Press 1972)

Groom, Nick, *The Union Jack. The Story of the British Flag* (London, Atlantic 2006)

Grossmith, George and Weedon, *The Diary of a Nobody* (1892. Harmondsworth, Penguin 1995)

Groves, Hilary, *Nuns, Buns and Green Uniforms. Memories of the School of St Helen & St Katherine, 1903-2003* (Abingdon, OGA 2003)

Gruneau, R, 'Somatic/Linguistic Turn', in Edelman and Wilson, *Handbook Sports History* (New York, Oxford University Press 2017)

Guha, Ramachandra, 'Cricket and Politics in Colonial India', *Past & Present* 161, November 1998

Guha, Ramachandra, *A Corner of a Foreign Field. The Indian History of a British Sport* (London, Macmillan 2003)

Gunn, Simon, 'People and the car: the expansion of automobility in urban Britain 1955-70', *Social History* 38, 2, 2013

Guttmann, Allen, *From Ritual to Record. The Nature of Modern Sports* (New York, Columbia University Press 1978)

H S, *Handbook to the Newcastle and Carlisle Railway* (Newcastle, Christie printer, 1851)

Hailstone, Alfred G, *One Hundred Years of Law Enforcement in Buckinghamshire* (Richmond, Dimbleby 1957)

Hale, Sir Matthew, *The History of the Common Law of England* (1713. Chicago, University of Chicago Press 1971)

Halevy, Elie, *History of the English People in the 19C. England in 1815* (1913. Trans. 1949. London, Ernest Benn 1960)

Hall, Brian, *Life of Brian in Black and White* (Bishop Auckland, Northern Writers 2007)

Hall, G. Stanley, *Adolescence* (New York, D Appleton 1911)

Hall, S C, *Retrospect of a Long Life: from 1815–1883* (New York, D Appleton 1883)

Hall, Stuart, 'Notes on Deconstructing the Popular', in Samuel, ed., *People's History and Socialist Theory* (London, RKP 1981)

Hamilton, Duncan, *The Great Romantic. Cricket and the Golden Age of Neville Cardus* (London, Hodder & Stoughton 2019)

Hamilton, Duncan, *Harold Larwood* (London, Quercus 2009)

Hamilton, Duncan, For the Glory. *The Life of Eric Liddell from Olympic Hero to Modern Martyr* (London, Doubleday 2016)

Hammond, J L & B, *The Village Labourer* (1911. London, Longman 1978)

Hammond, J L & B, *Lord Shaftesbury* (1923. London, Frank Cass 1969)

Hammond, J L & B, *The Age of the Chartists 1832–54* (London, Longmans, Green 1930)

Hammond, J L & B, *The Bleak Age* (1934. West Drayton, Penguin 1947)

Hanlon, Gregory, review: 'The Decline of Violence in the West', *English Historical Review* 128, 531, April 2013

Harding, John, *Lonsdale's Belts* (London, Robson Books 1994)

Harding, John, *Behind the Glory. History of the Professional Footballers' Association* (Derby, Breedon Books 2009)

Hardy, James, *Harvest Customs in Northumberland* (Newcastle, M A Richardson 1844)

Hargreaves, J A, 'Methodism and Luddism in Yorkshire 1812-13', *Northern History* 26, 1990

Harris, Ruth, and Lyndal Roper, 'Introduction to volume on Gender', *Past & Present* supplement, January 2006

Harrison, Brian, 'Animals and the State in 19c England', *English Historical Review* 88, 349, October 1973

Harrison, Brian, *Seeking a Role* (Oxford, Oxford University Press 2011)

Harrison, Mark, 'The Ordering of the Urban Environment. Time, Work and the Occurrence of Crowds 1790-1835', *Past & Present* 110, Feb 1986

Harrop, Peter, *Mummers' Plays Revisited* (London, Routledge 2020)

Hartmann, D, 'Sport and Social Theory', in Edelman and Wilson, *Handbook Sports History* (New York, Oxford University Press 2017)

Harvey, Adrian, *The Beginnings of a Sporting Commercial Culture in Britain 1793–1850* (Aldershot, Ashgate 2004)

Harvey, Adrian, 'Playing by the Rules', *Sport in History* 31, 3, 2011

Harvey, Alfred, *Bristol. A historical and topographical account* (London, Methuen 1906)

Harvey, Karen, 'Ritual Encounters. Punch Parties and Masculinity in the 18th Century', *Past & Present* 214 (1), 2012

Hasbach, Wilhelm, *A History of the English Agricultural Labourer* (1894. London, P S King 1908)

Hassan, David, 'What Makes a Sporting Icon?' *Sport in History* 33, 4, 2013

Hatcher, John, 'Labour, Leisure and Economic Thought before 19c', *Past & Present* 160, August 1998

Hattersley, R, *A Brand from the Burning. Life of John Wesley* (London, Little Brown 2002)

Hatton, Timothy, 'Infant mortality and the health of survivors in Britain 1910-50', *Economic History Review* 64, 3, 2011

Hawker, James, *A Victorian Poacher* (Oxford, Oxford University Press 1961)

Hawkes, John, *The Meynellian Science, or Fox Hunting upon System* (1808–09 privately printed; reprinted 1846, 1848, 1851, 1907; Leicester, Edgar Backus 1932)

Hawthorn R W, *Brief Historical Sketch & Catalogue, Forth Bank Locomotive Works* (Newcastle upon Tyne, Hawthorn, Leslie & Co 1921)

Haxall, Daniel, ed., *Picturing the Beautiful Game. A History of Soccer in Visual Culture and Art* (London, Bloomsbury 2018)

Hay, D, P. Linebaugh and E. P. Thompson, eds., *ALBION's Fatal Tree. Crime and Society in Eighteenth Century England* (LONDON, ALLEN LANE 1975)

Hayes, Alice M, *The Horsewoman. A Practical Guide to Side-Saddle Riding* (London, Hurst & Blackett 1903)

Hayter, Tony, *The Army and the Crowd in Mid-Georgian England* (London, Macmillan 1978)

Hazlitt, William, 'Whether the Fine Arts are Promoted by Academies?', *The Champion*, 11 September 1814, in P P Howe, ed., *Complete Works of William Hazlitt* (London, J M Dent 1933) vol. xviii

Hazlitt, William, *Character of John Bull* (1817) (Staplehurst, Florin Press 1978)

Hazlitt, William, 'Character of Cobbett', first published in *Table Talk* (1821); 'The Fight', first published in *New Monthly Magazine* (1822); 'Jack Tars', first published as 'English and Foreign Manners' (1825): all in Tom Paulin and D Chandler, eds., *The Fight and Other Writings* (London, Penguin 2000)

Hazlitt, William, 'Spirit of Monarchy' (1823), in *Hazlitt's Selected Essays* (London, Nonesuch Library 1946)

Headmasters' Conference, *Report* 1912 (London, Waterlow & Sons 1913)

Headmasters' Conference, *Curriculum of the Preparatory Schools. Report* (Winchester, Warren 1926)

Heath, Francis George, *Peasant Life in the West of England* (1872. London, Sampson Low 1883)

Heeney, Brian, *Mission to the Middle Classes. The Woodard Schools 1848–91* (London, SPCK 1969)

Heggie, Vanessa, 'Bodies, Sport and Science in the 19c', *Past & Present* 231, May 2016

Helias, Pierre-Jakez, *The Horse of Pride. Life in a Breton Village* (New Haven, Yale University Press 1975)

Heller, Benjamin, 'The Menu Peuple and the Polite Spectator: the individual in the crowd at 18c London fairs', *Past & Present* 208, August 2010

Heller, Peter, 'In this Corner'. *Forty World Champions Tell Their Stories* (London, Robson Books 1975)

Hempton, David, *Methodism. Empire of the Spirit* (New Haven, Yale University Press, 2005)

Henderson, James, *Irregularly Bold. A Study of Bedales School* (London, Andre Deutsch 1978)

Henderson, Michael, *That Will Be England Gone* (London, Constable 2020)

Henderson, William, *The Folk-Lore of the Northern Counties of England and the Borders* (London, Longmans, Green 1866)

Hennessey, Peter, *The Hidden Wiring. Unearthing the British Constitution* (London, Gollancz 1995)

Henricks, Thomas S, *Disputed Pleasures. Sport and Society in Pre-Industrial England* (New York, Greenwood Press 1991)

Herbage Committee, *List of Tents and Stands* (Newcastle 1847)

Heslop, Harold, *The Earth Beneath* (London, Boardman 1946)

Heslop, Harold, *Out of the Old Earth* (Newcastle, Bloodaxe, 1994) eds. Andy Croft and Graeme Rigby

Hewison, Robert, *Ruskin, Turner and the Pre Raphaelites* (London, Tate Gallery 2000)

Hey, David, *Oxford Companion to Local and Family History* (Oxford, Oxford University Press 1996)

Hibbert, Christopher, *Destruction of Lord Raglan* (1961. Ware, Wordsworth 1999)

Hickling, 'A letter to the Members of the Methodist Society in Sunderland and its Vicinity with an Address on Family Religion' (Sunderland 1808)

Higgins, Charlotte, 'An insight into the methods of an artistic revolutionary', *The Guardian*, 4 February 2006

Hill, Christopher, 'The Myth of the Norman Yoke', in *Puritanism and Revolution* (London, Secker & Warburg 1965)

Hill, Graham, *Graham* (Book Club Associates 1977)

Hilton, Boyd, *A Mad, Bad, and Dangerous People? England 1785–1846* (Oxford, Oxford University Press 2006)

Hindle, Steve, *The State and Social Change in Early Modern England 1550–1640* (Basingstoke, Macmillan 2000)

Hindle, Steve, et al., *Remaking English Society. Social Relations and Social Change in Early Modern England* (Woodbridge, Boydell Press 2013)

Hindley, C, *Curiosities of Street Literature* (London, Reeves & Turner 1871)

Hindmarsh, Bruce D, 'My Chains Fell Off, My Heart Was Free, Early Methodist Conversion Narrative', *Church History* 68 (4), 1999

Hines, Barry, *A Kestrel for a Knave* (1968. Penguin London 1969)

Hobhouse, Leonard, *Democracy and Reaction* (1905. London, T F Unwin 1909)

Hobsbawm, E J, *Bandits* (London, Weidenfeld & Nicolson 1969)

Hobsbawm, E J and Rude, G, *Captain Swing* (1969. Harmondsworth, Penguin 1973)

Hobsbawm, E J, *Primitive Rebels* (Manchester, Manchester University Press 1978)

Hobsbawm, E J, *Nations and Nationalism since 1870* (1990. Cambridge, Canto 2005)

Hobsbawm, E J, *Uncommon People. Resistance, Rebellion and Jazz* (London, Abacus 1998)

Hobsbawm, E J, 'A Life in History', *Past & Present* 177, November 2002

Hobson, J A, *Imperialism. A Study* (1902. London 1905)

Hodgkinson, E, and Laurence Tebbutt, *Stamford in 1850* (Stamford, Dolby Bros 1954)

Hodgson, George B, *The Borough of South Shields* (1903. Newcastle, Andrew Reid 1924)

Hoggart, Richard, *The Uses of Literacy* (Harmondsworth, Pelican 1958)

Hoggart, Richard, *A Local Habitation. Life and Times*, vol. i, 1918–40 (London, Chatto & Windus 1988)

Holcroft, Thomas, *Memoirs of Thomas Holcroft, written by himself*, book i and continued by William Hazlitt books ii to v (1816. Oxford, Oxford University Press 1926)

Holdenby, Christopher, *Folk of the Furrow* (London, Thomas Nelson 1913)

Holderness, B A, 'Open and Close Parishes in England in 18c and 19c', *Agricultural History Review* 70, 1972

Hole, Robert, *Pulpits, Politics and Public Order in England 1760–1832* (Cambridge, Cambridge University Press 2004)

Hollingshead, John, 'The Great Pugilistic Revival', *All the Year Round*, 19 May 1860

Holt, Richard, *Sport and Society in Modern France* (London, Macmillan 1981)

Holt, Richard, *Sport and the British. A Modern History* (Oxford, Oxford University Press 1990)

Holt, Richard, 'An Englishman in the Alps: Arnold Lunn, Amateurism and the Invention of Alpine Ski Racing', *International Journal History of Sport* 9, 3, December 1992.

Holt, Richard, Introduction to *British Sporting Heroes* (London, National Portrait Gallery Publications 1998)

Holt, Richard, 'Tony Mason's "Association Football and English Society"', *The Sports Historian* 22, i, May 2002

Holt, Richard, 'The Amateur Body and the Middle Class Man', *Sport in History* 26, 3, 2006

Holt, Richard, 'Sport and the British: Response to Comments', *Sport in History* 31, 2, 2011

Holt, Richard, 'Historians and the History of Sport', *Sport in History* 34, 1, 2014

Holt, Richard, 'C W Alcock (1842–1907)', *Oxford Dictionary National Biography* (Oxford, Oxford University Press 2004)

Holt, Richard, and Tony Mason, *Sport in Britain 1945–2000* (Oxford, Blackwell 2000)

Holt, Richard, and Ray Physick, 'Sport on Tyneside', in Robert Colls and Bill Lancaster, eds., *Newcastle upon Tyne. A Modern History* (Chichester, Phillimore 2001)

Hopcraft, Arthur, *The Football Man* (1968. London, Readers' Union, Collins 1970)

Hopkins, Harry, *The Long Affray. The Poaching Wars 1760–1914* (London, Macmillan 1986)

Hoppit, Julian, *A Land of Liberty? England 1689–1727* (Oxford, Oxford University Press 2002)

Hornblower, S, and A Spawforth, eds., *Oxford Companion to Classical Civilization* (Oxford, Oxford University Press 2004)

Hornby, Nick, *Fever Pitch* (London, Gollancz 1992)

Hornung, E W, *Fathers of Men* (London, Smith, Elder & Co 1912)

Horsley, J E, *Jottings about Old Time Penrith* (Penrith, Reed's Printers 1926)

Hoskins, W G, *Devon* (London, Collins 1954)

Hoskins, W G, *The Making of the English Landscape* (1955. Harmondsworth, Penguin 1979)

Hoskins, W G, *Old Devon* (Newton Abbot, David & Charles 1966)

Hoskins, W G, *One Man's England* (London, BBC 1978)

Hotten, J C, *A Dictionary of Modern Slang* (London, J C Hotten 1860)

Hovell, Mark, *The Chartist Movement* (1918. Manchester, Manchester University Press 1966)

Howard, Ebenezer, *Garden Cities of Tomorrow* (London, Swan Sonnenschein 1898)

Howgrave, Francis, *An Essay of the Ancient and Present State of Stamford* (Stamford, W Thompson 1726)

Hudson, Derek, *Munby. Man of Two Worlds. Life and Diaries of Arthur J Munby 1828–1910* (London, Abacus 1974)

Hudson, Kerry, *Lowborn. Growing Up, Getting Away, and Returning to Britain's Poorest Towns* (London, Chatto & Windus 2019)

Huggins, Mike, *Horseracing and the British 1919–1939* (Manchester, Manchester University Press 2003)

Huggins, Mike, *The Victorians and Sport* (London, Hambledon 2004)

Huggins, Mike, 'Sport and the British Upper Classes c. 1500-2000', *Sport in History* 28, 3, 2008

Hughes, Thomas, *Tom Brown's Schooldays* (1857. Oxford, Oxford University Press 1999)

Huizinga, Johan, *Homo Ludens* (Haarlem, Willink 1938)

Hulsker, Jan, *The Complete Van Gogh. Paintings, Drawings, Sketches* (Oxford, Phaidon 1980)

Humanitus, *Stamford Bull Running* (Peterborough, Robertson 10 November 1830) handbill

Hume, David, *History of England* (1778. Indianapolis, Liberty Fund 1983) vol. vi

Humphreys, R, *Tate Companion to British Art* (London, Tate 2001)

Humphries, Jane, *Childhood and Child Labour in the British Industrial Revolution* (Cambridge, Cambridge University Press 2011)

Hunt, B, *Northumbrian Goalfields* (Northern League 1989)

Hunt, C J, *The Lead Miners of the Northern Pennines* (Manchester, Manchester University Press 1970)

Hunt, Henry, *Memoirs of Henry Hunt Esq, Written by Himself, In His Majesty's Jail at Ilchester* (London, Dolby 1820) 3 vols.

Hunt, Tristram, *Building Jerusalem. The Rise and Fall of the Victorian City* (New York, Metropolitan Books 2005)

Hunter, Lisa, Wayne Smith, and Elke Emerald, eds., *Pierre Bourdieu and physical culture* (London, Routledge 2015)

Hunter, Sir Robert, *The Preservation of Open Spaces and of footpaths and other rights of way* (London, Eyre & Spottiswood 1896)

Hurd, Clarissa, 'An Address to Women: or, How to Make Home Happy' (Demerara 1862)

Hutchins, B L, and A Harrison, *A History of Factory Legislation* (1903. London, Frank Cass 1971)

Hutchinson, Roger, *The Toon. A Complete History of Newcastle United FC* (Edinburgh, Mainstream 1997)

Hutchinson, William, *View of Northumberland* (Newcastle, Charnley, and Vesey & Whitfield 1778)

Hutchinson, William, *The History of the County of Cumberland* (1794–97. Wakefield, E P Publishing 1974)

Hutton, Ronald, *The Stations of the Sun. A History of the Ritual Year in Britain* (Oxford, Oxford University Press 1996)

Huxley, Aldous, *Crome Yellow* (1921. London, Vintage 1994)

Huxley, Aldous, *Brave New World* (1932. London, Vintage 2014)

Inglis, K, *Churches and the Working Classes in Victorian England* (London, Routledge 1974)

Inglis, Simon, *Engineering Archie* (English Heritage 2007)

Iredale, Dinah, *Bondagers. The History of Women Farmworkers in Northumberland and S E Scotland* (Glendale Local History Society 2008)

Ireland, Jonathan, *The Street Preacher. An Autobiography* (London, John Dickenson, nd, 1886?)

Ireland, Sam, 'Captain Barclay' in *Graphic Illustrations of Hogarth* (London 1799) vol. ii, p.122

Isaac, Rhys, *The Transformation of Virginia 1740–1790* (Chapel Hill, University of North Carolina Press 1982)

Ito, Kota, 'Municipalization of Memorials: Progressive Politics and the Commemoration Schemes of the LCC 1889-1907', *London Journal* 42, 3, 2017

Itzkin, Elissa S, 'The Halevy Thesis A Working Hypothesis? *Church History* 44, 1, 1975

Itzkowitz, David, *Peculiar Privilege. A Social History of English Foxhunting 1753–1885* (Hassocks, Harvester 1977)

J Y, *The Coloured Evangelist or, a sketch of the life and work of Samuel J C Edwards of West Indies* (Manchester, Matthews 1884)

Jackson, Brian, and Dennis Marsden, *Education and the Working Class* (London, Routledge, Kegan Paul 1962)

Jackson, N. Lane ('Pa'), *Sporting Days and Sporting Ways* (London, Hurst & Blackett 1932)

Jacobs, Barbara, *The Dick, Kerr Ladies* (London, Robinson 2004)

Jaffe, J A, 'The Chiliasm of Despair reconsidered: revivalism and working-class agitation', *Journal of British Studies* 28, (1), 1989

James, C L R, *Beyond a Boundary* (London, Stanley Paul 1963)

James, Clive, *Unreliable Memoirs* (1980. London, Picador 2004)

James, Gary, and Dave Day, 'The Emergence of an Association Football Culture in Manchester 1840-84', *Sport in History* 34, 1, 2014

Jardine, Lisa, *Going Dutch. How England Plundered Holland's Glory* (London, Harper 2008)

Jarrett, John, *Byker to Broadway. The Fighting Life and Times of Seaman Tommy Watson* (Whitley Bay, Bewick Press 1997)

Jeffries, Richard, *Hodge and his Masters* (1880. London, Eyre & Spottiswoode 1949)

Jenkins, J Gilbert, *A History of the Parish of Penn* (London, St. Catherine's Press 1935)

Jenks, Edward, *Stephen's Commentaries on the Laws of England* (London, Butterworth 1922)

Jennings, Sir Ivor, *The Queen's Government* (1934. Harmondsworth, Penguin 1961)

Jerome, Jerome K, *Three Men in a Boat. To say nothing of the Dog* (1889. London, J M Dent 1952)

Jerram, Leif, *Streetlife. The untold history of Europe's Twentieth Century* (Oxford, Oxford University Press 2011)

Johnes, Martin, and Matthew Taylor, 'Boxing in History', *Sport in History* 31, 4, 2011

Johnson, Alan, *This Boy. Memoir of a Childhood* (London, Transworld 2014)

Johnson, Nevil, *In Search of the Constitution* (Oxford, Pergamon 1977)

Johnson, R W, *The Making of the Tyne. A Record of 50 Years Progress* (London, Walter Scott 1895)

Johnson, W, *Eton Reform* (London, Longman, Green 1861)

Johnston, Alexandra F and Wim Husken, eds., *English Parish Drama* (Amsterdam, Rodopi 1996)

Johnston, Ronnie and Arthur McIvor, 'Dangerous Work, Hard Men...Masculinity in Clydeside Heavy Industries 1930s–70s', *Labour History Review* 69, 2, August 2004

Jollie, F, *Jollie's Sketch of Cumberland Manners and Customs partly in the Provincial Dialect, in Prose and Verse* (1796. Beckermet Bookshop, 1974)

Jones, Colin, *The Smile Revolution in 18c Paris* (Oxford, Oxford University Press 2014)

Jones, Gareth Stedman, *Languages of Class. Studies in English Working Class History 1832–1982* (Cambridge, Cambridge University Press 1983)

Jones, Gareth Stedman, 'The Redemptive Power of Violence? Carlyle, Marx and Dickens', *History Workshop Journal* 65, (2008)

Jones, Owen, *Chavs. The Demonization of the Working Class* (London, Verso 2012)

Jones, Rhian, 'Symbol, Ritual and Popular Protest in early 19th century Wales: Scotch Cattle Rebranded', *Welsh History Review* 26, I, 2012.

Jones, Rosemary, 'Women, Community and Collective Action: the Ceffyl Pren', in Angela John ed., *Our Mother's Land. Chapters in Welsh Women's History 1830–1939* (Cardiff, University of Wales Press 1991)

Jones, Tobias, *Ultra. The Underworld of Italian Football* (London, Head of Zeus 2020)

Jones-Baker, Doris, *Old Hertfordshire Calendar* (Chichester, Phillimore 1974)

Joyce, Patrick, *Visions of the People* (Cambridge, Cambridge University Press 1991)

Joyce, Patrick, *Democratic Subjects* (Cambridge, Cambridge University Press 1994)

Joyce, Patrick, *The Rule of Freedom. Liberalism and the Modern City* (London, Verso 2003)

Joyce, Patrick, *State of Freedom. A Social History of the British State since 1800* (Cambridge, Cambridge University Press 2013)

Joyce, Patrick, 'The Journey West', *Field Day Review* (University of Notre Dame 2014)

Jubb, Rev. Arthur, *The Life Story of Albert Shakesby. A converted athlete* (Hull, Burtt Bros 1906)

Kamm, Josephine, *How Different from Us. A biography of Miss Buss and Miss Beale* (London, Bodley Head 1958)

Katzer, Nikolaus, 'Soviet physical culture', in Tomlinson et al., eds., *Sport and the Transformation of Modern Europe* (London, Routledge 2011)

Kay, Joyce, '"It Wasn't Just Emily Davison!" Sport, Suffrage and Society in Edwardian Britain', *International Journal of the History of Sport* 25, 10, September 2008

Keating, Frank, *Sporting Century* (London, Robson Books 1997)

Keeble, N H, *Richard Baxter. Puritan Man of Letters* (Oxford, Clarendon Press 1982)

Keegan, John, *The Face of Battle* (1976. Dorset Press, USA 1986)

Keeton, G W, *The Norman Conquest and the Common Law* (London, Ernest Benn 1966)

Keir, D L, *Constitutional History of Modern Britain since 1485* (1938. London, A & C Black 1969)

Kelman, John, *Prophets of Yesterday. And their Message for Today* (London, Hodder & Stoughton 1924)

Kendall, C, *Life of the Rev W Sanderson, Primitive Methodist* (London, G Lamb 1875)

Kendall, Rev. H B, *The Origin and History of the Primitive Methodist Church* (London, Edwin Dalton 1905) 2 vols.

Kent, John, *Holding the Fort. Studies in Victorian Revivalism* (London, Epworth Press 1978)

Kerrigan, Colm, 'Teachers and the origins of elementary school football', *History of Education* 29, 6, 2000

Kerrigan, Colm, 'Missing men and missing evidence', *Soccer & Society* 10, 6, November 2009

Kerrigan, Colm, 'Athleticism and Elementary School Football Associations', *International Journal of the History of Sport* 29, 18, December 2012

Key, Rev. Robert, *The Gospel Among the Masses* (London, R Davies 1872)

Kidambi, Prashant, *Cricket Country. An Indian Odyssey in the Age of Empire* (Oxford, Oxford University Press 2019)

Kipperman, Mark, 'Shelly Becomes a Romantic', *Nineteenth Century Literature* 42, September 1992

King, Peter, 'The Rise of Juvenile Delinquency in England 1740–1840', *Past & Present* 160, August 1998

King, M and R, *Street Games of North Shields Children* (Tynemouth, Priory Press 1926, 1930)

King, W M, 'Hugh Price Hughes and the British "Social Gospel"', *Journal of Religious History* 13, 1984

Kirkup, ` Mike, *Pit Ponies* (Newcastle, Summerhill 2008)

Kitching, Gavin, 'The Origins of Football', *History Workshop Journal* 79, 1, February 2015: https://doi.org/10.1093/hwj/dbu023

Klemperer, Victor, *The Diaries 1942–45* (London, Weidenfeld & Nicolson 1999)

Knights, Ben, 'Men from the Boys: Writing on the Male Body', *Literature & History* 3, 13, i, Spring 2004

Knox, V, *Winter Evenings, or, Lucubrations on life & letters* (New York, Duyckinck 1805)

Knudsen, K A, *A Text Book of Gymnastics* (London, Wm Heinemann 1920)

Korr, Charles, *West Ham United. The making of a football club* (Urbana, University of Illinois Press 1986)

Koven, Seth, *Slumming. Sexual and Social Politics in Victorian London* (Princeton, Princeton University Press 2005)

Kramer, D, ed., *The Cambridge Companion to Thomas Hardy* (Cambridge, Cambridge University Press 2005)

Krasnoff, Lindsay, 'Resurrecting the nation: the evolution of French sports policy', in Tomlinson et al., eds., *Sport and the Transformation of Modern Europe* (London, Routledge 2011)

Kynaston, David, *Austerity Britain 1945–51* (London, Bloomsbury 2007)

Lancaster, Bill, 'Sociability and the City', in Robert Colls and Bill Lancaster, eds., *Newcastle upon Tyne. A Modern History* (Chichester, Phillimore 2001)

Land Rover Burghley Horse Trials, programme, 7–10 September 2006: 'The Equestrian Social Event of the Year'

Langford, Paul, *A Polite and Commercial People. England 1727–1783* (Oxford, Clarendon Press 1989)

Langford, Paul, *Englishness Identified. Manners and Character 1650–1850* (Oxford, Oxford University Press 2000)

Langford, Paul, ed., Introduction, *The Eighteenth Century 1688–1815* (Oxford, Oxford University Press 2002)

Langley, Rev. A P, Vicar, *Annals of Olney* (Olney, Lyon & Knight 1892)

Laslett, Peter, *The World We Have Lost* (London, Methuen 1971)

Latimer, John, *The Annals of Bristol in the 18th Century* (for the author, Bristol 1893)

Laver, James, 'Old Boxing Prints', *The Antique Collector*, January 1939, pp.350–2, 364

Lawrence, D H, *Sons and Lovers* (1913. Harmondsworth, Penguin 1965)

Lawrence, Jon, *'Speaking for the People'. Party, Language and Popular Politics in England 1867–1914* (Cambridge, Cambridge University Press 1998)

Lawrence, Jon, *Me, Me, Me: the search for community in post-war England* (Oxford, Oxford University Press 2019)

Lawson's Tyneside Celebrities (Newcastle upon Tyne, W D Lawson 1873)

Le Bon, Gustave, *The Crowd. A Study of the Popular Mind* (London, Fisher Unwin 1896)

Le Carre, John, *A Perfect Spy* (London, Hodder & Stoughton 1986)

Leach, Arthur F, *A History of Winchester College* (London, Duckworth 1899)

Leach, Jonathan, *Morris Dancing in Abingdon to 1914* (Eynsham, Chandler 1987)

Lee, John, *Wrestling in the North Country* (Consett, Ramsden Williams 1953)

Lee, J, 'Crouch End', 'A National Game for Girls as for Boys', *International Journal of the History of Sport* 24, 11, 2007

Lee, Robert, *Unquiet Country. Voices of the Rural Poor 1820–80* (Macclesfield, Windgather Press 2005)

Leese, Rev. David, 'Images of Methodism. W H Y Titcomb: an artist of faith', *Heritage*, Journal of East Midlands WHS 7, 1, 2005

Lefebure, Molly, *Cumberland Heritage* (nd)

Legg, Rodney, *Dorset Sporting Runs* (Tiverton, Halsgrove 2001)

Leicester YMCA, *Association Echoes* (October 1888, March 1897)

Leighton, James, *Duncan Edwards. The Greatest* (London, Simon & Schuster 2012)

Lenton, John, 'John Wesley and the Travelling Preachers', *Bulletin* of John Rylands University Library of Manchester 85, 2003

Levenson, Cyra, et al., 'Haptic Blackness: the double life of an 18th century bust', *British Art Studies* i, Autumn 2015, YCBA online

Lever, Janet, *Soccer Madness* (Chicago, University of Chicago Press 1984)

Levett, Geoffrey, 'Degenerate days: colonial sports tours and British manliness 1900–10', *Sport in History* 38, 1, 2018

Levi, Leone, *Our Workmen* (Newcastle, M & M W Lambert 1868), paper read to *Newcastle Literary & Philosophical Society* 1868

Lewis, Wyndham, *Tarr* (1918. Oxford University Press 2010)

Lewis-Stempel, *John, Six Weeks* (London, Orion Books 2011)

Lidgett, Thomas L, *The Life of Thomas L Lidgett As Written by Himself* (Lincoln, Chronicle Office 1908)

Liebling, A J, *The Sweet Science* (1951. New York, North Point Press 2004)

Lindsay, J, *Death of the Hero. French Painting 1780–1830* (London, Studio 1960)

Litherland, Benjamin, 'Sporting Entertainments, Discarded Possibilities and the Case of Football as Variety Sport 1905-06', *Sport in History* 35, 2015

Lloyd, Alan, *The Great Prize Fight* (London, Cassell 1977)

Lobban, Michael, *The Common Law and English Jurisprudence 1760–1850* (Oxford, Clarendon Press 1991)

Logan, Joyce, 'Blackpool. A miner's daughter reflects on her first visit in 1930', R Turner and A Wingfield, Introduction, *North West Labour History* 38, 2013

London Antiquary, (A) *A Dictionary of Modern Slang, Cant and Vulgar Words* (London, J C Hotten 1860)

London, Jack, *The People of the Abyss* (1903. London, Journeyman Press 1980)

London, Jack, *The Game* (New York, Macmillan 1905)

Lopez, Sue, *Women on the Ball* (London, Scarlet Press 1997)

Loveless, George, *The Victims of Whiggery* (London, Central Dorchester Committee, 1837)

Lover of Freedom, *Poetical Remarks on the Game Laws showing how far they are Badges of Slavery and inconsistent with Real Liberty* (London, T N Longman 1791)

Lowe, Emma, 'Trade Unionism and Labour Representation' (Englesea Brook, Chapel and Museum 2008)

Lowe-Lauri, Richard, 'Bull by the Horns', *History Today* 62, 10, October 2012

Lowerson, J, *Sport and the English Middle Classes* (Manchester, Manchester University Press 1993)

Lowth, Robert, *Billesdon Coplow Hunt 24 February 1800* (Melton Mowbray, Clementson 1800)

Lubenow, W C, 'Lytton Strachey's *Eminent Victorians*', in M Taylor and M Wolff, eds, *The Victorians since 1901* (Manchester, Manchester University Press 2004)

Lyles, Albert M, *Methodism Mocked. The Satiric Reaction to Methodism in the 18c* (London, Epworth Press 1960)

Lynch, Bohun, *The Prize Ring, illustrated by Reproductions of Old Prints, Several Oil Paintings, and of the famous Byron Screen* (London, Country Life 1925)

Lynch, Kevin, *Image of the City* (Cambridge, Massachusetts Institute of Technology 1960)

Lysons, Daniel and Samuel, *Magna Britannia Cambridgeshire* (1808. Wakefield, E P, 1978)

MacAloon, J J, *This Great Symbol. Pierre de Coubertin and the Origins of the Modern Olympic Games* (1983. London, Routledge 2008)

Macdonald, Murdo, *Scottish Art* (London, Thames & Hudson 2000)

MacDonald, David, 'Sport, History and the Historical profession', in Edelman and Wilson, eds., *Sports History* (New York, Oxford University Press 2017)

Macdonell, A G, *England, their England* (1933. London, Pan 2017)

MacFarlane, Charles, *The Great Battles of the British Army* (London, Geo Routledge 1854)

MacFarlane, Charles, *Life of the Duke of Wellington* (London, Geo Routledge 1886)

Machell, Hugh, *John Peel. Famous in Sport and Song* (London, Heath Cranton 1926)

Mackenzie, Eneas, *A Descriptive and Historical Account of the Town and County of Newcastle upon Tyne inc the Borough of Gateshead* (Newcastle, Mackenzie & Dent 1827)

MacKenzie, John, *The Empire of Nature. Hunting, Conservation and British Imperialism* (Manchester, Manchester University Press 1988)

Mackenzie, Scott, 'Stock the Parish with Beauties'. Henry Fielding's Parochial Vision, *Modern Languages Association* 125, 3, May 2010

Maclean, John, *Parochial and Family History of the Parish and Borough of Bodmin* (London, Nichols & Sons 1870)

MacMillan, Margaret, *Women of the Raj* (London, Thames & Hudson 1988)

Macrae, Elidh, *Exercise in the Female Life Cycle in Britain* (London, Palgrave 2016)

Magnus, Laurie, *Jubilee Book of the Girls' Public Day School Trust 1873–1923* (Cambridge, Cambridge University Press 1923)

Magriel, Paul, ed., *The Memoirs of the Life of Daniel Mendoza* (1808. London, Batsford 1951)

Maguire, T Miller, *The Development of Tactics since 1866* (London, Hugh Rees 1904)

Maguire, T Miller, *The British Army under Wellington 1813–14* (London, Wm Clowes 1907)

Mahomet, Albert John, Evangelist, *From Street Arab to Pastor* (Fakenham, Miller 1894)

Mailer, Norman, 'Punching Papa', *New York Review of Books*, 1 February 1963

Maine, Rev. L G, *Two Lectures on The History and Antiquities of Stanford-in-the-Vale, Berks* (Oxford, James Parker 1866)

Malcolmson, R W, *Popular Recreations in English Society 1700–1850* (Cambridge, Cambridge University Press 1973)

Malekow, H L, *Gothic Images of Race in 19c Britain* (Stanford, Stanford University Press 1996)

Mallett, Ashley, 'Lords of the Bush', *The Cricketer*, December 1997.

Malpass, Peter, 'Rebuilding Byker': report, University of Edinburgh 1975–76

Manders, F W D, *A History of Gateshead* (Gateshead Corporation 1973)

Mandle, W F, *The GAA and Irish Nationalist Politics 1884–1924* (Dublin, Macmillan 1987)

Mandler, Peter, 'Revisiting the Olden Time', in T C String and M Bull, eds., *Tudorism. Historical Imagination and the Appropriation of the Sixteeenth Century* (Oxford, Oxford University Press 2011)

Mangan, J A, *Athleticism in the Victorian and Edwardian Public School* (1981. London, Routledge 2000)

Mangan, J A, 'Missing men: schoolmasters and the early years of Association Football', *Soccer & Society* 9, 2, April 2008

Marchand, Leslie, ed., *Byron's Letters and Journals* (London, John Murray 1973) 12 vols.

Markham, *The Nineteen Hundreds, being the story of the Buckinghamshire towns of Wolverton and Stony Stanford 1900–11* (Buckingham, Markham 1951)

Markovits, Stefanie, *The Crimean War in the British Imagination* (Cambridge, Cambridge University Press 2009)

Marquess of Queensberry, *The Sporting Queensberrys* (London, Hutchinson 1942)

Marshall, J D, and Walton, J K, *The Lake Counties from 1830 to the mid 20th Century* (Manchester, Manchester University Press 1981)

Martin, Simon, 'Bikila's aria: the 1960 Rome Olympics', in Tomlinson, et al., eds., *Sport and the Transformation of Modern Europe* (London, Routledge 2011)

Martin, Simon, *Sport Italia. The Italian Love Affair with Sport* (London, I B Tauris 2011)

Martin, William, *The Book of Sport, Athletic Exercises and Amusements* (London, Darton & Clark 1837)

Martin, William, *The Book of Sports* (London, Darton 1857)

Marx, Karl, Inaugural Address of the International Working Men's Association', October 1864, in D Fernbach, ed., *The First International and After* (Harmondsworth, Penguin & New Left Review 1974)

Marx, Karl, *Capital. A Critique of Political Economy* (1867. 1886 English edition. New translation: Harmondsworth, Penguin and London, New Left Review 1976)

Marx, Karl, 'The English Ten Hours Bill', for *Neue Rheinische Zeitung*, in Marx & Engels, *Collected Works* (London, Lawrence & Wishart 1978) vol. x

Mason, Tony, *Association Football and English Society 1863–1915* (Sussex, Harvester 1980)

Mason, Tony, ed., *Sport in Britain. A Social History* (Cambridge, Cambridge University Press 1989)

Mason, Tony, 'Football', in Mason ed., *Sport in Britain. A Social History* (Cambridge, Cambridge University Press 1989)

Mason, Tony, and E Riedi, *Sport and the Military. The British Armed Forces 1880–1960* (Cambridge, Cambridge University Press 2010)

Mason, William, *A Primitive Methodist Soldier in the British Army* (Leeds, James Strafford 1877)

Masterman, C E G, *The Condition of England* (London, Edward Arnold 1911)

Masters, Charles Walter, 'Rugby, Football and the Working Classes in Victorian and Edwardian York', *Borthwick Paper*, 123 & 124, 2014

Matthew, Colin, *The Nineteenth Century* (Oxford, Oxford University Press 2000)

Maurice, F D, *Learning and Working* (1855. Oxford, University of Hull 1968)

Mauss, Marcel, *The Gift. The form and reason for exchange in archaic societies* (1950. London, Routledge 2002)

Maxwell, William Hamilton, *Hill-Side and Border Sketches* (London, Bentley 1847) 2 vols.

May, Allyson N, *The Fox-Hunting Controversy 1781–2004. Class and Cruelty* (Farnham, Ashgate 2013)

May, Jonathan, *Mde Bergman-Osterberg* (London, Harrap 1969).

Mayhew, Henry, *London Labour and the London Poor*, select edition 1851. (Oxford, Oxford University Press 2010)

Maynard, Rev. John, *From Prison to Pulpit: The life story of the late Rev J Maynard. A Pioneer of the Primitive Methodist Connexion and Minister of the Gospel nearly 60 years* (Bingley, Harrison *c.* 1896)

McConnell II, James E, 'The Character of Methodism in George Eliot's Adam Bede', *Methodist History* 45, 4, 2007

McCormack M, ed., *Public Men. Masculinity and Politics in Modern Britain* (Basingstoke, Palgrave 2007)

McCreery, Cindy, *The Satirical Gaze. Prints of Women in Late 18c England* (Oxford, Clarendon Press 2004)

McCrone, Kathleen, *Playing the game. Sport and the Physical Education of English Women* (London, Routledge 1988)

McCrum, Robert, 'Alpha Mailer', *The Observer*, 4 February 2007

McDonald, David, 'Sports History and the Historical Profession', in Edelman and Wilson, eds., *Handbook Sports History* (New York, Oxford University Press 2017)

McKibbin, Ross, 'Working Class Gambling in Britain 1880-1939', *Past & Present* 82, February 1979

McKibbin, Ross, 'Work and Hobbies in Britain 1880-1950', in J Winter, ed., *The Working Class in Modern British History. Essays in Honour of Henry Pelling* (Cambridge, Cambridge University Press 1983)

McKibbin, Ross, *Classes and Cultures 1918–51* (Oxford, Oxford University Press 1998)

McKibbin, Ross, 'Class, Politics, Money: British Sport since the First World War', *20th Century British History* 13, 2, 2002

McKibbin, Ross, 'Sports History: Status, Definitions, and Meanings', *Sport in History* 31, 2, 2011

McKibbin, Ross, *Democracy and Political Culture. Studies in Modern British History* (Oxford, Oxford University Press 2019)

Mee, Arthur, ed., *The King's England. Leicestershire and Rutland* (1937. Rotherham, King's Press 1997)

Melling, Althea, 'Ray of the Rovers', The Working-Class Heroine in Popular Football Fiction 1915–25', *International Journal of the History of Sport* 15, i, 1998

Melling, Althea, '"Plucky Lasses", "Pea Soup" and Politics: the roles of ladies' football during the 1921 miners' lock-out in Wigan and Leigh', *International Journal of the History of Sport* 16, i, 1999

Mellon, Paul, *Bequest: Treasures of a Lifetime* (New Haven, YCBA 2001)

Mellor, Gavin, 'Football Crowds in NW England 1946-62', *Sports Historian* 19, 2, 1999

Mendoza, Daniel, *Memoirs of the Life of Daniel Mendoza* (1808. London 1816)

Mess, H A, *Factory Legislation and Its Administration 1891–1924* (London, P S King 1926)

Mess, H A, *Industrial Tyneside. A Social Survey* (London, Ernest Benn 1928)

Metcalfe, Alan, 'Organized Sport in the Mining Communities of South Northumberland 1800-1889', *Victorian Studies* 25, 4, 1982

Metcalfe, Alan, 'Sport and Space. A Case Study of the Growth in Recreational Facilities in East Northumberland 1850-1914', *International Journal of the History of Sport* 7, 3, 1990

Metcalfe, Alan, *Leisure and Recreation in a Victorian Mining Community* (London, Routledge 2006)

Middleton, Iris M, 'Origins of English Fox Hunting and the Myth of Hugo Meynell and the Quorn', *Sport in History* 25, i, 2005

Middleton, W H, *Willie Long. The Fisherman Evangelist* (London, Epworth Press 1950)

Milburn, Geoffrey E, 'H B Kendall's Origin and History of the Primitive Methodist Church', *Proceedings WHS* 50, 1995

Milburn, T A, *Life and Times in Weardale 1840–1910* (High House Chapel, Weardale Museum 1989)

Miles, Henry Downes, *Pugilistica* (Edinburgh, John Grant 1906)

Mill, John Stuart, *Coleridge* (1840), in J M Robson, ed., *Collected Works*, vol. x (Toronto, University of Toronto Press 1969)

Mill, John Stuart, *On Liberty* (1859. Harmondsworth, Penguin 1981)

Miller, S G, *Ancient Greek Athletics* (New Haven, Yale University Press 2004)

Mills, Dennis, 'The Poor Laws and the distribution of population 1600-1800', *Transactions of the Institute of British Geographers* 26, 1959

Mills, Dennis and Brian Short, 'The Use of the Open-Closed Village Model', in Mick Reed and Roger Wells, eds., *Class, Conflict and Protest in the English Countryside 1700–1880* (London, Frank Cass 1990)

Milne, Graeme, *North East England 1850–1914* (Woodbridge, Boydell 2006)

Mitchell, Ena, *Notes on the History of Parker's Piece, Cambridge* (Cambridge, Mitchell 1985)

Mitchell, Rosemary, *Picturing the Past. English History in Text and Image 1830–70* (Oxford, Oxford University Press 2000)

Mitchell, Thomas, *Christian Manhood . . . biographical sketches of Rev R S Blackburn, Missionary to Fernando Po, West Africa* (London, John Dickenson, nd)

Mitchell, William Cranmer, *History of Sunderland* (Sunderland, Hills Press 1919)

Mitchell, W R, *Men of Lakeland* (London, Phoenix House 1966)

Mitchell, W R, *The John Peel Story* (Lancaster, Dalesman 1968)

Mitford, Mary Russell, *Selected Stories from Our Village* (1824–32. London, Blackie, nd, 1916?)

Moffatt, F C, *Northern Sportsman* (Newcastle, Moffatt 1999)

Monkwearmouth Wesleyan Sabbath Schools, *Narrative of Facts relative to The Expulsion of Officers, Teachers & Scholars from the above Institution on April 27, 1851* (Bishopwearmouth, Jos Huntley 1851)

Moore, Henrietta, 'The problem of explaining violence in the social sciences', in P Harvey and P Gow, eds., *Sex and Violence. Issues in Representation and Experience* (London, Routledge 1994)

More, Hannah [anon], *Black Giles, The Poacher: with some account of A Family who had rather live by their Wits than their Work* (London, Cheap Repository for Moral & Religious Tracts 1820)

Moritz, C P, *Travels in England* (1782. London, Cassell 1886)

Morgan, Marjorie, *Manners, Morals, and Class in England 1774–1858* (Basingstoke, Macmillan 1994)

Morgan, N J, and A Pritchard, *Power and Politics at the Seaside. The development of Devon's resorts in the 20c* (Exeter, University of Exeter Press 1999)

Morgan, R C, *The Life of Richard Weaver. The converted collier* (London, Morgan & Chase, nd, 1860s?)

Morley, Charles, *Studies in Board Schools* (London, Smith, Elder 1897)

Morris, Jan (James), 'Patriotism', *Encounter*, January 1962

Morris, William, *News from Nowhere or, An Epoch of Rest* (1890. London, Longman's Green 1910)

Morrison, J, *Painting the Nation. Identity and Nationalism in Scottish Painting 1800–1920* (Edinburgh, Edinburgh University Press 2003)

Mosse, George, *Masses and the Man: Nationalist and Fascist Perceptions of Reality* (New York, Howard Fertig 1980)

Mott, Frank Luther, *History of American Magazines 1830–1865* (Cambridge, MA, Harvard University Press 1938)

Mount, Ferdinand, *The British Constitution Now* (London, Heinemann 1992)

Mudie-Smith, Richard, ed., *Sweated Industries* (London, Daily News Exhibition Handbook 1906)

Mullin, Janet, *A Sixpence at Whist: Gaming and the English Middle Class 1680–1830* (Woodbridge, Boydell Press 2015)

Munkwitz, Erica, 'The Master is the Mistress: women and fox hunting as sports coaching in Britain', *Sport in History* 37, 4, 2017

Munsche, P B, *Gentlemen and Poachers. The English Game Laws 1671–1831* (Cambridge, Cambridge University Press 1981)

Murphy, Michael J, *Cambridge Newspapers and Opinion 1780–1850* (Cambridge, Oleander Press 1977)

Murray, A Victor, *A Northumbrian Methodist Childhood* (Morpeth, County Library 1992)

Murray, Nicholas, *Aldous Huxley. English Intellectual* (London, Little Brown 2002)

Muthesius, Stefan, *The English Terraced House* (New Haven, Yale University Press 1982)

Myrone, M, ed., *Gothic Nightmares. Fuseli, Blake, and the Romantic Imagination* (London, Tate 2006)

Nairn, Tom, *The Break-Up of Britain* (London, Verso 1981)

National Council of Labour Colleges, *Labour and Leisure* (NCLC, Tillicoultry 1944)

National Playing Fields Association, *Jubilee Handbook* (1953)

Naughton, W W, *Kings of the Queensberry Realm* (Chicago, Continental 1902)

Neeson, J M, *Commoners: common right, enclosure and social change in England* (Cambridge, Cambridge University Press 1996)

Nelson, Claudia, 'Sex and the Single Boy. Ideals of Manliness in Victorian Literature for Boys', *Victorian Studies* 32, 1989

Neuberg, V, ed., *Mayhew. London Labour and the London Poor* (Harmondsworth, Penguin 1985)

Neuheiser, Jorg, *Crown, Church, and Constitution: Popular Conservatism in England 1815–67* (Oxford, Berghahn 2016)

Nevill, Ralph, *Sporting Days and Sporting Ways* (London, Duckworth 1910)

Nevill, Ralph, *Connoisseur (The)* xii, 48, August 1948

Nevinson, Rev. C, *History of Stamford* (Stamford, Henry Johnson 1879)

Newcastle Architecture Workshop, 'Housing in Byker', 'Housing in Elswick', Newcastle City Council, nd (1974?)

Newcastle Sunday School Union, *Rules* (Newcastle, SSU 22 May 1816)

Newman, Gerald, *The Rise of English Nationalism. A Cultural History 1740–1830* (London, Weidenfeld & Nicolson 1987)

Newton, David and Martin Smith, *The Stamford Mercury* (Stamford, Tyas 1999)

Newton, Francis (E J Hobsbawm), *The Jazz Scene* (London, MacGibbon & Kee 1959)

Newton J. P., F W, *A Letter on The Game Laws advocating the repeal of them* (London, Jarrold & Son, nd, 1862?)

Newton, Rev. D, *True to Principle. The Story of John Kent. An Agricultural Labourer in the County of Norfolk* (London, Dickenson 1894)

Nichols, John, *The History and Antiquities of the County of Leicester* (London, John Nichols 1795) vol i., pt. i

Nichols, John, *The History and Antiquities of the County of Leicester, East Goscote Hundred* (London, John Nichols 1800) vol. iii, pt. i

Nicholson, William, *An Almanac of Twelve Sports. Words by Rudyard Kipling* (London, Wm Heinemann 1898)

Nicolson, Adam, *Earls of Paradise. England and the Dream of Perfection* (London, Harper Press 2008)

Nicolson, Adam, *The Gentry. Stories of the English* (London, Harper Press 2011)

Nicolson, Adam, *Men of Honour* (London, Harper Collins 2015)

Nightingale, Florence, *Notes on Matters affecting the Health, Efficiency and Hospital Administration of the British Army* (London, Harrison 1858) 2 vols.

Nightingale, Florence, *Hospitals and Patients* (HMSO 1880)

Nimrod [Charles James Apperley], *The Life of a Sportsman by Nimrod with 36 coloured illustrations by Henry Alken* (London, Rudolph Ackermann 1842)

Nimrod, *Nimrod's Hunting Reminiscences, comprising Memoirs of Masters of Hounds, Notices of the Crack Riders and Characteristics of the Hunting Countries of England* (1843. London, John Lane at The Bodley Head 1926)

Nimrod, *Nimrod's Hunting Tours interspersed with characteristic anecdotes, sayings, and doings of sporting men including notices of the Principal Crack Riders of England* (1903. London, The Bodley Head 1926)

Nimrod, *The Chace, The Road, and The Turf* (1837. London, The Bodley Head 1927)

Noel, Conrad, *Byways of Belief* (London, Frank Palmer, nd, 1912?)

Noel, Susan, ed., *Sportswoman's Manual* (London, Hutchinson 1950)

Norwood, Janice, 'Pugilists and Greasepaint. Theatrical Encounters with a Bare-knuckle Fighter and Pantomime Clown', *Nineteenth Century Theatre and Film* 36, 2, 2009, 63–73

Nott, James, *Going to the Palais. Dancing and Dance Halls in Britain 1918–60* (Oxford, Oxford University Press 2015)

Oastler, Richard, *Eight Letters to the Duke of Wellington*, in K E Carpenter, ed., *King of the Factory Children* (1835. New York, Amo 1972)

Oates, Joyce Carol, *On Boxing* (New York, Harper 2006)

Obelkevich, James, *Religion and Rural Society: South Lindsey 1825–75* (Oxford, Oxford University Press 1976)

'Old Boy, An', *Early Days at Uppingham under Edward Thring* (London, Macmillan 1904)

Oliver, Thomas, *A New Picture of Newcastle upon Tyne* (Newcastle, Oliver 1831)

Olsen, Stephanie, *Juvenile Nation. Youth, Emotions and the Making of the Modern British Citizen* (London, Bloomsbury 2014)

Onslow, R, *The Squire. George Alexander Baird 1861–93* (London, Harrap 1980)

Oriard, M, 'In the beginning was the Rule', in S W Pope, ed., *The New American Sports History* (Urbana, University of Illinois Press 1997)

Orwell, George, 'Boys' Weeklies' (*Horizon* 1940), in S. Orwell and I. Angus, *Collected Essays, Journalism and Letters of George Orwell*, vol. i, 1920–40 (Penguin, Harmondsworth 1970)

Osbaldeston, George, *Squire Osbaldeston: His Autobiography*, E D Cuming, ed. (1856. London, John Lane, The Bodley Head 1926)

Osborne, Carole and Fiona Skillen, 'The State of Play: Women in British Sport History', *Sport in History* 30, 2, 2010

Owen, Robert, *Two Rooms and a View* (Glasshoughton, Owen 2005)

Owen, Robert, *The Reyrolle Story* (Mappleton, Write Good Books 2007)

Page, William, ed., *Victoria History of the county of Rutland* (London, IHR 1908), and supplement, E D Cuming and E E Dorling 'Ancient and Modern Sport'.

Paget, Guy, *Sporting Pictures of England* (London, Collins 1945)

Paine, Thomas, *The Rights of Man* (1791–92. Penguin, Harmondsworth 1977)

Palmer, Major James, *Detail of the Line Movements prescribed in Part Four of His Majesty's Regulations for the British Army* (London, Military Library Whitehall 1812)

Palmer, W J, *The Tyne and its Tributaries* (London, George Bell 1882)

Palmer, W M, and Rev. H H McNeice, *Notes on Cambridgeshire Villages; no. 1, Melbourn* (*Cambridge Chronicle* 1925); *no. 2, Caxton* (1927)

Palmer Heathman, Katie, ' "Lift Up a Living Nation": Community and Nation, Socialism and Religion in *The English Hymnal* 1906', *Cultural and Social History*, online 25 February 2017

Parker, Claire, 'Swimming? The "Ideal" Sport for 19c British Women', *International Journal of the History of Sport* 27, 4, 2010

Parker, Peter, *The Old Lie, The Great War and the Public School Ethos* (London, Constable 1987)

Parkin, George, ed., *Edward Thring. Headmaster of Uppingham School. Life, Diary and Letters* (London, Macmillan 1900)

Parkinson, George, *True Stories of Durham Pit Life* (London, Chas H Kelly 1912)

Parrott, Rev. John, *A Digest of the History, Polity and Doctrines of the Primitive Methodists* (London, Lister 1866)

Pasquin, Peter, *A Day's Journal of a Sponge* (London, Rowney & Forster 1824)

Patrick, John, *Thoroughly Commonplace. A History of Teversham 1850–1900* (Cambridge, John Patrick 1996)

Patterson, A Temple, *Radical Leicester 1780–1850* (1954. Leicester, Leicester University Press 1975)

Patterson, W M, *Northern Primitive Methodism* (London, E Dalton 1909)

Patterson, W M, *Behind the Stars* (Queensland, Samuel Lee, 1911)

Paulin, Tom, *The Day Star of Liberty. William Hazlitt's Radical Style* (London, Faber & Faber 1998)

Pearce, Rev. Joseph, *Dinna Forget. A Souvenir of Primitive Methodist Soul Winning Personalities* (Leominster, Orphan's Press 1932)

Pears, Ian, 'Gentleman and Hero', in Roy Porter, ed, *Myths of the English* (Cambridge, Cambridge University Press 1994)

Pearson, Harry, *The Far Corner. A Mazy Dribble through North East Football* (London, Little, Brown 1994)

Pearson, Harry, *Racing Pigs and Giant Marrows. Travels around North Country Fairs* (1966. London, Abacus 1997).

Pearson, Harry, *Slipless in Settle. A Slow Turn Around Northern Cricket* (London, Abacus 2012)

Peatling, G R, 'Re-thinking the History of Criticism of Organized Sport', *Cultural and Social History* 2, 3, 2005

Peck, Rev. Francis, *The History of the Stamford Bull-Runnings: containing the Original and Progress of that Elegant Diversion* (Stamford, Baily & Thompson 1726?)

Peck, Rev. Francis, *Academia tertia Anglicana; or, the Antiquarian Annals of Stamford, in Lincoln, Rutland and Northampton Shires* (London, James Bettenham 1727)

Pedersen, J S, 'Enchanting Modernity. The Invention of Tradition at Two Women's Colleges in late 19c and early 20c Cambridge', *History of Universities* 17, 2002

Peel, George, *The Future of England* (London, Macmillan 1911)

Pemberton, Neil, 'The Burnley Dog War. The Politics of Dog-Walking and the Battle over Public Parks in Post-Industrial Britain', *20c British History* 28, 2, June 2017

Pendleton, John, *A History of Derbyshire* (London, Elliot Stock 1886)

Pennell-Elmhirst, Capt [Brooksby], *The Cream of Leicestershire. Eleven Seasons Skimmings; Notable Runs and Incidents of the Chase*, Portraits and Map by John Sturgess (London, Routledge 1883)

Perkin, Harold, *Origins of Modern English Society* (London, RKP 1986)

Petty, Rev. John, *The History of the Primitive Methodist Connexion from its origins to the Conference of 1859* (London, Richard Davies 1860)

Phillips, Grace W, *Smile, Bow and Pass On. A biography of an avant-garde headmistress Miss Iris M Brooks MA (Cantab)* (Phillips, printed by Acer 1980)

Phillpotts, Eden, *The Virgin in Judgement* (1908. London, Westaway Books 1949)

'Philotheos', 'A letter to the People called Methodists on their unscriptural mode of addressing God at their Prayer Meetings, with brief remarks on females speaking and praying in public' (Manchester 1826)

Physical Deterioration, Interdepartmental Committee (London, HMSO 1904) vol. i, cmnd. 2175.

Physick, Ray, 'Imagining Reality. Artistic Responses to the Commercialization of the Beautiful Game', in Daniel Haxall, ed., *Beautiful Game* (London, Bloomsbury 2018)

Phythian-Adams, Charles, *Continuity, Fields and Fission* (Leicester, Dept English Local History 1978)

Piaget, Jean, *The Language and Thought of the Child* (London, RKP 1926)

Pick, Daniel, *Faces of Degeneration. A European Disorder 1848–1918* (Cambridge, Cambridge University Press 1989)

Pickford, W, *A Few Recollections of Sport* (Bournemouth, Bournemouth Guardian 1939)

Pickstone, John V, *Ways of Knowing. A new history of Science, Technology and Medicine* (Manchester, Manchester University Press 2000)

Pierce, G A, and W A Wheeler, eds., *The Dickens Dictionary* (London, Chapman & Hall 1878)

Pinfold, John, 'Horse Racing and the Upper Classes in 19c', *Sport in History* 28, 3, 2008

Pittman, M A, ed., *Nimrod's Hunting Tours* (Philadelphia, Museum of Foreign Literature 1835)

Plomer, William, ed., *Kilvert's Diary. Selections from the Diary of Rev Francis Kilvert* (1938. London, Jonathan Cape 1969) vol. i, Jan 1870–19 Aug 1871

Podeschi, J B, *Books on the Horse and Horsemanship* (London, Tate, YCBA 1981)

Pollock, Maj. C E, 'Florence Nightingale' *Journal Royal Army Medical Corps* xv, October 1910

Pond, Allen, 'Beyond Memory's Reach: The Particularities of English Radicalism', *The Quarterly Review* (Winter 2008)

Poole, Robert, *Tyneside Memories* (Newcastle, Word of Mouth 1988)

Poole, Robert, 'The March to Peterloo. Politics and Festivity in late Georgian England', *Past & Present* 192, August 2006

Pooley, W. G, 'Native to the Past: History, Anthropology and Folklore in *Past & Present*', *Past & Present* 239, May 2019

Poovey, Mary, *Making a Social Body. British Cultural Formation 1830–1864* (Chicago, University of Chicago Press 1995)

Pope, S W, ed., *The New American Sports History* (Urbana, University of Illinois Press 1997)

Porter, Dilwyn, 'Sport and National identity', in Edelman and Wilson, *Handbook Sports History* (New York, Oxford University Press 2017)

Porter, Enid, *Cambridgeshire. Customs and Folklore* (London, RKP 1969)

Porteous, Crichton, *The Ancient Customs of Derbyshire* (Derby, Derbyshire Countryside 1976)

Porter, Roy, *Flesh in the Age of Reason* (New York, W W Norton 2004)

Postema, G J, *Bentham and the Common Law Tradition* (Oxford, Clarendon Press 1986)

Pounds, N J G, *A History of the English Parish* (Cambridge, Cambridge University Press 2000)

Powell, H C, ed., *Amateur Athletic Annual* (London, Simpkin Marshall 1879)

Powicke, Frederick J, *A Life of Rev Richard Baxter 1615–1691* (London, Jonathan Cape 1924)

Prettejohn, Elizabeth, *Beauty and Art 1750–2000* (Oxford, Oxford University Press 2005)

Price, John, *Everyday Heroism. Victorian Constructions of the Heroic Civilian* (London, Bloomsbury 2014)

Primitive Methodist Connexion, *Rules, Regulations, Arrangements and Orders for Sunday Schools* (no publisher, nd, PM Book Room? 1832?)

Primitive Methodist Connexion, *Rules for Members* (London, F H Hurd, nd, 1850?)

Primitive Methodist Local Preacher, *The Heroes of the Cross and the Champions of Infidelity Contrasted* (London, J B Cooke 1858)

Pritchard, Rev. J, *Memoirs of the Life, Literary and Itinerant Labours of Rev Philip Pugh* (London, George Lamb 1871)

Proctor, R W, *Our Turf, Our Stage, Our Ring* (Manchester, Dinham 1862)

'Professor, A', *Confessions of a Methodist*, (London, Samuel Tipper 1810)

Prothero, I, 'William Benbow and the concept of the General Strike', *Past & Present* 63, (1974).

Protherough, R, 'Shaping the Image of the Great Headmaster', *British Journal Educational Studies* xxxii, October 1984

Prown, Jules David, 'Style as Evidence', *Winterthur Portfolio* 15, Autumn 1980

Pryce, George, *A Popular History of Bristol, antiquarian, topographical, and descriptive* (Bristol, W Mack 1861)

Pugh, R B, ed., *Victoria History of the Counties of England. Leicestershire* (London, IHR, Oxford University Press 1955)

'Pupil of the late Tom Cribb', *The British Boxer; or Guide to Self Defence* (London, Winn 1850)

Queensberry, 10th Marquess, *The Sporting Queensberrys* (London, Hutchinson 1942)

Quennell, Peter ed., *Mayhew's London; being selections from 'London Labour and the London Poor' by Henry Mayhew (1851)* (London, Spring Books, nd, 1960s)

Quennell, Peter, ed., *London's Underworld*; being selections from 'Those That Will Not Work' by Henry Mayhew (1862) (London, SpringBooks 1966)

Quin, Gregory, N Bancel, and P Vonnard, *Building Europe with the Ball* (Bern, Peter Lang 2016)

Rack, Henry, 'James Crawfoot and the Magic Methodists', in Rack et al., *Four Lectures on the 150th Anniversary of the funeral of Hugh Bourne* (Methodist Chapel Aid Association 2002)

Radford, Peter, 'British Boxers and the Emergence of the National Sporting Hero at the Time of the Napoleonic Wars', *Identities* 12, 2, 2005

Rankin, Stuart et al., *Newcastle Central Station* (Newcastle, nd, 1986?)

Raven, Simon, 'Perish by the Sword', in H Thomas, ed., *The Establishment* (London, Anthony Blond 1959)

Rawnsley, H D, 'The True Story of "D'ye Ken John Peel"?', *Baily's Magazine of Sports and Pastimes* lxvii, March 1897

Ray, Gordon N, *The Illustrator and the Book in England from 1790 to 1914* (Pierpont Morgan Library, Oxford University Press 1976)

Readman, Paul, *Land and Nation in England* (Royal Historical Society, Boydell Brewer 2008)

Readman, Paul, and Matthew Cragoe, eds., *The Land Question in Britain 1750–1950* (Basingstoke, Palgrave Macmillan 2010)

Redmayne, Sir Richard, *Men, Mines, and Memories* (London, Eyre & Spottiswoode 1942)

Reeder, David, 'Predicaments of City Children', in Reeder, ed., *Urban Education in the 19c* (1977. Abingdon, Routledge 2018)

Rees, Rev. Arthur Augustus, 'Reasons for not cooperating in the alleged Sunderland Revivals in an address to his congregation' (Sunderland 1859)

Reeves, Richard, 'Society's Challenge to Build "Character"', *Prospect*, August 2008

Regis, Amber, ed., *The Memoirs of John Addington Symonds* (London, Palgrave Macmillan 2016)

Reid, D A, 'The Decline of St Monday 1766–1866', *Past & Present* 71, 1976

Reid, D A, 'Weddings, Weekdays, Work and Leisure. St Monday Re-visited', *Past & Present* 153, 1996.

Reid, D B, *Health of Towns Commission. Report on the State of Newcastle upon Tyne and other towns* (London, HMSO by W Clowes 1845)

Reid, J C, *Bucks and Bruisers. Pierce Egan and Regency England* (London, Routledge Kegan Paul 1971)

Remnick, David, *King of the World. Muhammad Ali and the Rise of an American Hero* (London, Picador 1998)

Renton, Alex, *Stiff Upper Lip. Secrets, Crimes, and the Schooling of a Ruling Class* (London, Weidenfeld & Nicolson 2017)

Reynolds, Sir Joshua, *Discourses delivered to the students of the Royal Academy* (1769. London, Seeley & Co 1905)

Reynolds, Margaret, 'In Chancery Again: Dickens and Prizefighting': *Dickens Studies Newsletter* 14, 2, June 1983

Rice, Margery Spring, *Working-Class Wives. Their Health and Conditions* (1939. London, Virago 1981)

Richardson, M. A, *The Local Historian's Table Book of remarkable occurrences* (Newcastle, M A Richardson 1843)

Riches, Adam, *Football's Comic Book Heroes* (London, Mainstream 2009)

Ridley, George, 'The Blaydon Races', Ms 1862, in *Allan's Illustrated Edition of Tyneside Songs* (1862. Newcastle, Frank Graham 1972)

Riedi, E, and T Mason, 'Leather and Fighting Spirit', *Canadian Journal of History* 41, Winter 2006

Riess, Steven, *Sport in Industrial America 1850–1920* (Wheeling, Ill, Harlan Davidson 1995)

Riley, Charlotte, 'Rethinking Modern British Studies', July 2015, *20c British History* 27, 2, June 2016

Ritson, Joseph, *The Romance of Primitive Methodism* (London, PM Publishing House 1909)

Rivers, Isabel, 'John Wesley and the Language of Scripture, Reason and Experience', *Prose Studies* 4, 3, 1981

Roberts, Henry, *The Dwellings of the Labouring Classes* (Exeter Hall, London, Society Improving Condition Labouring Classes 1850)

Robertson, J M, *The Saxon and the Celt* (London, University Press 1897)

Robertson, J M, *Patriotism and Empire* (London, Grant Richards 1899)

Robins, David, and Philip Cohen, *Knuckle Sandwich. Growing Up in the Working Class City* (Harmondsworth, Penguin 1978)

Robinson, Emily, 'Telling Stories about Post-War Britain: Popular Individualism and the Crisis of the 1970s', *20c British History* 28, 2, June 2017

Robinson, R, and J Gallagher, *Africa and the Victorians* (London, Macmillan 1961)

Robson, Edward R, *School Architecture. Practical remarks on the planning, designing, building and furnishing of school-houses* (London, John Murray 1874)

Rodger, N. A. M, *The Wooden World. An Anatomy of the Georgian Navy* (London, Fontana 1988)

Rodriguez, R G, *The Regulation of Boxing* (Jefferson NC, McFarland 2008)

Rogers, Alan, *The Making of Stamford* (Leicester, Leicester University Press 1965)

Rogers, Ben, *Beef and Liberty. Roast Beef, John Bull and the English Nation* (London, Vintage 2004)

Rogers, Hugh, *Bottisham Enclosed 1801* (Staine Hundred Local History Society 1992)

Rogers, Nicholas, *Crowds, Cultures and Politics in Georgian Britain* (Oxford, Oxford University Press 1998)

Rollinson, William, *A History of Man in the Lake District* (London, J M Dent 1967)

Roper, Lyndal, and Chris Whickham, '*Past & Present* After Fifty Years', *Past & Present* 176, August 2002

Roper, M and John Tosh, eds., *Manful Assertions. Masculinities in Britain since 1800* (London, Routledge 1991)

Rose, Jonathan, *The Intellectual Life of the British Working Classes* (New Haven, Yale University Press 2001)

Rose, Karen, Introduction, in Patrick Collinson, *The Puritan Character. Polemics and Polarities in Early 17th Century English Culture* (Berkeley, University of California Press 1989)

Rosman, Doreen M, *Evangelicals and Culture* (London, Croom Helm 1984)

Rotella, Carlo, *Good with Their Hands. Boxers, bluesmen, and other characters from the rust belt* (Berkeley, UCP 2002)

Rotella, Carlo, *Cut Time. An Education at the Fights* (Chicago, UCP 2005)

Rotella, Carlo, 'The Biggest Entertainer in Entertainment', Play Magazine, *New York Times*, 1 June 2008

Rouse, Paul, *Sport in Ireland. A History* (Oxford, Oxford University Press 2015)

Rowbottom, William, *William Rowbottom's Diary 1787–1789* (Oldham Education 1996) introduction by Michael Winstanley

Rowe, John, *Cornwall in the age of the Industrial Revolution* (1953. St. Austell, Cornish Hillside 1993)

Royal Society for the Prevention of Cruelty to Animals, *Annual Reports Newcastle Branch 1873–1883* (Newcastle, Cail Printers 1874)

Ruggles-Brise, Sir Evelyn, *The English Prison System* (London, Macmillan 1921)

Rule, John, 'Explaining Revivalism. The case of Cornish Methodism', *Southern History* 20–1, 1998–9

Runciman, W G, *Very Different but Much the Same: the evolution of English Society since 1714* (Oxford, Oxford University Press 2015)

Ruskin, John, *The Two Paths. Lecture 1: The Deteriorative Power of Conventional Art over Nations* (London, Kensington Museum January 1858)

Russell, Dave, R Cox, and W Vamplew, *Encyclopedia of British Football* (London, Cass & NFM 2002)

Russell, Dave, *Looking North. Northern England and the National Imagination* (Manchester, Manchester University Press 2004)

Russell, W H, *The British Expedition to the Crimea* (London, Routledge 1858)

Sadler, M E, *Report on Secondary and Higher Education in Derbyshire* (Derby, Bemrose 1905)

Sala, George Augustus, *Twice Round the Clock or the Hours of the Day and Night in London* (1858. Leicester, Leicester Univ Press 1971)

Salmon, Thomas, *South Shields: Its Past, Present and Future: being a lecture delivered at the Central Hall, South Shields on Wednesday 9 April 1856 to a crowded audience* (South Shields, Henry Hewison 1856)

Samuel, Raphael, 'Workshop of the World. Steam Power and Hand Technology in mid-Victorian Britain', *History Workshop Journal* 3, Spring 1977

Samuel, Raphael, ed., *People's History and Socialist Theory* (London, RKP 1981)

Samuel, Raphael, ed., *East End Underworld. Chapters in the Life of Arthur Harding* (London, Routledge Kegan Paul 1981) vol. ii

Sandbrook, Dominic, *The Great British Dream Factory* (London, Penguin 2015)

Sandbrook, Dominic, *Who Dares Wins. Britain 1979–1982* (London, Allen Lane 2019)

Sandiford, Keith, *Cricket and the Victorians* (Aldershot, Scolar 1994)

Sargent, Dudley A, *John L Sullivan, Life and Reminiscences of a 19c Gladiator, 'Champion of the World'* (London, Routledge 1892)

Sargent, W C, 'Young England at School', *The Ludgate Monthly* vi, Nov 1893–April 1894

Sassoon, Siegfried, *Memoirs of a Fox-Hunting Man* (London, Faber & Gwyer 1928)

Saul, William, *The Class-Meeting Manual* (London, Davies, Conference Offices 1863)

Savage, Mike, *Identities and Social Change in Britain since 1940* (Oxford, Oxford University Press 2010)

Savage, Jon, *Teenage. The creation of Youth 1875–1945* (London, Chatto & Windus 2007)

Savage, Jon, *1966. The Year the Decade Exploded* (London, Faber & Faber 2015)

Sawyer, Tom, *Noble Art* (London, Unwin Hyman 1989)

Schama, Simon, *The Face of Britain. The Nation through its Portraits* (London, Viking 2015)

Schechter, Ronald, and Liz Clarke, *Mendoza the Jew. Boxing, Manliness and Nationalism. A Graphic History* (New York, Oxford University Press 2014)

Scheckner, P, ed., *Anthology of Chartist Poetry* (London, AUP 1989)

Schehr, Lawrence R, *Parts of an Andrology. On Representations of Men's Bodies* (Stanford, Stanford University Press 1997)

Schiller, Kay, 'Communism, youth, and sport: the 1973 World Youth Festival in East Berlin', in Tomlinson et al., eds., *Sport and the Transformation of Modern Europe* (London, Routledge 2011)

Schofield, Derek, 'Sowing the Seeds. Cecil Sharp and Charles Marson in Somerset 1903', *Folk Music Journal* 8, 4, 2004

Scott, Daniel, *Bygone Cumberland and Westmorland* (London, William Andrew 1899)

Scott, David, 'Boxing and Masculine Identity', in Dine and Crosson, eds., *Sport, Representation and Evolving Identities in Europe* (Bern, Peter Lang 2010)

Scott, David, ed., *Cultures of Boxing* (Oxford, Peter Lang 2015)

Scott, Joan W, 'Gender. A Useful Category of Historical Analysis', *American Historical Review* 91, 5, (1986)

Scriven, Tom, 'The Dorchester Labourers and Swing's Aftermath in Dorset 1830–38, *History Workshop Journal*, 31 July 2016, https://doi.org/10.1093/hwj/dbw020

Seaborne, Malcolm, *The English School. Its architecture and organization 1370–1870* (London, Routledge Kegan Paul 1971)

Sealle, C E, 'Custom, Class Conflict and Agrarian Capitalism: the Cumbrian customary economy in the 18th century', *Past & Present*, 110, Feb 1986

Seed, John, 'Secular' and 'religious' historical perspectives, *Social History* 39, 1, 2014

Seldon, Anthony, and David Walsh, *Public Schools and The Great War. The Generation Lost* (Barnsley, Pen & Sword 2013)

Selwyn, David, *Jane Austen and Leisure* (London, Hambledon Press 1999)

Semmel, Bernard, 'The Halevy Thesis'. Methodism and Revolution, *Encounter* 37, 1, 1971

Semmel, Bernard, *The Methodist Revolution* (London, Heinemann 1974)

Semmel, Stuart, 'British Radicals and Legitimacy: Napoleon and the mirror of history', *Past & Present* 167, May 2000

Shakesby, Albert, *From Street Arab to Evangelist. The Life Story of Albert Shakesby, A Converted Athlete, by Himself* (Hull, Burtt Bros 1910)

Shakespeare, Nicholas, *Six Minutes in May. How Churchill Unexpectedly Became Prime Minister* (London, Harvill Secker 2017)

Sharp, Cecil, *English Folk Song. Some Conclusions* (1907. Belmont, Ca, Wadsworth 1965)

Sharp, Cecil, *The Sword Dances of Northern England* (1911. London, Novello & Co 1951) 2nd ed., parts i, ii, iii

Sharp, Samuel, *Letters from Italy 1765–66* (London, R Cave 1766)

Sharpe, Pamela, 'Explaining the short stature of the poor: childhood disease and growth in 19c England', *Economic History Review* 65, 4, 2012

Shaw, Charles ('An Old Potter'), *When I was a Child* (London, Methuen 1903)

Shaw, Rev. George, *Our Filey Fishermen* (London, Hamilton Adams 1867)

Shaw, Rev. George, *John Wyndham; or the Gospel among the Fishermen* (London, Simpkin Marshall 1878)

Shaw, Philip, *Waterloo and the Romantic Imagination* (Basingstoke, Palgrave 2002)

Shepard, Alexandra, *Accounting for Oneself. Worth, Status and the Social Order in Early Modern England* (Oxford, Oxford University Press 2015)

Shipley, Stan, 'Tom Causer of Bermondsey', *History Workshop Journal* 15, 1983

Shipley, Stan, 'Boxing', in Mason, ed., *Sport in Britain* (Cambridge, Cambridge University Press 1989)

Shipley, Stan, *Bombadier Billy Wells* (Whitley Bay, Bewick Press 1993)

Shoemaker, Robert B, 'Male honour and the decline of public violence in 18c London', *Social History* 26, 2001

Shoemaker, Robert B, 'Worrying about Crime: Experience, Moral Panics and Public Opinion in London 1660-1800', *Past & Present* 234, February 2017

Shore, Heather, 'Criminality and Englishness in the Aftermath. The Racecourse Wars of the 1920s', *20c British History* 22, 4, December 2011

Short Time Committees, 'Address to the Friends of Justice', James Bedford, Chair, (1833. New York, Amo Press 1972)

Shuttleworth, J P Kay, *The Moral and Physical Condition of the Working Classes employed in the cotton manufacture in Manchester* (London, James Ridgway 1832)

Sillitoe, Alan, *The Loneliness of the Long Distance Runner* (London, Signet 1959)

Simmel, George, 'Fashion', *American Journal of Sociology* lxii, 6, May 1957

Simon, Brian, 'David Reeder's "alternative system": School Boards in the 1890s', in Colls and Rodger, eds, *Cities of Ideas* (Aldershot, Ashgate 2004)

Simon, Brian, and Ian Bradley, eds., *The Victorian Public School* (Dublin, Gill & Macmillan 1975)

Simon, Robin, 'The Eyes Have It', *Literary Review*, October 2019

Simonin, L, *Mines and Miners; or, underground life* (London, W Mackenzie 1869)

Simpson, A E, 'Duelling and the Law in 19c England', *Criminal Justice History* 9, 1998

Sindall, Rob, *Street Violence in the 19c. Media Panic or Real Danger?* (Leicester, Leicester University Press 1990)

Singleton, John, 'Britain's Military Use of Horses 1914-1918', *Past & Present* 139, May 1993

Skillen, Fiona, *Women, Sport and Modernity in Interwar Britain* (Oxford, Peter Lang 2013)

Slater, Michael, ed., *Dickens' Journalism* vol. 2 (London, Dent 1996)

Slater, Michael, ed., *Dickens' Journalism* vol. 3 (London, Dent 1998)

Sleight, Simon, *Young People and the Shaping of Public Space in Melbourne 1870–1914* (Farnham, Ashgate 2013)

Sloane, 'The Economics of Professional Football', *Scottish Journal of Political Economy*, June 1971

Smiles, Samuel, *The Life of George Stephenson. Railway Engineer* (London, John Murray 1857)

Smiles, Samuel, *Self Help. With illustrations of Conduct and Perseverance* (1859. London, Sphere 1968)

Smillie, Robert, *My Life for Labour* (London, Mills & Boon 1924)

Smith, G, *Gypsy Smith. His Life and Work, by Himself* (London, National Council Evangelical Free Churches 1910)

Smith, Horatio, *Festivals, Games and Amusements Ancient and Modern* (London, Colburn & Bentley 1831)

Smith, Martin, *Stamford Myths and Legends* (Stamford, Watkins 1991)

Smith, Martin, *Stamford Then and Now* (Stamford, Watkins 1992)

Smith, Martin, *The Story of Stamford* (Stamford, Martin Smith 1994)

Smith, Thomas, *Life of a Fox Written by Himself* (London, Whittaker 1843)

Snape, M F, *The Church of England in Industrializing Society. The Lancashire Parish of Whalley in the 18th Century* (Woodbridge, Boydell Press 2003)

Snelgrove, Dudley, *British Sporting and Animal Prints 1658–1874. The Paul Mellon Collection* (Tate Gallery, YCBA 1981)

Snell, K D M, 'The culture of local xenophobia', *Social History* 28, 1, 2003

Snell, K D M. *Parish and Belonging. Community, Identity and Welfare in England and Wales 1700–1950* (Cambridge, Cambridge University Press 2006)

Snell, K D M, *Spirits of Community. English senses of Belonging and Loss 1750–2000* (London, Bloomsbury 2016)

Snowdon, David, Drama *Boxiana*. Spectacle and Theatricality in Pierce Egan, *Romanticism on the Net* 46, May 2007: https://ronjournal.org/articles/n46/drama-boxiana-spectacle-and-theatricality-in-pierce-egans-pugilistic-writing/#paper-fulltext

Sokoll, Thomas, *Essex Pauper Letters 1731–1837* (Oxford, British Academy Oxford University Press 2001)

Sopwith, T, *The Stranger's Pocket Guide to Newcastle upon Tyne and its environs* (Newcastle, Currie & Bowman 1838)

Southey, Robert, *The Life of Wesley; and the Rise and Progress of Methodism* (London, Longman, Hurst 1820) vols. i, ii

Southey, Robert, *The Life of Wesley; and the Rise and Progress of Methodism* (London, Longman, Brown 1846) 3rd ed., 2 vols.

Souvenir of the Primitive Methodist Chapel, and Schools, Henshaw St, Oldham 24–27 November 1909 (Oldham, Sam Fish 1909)

Speight, Harry, *Chronicles and Stories of Old Bingley* (London, Elliot Stock 1899)

Spencer, David, 'Reformulating the closed parish thesis: associations, interests, and interaction', *Journal of Historical Geography* 26, i, Jan 2000

Spierenburg, Peter, *Men and Violence* (Columbus, Ohio State UP 1998)

Stanhope, Philip Henry, *Notes of Conversations with the Duke of Wellington* (London, John Murray 1888)

Staff Sergeant, A late, of the 13th Light Infantry, *Camp and Barrack-Room; or, the British Army as it is* (London, Chapman & Hall, 1846)

Stead, Peter, and Gareth Williams, eds., *Wales and its Boxers. The Fighting Tradition* (Cardiff, University of Wales Press 2008)

Steadman, F Cecily, *In the Days of Miss Beale. A study of her work and influence* (London, Ed J Burrow, nd, 1931?)

Steedman, Carolyn, *An Everyday Life of the English Working Class. Work, Self and Sociability in the Early 19th Century* (Cambridge, Cambridge University Press 2013)

Stein, Peter, *The Character and Influence of Roman Civil Law* (London, Hambledon 1988)

Steinkvaus, William, *The Thoroughbred. Born to Run and Jump* (Bruce Museum, Connecticut 1999)

Stephenson, J, *The Man of Faith and Fire or, the life and work of Rev G Warner* (London, R Bryant 1902)

Stockdale, Percival, *A remonstrance against inhumanity to animals, and particularly against the savage practice of Bull Baiting* (Alnwick, M & J Graham 1802)

Stokes, Francis Griffin, *The Bletcheley Diary of Rev William Cole 1765–67* (London, Constable 1931)

Stokes, J & A E, *Just Rutland* (Uppingham, John Hawthorn 1953)

Stone, Duncan, and John Hughson and Rob Ellis, *New Directions in Sport History* (Abingdon, Routledge 2015)

Stone, Rev. James S, *Woods and Dales of Derbyshire* (Derby, Frank Murray 1894)

Storch, Robert, ed., 'Introduction', *Popular Culture and Custom in 19th Century England* (London, Croom Helm 1982)

Storey, Mark, *The Poetry of John Clare* (London, Macmillan 1974)

Storey, David, *This Sporting Life* (1960. London, Vintage 2000)

Strachan, Hew, *The Reform of the British Army 1830–54* (Manchester, Manchester University Press 1984)

Strachan, Hew, *The First World War.* Vol i. *To Arms* (Oxford, Oxford University Press 2003)

Strachey, Lytton, *Eminent Victorians* (1918. London, Penguin 1986)

Strachey, Lytton, *The Letters of Lytton Strachey*, ed., Paul Levy, (London, Viking 2005)

Stratmann, Linda, *9th Marquess of Queensberry* (New Haven, Yale University Press 2011)

Strauss, Gerald, 'Viewpoint. The Dilemma of Popular History', *Past & Present* 132, August 1991

Strutt, Joseph, *The Sports and Pastimes of the People of England; including the Rural and Domestic Recreations, May Games, Mummeries, Shows, Processions, Pageants, and Pompous Spectacles, from the earliest period to the present time, edited by William Hone, illustrated by 140 engravings from ancient manuscripts in the Bodleian Library, Oxford, Cambridge University Library, British Museum Cottonian Library, Royal Library, Harleian Library, Sir Hans Sloane's Library etc etc* (1801. London, Chatto & Windus 1876 repr.)

Stuart, T, *The Bloodless Revolution. A Cultural History of Vegetarianism from 1600 to Modern Times* (New York, Norton 2006)

Stubbs, George, *Stubbs and the Horse*, catalogue and exhibition (National Gallery 29 June– 25 September 2005)

Subaltern, A Civil, *Civil Service Reform. Observations upon the Report by Sir C E Trevelyan and Sir S H Northcote on the Organization of the Civil Service* (London, W E Painter 1854)

Sugden, Peter, *Boxing and Society* (Manchester, Manchester University Press 1996)

Sulley, Philip, *History of Ancient and Modern Birkenhead* (Liverpool, Murphy 1907)

Sullivan, J, *Cumberland and Westmorland Ancient & Modern. The People, Dialect, Superstitions and Customs* (Kendal, Hudson, Dawson & Robinson; London, Whittaker 1857)

Summers, Leigh, *Bound to Please. A History of the Victorian Corset* (Oxford, Berg 2001)

Sumner, William Graham, *Folkways. A Study of the Sociological Importance of Usages, Manners, Customs, Mores, and Morals* (1906. New York, Mentor Books 1960)

Surtees, Robert Smith, *Handley Cross; or Mr Jorrocks's Hunt.* Illustrations by John Leech (London, Bradbury & Evans 1854)

Surtees, Robert, *Hunts with Jorrocks. From Handley Cross* (1854. London, Hodder & Stoughton 1908)

Surtees, Robert, *Mr Sponge's Sporting Tour* (1853. Oxford, Oxford University Press 1982)

Surtees Society, *North Country Diaries* (Newcastle 1910) vol i

Sutherland, Douglas, *The Mad Hatters. Great Sporting Eccentrics of the 19c* (London, Robert Hale 1987)

Swain, Peter, 'Cultural Continuity and Football in 19c Lancs', *Sport in History* 28, 4, 2008

Swain, Peter, 'The Grander Design and the Involvement of the Lower Classes 1818–40', *Sport in History* 34, 1, 2014

Sweet, Rosemary, 'Freemen and Independence in English Borough Politics', *Past & Present* 161, November 1998

Sweet, Rosemary, 'British perceptions of Florence in the long 18c', *Historical Journal* 50, 4, 2007

Sweet, Rosemary, '"Truly Historical Ground": Antiquarianism in the North', in Colls, ed., *Northumbria. History and Identity 547–2000* (Chichester, Phillimore 2007)

Sweetman, John, *War and Administration. The significance of the Crimean War for the British Army* (Edinburgh, Scottish Academic Press 1984)

Sylvester, David, *About Modern Art* (London, Chatto & Windus 1996)

Symonds, John Addington, *Studies of the Greek Poets* (London, Smith Elder 1873)

Symonds, John Addington, *Memoirs* (Basingstoke, Palgrave Macmillan 2016) ed. A K Regis

Szreter, Simon, and Graham Mooney, 'Urbanization, mortality and the standard of living debate: new estimates of expectation of life at birth in 19c British cities', *Economic History Review*, second series, li, 1998

Taft, Z, *Thoughts on Female Preaching* (Dover, Taft 1803)

Taft, Z, *A Reply To An Article inserted in the Methodist Magazine for April 1809, entitled Thoughts on Women's Preaching extracted from Dr James McKnight* (Leeds, Wilson 1809)

Tagg, William W, *A Vagrant's career: being a Sketch of the life and experiences of William Trewhitt Herdman, better known as Billy the Rope Performer* (North Shields, Whitecross & Yorke 1891)

Taine, Hippolyte, *Notes on England* (1860–71. London, Thames & Hudson 1957) and (New York, Henry Holt 1885)

Taylor, Alison, *Cambridge. The Hidden History* (Stroud, Tempus 1999)

Taylor, Antony, *Lords of Misrule. Hostility to Aristocracy in late 19c and early 20c Britain* (London, Palgrave 2004)

Taylor, Barbara, *Mary Wollstonecraft and the Feminist Imagination* (Cambridge, Cambridge University Press 2004)

Taylor, D G, *On the Corinthian Spirit. The Decline of Amateurism in Sport* (London, Yellow Jersey Press 2006)

Taylor, John, *Poetical Sketches of English Heroes and Heroines or, The Rifle Defenders* (London, A M Pigott 1860)

Taylor, Matthew, 'Work and Play: the professional footballer in England 1900–50', *The Sports Historian* 22, i, May 2002

Taylor, Matthew, 'The Football League and the North of England 1888-1939', *International Journal of Regional and Local Studies* 2, i, i, 2005

Taylor, Matthew, *The Leaguers. The Making of Professional Football in England 1900–1939* (Liverpool, Liverpool University Press 2005)

Taylor, Matthew, 'Football's Engineers? British Football Coaches, Migration and Intercultural Transfer 1910–1950s', *Sport in History* 30, 1, 2010

Taylor, Matthew, *The Association Game* (Abingdon, Routledge 2013)

Taylor, Matthew, 'The Global Spread of Football', in Edelman and Wilson, *Handbook Sports History* (New York, Oxford University Press 2017)

Taylor, Miles, 'John Bull and the Iconography of Public Opinion in England 1712–1929', *Past & Present* 134, February 1992

Taylor, Stephen, *Sons of the Waves. The Common Seaman in the Heroic Age of Sail 1740–1840* (New Haven, Yale University Press 2020)

Tebbutt, Melanie, *Women's Talk? A Social History of Gossip in Working-class Neighbourhoods 1880–1960* (Aldershot, Scolar Press 1995)

Tebbutt, Melanie, *Being Boys. Youth, Leisure and Identity in the Inter War Years* (Manchester, Manchester University Press 2012)

Tebbutt, Melanie, *Making Youth. A History of Youth in Modern Britain* (London, Palgrave 2016)

Tebbutt, Melanie, 'Listening to Youth: BBC Broadcasts during the 1930s and Second World War', *History Workshop Journal* 84, i, 2017

Tegg, John, printer, 'Britons Strike Home', print, aquatint (London, Tegg, Cheapside 1819)

Telford, John, *The Methodist Hymn Book Illustrated* (London, Chas H Kelly 1906)

Temperance Society Committee, *Newcastle As It Is; reviewed in its moral aspects* (Newcastle On Tyne, T P Barkas 1854)

Temperley, Nicholas, *The Music of the English Parish Church* (Cambridge, Cambridge University Press 1983) vol. i.

Temple, David, *The Big Meeting. A History of the Durham Miners' Gala* (Washington, TUPS Books 2011)

Tennant, John, *Football. The Golden Age 1900–85* (London, Bounty Books 2005)

Thackeray, William Makepeace, *Book of Snobs* (1848. St. Lucia, Univ Queensland Press 1978)

Thackeray, William Makepeace, *A Lay of Ancient London: Heenanus v Sayerius*, supposed to be recounted to his Great Grand Children April 17 AD 1920 by an Ancient Gladiator, *Punch*, 28 April 1860

Thain, Louise M, *'Through the Ages'; the story of Nenthead* (1957. Alston, N Pennines Heritage Trust 1988)

Thane, Pat, *Old Age in English History* (Oxford, Oxford University Press 2000)

Thiselton-Dyer, Rev. T F, *British Popular Customs Present and Past Illustrating the Social and Domestic Manners of the People* (1875. London, George Bell 1900)

Thomas, Hugh, ed., *The Establishment* (London, Anthony Blond 1959)

Thomas, Hugh, 'The Establishment and Society', in Thomas, ed., *The Establishment* (London, Anthony Blond 1959)

Thomas, Keith, *Man and the Natural World. Changing Attitudes in England 1500-1800* (Harmondsworth, Penguin 1984)

Thomas, Keith, *The Ends of Life. Roads to Fulfilment in Early Modern England* (Oxford, Oxford University Press 2009)

Thomas, Keith, *In Pursuit of Civility. Manners and Civilization in Early Modern England* (New Haven, Yale University Press 2018)

Thomas, Peter, & M A Nicholson, *The English Style of Rowing* (London, Faber & Faber 1958)

Thompson, E P, *The Making of the English Working Class* (London, Gollancz 1963)

Thompson, E P, 'Time, Work Discipline, and Industrial Capitalism', *Past & Present* 38, December 1967

Thompson, E P, 'The Moral Economy of the English Crowd in the 18th Century', *Past & Present* 50, February 1971.

Thompson, E P, *Whigs and Hunters. The Origin of the Black Act* (London, Allen Lane 1975)

Thompson, E P, *Customs in Common* (London, Penguin 1993)

Thompson, F M L, 'English Landed Society in 20c: ii, New Poor and New Rich', Presidential Address, *Transactions, Royal Historical Society*, 16 November 1990; iii, 'Self Help and Outdoor Relief', 22 November 1991; iv, 'Prestige without Power?', 20 November 1992

Thompson, Flora, *Lark Rise to Candleford* (1939. London, Reprint Society 1948)

Thomson, Robert, *The Pelican History of Psychology* (Penguin, Harmondsworth 1968)

Thornely, Thomas, *Cambridge Memories* (London, Hamish Hamilton 1936)

Thring, Edward, *Edward Thring. Headmaster of Uppingham School. Life, Diary and Letters* (London, Macmillan 1900) ed., George Parkin

Thring, J C, *The Winter Game. Rules of Football, to which are added The Rules of the Cambridge University Committee and London Association* (Uppingham, Hawthorn, Printer, High St 1863 & London, Hamilton, Adams 1863)

Throsby, John, *Selected Views in Leicestershire* (London, Wm Richardson, The Strand 1791)

Tidal Harbours Commission, *Evidence taken by the Commissioners on the condition of the River Tyne, with Reports on the Improvement of the River* (McColl, South Shields 1849)

Timbs, John, *Curiosities of London* (1855. London, J S Virtue 1867)

Todd, Selina, 'Young Women, Work and Leisure in inter-war England' *Historical Journal* 48, 3, 2005

Tomalin, Claire, *Charles Dickens. A Life* (London, Viking 2011)

Tombs, Robert, *The English and Their History* (London, Allen Lane 2014)

Tomlinson, Alan, Christopher Young, and Richard Holt, eds., *Sport and the Transformation of Modern Europe. States, media, and markets 1950–2010* (Abingdon, Routledge 2011)

Tomlinson, Jim, 'De-Industrialization Not Decline: a New Meta-Narrative for Post-War British History', *20c British History* 27, i, March 2016

Tomlinson, W W, *The North Eastern Railway* (Newcastle, Reid 1914)

Tonks, Rev. W C, *Victory in the Villages. The history of the Brinkworth Circuit* (Aberdare, Wilcox 1907)

Topping, George, and J J Potter, *Memories of Old Carlisle* (Carlisle, Steel Bros 1922)

Townsend, James, *News of a Country Town. Being Extracts from Jackson's Oxford Journal relating to Abingdon 1753–1835* (Oxford, Oxford University Press 1914)

Toynbee, Arnold, *Lectures on the Industrial Revolution of the 18c in England* (1884. London, Longmans, Green, 1919)

Tranter, Neil, *Sport, Economy and Society in Britain 1750–1914* (Cambridge, Cambridge University Press 1998)

Travis, John F, *The Rise of the Devon Seaside Resorts 1750–1900* (Exeter, University of Exeter Press 1993)

Trollope, Anthony, ed., *British Sports and Pastimes* (London, Virtue & Co 1868)

Trollope, Anthony, 'Mr Freeman on the Morality of Hunting', in John Morley, ed., *Fortnightly Review* xxxvi, December 1869

Trollope, Anthony, 'In the Hunting Field', *Good Words*, February 1879

Trotter, Wilfred, *Instincts of the Herd* (London, Fisher Unwin 1916)

Trumble, Angus, 'Diversions of the Field', *Apollo*, April 2007

Tucker, Geraint, 'Evan Roberts and the 1904-05 Revival', *Journal of Welsh Religious History* 4, 2004

Tumblety, Joan, *Remaking the Male Body. Masculinity and the Uses of Physical Culture in Interwar and Vichy France* (Oxford, Oxford University Press 2012)

Tunney, Gene, reviews James J Corbett's 'The Roar of the Crowd' (1925 reprint), *The Observer*, 14 February 1954

Turner, E S, *Boys Will Be Boys* (London, Michael Joseph 1948)

Turner, J Munsey, 'Robert Featherstone Wearmouth (1882–1963)' *Proceedings WHS* 43 (5) 1982

Turner, Thomas, *The Diary of Thomas Turner* (1754–65. East Hoathly, CTR Publishing 1994) ed., David Vaisey

Tylor, E B, *Primitive Culture* (London, Murray 1871)

Underdown, David, *Fire from Heaven. Life in an English Town in the 17c* (London, Fontana 1993)

Underdown, David, *Start of Play. Cricket and Culture in 18c England* (London, Allen Lane 2000)

Ungar, Ruti, 'Boxing as a Battle Ground for Conservatives and Radicals in late Georgian London', *Sport in History* 31, 4, 2011

Urdank, Albion M, 'The Rationalization of Rural Sport: British Sheepdog Trials 1873–1946', *Rural History* 17, 2006, pp. 65–82

Ure, Andrew, *The Philosophy of Manufactures or, an exposition of the scientific, moral and commercial economy of The Factory System of Great Britain* (1835. London, Frank Cass 1967)

Urwick, E J, *Studies of Boy Life in our Cities* (London, Dent 1904)

Vaizey, John, 'The Public Schools', in Thomas, ed., *The Establishment* (London, Anthony Blond 1959)

Valenze, Deborah M, *Prophetic Sons and Daughters. Female Preaching and Popular Religion in Industrial England* (Princeton New Jersey, Princeton University Press 1988)

Vamplew, Wray, 'Horse-Racing', in Mason, T, ed., *Sport in Britain* (Cambridge, Cambridge University Press 1989)

Vamplew, Wray, 'Empiricist versus Sociological History: Some Comments on the Civilizing Process', *Sport in History* 27, 2, 2007

Van Caenegem, R C, *The Birth of the English Common Law* (Cambridge, Cambridge University Press 1973)

Vandervell, Anthony, and Charles Coles, *Game and the English Landscape* (Debrett's Peerage 1980)

Vasili, Phil, *The First Black Footballer. Arthur Wharton 1865–1930* (London, Frank Cass 1998)

Veblen, Thorstein, *The Theory of the Leisure Class. An Economic Study in the Evolution of Institutions* (London, Macmillan 1899)

'Veritas', 'Dangerous Sportsmen' (tract, May 1861)

Vernon, James, *Politics and the People 1815–67* (Cambridge, Cambridge University Press 1993)

Vernon, James, ed., 'Introduction', *Re-Reading the Constitution. New narratives in the political history of England's long nineteenth century* (Cambridge, Cambridge University Press 1996)

Vertinsky, Patricia, 'Gender Matters in Sport History', in Edelman and Wilson, *Handbook Sports History* (New York, Oxford University Press 2017)

Vicar, 'A Late', *A Short History with Description of the Parish of West Wycombe, County of Bucks, Diocese of Oxford* (High Wycombe, Bucks Free Press 1925)

Vincent, Col. Sir Howard, *Police Code and General Manual* (London, Butterworth 1885)

Vipond, W, *The Scriptural Method of Governing and Instructing Children* (Canterbury, Saffery 1807)

Vlaeminke, Mel, 'Leicester City. The early years 1884-1919' (Leicester, University of Leicester School of Education 2005)

Waal, Kit de, *Common People. An anthology of working-class writers* (London, Unbound 2019)

Waddington, Ivan, 'Changing Patterns of Drug Use in British Sport from the 1960s', *Sport in History* 25, 3, 2005

Wagg, Stephen, *The Football World* (Brighton, Harvester 1984)

Wahrman, Dror, *The Making of the Modern Self. Identity and Culture in 18c England* (New Haven, Yale University Press 2004)

Walcott, Mackenzie E C, *Memorials of Stamford Past and Present* (Stamford, Henry and James Johnson 1867)

Walker, George, *Costume of Yorkshire* (1814. Caliban, Firle 1978)

Walker, J, *The History of Penrith from the Earliest Period to the Present Time* (Penrith, B T Sweeten 1858)

Walker, Julian, ed., *The Roar of the Crowd. A Sporting Anthology* (London, British Library 2016)

Walley, Phil, *Accrington Stanley. The club that wouldn't die* (Cheltenham, Sports Books 2006)

Walsh, John, 'The Bane of Industry'. Popular Evangelicalism and Work in the 18c, in R N Swansonson, ed., *The Use and Abuse of Time in Christian History* (London, Boydell Press 2002)

Walsh, John, and David Hempton, 'E P Thompson and Methodism', in M A Noll, ed., *God and Mammon. Protestants, Money and the Market 1790–1860* (Oxford, Oxford University Press 2002)

Walsham, Alexandra, 'The Godly and Popular Culture', in J Coffey and P C H Lim, eds., *The Cambridge Companion to Puritanism* (Cambridge, Cambridge University Press 2008)

Walsham, Alexandra, *The Reformation of the Landscape. Religion, Identity and Memory in Early Modern Britain and Ireland* (Oxford, Oxford University Press 2011)

Walsham, Alexandra, 'Rough Music and Charivari. Letters Between Natalie Zemon Davis and Edward Thompson 1970–72', *Past & Present* 235, May 2017

Walton, J. K, *The Blackpool Landlady* (Manchester, Manchester University Press 1986)

Walton, J K, *Lancashire. A Social History 1558–1939* (Manchester, Manchester University Press 1987)

Walton, J. K, *Fish and Chips and the British Working Class 1870–1940* (Leicester, Leicester University Press 1994)

Walton, J. K, *The British Seaside* (Manchester, Manchester University Press 2000)

Walton, J R, 'Pedigree and the National Cattle Herd 1750–1950', *Agricultural History Review* 34, 1986

Walvin, James, *The People's Game. A Social History of British Football* (London, Allen Lane 1975)

Walvin, James, *Football and the Decline of Britain* (London, Palgrave 1986)

Walvin, James, *Different Times. Growing up in post-war England* (York, Algie Books 2014)

Ward, Andrew, and John Williams, *Football Nation* (London, Bloomsbury 2009)

Ward, Geoffrey C, *Unforgivable Blackness. The Rise and Fall of Jack Johnson* (London, Pimlico 2006)

Ward, J T, *The Factory Movement 1830–1855* (London, Macmillan 1962)

Ward, Valentine, *A Miniature of Methodism; or, A Brief account of the History, Doctrines, Discipline and Character of the Methodists* (London, John Mason 1829)

Ward, W R, *Religion and Society in England 1790–1850* (London, Batsford 1972)

Wark, Robert, ed., *Sir Joshua Reynolds. Discourses on Art* (New Haven, Yale University Press 1975)

Warner, Malcolm, and Robin Blake, *Stubbs and the Horse* (London, YCBA & YUP 2004)

Warren, Ian, 'The English Landed Elite and the Social Environment of London 1580–1700', *English Historical Review* cxxvi, 518, February 2011

Waters, Chris, *Fred Trueman* (London, Aurum Press 2011)

Watkins, Carl, *The Undiscovered Country. Journeys Among the Dead* (London, Bodley Head 2013)

Watkins, Christopher, 'Inventing International Citizenship. Badminton School', *History of Education* 36, 3, 2007.

Watson, A E T, 'The Badminton Library', in Hedley Peek, ed., *The Poetry of Sport* (London, Longmans Green 1896)

Watson, Alexander, *Enduring the Great War. Combat, Morale and Collapse in the German and British Armies 1914-1918* (Cambridge, Cambridge University Press 2009)

Watson, G, 'England Women's Hockey Tour of Australia and New Zealand 1914', *International Journal History of Sport* 33, 17, 2016.

Watts, Diana, *The Renaissance of the Greek Ideal* (London, Wm Heinemann 1922)

Waugh, Alec, *The Loom of Youth* (1917, London, Methuen 1984)

Wawn, C N, *Thomas Curry the Pious Keelman (an authentic narrative)* (Newcastle, Edward Walker 1822)

Weardale Miners' Improvement Society, *Pledge* and 112 Signatures taken [at the] Newhouse, St John's, 30 September 1847, and Thomas Sopwith, *Address*, 1848

Wearmouth, R F, *Methodism and the Working Class Movements of England 1800-1850* (London, Epworth Press 1937)

Wearmouth, R F, *Some Working Class Movements of the 19c* (London, Epworth Press 1948)

Webb, Sidney, *The Story of the Durham Miners 1662-1921* (London, Fabian Society & Labour Publishing 1921)

Weisser, H, 'Chartism in 1848', *Albion* 13 i, 1981

Welbourne, E, *The Miners' Unions of Northumberland and Durham* (Cambridge, Cambridge University Press 1923)

Welford, Richard, *Men of Mark Twixt Tyne and Tweed* (London, Walter Scott Ltd 1895)

Werner, Julia Stewart, *The Primitive Methodist Connexion* (Wisconsin, University Wisconsin Press 1984)

Wesley, Rev J, *The Journals of the Rev John Wesley AM*, ed., Nehemiah Curnock (1909. London, Epworth Press 1938)

Westmann, Stephen K, *Sport. Physical Training and Womanhood* (London, Bailliere 1939)

Whannel, Garry, *Fields in Vision. Television Sport and Cultural Transformation* (London, Routledge 1992)

Whellan, William, *History, Topography, and Directory of Northumberland* (London, Whellan & Co. 1855)

White, Gilbert, *The Natural History and Antiquities of Selborne* (London, B. White 1789)

Whitefield, George, *Journals* (1737–41 (London, Henry J Drane 1905)

Whitehead, Ian, *James Renforth of Gateshead* (Newcastle, Tyne Bridge 2004)

Whitney, C E, *Dover College* (Dover, Corporation of Dover College 1982)

Whittle, Rev. John, *'Owd Roger', Bible Colporteur and Primitive Methodist Lay Preacher* (Blackburn, Toulmin 1912)

Whyte, William, 'Building a public school community 1860-1910', *History of Education* 32, 2003

Whyte, William, *Oxford Jackson. Architecture, Education, Status and Style 1835-1924* (Oxford, Oxford University Press 2006)

Whyte, William, *Redbrick. A social and architectural history of Britain's civic universities* (Oxford, Oxford University Press 2015)

Whyte-Melville, G J, *Market Harborough or How Mr Sawyer went to the Shires* (1861. Feltham, Country Life 1984)

Widnall, S P, *A History of Grantchester* (Grantchester, Widnell 1875)

Wiener, Joel H, *Papers for the Millions. The New Journalism in Britain 1850–1914* (New York, Greenwood Press 1988)

Wiener, Martin J, *Men of Blood. Violence, Manliness and Criminal Justice in Victorian England* (Cambridge, Cambridge University Press 2004)

Williams, G A, 'Introduction' to John Gorman, *Banner Bright. An illustrated history of the banners of the British trade union movement* (Harmondsworth, Penguin 1976)

Williams, Jack, *Cricket and England* (London, Cass 2000)

Williams, Jean, *A Game for Rough Girls? A History of Women's Football in Britain* (London, Routledge 2003)

Williams, John, *Into the Red. Liverpool FC and the Changing Face of English Football* (London, Mainstream 2001)

Williams, John, *Liverpool Radicals* (Liverpool 2011)

Williams, W M, *The Sociology of an English Village: Gosforth* (London, RKP 1969)

Williamson, David J, *Belles of the Ball* (Devon, R&D 1991)

Williamson, Henry, *Life in a Devon Village* (London, Right Book Club 1947)

Williamson, Tom and Liz Bellamy, *Property and Landscape. A Social History of Land Ownership and the English Countryside* (London, George Philip 1987)

Willis, Donald, *A Song on a Bugle Blown* (Oxford, Kenton 1983)

Willmott, Peter, *Adolescent boys of East London* (London, Routledge & Kegan Paul 1966)

Willmott, Peter, and Michael Young, *Family and Kinship in East London* (1957. Penguin, Harmondsworth 1967)

Wilson, G W, *Chronicles of Whitchurch, Bucks* (Whitchurch, Wilson 1909)

Wilson, J Bastow, *A Primitive Methodist Diamond Field, The story of a Northumbrian Mining Circuit* (Newcastle, Mark Taylor 1909)

Wilson, James, ed., *Victoria History of the Counties of England. Cumberland* (London, Archibald Constable 1905)

Wilson, Joe, *Tyneside Songs, Ballads and Drolleries* (Newcastle, Allan 1873)

Wilson, John, *A History of the Durham Miners' Association 1870–1914* (Durham, J H Veitch 1907)

Wilson, Jonathan, *The Outsider. A History of the Goalkeeper* (London, Orion 2012)

Wilson, Kathleen, *The Sense of the People. Politics, Culture and Imperialism in England 1715–85* (Cambridge, Cambridge University Press 1995)

Wilson, Linda, 'Conversion Amongst Female Methodists 1825–75', *Proceedings WHS* 51, 6, 1998

Wilton, Iain, '"A galaxy of sporting events": Sport's role and significance in the Festival of Britain', *Sport in History* 36, 4, 2016

Wilton, Rt. Hon. Earl of, Thos Grosvenor (Egerton), *On the Sports and Pursuits of the English. As bearing upon their national character* (London, Harrison 1868)

Winchester, Angus J L, *The Harvest of the Hills. Rural Life in Northern England and the Scottish Borders 1400–1700* (Edinburgh, Edinburgh University Press 2000)

Wing, Charles, *Evils of the Factory System demonstrated by Parliamentary Evidence* (London, Saunders & Otley 1837)

Winks, J F, *The Bull Running at Stamford. A Sermon delivered in the General Baptist Meeting House on Lord's Day Evening 15 Nov 1829* (London, Geroge Wightman 1829) 6d each, 5s per dozen

Winlaton & District Local History Society, *A History of Blaydon* (Gateshead, Metropolitan Borough 1975)

Winstanley, Michael, 'News from Oldham. Butterworth and the Manchester Press 1829–48', *Manchester Region History Review* 14, i, 1990

Winstanley, Michael, 'Researching a County History: Edwin Butterworth, Edward Baines and the History of Lancashire (1836)', *Northern History* xxxii, 1996

Winstanley, Michael, and Osborne, Harvey, 'Rural and Urban Poaching in Victorian England', *Rural History* 17, 2, 2006

Winter, Canon G R, *Eton and Oxford. A Few Familiar Scenes* (Oxford, Ryman 1852)

Winterbottom, Walter, *Soccer Coaching* (London, Naldrett Press for FA 1952)

Witts, Rev. Francis Edward, *The Diary of a Cotswold Parson*, ed., David Verey (Gloucester, Alan Sutton 1979)

Wolfenden, John, *The Public Schools Today* (London, University of London Press 1948)

Wolfenden, John, *Turning Points. The Memoirs of Lord Wolfenden* (London, Bodley Head 1976)

Wolfreys, Julian, *Writing London* (London, Palgrave 1999)

Wolfreys, Julian, *Victorian Hauntings* (London, Palgrave Macmillan 2001)

Wolseley, Col G J, *The Soldier's Pocket Book for Field Service* (London, Macmillan 1869)

Wolstenholme, Kenneth, *Sports Special* (London, Stanley Paul 1956)

Wood, Andy, 'Custom, Identity and Resistance: English Free Miners and Their Law 1550–1800', in P Griffiths, et al., *The Experience of Authority in Early Modern England* (London, Macmillan 1996)

Woodruff, William, *The Road to Nab End* (1993. London, Abacus 2003)

Woolridge, Joyce, 'These Sporting Lives. Football Autobiographies 1945–80', *Journal of British Society for Sports History*, 28, 4, 2008

Woolridge, Joyce, 'English Football Magazine Cover Portrait Photos 1950–75', *Sport in History* 30, 4, 2010

Wordsworth, William, 'Simon Lee: The Old Huntsman', in 'Poems of Sentiment and Reflection', *Poetical Works* (Oxford, Oxford University Press 1969)

Worsley, Lucy, 'Reining Cavaliers', *History Today* 54, September 2004

Wren, Percival, *The Indian Teacher's Guide to . . . Mental, Moral and Physical Education* (Bombay, Longman's Green 1910)

Wren, Percival, *Indian School Organization* (Bombay, Longman's Green 1911)

Wright, A R, *English Folklore* (London, Ernest Brown 1928)

Wrightson, Keith, 'The Politics of the Parish in Early Modern England', in P Griffiths et al., *The Experience of Authority in Early Modern England* (Basingstoke, Macmillan 1996)

Wrightson, Keith, 'Elements of Identity. The re-making of the North East 1500–1760', in Colls, ed., *Northumbria. History and Identity 547–2000* (Chichester, Phillimore 2007)

Wrightson, Keith, and David Levine, *The Making of an Industrial Society. Whickham 1560–1765* (Oxford, Clarendon Press 1991)

Yeandle, Peter, Katherine Newey, and Jeffrey Richards, eds., *Politics, Performance and Popular Culture. Theatre and Society in 19c Britain* (Manchester, Manchester University Press 2016)

Yeo, Eileen, 'Christianity in Chartist Struggle 1838–42', *Past & Present* 91, May 1981

Yeo, Eileen and Stephen, eds., *Popular Culture and Class Conflict 1590–1914* (Brighton, Harvester 1981)

Yeo, Eileen Janes, *The Contest for Social Science* (London, Rivers Oram 1996)

Yeo, Eileen Janes, ed., *Radical Femininity. Women's Self-Representation in the Public Sphere* (Manchester, Manchester University Press 1998)

Yeo, Eileen Janes, 'Taking It Like A Man', editorial, *Labour History Review* 69, 2, August 2004

Yeo, Eileen Janes, 'Moral Panics Over Working-Class Youth 1850–Present', *Labour History Review* 69, 2, August 2004

Yeo, Stephen, *Religion and Voluntary Organizations in Crisis* (London, Croom Helm 1976)

Yeo, Stephen, *Who Was J T W Mitchell?* (Manchester, CWS 1995)

Yeo, Stephen, 'Coops and Mutual Enterprises in Britain', LSE, June 2002

Yeo, Stephen, *A Usable Past. The History of Association, Cooperation and un-State Socialism in 19c and early 20c Britain* (Brighton, EER 2018)

Yeo, Stephen, *A New Life. The Religion of Socialism in Britain 1883–96* (Brighton, EER 2018)

York Minster Mystery Plays (York Minster 2016)

Young, Christopher, 'On Gumbrecht's "In praise of athletic beauty"', *Sport in History* 28, i, 2008

Young, Percy M, *Football through the Ages* (London, Methuen 1959)

Young, Rev. Frank, *Early History of Methodism around Houghton le Spring* (Hetton, Young 1927)

Young, Robert, *The Entranced Female; or, the Remarkable Disclosures of A Lady, concerning another world* (London, Inchbold 1842) 27th ed.

Yoxall, J H, and Ernest Gray, *The New Code. NUT Edition* (London, National Union of Teachers 1903)

Zervundachi, M, Introduction, Exhibition by British Sporting Art Trust, Vestey Gallery, Newmarket, *Noble Art. Prize fighting in England* 1738–1860 (2005)

Zouche, Dorothy E de, *Roedean School 1885–1955* (Brighton, Dolphin 1955)

Zweig, Ferdynand, *Men in the Pits* (London, Gollancz 1948)

2. Football Lives

Allison, Malcolm, *Colours of My Life* (London, Everest Books 1975)

Atkinson, Ron, *United to Win* (London, Sidgwick & Jackson 1984)

Banks, Gordon, *Banks of England* (London, Arthur Barker 1980)

Baxter, Jim, *Baxter* (London, Stanley Paul 1984)

Burgess, Ron, *Football My Life* (London, Souvenir Press, nd, 1952?)

Burn, Gordon, *Best and Edwards. Football, Fame and Oblivion* (London, Faber 2006)

Busby, Matt, *My Story* (London, Souvenir Press 1957)

Carter, Raich, *Footballer's Progress* (London, Sporting Handbooks 1950)

Chapman, Herbert, *Herbert Chapman on Football* (London, Garrick 1934)

Charlton, Bobby, *My Manchester United Years* (London, Headline 2007)

Charlton, Jackie, *For Leeds and England* (London, Stanley Paul 1967)

Cullis, Stan, *All For The Wolves* (London, Rupert Hart-Davies 1960)

Doherty, Peter, *Spotlight on Football* (London, Art & Educational 1947)

Dunphy, Eamon, *Only a Game? Diary of a Professional Footballer* (1976. Harmondsworth, Penguin 1987)

Finney, Tom, *Football round the World* (London, Museum Press 1953)

Football Who's Who and Guide to Association Clubs and Players with biographies of nearly 1000 players Season 1900–01 (London, Arthur Pearson 1901)

Gibson, John, *Wor Jackie* (Edinburgh, Sportsprint 1990)

Gowling, Alan, *Football Inside Out* (London, Souvenir Press 1977)

Hamilton, Duncan, *Twenty Years with Brian Clough. Provided You Don't Kiss Me* (London, 4th Estate 2007)

Hapgood, Eddie, *Football Ambassador* (London, Sporting Handbooks 1945)

Harding, John, *Alex James* (London, Robson Books 1988)

Heald, Tim, *Denis Compton* (London, Aurum 2006)

Heighway, Steve, *Liverpool. My Team* (London, Souvenir Press 1977)

Hornby, Nick, *Fever Pitch* (London, Gollancz 1992)

Imlach, Gary, *My Father and Other Working-Class Football Heroes* (London, Yellow Jersey Press 2006)

Izzet, Muzzy, *Muzzy* (Liverpool, Sport Media 2015)

Jack, David R, *Len Shackleton* (London, Nicholas Kaye 1955)

Johnston, Willie, *On the Wing* (London, Arthur Barker 1983)

Keith, John, *Cally. A Football Phenomenon* (London, Duckworth 1977)

Kirkup, Mike, *Jackie Milburn in Black and White* (London, Stanley Paul 1990)

Lawton, Tommy, *Football is My Business* (London, Sporting Handbooks 1946)

Leighton, James, *Duncan Edwards. The Greatest* (London, Simon & Schuster 2012)

Lennox, Bobby, *A Million Miles for Celtic* (London, Stanley Paul 2007)

Liddell, Billy, *My Soccer Story* (London, Stanley Paul 1960)

Lofthouse, Nat, *Goals Galore* (London, Stanley Paul 1954)

Matthews, Stanley, *Feet First* (London, Ewen & Dale 1948)

McKinstry, Leo, *Jack & Bobby* (London, Collins Willow 2002)

Milburn, Jackie, *Golden Goals* (London, Stanley Paul 1957)

Milburn, Jackie, *Jackie Milburn* (Edinburgh, Mainstream 2003)

Mortensen, Stanley, *Football Is My Game* (London, Simpson Low 1949)

Paisley, Bob, *A Lifetime in Football* (London, Arthur Barker 1983)

Perryman, Steve, *A Man for All Seasons* (London, Arthur Barker 1985)

Powell, Jeff, *Bobby Moore* (London, Everest Books 1976)

Ramsey, Alfred, *Talking Football* (London, Stanley Paul 1952)

Rathbone, Mick, *The Smell of Football* (Kingston on Thames, VSP 2011)

Raynor, George, *Football Ambassador at Large* (London, Stanley Paul 1960)

Revie, Don, *Soccer's Happy Wanderer* (London, Museum Press 1955)

Robson, Bobby, *Time on the Grass* (London, Arthur Barker 1982)

Robson, Bryan, *United I Stand* (London, Pelham Books 1984)

Seddon, Peter, *A Football Compendium. Comprehensive Guide to the Literature of Association Football* (British Library 1995)

Seed, Jimmy, *Soccer from the Inside* (London, Thorsons 1947)

Shackleton, Len, *Clown Prince of Soccer* (London, Nicholas Kaye 1955)

Sharpe, Ivan, *Forty Years in Football* (London, Hutchinsons 1952)

Smith, Tommy, *I Did it the Hard Way* (London, Arthur Barker 1980)

Souness, Graeme, *No Half Measures* (London, Willow Books 1985)

Taylor, Rogan, with Klara Jamrich, eds., *Puskas on Puskas* (London, Robson Books 1997)

Vasili, Phil, *The First Black Footballer. Arthur Wharton 1865–1930* (London, Frank Cass 1998)

Walsh, Nick, *Dixie Dean* (London, Macdonald & Janes 1977)

Watson, Penny, *My Dear Watson. Story of a Football Marriage* (London, Arthur Barker 1981)

Wright, Billy, *Captain of England* (London, Stanley Paul 1950)

3. Schools and Colleges

Abingdon

Charity Commission, In the Matter of the Foundation known as the Free School of the Holy Trinity (Roysse's) . . . In the Matter of the Endowed Schools Acts 1869, 1873 and 1874, *Scheme for the Administration of the Above-Mentioned Foundation* (29 June 1878)

The Griffin, 1563-1963 (Abingdon, Abbey Press 1963)

Cobban, James, *Abingdon School 1870-1970. A photographic record* (Abingdon School 1970)

Townsend, James, *A History of Abingdon* (London, Henry Frowde 1910)

Willis, Donald, *A Song on a Bugle Blown* (Oxford, Kenton 1983)

Altrincham

Kendrick, Myra, *Short History of Altrincham Grammar School for Girls 1910-1974* (Altrincham, AGS 1974)

Beaumont

Frs Lattey and Devas, *History of St Stanislaus' College 1861-1911* (Old Windsor 1911)

Levi, Peter, *Beaumont 1861-1961* (London, Andre Deutsch 1961)

Bedford

Anon, *History, Topography and Directory of Bedfordshire and Hunts* (London, Casey 1862)

Anon, Harpur Trust, *Town of Bedford and Its Schools* (Bedford 1896)

Barlen, M E, et al., *Bedford School and the Great Fire* (London, Quiller Press 1984)

Broadway, Constance M, and Esther I Buss, *The History of the School. 1882 Bedford Girls' Modern School—Dame Alice Harpur School 1982* (Bedford 1982)

Conisbee, L R, *Bedford Modern School* (Bedford, Modern School 1964)

Godber, Joyce, *History of Bedfordshire 1066-1888* (Beds, County Council 1969)

Godber, Joyce, *The Harpur Trust 1552-1973* (Bedford, Harpur Trust 1973)

Godber, J, and I Hutchins, eds., *A Century of Challenge. Bedford High School 1882-1982* (Bedford 1982)

Kelly, A D, *Kelly's Directory of Beds* (London, Kelly's 1924)

Lysons, D & S, *Magna Britannia. Bedfordshire* (1806. Ilkley, Scolar 1978)

Meynell, Laurence, *Bedfordshire* (London, Robert Hale 1950)

Sargeaunt, John, *History of Bedford School* (Bedford, Fisher Unwin 1925)

Westaway, Katherine, *History of Bedford High School* (Bedford, Hockliffe 1932)

Weston, S J, *The Organ and Organists of Bedford High School* (Bedford 1998)

Underwood, Andrew, *Bedford Modern School of the Black and the Red* (Underwood 1981)

St Bees

Old St Beghians' Club, *The Story of St Bees 1583-1939* (London, Buck & Wootton 1939)

Bideford

Shaw, A Mary, *When You Were There. Edgehill College 1884-1984* (S Molton, Shaw 1983)

Birmingham

Candler, W I, and A M Jacques, *King Edward VI High School for Girls* (London, Ernest Benn 1971)

Whitcut, Janet, *Edgbaston High School 1876-1976* (Governing Body 1976)

Bradfield

Leach, Arthur F, *History of Bradfield College* (London, Henry Frowde, Oxford U P 1900)

Brentwood

Lewis, R R, *History of Brentwood School* (Brentwood, Governors 1981)

Bristol

Hill, C P, *History of Bristol Grammar School* (London, Pitman's 1951)

Cambridge, Girton and Newnham College

Smalley, Alice, 'Student Life at Newnham and Girton College 1869-1926: a study in social negotiation', University of Leicester MA Victorian Studies dissertation 2010

Cambridge, The Perse School

Gray, J M, *History of The Perse School, Cambridge* (Cambridge, Bowes & Bowes 1921)
Mitchell, S J D, *Perse. A History 1615–1976* (Cambridge, Oleander Press 1976)

Charterhouse

The Carthusian, July 1921, June 1931
Charterhouse Magazine, June 1931

Chelmsford

Kenyon, Mary, *History of Chelmsford County High School* (Chelmsford, Essex Libraries 1982)

Cheltenham Ladies' College

Cheltenham Ladies' College Magazine, 1880–1968
Clarke, A K, *History of Cheltenham Ladies' College 1853–1953* (London, Faber & Faber 1953)
Kamm, Josephine, *How Different From Us. A biography of Miss Buss and Miss Beale* (London, The Bodley Head 1958)
Morgan, M C, *Cheltenham College. The First Hundred Years* (Chalfont St. Giles, Sadler 1968)
Steadman, F Cecily, *In the Days of Miss Beale. A study of her work and influence* (London, Ed J Burrow, nd, 1931?)
Anon, 'History of games in College' (Ts)
Constitution of the Cheltenham Ladies' College Captains' Club (CLCCC), December 1921
Minute book, CLCCC, 1903–1917
Minute book, CLCCC, 1917–1920
Minute book, CLCCC, 1921–1939
Members, CLCCC, 1907–29
Interview with Rachel Roberts, College Archivist, 7 November 2019 Chigwell (see also Collections)
Stott, Godfrey, *History of Chigwell School* (Ipswich, Cowell 1960)

Chigwell School Archive

The Chigwellian 1882–83
Games Books 1890–97
Levee Minute Book 1903–17

Crosby, Merchant Taylors'

Harrop, Sylvia with Joan Stubbs, *The Merchant Taylors' School for Girls, Crosby. One Hundred Years of Achievement 1888–1988* (Liverpool, Liverpool University Press 1988)

Dover, Dover College

Whitney, C E, *Dover College Junior School* (Dover, Corporation of the College 1982)

Dulwich, James Allen's

Green, Brian, *To Read and Sew: James Allen's Girls' School 1741–1991* (Dulwich, The Governors 1991)

Eastbourne, Queenwood

Carew, Dorothea Petrie, *Many Years, Many Girls* (Dublin, Carew 1967)

Edgbaston

Whitcut, Janet, *Edgbaston High School 1876–1976* (Governing Body 1976)

Ely

Saunders, R G, *King's School, Ely* (Ely 1970)

Eton

Anon, *Edinburgh Review* 230, April 1861
Byrne, L S R and E L Churchill, *Changing Eton* (London, Jonathan Cape 1940)
Chattock, R S, *Sketches of Eton* (London, Seeley Jackson Halliday 1874)
Clutton-Brock, A, *Eton* (London, Geo Bell 1900)
Connolly, Cyril, *Enemies of Promise* (1938. London, Routledge, Kegan Paul 1949)
Johnson, W, *Eton Reform* (London, Longman's Green 1861)
Jones, L E, *A Victorian Boyhood* (London, Macmillan 1955)
Ollard, Richard, *An English Education. A Perspective of Eton* (London, Collins 1982)
Song, *Ye Mariners of Eton* (29 July 1847)

Felsted

Craze, Michael, *History of Felsted School 1564–1947* (Ipswich, Cowell 1955)
Sadler, Michael, *Report on Secondary and Higher Education in Essex* (Chelmsford, Essex C C 1906)

Gerrard's Cross

Prospectus, Innisfree School for Girls (nd 1920s)

Girls' Public Day School Trust

Magnus, Laurie, *The Jubilee Book of the GPDST* (Cambridge, Cambridge University Press 1923)
Sondheimer, Janet, and P R Bodington, eds., *The Girls' Public Day School Trust 1872–1972. A Centenary Review* (London, GPDST 1972) including girls' high schools in Bath, Birkenhead, Blackheath, Brighton & Hove, Bromley, Croydon, Ipswich, Kensington, Liverpool Belvedere, Newcastle Central. Norwich, Nottingham, Notting Hill & Ealing, Oxford, Portsmouth, Putney, Sheffield, Shrewsbury, South Hampstead, Streatham Hill & Clapham, Sutton, Sydenham, Wimbledon

Gloucestershire

Hornsby, F W D and P K Griffin, *Katharine, Lady Berkeley's School* (Wotton Under Edge, The Governors 1984)
Robertson, David, *The King's School Gloucester* (Chichester, Phillimore 1974)

Hampstead

Bodington, Prunella R, *The Kindling and the Flame. A Centenary Review of the History of South Hampstead High School* (Hampstead, Bodington 1976)

High Wycombe
Ashford, L J and C M Haworth, *History of the Royal Grammar School 1562–1962* (High Wycombe, RGS 1962)

Ilminster
Prospectus (1895)

Kingswood
Ives, A G, *Kingswood School* (London, Epworth 1970)

Laygate Lane School, South Shields
Boys' Punishment Book 1900–1933
School Diary, or Log Book 1883–1906
School Diary, or Log Book (Infants School) 1911–1951

Leeds
Jewell, Helen M, *A School of Unusual Excellence. Leeds Girls' High School 1876–1976* (Leeds, LGHS 1976)

London North Collegiate
Ridley, Annie E, *Frances Mary Buss. And her work for education* (London, Longman's Green 1896)

Malvern
James, Rev. S R, *The Malvern College. 21 Views* (Malvern, Norman May 1902)

Malvern Girls' College
Phillips, Grace W, *Smile, Bow and Pass On. A biography of an avant-garde headmistress Miss Iris M Brooks MA (Cantab)* (Phillips, printed by Acer 1980)

Manchester
France, E, *The Story of Central High School for Girls 1844–1970* (Manchester, CHSG Magazine Committee 1970)

North Collegiate, London
Kamm, Josephine, *How Different from Us. A biography of Miss Buss and Miss Beale* (London, The Bodley Head 1958)
Ridley, Annie E, *Frances Mary Buss. And her work for education* (London, Longmans, Green 1896)

Notting Hill and Ealing
Flett, Kathryn, 'Please Miss I'm Back', *The Observer*, 25 August 2001.
Sayers, Jane E, *The Fountain Unsealed. A History of the Notting Hill and Ealing High School* (Welwyn Garden City, Sayers 1973)

Oundle
Anon, *Sanderson of Oundle* (London, Chatto & Windus 1923)

Queen's College
Grylls, Rosalie Glynn, *Queen's College 1848–1948* (London, George Routledge 1948)
Kaye, Elaine, *History of Queen's College, London* (London, Chatto & Windus 1972)

Radley

Boyd, A K, *History of Radley College 1847–1947* (Oxford, Basil Blackwell 1948)
Raikes, Rev. T D, *Fifty Years of St Peter's College, Radley* (Oxford, Parker 1897)

Roedean

Sidgwick, Mrs., 'An Address by... (Principal of Newnham) on the occasion of laying the foundation stone of Roedean School, 26 July 1895'
de Zouche, Dorothy E, *Roedean School 1885–1955* (Brighton, Dolphin 1955)

Rugby

Copley, T, *Black Tom. Arnold of Rugby* (London, Continuum 2002)
Stanley, Arthur Penrhyn, *The Life and Correspondence of Thomas Arnold DD* (London, B Fellowes 1846)

Sherborne

Gourley, A B, *History* of Sherborne School (Winchester, Wykeham Press 1951)
Waugh, Alec, *The Loom of Youth* (1917, London, Methuen 1984)
Shropshire, Adcote School (various county locations)
Lowe, Rachel, History of Adcote School (AOG Association 1987)

Taunton

Spooner, H, A *History of Taunton's School 1760-1967* (Southampton, Taunton's 1968)
Uppingham (see also Collections)
An Old Boy, *Early Days at Uppingham under Edward Thring* (London, Macmillan 1904)
Songs of Uppingham School composed by Music Masters (London, Novello, Ewer, nd)
Graham, John P. *Forty Years of Uppingham* (London, Macmillan 1932)
Hornung, E W, *Fathers of Men* (1912. London, John Murray 1919)
Jessel, Penelope, *Owen of Uppingham* (London, A R Mowbray 1965)
J.P.W.M, A New Campus (June 1967)
Matthews, Bryan, *By God's Grace. A History of Uppingham School* (Maidstone, Whitehall Press 1984)
Metcalfe, Warwick, *A Picture Book of a Unique School* (Stamford, Spiegl 1995)
Newton, W G, *The Work of Ernest Newton RA* (London, Architectural Press 1925)
Parkin, G R, 'An Ancient School Worked on Modern Ideas', `The Century Magazine* xxxvi, No. 5, September 1888
Parkin, G R, ed., *Edward Thring. Headmaster of Uppingham School. Life, Diary and Letters* (London, Macmillan 1900)
Patterson, William Seeds, *Sixty Years of Uppingham Cricket* (London, Longman's Green 1909)
Sargent, W C, 'Young England at School', *The Ludgate Monthly* vi, Nov 1893-April 1894
Tozer, Malcolm, *Physical Education at Thring's Uppingham* (Uppingham School 1976)
Tozer, Malcolm, 'The Magnetism of Edward Thring': talk to Uppingham Local History Study Group (July 2016)
Willison, Sir John, *Sir George Parkin* (London, Macmillan 1929)
Wolfenden, J, *The Public Schools To-Day* (London University Press 1948)
Wolfenden, John, *Turning Points. The Memoirs of Lord Wolfenden* (London, Bodley Head 1976)

Wantage

Sugden, K A R, *Short History of Wantage School* (Oxford, Oxford University Press 1924)

Watford

Hughes, W G, and M Sweeney, *Watford Grammar School for Boys and Girls 1704–1954* (Watford, WGS 1954)

Wigton

Loveday, L C, *A History of the Nelson Thomlinson School, Wigton, Cumbria* (Wigton 1976)
Wigton Old Scholars Assoc, *A History of Wigton School 1815–1915* (WOSA 1916)

Winchester

Bain, Priscilla, *St Swithun's. A Centenary History* (Chichester, Philliomore 1984)
Custance, Roger, ed., *Winchester College. Sixth-centenary Essays* (Oxford, Oxford University Press 1982)
Dike, Christopher, *Dr Moberly's Mint Mark. A Study of Winchester College* (London, Heinemann 1965)
Dolling, R, *Ten Years in a Portsmouth Slum* (London, Swan Sonnenschein 1896)
Furley, J S, *Winchester in 1867* (Winchester, Warren, nd)
Kitchin, G W, *Historic Towns. Winchester* (London, Longman's Green 1890)
Leach, Arthur F, *A History of Winchester College* (London, Duckworth 1899)
Firth, J D'E, *Winchester College* (London, Winchester Pubs 1949)
Moody, Henry, *Information for Hampshire Folk. Part II. Winchester College. As it is, and as it ought to be* (Winchester, Moody, nd, 1820?)

Woodard Schools

Kirk, K E, *The Story of the Woodard Schools* (Abingdon, Abbey Press 1952)
Worksop: see Collections

Worksop College Archive

College postcard Dining Hall, 1910?
Talbot Annals, v, 1933–36; vi, 1941
Captain of School Report, TS, Christmas 1970
Christopher Warner, Note on the College's History (2011)
Blazers and colours, cups and medals

York

Lloyd, Jean F, *Story of a School 1910–85. Brook Street to Queen Anne* (York, Queen Anne School 1985)

4. Film

British Pathe News, Wembley Cup Final (1963)
Fletcher, John, director: *The Saturday Men* (1962)
Reisz, Karel, and Tony Richardson, directors: *Momma Don't Allow* (1956)
Reisz, Karel, director: *We are the Lambeth Boys* (1959)
Whitter, Winstan, director: *You Can't Move History* (vimeo 2016)

5. Newspapers, Journals, Pamphlets, Guides, etc

Abingdon Herald, 25 June 1870

Abingdonian, December 1922; July, December 1923; March, July 1924

All the Year Round, 19 May 1860

Alnwick Gazette, 21 February 1914

Answers, 1 August 1903

Architectural Review, clvi, 934, December 1974

Ashton Register, 23 August 1856

Association Echoes (YMCA), 90, 8, March 1897

Athletic News, 8 March 1909

Athletic News, Who's Who in League Football. Pocket Guide (Manchester, AN1928)

Barnsley Sporting News, Saturday 11 July, 29 August, 20 October 1894

Beau Monde, Le, July–January 1807, 'Epping Hunt'

Bell's Life in London and Sporting Chronicle, April, 12 September, 10 October 1824; 15 November 1846; 3, 10, 17 January, 14, 21 February, 7, 14, 21 March, 4, 18 April, 2, 30 May, 20 June 1858; 1, 15, 23, 29 January, 5, 12, 19, 26 February, 4, 11, 18, 25 March, 1, 8, 15, 17, 22 April 1860

Bere Regis Parish Magazine 1887–1935: https://discovery.nationalarchives.gov.uk/browse/r/h/8fdd314c-7be7-4f01-9796-3fcd61a2e9e4

Blackwood's Edinburgh Magazine, lvi, viii, January 1821

Boys' Own Paper, lithograph, 'Famous English Football Players' 1881 (Willatt & Grover)

Brown, H. Ross, *Football Who's Who 1907–08* (London, Collier & Co 1908)

Carlisle Journal, 18 October 1929

Carlisle News and Star, 15 November 2004

Carlisle Patriot, 18 November 1854

Century Magazine, The, xxvi, No. 5, September 1888

Chuckles, 10, 17 January 1914

Connoisseur, The, 22 August 1754

Cornhill Magazine, The, July 1860, October 1919,

Country Life, 24 January 1925, 28 October 1954

Country Gentleman, 24 December 1904

Cricketer, The, December 1997

Cumberland News, 1 August 1912, 14 November 1914

Cumbria Life, October 1954

Daily Express, The, 21 August 2103

Daily Graphic, The, 11 November 1919

Daily Mail, The, 1 September 1896

Daily Mirror, The, 18 February 2005

Daily News, The, 10 September 1875

Daily Sketch, The, 2 April 1925

Daily Telegraph, The, 1 October 1861, 26 May 1864, 10 May, 10 November 1865, 4, 8, 10, 31 January, 7, 8 15, February 14, 7, 30 March, 1 April 1867, 15 October 1888, 4 April 1895, 15 January 1897, 19 February 1990

Daily Telegraph, The, 1 September 2015, Obituary, Joy Beverley (1924–2015)

Daily Telegraph, The, 17 March 2017, Oliver Brown, 'Rio's Olympic legacy lies in ruins'

Dorset County Chronicle & Somersetshire Gazette, 2 August 1866

Durham Chronicle, 8 November 1823, 26 June 1846

Durham County Advertiser, Saturday 24 October, 14 November, 28 November, 19 December 1818, 2, 9, 16, 23, 30 January, 27 February, 24 April 1819, 15 November 1828

East Lancs Echo, 8 December 1881

Echoes, The Strand, The Girl of the Period Almanack 1869

Eclipse, and Sporting Calendar, 5, 12 January, 10 August 1863

Edinburgh Review, 230, April 1861

English Illustrated Magazine 1888–1889, Louise Davis, 'Abingdon'

Era, The, 12 November 1850, 29 April, 6 May, 1860, 12 October 1862, 9 December 1893

Essex Standard, 24 November 1837

Fancy; or True Sportsman's Guide, The, (London, McGowan 1826), vol i, 1–28, 1821–22

Field, The, 12 October 1861, 31 May 1919

Football Association, *Rules of Association Football* (1863. Bodleian Library Oxford 2006) Introduction by Melvyn Bragg

Football Association, *Rules of the Association and Laws of the Game* (London, FA 1955)

Football Association, FA Vase Final programme, 21 May 2017

FIFA Mission Statement, May 2008

Football Field and Sports Telegram, iii, 68, Saturday 2 January 1886

Funny Folks, 12 December 1874, 13, 20, 27 February, 27 March, 17 April, 1, 29 May 1875

Gazetteer, The, 22 December 1787

Gentleman's Magazine, The, December 1802

Geographical Magazine, May 1961

Good Words, February 1879

Graphic, The, 4 June 1881

Grimsby Evening Telegraph, 'Old Timer', 28 August 1942

Guardian, *The*, 1 August 2010, 20 June 2012

Guardian, *The*, 1 March 1962

Guardian, *The*, 7 December 1968, Eric Todd interviews Bill Shankly

Guardian, *The*, 9 January 1999, Ted Hughes reprint from 'Wild Steelhead & Salmon Magazine'

Guardian, *The*, 25 March 2000, James Davidson, 'The beef that made John Bull'

Guardian, *The*, 7 December 2002, Mark Glanville, 'Seeing Red'

Guardian, *The*, 11 January 2003, Jim White, 'Pitch Battle'

Guardian, *The*, 11 June 2005, Gordon Burn, 'Living memories'

Guardian, *The*, 21 June 2005, obituary of Albert Marshall (1897–2005)

Guardian, *The*, 24 January 2006, Frank Keating, 'Last days of Pinks and Greens'

Guardian, *The*, 24 January 2006, 'ESRC study into play'

Guardian, *The*, 4 February 2006, 'An insight into the methods of an artistic revolutionary'

Guardian, *The*, 11 March 2006, Ian Jack, 'Lost Sundays'

Guardian, *The*, 25 April 2006, Frank Keating, 'Raising a glass to the lions of the Long Room'

Guardian, *The*, 31 May 2006, Maev Kennedy, 'Football manuscript published'

Guardian, *The*, 1 July 2006, D J Taylor, 'A good sport'

Guardian, *The*, 9 September 2006, Michael Walker, 'Keane embraces the emotion'

Guardian, *The*, 25 April 2007, Barney Ronay, 'Anyone want to play on the left?'

Guardian, *The*, 24 March 2008, Germaine Greer, 'Football counts as culture'

Guardian, *The*, 6 May 2008, Ken Worpole, 'The Child on the Street'

Guardian, *The*, 20 August 2008, Rachel Johnson, 'New Tory Stories'

Guardian, *The*, 21 October 2009, Ian McMillan, 'United front that led to footballers' riches'

Guardian, *The*, 3 April 2010, Andrew Martin, 'Only game in town'

Guardian, *The*, 13 April 2010, Jonathan Wilson, on football offside law

Guardian, The, 11 November 2011, David Conn, 'Madness of St James'...'

Guardian, The, 9 July 2012, George Monbiot, 'Enclosure and dispossession have driven us like John Clare, all a little mad'

Guardian, The, 18 December 2012, Helena Smith, 'LIBOR. System was set up in a more honest age, says its inventor'

Guardian, The, 21 March 2013, Paul Rees, 'Scrum reform'

Guardian, The, 20 August 2013, Louise Taylor, 'Premier Leagure reaches all-time low for English players'

Guardian, The, 11 September 2014, Roger Scruton, 'Why it's so much harder to think like a Conservative'

Guardian, The, 11 September 2015, Donald McCrae, 'The terrifying night Griffith answered gay taunts with a deadly cortege of punches'

Guardian, The, 26 May 2017, Giles Fraser, 'The parish is the perfect scale for moral community'

Guardian, The, 12 May 2018, Johann Cruyff on street football

Hansard, Commons, 23 March 1848, vol. 97, c.945, c.960; 15 May 1860, vol. 158, cc.1319–1325.

Horse & Hound, 3 December 1904

Hunting and Polo Journal, i, 4, October 1925

Illustrated Chips, 3 January to 19 December 1891

Illustrated London News, 25 May 1844, 29 March, 25 October, 29 November 1845, 5 February 1859, 1 November 1862

Illustrated London Times, 21 April 1860

Illustrated Sporting and Dramatic News, 1882

Independent, The, 5 August 2004, 'England's unseen urban poor'

Jackson's Oxford Journal, 29 April 1780

Joker, The, 18, 25 July, 1, 5, 15, 22, 29 August 1891

Labour League Examiner, 4 July 1874

Leeds Mercury, 7 March, 30 April 1864, 17 September 1875

Leicester Chronicle, 9 December 1837, 27 June 1863, 21 February 1880

Leicester & District Mutual Sunday School Football League 1935–36, rules and records, officials and functions

Leicester Football Mail, Saturday 3 January 1920

Leicester Mercury, 8 October 1842, 22 June 1850

Leicester Mercury, 22 June 1850, 'Hurrah for Our Ancient Pathways' by William Jones, framework knitter

Licensed Victuallers' Mirror, 20 September 1889

Lincoln & Stamford Mercury, 16 November 1838

London Review of Books, The 5 January, 16 November 2017

Literary Review, December 2018, January 2019, October 2019

Ludgate Monthly, The, vi, November 1893–April 1894

Lydney Observer, Newnham and Blakeney Herald, Forest of Dean News and County of Gloucester Record, Saturday 27 January 1894

Management Today, January 2003

Manchester Chronicle, 6 September 1834

Manchester Gazette, 11, 26 December 1885

Manchester Guardian, The (*The Guardian* from 1959): 16, 23 June 1821, 7 March 1840, 10 June 1848, 4 August 1849, 11 August 1852, 13, 30 September 1858, 21 March 1892, 11 December 1899, 12 December 1900, 24, 25 June 1924, 21 May 1932, 2 May 1953, 26 July 1954

Manchester United Official Programme, 3, 12, 1 January 1913, 27 August, 10 September 1927, 25 August 1928

Marvel, The, 26 February 1910

Medusa; or Penny Politician, The, 6 March 1819

Methodist Magazine, 'Historical reminiscences of the Book Room', December 1842

Methodist Recorder, 3 March 1910, 'Following the People. A Modern Durham Colliery Village'

Mirror of literature, amusement and instruction, The, 27 February 1836

Monthly Chronicle of North Country Lore & Legend, The, March–November 1887, June, July 1888, February–April, August 1889, March 1890, June, September 1891

Morning Herald, The, 8 November 1833, 16 November 1838

Morning Post, The, 19 November 1840, 17 September 1875

National Geographic, June 2006, 'The Beautiful Game'

New Newcastle Magazine, vol. i, no vii, July 1822

New Statesman, 2–15 August 2019

New Statesman, 18 October 2019, Michael Prodger, 'What Lies Beneath?'

New Statesman, 25 October 2019, Amelia Tait, 'Out of the Ordinary'

New Statesman, 8–14 May, 19–25 June 2020, Jonathan Liew, 'Left Field'

New York Times 30 April 1860

Newcastle Advertiser & Commercial Herald, 14 January 1845

Newcastle Chronicle, 28 January 1766, 22 June, 27 July, 14 September 1782, 28 December 1811, 16 January 1819, 29 September 1832, 8 January, 7 May, 12 November 1858, 11 March 1868, 18 February 1875, 10 April 1909

Newcastle Courant 1820–22

Newcastle Daily Chronicle, 26 June 1861, 1 January, 11 March, 5, 9 June, 28 September 1868, 18 August 1869, 18 July 1870, 24 August 1871, 28 September 1875, 10 May 1887, 29 October 1890

Newcastle Journal, 10 February 1880, 4 October 1930

Newcastle Song Book (Newcastle, W & T Fordyce 1842)

Newcastle Weekly Chronicle, 26 December 1818, 23, 30 January 1819, 31 August 1872, 12 May 1906

Newcastle Weekly Leader, 3 November 1906

Northampton Herald, 21 April 1860, 9 June 1894

Northampton Mercury, 7 February 1785, 5 August 1765

Northern Echo, 7 August, 23 September 1875

Northumberland and Newcastle Monthly Magazine, 15 Feb, 16, March, 19, June 1819

Observer, The, 27 April 1952, 14 February 1954, 4 February 2007

Observer, The, 25 August 2001, Kathryn Flett, 'Please Miss I'm Back'

Observer, The, 2 May 2010, Paul Hayward, 'Fair Play'

Observer, The, 15 December 2013, Andy Bull, 'Concussion'

Observer Sports Magazine, The, March 2007

Official Programme. The only official programme of Manchester City, Newton Heath, Broughton Rangers & Salford Clubs, no 1, 3 September 1898

Omnibus, April 1862

Oriental Notes. Official Organ of the Clapton Orient Football Club, i, 2 September 1907

Oxford Journal, 7 August 1819

Pall Mall Gazette, 1 March, 3 April 1895, 'Football. Some Points In Its Decadence'

Pearson's Weekly, 12 January 1929

Political Register, The, 29 January 1803, 21 August 1824, 3 August 1833, 20 February 1834

Polo and Hunting Journal, The, i, 3, September 1925

Primitive Methodist Magazine 1819–1907

Punch, or the London Charivari, 28 April 1860, 21 December 1861, 22 November 1862

Racing Times, The, 5 January, 9, 16 March 1863, 18, 25 May, 21, 28 December 1863

Referee, The, 3 February 1924

Salford Reporter, 25 October 1884, 12 June 1886, 25 January 1890, 24 August 1895, 20 June, 15 August 1896, 24, 29 August, 5, 26 September 1903, 1 July, 5 Aug 1905, 6 September 1913

Salford Weekly News, 12 December 1863, 29 July 1871, 7 July 1877

Saturday Review, 28 April 1860

Shields Gazette, The, 2 July 1993, Linda Colling, on Wilf Archer, 'Booting the ball for colliery'

Shields Gazette, 10 March 2006, on Bob Bates the boxer and Leigh Rose the goalkeeper

Shields Gazette, 9 May, 13 December 2012 on street team origins SS Adelaide FC

South Wales Star, Friday 19 January 1894

Southend Echo & Prittlewell, Leigh, Shoebury, and Rockford Argus, 21 November 1894

Spectator, The, 10 February 1866

Sporting Chronicle, 5, 8, 13, 15, 26 January, 2 February, 13 August, 24 November 1875, 1, 4, 6 January, 5, 7, 8, 9, 10, 11, 12, 14 September 1908

Sporting Gazette, 2 October 1869, 25 November 1876

Sporting Magazine, 1862–63

Sporting Times, 30 January 1875

Sporting World, or Life in London, This, March–May 1845

Sporting Life, The, 21 August 1847, 11 November 1865, 24 November 1875

Sports Mercury Football Annual, ed. H E Adcock (Leicester, Hewitt & Sons 1925)

Sportsman, The, 18 November 1865

Sportsman's Magazine & Life in London, 7 June, 5 July 1845, 30 December 1846, 9, 16, 23 January, 6, 27 February 1847

Standard, 12 October 1869

Stockton & Darlington Times, 4 September 1875

Strand Magazine, February 1905, 'Has the Public School Boy Deteriorated?' (The Opinion of the Head Masters) November 1905, 'English Sports Amongst Savages' (Rupert J King)

Suffragette, The, ed. C Pankhurst, 21 March 1913

Sunday Telegraph, The, 9 May 2004, Jane Shilling, 'My First Hunt'

Sunday Telegraph, The, 13 March 2005, letter of Lytton Strachey

Sunday Telegraph, The, 20 January 2008, Keegan's return to Newcastle

Sunday Telegraph, The, 28 September 2008, interview with Eddie Jones

Sunderland Daily Post, 3 November 1879, 22 October, 14, 16 November 1881

Sydney Morning Herald, 18 June 1860

Times, The, 19, 31 December 1787, 5, 8, 9, 15, 16 January, 9, 16 February, 10 June, 9 August, 27 November 1788, 12 February 1789, 3 July 1797, 17 November 1838, 8 April, 31 May 1860, 5–10 October 1863, 31 July 1911, 14 September 1950, 7 March 1952, 27 August 2018

Times, The, 6 January 2006, Simon Barnes, 'Baffling culture of vileness'

Times, The, 31 October 2009, Tim Coates, 'How The Times went to war with a Government'

Times, The, 22 April 2010, Matthew Syed, 'The man who stole the Olympics' innocence'

Times, The, 16 July 2010, Simon Barnes, 'Profit and dross: story of the World Cup'

Times, The, 8 October 2010, Alan Sugar, 'Buying a football league club just doesn't make any sense...'

Times, The, 5 November 2010, James Ducker, 'Red rebels...'

Times, The, 4 February 2012, Richard Scudamore, 'Pay up and play...'

Times, The, 22 May 2018, Paul Hirst, 'Mourinho wants squad to do less work with sponsors'.

Times, The, 7 July 2018, Editorial 'Gareth Southgate's side has restored faith in the national game'

Times, The, 27 August 2018, 'You Tube stars hit jackpot as millions watch grudge match'

Times, The, 27 August 2018, Matthew Syed, 'Abramovich used Chelsea to sanitize his image'

Times Higher Education Supplement, The, 9 January 2004

Times Literary Supplement, The, 27 March 2018, John Gray, 'The problem of hyper-liberalism'

Tom Spring's Life in London, 4 October 1840, 6 June, 5 September, 3 October, 7 November 1841, 13, 20 March, 24 April, 29 May, 10, 24 July 1842, 18 June 1843

Toronto Globe and Mail, 3 July 1971

Tyne Mercury, 12, 15 December 1818, 5 January 1819, 2, 16, 23 February 1819, 17 August 1824; collections relating to Newcastle upon Tyne inc. Letters of Peter Putright, 3, 5 April, 1, 15, 29 May, 2, 3, 10 July 1838, 19 January, 4 May, 14 December 1841, 26 July 1842

Votes for Women, ed., F & E Pethick Lawrence, vi, 287, 5 September 1913

Weekly Dispatch, 13 April 1913

West Cumberland Times, 9, 16 October 1886

Wimledon FC programme, Yellow & Blue, 29 December 2001

Wimbledon Independent Supporters Assoc, 'It's a Community Thing...' (2001)

Women's Beauty & Health, B MacFadden, April 1902

6. Academic Papers and Unpublished Sources

Adams, Iain, 'The Volunteer Soldier', British History of Sport Society, Leicester Conference 17 April 2004

Arthur, Janet, Church Broughton oral history transcripts 1974

Arthur, Janet, 'Church Broughton Parish, Derbyshire: an oral history 1900–1940', De Montfort University PhD 2020

Bale, John, 'Anti-Sport, John Betjeman and Heterotopia', paper given to ICSHC, DMU, 8 October 2005

Bateman, Tony, 'Neville Cardus and the Moment of Scrutiny', paper given to International Centre for Sports History & Culture, DMU, 8 October 2005

de Belin, Mandy, 'The Landscape of Foxhunting' MA University of Leicester 2006

de Belin, Mandy, 'The Hunting Transition', PhD inaugural, University of Leicester 2012

Blaxland, Dougie, 'The Long Walk Back', play performed at Leicestershire County Cricket Club, Grace Road, Leicester, 20 April 2019

Boddy, Kasia, 'Boxing and Cultural History', paper given to International Centre for Sports History and Culture, DMU, 25 October 2008

Bourdieu, Pierre, Plenary on 'Aristocracies', Toulouse, 24 September 1994

Brader, Christopher, 'Timbertown girls. Gretna female munitions workers in World War I', University of Warwick PhD 2001

Bradshaw, Jack, 'R S Surtees' MA University of Leicester 2002

BBC Radio 4, 'Hop, Skip and Jump: the story of children's play', 8 December 2009

Breward, Christopher, 'Sport and Fashion', paper given to ICSHC, DMU, 25 October 2008

Buckland, Theresa, 'Rise of Modern Dancing' professorial inaugural, DMU, October 2012

Carter, Neil, 'Amateurism and Coaching', paper given to Boston College, Dublin, 30 Nov 2012

Carter, Paul, 'Enclosure Resistance in Middlesex 1656–1889: a study of common right assertion', University of Middlesex PhD 1998

Cawthorne, Sophie, 'Creation of a Football Museum at Wolves', paper given to ICSHC, DMU, 25 January 2013

Cecil, Lord Charles, 'Surtees Crossing the Country', lecture to Surtees Society: https://www.rssurtees.com/lord-charles-cecils-lecture-at-the-bowes-museum-16th-march-2014-2/

Cohen, Phil, 'Public sociology and the ethnographic stake in community studies'. Michael Young 100 Conference, ICS, Barbican, 11 September 2011

Collins, Tony, 'Amateurism in Rugby', paper given to Boston College, Dublin, 30 November 2012

Collins, Tony, 'Football before 1871', unpublished Ms (2018)

Crump, Jeremy, 'Amusements of the People. Popular Culture in Leicester 1850–1914', University of Warwick PhD 1985

Crump, Jeremy, 'Revisiting popular culture in 19c Leicester, paper given to the ICSHC, DMU, 18 Nov 2015

Curry, Graham, 'Football. A study in diffusion', University of Leicester PhD 2001

D'Arcy, Julian, 'Ivy League Football in Early 20c. Scott Fitzgerald's *Great Gatsby*', paper given to ICSHC, DMU, 8 October 2005

Day, David, 'Selecting and Shaping the Athletic Body', paper given to ICSHC, DMU, 27 April 2012

Dee, Dave, 'The Estranged Generation, Inter-War Jewish Community', paper given to ICSHC, DMU, 28 February 2018

Dyhouse, Carol, 'Glamour, Fashion and Femininity in 1950s', paper given to ICSHC, DMU, 28 November 2012

Eadie, Emma Claire, 'The Structure and Organization of English Horse-Racing 1830–60. The development of a national sport', University of Oxford DPhil 1993

Fensham, Rachel, 'Designing for Movement. Art Schools and the New Body Culture', paper given to 'Natural Body' conference, ICSHC, DMU, 27 April 2012

Garratt, Delia, 'Primitive Methodism in Shropshire 1820–1900' University of Leicester PhD 2002

Gibbs, Stephen, 'The development of Association Football in Leeds 1864–1905', ICSHC, DMU, De Montfort University MA 2015

Goldblatt, David, 'What is Football?' lecture to CIES Master's, ICSHC, DMU, 10 October 2012

Greenhalgh, Paul, 'The History of the Northern Rugby Football Union 1895–1915', Lancaster University PhD 1992

Griffin, Emma, 'Sport in the Long 18th Century', paper given to ICSHC, DMU, 27 October 2007

Harvey, Adrian, 'The Evolution of Modern British Sporting Culture 1793–1850', University of Oxford DPhil 1996

Hearty, Conor, 'To what extent did Liverpool and Everton football clubs foster community ties in the inter-war years?' ICSHC, DMU MA 2020

Heffernan, Conor, 'Indian Clubs in Britain', paper given to Conference of European Sports Historians, ICSHC, DMU, 5 September 2016

Heiny, Henrietta A, 'Boxing in British Sporting Art 1730–1824', University of Oregon PhD 1987

Holt, Jenny, 'The Influences of Public School Literature and Culture on 19c and early 20c Concepts of Adolescence', University of Oxford DPhil 2000

Honey, J R de S, 'The Victorian Public School 1828–1902', University of Oxford DPhil 1970

Huggins, Mike, 'Robert Anderson, the Cumbrian Bard 1770–1833', paper given to ICSHC, DMU, 5 May 2007

James, Gary, 'Changing Emblems. Consultation at Manchester City', Conference European Sports Historians, ICSHC, DMU, 5 September 2016

Keiko, Ikeda, 'Japanese Sporting Tradition', paper to ICSHC, DMU, 9 July 2012

Kidambi, Prashant, 'The First All Indian Cricket Tour of England 1911', paper given to ICSHC, DMU, 15 October 2014

Kitching, Gavin, 'Playing Football in the Victorian North East', paper given to ICSHC, DMU, 31 October 2009

Kitching, Gavin, 'A Winter Game for the People. The Old Football and the Proto-Modern Codes in *Bell's Life* and *The Sporting Gazette* 1860–80', ICSHC, DMU, Ms 2014

Kitching, Gavin, 'Wittgenstein for Historians', ICSHC, DMU, December 2014

Kitching, Gavin, 'Detecting a Narrative in a Tremulous Press: causes of the Sunderland AFC / Sunderland Albion Split of 1888', paper given to ICSHC, DMU, 5 May 2017

Kitching, Gavin, 'Crook Town FC and the Durham Football Association 1927–31', ICSHC, DMU, Ms February 2018

Kitching, '"There is no such thing as society". Mrs Thatcher, Wittgenstein and Social Science', Ms 2018.

Lee, Robert James, 'Encountering and Managing the Poor. Rural Society and the Anglican Clergy in Norfolk 1815–1914' University of Leicester PhD 2003

Lewis, Robert William, 'The Development of Professional Football in Lancashire 1870–1914', Lancaster University PhD 1993

Mackenzie, J M, 'Sport and Empire', paper given to ICSHC, DMU, 26 October 2002

Marshall, Gail, 'Custom or Liberty?' professorial inaugural, University of Leicester, 22 March 2011

McLeod, Hugh, 'Religion and Sport in 19c Britain', paper given to ICSHC, DMU, 25 October 2008

Meller, Helen, 'Green Open Spaces in Europe 1850–1950', paper given to the Centre for Urban History, University of Leicester 20 February 2004

Metcalfe, Alan, 'Working Class Free Time Activities in Newcastle and South Northumberland 1780–1880', University of Wisconsin PhD 1968

Metcalfe, Chloe Elizabeth, 'A Shameful Conquest of Itself', An investigation into the non-existence of England's national costume' Bath Spa University MA 2013

Mettele, Gisele, 'The World as Village. The Transnational Community of Moravian Bretheren', paper given to School of Historical Studies, University of Leicester, 21 January 2009

Munkwitz, Erica, 'Riding Habits. Equestrianism, Fox Hunting and Female Sporting Emancipation', paper delivered at Conference of European Sports Historians, ICSHC, De Montfort University, 6 September 2016

Nead, Lynda, 'Ringcraft. Under the spell of boxing', paper given to ICSHC, DMU, 24 October 2008

Newell, Des, 'Disrobement in the Georgian Plebeian Honour Fight', paper delivered at RHS Symposium, Masculinity and the Body in Britain 1500–1900, University of Northampton, 18 June 2015

North East Rowing online: www.hastie.org.uk/nern/row/hist/

Norwood, Janice, 'The Britannia Theatre, Hoxton 1840–99' University of Leicester PhD 2006

Pantelides, Katerina, 'Self-Expression through classical form: Russian Ballet Body of the 1920s', paper given to 'Natural Body' conference, ICSHC, DMU, 27 April 2012

Pickering, Andrew, 'Methodism and the Royal Navy, 1793–1815', Ecclesiastical History Society Conference, DMU, 6 November 2019.

Pocock, Christine, 'The Origins, Development and Significance of the Circuit in Wesleyan and Primitive Methodism in England 1740–1914', University of Nottingham PhD 2015

Polley, Martin, 'Sweaters and Swimsuits', paper given to ICSHC, DMU, 27 April 2012

Polley, Martin, 'Olimpick Games and Olympian Games', paper given to ICSHC, DMU, 21 November 2017.

Polley, Martin, 'A Rational means of Relating Athleticism to Life: the Ashbees, the Guild of Handicraft, and Sport in the Cotswolds 1902–1907' (2019) Ts

Poole, R J R, 'Wakes Holidays and Pleasure Fairs in the Lancashire Cotton District c. 1790–1890' Lancaster University PhD 1985

Poole, Steve, 'The Murder of William Claypole. Foreign Sailors and Knife Crime in 19c Bristol', paper given to Centre for Urban History, University of Leicester, 24 February 2012

Porter, Dilwyn, 'Amateurism in English and Irish Sport', paper given to Boston College, Dublin, 30 November 2012

Porter, Dilwyn, 'B S Johnson. Sportswriter', paper given to ICSHC, DMU, 20 January 2016

Porter, Dilwyn, 'The Corinthians in English Soccer', Ms, September 2017

Russell, Dave, 'Sport and Music 1880–1939', paper given to International Centre for Sports History and Culture, DMU, 25 October 2013

Rouse, Paul, 'Amateurism and the GAA', paper given to Boston College, Dublin, 30 November 2012

Sandall, Simon, 'Custom and Popular Memory in the Forest of Dean 1580–1790', paper given to School of Historical Studies, University of Leicester, 11 January 2012

Searle, C E, 'The Odd Corner of England'. A Study of Rural Social Formation in Transition in Cumbria 1700–1914', University of Essex PhD 1983

Smalley, Alice, 'Student Life at Newnham and Girton College 1869–1926: a study in social negotiation', University of Leicester MA Victorian Studies dissertation 2010

Snell, K D M, 'Xenophobia and Local Communities', professorial inaugural, University of Leicester 15 October 2002

Strozek, P, 'Sport and Modernity in Central and Eastern Europe from avant-garde magazines', Conference European Sports Historians, ICSHC, DMU, 5 September 2016

Thomas, Keith, 'What was it to be civilized in 17c England?', paper given at University of Leicester, 14 May 2012

Tozer, Malcolm, 'Physical Education at Uppingham School 1850–1914', University of Leicester, MEd 1974

Turner, Mark, 'Cruising and Everyday Life in the late 19c City', paper given at the University of Leicester, 5 May 2004

Veitch, Colin, 'Play Up! Play Up! And Win the War! Football, the Nation and the First World War 1914–15', paper given to British History Seminar, University of Alberta, 14 March 1983

Warren, Phillip, 'The Transformation of Fashion. Early Sportswear 1860–1940', paper given to 'Natural Body' conference, ICSHC, DMU, 27 April 2012

Watts, Ian, 'Fields and Commons in English Landscape Art 1730–1850', paper given to Centre for English Local History, University of Leicester, 1 February 2007

Wessel, Caroline, 'Associational Life in Late Victorian Leicester', University of Leicester, MA Victorian Studies 2003

West, Shearer, 'Urban Degeneration in *Fin de Siecle* Art 1870–1914', paper given to the Centre for Urban History, University of Leicester, 28 February 1992

Williams, Jean, 'Aquadynamics and the revealed body of Jennie Fletcher 1912', paper given to 'Natural Body' conference, ICSHC, DMU, 27 April 2012

Williams, J T, 'Bearers of Moral and Spiritual Values. The social roles of clergymen and women in British society 1790–1880, as mirrored in attitudes to them as foxhunters', University of Oxford DPhil 1988

Wrightson, Keith, 'Mutualities and Obligations in Early Modern England', lecture to the North of England Institute of Mining Engineers, 24 November 2005

Yokoyama, Kensuke, 'Youth Culture and Total Fighting in Japan', paper given to ICSHC, DMU, 17 April 2004

7. Collections, Manuscript Sources

Alfred Lane Crauford's Cuttings File

In possession of Dr. Janice Norwood

British Library

Theatre Cuttings, 65, unidentified newspaper 31 March 1863; 67, 'The Late Tom Sayers'

British Museum

William Hogarth (1697–1764), *Beer Street, Gin Lane*, 1751, engravings

Carlisle Record Office

Brash Bros Ltd, zinc blocks for engraving for printed newspapers: women's football teams DB 20/521/10

Title deeds Carleton Hall Estate, pre 1751 D CC 2/43

Brampton, Coursing Club Cards 1844–65 D/CL/P/9/1; papers and lists of members, D ING/164, D/CL/P/9/4; open meeting, 17 & 18 March 1870, D/CL/P/9/2; balance sheets 1867–68, D/CL/P/9/3

Green, Ethel, Hunting Diary 1895–1901 DE 2101/128

Howard family papers, letter of William Patterson, 24 November 1842, D HC 1/18

Huddleston family papers, of Hutton John, examination of John Wright by Andrew Huddleson magistrate, 30 November 1747 D HUD 8/10/9 and information of John Lancaster and Joseph Edmondson before Andrew Huddlestone, 20 May 1747 D HUD 8/19/2; advice proffered by Mr Warren, attorney, on the property, 17, 19 June 1772 D HUD/8/44; letters to and from his mother, Andrew Fleming-Huddlestone, 26 December 1827, 5 December 1828 D HUD 15/5

Grainger, Henry, Schedule of Title Deeds, Ireby Grange estate papers, Portland Meadow, 9 October 1845 D/IG/8

Peel, John and Mary, Ireby Grange estate papers 1816–60, D/IG/31

Lawson family papers, deeds of enfranchisement, D LAW/1/155–77, D LAW/3/18/1–19, D LAW/1/118–238

Lonsdale family papers, estate letters and correspondence D LONS/L1/2/54, D LONS/L1/3/ 34; letter from Hugh Wharton to inform Sir John Lowther, 3 January 1680 D LONS/LI/3/ 2; letters from H Ainslie, 1829–33, D LONS/LI/2/63; petition on behalf of John Burn, and request to Lord Lonsdale from Rev John Rowlandson and Walter Parker, overseer, 26 December 1833 D LONS/L5/2/36/29; various correspondence appertaining to a breach of hunting etiquette in Bedfordshire: from Major Hope, 28 November 1849; from Lord Lonsdale, 30 November 1849; from John Brown, 31 November, 5 December 1849; from B Harrison, nd, and 2 December 1849, D LONS LI/2/154; letters to and from William, 2nd Earl Lonsdale and George Lumb, agent, March–April 1863 D LONS/LI/3/486

Cumberland and Westmoreland Association on Tyneside (f 1904) programme, nd, c1910 DSO 34/17

Walton family papers, 'Bond to refrain from poaching', 24 December 1830 D/WAL/2; title deeds showing perambulation of Priorsdale, 1848, D/WAL/2

Durham County Record Office

North Riding of Yorkshire, Michaelmas Quarter Sessions, 1836, King against Peter Dent for trespass D/HH/2/13/4–67; and Epiphany Sessions, appeal of John Barker against conviction for trespass D/HH/2/13/68–115

Association of the Noblemen and Gentlemen interested in the suppression of poaching and other lawless acts, 16 August 1822 D/HH/2/13/114

Greta Bridge Police Court, 19 June 1895, Wm Miller's deposition D/HH/2/13/116–131

York Lent Assizes, Game Prosecutions 1822 D/HH/2/13/130

Deposition of Joseph Longstaff against Robert Thirlkeld, for poaching, sworn at Barnard Castle, 1850 D/HH/2/13/145

Letter of Thos Keighley to John Keighley, his brother, at Catherstone, Barnard Castle, 5 Nov 1842 D/HH/2/13/151

Letter, Arthur Aylmer, Durham, and other JPs to Cuthbert Rippon et al., 6 August 1818 D/ X 1369/22; letters, T H Faber, Auckland Castle, to Arthur Aylmer, 28 September and 4 December 1818 D/X 1369/24 (i), 24 (ii); letter, Col. Beaumont, Hexham Abbey, to Arthur Aylmer, 4 October 1818 D/X 1369/25; letter, Lord Darlington, Newton House, to Arthur Aylmer, 14 December 1818, D/X 1369/26; letters, Arthur Aylmer, Walworth Castle, to Rev. W Wilson, Wolsingham, 15 December 1818, and Wilson to Aylmer, same date, D/X 1369/23 (i), 23 (iii)

Quarter Sessions Order Books April 1733 to 1743, Q/S/OB 9; deputations of gamekeepers 1814–18; Michaelmas Sessions, warrants, indictments, and reports, June–October 1818; Adjourned Michaelmas Sessions, warrants, 19 December 1818; Epiphany Sessions, prosecutions, 11 January 1819; Adjourned Epiphany sessions, 16 January 1819; Easter Sessions, 19 April 1819—all Q/S/OB 18; Chief Constable's Report, presented to Quarter Sessions, Winter 1840, Q/S/OB 25

Durham University, Palace Green Library, Bishop's Visitations 1814, including

Articles to be Enquired of the Churchwardens and Sidesmen of Every Parish...at the Ordinary Visitation of Rt Rev. Father in God Shute, Lord Bishop of that Diocese (Durham, G Walker 1814) DDR/UP/1806/4

Englesea Brook Primitive Methodist Chapel and Museum, Cheshire

Primitive Methodist printed works (under Printed Works) and virtually all works cited in 'War on the Parish', in ch 5 of this volume

Primitive Methodist Magazine 1819–1907

Football Association, Soho Square, London W1 D 3QN (before 2010)

Minutes of the Football Association, vol. i, 1863–75
History of the Football Association (FA, Naldret Press 1953)

Hackney Archives, C L R James Building

playbill, 'Engagement of Tom Sayers at The Britannia' (27 February 1863)
playbill, 'Four Champions of the World at The Britannia' (11 November 1868)
playbill, 'Champion of England', New Dramatic Fancy Sketch at the Britannia Theatre
   Hoxton by Mr C F Hazlewood (28 May 1860)
playbill, New Britannia Theatre Hoxton, handbill, 'Abou Hassan . . . Tom Sayers as Clown!
   with his wonderful Performing Mules' (27 February 1863)

Harris Library, Preston

Butterworth Papers: fair copy returns of Edwin Butterworth's' Parish Field Notebooks
   (1831–36) for Edward Baines' *History of Lancashire*, BAI/B/59–69
Edwin Butterworth's 'Journal of Excursions in Lancashire to collect historical information
   for Mr Baines' History of Lancashire 1831–36', vol ii

Hugh Lane Gallery, Dublin

Francis Bacon Exhibition, 17 February 2008

John Johnson Collection of printed ephemera, Bodleian Library, University of
   Oxford

Bodleian Exhibition, June to November 2003, including Cruikshank, I, 'Charles James Fox
   in two costumes', 1792; Cruikshank, I, 'How to Invade England', 1803; Gilray, J, 'French
   Liberty, English Slavery', 21 December 1792; Gilray, J, 'Britannia between rock and
   whirlpool', 1793; Rowlandson, T, 'British Liberty and French Liberty', 1792 and Folder
   6, John Bull and Bonaparte cartoon prints –
Isaac Cruikshank, 'John Bull tipping all nine', 28 May 1803
Isaac Cruikshank, 'John Bull peppering Bonaparte in the front and rear', 1801 or 1802
Isaac Cruikshank, 'Olympic Games or John Bull Introducing his new Ambassador to the
   Grand Consul', 16 June 1803
Isaac Cruikshank, 'Selling the skin before the bear is caught, or cutting up the bull before he
   is killed', 24 December 1803
Isaac Cruikshank, 'The scare crow's arrival or Honest Pat giving them an Irish welcome',
   10 June 1803
Animals on Show Box 1—
Various handbills and pamphlets inc 'Wonderful Pig to be seen Alive' (nd), 'Wild Beasts of
   Both Sexes' (1795), 'Destroying the Elephant' (1826)
Beer Box 1—
Various brewers' cards and handbills: Imperial Lager, Tottenham Lager, Mason's Non-
   Intoxicating Beers, Shillingford & Co, Bass East India Pale, Allsopp's Pale Ale, Guiness,
   Flower & Sons, Waltham's English, Elliott's Ale & Stout, Crown Light Invalid Stout,
   Raggett's Nourishing Stout
Inn Signs. Their History and Meaning (London, Brewers' Society 1939) inc. Bear, Bull,
   Cock, Dog, Falcon, Fox, White Hart
Bewick Box 1, 2—
Thomas Bewick's woodcuts, cheap prints, and engravings of animals for every conceivable
   occasion, including

A Pretty Book of Pictures for Little Masters and Misses, or Tommy Trip's History of Beasts and Birds (Newcastle 1779)

The Chillingham Wild Bull (Newcastle 1789) 9×7 in

The Whitley Large Ox (Newcastle 1789) 11×8 in

A General History of Quadrupeds (Newcastle 1790) various sizes

The Chase, a poem by William Somerville (1796)

History of British Birds (Newcastle and London, 1797 and 1804)

The Sportsman's Friend (Newcastle 1801)

The Sportsman's Cabinet (London 1803)

Boxing, Large—

Broughton's Amphitheatre, Tottenham Court Road (August 16, 1743) plaque or notice board

Bungaree v McGinty Joint Benefit (J W Peel, Lambeth 1843) poster

Eight of the Best Lads in England' (Wonderland, Mile End, London, nd, late 19th c) handbill

Empress Theatre of Varieties, Brixton, Jem Mace, Retired Champion of the World showing his Belts Cups and Trophies Medals etc, handbill, (24 July 1903)

Fight between Jack Brown and Bob Forbester, Lead Gate, Co. Durham (Boag & Nelson, Newcastle 22 May 1838) handbill

Full Account…Molyneux v Renwick, Eldon Bridge, Northumberland (Stephenson, Gateshead 31 October 1837) handbill

Prints of boxers: Deaf Burke (London, J Moore 1839); John Langan (London, Fores 1824), Jack Randall (London, Fores 1820), Edward Stockman (London, Fores 1827)

Pugilism…Randall v Martin, Crawley Down, East Grinstead (*The Traveller* September 1821)

Pugilism on Barlow Fell, Wallace v Dunn, Ryton (25 October 1824) handbill

Account of the Battle…Jem Wallace and Tom Dunn, Barlow Fell, Ryton (Blagburn, Newcastle, 25 October 1824) handbill

Pugilism. True Account…Crow v Davidson (Blagburn, Newcastle, 13 September 1824) handbill

Rules to be observed in all battles on the stage…as agreed by several Gentlemen

T W Spring, broadsheet with woodcut (1824?)

Stephen Pearce, The Chicken, v Bourke, at Wimbledon (23 January 1804) broadsheet

Cigarette Cards vol. 2

Circuses Box 4—

'1867 Dangerous Performances Act'

Crime Box 1—

Last Speech, Dying Words and Confessions of James Chambers and William Collins, executed Town Moor, 27 August 1784 (Newcastle 1784) handbill

Last Dying Words, Speech, and Confession of the 5 Malefactors executed Tyburn, York, 14 April 1792 (York 1792) handbill

Crime Box 2—

Last Speech, Confession and Dying Words of Griffith Williams executed 12 March 1800 (Newcastle 1800)

Education Box 1, 2, 5, 6, 7, 8—

Various school prospectuses, booklets, magazines, regulations, speech day programmes, duties, privileges etc, inc. Aspley, Bedford, Bembridge, Blackheath, Brecon, Monkton Wyld, Coventry High, Keswick, Heath (Wakefield), Eton, Taunton, Harrow, Oxford Prep ('Dragon'), Manchester Grammar, Newnham College, Lancing, Stamford, Seaford

Prep, Clayesmore, St Paul's, Westminster, Wellington, Charterhouse, 'Innisfree' at Gerards Cross, Birchington, Birkenhead, Frensham Heights, Malvern, Cranley ('Middle Class School'), Wimbledon ('Middle Class School for Young Ladies'), Bath, Bedford St. Peter's, Bishop Stortford, Chelmsford, All Hallows (Honiton), and Bedales

Girls Public Day School Company Ltd (Oxford 1895)

Address by Mrs Sidgwick (Principal, Newnham College) on the occasion of laying the foundation stone of Roedean School, 26 July 1895

Sermon preached by Bishop of Salisbury at the Opening of the School at Marlborough (1843)

Retrospect. Being an appreciation of Fifty Years of the Old Boys' Club of the City of Oxford High School (1953)

Strand Magazine, iv, 1892, 'Illustrated Interviews', Rev. Weldon, Head Master of Harrow,

Strand Magazine, xii, 1896, 'Public School Traditions'

Montem Ode (handbill: 1820)

Account of Mr Boucher, for Mr Harris, Assistant Master, Harrow (1857)

'Theses of Orations to be spoken by the Senior Scholars of St Paul's' (6 April 1785)

Herbert Chitty, *Medal Speaking at Winchester College 1761-1815* (Wykehamist Society, Winchester 1905)

'Short Account of the Discipline, Studies, Examinations, Prizes etc of Westminster School' (London, Woodfall 1845)

Sir John Coleridge, Public School Education (1860)

Fairs and Festivals Box 2—

Convivial Magazine December 1775

A List of Fairs and Markets (Langdon, Sherborne, nd, 18c)

Whitsuntide Revel on Marlborough Common, 1795, handbill

Innocent Amusements of the Poor, 1795, handbill

Byelaws with respect to Markets and Fairs (Burton upon Trent 1895)

Food Box 1—

Beef. New Portable Soup of Beunos Ayres (sic), nd, late 18th c

French Revolution Box 2—

Napoleon Bonaparte, various portrait prints 1816-1899

French Revolution Box 3—

Napoleon Bonaparte, various portrait prints inc H A Dahling (1807) engraved by Lehmann and Isaac Cruikshank, James Gilray (Consequences of a Successful Invasion'), and John Cawse ('The Grand Consul of the Nation Perusing John Bull's Dispatches')

Armee des Souverains Alles Annee 1814 (A Paris chez Martinel, Libraire, Rue du Coq No 15 1814)

Land & People Box 1—

'Home Colonization', 'A Brief for Rural England', 'How the People can best use the land' (London, English Land Colonization Society 1893)

First Annual Report, Bradford District Branch, English Land Restoration League (1884), and handbills for—

Scottish Single Tax League

Scottish Land Restoration Union

English League for Taxation of Land Values

Movement for Land Value Taxation and Free Trade

Henry George Foundation

Land Nationalization Society

Land & People Box 2—

D Lloyd George, 'The Limehouse Speech' (London, Budget Protest League 1909)

'Among the Agricultural Labourers with the Red Vans (London, English Land Restoration League 1893) and series 'With the Red Vans' (1896, 1897, 1893, 1895)

Land & People Box 3—

D Lloyd George, 'The Rural Land Problem. Speech at Bradford', 11 October 1913 (London, Liberal Publications Dept. 1913)

'Land Songs for the People' (Land Values Dept. 1910) 2pp

R L Outhwaite, 'Deer and Desolation. The Scottish Land Problem' (United Committee to Tax Land Values 1910)

Maria J Salzs, Land Nationalization Hymn, 14 January 1892 (Land Nationalization Society, nd)

Alexander Stewart, 'Deer Forests, National Wastefulness' (Liverpool, Financial Reform Association December 1888)

Anon, 'Among the Agricultural Labourers with the Red Vans' (London, Land Restoration League 1893)

Land & People Box 5—

Rt. Hon. H H Asquith, MP, Prime Minister, Speech at Earlston, 3 October 1908 (Scottish Liberal Association 1908)

Land & People Box 6—

'The Source of Unemployment' (United Committee for Taxation of Land Values 1906) leaflet 20

'Another Ducal Walbottle' (from *The Daily Chronicle* c.1906–14, Land Values Publication Department)

'The Duke's City. Sheffield's Toll to Arundel' (from *The Daily News* 1912? UCTLV)

Land & People Box 7—

Joseph Edwards, 'A Brief History of Landholding in England' (London, Land Values Publications 1909)

Samuel Milliken, 'A Tragedy of English History. Wage Condition of the English Labourer in Proportion to the Cost of Living 1260-1887' (Glasgow, Land Values Publication Department, nd, 1890s?)

Land & People Box 8—

James M Cherrie, 'On the Economic Conditions of Land Occupancy and the Depopulation of the Highlands of Scotland' (London, Reeves 1884)

Land & People Box 9—

Arthur Arnold, 'The Land and the People' (Manchester, CWS 1887)

Andrew Maclaren, 'Who Owns the Land? The Duke Runs Away' (Lansbury's Labour Weekly 1926)

Alexander MacKenzie, 'The Highland Clearances' (Inverness, Mackenzie 1881)

Law Box 7—

Personal warnings, printed with blanks for name, Doncaster and Sherborne

Magistrates' summonses, blanks

Summons to William East, of Dinmore, Herefordshire, for destroying game, 12 December 1827, Thomas Jay JP

Memorials Box 3—

Winchester College Cloister (1924)

Handbook to Prince Consort National Memorial (1872) Garibaldi reception (1864)

Men's Clothes Box 1—

Aertex, Men's Price List 1938 (Bolton's Piccadilly)

Catalogues for Burberry's, Daks, Dunlop's, Guinea Guards' Flannels

Men's Clothes Box 2—
Poster, Greenburg 'The noted Working Men's Tailor' (nd) 'For Flash Toggery'
Men's Clothes Box 3—
Catalogues for Rego Clothiers and Linia reinforced corsetted underpants
Men's Clothes Box 4—
Catalogues for Moss Bros
Men's Clothes Box 5—
Catalogues for Simpson's of Piccadilly, Daks and Lastex, Montague Burton, Hector Powe,
     Austin Reed and Horne Bros
Music Titles Box 5—
Sheet music covers including 'The Song my Mother Sang', 'The Gay Young Spring', 'Rose of
     Kildare', 'Bonnie Annie Laurie', 'Rose of Tralee', etc
Political Folder 1—
A Letter from General Fielding to Sir C. D. (nd, 18c) flyer
Public Service Box 12—
'Norfolk Association for the Preservation of the Game', 5 May 1788
Sport Box 1—
Good Words, August 1979
Handbills 'Great professional meeting at . . . Stamford Hill' and 'South London Harriers . . .
     Kennington Oval' (1903)
Handbill District Railway to Lillie Bridge Grounds, W. Brompton (1880)
Programme 1st Batt Worcs Regt Sports, Polo Ground, Nasirabad, 11 Nov 1920
Sport Box 2—
Appeal to the Patrons of the Ring for the benefit of Mrs Richmond and her family under the
     sanction of the Old and New School, A Grand Exhibition of the art of Self Defence . . .
     9 February 1830
Gilbey, Sir Walter, review by Ralph Nevill of his *Animal Painters* (1905), in *The
     Connoisseur*, xii, 48, 1905
Great Booth at Tottenham Court, newspaper cuttings for 1742
Great Fight for the Bowburn Cup (1865) handbill
Invitation, Coursing Meeting, 20 November 1928
Pugilistic Club, 1 December 1789, cartoon print
Programme of Amateur Boxing Association, Olympic Games of London 1908, at
     Northampton Institute, Clerkenwell, 27 October 1908
Programme, Kings Hall, London Rd. Two Contests of Twenty 3 minute Rounds, 19
     October 1910
Sala's Journal, A Weekly Magazine for All, 24 September 1892
Sparring. The Two Champions, Spring & Cribb, Theatre Royal Newcastle (17, 18
     September 1824), handbill
Wensleydale Coursing Meeting, 3 November 1831, handbill and rules
Wriothesley, Noel, *The fight between Sayers and Heenan. A LETTER to the Noblemen and
     Gentlemen who attended the fight* (London, James Nisbet 1860)
Sport Box 3—
A Great Fight (Pitts, Seven Dials 1824) and (Newcastle, Thompson 8 June 1824)
'Battle between Tom Spring and Pat Langan' (Newcastle, Thompson 1824)
Churchman's cigarette cards, Jack 'Kid' Berg, Joe Beckett, Boy McCormick (1930s)
Boxing & Athletic Carnival, Royal Albert Hall, 20 January 1888
Boxing Advert, Salvation Army Citadel Birmingham, visit of Billy McLeod, ex Champion
     Pugilist (nd, early twentieth century)

Boxing Matinee, Holborn Empire, High Holborn (1909–10)

Boxing Programme, Empire Pool, Wembley (1935)

Boxing Programme, National Sporting Club, Empress Stadium, Earls Court (7 November 1938)

Boxing Programme, Royal Albert Hall, 12 October 1922, 15 February 1923

Joe Elvin's Grand Testimonial (Wilkes, Walworth Rd. 1899)

Johnson, T B, Sportsmen's Cyclopaedia, 1831

Judean Athletic Club, programme, 54 Princes Square, Cable St, East London (1920s)

Tableau de la Grand Bretagne, vol. iv, p.206, Combat de Boxers a Odiham, French print

'Where Sporting Writers Dine', Harry Chiltern's, Fleet St., and other adverts for sporting restaurants

Sport Box 6—

Poster: 'African Students Garden Party, African Institute, Colwyn Bay, 31 July 1899'

'Heroes of the Cricket Field' Grace, Ranji, Maclaren, Fry: *The Young Men*, December 1900

B Macfadden, *Women's Beauty & Health* magazine, April 1902

Poster: City of London Ladies Amateur Swimming Club, 27 September 1912

Sport Box 7—

'To...all lovers of that Manly Exercise of Football Playing...TEN HATS to be played for ...' (Bury, 17 May 1755)

Alfred Gibson & W Pickford, *Association Football and The Men Who Made It* (London, Caxton 1906) 4 vols.

Various programmes

W D & H O Wills, Association Footballers 1935–36, 1d, plus cigarette cards

Sport Box 8—

Budd, Arthur, *Football. New Penny Handbooks* (London, Ward, Lock & Co 1899)

Sport Box 9—

A List of Mr. Parry's Fox Hounds (Bishop Stortford, November 1870)

Printed letter from F Lechmere Charlton to selected gentlemen, 'Sir', Worcester, 29 March 1819

Anthony Trollope, 'In the Hunting Field' *Good Words*, February 1879

Girls Gymnastics Exercises, Kensington Town Hall, *Illustrated Sporting & Dramatic News*, 15 March 1884

Printed letter on behalf of Blackmore Vale Hunt, 22 May 1896

Handbill: Sandow's School of Physical Culture, 32 St. James' Street, Piccadilly, December 1898

English Life, 'A journal of lovely and pleasant things' 1925

Greyhound Racing Trap Guide (London, Robbins 1932)

Pearson's Greyhound Race Game (*Pearson's Weekly*, 12 January 1929)

Dunse Gymnastic Games (4 August 1852)

Guide to Gymnastic Exercises (London, Duncombe, nd, 1850s)

Hunt fixture and calling cards, various (1799, 1828, 1832, 1833, 1842) 'It is requested that no Gentleman will cross Corn Fields' (Kilkenny Hunt 1833)

Royal Hunt card (nd)

Variety of nineteenth-century prints by Alken, Morland, Fuller, Beccles, and from *The Connoisseur*

Sport Box 10—

'Queer Feelings', print (J W Laird, Leadenhall St., 1836)

Various satirical prints—'A Day's Sport', 'London Sportsmen finding a hare', 'London sportsmen recharging'. 'Mr Jogglebury Crowdey with his dog and gun'

Alphabet book: *Trades and Characters* (London, J Innes, Oxford St nd 1850s?)

Record of Game killed by Earl de Grey 1867–89

Scorecards, Marquis of Londonderry 1894

The Shooter's Diary (London, Horace & Cox 1866)

Coop Society Gun Department, handbill (1897)

Sport Box 11—

Oxoniensia, xiii, 1948

Present State of the Arts in England (1755)

Racing Calendar and General Stud Book (Jockey Club 1773)

Ascot Races 1925 Official Programme, Third Day Thursday 18 June, 6d

Sporting Snips, Racing Tips, Turf Times, Lotinga's Weekly, Racing Post, betting books, manuals, systems calendars, cards, and circulars

Sport Box 12—

Race cards, various, Richmond, Epsom, and Kempton Park (1771, 1813, 1843, 1873, 1878, 1886, 1903)

J Pollard, 'The Winner of the Derby Race', engraving R G Reeves (Thomas Maclean 1 November 1836)

Sport Box 13—

A Cup and A Cover, King's Theatre Richmond, Richmond annual Rowing Match, 19 August 1822, poster and handbill

Hill, W W, *One Hundred Years of Boat Racing* (London, Albion 1926)

Sport Box 14—

'Women's Kit', by GG, *The Polo and Hunting Journal* I, 3, September 1925

Sport Box 15—

Engravings of famous pedestrians: Capt. Barclay by R S Kirby and 'Narrative of Life and Extraordinary Pedestrian Performances' (1813), Daniel Crisp (1818), James Davey (1889), Foster Powell (1773), William Gale (1877), George Wilson (1815), prints

Lunn & Co, Annual Catalogue (1887)

Sport Large—

A Compleat Sporting Table gives the state of the law as from the time of John for Deers, Hares, Conies, Beasts of Prey, Birds, Fish, Persons Qualified, Forest, Chases, Perlieus, Parks, Warren, Fishponds, Penalties of Game Laws, Published According to Act of Parliament (F Patton 1741)

Bailey's Magazine of Sports and Pastimes List of Hounds 1894–95

Full Cry; The Death (London, S & J Fuller, Sporting Gallery, Rathbone Place, 1828)

Interior of the Fives Court with Randall and Turner sparring (London, Turner, Warren Street 1821)

Grand Leicestershire Fox Hunt (London, Laird, Leadenhall St., 1839) Plate 1

Grand Leicestershire Fox Hunt Plate 3

Grand Leicestershire Fox Hunt Plate 4

Hunt in five prints, H Alken and C Bentley: The Meet; Going to Cover; Breaking Cover

Illustrated Sporting News and theatrical and musical review, Saturday 30 May 1863

Lambeth Baths Gymnasium, poster (nd, late nineteenth century)

Rules Agreed by several gentlemen at Broughton's Amphitheatre, Tottenham Court Road, 16 August 1743

'St Monday or the Humours of a Skittle Ground' (1802)

'Real Christmas Holiday', print, John Leech, in Illustrated London News, 19 December 1857

'The Death', print, Henry Alken (1828)

Box of cardboard figures, horse riders: Hurdle Riders, Royal Art Novelty Series

Street Ballads Box 13

handbill, 'Gallant Poachers' (Manchester, Bebbington, nd); 'We shall never see his like again' (Manchester, Swindell's 1837?)

Trade in Prints and Scraps Box 2—

Thos Rowlandson: A Paviour!! A Devotee!! A Loiterer!! A Minuet dancer!! A Vaulter!! (London, Ackermann, Strand 1799)

Cartoon of horses and riders (London, Ackermann, Strand 1799)

Robert Cruikshank: inc. well-known social types playing skittles, eg 'Bull & Bush. Hampstead Characters' (London, Allen & West, Paternoster Row, 1796)

'Babraham, A Fine stallion in high esteem, belonging to the Earl of Godolphin' (London, Bowles & Carver, St. Paul's Churchyard, nd) and various other pictures of record as prints, including:

'[Blank], the Property of his Grace the Duke of Ancaster' London, Bowles & Carver, St. Paul's Churchyard, nd)

'Hunters & Running Horses, taken in Various Actions' (London, Carrington Bowles, St. Paul's Churchyard, nd) inc. L Seymour's 'The Stables, & two famous Hunters belonging to HRH Duke of York', and 'Old Partner beat the following Horses at great Odds viz Sir Robert Fagg's Horse 'Barter', Lord Drogheda's Horse 'Tipler' and the Duke of Bolton's Horse 'Sloven' he beat twice'

Trade in Prints and Scraps Box 6—

Harry Payne, Sgt. H Ramage, Scots Greys, dashing to assistance Trooper MacPherson (London, R Harrild, Victoria Cross Gallery, Great Eastcheap, c.1857)

Horsed figures, all types, historic and satirical inc. Dandies and Hunters, Actresses, Knights, and Cavalrymen (London, Orlando Hodgson, Cloth Fair, c.1830s)

Geo Hunt, engraver, Chances of the Steeple Chase, eg 'Mr Rice and Red Deer', 'Mr Seffert and Grimaldi', (London, Lewis & Johnson, Cheapside 1820s)

Trade in Prints and Scraps Box 8—

Prints celebrating The Horse (H Alken: Haymaket, Mclean 1820)

Prints celebrating The Hounds (H Alken: Haymarket, Mclean 1820)

Prints mocking riders (H Alken: Haymarket 1822) inc '. . . of learning to trot'; 'of a hard mouth'; 'off to be sold'; 'of sold and had him a week'; 'of just got over the gate'; 'of taking a cooler'; 'of very fast but showy'; 'of very showy but not fast' etc

Trade Cards—

Hunting scenes are common in trade cards as a badge of the goods and services such as: Hoare & Reeves (Grays Inn Road), brush makers, showing a wild boar at the kill. Sporting analogies are also frequent, such as: Robert Cruikshank, A Magisterial Visit [to the punch bowl], Cartoon No 17 (London, Fores, Piccadilly Corner 1795); Thomas Rowlandson, Five to One—the young cock wins (London, Ackermann 1799)

Sporting writing as a particular kind of writing is recognized in: Thomas Rowlandson, Sentimental. Sporting (London, Ackermann 1799)

Women's Suffrage Box 3—

The Girl of the Period Almanack for 1869, ed., 'Miss Echo' (Echoes Office, The Strand 1869)

Votes for Women, vi, 287, 5 September 1913, eds., Frederick & Emmeline Pethick Lawrence

Women's Suffrage Box 7—

The Suffragette, 23, i, 21 March 1913, ed., Christabel Pankhurst

John Rylands Library, University of Manchester

Bunting, Rev. Dr. J, Speech to United Committee of Wesleyan Methodists on proposed plan of National Education, Monday 10 June 1839 (Manchester 1839)

Campbell, Rev. Chas, *Conversations with a Ranter* (London 1835)

Coke, Rev. Dr. T, *A Plain Catechism: or familiar instructions for children in the truths of Christianity* (London 1807)

'Great Fight at Gateshead between Cumberland Hodge and Brimstone Harry' (Gateshead 1829) tract

'H', Ann, *The Christian's Duty with regard to Dress... especially to The Female Sex* (Rochdale 1809)

Hurd, Clarissa, *An Address to Women; or, How to Make Home Happy* (Demerara 1862)

'For the Ministers Forming the General Union' (Newcastle 1832)

Philotheos, A Letter to the People called Methodists on their unscriptural mode of addressing God at their Prayer Meetings with brief remarks on females speaking and praying in public (Manchester 1826)

Rees, Rev. Augustus, Reasons for not cooperating in the alleged 'Sunderland Revivals' in an address to his congregation (Sunderland 1859)

Report on Sunday and Other Schools, presented to The Conference 1837 (London, Wesleyan Methodist Connexion 1871)

Rules and Regulations of the Sunderland Reading Society (Sunderland 1803)

Rules and Regulations for the Management of the Sunday School, agreed upon, and entered into, 26 July 1821 (Tunstall Wesleyan Methodist Connexion, 1822)

Sermon preached at Hebburn Colliery on Thursday October 10 1805 (Newcastle 1805)

Wesley College Prospectus, Sheffield, 1850

Wesleyan Local Preacher, *Remarks on Preaching* (Manchester 1844)

Wesleyan Penny Almanack (1850)

White, Dr. D B, *Remarks on the Precautionary Means best adapted for guarding against an attack of the Malignant Cholera addressed to the poorer classes* (Newcastle 1832)

Kendal Record Office

Deed, Kirkby Thore Parish, 1844 WPR 36/2/7

Lease for Hill Estate farm, Manor of Broughton, 15 April 1790 BD/8/15/2

Lancashire County Record Office, Preston

Forest of Pendle, football on Sunday, 1699, QSP/831/16

Leach, Samuel, b. Preston 1829, recollections (Ms October 1916) P160/2

Hoyle, E, b. Failsworth 1896, and Mr. T Parr, b. Failsworth 1900, recollections (recorded 1963) DOX 978/1/20

Ince Blundell Estate Papers: fishing rights and rentals to do with lords of the manor of Great Crosby Foreshore and the Fishermen's Association (1891–96) DDWW 3/3/1

Order against John Marsden, for using a snare, Clayton-le-Moors, 1813, UDCL/9/3

Penalty on George Monk, for playing 'foot ball', Clayton-le-Moors, 1810, UDCL/9/3

Release of Thos Sharrock, for assault during football, Lancaster, 1679/80, QSP/511/9

Prosecution of men for football and profaning the Sabbath, three lists, Lancaster, 10 May 1699, QSP/83/16

Newspaper cuttings, Lancashire Quarter Sessions 1852–74, QEV/18

Leicestershire Record Office

William Willoughby, farmer, High Court action against the Quorn, Queen's Bench, March 1894, DE 603

Martin family Ms, of Anstey and Woodhouse Eaves, letter from sister of Thomas Frewen Turner, nd, DE 718/D/96/iii

Quorn Hunt Minute Book, 1884–1913, DE 857/1

Quorn Hunt Minute Book, 1913–1932, DE 857/4

Curzon family Ms, of Lockington Hall, letter to Mrs Curzon, 13 March 1770, DE 1536/390

Letter from G A Legh-Keck to Earl of Denbigh, 11 February 1820, and from George Osbaldeston to Legh-Keck, 20 February 1820, DE 2515/2/14, 15

Correspondence of Lt. Col. D L Weir, Leicestershire Regt., 1909–1914, DE 2913/1/2–6

Quorn Hunt Accounts 1887–92, DE 3030/6/1–4

Letter from Mr. Phillips and Mr. Peacock to Secretary, Hunt Committee, 21 February 1920, DE 3030/15

Quorn Hunt Scrap Book, DE 3030/29

Bills for Capt. Warner, 1868, 1888–89, DE 3030/148

Packe family Ms, of Prestwold Hall, letter from Mr. Clowes to Mr. Packe, 26 December 1860; letter from Mr. Packe to Mr. Clowes, 5 January 1861, DE 5047/113/1–2

Secret Instructions, 2nd Battalion Leicester Regiment, April 1926, DE 6007/175A

Ts account, 8th Leicestershire Somme Bugle, 28 November 1974, DE 6007/376

Army sports photographs, DE 6007/172

Cottesmore Hunt Minutes 1883, DG 37/194

Idbury book of payments, defalcations and arrears, 1736–46, DG 39/840

Fortescue-Turvile family Ms, of Bosworth Hall, letter from Charles Dormer, 11 January 1797, DG 39/1096; letter from George Talbot, 12 March 1782, DG 39/1111; from T Potts, 27 September 1785, DG 39/1158; from W Ward, 3 September 1800, DG 39/1496; from Duke of Beaufort, 5 Nov 1803, DG 39/1602, 2 July 1807, DG 39/1725; from Charles Dormer, 17 March 1805, DG 39/1666; from Francis Turvile, 23 December 1897, DG 39/1741; from G Fortescue Turvile, 15, 18 October 1808, DG 39/1542, DG 39/1763

Mrs. M Burnaby's hunting diary 1909–21 DG 51/2, 51/3, 51/4, 51/6, 51/851/9

Mrs M Burnaby's journal and scrapbook 1932–37 DG 51/19

Letter from Harold Nutting, Quenby Hall, to A E Burnaby, Baggrave Hall, 8 December 1930, DG 51/31

Mr. A E Burnaby, note on the 'Christian Knight', DG 51/32

Mr. A E Burnaby, note on will, 'Rock Lodge, York, Maine, 8 July 1911, DG 51/33

Obituary of Mr. A E Burnaby by Guy Paget, 1938, DG 51/36

Handbook, Quorn Hounds, 1918; hunting appointment cards 1938; Baggrave Hall Auction 8 December 1938 DG 51/109–21

Henry Field, The Quorn Hunt, Ts, 11 March 1954, DG 51/123

Leicester Museum & Art Gallery: Ferneley, John, (possibly 1782–1860) *Henry John and Francis Grant at Melton Mowbray* (1823), oil on canvas, 52×77 inches

London Metropolitan University

Women's Library

Cicely Hamilton, *A Matter of Sport* (nd 1908–14? no publisher), a pull-out frieze illustrated by Hope Joseph

Box 4 Photographic Collection

Girls playing hockey: TWL 2004.170

Royal Holloway Rowing Crew 1891–92: TWL 2004.169

Female pilots, including Amy Johnson, 191433: TWL 2004.172
Royal Holloway Hockey Team 1892–93: TWL 2004.192
Cheltenham Ladies' College Cricket First XI 1907: TWL 2004.194

Museum of London
'Sayers' & Heenan's Great Fight for the Championship' (Disley, St. Giles, London 1860)
'Tom Sayers as Clown in Abou Hassan at the Brittannia (sic) Theatre' (Redington, Hoxton 1863)
Astley's 'The Brute Tamer of Pompeii' etc (nd)

National Archives, London
Assize Papers:
Northumberland Assizes, 1836–42: ASSI/41/15–16, ASSI/45/24; night poaching prosecutions 1838–42: ASSI 45/24; Northern Circuit depositions 1784–86, depositions of William Taylor, 28 February 1785, Andrew Murdue and George Humble, 15 July 1785, and Thomas Johnson, 21 July 1785: ASSI 45/35; depositions, Newcastle Races, anti-Irish riot, June 1847: ASSI/45/67
Home Office Papers:
British Convict Transportation Registers 1787–1867: HO 11/2/363–67
Pardons and Remissions, 1 July 1819–4 April 1820, remission of Ralph Buddle, 6 November 1819: HO 13/34
Criminal Registers, Durham and Northumberland, 1818–1820, HO 27/15–20
'A Plan for Establishing a Repository of Cheap Publications', tract, 21 March 1795, Manchester: HO 42/34
Northern Political Union, 'Address to Middle Classes of the North of England', handbill, 1839: HO 40/42
Home Office Disturbance Entry Book, letter, Sidmouth to Mayor of Newcastle, 10 October 1818: HO 41/44
Letter, Messrs. Newburn, Richmond, Dent and Shafto, to Duke of Northumberland, 3 December 1816, and letter, Duke of Northumberland to Sidmouth, 7 December 1816, with information of Edward Johnson, taken 2 December 1816, and George Johnson taken 3 December 1816: HO 42/156
Letter, 'Poacher' to Thomas Clennell, JP, Newcastle or at Harbottle, Northumberland, 20 January 1817; letter, Duke of Northumberland to Sidmouth, 22 January 1817: HO 42/158
Letter, Thomas Leaton, Whickham House, Newcastle, to Sidmouth, 24 February 1817: HO 42/160
Letters, Joseph Forster, Mayor of Newcastle to Sidmouth, 6, 16 October 1818: HO 42/181
Sherwin's Political Register, Saturday 28 November 1818, 'On the Right and Necessity of Every Englishman Carrying and Knowing the Use of Arms': HO 42/182
General Quarter Sessions of the Peace, Durham, 19 December 1818, and letter Arthur Aylmer, Chair Quarter Sessions, Walworth Castle, Darlington, to Sidmouth, 19 December 1818, and letter, May Gen Byng to Hobhouse at the Home Office, 21 December 1818, and letter, Aylmer, Walworth Castle, to Sidmouth, 21 December 1818, and letter Byng at Pontefract to Aylmer, 25 December 1819: HO 42/182 (ii) (iii); letter, Aylmer to Byng, 1 January 1819, and Byng to Aylmer, 3 January 1819, and Earl of Darlington to Sidmouth, 7 January 1819: HO 42/183 (iv)
Parliamentary Papers:
Census of Great Britain. Religious Worship. England & Wales. Report and Tables. Parliamentary Papers, vol. lxxxix, 1852–53

Return of Owners of Land 1873, vol. i, England and Wales (Exclusive of the Metropolis) Presented to both Houses of Parliament by John Lambert, Secretary of the Local Government Board (HMSO 1875)

Report of Select Committee on the Game Laws; together with the Proceedings of the Committee, Minutes of Evidence and Appendix (House of Commons 1872)

Report of Commissioners [known as the Clarendon Commssion] appointed to inquire into the Revenues and Management of Certain Colleges and Schools and the Studies Pursued and Instruction given therein, vol. i, Report (HMSO 1864) vol. xx

Appendix to the [above] Report (HMSO 1864) vol. xx

Evidence [Part I] to the [above] Report (HMSO 1864) vol. xxi

Evidence [Part II] to the [above] Report (HMSO 1864) vol. xxi

Report of Schools' Enquiry Commission on the Education of Girls (1867–68): D. Beale, Principal, Ladies' College Cheltenham (1870)

Report of Select Committee on Act for Regulation of Mills and Factories PP 1840 (314) vol. x

Report on the Sanitary Condition of the Labouring Population... by Edwin Chadwick: PP 1842 (HL) vol. xxvi

Reports of the Inspectors of Factories for the half year ending 30 April 1863: PP 1863 (3206) vol. xviii

Children's Employment Commission (1862), Fourth Report of the Commissioners 1865: PP 1865 (3548) vol. xx

Reports from the Select Committee on the Shop Hours Regulation Bill (1886): PP 1886 (155 Session 1) vol. xii & Proceedings 10 May 1886

Report of the Inter-Departmental Committee on Physical Deterioration (HMSO 1904) vol. i Report and Appendix (cd 2175) vol. xxii

War Office Papers:

Correspondence and papers relating to the Victoria Cross: WO 98/2

National Gallery, London

William Hogarth (1697–1764) *The Shrimp Girl*, 1740–43, oil on canvas, 63 × 52 cms

Thomas Gainsborough (1727–1788) *Mr Mrs Andrews*, 1750, oil on canvas, 70 × 119 cms

National Society for the Prevention of Cruelty to Animals, Horsham

Minutes of monthly meetings 26 May 1832–4 December 1843, vols. i–iv

Annual Reports

Windham's Speech to the House of Commons, 24 May 1802, vol. i, 1800–22

Newcastle City Library

Bell Collection, vol. ii, small posters: 'Ascension Day Sports 23 May 1811'; 'Boat Race 19 July 1821'; 'Addresses of the Keelmen', 9 October–25 November 1822; letters and notices regarding recruitment for Royal Navy, July–November 1803

Bell Collection, vol. iv: poster: 'Ascension Day Boat Races' 17 May 1841; 'Grand Tyne Regatta' 7 & 8 August 1843; Moorings and River Police (Newcastle 29 August 1844); Act for granting further Powers for establishing an efficient River Police, 30 June 1845; Jarrow Docks & Railway Prospectus 1845; Northumberland Docks Prospectus 1845; W Fordyce, Maritime Chart of the River Tyne Patronized by the Admiralty (Newcastle, July 1846); I T W Bell, Plan of part of the Newcastle Coal District 1847; Report of the Engineer (1848); I T W Bell, Plan of the River Tyne between Hedwin Streams, above

Newcastle upon Tyne, and the place called Spar Hawke, in the Sea (1849); Tidal Harbour Commission (1849); Bill for Conservancy (1849).

Hayler Cuttings, vol. ii

Martin Cuttings, vol. i

Seymour Bell Portfolio 10, Newcastle Forth: valuations, articles of agreement, reports, handbills, plans, and enclosure and Improvement Acts; inc. W Chapman, Report on the Cost and Separate Advantages of a Ship Canal and of a Rail-Way from Newcastle to Carlisle (Newcastle, Ed Walker, October 1824), with Additional Supplement (Newcastle, Ed Walker, July 1824)

Wilson Collection, vol. 5, part I, May–December 1835: vol. 10, 1842–45, handbill, 'Wylam Hoppings' (Newcastle, Marshall 28 July 1828); handbill, 'Topliff's Merry Night' (Newcastle Nov 1844); poster, 'Encroachment on the Land. Enclosure of the Ropery Banks' (Newcastle 12 July 1844); *Newcastle Advertiser & Commercial Herald*, 14 January 1845

Tyne Conservancy Commissioners, Bill for Conservancy of the River Tyne (London, 1849)

Tyne Hat Manufactory, Gateshead, bill for 9s 6d, 18 May 1872

Tyne Improvement Commissioners, Proceedings 1875–76 (Newcastle, Daily Journal Office 1876); public notices inc memos, bye-laws, instructions, rates, and regulations

Borough of Newcastle upon Tyne: various Acts and bye-laws; Newcastle Races Herbage Committee List of Tents and Stands 1847; Town Moor Management Committee, Report 21 March 1881; Memorandum prepared by Town Clerk for submission to the Royal Commission on Common Land, Appendix, Newcastle City Council Proceedings 6 February 1957, The Town Moor; Proceedings and Reports of the Town Council of the Borough of Newcastle for 1840, being their fifth year after the Municipal Reform Act (Newcastle, Emerson Charnley 1841); Town Council, Debate on a motion to assent to the Newcastle & Berwick Railway with a High Level Bridge (Wednesday 8 January 1845)

Rules of the Sunday School Union of Newcatle upon Tyne established May 1816 (Newcastle, SSU, 22 May 1816); First Annual Report of the Newcastle RSPCA for 1873 (Newcastle, Cail Printers 1874)

R W Hawthorn Leslie & Co. Ltd, Brief Historical Sketch & Catalogue (Newcastle, Hawthorn Leslie 1921)

F C Moffat, 'Northern Sportsman' (Newcastle, Moffat 1999)

Percival Stockdale, 'A Remonstrance against Inhumanity to Animals and particularly against the savage practice of Bull Baiting' (Alnwick, M & J Graham 1802)

Ordnance Survey, Ministry of Transport Road Map of Newcastle upon Tyne (1924–25)

Northumberland Archives Service, Woodhorn

Northumberland Quarter Sessions, 1817: QS1/521/36

Northumberland Estates: Percy Papers

Uncatalogued collection: receipts, 13 July–31 December 1778

Sir John Soane's Museum, London

William Hogarth (1697–1764), *A Rake's Progress*, 1733–35, eight paintings; also *A Harlot's Progress*, 1731–32, six paintings destroyed by fire 1755: both engraved and reproduced as prints

South Shields Public Library

Ordnance Survey Tyneside, South Shields (1894–96); Mouth of the Tyne (1898)

Spellman Collection, University of Reading

'Stout and Bitter' sung by Harry Rickards (1868–71)
'Old England and the New' sung by Alfred Concanen (1884)

Stamford Town Hall

Mayor's Wand 1461
Charters from Ed IV 1462
Mayor's Mace 1678
Two bull's horns, silver-plated, 13 November 1836, presented by W Haycock Esq.
Painting of the last bull running, 13 November 1839, identifying main protagonist
Painting of the bull running presented by Rev. Carroll of Tallington, May 1891
Phillips' Collection relating to the running, vol. 183—
folio 3 from MS Diary Maurice Pollard, resident 1788–90
folios 4, 6 handbills from the Mayor, Aldermen, and Burgesses October 1788, October 1789,
    27 March 1835
folio 5, Stamford Bull Running. Report of a Criminal Prosecution and Trial at Lincoln,
    Summer Assizes 1837
folio 7 handbill Roger Burton, 'To the Worthy Independent Electors of the Town and
    Borough of Stamford', 24 July 1796
folio 8 song 'The Bullards' Frolicks', 1802
folio 9 handbill 'The Independent Electors of Stamford and 'A New Song', 1809, and 'Free
    Election, Bull Running, Oddy for Ever'
folio 10 handbill 'To the Worthy Electors...etc', Mr. G N Noel, Exton Park, 1 March 1809
folio 11 'To the Worthy Electors...etc' second address from Mr. Noel, 1 March 1809
folio 12 'To the Worthy Electors...etc' third address from Mr. Noel, 2 March 1809
folio 13 'To the Worthy and Independent Electors etc' from 'An Elector', 2 March 1809
folio 14 'To the Editor of the Stamford Mercury', from Mr. Noel, 9 March 1809
folio 16 handbill from Sir Gerard Noel, 8 November 1813 'for substituting a Plan of
    Amusement more congenial to the mild and enlightened Times in which we live'
folio 17 poster 'Bull Running' (Leicester, Tebbutt 1833) running 'utterly incompatible with
    Christianity'
folio 18 handbill 'To the Inhabitants of Stamford' from 'A Bullard', 1833
folio 19 handbill 'Stamford Bull Running' from 'Fairplay' 6 November 1830
folio 20 handbill 'Stamford Bull Running' from 'Humanitus' 10 November 1830
folio 21 song 'The Luffenham Bull' 13 November 1816; and song 'Stamford Bull Running'
    'Bold William is our King Boys / he will protect our ancient right'
folio 22 handbill 'Public Caution', Horse Guards, 27 March 1835
folio 23 large poster 'Stamford Bull Running...designated by certain Fanatics as Brutal'
    (Stamford 1835)
folio 24 handbill 'Extract from Morning Herald' 8 November 1833, and poster 'The Bull
    Running' offering £20 to the Poor to desist
folio 25 handbill 'Stamford Bull Running', 14 March 1837
folio 27 handbill 'To the inhabitants of Stamford' 13 June 1837
folio 28 handbill 'Stamford Bull Running' 1837 'deemed by some objectionable'
folio 29 poster 'Bull Running Stamford' signed Mayor and Magistrates 9 November 1837
folio 30 handbill 'Stamford Bull Running' 1837 'People's Rights' upheld

folio 31 poster 'Stamford Bull Running' 7 November 1838 troops 'to enforce obedience'

folio 32 poster 'Bull Running Stamford' 4 November 1839 'absolute directions' to suppress it

folio 33 leaflet 'Instructions' to Special Constables (Town Hall 12 November 1839)

folio 35 poster 'Bull Running Prosecutions' 27 December 1839

folio 36 poster 'Borough of Stamford' 3 November 1840 meeting of inhabitants, and poster from F Mantle, Mayor, 9 November 1840, with 'Memorial of Inhabitants' asking for expenses towards suppression

folio 37 poster from H Gilchrist, Mayor 14 November 1840

folio 39, song sheet, 'Songs', 13 November 1843, as sung by James Woodhall at supper at Stamford Arms 'on the 626th anniversary of the sport'

folio 40, unidentified newspaper cutting 28 May 1802, Mr. Windham's speech against Mr. Dent's bill for the abolition of bull-baiting and running

folio 41 unidentified newspaper cutting 'Stamford Bull Running 1209-1839'

chapbook, *Stamford Bull Running. Report of a Criminal Prosecution (Rex v Richardson and others) Trial at Lincoln Summer Assizes 18 July 1837* (Stamford 1837)

folio 42 chapbook, *A Christmas Box for the Advocates of Bull-Baiting particularly addressed to the inhabitants of Uppingham* (London, Darton & Harvey printers 1809)

folio 44 tract, Percival Stockdale, *A Remonstrance against Inhumanity to Animals and particularly against the savage practice of Bull Baiting* (Alnwick, M & J Graham 1802)

folio 48 deposition, 17 November 1838

folio 51 Anon, *Stamford Bull Running* (London, Wightman 1830)

Sussex University, Mass Observation Archive

'The Finest Person That Ever Lived' (1937): 512 essays from boys at private schools

Report on Sport, July 1949: file 3141

Tate Britain

William Hogarth (1697-1764), *The Gate of Calais*, 1748, exhibition 'Re-Presenting Britain, Roast Beef and Liberty', March 2000

Tyne Wear Museums, Blandford Square, Newcastle upon Tyne

Ordnance Survey map of Newcastle upon Tyne (1879), xcvii.ii

Uppingham School Archive and Library

Diary of Edward Thring, Headmaster (1854-1887)

Uppingham School XI, photograph 1858: 'This belongs to John Whitehead Moore'

Uppingham School Roll 1853-1947, C E Green (London, Deacon & Sons 1948)

Uppingham School Magazine, vols. 1-8, 11, 16, 17, April-December, 1863, April, November-December 1864; 335, July 1907

Uppingham Tercentenary 26 June 1884

Memoirs of G R Turner Ms (1933)

Memoirs of Henry Walker Ms (1957)

Photograph Album, mainly sports teams

Ludgate Monthly, vii, November 1893-April 1894

Century Magazine, xxxvi, September 1888

Guide Book (Uppingham, Hawthorn 1870)

History of Uppingham School Ts, by J D Shipton (nd)

General Rules passed by the Committee of Games, November 1877 (Northampton, 1877), and subsequent 1968, 1983

Records of the Old Uppinghamian Football Club (Uppingham, Hawthorn 1913?)

John P Graham, *Forty Years of Uppingham* (London, Macmillan 1932)

Uppingham Association and School Society, 96, June 1942–November 1943

Letters, Mr. Hawley and Mr. Bothamley 1, 13 November 1948

Oliver Hill file on War Memorial, and notes by Belk

J P W M [headmaster], 'A New Campus' (June 1967)

T G Jackson, Architect's report on the Proposed New Buildings for Uppingham (1895)

R C Rome, History of Uppingham School Ms (1950)

Uppingham Local History Group, Uppingham in 1851 (2001)

Heath, P, Early Buildings (nd)

'Old Boy', An, *Early Days at Uppingham under Edward Thring* (London, Macmillan 1904)

Victoria State Library

Jerilderie Letter, Ned Edward Kelly, 10 February 1879: https://trove.nla.gov.au/newspaper/article/199362803?afterLoad=showCorrections

Beinecke Library, Yale University

Anon, *Life and Extraordinary Career of John Gully. Butcher Boy. Prize Fighter. Great Betting Man. Publican and MP for Pontefract* (London, 'at eight shops' 1863)

Anon, *Prize Ring Heroes. Life and Battles* (New York, Richard K Fox 1889)

Famous Sporting Prints, vi, Boxing (London, The Studio Ltd. 1930)

Cox, W D, *Boxing in Art and Literature* (New York, W D Cox 1935)

Fleischer, Nat, *Reckless Lady. The Life Story of Adah Isaacs Menken* (New York, Ring Magazine 1941)

Hughes, Rupert, *The Patent Leather Kid* (New York, Grosset & Dunlap 1927)

New York Clipper, *Life and Battles of John Morrissey with portraits from life of John Morrisey, John C Heenan, Yankee Sullivan and Bill Poole* (New York, 1879)

Prints—'A Slap at Charley's or a Tom & Jerry lark—vide New Police Bill' (Mclean, Haymarket 26 May 1829); 'Oh Murther its mancipation we're getting now aneyhow' (nd); I R & G Cruikshank, 'Tom & Jerry Receiving Instructions from Mr Jackson at his rooms in Bond street' (nd)

Boxing Print Collection Gen Mss 402—aquatint engravings of boxers 1810s–1870s, mostly published by Fores of Piccadilly: Tom Sayers, John C Heenan, John L Sullivan ('The Champion Slugger', New York, Currier 1883), Tom Cribb, David Hudson, E Baldwin, Edward Stockman, Edward Turner, Jack Randall, James Belcher, James Ward, John Langan, John Martin, Reuben Martin, Richard Curtin, Thomas Shetton, Johnny Walker, Tom Spring, Arthur Chambers, 'Molineaux'

Beinecke Papers, Yale University

Percy family MS, letter from Duchess of Northumberland, 6 October 1789, OSB Mss 88, Box 1, folder 5

Paul Mellon Collection, Yale Centre for British Art

All sizes approximate

Agasse, Jacque-Laurent (1767–1849), *Lord Rivers' Stud Farm, Stratfield Saye*, 1807, oil on canvas

Alken, Henry Thomas (1785–1851), *Hunting Scene: The Meet*, oil on canvas, 18 × 24 inches

Alken, Henry Thomas, *Pheasant Shooting*, c.1820–30, oil on panel, 9 × 11 inches

Alken, Henry Thomas, *Grouse Shooting: The Right Sort, The Wrong Sort*, c.1815, watercolour, 8 × 11 inches

Alken, Henry Thomas, *Partridge Shooters: The Right Sort, The Wrong Sort*, c.1815, watercolour, 8 × 11 inches

Alken, Henry Thomas *Hunting Scene: Drawing the Cover*, oil on canvas, 18 × 24 inches

Alken, Henry Thomas *Hunting Scene: In Full Cry*, oil on canvas, 18 × 24 inches

Alken, Henry Thomas *Hunting Scene: The Kill*, oil on canvas, 18 × 24 inches

Alken, Henry Thomas, *How To Qualify for a Meltonian*, 1819, six engravings, 16 July 1819

Alken, Henry Thomas, or 'Ben Tally-Ho', *Some Do and Some Don't; It is All a Notion*, set of seven engravings, large book, 1 January 1820

Alken, Henry Thomas, *Comparative Meltonians, as they Are, and as they Were*, six aquatints, 1823

Alken, Henry Thomas, scenes of Cricket, 1821, oil on canvas, 6 × 10 inches

Alken, Henry Thomas, *G Osbaldeston Esq Performing His Wonderful and Unprecedented Feat of 200 Miles against Time*, print (Stregear, Cheapside, 15 November 1831)

Alken, Henry Thomas, set of three Fores's Contrasts: *Driver of the Mail 1852 and 1832, The Guard of 1852 and 1832, The Driver of 1852 and 1832*, 1852, prints (Fores, 41 Piccadilly 18 November 1852)

Alken, Henry Thomas, 'Skittle Alley with Players', 1823, pencil and red chalk, 7 × 9 inches

Anon, after Francis Hayman, *A Game of Cricket (The Royal Academy Club in Marylebone Fields, now Regent's Park)*, c.1799, oil on panel, 10 × 11 inches

Anon, *First Grand Match of Cricket played by members of the Royal Amateur Society on Hampton Court Green*, 1836, oil on canvas, 22 × 32 inches

Burney, Edward Francis (1760–1848), *View at Chelsea of the Annual Sculling Race for Doggett's coat and badge, 1 August*, nd, drawing and watercolour, 11 × 17 inches

Cawthorne, Neil (1936–), *Full Cry: The Quorn*, oil on canvas, 18 × 24 inches

Chalon, Henry Bernard (1771–1849), *The Start of the Race for the Clarence Gold Cup at Hampton, Wednesday 21 June 1815*, 1815, oil on four-fold mahogany screen, 70 × 94 inches

Clausen, George (1852–1944), *Schoolgirls—Haverstock Hill*, 1880, oil on canvas, 20 × 30 inches

Closterman, John (1660–1711), *John, 1st Earl Poulett, of Hinton St George, Somerset* (c.1680), oil on canvas, 76 × 52 inches

Cooper, Abraham (1787–1868), *Elis at Doncaster, Ridden by John Day, with his Van in the Background*, c.1836–37, oil on canvas, 35 × 43 inches

Cooper, Edwin W, of Beccles (1785–1833), *A Sportsman with Shooting Pony and Gun Dogs* (1832), oil on canvas, 25 × 30 inches

Cotes, Francis (1726–1770), *Charles Collyer as a Boy, with a Cricket Bat*, 1766, oil on canvas, 36 × 28 inches

Cruikshank, Isaac (1756–1810), 'Rights of Man alias French Liberty alias Entering Volunteers for the Republic', 1791, etching

Cruikshank, Isaac, 'Resist unto Blood (a Clerical Boxing Match)', 1791, etching

Cruikshank, Isaac, 'False Liberty Rejected', 1793, etching

Cruikshank, Isaac Robert (1789–1856), 'Foot Ball', c.1820, print (London, Charles Hunt, Covent Garden, nd)

Dalby, John (active 1826–1853), *The Quorn Hunt in Full Cry: Second Horses*, after Henry Alken, 1835, oil on canvas, 15 × 20 inches

Dalby, John, *Foxhunting: Clearing a Bank*, 1840, oil on millboard, 5 × 6 inches

Davis, Richard Barrett (1782–1854), *George Mountford, Huntsman to the Quorn, and W Dery, Whipper In, at John O' Gaunt's Gorse, near Melton Mowbray*, 1836, oil on canvas, 28 × 34 inches

Edwards, Lionel (1878–1966), *Taking Out the Hounds*, oil on panel, 15 × 24 inches

Ferneley, John, Lord Edward Thynne's snuff box painted with fox-hunting scenes, 1832 or 1833, *The Death* on the lid, *The Meet* on the base, *Full Cry* around, oil on gold, 1 1/2 × 3 3/8 inches

Ferneley, John, Count Sandor's Hunting Exploits in Leicestershire', 1829, oil on canvas, set of ten

Garrard, George, *Duke of Hamilton's Disguise, with jockey up*, 1786, oil on canvas, 33 × 42 inches

Gillray, James (1757–1815), 'A View in Perspective. The Zenith of French Glory. The Pinnacle of Liberty' 1793, engraving

Gillray, James, 'The Tree of Liberty. With the Devil. (Fox) Tempting John Bull', 1798, etching

Gillray, James, 'Sans Culottes. Feeding Europe with the Bread of Liberty', 1793, etching

Gillray, James, 'French Liberty. British Slavery', 1792, etching

Gott, Joseph (1786–1860), 'A Great Boxer Waiting his Turn', 1838, marble sculpture

Gravelot, H. F (1699–1773), 'The Sporting Lady', nd, pen, ink, watercolour

Harwood, Francis (active 1748–83), 'Bust of a Man', reputedly 'Psyche', allegedly 1758, black marble 27 × 20 inches: correspondence regarding its provenance: B.2006.14.11

Haytley, Edward (active 1740–61), *A Sportsman* (1752), oil on canvas, 21 × 15 in

Healy, Robert, *The Death of the Hare*, c.1760–70, oil on canvas, 60 × 99 inches

Herring, John Frederick (1795–1865), *Memnon, with William Scott Up*, 1825, oil on canvas, 26 × 33 inches

Herring, John Frederick, *Margrave with James Robinson Up*, 1833, oil on canvas, 26 × 38 inches

Herring, John Frederick, *Study of Three Steeplechase Cracks: Allen McDonough on Brunete, Tom Oliver on Discount, and Jem Mason on Lottery*, 1846? oil on canvas, 28 × 36 inches

Hunt, William Henry (1790–1864), *The Gamekeeper*, 1834, watercolour and ink, 15 × 10 inches

Marshall, Benjamin (1767–1835), *Diamond, with Dennis Fitzpatrick Up*, 1799, oil on canvas, 34 × 41 inches

Marshall, Benjamin, *George, 5th Duke of Gordon, on Tiny*, 1806–07, oil on canvas, 40 × 50 inches

Marshall, Benjamin, *Foxhunting Scene: Two Gentlemen with Groom at the Edge of a Wood*, 1808, oil on canvas, 40 × 50 inches

Mortimer, John Hamilton (1740–79), *Broughton the Boxer*, 1767, oil on canvas, 30 × 25 inches

Munnings, Alfred J (1878–1959), *Portrait of a Sporting Lady*, 1929, oil on canvas, 41 × 50 inches

Munnings, Alfred J, *Paul Mellon on Dublin*, 1933, oil on canvas, 30 × 37 inches

Newton, Richard (1777–98), 'Political Boxing; or an attack at the Woolsack', 1792, etching

Nimrod, *Sporting Oracle*, 'the Few' and 'the Funker', nd

Pollard, James (1792–1867), *Epsom Races: The Betting Post*, 1834–35, oil on canvas, 12 × 18 inches

Rowlandson, Thomas (1756–1827), *A Stag Hunt in the West Country*, watercolour, 5 × 9 inches

Rowlandson, Thomas, 'How to Twist Your Neck', nd, 1799?, verso, colours from artist's palette

Rowlandson, Thomas, *A Crowded Race Meeting*, 1805–10, pen, ink, watercolour, 6 × 9 inches

Rowlandson, Thomas, *A Sporting Cove*, 1815–20, pen, brown ink, and watercolour over graphite, 8 × 6 inches

Seymour, James (1702–52), set of thirty-four racehorses, including No 1, *The Portraiture of Starling, late the property of His Grace the Duke of Bolton*, and No 34, *The Portraiture of Othello, the property of Sir Ralph Gore, Baronet, c.*1749, pedigree and prize money, prints

Seymour, James, *Sir Roger Burgoyne Riding Badger*, 1740, oil on canvas, 49 × 69 inches

Sickert, Walter (1880–1942), *Gatti's Hungerford Palace of Varieties. Second Turn of Miss Katie Lawrence*, 1903, oil on canvas

Stubbs, George (1724–1806), *Lustre, held by a groom*, 1760–62, oil on canvas

Stubbs, George, *Turf, with jockey up, at Newmarket*, c 1765, oil on canvas, 38 × 49 inches

Stubbs, George, *A Phaeton with Pair of Cream Ponies in charge of a Stable Lad*, 1780–85, wax and resin

Stubbs, George, *Two Gentlemen Going Shooting and three others—now on foot, ready to fire, end of day*, 1767? oil on canvas

Thornycroft, Thomas (1848–1937), *Queen Victoria on Horseback*, 1853, bronze sculpture

Tillemans, Peter (1684–1734), *The Round Course at Newmarket, Cambs, preparing for the King's Plate*, 1725, oil on canvas, 34 × 39 inches

Tillemans, Peter, *Rev Jemmet Browne at a meet of foxhounds*, 1730–32, oil on canvas, 38 × 48 inches

Turner, Charles (1773–1857), *An Extensive View of the Oxford Races*, oil on canvas, 25 × 36 inches

Turner, Francis Calcraft (1782–1846), *Bachelors' Hall: The Hunt Breakfast*, 1835–36, oil on canvas, 14 × 19 inches

Turner, Francis Calcraft, *Bachelors' Hall: Full Cry*, 1835–36, oil on canvas, 14 × 19 inches

Ward, James (1769–1859), *Portrait of Rev T Levett and Favourite Dogs, Cock Shooting* (1811), oil on canvas, 28 × 36 inches

Wheatley, Francis (1747–1801), *Portrait of a Sportsman with his son* (1779), oil on canvas, 36 × 28 inches

Wissing, Willem (*c.*1656–87), *Portrait of a Boy* (c 1685), oil on canvas, 81 × 49 inches

Wolstenholme, Dean (1757–1837), *Lord Glamis and his Staghounds*, 1823, oil on canvas, 51 × 81 inches

Wootton, John (1682–1764), *Duke of Rutland's Bonny Black*, 1715, oil on canvas, 30 × 48 inches

Wootton, John, *George I at Newmarket, 4 or 5 October 1717*, 1717, oil on canvas, 50 × 67 inches

Wootton, John, *Lamprey, with his owner Sir William Morgan at Newmarket*, 1723, oil on canvas, 41 × 49 inches

Wootton, John, *Duke of Hamilton's Grey Racehorse Victorious at Newmarket, c.*1725, oil on canvas, 113 × 127 inches

Wootton, John, *Lord Portmore Watching Racehorses at Exercise on Newmarket Heath*, 1735, oil on canvas, 26 × 49 inches

Wootton, John, *A Fox Hunt, c.*1730–40, oil on canvas, 45 × 69 inches

Wootton, John, *Preparing for the Hunt, c.*1740–50, oil on canvas 47 × 49 inches

Wyck, Jan (1640–1700), *A Hawking Party*, c.1690, oil on canvas, 20 × 27 inches

Wyck, Jan , *Hare Hunting*, c.1690, oil on canvas, 56 × 48 inches

Yeats, Jack Butler (1871–1957), *On the Old Racecourse, Sligo*, 1921, oil on canvas, 24 × 36 inches

Sporting 'conversation pieces', or, smaller paintings for placing in rooms where family and friends would be at their more personal and at ease—

Devis, Arthur (1712–87), *John Orde, His Wife Anne and His Eldest Son William*, 1754, oil—son returns from hunting trip

Devis, Arthur, *Portrait of a Family, the Swaine Family of Fencroft, Cambs*, 1749, oil—father and son with rods and carp at their feet

Hagman, Francis (1708–76), *George and Margaret Rogers, with his Sister Margaret*, 1748, oil—George has gun and holds game aloft while wife pets dog

Hogarth, William (1697–1764), *John and Elizabeth Jeffreys, and their Children*, 1730, oil—by a lake, rod, dog, and duck

Ward, James (1769–1859), *The Day's Sport*, 1826, oil—cold slaughter of a day's shooting in a different interpretation of sport from an Evangelical Christian

YCBA Rare Books and Manuscripts—

Alken, Henry Thomas, *A Turn Up with the Lads of the Village*, pencil, red chalk, nd

Alken, Henry Thomas, *Grouse Shooting: The Right Sort*, c.1815, watercolour

Alken, Henry Thomas, *Grouse Shooting: The Wrong Sort*, c.1815, watercolour

Alken, Henry Thomas, *Set of Six Comparative Meltonians*, 1823, prints

Alken, Henry Thomas, *Sporting Discoveries, or the Miseries of Driving*, nd, graphite and watercolour,

Alken, Henry Thomas, *Set of Four. Comparative Sporting*, nd, soft ground etchings

Alken, Henry Thomas, *The Quorn Hunt. Snob is Beat*, nd, watercolour

Alken, Henry Thomas, *Sporting Notices*, 1831–33, graphite

Alken, Henry Thomas, *Sporting Satirist*, 1834, hand coloured, set of twelve in book

Anon, *Boxiana-or-the-Fancy*, aquatint, London 1815

Blake, C, *The Poacher's Progress: stalking for partridges*, nd, pencil on watercolour

Blake, C, *The Poacher's Progress: poachers scuffling with the Constables in the Skittle Ground*, 1825–26, set of five, pencil and watercolour

Blake, T, *Interior of the Fives Court with Randall and Turner Sparring*, 1821, aquatint

Bromley, William, *William Howitt (Better known by the Name of Jackson the American Deer)*, mezzotint, London 1845

Brown, Hablot Knight, 'Phiz', *The Sporting Parson* series, nd, black chalk

Cruikshank, George (1792–1878), Tom and Jerry series, *Sporting their 'bits o' blood'*, 1820

Cruikshank, I R, *Going to a Fight*, pen and ink watercolour, on a roller, forty-one frames, 1819

Darly, Mary (active 1762–72), *The Timorous Sporting Macaroni*, nd, etching

Davis, Richard Barrett (1782–1854), *Foxhunting: the few not the funkers*, 1840, oil on canvas

Davis, Richard Barrett, *Foxhunting: Road Riders or Funkers*, 1840, oil on canvas

Gillray, James (1757–1815), *Two Men at Fisticuffs*, pen and ink, nd

Samuel Howitt (1756/7–1822), *Bull Attacking Mastiff*, pen and ink watercolour (nd); *Bull Attacking Dog*, pen and ink watercolour (nd); *Village Inn*, 1793, pen and ink watercolour

Hull, Edward (1823–1906), *Fox Hunting at Melton Mowbray, Taking the Gate at the Hinge Post while Snob walks thro*, 1835, watercolour and gum Arabic

Hunt, William Henry (1790–1864), *The Gamekeeper*, 1826, pencil on watercolour

Jones, Thomas, *Sporting Idealities, A Flattering Idea, A Not So Flattering Idea*, 1828, etchings

Locke, William (1761–1847), *Portrait of the pugilist Johnson*, 1790

Marshall, Benjamin (1767–1835), *Mr John Jackson*, 1810, aquatint engraving

Payne, Charles Johnson ('Snaffles') (1884–1967), *The Bullfinch*, nd, charcoal on watercolour

Podeschi, J B, *Books on the Horse and Horsemanship* (London, Tate, YCBA 1981)

Rooker, Michael (1743–1801), *Game of Bowls on the Bowling Green outside the Bunch of Grapes Inn, Hurst, Berkshire*, nd, watercolour

Rowlandson, Thomas (1756–1827), *The Prize Fight*, Humphries v Martin, 1787, pen and ink and watercolour

Rowlandson, Thomas, *A Sporting Cove*, 1815–20, watercolour

Rowlandson, Thomas, *Tour of Dr Syntax in Search of the Picturesque*, 1813

Rowlandson, Thomas, *A Fair in the Country*, nd, watercolour

Rowlandson, Thomas, *Scene outside an Inn*, 1816, watercolour

Rowlandson, Thomas, *The Woolpack Inn*, nd, watercolour

Rowlandson, Thomas, *Village Square*, nd, watercolour

Rowlandson, Thomas, *Two Girls Tippling*, nd, watercolour

Rowlandson, Thomas, *Elegant Company Dancing*, nd, watercolour

Rowlandson, Thomas, *The Ballad Singers*, 5 × 4 inches, and *The Opera Singers*, diptych, (1790–95), watercolour

Rowlandson, Thomas, *How To Twist Your Neck*, nd, watercolour

Smith, John Raphael, *Enamour's Sports*, 1801, mezzotint

Turner, Charles (1774–1857), *Portrait for study for engraving of Gentleman Jackson, Pugilist*, nd

Turner, Charles, *Backswords*, 1810, ink and watercolour

Turner, Charles, *Wrestling*, 1810, ink and watercolour

Un Francais Prisonnier de Guerre, *Le Boxeur Busse et Ses Parieurs Consternes*, Paris Martinet Libraire Rue du Coq St Honore, (nd),

YCBA Reference Library—

Emily Love Gallery, Hempstead, New York, *The Art of Boxing* catalogue, The J Terry Bender Collection 22 February–1 April 1978

Vestey Gallery, Newmarket, Cambs, *Noble Art. Prize Fighting in England* catalogue March–October 2005 inc. etching with hand colouring, *A Striking View of Bill Richmond* (Dighton, Charring Cross, March 1810)

8. Personal

Tegg, John, printer, 'Britons Strike Home', print, aquatint (London, Tegg, Cheapside 1819)

Index

For the benefit of digital users, indexed terms that span two pages (e.g., 52–53) may, on occasion, appear on only one of those pages.